THE CHILD IN INTERNATIONAL REFUGEE LAW

Children are the victims of some of the most devastating examples of state-sanctioned and private human rights abuse. In increasing numbers, they are attempting to find international protection, and are forced to navigate complex administrative and legal processes that fail to take into account their distinct needs and vulnerabilities. The key challenges they face in establishing entitlement to refugee protection are their invisibility and the risk of incorrect assessment. Drawing on an extensive and original analysis of jurisprudence of leading common law jurisdictions, the book undertakes an assessment of the extent to which these challenges may be overcome by greater engagement between international refugee law and international law on the rights of the child. The result is the first comprehensive study on the manner in which these two mutually reinforcing legal regimes can interact to strengthen the protection of refugee children.

DR JASON M. POBJOY is a barrister at Blackstone Chambers, where he has a broad practice including public and human rights law, refugee and immigration law and public international law. He is a Research Associate at the Refugee Studies Centre at the University of Oxford.

CAMBRIDGE ASYLUM AND MIGRATION STUDIES

At no time in modern history have so many people been on the move as at present. Migration facilitates critical social, economic, and humanitarian linkages. But it may also challenge prevailing notions of bounded political communities, of security, and of international law.

The political and legal systems that regulate the transborder movement of persons were largely devised in the mid-twentieth century, and are showing their strains. New challenges have arisen for policymakers, advocates, and decision-makers that require the adaptation and evolution of traditional models to meet emerging imperatives.

Edited by a world leader in refugee law, this new series aims to be a forum for innovative writing on all aspects of the transnational movement of people. It publishes single or coauthored works that may be legal, political, or cross-disciplinary in nature, and will be essential reading for anyone looking to understand one of the most important issues of the twenty-first century.

Series Editor

James Hathaway, James E., and Sarah A. Degan Professor of Law, and Director of Michigan Law's Program in Refugee and Asylum Law, University of Michigan, USA

Editorial Advisory Board

Alexander Betts, Leopold Muller Professor of Forced Migration and International Affairs, and the Director of the Refugee Studies Centre, University of Oxford, UK

Vincent Chetail, Professor of Public International Law, and Director of the Global Migration Centre, Graduate Institute of International and Development Studies, Switzerland

Thomas Gammeltoft-Hansen, Research Director, Raoul Wallenberg Institute of Human Rights and Humanitarian Law, Sweden

Audrey Macklin, Professor and Chair in Human Rights Law, University of Toronto, Canada

Saskia Sassen, Robert S. Lynd Professor of Sociology, and Chair of the Committee on Global Thought, Columbia University, USA

Books in the Series

The Child in International Refugee Law Jason M. Pobjoy

THE CHILD IN INTERNATIONAL REFUGEE LAW

JASON M. POBJOY

Barrister, Blackstone Chambers

CAMBRIDGE
UNIVERSITY PRESS

CAMBRIDGE
UNIVERSITY PRESS

University Printing House, Cambridge CB2 8BS, United Kingdom

One Liberty Plaza, 20th Floor, New York, NY 10006, USA

477 Williamstown Road, Port Melbourne, VIC 3207, Australia

4843/24, 2nd Floor, Ansari Road, Daryaganj, Delhi – 110002, India

79 Anson Road, #06–04/06, Singapore 079906

Cambridge University Press is part of the University of Cambridge.

It furthers the University's mission by disseminating knowledge in the pursuit of education, learning, and research at the highest international levels of excellence.

www.cambridge.org
Information on this title: www.cambridge.org/9781107175365
10.1017/9781316798430

First published 2017

Printed in the United Kingdom by Clays, St Ives plc

A catalogue record for this publication is available from the British Library.

Library of Congress Cataloging-in-Publication Data
Names: Pobjoy, Jason M., 1982– author.
Title: The child in international refugee law / Jason M. Pobjoy.
Description: Cambridge [UK] ; New York : Cambridge University Press, 2017. |
Series: Cambridge asylum and migration studies | Includes bibliographical references and index.
Identifiers: LCCN 2017000011 | ISBN 9781107175365 (hardback)
Subjects: LCSH: Refugee children – Legal status, laws, etc. | Refugees – Legal status, laws, etc. | Children (International law) | International law and human rights. | Convention on the Rights of the Child (1989 November 20) | Convention Relating to the Status of Refugees (1951 July 28)
Classification: LCC KZ6530 .P63 2017 | DDC 341.4/86083–dc23
LC record available at https://lccn.loc.gov/2017000011

ISBN 978-1-107-17536-5 Hardback
ISBN 978-1-316-62740-2 Paperback

For my brother Luke,
and my best friend Mathew

CONTENTS

Preface		*page* xi
Series Editor's Preface		xv
Table of Cases		xvi
Table of Treaties and Other International Instruments		xxxiii
Table of Domestic Statutes and Instruments		xxxviii
Table of Abbreviations		xli
Frequently Cited Sources		xliii
Introduction		1
	The Child Refugee: Overlooked and Incorrectly Assessed	3
	A Child-Rights Framework	5
	Methodology and Research Design	8
1	**Situating the Refugee Child in International Law**	13
	Introduction	13
	1.1 The Refugee and the Child – The International Legal Framework	16
	1.1.1 The *Refugee Convention*	16
	1.1.2 The *Convention on the Rights of the Child*	19
	1.2 The Refugee Child – Signs of Alignment	22
	1.3 A Child-Rights Framework	27
	1.3.1 The *CRC* as a Procedural Guarantee	27
	1.3.2 The *CRC* as an Interpretative Aid	28
	1.3.3 The *CRC* as an Independent Source of Status	30
	1.4 A Systemic Approach to Interpreting the *Refugee Convention*	31

1.4.1 The Interpretation of an International Treaty in Domestic Fora   32

1.4.2 A General 'Rule' of Treaty Interpretation   33

1.4.3 A Human Rights *Object and Purpose*   35

1.4.4 The *CRC* as a *Relevant Rule of International Law*   37

Conclusions   43

2   **The Child and the Refugee Status Determination Process**   44

Introduction   44

2.1 The Invisibility of Refugee Children   46

2.1.1 Unaccompanied or Separated Children   47

2.1.2 Accompanied Children   49

2.2 The Individual Assessment of Status   52

2.2.1 The Duty of *Non-Refoulement*   54

2.2.2 A Child's Right to Be Heard   55

2.2.3 Implementing a Child-Centred Framework   60

2.3 Family Unity Procedures   69

2.3.1 Recommendation B   71

2.3.2 The Duty of Non-Separation   72

Conclusions   78

3   **An Age-Sensitive Assessment of Risk**   79

Introduction   79

3.1 The Refugee Definition and the *CRC*   79

3.2 The Well-Founded Fear Requirement   81

3.2.1 The Bipartite Understanding of Well-Founded Fear   82

3.2.2 Why Require a Child to Establish Subjective Fear?   84

3.3 Assessing the Objective Risk   89

3.3.1 A Shared Duty of Fact-Finding   90

3.3.2 Country of Origin Information   91

3.3.3 Similarly Situated Persons   93

3.3.4 A Liberal Benefit of the Doubt   93

Conclusions   99

4 A Child-Rights Framework for Identifying Persecutory Harm 101

Introduction 101

4.1 The Definition of 'Being Persecuted' 102

4.1.1 A Human Rights Framework 103

4.1.2 Taking Human Rights on Their Own Terms 105

4.1.3 The Role of State Protection 109

4.2 The Definition of 'Being Persecuted' in Claims Involving Children 116

4.2.1 The Persecution of Children 116

4.2.2 The *CRC* as a Benchmark 123

4.2.3 What Does the *CRC* Add? 126

4.3 Four Case Studies 131

4.3.1 Domestic Child Abuse 132

4.3.2 Education 139

4.3.3 Separation from the Family 144

4.3.4 Psychological Harm 149

Conclusions 156

5 Nexus to a *Convention* Ground 157

Introduction 157

5.1 The Causal Link – The Predicament of Childhood 157

5.1.1 An Intention Requirement 158

5.1.2 The Predicament Approach 160

5.2 The *Convention* Grounds 165

5.2.1 Political Opinion 166

5.2.2 Religion 169

5.2.3 Membership of a Particular Social Group 172

Conclusions 185

6 The *Convention on the Rights of the Child* as a Complementary Source of Protection 186

Introduction 186

6.1 *Non-Refoulement* Under the CRC 188

6.1.1 Right to Life, Survival and Development   192

6.1.2 Right to Liberty and Freedom from Torture and Cruel, Inhuman or
Degrading Treatment or Punishment   193

6.1.3 Freedom from Underage Military Recruitment   195

6.2 Article 3 as an Independent Source of Protection   196

6.3 An Overview of State Practice   203

6.3.1 International Models   203

6.3.2 Article 8 of the *ECHR*   206

6.3.3 The Removal of a Parent Where the Child Has a Right to Remain   213

6.3.4 The Discretionary Grant of Protection to Children on Humanitarian
Grounds   218

6.3.5 Special Protection Measures for Unaccompanied Children 221

6.4 The Application of Article 3 as an Independent Source of Protection   223

6.4.1 Stage One: Determining the Best Interests of the Child   225

6.4.2 Stage Two: The Balancing Exercise   234

Conclusions   238

Conclusions   239

Annex 1 CRC, *Preamble and Articles 1 to 41*   243

Annex 2 Refugee Convention, *Preamble and Article 1*   257

Annex 3 Final Act of the Conference of Plenipotentiaries, *Recommendation
B (Principle of Family Unity)*   260

Bibliography   261

Index   284

PREFACE

Today, more than half of the world's refugees are children. In Europe alone, more than 25 per cent of arrivals by sea during the 2015–16 refugee crisis were children. Some survived the journey; far too many did not. Many of these children will spend the majority, if not all, of their childhood away from their home country. These figures are devastating, particularly given the reality that childhood is a wasting asset – there are no second chances.

I witnessed first-hand the devastating impact of forced displacement while conducting fieldwork in Uganda in 2010. Working with the Refugee Law Project in Kampala, I compiled the stories of 82 unaccompanied refugee children, predominantly from the Democratic Republic of the Congo. Many of the children had witnessed the murder of parents and siblings; many of the girls had been raped repeatedly; several were pregnant as a result of sexual abuse. All faced countless obstacles in their search for a better life. Although the stories of these children do not feature in the pages that follow, they have provided the drive and inspiration both for this book and for my broader work on issues confronting refugee children.

This book explores the relationship between international refugee law and international law on the rights of the child. It is fitting, then, to begin with the three individuals who introduced me to these areas of law: Michelle Foster, Jim Hathaway and John Tobin. I owe a great personal and intellectual debt to each of them. In my formative academic years they provided a constant source of challenge and encouragement. They are both my harshest critics and my greatest source of inspiration. Together they have shaped much of the thinking contained in this book.

This book started its life as a doctoral thesis, completed at the University of Cambridge in 2015. My doctoral supervisor, Guglielmo Verdirame, was an engaged, thoughtful and always patient sounding board for the ideas explored in the book. He has read and commented upon numerous drafts, and challenged me to stand back and approach issues from a fresh angle. My thesis was examined by Colin Harvey and Sarah Nouwen, who, in addition to facilitating a stimulating and enjoyable viva, provided detailed comments, which assisted in preparing the thesis for publication.

The funding for my doctoral research was provided by the W M Tapp Studentship in Law (Gonville and Caius College) and the Poynton Cambridge Australia Scholarship (Cambridge Australia Trust). My doctoral studies would not have been possible without the generous support that these scholarships provided. A special thanks to Pippa Rogerson for her support and guidance during my time at Gonville and Caius, and to Alison Hirst for dealing with my many and varied administrative queries.

More generally, I have received support and encouragement from an extraordinarily giving community of refugee and human rights academics and practitioners. I am particularly grateful to the following for their guidance at various stages of the project: Deborah Anker, Syd Bolton, Jonathan Bonnitcha, Jason Corrall, Cathryn Costello, Catherine Dauvergne, Guy Goodwin-Gill, Rodger Haines, Barbara Harrell-Bond, Raza Husain, David Heaton, Catriona Jarvis, Jonathan Ketcheson, Stephen Kosmin, Tillman Löhr, Jane McAdam, Tony North, Katie O'Byrne, Kate Purcell, Cheryl Saunders, Marina Sharpe and Sarah Spencer. James Crawford and Zach Douglas provided generous feedback on my first-year doctoral paper. Special thanks are owed to David Heaton, Alexandra Whelan, Nick Petrie and Kara Connolly, who provided invaluable assistance in proofreading and indexing the manuscript.

One of the greatest challenges in researching this book was the identification and indexing of over 2,500 decisions involving refugee children. I am grateful to Tina Bridge, Catriona Jarvis and Sarah Marsden for their assistance in identifying cases from the Australian Refugee Review Tribunal, the United Kingdom Upper Tribunal and the Immigration and Refugee Board of Canada respectively. I am particularly grateful to the Princess Diana Trust for providing a generous grant to allow for the development of a web resource, which collates, in an indexed and readily searchable format, the case-law and primary material drawn upon throughout this book. The website – Childref.com – is due to be launched in 2017. I am grateful to Nathan Sampimon and his team at Inspire9 for their work in designing and developing the web resource.

During my doctoral research, I was fortunate enough to spend six months as a Hauser Visiting Doctoral Researcher at New York University School of Law under the supervision of Philip Alston. My time there provided a stimulating environment to develop and deepen my thinking, and I am grateful to Philip, and to Ryan Goodman, Joseph Weiler, Martin Guggenheim and the team at the Center for Human Rights and Global Justice for support and constructive feedback during my time in New York. In addition, I spent three months as a Research Associate at Makerere University, associated with the Refugee Law Project in Kampala. As noted above, this provided me with first-hand insight into the experiences of unaccompanied refugee children, and I am grateful to Chris Dolan for affording me the privilege of working with him and his team. More recently I have been appointed as a Research Associate at the Refugee Studies Centre at the University of Oxford. I am grateful to the RSC for providing me the opportunity to present a number of the ideas developed in this book, and look forward to continuing to work with the team at the Centre.

Since 2012, I have been practising as a barrister at Blackstone Chambers in London. A huge debt of thanks is owed to the team of staff and clerks in Chambers who have both supported this project and allowed me the time to complete it. Special thanks are owed to my colleagues, who have provided invaluable support, guidance and mentorship in my transition to practice: in particular, Shaheed Fatima, Mike Fordham, Kate Gallafent, Raza Husain, Brian Kennelly and Dinah Rose.

It has been a privilege to work with the team at Cambridge University Press on this project, and I am honoured to have been selected as the inaugural publication in the new *Cambridge Asylum and Migration Studies* series, edited by Jim Hathaway. I am grateful to Finola O'Sullivan for her confidence in the project, and to Puviarassy Kalieperumal, David Morris and Rebecca Roberts for their editorial assistance, and Helen Cooper and James Diggins for their copy-editing and indexing support.

My deepest gratitude is owed to my family and friends. My friends in London, Melbourne and New York have provided unconditional friendship and support. My mum, dad, brothers and grandparents have provided a constant source of love, friendship and encouragement. And my best friend and husband Derek, who, although he has yet to read a word of the manuscript (despite a wedding vow that he would do so), has provided support in more ways than I can possibly capture in words.

The book is dedicated to my brother Luke and to my best friend Mathew.

J.M.P.
Temple, London
December 2017

SERIES EDITOR'S PREFACE

It is fitting that we launch the Cambridge Asylum and Migration Studies series with this ground-breaking analysis of the challenges faced by children seeking protection as refugees.

Children are today the majority of the world's refugees. Globally, the number of child refugees has increased from 41% of the refugee population in 2009 to 51% in 2015. The upward trajectory in states with formal asylum procedures is even more stark, with nearly three times as many children making protection claims in 2015 as in 2014.

When these children arrive, they too often encounter a protection apparatus that is oriented to adults. Many refugee children are simply invisible during the asylum procedure – assumed to be no more than an appendage of their parent, with little or no attention paid to their independent needs and rights. And even when their own claims are scrutinized – in particular when children arrive unaccompanied – the standards against which their entitlement to protection is evaluated often fail to take account of their particular vulnerabilities as children.

Jason Pobjoy's important book provides a legally compelling and creative answer to the twin challenges of invisibility and adult-centrism. Drawing on a fusion of progressive understandings of refugee law and relevant international human rights law – in particular, as codified in the Convention on the Rights of the Child – Pobjoy maps out a principled and practical approach to ensuring that children receive the protection they need and deserve.

First, Pobjoy makes the case for a legal imperative to reconceive procedural guarantees to do justice by children. Second, he addresses the three most pressing substantive challenges of navigating the refugee assessment process – showing a "well-founded fear," demonstrating that the risk rises to the level of "being persecuted," and linking the risk to a protected form of status. This part is the heart of the book – drawing on an entirely original and painstaking analysis of some 2500 refugee status decisions from leading jurisdictions. Third, Pobjoy argues convincingly that there is a duty to protect children that goes beyond refugee law, born of both the free-standing *non-refoulement* obligation and best interests of the child principle set by the Convention on the Rights of the Child.

Despite the clear logic of reading the Convention on the Rights of the Child and the Refugee Convention together when assessing the protection claims of children, Jason Pobjoy finds that fewer than 5% of the asylum decisions he analyzed did so. This is a shockingly low number. It should serve as a wake-up call to scholars, policymakers, advocates, and adjudicators – all of whom will be much better prepared to protect at-risk children after engaging with Jason Pobjoy's thoughtful and compelling *The Child in International Refugee Law*.

James C. Hathaway
Editor, Cambridge Asylum and Migration Studies

TABLE OF CASES

International Decisions

International Court of Justice

Gabčíkovo-Nagymaros Project (Hungary/Slovakia) (Judgment) [1997] ICJ Rep 7 38
Legal Consequences for States of the Continued Presence of South Africa in Namibia (South West Africa)
 Notwithstanding Security Council Resolution 276 (1970) (Advisory Opinion) [1971] ICJ Rep 16 40
Oil Platforms (Iran/US) (Merits) [2003] ICJ Rep 161 38
Territorial Dispute (Libyan Arab Jamahiriya/Chad) (Judgment) [1994] ICJ Rep 6 32

United Nations Human Rights Committee

HRC, *Communication No 886/1999*, CCPR/C/77/D/886/1999 (2003) (*'Schedko v Belarus'*) 150
HRC, *Decision: Communication No 820/1998*, CCPR/C/78/D/820/1998 (2003) (*'Rajan v New
 Zealand'*) 207
HRC, *Views: Communication No 1011/2001*, CCPR/C/81/D/1011/2001 (2004) (*'Madafferi
 v Australia'*) 207
HRC, *Views: Communication No 1069/2002*, CCPR/C/79/D/1069/2002 (2003) (*'Bakhtiyari
 v Australia'*) 73, 207
HRC, *Views: Communication No 107/1981*, CCPR/C/19/D/107/1981 (1983) (*'Quinteros Almeida
 v Uruguay'*) 150
HRC, *Views: Communication No 1222/2003*, CCPR/C/82/D/1222/2003 (2004) (*'Byahuranga
 v Denmark'*) 207
HRC, *Views: Communication No 1557/2007*, CCPR/C/102/D/1557/2007 (2011) (*'Nystrom
 v Australia'*) 73, 207
HRC, *Views: Communication No 265/1987*, CCPR/C/35/D/265/1987 (1989) (*'Vuolanne
 v Finland'*) 151, 194
HRC, *Views: Communication No 887/1999*, CCPR/C/77/D/887/1999 (2003) (*'Staselovich
 v Belarus'*) 150
HRC, *Views: Communication No 893/1999*, CCPR/C/77/D/893/1999 (2003) (*'Sahid v New
 Zealand'*) 207
HRC, *Views: Communication No 900/1999*, CCPR/C/76/D/900/1999 (2002) (*'C v Australia'*) 150,
 188
HRC, *Views: Communication No 930/2000*, CCPR/C/72/D/930/2000 (2001) (*'Winata
 v Australia'*) 73, 207
HRC, *Views: Communication No 983/2001*, CCPR/C/77/D/983/2001 (2003) (*'Love v Australia'*) 177

World Trade Organization

Panel Reports, *European Communities – Measures Affecting the Approval and Marketing of Biotech Products*, WT/DS291-3/R, WT/DS332-4/R (29 September 2006) 38, 40, 42

Regional Decisions

European Court of Human Rights

A v UK (1999) 27 EHRR 611 134
AA v UK [2012] INLR 1 209
Al-Adsani v UK (2002) 23 EHRR 11 38
Demir v Turkey (2009) 48 EHRR 54 38
E v UK (2003) 36 EHRR 519 134
Fogarty v UK (2002) 34 EHRR 12 38
Gül v Switzerland (1996) 22 EHRR 93 207
IAA v UK (2016) 62 EHRR SE19 209
Ireland v UK (1979–80) 2 EHRR 25 151
Jakupovic v Austria (2004) 38 EHRR 595 209
Jeunesse v Netherlands (2015) 60 EHRR 17 209
Loizidou v Turkey (Merits) (1996) 23 EHRR 513 38
Maslov v Austria [2009] INLR 47 207, 209
Mayeka and Mitunga v Belgium (2008) 46 EHRR 23 151, 191
McElhinney v Ireland (2002) 34 EHRR 13 38
National Union of Rail, Maritime and Transport Workers v UK (2015) 60 EHRR 10 38
Neulinger v Switzerland (2012) 54 EHRR 31 38, 208
Nunez v Norway (2014) 58 EHRR 7 209
Omojudi v UK (2010) 51 EHRR 10 209
Osman v UK (2000) 29 EHRR 245 114
Rodrigues da Silva v Netherlands (2007) 44 EHRR 34 208
Şen v Netherlands (2003) 36 EHRR 81 207, 208
Tuaquabo-Tekle v Netherlands (Application No. 60665/00, 1 December 2005) 207, 208
Üner v Netherlands (2007) 45 EHRR 14 207, 208
Z v UK (2002) 34 EHRR 97 134

Court of Justice of the European Union

'Opinion of Advocate General Cruz Villalón', Opinion in *R (MA) v SSHD*, C-648/11, EU:C:2013:367 (21 February 2013) 199
R (MA) v SSHD, C-648/11, EU:C:2013:367 (6 June 2013) 199
Zambrano v Office national de l'emploi, C-34/09, EU:C:2011:124 (8 March 2011) 207, 230

Inter-American Court of Human Rights

Juridical Status and Human Rights of the Child, Advisory Opinion OC-17/02, 28 August 2002, IACHR (Ser A) No 17 55
Rights and Guarantees of Children in the Context of Migration and/or in Need of International Protection, Advisory Opinion OC-21/14, 19 August 2014, IACHR (Ser A) No 21 227
Smith v US, Case 12.562, IACHR (Ser C) No 81/10, 12 July 2010 217

Domestic Decisions

Australia

060741183 [2006] RRTA 185 76, 176
071687786 [2007] RRTA 318 170
071775230 [2007] RRTA 343 179
0800288 [2008] RRTA 133 179
0803919 [2008] RRTA 333 176
0806954 [2009] RRTA 264 179
0807174 [2009] RRTA 1060 184
0900423 [2009] RRTA 191 179
0903098 [2009] RRTA 113 179
0903733 [2009] RRTA 1067 76
0906142 [2009] RRTA 955 141
0906198 [2009] RRTA 891 141
0909848 [2010] RRTA 216 169
1000003 [2010] RRTA 400 141
1004339 [2010] RRTA 816 141
1004814 [2010] RRTA 862 122
1004817 [2010] RRTA 862 122
1007384 [2010] RRTA 1050 179
1009355 [2011] RRTA 120 133
1100862 [2011] RRTA 291 218
1102118 [2011] RRTA 415 218
1103115 [2011] RRTA 434 218
1103242 [2011] RRTA 517 179
1106185 [2011] RRTA 844 120, 179
1113067 [2012] RRTA 982 218
1201414 [2012] RRTA 410 218
1206440 [2013] RRTA 102 218
1209930 [2012] RRTA 802 76
1211431 [2012] RRTA 975 120, 153
1304507 [2013] RRTA 342 120
Abebe v Commonwealth (1999) 197 CLR 510 98
Al Raied v MIMA [2000] FCA 1357 86
Al Raied v MIMA [2001] FCA 313 86
Appellant S395/2002 v MIMA (2003) 216 CLR 473 93
Applicant A v MIEA (1997) 190 CLR 225 30, 33, 34, 172, 174, 179
Applicant NABD of 2002 v MIMIA (2005) 216 ALR 1 28, 108
Applicant S v MIMA (2004) 217 CLR 387 174, 179
Applicant SBAP of 2001 v MIMIA [2003] FCAFC 79 154
AZAEF v MIBP [2016] FCAFC 3 50
Basile v MIAC (2011) 193 FCR 329 214
C and S v MIMA [1999] FCA 1430 183, 184
Cebreros v MIMIA [2002] AATA 213 229

Chan v MIEA (1989) 169 CLR 379 102

Chan Yee Kin v MIEA (1989) 169 CLR 379 89

Chen Shi Hai v MIMA (2000) 201 CLR 293 53, 85, 86, 101, 122, 130, 141, 158, 160, 161, 179, 180

Chen Shi Hai v MIMA [1998] FCA 622 85

Giraldo v MIMA [2001] FCA 113 184

Griffiths v Minister for Immigration [2003] FMCA 249 224

Jaffari v MIMA [2001] FCA 985 62

Lesianawai v MIAC [2012] FCA 897 214, 225

M93 of 2004 v Minister for Immigration [2006] FMCA 252 122, 142, 143, 162, 179

MIAC v SZJGV (2009) 238 CLR 642 82

MIAC v SZLSP (2010) 187 FCR 362 102

MIEA v Teoh (1995) 183 CLR 273 213, 214, 217, 224

MIMA v Chen Shi Hai (1999) 92 FCR 333 53, 85, 86, 121, 122

MIMA v Khawar (2002) 210 CLR 1 28, 104, 110, 112, 177

MIMA v Respondents S152/2003 (2004) 222 CLR 1 82, 110, 111, 114, 115, 134

MIMA v Sarrazola (No 2) (2001) 107 FCR 184 182, 183

MIMIA v SGLB (2004) 207 ALR 12 98

MIMIA v VFAY [2003] FCAFC 191 178

N03/46545 [2003] RRTA 670 142

NACM v MIMIA [2003] FCA 1554 161

Nweke v MIAC [2012] FCA 266 214, 224, 225

Odhiambo v MIMA [2002] FCAFC 194 62, 94

Paramananthan v MIMA (1998) 94 FCR 28 179

Re MIMIA; Ex parte Lam (2003) 214 CLR 1 214

Santhirarajah v Attorney-General [2012] FCA 940 214, 229, 236

Sarrazola v MIMA [1999] FCA 101 183

SBAH of 2001 v MIMIA [2002] FCAFC 426 50

SBAS v MIMIA [2003] FCA 528 142, 171

SFTB v MIMIA [2003] FCAFC 108 62

SGBB v MIMIA [2003] FCA 709 179

SHBB v Minister for Immigration [2003] FMCA 82 165

Spruill v MIAC [2012] FCA 1401 225

SZDAG v MIMIA [2006] FMCA 987 153

SZRLY v MIAC [2012] FCA 1459 224

Tauariki v MIAC [2012] FCA 1408 214, 225

Uelese v MIBP [2015] HCA 15 224

V95/03256 [1995] RRTA 263 183

Vaitaiki v MIEA (1998) 150 ALR 608 213, 214, 230

VFAY v Minister for Immigration [2003] FMCA 35 176, 178, 179

WAEF v MIMIA [2002] FCA 1121 94

WALT v MIMIA [2007] FCAFC 2 170

Wan v MIMA (2001) 107 FCR 133 214, 224, 229, 230, 231, 234, 235

Win v MIMA [2001] FCA 132 88, 89

WZAOT v Minister for Immigration [No 3] [2011] FMCA 967 64

X v MIMA (1999) 92 FCR 524 57, 61, 62

X v MIMA [2000] FCA 702 62

Y v MIMA [2000] FCA 703 62

Canada

A95-00633 (IRB, 28 January 1998) 163, 176, 179

A99-00215, A99-00256 and A99-00258 (IRB, 30 September 1999) 145, 147

A99-00575, A99-00576 and A99-00577 (IRB, 29 December 2000) 67, 68

A99-00789, A99-00790, A99-00791, A99-00792 and A99-00793 (IRB, 8 April 2002) 137

A99-00918 and A99-00919 (IRB, 20 March 2000) 70, 147

AA0-00661, AA0-00662, AA0-00663, AA0-00664 and AA0-00665 (IRB, 11 January 2001) 67, 68, 183

Ahmad v Canada (MCI) [2008] FCJ No 814 225

Akhter v Canada (MCI) [2000] FTR LEXIS 561 65

Akyol v Canada (MCI) 2014 FC 1252 228, 229, 232

Al Asali v Canada (MPSEP) 2007 FC 991 65

Alcocer v Canada (MCI) [2013] FCJ No 2 229

Ali v Canada (MCI) (1996) 119 FTR 258 142

AMC v Canada (MCI) 2011 FC 1012 65

Awolope v Canada (MCI) [2010] FCJ No 645 230

Badran v Canada (MCI) (1996) 111 FTR 211 184

Baker v Canada (MCI) [1999] 2 SCR 817 57, 75, 214, 215, 217, 220, 225, 234

Basak v Canada (MCI) [2005] FCJ No 1839 88

Bautista v Canada (MCI) 2014 FC 1008 232

Bueckert v Canada (MCI) 2011 FC 1042 67, 76, 126, 135, 139

C95-00441 (IRB, 17 December 1996) 86

Cadena v Canada (MPSEP) 2012 FC 67 241

Canada (Attorney General) v Ward [1993] 2 SCR 689 28, 35, 36, 91, 104, 109, 111, 165, 173, 174, 177

Canada (MCI) v Li [2001] FCJ No 620 176

Canada (MCI) v Lin [2001] FCJ No 1574 118

Canada (MCI) v Lin [2001] FCJ No 609 133

Canada (MCI) v Oh [2009] FCJ No 640 179

Canada (MCI) v Patel 2008 FC 747 84, 85, 96, 132, 149, 230

Canada (MCI) v Smith [1999] 1 FC 310 133

Casetellanos v Canada (Solicitor General) [1995] 2 FC 190 67, 68, 70, 182

Charles v Canada (MCI) 2007 FC 103 137, 139

Chandidas v Canada (MCI) 2013 FC 258 232

Chehar v Canada (MCI) [1997] FTR LEXIS 3234 64

Cheung v Canada (MEI) [1993] 2 FC 314 65, 68, 129, 179

Children's Aid Society of Toronto v MM [2010] OJ No 2550 237

Cho v Canada (MCI) 2009 FC 70 137

Coomaraswamy v Canada (MCI) 2002 FC 501 64

Cordeiro v Canada (MCI) [2004] FCJ No 179 215

Cruz v Canada (MCI) [2012] FCJ No 650 64

Csonka v Canada (MEI) 2001 FCT 915 64, 65

De Guzman v Canada (MCI) [2006] 3 FCR 655 70, 215

Denis v Canada (MCI) 2015 FC 65 215

Diakité v Canada (MCI) [2009] FCJ No 217 220, 229, 230

Duka v Canada (MCI) [2010] FCJ No 1334 220

EB v Canada (MCI) [2011] FCJ No 134 220

Ek v Canada (MCI) [2003] FCJ No 680 220, 231

Elmi v Canada (MEI) [1999] FCJ No 336 240

Espinoza v Canada (MCI) [1999] 3 FC 73 64

Etienne v Canada (MCI) 2014 FC 937 229, 232

Ezedunor v Canada (MCI) 2015 FC 783 160

Feng Chai Li v Canada (MCI) [2001] FCJ No 1710 97, 98

Ferrer v Canada (MCI) [2009] FCJ No 440 220, 225

Ganji v Canada (MCI) (1997) 135 FTR 283 65, 67, 91

Garasova v Canada (MCI) (1999) 177 FTR 76 215, 224

Garcia v Canada (MCI) 2011 FC 1080 65

Gengeswaran v Canada (MCI) (1999) 169 FTR 148 65

Gilbert v Canada (MCI) 2010 FC 1186 65

Gill v Canada (MCI) [2008] FCJ No 780 220

Gonsalves v Canada (MCI) 2008 FC 844 65

Gordon v Goertz [1996] 2 SCR 27 223

Gutierrez v Canada (MCI) [2000] FCJ No 636 183

Hawthorne v Canada (MCI) [2003] 2 FC 555 215, 216, 225, 227, 229

Hernandez v Canada (MCI) 2010 FC 179 144

Hinzman v Canada (MCI) [2009] FCJ No 521 220

Houareau v Canada (MCI) (1996) 108 FTR 71 50

IECC v Canada (MCI) [2006] FCJ No 409 138

Inniss v Canada (MCI) 2015 FC 567 232

Iruthayathas v Canada (MCI) (1994) 82 FTR 154 65

Jabari v Canada (MCI) [2008] FCJ No 295 85

Jaroslav v Canada (MCI) 2011 FC 634 143

JB v Canada (MCI) 2011 FC 210 137, 143

Jean v Canada (MCI) [2010] FCJ No 769 177

Jiminez v Canada (MCI) 2015 FC 527 232

JNJ v Canada (MPSEP) 2010 FC 1088 132, 137

Joe v Canada (MCI) [2009] FCJ No 176 220

Jones v Canada (MCI) 2015 FC 419 224, 225

Joseph v Canada (MCI) 2013 FC 993 232

Judnarine v Canada (MCI) [2013] FCJ No 61 229

Kalu v Canada (MCI) [2008] FCJ No 488 97

Kamalraj v Canada (MCI) [2000] Fed Ct Trial LEXIS 932 65

Kambo v Canada (MCI) [2012] FCJ No 936 232

Kaneza v Canada (MCI) 2015 FC 231 220

Kaniz v Canada (MCI) [2013] FCJ No 63 64

Kanthasamy v Minister of Citizenship and Immigration [2015] 3 SCR 909 220, 223, 225, 229, 230

Katwaru v Canada (MCI) 2007 FC 612 137

Katwaru v Canada (MCI) 2010 FC 196 82

Khader v Canada (MCI) [2013] FCJ No 359 227

Khadra Hassan Farah (IRB, 10 May 1994) 126, 133, 135, 145, 146, 176

Kim v Canada (MCI) [2007] FCJ No 1399 198, 230

Kim v Canada (MCI) [2011] 2 FCR 448 47, 116, 123, 125, 156

Kisana v Canada (MCI) [2009] FCJ No 713 220

Kobita v Canada (MCI) [2012] FCJ No 1580 220

Kolosovs v Canada (MCI) [2008] FCJ No 211 215, 225, 230

Koud v Canada (MCI) 2001 FCT 856 220

Kukunov v Canada (MCI) 2001 FCT 1377 67

Legault v Canada (MCI) [2002] 4 FC 358 215, 225

Leobrera v Canada (MCI) [2010] FCJ No 692 220

Li v Canada (MCI) (2000) 198 FTR 81 128, 133, 176,

Li v Canada (MPSEP) 2016 FC 451 224, 225

Lorne v Canada (MCI) 2006 FC 384 88, 133, 138, 139

Lu v Canada (MCI) 2004 FC 1517 64

Lu v Canada (MCI) 2016 FC 175 220

Lauture v Canada (MCI) 2015 FC 336 220

M99-04586, M99-04587, M99-04588 and M99-04589 (IRB, 21 December 1999) 67

M99-07094, M99-07096 and M99-07098 (IRB, 31 May 2001) 126, 145, 146, 184

MA0-10045 and MA0-10446 (IRB, 7 December 2001) 67

MA0-10528 and MA0-10529 (IRB, 29 October 2001) 138

MA1-00356, MA1-00357 and MA1-00358 (IRB, 18 December 2001) 133, 137, 146

MA1-07929 (IRB, 13 March 2002) 133

MA1-11675, MA1-11676 and MA1-11677 (IRB, 16 June 2003) 126, 152, 184

MA2-10373 (IRB, 12 June 2003) 133

MA3-08450 and MA3-08451 (IRB, 4 April 2004) 67, 76

Macias v Canada (MCI) 2004 FC 1749 183

Makias v Canada (MPSEP) [2008] FCJ No 1534 220

Malchikov v Canada (MCI) 120 FTR 138 117

Mangru v Canada (MCI) [2011] FCJ No 978 215

Manoharan v Canada (MCI) 2003 FC 871 65

Matthews v Canada (MCI) 2008 FC 770 148

MFD v Canada (MCI) [2001] FCJ No 771 97

Mikiani v Canada (MCI) 2005 FC 1285 65

Mileva v Canada (MEI) [1991] 3 FC 398 68

Mohacsi v Canada (MCI) [2003] 4 FC 772 64, 65

Mulaja v Canada (MCI) 2004 FC 1296 65

Nahimana v Canada (MCI) [2006] FCJ No 219 96

Nam v Canada (MCI) 2010 FC 783 65

Naredo v Canada (MCI) [2000] FCJ No 1250 220

Neethinesan v Canada (MCI) 2004 FC 138 65

Newton v Canada (MCI) (2000) 182 FTR 294 50

Ngani v Canada (MCI) 2016 FC 167 97

Ni v Canada (MCI) [2001] FCJ No 1711 96

Nikolov v Canada (MCI) 2003 FCT 231 65

Noh v Canada (MCI) 2012 FC 529 220

Norbert v Canada (MCI) 2014 FC 409 220

Okoloubu v Canada (MCI) [2008] FCJ No 1495 215

Pacificador v Canada (MCI) [2003] FCJ No 1864 93

Patel v Canada (MCI) [2005] FCJ No 1305 198, 220

PGS v Canada (MCI) [2012] FCJ No 10 225

Pour-Shariati v Canada (MEI) (1997) 215 NR 174 68

Pour-Shariati v Canada (MEI) [1995] 1 FC 767 68, 82

Pushpanathan v Canada (MCI) [1998] 1 SCR 982 36

Qiu v Canada (MCI) [2009] FCJ No 790 94, 170

Rafizade v Canada (MCI) (1995) 92 FTR 55 67

Ramsawak v Canada (MCI) [2009] FCJ No 1387 220

Raposo v Canada (MCI) [2005] FCJ No 157 215

Richards v Canada (MCI) 2011 FC 1391 50, 97

Ruiz v Canada (MCI) 2012 FC 258 88, 126

SA v Canada (MCI) 2010 FC 344 132

SBG v Canada (MCI) 2001 FC 648 142

Sebbe v Canada (MCI) [2012] FCJ No 842 229

Seevaratnam v Canada (MCI) (1999) 167 FTR 130 64, 65

Selvarajah v Canada (MCI) (1997) 138 FTR 237 65

Shanmuganathan v Canada (MCI) 2000 FTR LEXIS 1699 120, 122

SI v Canada (MCI) [2004] FCJ No 2015 97

Simoes v Canada (MCI) 2000 FTR LEXIS 948 75

SRH v Canada (MCI) [2012] FCJ No 1372 64

SSPM v Canada (MCI) [2013] FCJ No 1391 121, 132

Sun v Canada (MCI) [2012] FCJ No 218 220, 229

Suppiah v Canada (MCI) 2008 FC 1170 65

Swartz v Canada (MCI) 2002 FCT 268 220

T91-01497 and T91-01498 (IRB, 9 August 1994) 126, 135, 152,
     164, 176, 177

T92-01497 and T91-01498 (IRB, 9 August 1994) 152

T93-02403 (IRB, 15 March 1994) 96

T93-09636, T93-09638 and T93-09639 (IRB, 26 January 1994) 126, 145, 146,
     164, 176, 177

T93-12579 and T93-12586 (IRB, 25 July 1995) 121, 176

T94-00001, T94-00002, T94-00003 and T94-00004 (IRB, 17 May 1994) 184

T94-00416, T94-00418 and T94-00419 (IRB, 25 August 1994) 152, 164, 176

T95-00479 (IRB, 5 July 1996) 85

T95-01010, T95-01011 and T95-01012 (IRB, 30 July 1996) 67, 68, 76

T95-01828 and T95-01829 (IRB, 1 October 1996) 142, 153

T95-05227 and T95-05228 (IRB, 2 July 1996) 152

T96-02166 and T96-02168 (IRB, 14 May 1997) 130, 180

T96-04645 (IRB, 25 August 1997) 179

T96-06291 and T96-06292 (IRB, 2 September 1997) 179

T97-00096, T97-00097 and T97-00098 (IRB, 22 January 1998) 67, 143

T97-05827 (IRB, 16 July 1998) 240

T98-00366 (IRB, 18 January 1999) 240

T98-03163, T98-03164 and T98-03165 (IRB, 7 May 2001) 121, 183

T98-09341 and T98-09342 (IRB, 16 September 1999) 133, 149

T98-09801 (IRB, 11 March 1999) 86

T99-11540 and T99-11541 (IRB, 31 May 2001) 139, 146

T99-11706, T99-11707 and T99-11708 (IRB, 26 January 2001) 97

T99-14088 (IRB, 17 July 2000) 133

TA0-03535 (IRB, 1 May 2001) 132

TA0-05472 (IRB, 30 May 2001) 136, 137, 179

TA1-03656, TA1-03657 and TA1-03658 (IRB, 19 December 2002) 101, 142,
  144, 153, 156
TA2-00795 (IRB, 2 December 2002) 98, 137
TA4-16915 (IRB, 16 March 2006) 164
TA6-06827 (IRB, 7 February 2007) 86, 98
Taj v Canada (MCI) [2004] FCJ No 880 88
Taylor v Canada (MCI) 2016 FC 21 225, 229, 232
Toney v Canada (MPSEP) [2009] FCJ No 1128 220
Trach v Canada (MCI) 2015 FC 282 232
U94-04870, U94-04871, U94-04872 and U94-04873 (IRB, 19 July 1996) 147, 184
U95-03968 and U95-03969 (IRB, 28 August 1996) 166
U97-00946 and U97-00947 (IRB, 21 January 1998) 67
Ultima v Canada (MCI) 2013 FC 81 240
Uthayakumar v Canada (MCI) [1999] FCJ No 1013 85, 98
V91-00998 (IRB, 15 November 1991) 144
V93-02093 (IRB, 4 May 1994) 155
V96-02102 and V96-02103 (IRB, 28 May 1999) 146
V97-00156 and V97-00962 (IRB, 23 July 1998) 137
V97-00156 and V97-00962 (IRB, 28 May 1998) 163, 176
V97-00708, V97-00709, V97-00710 and V97-00711 (IRB, 11 August 1998) 152, 179
V97-01419, V97-01420, V97-01421, V98-02335, V98-02345 and V98-02346 (IRB, 9 August 1999) 126,
  145, 146, 179
V97-03500 (IRB, 31 May 1999) 126, 135, 139, 147, 148, 163, 179
V98-00787 (IRB, 4 June 1999) 152, 155, 179, 180
V99-02926 and V99-02950 (IRB, 9 May 2000) 126, 133
V99-02929 (IRB, 21 February 2000) 126, 133, 137, 138, 164,
  176, 177
V99-02943 (IRB, 12 May 2000) 129
V99-03528 (IRB, 27 January 2000) 129
V99-03532 (IRB, 12 October 2001) 129, 176
VA0-00091 (IRB, 29 May 2000) 184
VA0-02635 (IRB, 22 March 2001) 86, 126, 132, 138, 176
VA1-00781 (IRB, 22 February 2002) 118
VA1-02828, VA1-02826, VA1-02827 and VA1-02829 (IRB, 27 February 2003) 67, 126,
  142, 143
VA1-03231, VA1-03232 and VA1-03233 (IRB, 12 March 2003) 67, 141
VA3-01886, VA3-01887, VA3-01888 and VA3-01889 (IRB, 5 February 2004) 67
VA8-04301 and VA8-04302 (IRB, 28 July 2009) 130
Vasquez v Canada (MCI) 2002 FCT 413 227
Voskova v Canada (MCI) [2011] FCJ No 1682 85, 86, 93, 97, 126
Williams v Canada (MCI) [2012] FCJ No 184 225, 229, 230
Xiao v Canada (MCI) [2001] FCJ No 349 159, 176
Yaabe v Canada (MCI) [1997] FCJ No 1633 91, 165
Yoo v Canada (MCI) 2009 FC 343 220
Yusuf v Canada (MEI) [1992] 1 FC 629 84, 89
Zakar v Canada (MCI) 2005 FC 1016 64, 65, 91, 135
Zhu v Canada (MCI) 2001 FCT 884 126, 133, 138, 159

Ireland

AN (Nwole) v Minister for Justice, Equality and Law Reform [2007] IESC 44 69
D (a minor) v Refugee Appeals Tribunal & Anor [2011] IEHC 431 141

New Zealand

A v Chief Executive, Department of Labour [2001] NZAR 981 75, 216
AB (Germany) [2012] NZIPT 800107 105, 170, 171
AC (Czech Republic) [2012] NZIPT 800183–186 147
AD (Czech Republic) [2012] NZIPT 500876 67, 76, 218, 232
AD (Nigeria) [2012] NZIPT 500451 218
AE (Hungary) [2012] NZIPT 800325–327 144
AF (South Africa) [2011] NZIPT 800100–102 155
AH (Iran) [2011] NZIPT 500395 67, 218
AH (South Africa) [2011] NZIPT 500228 218, 237
AI (South Africa) [2011] NZIPT 800050–53 153, 155
AK (Iraq) [2015] NZIPT 800716–720 147
AK (Brazil) [2016] NZIPT 800834–35 92, 137
AN (Pakistan) [2013] NZIPT 800422–426 183
BL (Iran) [2012] NZIPT 500963 67, 76, 218, 232
BP (Iran) [2012] NZIPT 500965 67, 76, 218, 232
Chief Executive, Ministry of Business, Innovation and Employment v Liu [2014] NZCA 37 75
CR (Iran) [2013] NZIPT 500795 230
DF (Iran) [2014] NZIPT 800646–647 170
Ding v Minister of Immigration (2006) 25 FRNZ 568 216
DQ (Iran) [2015] NZIPT 800868 126, 146, 171
DR (Iran) [2015] NZIPT 502356 237
Elika v Minister of Immigration [1996] 1 NZLR 741 216
Helu v Immigration and Protection Tribunal and Minister of Immigration [2015] NZSC 28 237
Huang v Minister of Immigration [2008] NZCA 377 75
Huang v Minister of Immigration [2009] NZSC 77 216
Liu v Chief Executive, Department of Labour [2012] NZHC 2753 74, 75
Loumoli v Minister of Immigration [2012] NZIPT 500442 237
Manase v Minister of Immigration [2012] NZIPT 500522 237
Puli'uvea v Removal Review Authority [1996] 3 NZLR 538 216
Puli'uvea v Removal Review Authority (1996) 14 FRNZ 322 216
Refugee Appeal No 70695/97 (RSAA, 30 April 1998) 198
Refugee Appeal No 71427/99 (RSAA, 16 August 2000) 110, 114, 115
Refugee Appeal No 72635/01 (RSAA, 6 September 2002) 161, 162
Refugee Appeal No 72668 (RSAA, 5 April 2002) 89
Refugee Appeal No 74665/03 [2005] INLR 68 106, 107
Refugee Appeal No 76344 (RSAA, 24 July 2009) 169, 171
Refugee Appeal No 77074 (RSAA, 17 September 1996) 89
Refugee Appeal Nos 72072/2000 and 72073/2000 (RSAA, 7 December 2000) 126
Refugee Appeal Nos 73898 and 73899 (RSAA, 9 November 2004) 183
Refugee Appeal Nos 73931, 73932 and 73933 (RSAA, 21 February 2005) 67

Refugee Appeal Nos 74046, 74047, 74048 and 74049 (RSAA, 30 June 2005) 183

Refugee Appeal Nos 74122, 74123, 74124 and 74125 (RSAA, 23 June 2005) 67

Refugee Appeal Nos 74580, 74579 and 74578 (RSAA, 13 October 2003) 67

Refugee Appeal Nos 74632 and 74633 (RSAA, 27 June 2003) 156

Refugee Appeal Nos 74862, 74863, 74864 and 74865 (RSAA, 19 February 2004) 67

Refugee Appeal Nos 74957 and 74958 (RSAA, 12 May 2004) 146

Refugee Appeal Nos 75045, 75046 and 75047 (RSAA, 6 September 2004) 67, 68

Refugee Appeal Nos 75186 and 75187 (RSAA, 30 November 2005) 147

Refugee Appeal Nos 75301, 75302 and 75303 (RSAA, 24 January 2006) 126, 136, 145, 146, 163, 176

Refugee Appeal Nos 75805 and 75806 (IRB, 30 November 2007) 135

Refugee Appeal Nos 75805 and 75806 (RSAA, 30 November 2007) 184

Refugee Appeal Nos 75829, 75830, 75831, 75832 and 75833 (RSAA, 7 March 2007) 144

Refugee Appeal Nos 75940, 75941, 75942 and 75943 (RSAA, 15 October 2007) 92

Refugee Appeal Nos 76083, 76084 and 76085 (RSAA, 27 June 2008) 170

Refugee Appeal Nos 76226 and 76227 (RSAA, 12 January 2009) 126, 131, 145, 163, 176

Refugee Appeal Nos 76305, 76306, 76307 and 76308 (RSAA, 30 June 2010) 92, 142, 143, 176

Refugee Appeal Nos 76352, 76353 and 76354 (RSAA, 26 January 2010) 141

Refugee Appeal Nos 76380, 76381, 76382 and 76383 (RSAA, 30 June 2010) 67, 126, 144

Refugee Appeal Nos 76410 and 76411 (RSAA, 14 December 2009) 137

Refugee Appeal Nos 76478, 76479, 76480 and 76481 (RSAA, 11 June 2010) 67

Refugee Appeal Nos 76485, 76486 and 76487 (RSAA, 17 June 2010) 67, 183, 184, 185

Refugee Appeal Nos 76494 and 76495 (RSAA, 23 November 2010) 126, 145, 163, 176

Singh v Minister of Immigration [2012] NZIPT 500067 237

Tavita v Minister of Immigration [1994] 2 NZLR 257 75, 216

Vaitaiki v Minister of Immigration [2012] NZIPT 500060 237

X v RSAA [2009] NZCA 488 30

Ye v Minister of Immigration [2008] NZCA 291 75, 216, 227, 229, 230, 233, 234

Ye v Minister of Immigration [2009] NZSC 76 57, 216, 224, 227, 229, 230, 234, 236

Zanzoul v Removal Review Authority [2009] NZHC 687 75

South Africa

M v State [2007] ZACC 18 47

United Kingdom

AA (AP) v SSHD [2014] CSIH 35 225

AA (unattended children) Afghanistan CG [2012] UKUT 00016 92, 96, 148, 169, 210, 230

AAN (Malawi) v SSHD [2012] CSOH 151 210

Abdul v SHHD [2016] UKUT 00106 202

Adan v SSHD [1999] 1 AC 293 33, 34, 110

AJ (Bangladesh) v SSHD [2013] EWCA Civ 493 211, 230

AJ (Liberia) v SSHD [2006] EWCA Civ 1736 155

Ali v Head Teacher and Governors of Lord Grey School [2006] 2 AC 363 139

Al-Sirri v SSHD [2013] 1 AC 745 30

AM and BM (Trafficked Women) Albania CG [2010] UKUT 80 147

Atkinson v SSHD [2004] EWCA Civ 846 114

CA v SSHD [2004] EWCA Civ 1165 51, 224

CW (Jamaica) v SSHD [2013] EWCA Civ 915 211

DK v SSHD [2006] EWCA Civ 682 114

DS (Afghanistan) v SSHD [2011] EWCA Civ 305 96, 148, 176, 179, 212, 222

E v Chief Constable of the Royal Ulster Constabulary [2009] 1 AC 536 191

E-A v SSHD [2011] UKUT 00315 207

EB (Kosovo) v SSHD [2009] 1 AC 1159 209

Eliassen v Eliassen [2011] EWCA Civ 361 210

EM (Lebanon) v SSHD [2009] 1 AC 1198 66, 144, 146

Entry Clearance Officer v T [2011] UKUT 00483 211

EU (Afghanistan) v SSHD [2013] EWCA Civ 32 222

EV (Philippines) and another v SSHD [2014] EWCA Civ 874 232, 233, 235

FA (Iraq) v SSHD [2010] 1 WLR 2545 222

FM (Afghanistan) v SSHD (Upper Tribunal, AA/01079/2010, 10 March 2011) 119, 120, 126, 135, 148, 166, 176, 184, 207, 211, 212, 229, 230

Fornah v SSHD [2005] 1 WLR 3773 118

Fornah v SSHD [2007] 1 AC 412 9, 28, 33, 36, 118, 126, 133, 138, 157, 158, 160, 161, 173, 174, 179, 183, 185

GS v SSHD [2012] UKUT 00397 191

H (H) v Deputy Prosecutor of the Italian Republic, Genoa [2013] 1 AC 338 57, 210, 227, 230, 231, 233, 234, 235, 236, 237

H v Lord Advocate [2013] 1 AC 413 210, 230

HJ (Iran) v SSHD [2011] 1 AC 596 28, 36, 104, 165

HK (Afghanistan) v SSHD [2012] EWCA Civ 315 96, 148

Horvath v SSHD [2000] INLR 15 102, 110, 158

Horvath v SSHD [2001] 1 AC 489 28, 104, 109, 110, 111, 112, 114, 136

HS (Homosexuals: Minors, Risk on Return) Iran [2005] UKAIT 00120 117

HS v SSHD [2010] CSIH 97 212

IE v SSHD [2013] CSOH 142 210, 232

In the matter of N (Children) [2016] UKSC 15 202

JA (child – risk of persecution) Nigeria [2016] UKUT 00560

Jakitay v SSHD (IAT, Appeal No 12658, 15 November 1995) 93, 176

Januzi v SSHD [2006] 2 AC 426 33, 34

JO and others (section 55 duty) Nigeria [2014] UKUT 00517 212, 225, 227

Johnson v SSHD 2005 SLT 393 118

JW (China) v SSHD [2013] EWCA Civ 1526 210

KA (Afghanistan) v SSHD [2013] 1WLR 615 148, 176, 222

KA (domestic violence – risk on return) Pakistan CG [2010] UKUT 216 146

Kacaj v SSHD [2001] INLR 354 189

King v Bristow Helicopters [2002] 2 AC 628 29

Kovac v SSHD (IAT, 15 February 2000) 114

LD v SSHD [2010] UKUT 278 209, 210, 229, 230, 231

KS (benefit of the doubt) [2014] UKUT 00552

Lee v SSHD [2011] EWCA Civ 348 211, 235

LQ (Age: immutable characteristic) Afghanistan [2008] UKAIT 0005 148, 176, 177, 179, 180, 181

Mathieson v Secretary of State for Work and Pensions [2015] 1 WLR 3250 196

MD (Guinea) v SSHD [2009] EWCA Civ 733 95

MK (best interests of child) India [2011] UKUT 00475 212, 224, 229, 230, 233, 238

MK (Lesbians) v SSHD [2009] UKAIT 0036 154

MK (section 55 – Tribunal options) Sierra Leone [2015] UKUT 00223 212, 223, 225

Moohan and another v Lord Advocate [2015] AC 901 38

MS (Somalia) v SSHD [2010] EWCA Civ 1236 68

Mukendi v SSHD [2002] UKIAT 06741 166

Mundeba v Entry Clearance Officer, Nairobi [2013] UKUT 00088 211

Muse v Entry Clearance Officer [2012] EWCA Civ 10 211

Noune v SSHD [2000] EWCA Civ 306 114

Ogundimu v SSHD [2013] UKUT 00060 211

Omotunde v SSHD [2011] UKUT 00247 211, 230

R (AA) v Upper Tribunal [2012] EWHC 1784 (Admin) 211, 226

R (ABC) (a minor) (Afghanistan) v SSHD [2011] EWHC 2937 (Admin) 199, 226

R (Al-Saadoon) v Secretary of State for Defence [2015] 3 WLR 503 38

R (AN) (a child) v SSHD [2012] EWCA Civ 1636 98, 236

R (B) v SSHD [2010] EWHC 2571 (Admin) 207

R (BN) v SSHD [2011] EWHC 2367 (Admin) 235

R (BT) v SSHD [2011] EWCA Civ 1446 199

R (Cheung Yew Mine) v SSHD [2011] EWHC 2337 (Admin) 207

R (EM) (Eritrea) v SSHD [2013] 1 WLR 576 212

R (European Roma Rights Centre) v Immigration Officer at Prague Airport [2005] 2 AC 1 34

R (Hoxha) v Special Adjudicator [2005] 1 WLR 1063 132

R (Mansoor) v SSHD [2011] EWHC 832 (Admin) 234, 235, 236

R (Meaza Asefa) v SSHD [2012] EWHC 56 (Admin) 210, 229, 234, 235

R (Mozaffar) v SSHD [2014] EWCA Civ 854 237

R (MXL) v SSHD [2010] EWHC 2397 (Admin) 209, 211, 234

R (Osmani) v Immigration Adjudicator [2001] EWHC 1087 (Admin) 87

R (Reece-Davis) v SSHD [2011] EWHC 561 (Admin) 211

R (SS) v SSHD [2011] EWHC 3390 (Admin) 211

R (SG and others) v Secretary of State for Work and Pensions [2015] 1 WLR 1449 6, 23, 38, 196, 197, 237

R (SQ) (Pakistan) v Upper Tribunal Immigration and Asylum Chamber [2013] EWCA Civ 1251 191

R (ST) v SSHD [2010] 1 WLR 2858 2

R (ST) v SSHD [2012] 2 AC 135 33

R (Tinizaray) v SSHD [2011] EWHC 1850 (Admin) 211, 229

R (TS) v SSHD [2010] EWHC 2614 (Admin) 199, 212, 229, 230

R (Ullah) v Special Adjudicator [2004] 2 AC 323 28, 104

R (ZAT and ors) v SSHD [2016] UKUT 61 199

R v Asfaw [2008] 1 AC 1061 33, 34

R v Edmundson (1859) 28 LJ MC 213 173

R v Immigration Appeal Tribunal; Ex parte Shah [1997] Imm AR 145 37

R v SSHD; Ex parte Adan [1999] 3 WLR 1274 30

R v SSHD; Ex parte Adan [2001] 2 AC 477 30

R v SSHD; Ex parte Sivakumaran [1988] AC 958 89

RA (AP) v SSHD [2011] CSOH 68 199, 240

RA v SSHD [2015] EWCA Civ 679 202

RA v SSHD [2015] UKUT 00242 66

RA v SSHD [2015] UKUT 00292 202, 212

Re E (a child) [2009] 1 AC 536 134

Re E (Children) (Abduction: Custody Appeal) [2012] 1 AC 144 210, 212

Re S (a minor) (Independent Representation) [1993] Fam 263 58

Re X (a minor) [1975] Fam 47 237

RG (Ethiopia) v SSHD [2006] EWCA Civ 339 133

RT (Zimbabwe) v SSHD [2013] 1 AC 152 28, 36, 166, 171

Sanade v SSHD [2012] UKUT 00048 211, 230, 235

SB v SSHD [2008] UKAIT 00002 164, 180

Sepet v SSHD [2001] EWCA Civ 681 31, 161

Sepet v SSHD [2003] 1 WLR 856 4, 28, 33, 37, 104, 161

Singh v Entry Clearance Officer, New Delhi [2005] QB 608 207

SQ (Pakistan) v Upper Tribunal Immigration and Asylum Chamber [2013] EWCA Civ 1251 151

SS (India) v SSHD [2010] EWCA Civ 388 207

SS (Nigeria) v SSHD [2014] 1 WLR 998 211

SS (Sri Lanka) v SSHD [2012] EWCA Civ 945 212, 224

SSHD v Fatemah Firouz Ranjbar (IAT, 28 June 1994) 138

SSHD v Nigerian Minor (IAT, Appeal No HX/27501/03, 26 January 2005) 179, 180

SSHD v ZAT and ors [2016] EWCA Civ 810 199

ST (Child Asylum Seekers: Sri Lanka) [2014] INLR 332 126

Svazas v SSHD [2002] 1 WLR 1891 12, 81, 107

SW (Lesbians) v SSHD [2011] UKUT 00251 154

T v SSHD (SIAC, Appeal No SC/31/2005, 22 March 2010) 211

TN (Afghanistan) v SSHD [2014] 1 WLR 2095 96, 222

TN v SSHD [2011] EWHC 3296 (Admin) 222

ZH (Tanzania) v SSHD [2011] 2 AC 166 38, 57, 74, 75, 210, 212, 214, 224, 227, 229, 230, 231, 234, 235, 236

ZJ (Afghanistan) v SSHD [2008] EWCA Civ 799 88, 96

Zoumbas v SSHD [2013] 1 WLR 3690 210, 233, 235

United States

Abay v Ashcroft, 368 F 3d 634 (6th Cir, 2004) 51, 85, 96, 98, 104, 133

Abebe v Ashcroft, 379 F 3d 755 (9th Cir, 2004) 51, 75, 77, 126

Abebe v Gonzales, 432 F 3d 1037 (9th Cir, 2005) 51, 52

Aguirre-Cervantes v INS, 242 F 3d 1169 (9th Cir, 2001) 132, 135, 183, 184

Air France v Saks, 470 US 392 (1985) 10

Argueta-Rodriguez v INS, 1997 US App LEXIS 29864, 12 (4th Cir, 1997) 152

Bah v Mukasey, 529 F 3d 99 (2nd Cir, 2008) 83

Barrios v Holder, 581 F 3d 849 (9th Cir, 2009) 159

Barry v Gonzales, 445 F 3d 741 (4th Cir, 2006) 50, 51

Beharry v Ashcroft, 329 F 3d 51 (2nd Cir, 2003) 217

Beharry v Reno, 183 F Supp 2d 584 (ED NY, 2002) 217

Benyamin v Holder, 579 F 3d 970 (9th Cir, 2009) 51, 52, 118

Bringas-Rodriguez v Lynch, 805 F 3d 1171, (9th Cir, 2015) 139

Brown v Board of Education of Topeka, 347 US 483 (1954) 139

Bucur v INS, 109 F 3d 399 (7th Cir, 1997) 140

Bueso-Avila v Holder, 663 F 3d 934 (7th Cir, 2011) 159

Bustami v Holder, 385 Fed Appx 719 (9th Cir, 2010) 52

Cabrera-Alvarez v Gonzales, 423 F 3d 1006 (9th Cir, 2005) 75, 217, 218

Calle v US Attorney General, 264 Fed Appx 882, 884 (11th Cir, 2008) 117

Canjura-Flores v INS, 784 F 2d 885 (9th Cir, 1985) 168

Castellano-Chacon v INS, 341 F 3d 533 (6th Cir, 2003) 172

Chen, 20 I & N Dec 16 (BIA, 1989) 83

Civil v INS, 140 F 3d 52 (1st Cir, 1998) 119, 155, 167, 168

Crespin-Valladares v Holder, 632 F 3d 117 (4th Cir, 2011) 183

Cruz-Diaz v INS, 86 F 3d 330 (4th Cir, 1996) 159, 165

Demiraj v Holder, 631 F 3d 194 (5th Cir, 2011) 159, 183, 184

Díaz Ruano v Holder, 420 Fed Appx 19 (1st Cir, 2011) 181

Dieng v Holder, 698 F 3d 866 (6th Cir, 2012) 51

Escobar v Gonzales, 417 F 3d 363 (3rd Cir, 2005) 177, 179, 180

Escobar-Batres v Holder, 385 Fed Appx 445 (11th Cir, 2010) 181

Fatin v INS, 12 F 3d 1233 (3rd Cir, 1993) 172

Firempong v INS, 766 F 2d 621 (1st Cir, 1985) 93

Fladjoe v Attorney General (US), 411 F 3d 135 (3rd Cir, 2005) 133

Flores-Cruz v Holder, 325 Fed Appx 512 (9th Cir, 2009) 181

Gatimi v Holder, 578 F 3d 611 (7th Cir, 2009) 51, 52, 175, 182

Gebremichael v INS, 10 F 3d 28 (1st Cir, 1983) 183

Gjerazi v Gonzales, 435 F 3d 800 (7th Cir, 2006) 166

Gomez-Guzman v Holder, 485 Fed Appx 64 (6th Cir, 2012) 181

Gomez-Romero v Holder, 2012 US App LEXIS 7521 (6th Cir, 2012) 159

Gonzales v Tchoukhrova, 549 US 801 (2006) 52

Gonzalez v Reno, 2000 US App LEXIS 7025 (11th Cir, 2000) 61

Gonzalez v Reno, 86 F Supp 2d 1167 (SD Fla, 2000) 48

Guaylupo-Moya v Gonzales, 432 F 3d 121 (2nd Cir, 2005) 217

Gumaneh v Mukasey, 535 F 3d 785 (8th Cir, 2008) 51

Hassan v Gonzales, 484 F 3d 513 (8th Cir, 2007) 51, 52

Hernandez-Montiel v Immigration and Naturalization Service, (2000) 225 F 3d 1084 (9th Cir, 2000) 117

Hernandez-Ortiz v Gonzales, 496 F 3d 1042 (9th Cir, 2007) 119, 120, 121, 151, 152

Hong v Attorney General, 165 Fed Appx 995 (3rd Cir, 2006) 159, 164, 180

INS v Cardoza-Fonseca, 480 US 421 (1987) 82, 89

Ixtlilco-Morales v Keisler, 507 F 3d 651 (8th Cir, 2007) 83, 178, 241

Joaquin-Porras v Gonzales, 435 F 3d 172, 174 (2nd Cir, 2006) 117

Jorge-Tzoc v Gonzales, 435 F 3d 146 (2nd Cir, 2006) 119, 121, 152

Kahssai v INS, 16 F 3d 323 (9th Cir, 1994) 120, 152, 155, 166

Kane v Holder, 581 F 3d 231 (5th Cir, 2009) 51

Kechichian v Mukasey, 535 F 3d 15 (1st Cir, 2008) 51

Khachaturyan v Ashcroft, 86 Fed Appx 207 (7th Cir, 2004) 122

Kholyavskiy v Mukassey, 540 F 3d 555 (7th Cir, 2008) 119, 142, 153

Kimumwe v Gonzales, 431 F 3d 319 (9th Cir, 2005) 94, 122

Kone v Holder, 596 F 3d 141 (2nd Cir, 2010) 51

Kone v Holder, 620 F 3d 760 (7th Cir, 2010) 51, 52

Kourouma v Holder, 588 F 3d 234 (4th Cir, 2009) 133

Lin v Ashcroft, 377 F 3d 1014 (9th Cir, 2004) 166, 183

Liu v Ashcroft, 380 F 3d 307 (7th Cir, 2004) 116, 119, 120, 122

Lopez-Soto v Ashcroft, 383 F 3d 228 (4th Cir, 2004) 184

Lukwago v Ashcroft, 329 F 3d 157 (3rd Cir, 2003) 159, 169, 177, 180

Lusingo v Gonzales, 420 F 3d 193 (3rd Cir, 2005) 93

Maerschalack v Gonzales, 159 Fed Appx 29 (10th Cir, 2005) 147

Mansour v Ashcroft, 390 F 3d 667 (7th Cir, 2004) 51, 52, 101, 102, 104, 119, 122, 126, 128, 135, 153, 170

Mashiri v Ashcroft, 2004 US App LEXIS 22714 (9th Cir, 2004) 117, 142

Matter of Chen (BIA, 1989) 170

Matter of Juan Carlos Martinez-Mejia (BIA, 1999) 132, 148

Matter of M-E-V-G-, 26 I & N Dec 388 (BIA, 2014) 182

Mejilla-Romero v Holder, 600 F 3d 63 (1st Cir, 2010) 85, 97, 99, 119, 120, 122, 148, 154, 166

Mejilla-Romero v Holder, 614 F 3d 572 (1st Cir, 2010) 85, 119

Mema v Gonzales, 474 F 3d 412 (7th Cir, 2007) 166

Mendoza-Pablo v Holder, 667 F 3d 1308 (9th Cir, 2012) 98, 119, 121, 123

Mohammed v Gonzales, 400 F 3d 785 (9th Cir, 2005) 83

Morgan v Mukasey, 529 F 3d 1202 (9th Cir, 2008) 66

Nabhani v Holder, 382 Fed Appx 487 (6th Cir, 2010) 119

N-A-M v Holder, 587 F 3d 1052 (10th Cir, 2009) 10

Ni v Holder, 635 F 3d 1014 (7th Cir, 2011) 51

Niang v Gonzales, 492 F 3d 505 (4th Cir, 2007) 51, 77

Nwaokolo v INS, 314 F 3d 303 (7th Cir, 2002) 51, 52

Oforji v Ashcroft, 354 F 3d 609 (7th Cir, 2003) 51, 52, 77

Olowo v Ashcroft, 368 F 3d 692 (7th Cir, 2004) 51, 52, 77

Olympic Airways v Husain, 540 US 644 (2004) 9

Ordonez-Quino v Holder, 760 F 3d 80 (1st Cir, 2014) 119

Perdomo v Holder, 611 F 3d 662 (9th Cir, 2010) 177

Polovchak v Meese, 774 F 2d 731 (7th Cir, 1985) 49, 50, 168

Poplavskiy v Mukasey, 271 Fed Appx 130 (2nd Cir, 2008) 119, 122

Razzak v Attorney General, 287 Fed Appx 208 (3rd Cir, 2008) 122

Re Acosta, 19 I & N Dec 211 (BIA, 1985) 172, 173, 183

Re A-K-, 24 I & N Dec 275 (BIA, 2007) 51, 52

Re A-T-, 24 I & N Dec 296 (BIA, 2007) 83

Re A-T-, 24 I & N Dec 617 (Attorney General, 2008) 83

Re Brus Funetes Ortega (BIA, 2001) 179

Re CA, 23 I & N Dec 951 (BIA, 2006) 175

Re Fauziya Kasinga, 21 I & N Dec 357 (BIA, 1996) 133, 160, 179

Re John Doe, 23 Immigration Reporter B1-159 (BIA, 2001) 132

Re Monreal-Aguinaga, 23 I & N Dec 56 (BIA, 2001) 217

Re O-Z and I-Z, 22 I & N Dec 23 (BIA, 1998) 153

Re R-A-, 22 I & N Dec 906 (BIA, 2001) 159

Re Recinas, 23 I & N Dec 467 (BIA, 2002) 217

Re S-A-, 22 I & N Dec 1328 (BIA, 2000) 132, 137, 171, 172

Re the Welfare of DAM (Minn Ct App, No A12-0427, 10 December 2012) 222

Rivera-Barrientos v Holder, 666 F 3d 641 (10th Cir, 2012) 159, 181

Rodriguez-Ramirez v Ashcroft, 398 F 3d 120 (1st Cir, 2005) 152

Rusak v Holder, 734 F 3d 894 (9th Cir, 2013) 121

S-A-K & H-A-H, 24 I & N Dec 464 (BIA, 2008) 83

Salaam v INS, 229 F 3d 1234 (9th Cir, 2000) 168

Salameda v INS, 70 F.3d 447 52

Sanchez-Trujillo v INS, 801 F 2d 1571 (9th Cir, 1986) 182

Seck v Attorney General, 663 F 3d 1356 (11th Cir, 2011) 51

S-E-G-, 24 I & N Dec 579 (BIA, 2008) 159, 169, 177, 180, 181, 182

Shi Chen v Holder, 604 F 3d 324 (7th Cir, 2010) 166, 179

Singh v Gonzales, 406 F 3d 191 (3rd Cir, 2005) 167

Singh v Holder, 638 F 3d 1264, (9th Cir, 2011) 90

Stenaj v Gonzalez, 227 Fed Appx 429 (6th Cir, 2007) 28, 104

Tchoukhrova v Gonzales, 404 F 3d 1181 (9th Cir, 2005) 50, 51, 52, 117, 120, 130, 134, 141, 144, 147, 179

Thomas v Gonzales, 409 F 3d 1177 (9th Cir, 2005) 184, 185

Timnit Daniel (BIA, 2002) 83, 119, 154, 155, 169

Unnamed File (BIA, 2003) 162

Valcu v Attorney General, 394 Fed Appx 884 (3rd Cir, 2010) 178, 241

Valdiviezo-Galdamez v Attorney General, 663 F 3d 582 (3rd Cir, 2011) 175, 181, 182

Velasquez v US Attorney General, 490 Fed Appx 266 (11th Cir, 2012) 181

Vicente v Holder, 451 Fed Appx 738 (10th Cir, 2011) 166

W-G-R-, 26 I & N 208 (BIA, 2014) 182

Winata v Holder, 2011 US App LEXIS 16962 (9th Cir, 2011) 119, 151, 152

Zhang v Gonzales, 408 F 3d 1239 (9th Cir, 2005) 166

TABLE OF TREATIES AND OTHER INTERNATIONAL INSTRUMENTS

African Charter on the Rights and Welfare of the Child, opened for signature 1 July 1990, OAU Doc CAB/LEG/24.9/49 (entered into force 29 November 1999) 125
    Art IV 196

American Convention on Human Rights, opened for signature 22 November 1969, 1144 UNTS 123 (entered into force 18 July 1978)
    Art 5 149
    Art 33 11

Cartagena Declaration on Refugees (in Inter-American Commission on Human Rights, *Annual Report of the Inter-American Commission on Human Rights*, OEA/Ser.L/V/II.66/doc.10, Rev.1 (1984–85) 186

Convention against Torture and Other Cruel, Inhuman or Degrading Treatment or Punishment, opened for signature 10 December 1984, 1465 UNTS 85 (entered into force 26 June 1987) 186, 189, 190, 191, 192, 196, 238, 241
    Art 3 188, 190
    Art 14 156
    Art 16 149

Convention Concerning the Prohibition and Immediate Action for the Elimination of the Worst Forms of Child Labor (ILO No 182), opened for signature 17 June 1999, 2133 UNTS 161 (entered into force 19 November 2000)
    Art 3 195

Convention for the Protection of Human Rights and Fundamental Freedoms, opened for signature 4 November 1950, 213 UNTS 221 (entered into force 3 September 1953), as amended 105, 151, 206, 208, 212
    Art 1 113
    Art 3 134, 149, 155, 188
    Art 8 73, 146, 206, 207, 208, 209, 210, 211, 212, 213

Convention on the Civil Aspects of International Child Abduction, opened for signature 25 October 1980, 1343 UNTS 89 (entered into force 1 December 1983) 208

Convention on the Elimination of All Forms of Discrimination against Women, opened for signature 18 December 1979, 1249 UNTS 13 (entered into force 3 September 1981) 29

Convention on the Rights of Persons with Disabilities, opened for signature 30 March 2007, 2515 UNTS 3 (entered into force 3 May 2008) 144
    Art 7 196
    Art 24 144

Convention on the Rights of the Child, opened for signature 20 November 1989, 1577 UNTS 3 (entered into force 2 September 1990) *passim*

Preamble 70, 145, 183, 226

Art 1 1, 6, 175

Art 2 6, 14, 20, 31, 113, 130, 140, 144, 157, 177, 183, 185, 188, 197, 230

Art 3 7, 8, 12, 21, 31, 46, 61, 73, 75, 80, 81, 96, 113, 124, 133, 140, 145, 146, 187, 196, 197, 198, 199, 200, 201, 202, 203, 205, 206, 209, 211, 212, 213, 217, 218, 223, 224, 225, 227, 228, 232, 234, 235, 237, 238, 240, 241

Art 4 57, 134, 140

Art 5 44, 58, 61, 83, 140, 231, 232

Art 6 7, 12, 30, 31, 128, 131, 133, 140, 148, 150, 186, 188, 189, 191, 192, 193, 196, 226, 230, 238, 241

Art 7 125, 145, 230

Art 8 230

Art 9 11, 15, 45, 46, 59, 67, 70, 72, 73, 74, 75, 76, 77, 78, 125, 127, 145, 146, 147, 196, 206, 231, 239, 240

Art 10 70, 74, 145, 231

Art 11 21, 127

Art 12 20, 28, 45, 46, 55, 56, 57, 58, 59, 60, 61, 62, 68, 75, 78, 140, 145, 146, 168, 226, 227, 239, 240

Art 13 20, 55, 108

Art 14 20, 55, 108, 140, 170, 171

Art 15 20, 55, 108, 127, 168

Art 16 46, 73, 145, 147, 207, 230, 231

Art 17 140

Art 18 61, 130, 140, 145, 147, 240

Art 19 21, 113, 130, 133, 134, 135, 136, 137, 138, 147, 150, 152, 192, 194, 230

Art 20 21, 46, 113, 130, 145, 148, 149, 196, 230, 240

Art 21 21, 46, 196

Art 22 14, 20, 21, 22, 46, 52, 54, 59, 96, 124, 197, 240

Art 23 130, 140, 144, 226

Art 24 21, 30, 113, 127, 128, 130, 133, 138, 140, 150, 152, 192, 193, 230

Art 25 230

Art 26 131, 147

Art 27 128, 131, 147, 193, 226, 230

Art 28 125, 128, 140, 141, 142, 143, 144, 193, 229

Art 29 128, 139, 140, 143, 144, 226, 229

Art 30 21, 127, 140, 143

Art 32 21, 125, 127, 133, 192

Art 34 21, 127, 133, 192, 230

Art 35 21, 127, 128, 133, 192, 230

Art 36 133, 192, 230

Art 37 7, 12, 30, 31, 46, 59, 126, 128, 129, 133, 138, 142, 150, 186, 188, 189, 191, 192, 193, 194, 196, 230, 238, 241

Art 38 21, 31, 127, 189, 191, 192, 195, 230

Art 39 46, 113, 130, 150, 155, 156

Art 40 129, 194, 196

Art 41 59, 127

Art 43 23

Art 44 23
Art 45 23
Convention Relating to the Status of Refugees, opened for signature 28 July 1951, 189 UNTS 150
   (entered into force 22 April 1954) passim
   Preamble 35
   Art 1 2, 16, 18, 22, 124, 178, 186, 188
   Art 1A 3, 4, 16, 25, 26, 33, 52, 80, 81, 88, 110, 114, 133, 145, 157, 161, 162, 164, 172, 173, 174, 182,
      185, 189, 240
   Art 1C 16, 80, 81, 240, 241
   Art 1D 16, 81
   Art 1E 16, 81
   Art 1F 16, 25, 26, 39, 50, 80, 81, 189, 241
   Art 3 10, 16
   Art 4 17, 74
   Art 5 32, 35
   Art 16 16
   Art 17 17
   Art 21 16
   Art 22 16, 17
   Art 26 16
   Art 33 11, 16, 45, 54, 188, 189, 239
   Art 34 10, 16
   Art 35 23
   Art 38 9
Council Directive 2004/83/EC of 29 April 2004 on Minimum Standards for the Qualification and Status
   of Third Country Nationals or Stateless Persons as Refugees or as Persons Who Otherwise Need
   International Protection and the Content of the Protection Granted [2004] OJ L 304/12 190, 200
Council Directive 2013/33/EU of the European Parliament and of the Council of 26 June 2013 laying
   down standards for the reception of applicants for international protection [2013] OJ L 180
   art 24 148
Council Regulation (EC) No 343/2003 of 18 February 2003 Establishing the Criteria and Mechanisms for
   Determining the Member State Responsible for Examining an Asylum Application Lodged in One of
   the Member States by a Third-Country National [2003] OJ L 50/1
   Art 6 199
Council Regulation (EC) No 604/2012 of 26 June 2013 Establishing the Criteria and Mechanisms for
   Determining the Member State Responsible for Examining an Application for International
   Protection Lodged in one of the Member States by a Third-Country National or a Stateless Person
   (Recast) [2012] OJ L 180/31
   Art 6 199
Declaration of the Rights of the Child, UNGA Res 1386 (XIV) (1959) 19
Declaration on the Protection of Women and Children in Emergency and Armed Conflict, UNGA Res
   3318 (XXIX) (1974) 19
Directive 2011/95/EU of the European Parliament and of the Council of 13 December 2011 on Standards
   for the Qualification of Third-Country Nationals or Stateless Persons as Beneficiaries of International
   Protection, for a Uniform Status for Refugees or for Persons Eligible for Subsidiary Protection, and for
   the Content of the Protection Granted [2011] OJ L 337/9 118
   Art 10 175

Art 15 190
Art 2 77
Art 4 120
Recital 18 227
Recital 27 149, 199, 240
Explanations Relating to the Charter of Fundamental Rights [2007] OJ C 303/17 202
Final Act of the United Nations Conference of Plenipotentiaries on the Status of Refugees and Stateless Persons, A/CONF.2/108/Rev.1 (1952) 17, 19, 71
Geneva Convention Relative to the Protection of Civilian Persons in Time of War, opened for signature 21 April 1949, 75 UNTS 287 (entered into force 21 October 1950) 17, 70
Geneva Declaration of the Rights of the Child (adopted 26 September 1924) [1924] LN OJ Spec Supp 21, 43 13, 19, 20, 149
International Convention on the Elimination of All Forms of Racial Discrimination, opened for signature 21 December 1965, 660 UNTS 195 (entered into force 4 January 1969) 29, 104, 106
International Covenant for the Protection of All Persons from Enforced Disappearance, opened for signature 6 February 2007, A/RES/61/177, (entered into force 12 December 2010), art 16 188
International Covenant on Civil and Political Rights, opened for signature 16 December 1966, 999 UNTS 171 (entered into force 23 March 1976) 11, 19, 20, 29, 59, 70, 104, 106, 113, 127, 128, 130, 150, 186, 188, 189, 190, 191, 192, 196, 238, 241
Art 2 113, 127, 177, 188
Art 4 20, 108, 128
Art 6 188, 190, 191, 192, 193
Art 7 113, 149, 150, 151, 188, 190, 191, 193, 194
Art 9 129, 194
Art 12 108, 127
Art 13 127
Art 14 59
Art 16 127
Art 17 73, 113, 207
Art 18 108, 127, 171
Art 19 108
Art 21 108
Art 22 108
Art 23 70, 127, 183
Art 24 19, 177
Art 26 113, 127, 177
International Covenant on Economic, Social and Cultural Rights, opened for signature 16 December 1966, 993 UNTS 3 (entered into force 3 January 1976) 11, 19, 20, 29, 104, 106, 108, 127, 128, 130, 140
Art 2 20, 113, 128, 140
Art 4 108
Art 10 19, 70, 183
Art 13 140, 143
Art 14 140
International Refugee Organization Constitution, opened for signature 15 December 1946, 18 UNTS 3 (entered into force 20 August 1948) 17, 18, 71, 203
Preamble 17

Art 2 17
Annexure 1 18
Annexure 2 17
OAU Convention Governing the Specific Aspects of Refugee Problems in Africa, opened for signature
   10 September 1969, 1001 UNTS 45 (entered into force 20 June 1974) 186
Optional Protocol to the Convention on the Rights of the Child on a Communications Procedure, opened
   for signature 28 February 2012, A/RES/66/138 (entered into force 14 April 2014) 22
*Optional Protocol to the Convention on the Rights of the Child on the Involvement of Children in Armed
   Conflict*, opened for signature 24 May 2000, 2173 UNTS 222 (entered into force
   12 February 2002) 22, 41, 106, 191, 195
Art 2 195
Art 3 31, 189, 195
Art 4 31, 189, 195
Art 7 156
*Optional Protocol to the Convention on the Rights of the Child on the Sale of Children, Child Prostitution
   and Child Pornography*, opened for signature 25 May 2000, 2171 UNTS 227 (entered into force
   18 January 2002) 22, 29, 41, 106, 128, 133
Art 1 133
Art 9 156
*Protocol Additional to the Geneva Conventions of 12 August 1949, and Relating to the Protection of
   Victims of International Armed Conflicts (Protocol I)*, opened for signature 8 June 1977, 1125 UNTS
   3 (entered into force 7 December 1978) 195
Protocol Relating to the Status of Refugees, opened for signature 31 January 1967, 606 UNTS 267
   (entered into force 4 October 1967) 9, 16, 22, 32, 53, 175, 187
Preamble 35
Rome Statute of the International Criminal Court, opened for signature 17 July 1998, 2187 UNTS 3
   (entered into force 1 July 2002) 195
Statute of the International Court of Justice, 26 June 1945, 961 UNTS 183 (entered into force
   24 October 1945) 9, 40
Art 38(1) 9, 40
Universal Declaration of Human Rights, GA Res 217(III)(A), A/810 (1948) 19, 20, 29, 35, 36, 104, 105
Art 7 59
Art 16 70, 78, 145, 183
Art 25 19
Art 26 140
Art 29 108
Vienna Convention on the Law of Treaties, opened for signature 23 May 1969, 1155 UNTS 331
   (entered into force 27 January 1980) 32, 33, 35, 36, 40
Art 4 32
Art 18 43
Art 26 32, 54
Art 27 32
Art 31 19, 23, 32, 33, 34, 35, 37, 38, 39, 40, 41, 42, 43, 106, 208, 228
Art 32 33, 39
Art 33 33

TABLE OF DOMESTIC STATUTES AND INSTRUMENTS

Australia

Migration Act 1958 (Cth) 190
  s 36 190
  s 351 218
  s 417 218
  s 501J 218
Migration Amendment (Complementary Protection) Act 2011 (Cth) 190, 191

Canada

Canada Act 1982 (UK) c 11, sch B pt I (*Canadian Charter of Rights and Freedoms*) 77
  s 15 77
Immigration Act, RSC 1985, c I-2 214
  s 114 214
Immigration and Refugee Protection Act, s 3 215
Immigration and Refugee Protection Act, SC 2001, c 27 68
  s 25 215
  s 97 190
  s 108 155
  s 167 64
Immigration and Refugee Protection Regulations, SOR/2002–227 76
  s 1 77
  s 66 77
  s 67 77
  s 68 77
  s 69 77
  s 176 76
Refugee Protection Division Rules, SOR/2012–256 64
  r 55 64
  r 56 64

Finland

Aliens Act (Finland 301/2004) 219
  s 6 219

HICOG

HICOG, *Law No 11* (reproduced in L W Holborn, *The International Refugee Organization: A Specialized Agency of the United Nations – Its History and Work, 1946–1952* (1956) 501) 204
 Art 14 204

New Zealand

Immigration Act 2009 (NZ) 216
 s 125 62
 s 130 190
 s 131 190
 s 133 62
 s 206 76, 77
 s 207 76, 77, 216,

Norway

Act No 30 of 21 May 1999 Relating to the Strengthening of the Status of Human Rights in Norwegian Law (The Human Rights Act) (Norway) 219
Act of 15 May 2008 on the Entry of Foreign Nationals into the Kingdom of Norway and Their Stay in the Realm (Immigration Act) 219
 s 29 118
 s 38 219

Sweden

Aliens Act (Sweden 2005:716) 56
 ch 1 s 10 62, 219
 ch 1 s 11 56

United Kingdom

Adoption and Children Act 2002, c 38 226
 s 1 226
Borders, Citizenship and Immigration Act 2009, c 11 209
 s 55 198, 202, 209, 211, 212,
Children Act 1989, c 41 229
 s 1 229
Immigration Rules 87
 para 351 87
 para 352ZC 221

United States

8 CFR §207 76
8 CFR §208 83, 190
8 USC §1101 82
8 USC §1229b 216

ABBREVIATIONS

Abbreviation	Term
AIT	Asylum and Immigration Tribunal (United Kingdom)
BIA	Board of Immigration Appeals (United States)
CIC	Citizenship and Immigration Canada
CJEU	Court of Justice of the European Union
DIAC	Department of Immigration and Citizenship (Australia)
DIMIA	Department of Immigration and Multicultural and Indigenous Affairs (Australia)
ECOSOC	United Nations Economic and Social Council
ECRE	European Council on Refugees and Exiles
ECtHR	European Court of Human Rights
EU	European Union
FGC	female genital cutting[1]
FGM	female genital mutilation
GLBTI	gay, lesbian, bisexual, transgender, intersex
HICOG	United States High Commission for Occupied Germany
HRC	United Nations Human Rights Committee
IACHR	Inter-American Court of Human Rights
IAT	Immigration Appeal Tribunal (United Kingdom)
ICJ	International Court of Justice
ICRC	International Committee of the Red Cross
IJ	Immigration Judge
ILC	International Law Commission
ILPA	Immigration Law Practitioners' Association (United Kingdom)
INS	United States Department of Justice Immigration and Naturalization Service
IRB	Immigration and Refugee Board of Canada
IRO	International Refugee Organization
JCHR	Joint Committee on Human Rights (United Kingdom)
MCI	Minister of Citizenship and Immigration (Canada)
MEI	Minister of Employment and Immigration (Canada)

[1] The use of the term 'female genital cutting' is adopted here rather than the more provocative alternative, 'female genital mutilation' (which appears in some quotations): see J Tobin, *The Right to Health in International Law* (2012) 315–16.

Abbreviation	Term
MIAC	Minister for Immigration and Citizenship (Australia)
MIBP	Minister for Immigration and Border Protection (Australia)
MIEA	Minister for Immigration and Ethnic Affairs (Australia)
MIMA	Minister for Immigration and Multicultural Affairs (Australia)
MIMIA	Minister for Immigration and Multicultural and Indigenous Affairs (Australia)
MPSEP	Minister of Public Safety and Emergency Preparedness (Canada)
MRT	Migration Review Tribunal (Australia)
NZIPT	New Zealand Immigration and Protection Tribunal
PTSD	post-traumatic stress disorder
RRT	Refugee Review Tribunal (Australia)
RSAA	New Zealand Refugee Status Appeals Authority
SIAC	Special Immigration Appeals Commission (United Kingdom)
SIJS	special immigrant juvenile status
SSHD	Secretary of State for the Home Department (United Kingdom)
UK	United Kingdom
UKBA	United Kingdom Border Agency
UKUT	United Kingdom Upper Tribunal
UN	United Nations
UNCEDAW	United Nations Committee on the Elimination of Discrimination against Women
UNCERD	United Nations Committee on the Elimination of Racial Discrimination
UNCESCR	United Nations Committee on Economic, Social and Cultural Rights
UNCRC	United Nations Committee on the Rights of the Child
UNHCR	United Nations High Commissioner for Refugees
UNHCR ExCom	Executive Committee of the High Commissioner's Programme
UNICEF	Fonds des Nations Unies pour l'Enfance (United Nations Children's Fund)
US	United States of America
USCIS	United States Citizenship and Immigration Services
USSR	Union of Soviet Socialist Republics
WTO	World Trade Organization

FREQUENTLY CITED SOURCES

Abbreviated Citation	Source
1924 Declaration	*Geneva Declaration of the Rights of the Child* (adopted 26 September 1924) [1924] LN OJ Spec Supp 21, 43
1951 Convention	*Convention Relating to the Status of Refugees*, opened for signature 28 July 1951, 189 UNTS 150 (entered into force 22 April 1954)
1967 Protocol	*Protocol Relating to the Status of Refugees*, opened for signature 31 January 1967, 606 UNTS 267 (entered into force 4 October 1967)
2004 Qualification Directive	*Council Directive 2004/83/EC of 29 April 2004 on Minimum Standards for the Qualification and Status of Third Country Nationals or Stateless Persons as Refugees or as Persons Who Otherwise Need International Protection and the Content of the Protection Granted* [2004] OJ L 304/12
Asylum Procedures Directive	*Council Directive 2013/32/EU of the European Parliament and of the Council of 26 June 2013 on common procedures for granting and withdrawing international protection* [2013] OJ L 180/60
CAT	*Convention against Torture and Other Cruel, Inhuman or Degrading Treatment or Punishment*, opened for signature 10 December 1984, 1465 UNTS 85 (entered into force 26 June 1987)
CEDAW	*Convention on the Elimination of All Forms of Discrimination against Women*, opened for signature 18 December 1979, 1249 UNTS 13 (entered into force 3 September 1981)
CERD	*International Convention on the Elimination of All Forms of Racial Discrimination*, opened for signature 21 December 1965, 660 UNTS 195 (entered into force 4 January 1969)
CRC	*Convention on the Rights of the Child*, opened for signature 20 November 1989, 1577 UNTS 3 (entered into force 2 September 1990)
Disability Convention	*Convention on the Rights of Persons with Disabilities*, opened for signature 30 March 2007, 2515 UNTS 3 (entered into force 3 May 2008)

Abbreviated Citation	Source
Dublin II	*Council Regulation (EC) No 343/2003 of 18 February 2003 Establishing the Criteria and Mechanisms for Determining the Member State Responsible for Examining an Asylum Application Lodged in One of the Member States by a Third-Country National* [2003] OJ L 50/1
Dublin III	*Council Regulation (EC) No 604/2012 of 26 June 2013 Establishing the Criteria and Mechanisms for Determining the Member State Responsible for Examining an Application for International Protection Lodged in one of the Member States by a Third-Country National or a Stateless Person (Recast)* [2012] OJ L 180/31
ECHR	*Convention for the Protection of Human Rights and Fundamental Freedoms*, opened for signature 4 November 1950, 213 UNTS 221 (entered into force 3 September 1953), as amended
EU Qualification Directive	*Directive 2011/95/EU of the European Parliament and of the Council of 13 December 2011 on Standards for the Qualification of Third-Country Nationals or Stateless Persons as Beneficiaries of International Protection, for a Uniform Status for Refugees or for Persons Eligible for Subsidiary Protection, and for the Content of the Protection Granted* [2011] OJ L 337/9
Home Office, *Processing Children's Asylum Claims*	Home Office, *Processing Children's Asylum Claims* (ver 1.0, 12 July 2016)
HRC, *GC6*	HRC, *General Comment No 6: Article 6 (Right to Life)*, HRI/GEN/1/Rev.8 (1982)
HRC, *GC13*	HRC, *General Comment No 13: Equality before the Courts and the Right to a Fair and Public Hearing by an Independent Court Established by Law*, HRI/GEN/Rev.8 (1984)
HRC, *GC15*	HRC, *General Comment No 15: The Position of Aliens under the Covenant*, HRI/GEN/1/Rev.8 (1986)
HRC, *GC17*	HRC, *General Comment No 17: Rights of the Child*, HRI/GRN/1/Rev.7 (1989)
HRC, *GC18*	HRC, *General Comment No 18: Non-Discrimination*, HRI/GEN/1/Rev.8 (1989)
HRC, *GC19*	HRC, *General Comment No 19: Protection of the Family, the Right to Marriage and Equality of the Spouses (Article 23)*, HRI/GEN/1/Rev.8 (1990)
HRC, *GC20*	HRC, *General Comment No 20: Article 7 (Prohibition of Torture, or Other Cruel, Inhuman or Degrading Treatment or Punishment)*, HRI/GEN/1/Rev.8 (1992)
HRC, *GC31*	HRC, *General Comment No 31: The Nature of the General Legal Obligation Imposed on States Parties to the Covenant*, HRI/GEN/1/Rev.8 (2004)

Abbreviated Citation	Source
ICCPR	*International Covenant on Civil and Political Rights*, opened for signature 16 December 1966, 999 UNTS 171 (entered into force 23 March 1976)
ICESCR	*International Covenant on Economic, Social and Cultural Rights*, opened for signature 16 December 1966, 993 UNTS 3 (entered into force 3 January 1976)
INS, *Guidelines*	Memorandum from Jeff Weiss, Acting Director, Office of International Affairs, INS, 'Guidelines for Children's Asylum Claims' (File No 120/11.26, 10 December 1998)
IRB, *Guidelines*	IRB, *Guidelines Issued by the Chairperson Pursuant to Section 65(3) of the Immigration Act: Guideline 3: Child Refugee Claimants: Procedural and Evidentiary Issues* (30 September 1996)
IRO Constitution	*International Refugee Organization Constitution*, opened for signature 15 December 1946, 18 UNTS 3 (entered into force 20 August 1948)
OPAC	*Optional Protocol to the Convention on the Rights of the Child on the Involvement of Children in Armed Conflict*, opened for signature 24 May 2000, 2173 UNTS 222 (entered into force 12 February 2002)
OPCP	*Optional Protocol to the Convention on the Rights of the Child on a Communications Procedure*, opened for signature 28 February 2012, A/RES/66/138 (entered into force 14 April 2014)
OPSC	*Optional Protocol to the Convention on the Rights of the Child on the Sale of Children, Child Prostitution and Child Pornography*, opened for signature 25 May 2000, 2171 UNTS 227 (entered into force 18 January 2002)
Refugee Convention or *Convention*	*1951 Convention* and the attendant *1967 Protocol*
UDHR	*Universal Declaration of Human Rights*, GA Res 217(III)(A), A/810 (1948)
UKBA, *Asylum Process Guidance*	UKBA, *Asylum Process Guidance: Processing an Asylum Application from a Child* (ver 6, 16 April 2013)
UNCESCR, *GC3*	UNCESCR, *General Comment No 3: The Nature of States Parties' Obligations (Art 2, Para 1 of the Covenant)*, HRI/GEN/1/Rev.8 (1990)
UNCESCR, *GC11*	UNCESCR, *General Comment No 11: Plans of Action for Primary Education (Art 14)*, HRI/GEN/1/Rev.8 (1999)
UNCESCR, *GC12*	UNCESCR, *General Comment No 12: The Right to Adequate Food (Art 11)*, HRI/GEN/1/Rev.8 (1999)
UNCESCR, *GC13*	UNCESCR, *General Comment No 13: The Right to Education (Art 13)*, HRI/GEN/1/Rev.8 (1999)
UNCESCR, *GC14*	UNCESCR, *General Comment No 14: The Right to the Highest Attainable Standard of Health (Art 12)*, HRI/GEN/1/Rev.8 (2000)

Abbreviated Citation	Source
UNCESCR, *GC15*	UNCESCR, *General Comment No 15: The Right to Water (Arts 11 and 12 of the Covenant)*, HRI/GEN/1/Rev.8 (2002)
UNCESCR, *GC16*	UNCESCR, *General Comment No 16: The Equal Right of Men and Women to the Enjoyment of All Economic, Social and Cultural Rights (Art 3)*, HRI/GEN/1/Rev.8 (2005)
UNCESCR, *GC18*	UNCESCR, *General Comment No 18: The Right to Work (Art 6)*, HRI/GEN/1/Rev.8 (2005)
UNCESCR, *GC20*	UNCESCR, *General Comment No 20: Non-Discrimination in Economic, Social and Cultural Rights (Art 2, Para 2 of the International Covenant on Economic, Social and Cultural Rights)*, E/C.12/GC/20 (2009)
UNCRC, 2012 *Discussion Day Report*	UNCRC, *Report of the 2012 Day of General Discussion: The Rights of All Children in the Context of International Migration* (2013)
UNCRC, *GC1*	UNCRC, *General Comment No 1: Article 29(1) – The Aims of Education*, CRC/GC/2001/1 (2001)
UNCRC, *GC3*	UNCRC, *General Comment No 3: HIV/AIDS and the Rights of the Child*, CRC/GC/2003/3 (2003)
UNCRC, *GC5*	UNCRC, *General Comment No 5: General Measures of Implementation of the Convention on the Rights of the Child (Articles 4, 42 and 44(6))*, CRC/GC/2003/5 (2003)
UNCRC, *GC6*	UNCRC, *General Comment No 6: Treatment of Unaccompanied and Separated Children outside Their Country of Origin*, CRC/GC/2005/6 (2005)
UNCRC, *GC7*	UNCRC, *General Comment No 7: Implementing Child Rights in Early Childhood*, CRC/C/GC/7/Rev.1 (2006)
UNCRC, *GC8*	UNCRC, *General Comment No 8: The Right of the Child to Protection from Corporal Punishment and Other Cruel or Degrading Forms of Punishment*, CRC/C/GC/8 (2007)
UNCRC, *GC9*	UNCRC, *General Comment No 9: The Rights of Children with Disabilities*, CRC/C/GC/9 (2007)
UNCRC, *GC10*	UNCRC, *General Comment No 10: Children's Rights in Juvenile Justice*, CRC/C/GC/10 (2007)
UNCRC, *GC12*	UNCRC, *General Comment No 12: The Right of the Child to Be Heard*, CRC/C/GC/12 (2009)
UNCRC, *GC13*	UNCRC, *General Comment No. 13: The Right of the Child to Freedom from All Forms of Violence*, CRC/C/GC/13 (2011)
UNCRC, *GC14*	UNCRC, *General Comment No 14 on the Right of the Child to Have His or Her Best Interests Taken as a Primary Consideration (Art 3, Para 1)*, CRC/C/GC/14 (2013)
UNHCR, 2009 *Guidelines*	UNHCR, *Guidelines on International Protection: Child Asylum Claims under Article 1A(2) and 1 F of the 1951 Convention and/ or 1967 Protocol Relating to the Status of Refugees*, HCR/GIP/ 09/08 (2009)

Abbreviated Citation	Source
UNHCR, *Handbook*	UNHCR, *Handbook on Procedures and Criteria for Determining Refugee Status under the 1951 Convention and the 1967 Protocol Relating to the Status of Refugees*, HCR/IP/4/Eng/REV.1 (1979, re-edited 1992)
UNHCR, *MPSG Guidelines*	UNHCR, *Guidelines on International Protection: 'Membership of a Particular Social Group' within the Context of Article 1A(2) of the 1951 Convention and/or Its 1967 Protocol Relating to the Status of Refugees*, HCR/GIP/02/02 (2002)
VCLT	*Vienna Convention on the Law of Treaties*, opened for signature 23 May 1969, 1155 UNTS 331 (entered into force 27 January 1980)

INTRODUCTION

It is a sad and chilling reality that children today remain the victims of some of the most devastating examples of state-sanctioned and private human rights abuse.[1] Infanticide, involuntary military recruitment, ritual sacrifice, child labour, surgical mutilation, child prostitution, and domestic abuse represent just some of the ways that children are maltreated in contemporary societies.[2] Millions of children around the world find themselves caught up in armed conflict, not only as civilian bystanders, but as specific targets and, in some instances, active participants.[3] Children are also often the first to suffer the less brutal but equally crippling effects of poverty, with more than one billion children deprived of one or more of the services essential to a child's survival and development.[4] In many of these cases, the child has become a victim purely by reason of her status as a child and the heightened vulnerabilities that flow from her more limited capacity for self-protection.

While the maltreatment of children cannot be regarded as a new phenomenon, children are increasingly attempting to remove themselves from the debilitating environments in which circumstances have placed them. Significant numbers of children are travelling thousands, sometimes tens of thousands of miles – often accompanied by family, sometimes not – in search of protection.[5] In leaving their home and their country of origin these children are triggering an often-silent appeal for substitute protection of their human rights. Sometimes that appeal is answered. In other cases, children are confronted with fresh

---

[1] '[A] child means every human being below the age of eighteen years unless, under the law applicable to a child, majority is attained earlier': CRC, art 1.

[2] See, e.g., UNICEF, *The State of the World's Children* (2015); UNICEF, *Annual Report on Child Protection* (2014); UNICEF, *Hidden in Plain Sight: A Statistical Analysis of Violence against Children* (2014).

[3] 'This is a space devoid of the most basic human values; a space in which children are slaughtered, raped and maimed; a space in which children are exploited as soldiers; a space in which children are starved and exposed to extreme brutality. Such unregulated terror and violence speak of deliberate victimization. There are few further depths to which humanity can sink': G Machel, *Impact of Armed Conflict on Children*, A/51/306 (1996), [3].

[4] UNICEF, *The State of the World's Children 2014 in Numbers: Every Child Counts* (2014); UNICEF, *Progress for Children: Beyond Averages, Learning from the MDGs* (2015); UNICEF (2015) *supra* n 2.

[5] According to UNHCR data, in 2015 children below 18 years constituted 51% of the refugee population, up from 41% in 2009 and the same as in 2014. In 2015, some 98,400 asylum applications were lodged by unaccompanied or separated children in 78 countries, the highest number on record since UNHCR started collecting data in 2006, and almost three times the number of applications in 2014 (34,300): UNHCR, *Global Trends 2015* (2016) 3, 8. In the context of the 2015–16 refugee crisis in Europe, approximately 27% of arrivals into Europe by sea were children (based on arrivals since 1 January 2016): see http://data.unhcr.org/mediterranean/regional.php (accessed 21 November 2016).

obstacles in their attempt to navigate domestic administrative and legal processes that fail to take into account their particular needs or vulnerabilities.[6]

Although a child may face difficulties at each stage of the asylum-seeking process, the oversight in protection is particularly striking at the qualification stage – the assessment of whether or not a child qualifies for protection as a refugee under the *Refugee Convention*.[7] The determination of refugee status lies at the heart of the asylum process, signifying a state's recognition of the legitimacy of an individual's claim to international protection.[8] But while there is a vast and mature body of literature addressing issues faced by refugee children generally, often with an emphasis on unaccompanied and separated children,[9] there has been relatively limited engagement with the legal challenges that a child may face in qualifying for international protection.[10] This is beginning to change, with scholarship focused on these

---

[6] 'The protection needs of children remain a paramount concern, but have not always been sufficiently prioritised. We are worried that many asylum systems are not 'child friendly', take no account of the special circumstances of child applicants, and legitimate the automatic repatriation of children, without resort to established protections, such as best interests of the child determinations': E Feller, Assistant High Commissioner – Protection, UNHCR, 'Rule of Law 60 Years On' (Statement, 61st Session of the UNHCR ExCom, 6 October 2010) 3. The challenges faced by children in the migration context have been the subject of increased attention in the international arena in recent years. See, e.g., Human Rights Council, *Study of the Office of the United Nations High Commissioner for Human Rights on Challenges and Best Practices in the Implementation of the International Framework for the Protection of the Rights of the Child in the Context of Migration*, A/HRC/15/29 (2010); J Bustamante, *Report of the Special Rapporteur on the Human Rights of Migrants*, A/64/213 (2009), [85], [97]; J Bustamante, *Report of the Special Rapporteur on the Human Rights of Migrants*, A/HRC/11/7 (2009), [57], [123]; UNCRC, '2012 Day of General Discussion: The Rights of All Children in the Context of International Migration' (Background Paper, August 2012); UNCRC, 2012 *Discussion Day Report*. At a domestic level see, e.g., Joint Committee on Human Rights, *Human Rights of Unaccompanied Migrant Children and Young People in the UK*, House of Lords Paper No 9, House of Commons Paper No 196, Session 2013–14 (2013).

[7] Art 1. Although this book is principally concerned with protection under the *Refugee Convention*, Chapter 6 considers the wider independent protection obligations under international human rights law.

[8] C Harvey, 'Is Humanity Enough? Refugees, Asylum Seekers and the Rights Regime' in S Juss and C Harvey (eds), *Contemporary Issues in Refugee Law* (2013) 68, 69–76. The declaratory nature of refugee status means, however, that status as a refugee under international law is not dependent on a domestic determination of refugee status: see *Handbook*, [28]; *R (ST) v SSHD* [2010] 1 WLR 2858, [31]–[32].

[9] As to terminology, the phrase 'refugee child' is adopted throughout the book to refer to children who qualify for protection as a refugee pursuant to the *Refugee Convention*. The phrases 'at-risk child' and 'child seeking international protection' are adopted to refer to a child who is seeking protection either as a refugee, or pursuant to a state's broader international human rights obligations. The book adopts UNHCR's definition of 'unaccompanied child' and 'separated child': an 'unaccompanied child' is a child who is separated from both parents and other relatives, and is not being cared for by an adult who is responsible for doing so, by law or custom; a 'separated child' is a child who is separated from both parents, or from a primary caregiver, but not necessarily from other relatives: UNHCR, *UNHCR Guidelines on Determining the Best Interests of the Child* (2008) 8.

[10] There are exceptions, in particular the seminal work of Jacqueline Bhabha and Mary Crock on unaccompanied and separated refugee children: see especially J Bhabha and M Crock, *Seeking Asylum Alone: A Comparative Study* (2007). Michelle Foster has considered the status of child refugees as part of her broader worker on refugee claims based on social and economic deprivation (M Foster, *International Refugee Law and Socio-Economic Rights: Refuge from Deprivation* (2007) 206–12, 329–39), and Jane McAdam has considered the relevance of complementary standards to the status of at-risk children as part of her broader work on complementary protection (J McAdam, *Complementary Protection in International Refugee Law* (2007) 173–96). See also C Smyth, *European Asylum Law and the Rights of the Child* (2014); D Anker, N Kelly, J Willshire Carrera and S Ardalan, 'Mejilla-Romero: A New Era for Child Asylum', 12–09 *Immigration Briefings* (September 2012) 1; T Löhr, *Die kinderspezifische Auslegung des völkerrechtlichen Flüchtlingsbegriffs* (2009).

challenges emerging at a rapid rate.[11] What remains missing is a comprehensive, comparative review of the procedural and substantive obstacles that a child – whether unaccompanied, separated or accompanied – may encounter in establishing refugee status, and a consideration of the manner in which these challenges might be resolved.

The Child Refugee: Overlooked and Incorrectly Assessed

The *Refugee Convention* is the primary instrument governing refugee status under international law. The core of the refugee definition, contained in art 1A(2), provides that a refugee is a person who has a 'well-founded fear of being persecuted for reasons of race, religion, nationality, membership of a particular social group or political opinion'. A person will thus be a refugee, and entitled to the protections afforded under the *Convention*, only if there is a genuine risk of the applicant 'being persecuted' that is causally connected to one of the five enumerated forms of civil or political status. The art 1A(2) definition makes no specific reference to or provision for children, although it is clear that the *Convention* applies to all individuals regardless of age.[12] It has been suggested that the absence of any child-specific provision has allowed the *Convention* to be interpreted through an 'adult-focused lens',[13] resulting in the development of an age-insensitive jurisprudence where 'the adult asylum seeker [is] the norm'.[14]

UNHCR – the lead agency responsible for supervising the application of the *Convention* – has recently apprised that the *Convention* definition has 'traditionally been interpreted in light of adult experiences' and that, as a result, many refugee claims made by children have been 'assessed incorrectly or overlooked altogether'.[15] UNHCR's diagnosis identifies the two core challenges that children face in establishing that they are entitled to refugee status. First, *invisibility*: a failure to consider a child as a refugee in her own right. Second, *incorrect assessment*: in cases where a child's claim is assessed independently, a failure to interpret the *Convention* in a manner that takes into account the fact that the applicant is in fact a child. Both challenges may have debilitating consequences for a child: most significantly, an incorrect determination of refugee status and the attendant risk that she will be returned to a risk of being persecuted in her country of origin.

Turning first to the challenge of invisibility, a review of state practice indicates that children are often overlooked in domestic asylum processes.[16] This is particularly acute where a child is accompanied, in which case her claim will generally be subsumed within the application of another family member. In the majority of cases, a child's status is treated as derivative: if a child's parent or guardian receives refugee status, the child's status will automatically follow. But the converse is also true: where the family member's claim is denied, the child will similarly be denied protection. This is problematic where a child faces an independent risk of persecutory harm. A child has a greater chance of having her claim

---

[11] This emerging body of scholarship is drawn upon throughout this book.
[12] Human Rights Council (2010) *supra* n 6, [12] ('[a]lthough there is no specific mention of child refugees in [the *Refugee Convention*], its provisions ... apply equally to the situation of children'); UNHCR, *Handbook*, [213] ('[t]he same definition of a refugee applies to all individuals, regardless of their age').
[13] M Crock, *Seeking Asylum Alone: Australia* (2006) 244.
[14] M Crock, 'Lonely Refuge: Judicial Responses to Separated Children Seeking Refugee Protection in Australia' (2005) 22(2) *Law in Context* 120, 157.
[15] UNHCR, 2009 *Guidelines*, [1].   [16] See Chapter 2.

individually assessed where she is unaccompanied or separated, although states have, in a limited range of circumstances, suggested that unaccompanied children lack the capacity to claim refugee status.

But even where a child's claim is individually assessed, she will then be required to navigate a jurisprudence that has, for the most part, failed to engage with the *Convention* from the perspective of a child. Article 1A(2) of the *Convention* comprises a set of discrete definitional requirements, each of which gives rise to a series of distinct doctrinal challenges when applied to children. In what circumstances is it reasonable to require a child to articulate a fear of being persecuted? To what extent must a decision-maker take into account the age of a child in determining whether the 'being persecuted' threshold has been satisfied? Are there child-specific forms of harm that may amount to persecutory harm? In what circumstances can a child secure protection where the agent of persecution is a family member rather than the state? To what extent is an applicant's status as a child relevant to determining whether a child is a member of a 'particular social group'? A distinct set of evidential issues will also be triggered when considering a child's refugee claim, particularly when assessing a child's credibility.

This book considers the extent to which the *Convention* is capable of responding to each of these challenges and the phenomenon of the involuntary movement of children more generally. A number of commentators have suggested that the *Convention* is not up to the task and that the reach of the instrument is curtailed by its historical context, favouring the (largely adult) political dissidents of the Cold War era. This has given rise to calls for an amendment to the refugee definition or the negotiation of a new treaty specifically addressing the movement of child refugees.[17] While it is certainly true that the *Convention* was strategically drafted to respond to a particular political climate,[18] these concerns fail to appreciate the proven resilience and malleability of the *Convention*. Over the past 60 years the *Convention* has established itself as a 'living instrument',[19] capable, through organic evolution and progressive interpretation, of accommodating claims not envisaged, and certainly not expressly addressed, by its drafters. This is evident in the context of refugee claims based on gender[20] and sexuality-related persecution,[21] where we have witnessed the development of a fast-evolving jurisprudence underlining the need to interpret the *Convention* in a gender- and sexuality-sensitive way. Indeed, although more nascent, we

---

[17] See, e.g., C Gates, 'Working toward a Global Discourse on Children's Rights: The Problem of Unaccompanied Children and the International Response to Their Plight' (1999) 7 *Indiana Journal of Global Legal Studies* 299, 332.

[18] J C Hathaway, 'A Reconsideration of the Underlying Premise of Refugee Law' (1990) 31(1) *Harvard International Law Journal* 129, 148.

[19] *Sepet v SSHD* [2003] 1 WLR 856, [6].

[20] See, e.g., D Anker 'Boundaries in the Field of Human Rights: Refugee Law, Gender and the Human Rights Paradigm' (2002) 15 *Harvard Human Rights Journal* 133; C Dauvergne and J Millbank, 'Forced Marriage as a Harm in Domestic and International Law' (2010) 73 *The Modern Law Review* 57; A Edwards, 'Transitioning Gender: Feminist Engagement with International Refugee Law and Policy 1950–2010' (2010) 29(2) *Refugee Survey Quarterly* 21.

[21] See, e.g., J C Hathaway and J Pobjoy, 'Queer Cases Make Bad Law' (2012) 44 *New York University Journal of International Law and Politics* 315; R Goodman, 'The Incorporation of International Human Rights Standards into Sexual Orientation Asylum Claims: Cases of Involuntary "Medical" Intervention' (1995) 105 *Yale Law Journal* 255; J Millbank, 'From Discretion to Disbelief: Recent Trends in Refugee Determinations on the Basis of Sexual Orientation in Australia and the United Kingdom' (2009) 13(2) *International Journal of Human Rights* 391.

are beginning to see the development of a similar jurisprudence in cases involving children. As the analysis that follows will demonstrate, although this jurisprudence is recent, and certainly underdeveloped, decision-makers are beginning to pay attention to the manner in which the *Convention* definition might be interpreted where the refugee applicant is a child. The relevance of these developments should not be underestimated, as they reflect a willingness on the part of decision-makers to test the authentic scope of the *Convention* definition in its application to refugee children.

The absence of any express reference to children in the *Convention* definition should be no impediment to a child seeking recognition as a refugee. The *Convention* applies to all refugees, irrespective of age, so there is, in principle, no reason for the child refugee to remain *invisible*. And we have seen that there is scope – evident in case-law concerning gender and sexuality – for the interpretation of the *Convention* definition to evolve to respond to contemporary challenges; so there is, again, at least in principle, no reason for a child's claim to be *incorrectly assessed* from an adult-centred perspective. Against this background, how, then, does one go about dismantling the related challenges of *invisibility* and *incorrect assessment* in the context of child refugee claims? How does one ensure that the *Convention* is interpreted and applied 'with the image of the child front and centre in the mind of the decision-maker'?[22]

A Child-Rights Framework

The hypothesis advanced in this book is that progressive developments in the interpretation of the *Refugee Convention*, coupled with a greater understanding of the relationship between international refugee law and international law on the rights of the child, enable the *Convention* to respond in a sophisticated and principled way to refugee claims brought by children.[23] This will require a creative alignment between refugee law and the fast-evolving body of international law on the rights of the child. Although by no means the only solution to the challenges produced by the involuntary movement of children,[24] the argument developed in this book focuses on the invocation of authoritative standards of international law as a means of advancing the interests and protection of refugee children.[25]

---

[22] Crock (2006) *supra* n 13, 170.

[23] Foster advanced a similar hypothesis in her monograph, which considered the capacity of the *Convention* to respond to claims based on the deprivation of economic and social rights – specifically, that contemporary developments in the interpretation of the *Convention*, in conjunction with developments in international human rights law and theory, would 'enable the Convention to respond in a more sophisticated manner to the claims of persons fleeing economic and social deprivation': Foster (2007) *supra* n 10, 20–1.

[24] It might be suggested, for example, that rather than a unified solution underscored by international law, one should 'let a thousand flowers bloom'; that a diverse range of legal, institutional and policy-oriented remedies – for example, campaigns to shift public attitudes, enhanced training for decision-makers, ad hoc protection options outside the *Convention* – might be developed in different domestic jurisdictions to ensure that any solution is appropriately tailored to meet a variety of protection needs. Ultimately, in fashioning the 'perfect' solution, there is a clear need for empirical research in the social sciences field, to gain a greater understanding of *why* it is that children are *overlooked* and *incorrectly assessed* in the context of child refugee claims. Such an exercise is beyond the scope of this book.

[25] See J C Hathaway, *The Rights of Refugees under International Law* (2005) 6–7, advancing a similar proposition in the context of refugee protection generally. See more generally B A Simmons, *Mobilizing for Human Rights* (2009).

The *Refugee Convention*, drafted in the years immediately following the Second World War, has grown up within, and now constitutes part of, a much broader international human rights regime. Within that regime, the *CRC* provides the most comprehensive articulation of the minimum obligations that a state owes to a child, both generally and within the asylum context.[26] The *CRC* is widely recognised as a 'critical milestone in the legal protection of children',[27] its authority underscored by its near-universal ratification.[28] The *CRC* gives children a 'seat at the international law table',[29] promoting a broader construction of the child as an individual rights-bearer, with distinct needs and distinct problems. This represents a fundamental shift away from the notion of a child as a passive dependent, instead codifying a vision of a child as an independent bearer of a unique, tailored set of human rights. While the *Convention* remains the 'cornerstone of the international refugee protection regime',[30] the *CRC* provides a critical moral and legal benchmark for the treatment of refugee children; a 'model of the achievable'.[31] As Goodwin-Gill has argued, the *CRC* provides an 'international set of rules, cogently and coherently supporting the work of those who would bring effective protection to refugee children'.[32]

In the chapters that follow I explore three contexts – or 'modes of interaction' – where the *CRC* might be engaged to assist in determining the status of an at-risk child.[33] First, the *CRC* might be invoked as a *procedural guarantee* to inform the refugee determination process. The *Convention* is silent on the procedures that a state should implement in designing a domestic system of refugee status determination. In contrast, the *CRC* comprises a number of provisions that may inform the determination process, including the principle that a child has a right to express views freely and to be heard in any judicial or administrative proceedings affecting her. Second, the *CRC* might be drawn upon as an *interpretative*

---

[26] The rights contained in the *CRC* apply to *all* children (art 1), without discrimination of *any* kind (art 2).

[27] G S Goodwin-Gill, 'Unaccompanied Refugee Minors: The Role and Place of International Law in the Pursuit of Durable Solutions' (1995) 3 *International Journal of Children's Rights* 405, 405.

[28] The *CRC* is the most widely ratified human rights treaty in the world. The United States is the only UN member state that has not ratified the *CRC*, although it has signed it. In *R (SG and others) v Secretary of State for Work and Pensions* [2015] 1 WLR 1449, Lord Kerr endorsed UNICEF's description of the *CRC* as 'the most complete statement of children's rights ever produced and ... the most widely-ratified international human rights Treaty in history' (at [256]).

[29] M Freeman, 'The Human Rights of Children' (2010) 63 *Current Legal Problems* 1, 20.

[30] UNHCR ExCom, *Conclusions on the Provision of International Protection Including through Complementary Forms of Protection*, No 103 (LVI) (2005) Preamble para 1.

[31] Goodwin-Gill (1995) *supra* n 27, 410. See also J Tobin, 'Judging the Judges: Are They Adopting the Rights Approach in Matters Involving Children' (2009) 33 *Melbourne University Law Review* 579, 584 ('the considerable thought that went into [the *CRC*'s] formulation and its almost universal ratification among states provides a compelling reason to consider the vision of children's rights that it offers'); UNCRC, '2012 Day of General Discussion' (2012) *supra* n 6, 11 ('[T]he CRC provides both a comprehensive catalogue of civil, political, social, economic and cultural rights, and clear principles regarding their application to all children, regardless of migration status. Thus, as a legally-binding instrument with virtually universal ratification, the CRC, as the most relevant international child rights instrument, has the potential to play a key role in the protection of children's rights in the context of migration').

[32] Goodwin-Gill (1995) *supra* n 27, 416. See J Bhabha and W Young, 'Not Adults in Miniature: Unaccompanied Child Asylum Seekers and the New US Guidelines' (1999) 11 *International Journal of Refugee Law* 84, 94: 'The [CRC] provides a new child-centred perspective on questions of rights and establishes a near universal set of internationally endorsed and validated standards and aspirations for children'.

[33] See generally J Pobjoy, 'A Child Rights Framework for Assessing the Status of Refugee Children' in S Juss and C Harvey (eds), *Contemporary Issues in Refugee Law* (2013) 91.

aid to inform the interpretation of the *Convention* definition. International law, and in particular international human rights law, has grown exponentially over the past 60 years. Many of the relatively nascent precepts contained within the *Convention* have now been re-articulated, re-contextualised and in some cases expanded in a comprehensive suite of international human rights treaties. It is now widely accepted that the *Convention* definition should be interpreted taking into account this broader international human rights framework, including the *CRC*. Third, the *CRC* might give rise to an *independent source of status* outside the international refugee protection regime. It is accepted that the *CRC* comprises a complementary source of protection via the principle of *non-refoulement* implicit in, at the very minimum, arts 6 and 37. There is also an argument that the 'best interests' principle, enshrined within art 3 of the *CRC*, may give rise to an independent source of international protection. These three modes of interaction provide an illustration of the potential role that the *CRC*, alongside the *Convention*, might play in facilitating a more child-centred approach to the status determination process. In practical terms, the three modes provide a platform for the development of a child-rights framework for determining the status of an at-risk child.

The proposition that there should be greater interaction between international refugee law and international law on the rights of the child is by no means novel. The argument has for some time been advanced by leading scholars and advocates. UNHCR and the UNCRC have also promoted the relationship between the two regimes. In its 1993 *Policy on Refugee Children*, UNHCR referred to the *CRC* as providing a 'comprehensive framework for the responsibilities of its States Parties to all children within their borders'.[34] In 1994 UNHCR revised its earlier guidelines on refugee children in order to combine 'the concept of "children's rights" with UNHCR's ongoing efforts to protect and assist refugee children'.[35] The UNCHR ExCom has also repeatedly underlined the relationship between the *Refugee Convention* and the *CRC* in its formal Conclusions. In its most recent Conclusion on refugee children, the Committee stressed the need for[36]

> [a] rights-based approach, which recognizes children as *active subjects of rights*, and according to which all interventions are consistent with States' obligations under relevant international law, including, as applicable, international refugee law, international human rights law and international humanitarian law, and acknowledgment that the CRC provides an important legal and normative framework for the protection of children.

Of more recent vintage, in 2009 UNHCR issued the 2009 *Guidelines*, which provide 'substantive and procedural guidance on carrying out refugee status determination in a child-sensitive manner'[37] and emphasise that the substantive and procedural aspects of a child's application of refugee status should be informed by the *CRC*.[38] The UNCRC has also acknowledged the relevance of the *CRC* in the refugee status determination process.

---

[34] UNHCR ExCom, *UNHCR Policy on Refugee Children*, EC/SCP/82 (1993), [17].

[35] UNHCR, *Refugee Children: Guidelines on Protection and Care* (1994) 14. The opening remarks to these *Guidelines* (at 13) state: 'This book of Guidelines has its ancestors. On one side of the family tree is the human rights branch, which includes the most recent forebear, the 1989 Convention on the Rights of the Child. On the other side is the UNHCR branch.'

[36] UNHCR ExCom, *Conclusion on Children at Risk*, No 107 (LVIII) (2007), [(b)(x)] (emphasis added).

[37] UNHCR, 2009 *Guidelines*, [1].   [38] *Ibid.*, [1].

In its *GC6*, the Committee underlined that states must adopt a '[c]hild-sensitive assessment of protection needs, taking into account persecution of a child-specific nature'.[39]

The relationship between the *Refugee Convention* and the *CRC* has also been recognised by states at a domestic level, with guidelines in Canada, the United Kingdom, Australia and New Zealand all referring to the relevance of the *CRC* in the refugee determination process. Even the United States – one of the two states *not* to have ratified the *CRC* – has issued guidance acknowledging the significance of obligations contained in the *CRC* in determining the status of a child refugee.[40]

But notwithstanding this clear international and domestic support for greater interaction between the *CRC* and the *Refugee Convention*, decision-makers have been reluctant to engage with the *CRC* and its associated jurisprudence when considering the status of refugee children. A review of more than 2,500 domestic decisions involving children since the adoption of the *CRC* revealed that the treaty was mentioned in less than 5 per cent of decisions.[41] There are certainly exceptions and, as noted above, there are nascent signs of a domestic refugee jurisprudence that does, in fact, engage with the framework provided in the *CRC*. But these cases are few and far between.

There may be a number of explanations for the apparent disinclination to draw on the *CRC*'s legal framework in assessing a child's refugee status. One possibility is the limited guidance on the precise role that the *CRC* might play in the refugee status determination process. Although the international community has strongly promoted greater engagement between the two international legal regimes, there have been limited attempts to outline what this relationship might mean in practical terms. What procedural guarantees does the *CRC* provide in the context of the refugee determination process? How might the obligations enshrined in the *CRC* impact on a decision-maker's interpretation of the *Convention*'s definitional requirements? And in what, if any, circumstances will the *CRC* provide a complementary or independent source of international protection? Each of these questions has, to varying degrees, been addressed in the growing body of scholarship and UNHCR and UNCRC guidance; however, the contours of the relationship between the two regimes are far from fully mapped. Throughout the book, I draw on the existing body of scholarship and institutional guidance, complemented by a comprehensive review of national refugee jurisprudence, to present a more detailed picture and encourage a deepened understanding of the relationship between the two international legal regimes.

Methodology and Research Design

This book represents an attempt to better understand the relationship between international refugee law and international law on the rights of the child, and what that relationship means in the context of determining the status of refugee children. In particular, I seek to

---

[39] UNCRC, *GC6*, 21.
[40] 'Many of the components of international policy regarding children also derive from the [*CRC*]. Adopted by the United Nations in November 1989, the CRC codifies standards for the rights of all children, including those who are refugees. Article 3(1) of the CRC provides that the "best interests of the child" should be the primary consideration in decisions involving children. Because the United States has signed but not ratified the CRC, its provisions, as noted above, provide guidance only and are not binding on adjudicators. Having signed the CRC, however, the United States is obliged under international treaty law to refrain from acts which would defeat the object and purpose of the Convention': INS, *Guidelines*, 2.
[41] See *infra* text accompanying n 52.

outline the authentic reach of the two international legal regimes and consider how a synthesis of the two regimes might be used to provide a 'child-rights framework' for the status determination process. In doing so, I test the capacity of the two regimes – individually and collectively – to respond to the particular needs and vulnerabilities of refugee children. This exercise is firmly anchored in existing international legal obligations; it is not driven by an idealistic aspiration grounded in policy considerations, nor is it a call for the creation of more international law. The book represents an attempt to make better use of, and to more creatively align, the authoritative international legal standards already in place.

Although the analysis is anchored in extant international legal obligation, it draws extensively on domestic refugee case-law in order to illustrate the actual and potential scope of the two legal regimes and, in particular, the authentic scope of the *Refugee Convention* definition. The reason for this is straightforward. In contrast to virtually every other UN human rights treaty, the *Convention* provides for no supervisory body to monitor compliance or to develop authoritative legal standards to guide states in determining the scope the legal obligations contained within it.[42] Rather, the task of interpreting the *Convention* has fallen almost exclusively on the shoulders of the 148 signatories to the *Convention* and/or the *Protocol*. In large part the task has fallen on national administrative agencies, courts and tribunals, particularly those in jurisdictions with the requisite infrastructure to adjudicate disputes concerning the scope of the *Convention*. In these circumstances, a review of domestic jurisprudence is critical to providing an applied understanding of the interpretation of the *Convention*.[43] A review of the accumulated thinking of national tribunals and courts is also particularly important in circumstances where decision-makers are increasingly referring to the reasoning adopted by their colleagues in other jurisdictions. Through this 'transnational judicial conversation'[44] we are beginning to see the emergence of a truly international refugee law jurisprudence aimed at promoting a common understanding of the *Convention*.[45]

---

[42] Article 38 of the *Convention* provides that a dispute between states parties relating to its interpretation or application may be referred to the ICJ; however, this provision has never been invoked.

[43] 'Since the Convention is an international instrument which no supra-national court has the ultimate authority to interpret, the construction put upon it by other states, while not determinative … is of importance': *Fornah v SSHD* [2007] 1 AC 412, [10] (Lord Bingham). See also art 38(1)(d) of the *Statute of the International Court of Justice*, which recognises 'judicial decisions' as 'subsidiary means for the determination of rules of law'.

[44] A Slaughter, 'A Typology of Transjudicial Communication' (1994) 29 *University of Richmond Law Review* 99.

[45] See J C Hathaway, 'A Forum for the Transnational Development of Refugee Law: The IARLJ's Advanced Refugee Law Workshop' (2003) 15 *International Journal of Refugee Law* 418, 419; E Benvenisti, 'Reclaiming Democracy: The Strategic Use of Foreign and International Law by National Courts' (2008) 102(2) *American Journal of International Law* 241, 264–7; M Kirby, 'Transnational Judicial Dialogue, the Internationalisation of Law and Australian Judges' (2008) 9 *Melbourne Journal of International Law* 171, 180–1. Superior courts in the United Kingdom have for some time been open to the citation of comparative case-law in the interpretation of the *Convention*: see G S Goodwin-Gill, 'The Search for the One, True Meaning' in G S Goodwin-Gill and H Lambert (eds), *The Limits of Transnational Law: Refugee Law, Policy Harmonization and Judicial Dialogue in the European Union* (2010) 204. The use of comparative material in this context has also received an imprimatur in Australian, Canadian and New Zealand courts: see generally Kirby (2008) *supra*. Even within the United States, there is some consensus – even amongst the staunchest opponents of the use of comparative material in constitutional law cases – supporting reference to foreign case-law in the interpretation of international treaties generally and the *Convention* specifically. Scalia J wrote in dissent in *Olympic Airways v Husain*, 540 US 644, 658 (2004): '[The] decision stands out for its failure to give any serious

There are two limitations to the scope of the analysis that follows. First, this is a study on refugee *status* and the procedural and substantive challenges that a child may face in establishing entitlement to that status. There is, in particular, no detailed consideration of refugee *rights* and the interplay between the framework of rights set out in arts 3 to 34 of the *Refugee Convention* and the framework of child-specific rights set out in the *CRC*. It is hoped, however, that the central argument developed in the book – that greater interaction between the two legal regimes has the capacity to enhance the protection afforded to refugee children – will have relevance and application well beyond the issue of qualification for refugee status.

Second, although intended to have a broader reach, this book is principally a study on the status of children arriving in the industrialised world. In circumstances where the global south hosts 86 per cent of the world's refugees,[46] this is a significant shortcoming. It reflects, however, the reality that recognition of refugee status is generally less of an issue for those arriving in the global south.[47] In these poorer countries the key challenge for children is their treatment subsequent to the recognition of status, with millions of children languishing in refugee camps or denied access to even the most basic services in urban settings.[48] Although the *CRC* will certainly be relevant to the plight of these children, these issues are beyond the more limited scope of this book.

Against this background, the first chapter traces the development of international law relating first to refugees and then to children. This largely expository exercise introduces the reader to the key international instruments operating within the respective regimes and illustrates the extent to which the fields of international refugee law and international law on the rights of the child have spoken to or disregarded each other over the past century. In circumstances where neither the *Convention* nor the *CRC* set out the full range of obligations owed by a state to a refugee child, the chapter suggests that there is a convincing argument for reimagining the relationship between the two regimes. The chapter reintroduces the three 'modes of interaction' where the *CRC* might be engaged to assist in assessing the status of an

---

consideration to how the courts of our treaty partners have resolved the legal issues before us … The Court's new abstemiousness with regard to foreign fare is not without consequence: Within the past year, appellate courts in both England and Australia have rendered decisions squarely at odds with today's holding. Because the Court offers no convincing explanation why these cases should not be followed, I respectfully dissent.' See also *Air France v Saks*, 470 US 392 (1985) (citations omitted): 'we "find the opinions of our sister signatories to be entitled to considerable weight."' In the refugee context, see *N-A-M v Holder*, 587 F 3d 1052, 1061 (10th Cir, 2009): 'We can also benefit from reference to international law, as it reveals how other tribunals have interpreted the exact same text. Although citing foreign law is at times controversial, the broad consensus, even among opponents of its use in constitutional law cases, supports its use when determining how other signatories on a treaty interpret that treaty.'

[46] UNHCR (2016) *supra* n 5, 2.

[47] This is a consequence of the fact that the majority of refugees in the developing world are granted status through the practice of prima face refugee status determination (essentially, a grant of status on a group basis): see M Albert, 'Governance and *Prima Facie* Refugee Status Determination: Clarifying the Boundaries of Temporary Protection, Group Determination, and Mass Influx' (2010) 29(1) *Refugee Survey Quarterly* 61. As Hathaway notes, '[f]or reasons born of both pragmatism and principle, poorer countries – which host the overwhelming majority of the world's refugees – have rarely contested the eligibility for those arriving at their borders': Hathaway (2005) *supra* n 25, 3.

[48] See G Verdirame and J Pobjoy, 'The End of Refugee Camps?' in S Juss (ed), *Ashgate Research Companion on Migration Theory and Policy* (2013) 91; B Harrell-Bond, 'Are Refugee Camps Good for Children?' (Working Paper No 29, New Issues in Refugee Research, UNHCR, August 2000).

at-risk child: as a *procedural guarantee*, as an *interpretative aid* and as an *independent source of status*. The chapter concludes with an outline of the key arguments supporting greater alignment between international refugee law and international law on the rights of the child, with a particular focus on the international rules of treaty interpretation.

Chapter 2 addresses the first mode of interaction: the *CRC* as a *procedural guarantee*. The first section of the chapter outlines the various ways in which children have been rendered invisible within domestic refugee status determination processes. Section 2.2 considers the circumstances in which a state is required individually to assess a child's eligibility for refugee status and develops an argument that the removal of a child, without a review of her independent claim for refugee status, may give rise to a risk of a violation of the duty of *non-refoulement* under art 33 of the *Convention* and a violation of the *CRC*'s procedural requirement that the child have an opportunity to express views freely in matters affecting her and be heard in judicial and administrative proceedings. Section 2.3 of the chapter considers the application of family unity obligations to the refugee status determination process, with a focus on the duty of non-separation contained in art 9 of the *CRC*.

Chapters 3 to 5 are the heart of the book. These three chapters consider the second mode of interaction: the *CRC* as an *interpretative aid* to inform the interpretation of the *Convention* definition. These chapters draw on contemporary understandings of that definition, combined with the broader child-rights framework enshrined in the *CRC*, to test the capacity of the *Convention* to respond to the specific needs and circumstances of children. From the very outset, it is important not to overstate the role of the *CRC* or its capacity to influence the interpretation of the *Convention*. In some circumstances, an age-sensitive interpretation may be obtained exclusively by adopting a principled interpretation of the *Convention*. In other cases, the invocation of the standards enshrined in the *CRC* may increase the likelihood of an age-sensitive interpretation.

The analysis in Chapters 3 to 5 draws principally on four key sources: first, the international treaties themselves, in particular the *Convention* and the *CRC*;[49] second, guidance produced by UNHCR and the UNCRC, including UNHCR's *Handbook*, UNHCR ExCom Conclusions, UNHCR Guidelines on International Protection and the UNCRC's General Comments;[50] third, the views advanced by scholars and advocates pertaining to the interpretation of both the *Convention* and the *CRC*; and finally, and perhaps most significantly, the emerging body of domestic case-law where the decision-maker has specifically addressed a claim brought by a child (in circumstances where the child is unaccompanied or has an independent claim from other members of the family).[51] The analysis focuses on decisions from all levels of judicial decision-making (including first-tier tribunals) in the five major common-law jurisdictions: the United Kingdom, the United States, Canada, Australia and New Zealand.[52] In total, more than 2,500 decisions (reported and unreported) have been identified and reviewed for the purposes of this project. Those cases have been

---

[49] Where relevant, the book will draw upon the Optional Protocols to the *CRC*, and the broader framework of international human rights law (for example, the *ICCPR* and *ICESCR*); however, the primary analytical focus will be the *Convention* and the *CRC*.

[50] See Chapter 1, Section 1.2.

[51] Although the book draws on regional and domestic case-law, it does not seek or attempt to provide a comprehensive account of the jurisprudence in any particular jurisdiction.

[52] Although the focus here is on decisions of domestic courts and tribunals, it is of course important to recognise that interpretation of a treaty also takes place in the day-to-day work of executive governments and legislatures. This is particularly true in the refugee context, where the executive or legislative

indexed and captured in a web resource (www.childref.org), which, consistent with the central argument developed in the book, is designed to promote greater interaction between the *Convention* and the *CRC*. Although I have drawn selectively on case-law from other jurisdictions, the focus is centred on common law jurisdictions given the more comprehensive engagement with the definitional requirements of the *Convention* in these jurisdictions.[53]

Chapters 3 to 5 address distinct elements of the *Refugee Convention* definition.[54] A decision was made to focus on aspects of the *Convention* definition that have caused particular difficulty for child claimants. This is not an exhaustive treatise on the refugee definition[55] and is certainly not an attempt to address every doctrinal obstacle that a child may face in demonstrating eligibility for refugee status. The selection of issues does, however, reflect the key challenges that have presented themselves to date and thus provides an appropriate illustrative platform to consider the capacity of the *Convention*, together with the *CRC*, to respond to claims brought by refugee children. The chapters address, in turn, the requirement that a child demonstrate a 'well-founded fear' of harm (Chapter 3); the requirement that a child be at risk of 'being persecuted', meaning that the child is at risk of serious harm that cannot or will not be rectified by her own country (Chapter 4); and the requirement that the risk be causally connected to one of the five enumerated forms of civil or political status (Chapter 5).

The final chapter of the book steps outside the international refugee protection regime and considers the third mode of interaction: the capacity of the *CRC* to provide an *independent source of status* for children seeking international protection. After a brief outline of the more traditional *non-refoulement* obligations contained in arts 6 and 37 of the *CRC*, the chapter examines the extent to which the best interests principle codified in art 3 of the *CRC* may provide an independent source of international protection. That protection may, for instance, proscribe the removal of a child notwithstanding the fact that the child is not eligible for protection as a refugee or protection under the *non-refoulement* obligations in international human rights law.

---

branches are often responsible for the initial decision regarding the status of any individual claiming refugee status.

[53] See Foster (2007) *supra* n 10, 23. Although still underdeveloped, there are signs of more detailed analysis occurring in courts in civil law jurisdictions: see generally G S Goodwin-Gill and H Lambert (eds), *The Limits of Transnational Law: Refugee Law, Policy Harmonization and Judicial Dialogue in the European Union* (2010).

[54] The separate treatment of the constituent elements of the *Convention* definition accords with the prevailing view that 'adjudicators and tribunals give better reasoned and more lucid decisions if they go step by step rather than follow a recital of the facts and arguments with a single laconic assessment which others then have to unpick': *Svazas v SSHD* [2002] 1 WLR 1891, [30].

[55] See J C Hathaway and M Foster, *The Law of Refugee Status* (2nd edn, 2014); G S Goodwin-Gill and J McAdam, *The Refugee in International Law* (3rd edn, 2007); J C Hathaway, *The Law of Refugee Status* (1991).

1

Situating the Refugee Child in International Law

Introduction

International law has long recognised that a refugee child is entitled to special care and protection. Since the *1924 Declaration* – which arose out of a concern about the particular problems faced by children during and subsequent to war – the need to prioritise the protection of refugee children has been affirmed repeatedly by the UN General Assembly,[1]

---

[1] '[The General Assembly] *notes with concern* the large number of . . . refugee or asylum seeking children . . . [and] internally displaced children . . . and stresses the need to incorporate special measures, in accordance with the principle of the best interests of the child . . . and calls upon states to provide special support and to ensure equal access to services for those children': *Rights of the Child*, A/RES/69/157 (2014), [8]; '[The General Assembly] *calls upon* all States to protect refugee, asylum-seeking and internally displaced children, in particular those who are unaccompanied, who are particularly exposed to violence and risks in connection with armed conflict and trafficking, and taking into account their gender-specific needs, stressing the need for States as well as the international community to continue to pay more systematic and in-depth attention to the special assistance, protection and development needs of those children': *Rights of the Child*, A/RES/68/147 (2014), [42]; '[The General Assembly] *calls upon* all States to protect refugee, asylum-seeking and internally displaced children, in particular those who are unaccompanied and who are particularly exposed to risks in connection with armed conflict and post-conflict situations, such as recruitment, sexual violence and exploitation': *Rights of the Child*, A/HRC/19/L.31 (2012), [22]; '[The General Assembly] *[a]ffirms* the importance of age, gender and diversity mainstreaming in analysing protection needs and . . . recognizing the importance of addressing the protection needs of women and children in particular': *Office of the United Nations High Commissioner for Refugees*, A/RES/ 65/194 (2011), [21]; '[The General Assembly] *[a]ffirms* that children, because of their age, social status and physical and mental development, are often more vulnerable than adults in situations of forced displacement, recognizes that forced displacement, return to post-conflict situations, integration into new societies, protracted situations of displacement and statelessness can increase child protection risks, taking into account the particular vulnerability of refugee children to forcible exposure to the risks of physical and psychological injury, exploitation and death in connection with armed conflict, and acknowledges that wider environmental factors and individual risk factors, particularly when combined, may generate different protection needs': *Assistance to Refugees, Returnees and Displaced Persons in Africa*, A/ RES/69/154 (2014), [9]. The need to prioritise the protection of refugee children was affirmed in similar resolutions under the title *Assistance to Refugees, Returnees and Displaced Persons in Africa* in 2013 (A/ RES/68/143), 2012 (A/RES/67/150), 2011 (A/RES/65/193), 2010 (A/RES/64/129), 2009 (A/RES/63/149), 2008 (A/RES/62/125), 2007 (A/RES/61/139), 2006 (A/RES/60/128), 2005 (A/RES/59/172), 2004 (A/RES/ 58/149), 2003 (A/RES/57/183), 2002 (A/RES/56/135), 2001 (A/RES/55/77), 2000 (A/RES/54/147), 1999 (A/RES/53/126), 1998 (A/RES/52/101), 1997 (A/RES/51/71), 1996 (A/RES/50/149), 1995 (A/RES/49/174), 1994 (A/RES/48/118) and 1993 (A/RES/47/107). The UN General Assembly has also adopted several resolutions addressing the particular needs of unaccompanied refugee children under the title *Assistance to Unaccompanied Refugee Minors*: A/RES/58/150 (2004); A/RES/56/136 (2002); A/RES/54/145 (2000); A/RES/53/122 (1999); A/RES/52/105 (1998); A/RES/51/73 (1997); A/RES/50/150 (1996); A/RES/49/172 (1995).

the UNCRC[2] and UNHCR.[3] The international community has also adopted two treaties that respond independently to the particular difficulties occasioned by involuntary alienage and to the special care and assistance required by children: the *Refugee Convention* and the *CRC*.

Attentiveness at the international level to the distinct needs of refugee children has not always found a counterpart in domestic practice. At the domestic level, there has been a tendency for states to focus on a child's status as a migrant (inevitably enlivening discourses of suspicion and immigration control) rather than their status as a child (more likely to evoke discourses of welfare and protection).[4] The child refugee, by reason of her asylum-seeking status, effectively ceases to be a child.[5] The tension between immigration control and the protection of children was evident throughout the drafting of the *CRC*, when a number of states sought, unsuccessfully, to limit the jurisdictional scope of the *CRC* to apply only to children 'lawfully' within a state's territory.[6] The United Kingdom subsequently entered a general reservation to the *CRC* to prevent the treaty from applying to migrant children.[7] This was withdrawn in 2008 following widespread international[8] and

---

[2] See *infra* text accompanying n 67–111.   [3] See *infra* text accompanying n 67–111.

[4] 'In spite of the manifest vulnerability of unaccompanied and separated children, the tendency of all the governments studied has been to treat them as migrants first, and children a distant second, placing the issue of border control above that of child protection': J Bhabha and M Crock, *Seeking Asylum Alone: A Comparative Study* (2007) 21. See also G Doná and A Veale, 'Divergent Discourses, Children and Forced Migration' (2011) 37 *Journal of Ethnic and Migration Studies* 1273.

[5] J Bhabha, 'Minors or Aliens? Inconsistent State Intervention and Separated Child Asylum-Seekers' (2001) 3 *European Journal of Migration and Law* 283, 293–4.

[6] The representative of the United States proposed that what is now art 2 of the *CRC* should read: 'Each State Party to the present Covenant shall respect and extend all the rights set forth in this Convention to all children *lawfully* in its territory' (emphasis added). The representative later amended the proposal to read: 'The States Parties to the present Covenant shall respect and extend all the rights set forth in this Convention to all children (lawfully) in their territories without distinction of any kind'. *Report of the Working Group on a Draft Convention on the Rights of the Child*, E/CN.4/L.1575 (1981), [40], [44]. Other delegates were uncomfortable with limiting the *CRC*'s application to children lawfully in the territory of a State Party: at [40]. An earlier Polish draft contained an express provision (then art 5) emphasising that '[t]he States Parties . . . recognize the right of alien children staying in their territories to enjoy the rights provided for in this Convention': *Note Verbale Dated 5 October 1979 Addressed to the Division of Human Rights by the Permanent Representation of the Polish People's Republic to the United Nations in Geneva*, E/CN.4/1349 (1979). The US representative ultimately agreed to withdraw the word 'lawfully' from its proposed text, but only on the understanding that the proposed art 5 would be deleted: E/CN.4/L.1575 (1981), [47]. Throughout the drafting the UK and German representatives repeatedly noted their concerns about the extension of the *CRC* to non-nationals: *Report of the Working Group on a Draft Convention on the Rights of the Child*, E/CN.4/1984/71 (1984), [9], [11].

[7] 'The United Kingdom reserves the right to apply such legislation, in so far as it relates to the entry into, stay in and departure from the United Kingdom of those who do not have the right under the law of the United Kingdom to enter and remain in the United Kingdom, and to the acquisition and possession of citizenship, as it may deem necessary from time to time': 1658 UNTS 682 (United Kingdom of Great Britain and Northern Ireland). Although this reservation is often referred to as a reservation to art 22, it is clear from its language that it applies to the application of the entire treaty. See N Blake and S Drew, 'In the Matter of the United Kingdom Reservation to the UN Convention on the Rights of the Child' (Opinion, 30 November 2001).

[8] UNCRC, *Concluding Observations: United Kingdom of Great Britain and Northern Ireland*, CRC/C/15/Add.188 (2002), [6]–[7].

domestic[9] criticism. Germany, Japan, Switzerland, Singapore and New Zealand also entered reservations or made declarations seeking to limit the rights available to non-citizen children.[10]

It has been suggested that the resolution of this 'Janus-like'[11] tension lies in treating each refugee child as a child first and a refugee second.[12] The more critical point is that the identity of a refugee child is layered and complex, and it is important that protection is tailored to respond both to the difficulties associated with refugeehood *and* the distinct needs and vulnerabilities of childhood.[13]

This chapter situates the refugee child in international law. It considers how international refugee law and international law on the rights of the child might be more creatively aligned to respond to the reality that the at-risk individual is both a child and a refugee. The focus of the chapter is on the capacity of the two legal regimes to respond to the distinct needs of a refugee child in the context of the status determination process. Notwithstanding this focus, the chapter's central thesis – that greater interaction between the two legal regimes has the capacity to enhance the protection afforded to refugee children – has application well beyond the issue of qualification. There is, in particular, extraordinary scope for greater alignment between the CRC and the full range of rights which follow from recognition of a child's *Convention* refugee status.

Against this background, Section 1.1 of the chapter traces the development of international law relating first to refugees and then to children. This exposition introduces the reader to the two key international instruments operating within the respective fields. Section 1.2 examines the manner in which the two international legal regimes have spoken

---

[9] '[T]he reservation sends out a powerful signal that the rights of asylum seeking children are less important than those of other children': JCHR, *The Treatment of Asylum Seekers*, HL 81-I, HC 60-I, Session 2006–07 (2007), [176].

[10] New Zealand has retained its reservation that '[n]othing in [the CRC] shall affect the right of the Government of New Zealand to continue to distinguish as it considers appropriate in its law and practice between persons according to the nature of their authority to be in New Zealand': 1719 UNTS 495, 495. Similarly, Singapore has retained its reservation reserving its 'right to apply such legislation and conditions concerning the entry into, stay in and departure from the Republic of Singapore of those who do not or who no longer have the right under the laws of the Republic of Singapore, to enter and remain in the Republic of Singapore': 1890 UNTS 526, 537. Switzerland has also retained its reservation that 'Swiss legislation, which does not guarantee family reunification to certain categories of aliens, is unaffected [by the CRC]': 1965 UNTS 505. Japan has maintained its initial declaration that the right to family unity in art 9(1) of the CRC is to be interpreted 'not to apply to a case where a child is separated from his or her parents as a result of deportation in accordance with its immigration law': 1775 UNTS 447. Germany's declaration (withdrawn on 15 July 2010) provided that '[n]othing in the [CRC] may be interpreted as implying that unlawful entry by an alien into the territory of the Federal Republic of Germany or his unlawful stay there is permitted; nor may any provision be interpreted to mean that it restricts the right of the Federal Republic of Germany to pass laws and regulations concerning the entry of aliens and the conditions of their stay or to make a distinction between nationals and aliens': 1669 UNTS 475, 479–80.

[11] S Melzac, 'The Emotional Impact of Violence on Children' in V Varma (ed), *Violence in Children and Adolescents* (1996) 1, 4.

[12] 'Refugee children are children first and foremost, and as children, they need special attention': UNHCR, *Refugee Children: Guidelines on Protection and Care* (1994) preface.

[13] 'It is therefore vital to view the rights of child-asylum seekers not only in the context of the Refugee Convention, but also in the specific framework of the CRC, in an attempt to fill the gaps and achieve the best possible combination of protection measures available under international law': J McAdam, 'Seeking Asylum under the Convention on the Rights of the Child: A Case for Complementary Protection' (2006) 14 *International Journal of Children's Rights* 251, 269.

to or disregarded each other over the past century. Section 1.3 sets out a framework for greater interaction between international refugee law and international law on the rights of the child. It does this by outlining three contexts – defined as 'modes of interaction' – where the *CRC* might appropriately be engaged to assist in determining the status of a refugee child: first, as a *procedural guarantee* to incorporate safeguards into the refugee status determination process; second, as an *interpretative aid* to inform the interpretation of the *Convention* definition; and, third, as an *independent source of status* outside the international refugee protection regime. Section 1.4 draws on the international rules of treaty interpretation to provide a principled anchor for that framework.

1.1 The Refugee and the Child – The International Legal Framework

1.1.1 *The* Refugee Convention

The *1951 Convention* and the attendant *1967 Protocol* are the primary instruments governing refugee status under international law. The *Convention* has been described as 'the cornerstone of the international refugee protection regime',[14] an elevation hardly surprising given the extensive and continued endorsement of the standards codified in the instrument. There are currently 145 states party to the *1951 Convention* and 146 states party to the *1967 Protocol*, with 98 states participating in the work of the Executive Committee of the High Commissioner's Programme ('UNHCR ExCom'), responsible for the *Convention*'s ongoing supervision. The *Convention* therefore provides the appropriate platform from which to consider the manner in which international law has attempted to address the challenges associated with the involuntary migration of children.

The *Convention* defines a refugee as an individual who satisfies the definition proscribed under art 1A(2) and is not otherwise excluded by operation of art 1. Article 1A(2) defines a refugee as a person who

> owing to a well-founded fear of being persecuted for reasons of race, religion, nationality, membership of a particular social group or political opinion, is outside the country of his nationality and is unable or, owing to such fear, is unwilling to avail himself of the protection of that country; or who, not having a nationality and being outside the country of his former habitual residence as a result of such events, is unable or, owing to such fear, is unwilling to return to it.

A person will thus be a refugee only if there is a genuine risk of the applicant 'being persecuted' that is causally connected to one of five enumerated forms of civil or political status. Article 1 also contains a number of carve-out provisions, for persons not deserving of protection (art 1F) and persons no longer needing protection (arts 1C–1E). Articles 3 to 34 of the *Convention* outline a comprehensive set of rights that attach to all refugees, including freedom from discrimination (art 3), access to courts (art 16), access to housing (art 21), access to public education (art 22), freedom of movement (art 26) and protection against *refoulement* (art 33).

---

[14] UNHCR ExCom, *Conclusions on the Provision of International Protection Including through Complementary Forms of Protection*, No 103 (LVI) (2005) Preamble para 1. See also UNHCR, *Ministerial Communique*, HCR/MINCOMMS/2011/6 (8 December 2011), [2], 'reaffirm[ing] that the [*1951 Convention*] and [*1967 Protocol*] are the foundation of the international refugee protection regime and have enduring value and relevance in the twenty-first century'.

The mandate of the *Refugee Convention* is age-neutral, applying to all individuals irrespective of age and containing no express reference to or provision for refugee children.[15] A number of commentators have suggested that this 'deficiency' is not surprising in light of the *Convention*'s historical context.[16] While it is certainly true that the *Convention* was strategically conceptualised to respond to a particular political climate,[17] it is not altogether self-evident why this political context obviated a need to recognise the fact that child refugees may require special protection.[18] At the time the *Convention* was drafted, a number of international instruments had already explicitly recognised the special needs of children, specifically refugee children.[19] Of particular salience, the mandate of the IRO – the first international agency created by the UN and the immediate predecessor to UNHCR – made express provision for 'unaccompanied children'.[20]

An examination of the *IRO Constitution* and a review of the IRO's operations in the period 1947–52 provide an interesting historical backdrop to the drafting of the *Refugee Convention*. The IRO was established in 1946 to coordinate the international action then required to respond to the 'urgent problem'[21] generated by the mass displacement and dislocation of populations following the Second World War.[22] The IRO's function was expressed in the following terms:[23] 'the repatriation; the identification, registration and classification; the care and assistance; the legal and political protection; the transport; and the resettlement and re-establishment, in countries able and willing to receive them, of

[15] The only references to children in the *Convention* itself relate to refugee parents' freedom as regards the religious education of their children (art 4) and the effect on an adult refugee's right to employment of having one or more children possessing the nationality of the country of residence (art 17(2)(c)). Even the article on public education fails to mention age or childhood specifically (art 22). See also *infra* text accompanying n 31 for discussion on Recommendation B of the *Final Act of the Conference of Plenipotentiaries*.

[16] G S Goodwin-Gill, 'Unaccompanied Refugee Minors: The Role and Place of International Law in the Pursuit of Durable Solutions' (1995) 3 *International Journal of Children's Rights* 405, 406 ('[c]onsidered in historical context, this deficiency is not surprising'); Bhabha and Crock (2007) *supra* n 4, 22 ('[The] Convention was focused from its inception on problems and conflicts familiar to the Cold War era in Europe, where the label of "refugee" was applied most readily to the political and intellectual dissidents escaping to the West from the Communist Bloc countries').

[17] J C Hathaway, *The Law of Refugee Status* (1991) 6; J C Hathaway, 'The Evolution of Refugee Status in International Law: 1920–1950' (1984) 33 *International and Comparative Law Quarterly* 348.

[18] Indeed, it seems arguable that the omission of protection measures is surprising because of the historical context, including the specific targeting of Jewish children during the Second World War. See E D Pask, 'Unaccompanied Refugee and Displaced Children: Jurisdiction, Decision-Making and Representation' (1989) 1(2) *International Journal of Refugee Law* 199.

[19] The idea that refugee children are entitled to special protection was, for example, firmly entrenched in the 1949 *Geneva Conventions*: see, e.g., *Geneva Convention Relative to the Protection of Civilian Persons in Time of War*, opened for signature 21 April 1949, 75 UNTS 287 (entered into force 21 October 1950), art 24(1). The 1977 *Additional Protocols* go even further. In total, 25 articles in the 1949 *Geneva Conventions* and the 1977 *Additional Protocols* deal specifically with children: Goodwin-Gill (1995) *supra* n 16, 413. See further D Plattner, 'Protection of Children in International Humanitarian Law' (1984) 24(240) *International Review of the Red Cross* 140.

[20] *IRO Constitution*, Annexure 2, Part I, [4].   [21] *IRO Constitution*, Preamble.

[22] Holborn describes the Second World War as causing 'the most formidable displacements of population ever experienced': 'At its outbreak there had been more than a million refugees in various parts of Europe and Asia. This number was swelled almost beyond calculation by mass movements which brought vast human misery and suffering in their wake': L W Holborn, *The International Refugee Organization: A Specialized Agency of the United Nations – Its History and Work, 1946–1952* (1956) 15.

[23] *IRO Constitution*, art 2.

persons who are the concern of the Organization under the provisions of Annex I'. A large number of children were separated from their families throughout the Second World War: many were forcibly removed from non-Germanic families and sent to special institutions for 'Germanization';[24] others found themselves separated as a consequence of the vicissitudes of the war and the deportation, kidnapping or execution of their families.

The definition of the term 'refugee' set out under Annexure 1, Part 1 of the *IRO Constitution* included the following category:

> (4) The term 'refugee' also applies to unaccompanied children who are war orphans or whose parents have disappeared, and who are outside their countries of origin. Such children, sixteen years of age or under, shall be given all possible priority assistance, including, normally, assistance in repatriation in the case of those whose nationality can be determined.

The *IRO Constitution* thus established a *priority* obligation to render all possible assistance to unaccompanied children. This proved to be one of the IRO's most politically divisive tasks, with divergent interests and views as to who ultimately had jurisdiction to make a determination about the repatriation or resettlement of an unaccompanied child.[25] Was it the IRO, the child's family (if they could be located), the government of the country of origin or the government of the host country? And to what extent, if at all, should the IRO take into account the wishes of any individual child?

One of the key debates during the drafting of what became art 1 of the *Refugee Convention* was whether the *Convention* should list categories of known refugee groups in a manner similar to the *IRO Constitution*, or whether a more general definition should be adopted based on what was perceived, at the time, to reflect the refugee experience.[26] The United States was the lead proponent of the former approach, proposing four categories of refugees that included, among others, '[a]ny unaccompanied child sixteen years of age or under, who is a war orphan, or whose parents have disappeared, who is unable or unwilling to avail herself of the protection of the government of his country of nationality or former nationality, and who has not acquired another nationality'.[27] A similar category was included in a provisional draft of the *Convention* definition,[28] but was removed after receipt of a cable from the then Director-General of the IRO, who noted his doubts about the 'continu[ed] usefulness' of the express inclusion of 'unaccompanied children' as a category in the refugee definition.[29] The observer for the IRO expanded on the Director-General's observation with the rather curious statement that the inclusion of 'unaccompanied minors' in the *IRO Constitution* 'purported mainly to give priority assistance to this group, i.e. physical assistance with regard to care and maintenance, repatriation and resettlement' and that '[t]he Director General doubts the continued usefulness of including this group in the

---

[24] Holborn (1956) *supra* n 22, 493.   [25] *Ibid.*, 495.

[26] G S Goodwin-Gill, 'Refugees and Their Human Rights' (Working Paper No 17, Refugee Studies Centre, August 2004) 6.

[27] Ad Hoc Committee on Statelessness and Related Problems, *United States of America: Memorandum on the Definition Article of the Preliminary Draft Convention Relating to the Status of Refugees (and Stateless Persons) (E/AC.32/2)*, E/AC.32/L.4 (1950) art 1A(3)(b).

[28] Ad Hoc Committee on Statelessness and Related Problems, *Provisional Draft of Parts of the Definition Article of the Preliminary Draft Convention Relating to the Status of Refugees, Prepared by the Working Group on This Article*, E/AC.32/L.6 (1950).

[29] Ad Hoc Committee on Statelessness and Related Problems, *Memorandum from the Secretariat of the International Refugee Organization*, E/AC.32/L.16 (1950).

Convention and in the mandate of the High Commissioner who will be concerned with international protection only'.[30]

Although the final text of the *Convention* contains no express provision on refugee children, the drafters' consideration of the special protection needs of this particular category of refugee is reflected in the summary of conference proceedings appended to the *Convention*. Recommendation B of the *Final Act of the United Nations Conference of Plenipotentiaries on the Status of Refugees and Stateless Persons* provides for '[t]he protection of refugees who are minors, in particular unaccompanied children and girls, with special reference to guardianship and adoption'.[31] Although not binding, the declaration contained in Recommendation B provides a compelling affirmation of the responsibility of states to take special measures to protect refugee children.[32]

1.1.2 *The* Convention on the Rights of the Child

International law has played an important role in advancing the rights of children. The League of Nations adopted the *1924 Declaration*, which provided that 'mankind owes to the [c]hild the best that it has to give'. In 1959 the UN adopted a more comprehensive declaration, which emphasised the 'special protection' needs of children.[33] The idea that children are entitled to special protection was also firmly entrenched in the 1949 Geneva Conventions.[34] And each of the *UDHR*,[35] the *ICCPR*[36] and the *ICESCR*[37] contain express provisions emphasising the obligations on states to provide special protection measures for children.

Although earlier accords had addressed the particular protection needs of children, the *CRC* – adopted by the UN General Assembly in 1989 and entering into force in 1990 – was the first international instrument to articulate the full set of rights applicable to children. The *CRC* was also the first international instrument to recognise children as individual rights-bearers, 'active in the construction and determination of their own social lives'.[38] In promoting a construction of children as 'social actors and active holders of their own rights',[39] the *CRC* represents a radical shift away from the conception of a child as a passive dependent tethered to a parent, evident in the earlier, largely protectionist instruments, which focused attention on a child's need to be cared for.[40] This attitudinal shift is

---

[30] E/AC.32/L.16 (1950).

[31] *Final Act of the United Nations Conference of Plenipotentiaries on the Status of Refugees and Stateless Persons*, A/CONF.2/108/Rev.1 (1952) Pt IV.

[32] The declaration constitutes an 'agreement relating to the treaty made by all the parties in connection with the conclusion of the treaty': *VCLT*, art 31(2).

[33] *Declaration of the Rights of the Child*, UNGA Res 1386 (XIV) (1959), Principle 2. See also *Declaration on the Protection of Women and Children in Emergency and Armed Conflict*, UNGA Res 3318 (XXIX) (1974).

[34] See *supra* n 19.   [35] *UDHR*, art 25(2).   [36] *ICCPR*, art 24(1). See also HRC, *GC17*.

[37] *ICESCR*, art 10(3).   [38] A James and A Prout, *Constructing and Reconstructing Childhood* (1990) 8.

[39] UNICEF, *The State of the World's Children: Celebrating 20 Years of the Convention on the Rights of the Child* (2009) 2.

[40] 'Underlying this change in focus is the rejection of perceptions of children as partly formed human beings and their acceptance in international law as individuals who are capable of being as rational as adults': G Van Bueren, *The International Law on the Rights of the Child* (1998) 137. 'The [CRC] recognizes the child as a subject of rights, and the nearly universal ratification of this international instrument by States parties emphasizes the status of the child, which is clearly expressed in article 12': UNCRC, *GC12*, [18]. This commitment was reaffirmed at the 27th special session of the UN General Assembly: *A World Fit for Children*, A/RES/S-27/2 (2002). This is not the place to trace the evolution of child rights nor to defend

most clearly illustrated by the inclusion in the *CRC* of traditional civil and political rights – freedom of expression,[41] freedom of religion[42] and freedom of association and assembly[43] – absent in both the *1924 Declaration* and the *Declaration of the Rights of the Child*.[44] The *CRC* also gives children a voice, containing an express provision affording a child the right to participate, and have her views respected, in all matters that affect her.[45]

The *CRC* applies to 'each child within [a state party's] jurisdiction' and prohibits any discrimination 'irrespective of the child's or his or her parent's or legal guardian's . . . birth or other status'.[46] The rights contained in the *CRC* thus apply to all children in the jurisdiction of a state party, including refugees, asylum seekers and refused asylum seekers, and these subcategories of children are entitled to benefit from the provisions of the *CRC* to the same extent as a citizen child.[47] The point has been emphasised by the UNCRC: '[t]he principle of non-discrimination, in all its facets, applies in respect to all dealings with unaccompanied and separated children. In particular, it prohibits any discrimination on the basis of the status of a child as being unaccompanied or separated, or as being a refugee, asylum seeker or migrant'.[48]

The obligations enshrined in the *CRC* can be categorised in the following way. First, the treaty *reaffirms* many of the core principles contained in the *UDHR*, the *ICCPR* and the *ICESCR*, and applies these principles directly to children. In contrast to the *ICCPR* and the *ICESCR*, the *CRC* is unique in that it covers the full spectrum of civil, political, economic, social and cultural rights in a single instrument. Second, the *CRC strengthens* the nature of a state's obligations to children, such that in some circumstances children will be eligible for greater protection than adults. Most significantly, the *CRC* does not permit derogation from any of its provisions at any time, including wartime situations.[49] And in contrast to the *ICESCR*, the *CRC* does not allow developing states to limit the extent to which economic rights would be guaranteed to non-nationals.[50] Third, the *CRC introduces* a number of rights specifically tailored to children. This includes the right for a child to participate in any decision involving them[51] and a requirement that the best interests of the

---

the concept of children as rights-bearers. Both issues have been addressed, in detail, elsewhere. The key point here is that the international community has, through the *CRC*, committed itself to recognising children as rights-holders. See generally J Tobin, 'Justifying Children's Rights' (2013) 21 *International Journal of Children's Rights* 395; M Freeman, 'The Value and Values of Children's Rights' in A Invernizzi and J Williams (eds), *The Human Rights of Children* (2011) 21; J Fortin, *Children's Rights and the Developing Law* (2009) 3–32; M Freeman, 'Why It Remains Important to Take Children's Rights Seriously' (2007) 15 *International Journal of Children's Rights* 5; P Alston and J Tobin, *Laying the Foundations for Children's Rights: An Independent Study of Some Key Legal and Institutional Aspects of the Impact of the Convention on the Rights of the Child* (2005) 3–8; J Eekelaar, 'The Emergence of Children's Rights' (1986) 6 *Oxford Journal of Legal Studies* 161; C P Cohen, 'The Human Rights of Children' (1983) 12 *Capital University LR* 369. Contra J Griffin, *On Human Rights* (2008) 83–94; M Guggenheim, *What's Wrong with Children's Rights* (2005).

[41] Art 13.   [42] Art 14.   [43] Art 15.

[44] *Declaration of the Rights of the Child*, UNGA Res 1386 (XIV) (1959).   [45] Art 12.   [46] Art 2(1).

[47] 'Article 2 emphasises that all the rights in the Convention on the Rights of the Child must apply to all children in the State, including visitors, refugees, children or migrant workers and those in the State illegally': UNICEF, *Implementation Handbook for the Convention on the Rights of the Child* (3rd ed, 2007) 23. See also *CRC* art 22, which provides that states shall take appropriate measures to ensure that a refugee child, or child seeking refugee status, 'shall . . . receive appropriate protection and humanitarian assistance in the enjoyment of applicant rights set forth in [the *CRC*]'.

[48] UNCRC, *GC6*, [18].   [49] *Contra ICCPR*, art 4.   [50] *Contra ICESCR*, art 2(3).   [51] *CRC*, art 12.

child be a primary consideration in any actions involving children.[52] There are also express provisions on the abduction and trafficking of children,[53] the role of parents, guardians and the state in the upbringing and development of children,[54] harmful traditional practices,[55] the right to engage in play and recreational activities,[56] child labour,[57] sexual exploitation[58] and the recruitment of children into armed forces.[59]

Throughout the drafting of the *CRC* there was acknowledgement of the specific protection needs of refugee children.[60] Although the first draft contained no express provision relating to refugee children, in 1981 the delegate for Denmark submitted a proposal to introduce a provision dealing specifically with protection and assistance to refugee children.[61] The proposal was generally well received, resulting in the inclusion of what is now art 22(1):

> States parties shall take appropriate measures to ensure that a child who is seeking refugee status or who is considered a refugee in accordance with applicable international or domestic law and procedures shall, whether unaccompanied or accompanied by his or her parents or by any other person, receive appropriate protection and humanitarian assistance in the enjoyment of applicable rights set forth in the present Convention and in other international human rights or humanitarian instruments to which the said States are Parties.

Article 22(2) requires that, where a refugee child has no family members, 'the child shall be accorded the same protection as any other child permanently or temporarily deprived of his or her family environment'.[62]

Article 22 remains the only provision in any international human rights treaty that deals expressly with the situation of refugee children and children seeking refugee status.[63] The provision transposes the international community's long-standing recognition that refugee children require special protection into a treaty-based mechanism to guarantee that protection. Far from simply guaranteeing beneficiaries of art 22 the enjoyment of applicable rights on a non-discriminatory basis – which is in any event mandated by the balance of the *CRC* – art 22 provides a rights-plus framework that requires states to take *appropriate* measures to ensure that a refugee child or child seeking refugee status receive the *appropriate* level of protection and humanitarian assistance. This framework requires states to take into account any additional protection and humanitarian assistance that a refugee child or child seeking refugee status may, on account of their distinct vulnerabilities and

---

[52] *Ibid.*, art 3.   [53] *Ibid.*, arts 11, 35.   [54] *Ibid.*, arts 7, 19–21.   [55] *Ibid.*, art 24(3).   [56] *Ibid.*, art 30.

[57] *Ibid.*, art 32.   [58] *Ibid.*, art 34.   [59] *Ibid.*, art 38.

[60] See, e.g., *Summary Record of the 1438th Meeting*, E/CN.4/SR.1438 (1978), [40]; *Question of a Convention on the Rights of the Child – Report of the Working Group*, E/CN.4/L.1468 (1979), [6]; *Summary Record of the 53rd Meeting (Second Part)*, E/CN.4/1985/SR.53/Add.1 (1985), [114], [117]; *Summary Record of the 56th Meeting*, E/CN.4/1988/SR.56 (1988), [50]; *Summary Record of the 54th Meeting*, E/CN.4/1989/SR.54 (1989), [8].

[61] This may have been prompted by the Women's International Democratic Federation's proposal that the *CRC* contain articles 'on the protection of the children of migrant workers and of the children of refugees': *Written Statement Submitted by the Women's International Democratic Federation*, E/CN.4/NGO/244 (1979) 4.

[62] See also arts 20–21.

[63] See generally J Pobjoy, 'Article 22' in P Alston and J Tobin (eds), *The UN Convention on the Rights of the Child: A Commentary* (2017) (forthcoming).

developmental needs, require in order to effectively enjoy the rights guaranteed under the *CRC* and other international human rights instruments.

Although significant in introducing a rights-plus framework for refugee children and children seeking refugee status, art 22, at least on its face, provides no substantive guidance in relation to the assessment of whether or not, and on what basis, a child qualifies for refugee status.[64] There were suggestions from a number of delegates that the provision be amended to contain a definition of the refugee child; however, these delegates appear to have been in the minority.[65] Van Bueren has suggested that a view was taken that any expansion of the refugee definition within the *CRC* would have required a corresponding amendment to the *1951 Convention* and *1967 Protocol*, which was 'something for which states ha[d] not demonstrated any enthusiasm'.[66]

The *CRC* has since been complemented by three Optional Protocols: the *OPAC*, the *OPSC* and, most recently, the *OPCP*.

1.2 The Refugee Child – Signs of Alignment

There is no single instrument in international law that sets out the full range of obligations that a state owes in respect of a refugee child. Although the mandate of the *Refugee Convention* extends to children, the *Convention* definition makes no express reference to or concession for refugee children. And while the *CRC* contains a provision guaranteeing 'appropriate protection and humanitarian assistance' to refugee children, it offers limited guidance on the assessment of a child's refugee status. In circumstances where neither the *Convention* nor the *CRC* independently provide an 'adequate or satisfactory basis' for the protection of refugee children,[67] there is clear merit in exploring the relationship between the two legal regimes and what this relationship might mean in the context of determining the refugee status of children.

This section examines the manner in which the international community – principally in the form of guidance from the UNCRC and UNHCR – has treated the relationship between international refugee law and international law on the rights of the child.[68] Although not binding on states as a matter of treaty interpretation,[69] this guidance has appropriately been

---

[64] This point is made in Japan's statement after the adoption of the *CRC*: 'the delegation of Japan accepted article 22 on the understanding that this provision was not intended to request the States to take further measures in addition to the present procedures for the recognition of refugees in accordance with their international obligations and their national laws on refugees': *Report of the Working Group on a Draft Convention on the Rights of the Child*, E/CN.4/1989/48 (1989), [722]. The Netherlands made a declaration expressly providing that its government 'understands the term "refugee" in [art 22(1)] as having the same meaning as in article 1 of the [*Refugee Convention*]': 1855 UNTS 420, 421 (Netherlands). Notwithstanding this view, there is a compelling argument that the duty to ensure that a child seeking refugee status receives 'appropriate protection' compels a state to give consideration to the circumstances of the intended beneficiary of protection and, hence, the relationship between the *Convention* definition and the rights protected under the *CRC*. See Chapter 4, text accompanying n 166.

[65] *Report of the Informal Open-Ended Working Group on the Rights of the Child*, E/CN.4/1982/30/Add.1 (1982), [94].

[66] Van Bueren (1998) *supra* n 40, 361.   [67] Goodwin-Gill (1995) *supra* n 16, 407.

[68] See generally J Pobjoy, 'A Child Rights Framework for Assessing the Status of Refugee Children' in S Juss and C Harvey (eds), *Contemporary Issues in Refugee Law* (2013) 91, 108–15.

[69] In circumstances where these policy documents are produced without the engagement or agreement of all states party to the *Convention* or *CRC*, they cannot properly be characterised as 'subsequent agreement

recognised as having clear persuasive value[70] and in the refugee context is often afforded considerable deference.[71] Indeed, given that the production of the guidance falls within the scope of the respective bodies' supervisory functions, there is an argument that a state could be required to explain treatment of child refugees that does not conform to the standards set by the two bodies.[72]

The most authoritative source of UNHCR guidance is found in the Conclusions on the International Protection of Refugees adopted by the agency's governing body, the UNHCR ExCom. The non-binding resolutions of the ExCom are particularly significant in that they reflect the consensus of representations from more than half of the signatories to the *Convention*.

The UNHCR ExCom first turned its attention to the situation of child refugees in 1986, noting that 'the situation of refugee children . . . required special consideration' and calling on the High Commissioner to report regularly to the ExCom on the 'needs of refugee children, and on existing and proposed programmes for their benefit'.[73] Following that session, UNHCR established a Working Group on Refugee Children at Risk and in 1987 published its first *Note on Refugee Children*. The opening paragraph of that note states:[74]

> Refugee children comprise approximately one-half of the world's refugee population, and as such benefit from general efforts on behalf of all refugees with respect to international protection, material assistance and durable solutions. Children, however, have special needs which must be identified and met. While refugee children have always been a major concern of UNHCR, they have received increasing attention in recent years. This is due both to the substantial number of children in the various large-scale refugee situations in different parts of the world and to the complexity of the problems to which their presence give[s] rise, as well as to the wider international attention now given to children in general and refugee children in particular.

The same year the ExCom published its first Conclusion specific to refugee children.[75] In that Conclusion, the ExCom noted the 'special needs and vulnerability'[76] of children within the broader refugee population and recognised that the situation in which children live 'often gives rise to special protection and assistance problems as well as to problems in the area of durable solutions'.[77] The ExCom stressed that 'all action taken on behalf of refugee children must be guided by the principle of the best interests of the child as well as by

---

between the parties' under *VCLT*, art 31(3)(a): J C Hathaway and M Foster, *The Law of Refugee Status* (2nd ed, 2014) 10.

[70] See, e.g., *R (SG and others) v Secretary of State for Work and Pensions* [2015] 1 WLR 1449, [105] (Lord Carnwath) (describing *GC14* as 'the most authoritative guidance now available on the effect of article 3.1 [of the *CRC*]').

[71] See, e.g., M Foster, *International Refugee Law and Socio-Economic Rights: Refuge from Deprivation* (2007) 72–5; J McAdam, 'Interpretation of the 1951 Convention' in A Zimmermann (ed), *The 1951 Convention Relating to the Status of Refugees and Its 1967 Protocol: A Commentary* (2011) 75, 112–14.

[72] For UNHCR, see *Statute of the Office of the United Nations High Commissioner for Refugees*, GA Res 428 (V), Annex, A/1775 (1950). Article 35(1) of the *Refugee Convention* further provides that '[t]he Contracting States undertake to co-operate with the [UNHCR] . . . in the exercise of its functions, and shall in particular facilitate its duty of supervising the application of the provisions of this Convention'. The importance of ensuring 'closer cooperation between States Parties and UNHCR' was affirmed by states in the *Declaration of States Parties to the 1951 Convention and/or Its 1967 Protocol Relating to the Status of Refugees*, HCR/MMSP/2001/09 (2001), [9]. For the UNCRC, see *CRC*, arts 43–5.

[73] UNHCR ExCom, *General*, No 41 (XXXVII) (1986), [(m)].   [74] *Ibid.*, [1].

[75] UNHCR ExCom, *Refugee Children*, No 47 (XXXVIII) (1987).   [76] *Ibid.*, [(a)].   [77] *Ibid.*, [(b)].

the principle of family unity'[78] and reaffirmed the need to promote expanded cooperation between UNHCR and other relevant organisations, including through the development of 'legal and social standards'.[79] Finally, the ExCom called upon the High Commission to develop, in consultation with these organisations, 'guidelines to promote cooperation between UNHCR and these organizations to improve the international protection, physical security, well-being and normal psychosocial development of refugee children'.[80]

The UNHCR Working Group convened a consultation on refugee children in March 1988, and in August 1988 issued the first edition of its *Guidelines on Refugee Children*.[81] The *Guidelines* identify the major issues affecting refugee children and provide guidance on how UNHCR will ensure that the special protection needs of refugee children are met.[82] In 1989 the UNHCR ExCom issued a second Conclusion on refugee children, reaffirming and expanding on the need for particular attention to be paid to the special protection needs of refugee children.[83]

After the adoption of the *CRC*, UNHCR began to promote the *CRC* as the appropriate framework for conceptualising the special protection needs of refugee children. Crisp has suggested that that agency's policies on refugee children 'owe a self-evident intellectual debt' to the *CRC*.[84] This intellectual debt is evident in the UNHCR *1993 Policy* published in August 1993,[85] which expressly notes that the *CRC*:[86] 'provides a comprehensive framework for the responsibilities of its States Parties to all children within their borders, including those who are of concern to UNHCR. Moreover, as a United Nations convention, it constitutes a normative frame of reference for UNHCR's action.' The *1993 Policy* was welcomed by the ExCom, which stressed the 'importance of the [CRC] as a normative framework for action to protect and care for children of [UNHCR's] concern'.[87] In its 1997 Conclusion on refugee children the ExCom reaffirmed 'the fundamental importance of the

---

[78] *Ibid.*, [(d)].   [79] *Ibid.*, [(s)].   [80] *Ibid.*, [(u)].   [81] UNHCR, *Guidelines on Refugee Children* (1988).
[82] J Crisp, 'Meeting the Needs and Realizing the Rights of Refugee Children and Adolescents: From Policy to Practice' (1996) 15(3) *Refugee Survey Quarterly* 1, 12.
[83] UNHCR ExCom, *Refugee Children*, No 59 (XL) (1989).
[84] 'Indeed, the UNHCR policy can legitimately be described as an attempt to operationalize the CRC in situations of human displacement. While only states can be parties to the CRC, UNHCR applies the Convention to all aspects of its work with refugee children and considers itself to be accountable for the implementation of CRC standards': Crisp (1996) *supra* n 82, 12.
[85] 'Although many of the components of this policy can be found in UNHCR's Guidelines on Refugee Children [which predated the *CRC*] or derive from the [CRC], their assimilation into the global policy of the Office reflects a new level of priority that the High Commissioner has come to meeting the specific protection and assistance needs of refugee children': UNHCR ExCom, *UNHCR Policy on Refugee Children*, EC/SCP/82 (1993), [6].
[86] UNHCR, *1993 Policy*, *supra* n 85, [17]. The UNHCR *1993 Policy* was followed by a revised set of operational guidelines on refugee children in 1994: UNHCR, *1994 Guidelines*, *supra* n 12. The *1994 Guidelines* were intended to combine 'the concept of "children's rights" with UNHCR's ongoing efforts to protect and assist refugee children' (at 14). In its introductory remarks, UNHCR refers to the two ancestral branches of the *Guidelines* (at 13): 'This book of Guidelines has its ancestors. On one side of the family tree is the human rights branch, which includes the most recent forebear, the [CRC]. On the other side is the UNHCR branch'. The introduction goes on to state (at 18–20): 'UNHCR [applies] the CRC to its own work by using the rights as guiding principles ... At the beginning of each chapter of these Guidelines, the rights in the CRC are stated as UNHCR's standards ... For the well-being of refugee children, UNHCR advocates the observance of CRC standards by all States, international agencies and non-governmental organizations.' See also UNHCR, *Guidelines on Policies and Procedures in Dealing with Unaccompanied Children Seeking Asylum* (1997).
[87] UNHCR ExCom, *General*, No 71 (XLIV) (1993), [(w)].

[CRC] to the legal framework for the protection of child and adolescent refugees and for promoting their best interests'[88] and called upon UNHCR to 'continue to integrate fully the rights of the child into its policies and programmes'.[89] In its most recent Conclusion on refugee children the ExCom emphasised the need for a:[90]

> rights-based approach, which recognizes children as *active subjects of rights*, and accord-ing to which all interventions are consistent with States' obligations under relevant international law, including, as applicable, international refugee law, international human rights law and international humanitarian law, and acknowledgment that the CRC provides an important legal and normative framework for the protection of children.

The Conclusion recommends the development of 'child and gender-sensitive national asylum procedures',[91] including consideration of 'an age and gender-sensitive application of the 1951 Convention through the recognition of child-specific manifestations and forms of persecution, including under-age recruitment, child trafficking and female genital mutilation'.[92]

The Conclusions of the UNHCR ExCom are complemented by UNHCR's *Handbook*, which was produced at the behest of – although never formally adopted by – the ExCom.[93] The *Handbook* was intended to provide a comprehensive analysis of the interpretation of the definition of a refugee and has traditionally been afforded a high degree of deference by domestic decision-makers.[94] Although the *Handbook* contains a number of references to children, given that it predates the *CRC* by a decade it is unsurprisingly silent on the relationship between the *Convention* and the *CRC*. Some guidance, however, can be gleaned from the more recent *Guidelines on International Protection*, which UNHCR's Department of International Protection began publishing in 2003 to complement the standards set in the *Handbook*.[95] Although these *Guidelines* are not formally adopted by the ExCom – and are therefore unlikely to be treated to the same degree of deference as the state-generated Conclusions – they nonetheless represent persuasive guidance on the interpretation of the *Convention*.[96]

Of particular salience to this project, UNHCR has issued the 2009 *Guidelines* which address the application of arts 1A(2) and 1F of the *Convention* to child asylum claims. The 2009 *Guidelines* emphasise that the substantive and procedural aspects of the assess-ment of a child's application for refugee status should be informed by the *CRC*. The 2009 *Guidelines* provide 'substantive and procedural guidance on carrying out refugee status

---

[88] UNHCR ExCom, *Conclusion on Refugee Children and Adolescents*, No 84 (XLVIII) (1997).
[89] *Ibid.*, [(c)].
[90] UNHCR ExCom, *Conclusion on Children at Risk*, No 107 (LVIII) (2007), [(b)(x)] (emphasis added). See also UNHCR ExCom, *Conclusion on Women and Girls at Risk*, No 105 (LVII) (2006).
[91] UNHCR ExCom, *Conclusion on Children at Risk*, No 107 (LVIII) (2007), [(g)(viii)].
[92] *Ibid.*, [(g)(viii)].   [93] UNHCR ExCom, *Determination of Refugee Status*, No 8 (XVIII) (1977), [(g)].
[94] G S Goodwin-Gill, 'The Search for the One, True Meaning . . .' in G S Goodwin-Gill and H Lambert (eds), *The Limits of Transnational Law: Refugee Law, Policy Harmonization and Judicial Dialogue in the European Union* (2010) 204, 209–13, 224–7.
[95] V Türk, 'Introductory Note to UNHCR Guidelines on International Protection' (2003) 15 *International Journal of Refugee Law* 303.
[96] Foster (2007) *supra* n 71, 71–2; Goodwin-Gill (2010) *supra* n 94, 219–20; J C Hathaway, *The Rights of Refugees Under International Law* (2005) 116–18.

determination in a child-sensitive manner',[97] including guidance on the interpretation of the definitional elements of arts 1A(2) and 1F of the *Convention*. This includes the assessment of the 'well-founded fear of being persecuted' standard,[98] the relevant agents of persecution,[99] the *Convention* grounds ('race and nationality or ethnicity',[100] 'religion',[101] 'political opinion',[102] 'membership of a particular social group'),[103] the issue of internal flight alternatives[104] and the application of the exclusion provisions to children.[105] The 2009 *Guidelines* also provide guidance on a number of evidentiary and procedural issues.[106]

The UNCRC has also issued a General Comment specifically addressing the treatment of unaccompanied and separated children outside their country of origin.[107] The General Comment seeks to 'provide clear guidance to States on the obligations deriving from the [CRC] with regard to this particular vulnerable group of children'.[108] In the context of status determination, the General Comment provides that states must adopt a '[c]hild-sensitive assessment of protection needs, taking into account persecution of a child-specific nature':[109]

> When assessing refugee claims of unaccompanied or separated children, States shall take into account the *development of, and formative relationship between, international human rights and refugee law*, including positions developed by UNHCR in exercising its supervisory functions under the 1951 Refugee Convention. In particular, the refugee definition in that Convention must be interpreted in an age and gender-sensitive manner, taking into account the particular motives for, and forms and manifestations of, persecution experienced by children. Persecution of kin; under-age recruitment; trafficking of children for prostitution; and sexual exploitation or subjection to female genital mutilation, are some of the child-specific forms and manifestations of persecution which may justify the granting of refugee status if such acts are related to one of the 1951 Refugee Convention grounds. States should, therefore, give utmost attention to such child-specific forms of manifestations of persecution as well as gender-based violence in national refugee status determination procedures.

The General Comment provides that the rights of a refugee child are not limited to those provided under the *Convention*, but instead extend to 'all human rights granted to children in the territory or subject to the jurisdiction of the State'.[110] In circumstances where a child does not satisfy art 1A(2) of the *Convention*, the General Comment provides that that child 'shall benefit from available forms of complementary protection to the extent determined by their protection needs'.[111]

The above discussion evinces clear endorsement, at an institutional level, of greater alignment between international refugee law and international law on the rights of the child. UNHCR's 2009 *Guidelines* and UNCRC's *GC6* are particularly significant in that they move beyond the mere articulation of general principles in support of alignment and provide guidance on the manner in which the *CRC* might be substantively relevant in the refugee determination context.

---

[97] UNHCR, 2009 *Guidelines*, [1].   [98] *Ibid.*, [10]–[36].   [99] *Ibid.*, [37]–[39].   [100] *Ibid.*, [41].
[101] *Ibid.*, [42]–[44].   [102] *Ibid.*, [45]–[47].   [103] *Ibid.*, [48]–[52].   [104] *Ibid.*, [53]–[57].
[105] *Ibid.*, [58]–[64].   [106] *Ibid.*, [65]–[77].   [107] UNCRC, *GC6*.   [108] *Ibid.*, [4].
[109] *Ibid.*, [74] (emphasis added).   [110] *Ibid.*, [76].
[111] *Ibid.*, [77]–[78]. See also UNCRC, 2012 *Discussion Day Report*, 'emphasis[ing] the primacy of the [CRC] in addressing the rights of the child in the context of international migration' (at [12]) and '[t]he need for clear guidance and frameworks that ensured Convention-compliant treatment of a child at all stages of the asylum-seeking procedure' (at [47]).

1.3 A Child-Rights Framework

The proposition that both the *Refugee Convention* and the *CRC* are relevant when determining the status of a refugee child is not new. The argument for greater interaction between the two regimes has for some time been advanced by scholars and advocates[112] and, as the above discussion demonstrates, by the UNHCR and the UNCRC. The relationship between the two regimes has also been recognised in domestic guidelines and policy documents.[113] Notwithstanding this clear in-principle support, decision-makers have been reluctant to engage with the *CRC* and associated jurisprudence when considering the status of refugee children. A review of more than 2,500 national decisions involving children seeking international protection since the adoption of the *CRC* revealed that the treaty was applied explicitly in a very limited number of cases. There are certainly exceptions and, as the analysis that follows will demonstrate, embryonic signs of domestic refugee jurisprudence that draws on the *CRC*'s normative framework in assessing a child's refugee status. But these cases remain the exception rather than the norm.

There are at least three ways in which the *CRC* may be relevant when considering the status of a refugee child. First, the *CRC* may provide *procedural guarantees* not otherwise provided under international refugee law. Second, the *CRC* may be invoked as an *interpretative aid* to inform the interpretation of the *Refugee Convention*. Third, the *CRC* may give rise to an *independent source of status* outside the international refugee protection regime. These three modes of interaction provide a child-rights framework for assessing the status of an at-risk child.

1.3.1 The CRC as a Procedural Guarantee

There are a number of scenarios in which a child's refugee claim may come before a decision-maker. If the child is accompanied, her claim will generally be subsumed within the application of the 'head of the family'. If the parent or guardian receives refugee status, it is common practice for any dependent children to automatically receive derivative refugee status. But the converse is also true: if the parent or guardian is denied refugee status, the

---

[112] 'The fact that [the *CRC*] reflects a near-universal consensus is a major advantage of child advocates throughout the world, seeking to initiate protection and assistance programmes, to monitor existing practices, and to reform those that do not work. The arguments from experience can now, in many cases, be backed up or grounded in, this international set of rules, cogently and coherently supporting the work of those who would bring effective protection to refugee children': Goodwin-Gill (1995) *supra* n 16, 416. For further examples see, e.g., J Bhabha and W Young, 'Not Adults in Miniature: Unaccompanied Child Asylum Seekers and the New US Guidelines' (1999) 11 *International Journal of Refugee Law* 84; Bhabha and Crock (2007) *supra* n 4; Foster (2007) *supra* n 71, 64–6, 207–12; M Crock, 'Re-Thinking the Paradigms of Protection: Children as Convention Refugees in Australia' in J McAdam (ed), *Forced Migration, Human Rights and Security* (2008) 155, 155; T Löhr, *Die kinderspezifische Auslegung des völkerrechtlichen Flüchtlingsbegriffs* (2009); G Sadoway, 'Refugee Children before the Immigration and Refugee Board' (1996) 15(5) *Refuge* 17; J McAdam, *Complementary Protection in International Refugee Law* (2007) 173–96; A Edwards, 'Age and Gender Dimensions in International Refugee Law' in E Feller, V Türk and F Nicholson (eds), *Refugee Protection in International Law: UNHCR's Global Consultations on International Protection* (2003) 46.

[113] Canadian, UK and Australian government guidelines all refer to the relevance of the *CRC* in refugee status determination. Even the United States – one of the two states that has *not* ratified the *CRC* – has issued guidance noting the significance of the obligations in the *CRC* in determining a child refugee's status: INS, *Guidelines*, 2.

child will similarly be denied protection. This is notwithstanding the fact that the child might have an independent, and potentially conflicting, claim for refugee protection. If a child is unaccompanied or separated, there is a greater chance that her claim will be independently assessed, although in a limited range of circumstances states have suggested that an unaccompanied child lacks the capacity to claim refugee status independently.

The *Refugee Convention* is silent on the procedures that a state should implement in designing a domestic system of refugee status determination. In contrast, the *CRC* contains a number of provisions that may be relevant to the determination process, including the principle that a child has a right to right to express views freely and to be heard in any judicial or administrative proceedings affecting her.[114] In promoting a construction of the child as an independent social actor, the *CRC* provides a solid legal basis for developing a participatory framework to ensure that children are not rendered invisible in domestic asylum processes.

1.3.2 The CRC as an Interpretative Aid

International law, and in particular international human rights law, has grown exponentially over the past 60 years. Many of the relatively nascent precepts contained within the *Refugee Convention* have since been re-articulated, re-contextualised and in many cases expanded in a comprehensive suite of international human rights treaties. There is widespread acceptance, both at an international and a domestic level, that the open-textured provisions of the *Convention* definition should be interpreted taking into account this broader international human rights framework.[115] In these circumstances there is a clear, principled basis for drawing on the *CRC* – the most authoritative articulation of the obligations that a state owes to a child – as an aid to inform the interpretation of the *Convention* definition in claims involving children.

The alignment of international refugee law with international human rights law is generally attributed to the work of James Hathaway, who in *The Law of Refugee Status* advanced a vision of refugee law linked to the emerging corpus of international human rights law.[116] Although Hathaway advocates this vision in a more general sense,[117] the link

---

[114] *CRC*, art 12.

[115] The link between international human rights law and the interpretation of the *Refugee Convention* has been endorsed by senior courts in the common law world, increasingly by decision-makers in the civil law world, by UNHCR, and by the majority of refugee scholars. For an excellent, comprehensive discussion on the extent of this endorsement, see Foster (2007) *supra* n 71, 27–35. For examples of case-law see, e.g., *Canada (A-G) v Ward* [1993] 2 SCR 689; *R v Immigration Appeal Tribunal; Ex parte Shah* [1999] 2 AC 629, 653 (Lord Hoffmann); *Horvath v SSHD* [2001] 1 AC 489, 495 (Lord Hope for the majority), 512 (Lord Clyde); *Sepet v SSHD* [2003] 1 WLR 856, [6]–[7] (Lord Bingham); *R v Special Adjudicator; Ex parte Ullah* [2004] 2 AC 323, 355 (Lord Steyn); *Fornah v SSHD* [2007] 1 AC 412, [10] (Lord Bingham); *HJ (Iran) v SSHD* [2011] 1 AC 596, [13] (Lord Hope); *RT (Zimbabwe) v SSHD* [2013] 1 AC 152, [29]–[31]; *MIMA v Khawar* (2002) 210 CLR 1, [111] (Kirby J); *Applicant NABD of 2002 v MIMIA* (2005) 216 ALR 1, [108]–[111]; *Stenaj v Gonzalez*, 227 Fed Appx 429 (6th Cir, 2007).

[116] Hathaway, *The Law of Refugee Status* (1991) *supra* n 17.

[117] The argument that refugee law should be reconceived as human rights protection runs as a red thread throughout Hathaway's scholarship: see generally J C Hathaway, 'Reconceiving Refugee Law as Human Rights Protection' 4(2) *Journal of Refugee Studies* (1991) 113; J C Hathaway, 'The Relationship between Human Rights and Refugee Law: What Refugee Judges Can Contribute' in International Association of Refugee Law Judges, *The Realities of Refugee Determination on the Eve of a New Millennium: The Role of*

has been most readily embraced by domestic courts in the context of the 'being persecuted' inquiry. Hathaway considers that the phrase 'being persecuted' should be understood as the 'sustained or systemic violation of basic human rights demonstrative of a failure of state protection',[118] identifying the rights enumerated in the *UDHR* and subsequently translated into the *ICCPR* and *ICESCR* as the appropriate reference points for the range of circumstances where the action or inaction of a state will constitute persecutory harm. More recently Hathaway has acknowledged that other widely ratified treaties may be relevant in defining what might be appropriately recognised as persecutory harm.[119] Treaties that may be relevant include the *CRC, OPSC, OPCP, CERD* and *CEDAW*. Hathaway considers that the specialised treaties have the capacity to act as valuable interpretive aids to decision-makers when applying the *Convention* definition.[120]

There are a number of principled benefits that flow from interpreting the *Convention* definition by reference to authoritative international human rights standards including the *CRC*.[121] First, it promotes objective and consistent decision-making.[122] In circumstances where the *Convention* is applied to thousands of individual refugee claims every day,[123] across more than 150 jurisdictions and without any overarching supervision, the issue of consistent interpretation is invariably raised. The general proposition that an international treaty should be accorded the 'same meaning by all who are party to it'[124] is largely uncontroversial. The need for international uniformity is particularly evident in the context of the *Convention*, a treaty which by its very design is intended to facilitate a minimum level of protection to a refugee regardless of the state party in which they seek refuge.[125] Notwithstanding practical difficulties,[126] the desirability of uniformity in the interpretation of the *Convention* has found favour in superior domestic courts, particularly within the

---

the Judiciary (1998) 80. In addition to conceptualising the 'being persecuted' inquiry by reference to international human rights law, Hathaway has drawn on international human rights standards: to define the scope of the 'membership of a particular group' *Convention* ground (Hathaway, *The Law of Refugee Status* (1991) *supra* n 17, 161); to limit the reach of the 'internal protection alternative' doctrines (J C Hathaway and M Foster, 'International Protection/Relocation/Flight Alternative as an Aspect of Refugee Status Determination' in E Feller, V Türk and F Nicholson (eds), *Refugee Protection in International Law: UNHCR's Global Consultations on International Protection* (2003) 353); to consider the circumstances when risk following from behaviour will warrant refugee status (J C Hathaway and J Pobjoy, 'Queer Cases Make Bad Law' (2012) 44(2) *New York University Journal of International Law and Politics* 315); and to adumbrate the authentic scope of the obligations that a state owes to refugees (Hathaway (2005) *supra* n 96).

[118] Hathaway, *The Law of Refugee Status* (1991) *supra* n 17, 104–5.

[119] Hathaway, (1998) *supra* n 117, 80.   [120] Hathaway (1998) *supra* n 117.

[121] This discussion derives in part from Hathaway and Pobjoy (2012) *supra* n 117, 382–4.

[122] 'Not only are states interpreting key criteria of the refugee definition in light of human rights principles, but international human rights law is providing the unifying theory binding different bodies of national jurisprudence': D Anker, 'Boundaries in the Field of Human Rights: Refugee Law, Gender and the Human Rights Paradigm' (2002) 15 *Harvard Human Rights Journal* 133, 136.

[123] In 2014, more than 1.66 million individual applications for asylum or refugee status were submitted to states or UNHCR in 157 countries or territories: UNHCR, *Global Trends 2014* (2015) 27. In 2015 this figure increased to 2.45 million individual applications in 174 countries or territories: UNHCR, *Global Trends 2015* (2016) 37.

[124] *King v Bristow Helicopters* [2002] 2 AC 628, [81].   [125] Foster (2007) *supra* n 71, 36.

[126] '[W]e may never know, or in some cases, we may not know for a time, which autointerpretation was correct ... This is, for better or worse, the situation resulting from the organizational insufficiency of international law': L Gross, 'States as Organs of International Law and the Problem of Autointerpretation' in G A Lipsky (ed), *Law and Politics in the World Community: Essays on Hans*

common law world.[127] The framework of international human rights law, particularly the core international human rights treaties, provides a principled and objective anchor to assist decision-makers in the task of ascertaining the international meaning of the key definitional elements of the *Convention*, and thus promotes transparent and predictable decision-making.

Second, reliance on internationally agreed human rights treaties promotes an interpretation of the *Convention* that is sensitive to the reality that states can only be bound by what they themselves have agreed to. Apart from anything else, interpreting the *Convention* by reference to the same extrinsic standards agreed to by states is 'strategically wise'.[128] Decision-makers are likely to be more comfortable grounding an interpretation of the *Convention* definition in standards to which states themselves have agreed. Consider for instance the case of a 15-year-old girl claiming refugee status on the basis that she will be subjected to FGC if returned to her country of origin. In circumstances where FGC has been widely condemned as a violation of international human rights law,[129] it would be incongruous for a government that claims to act consistently with its obligations under international human rights law to assert that the practice of FGC does *not* constitute persecutory harm for the purposes of the *Convention* definition.

Finally, recourse to internationally agreed standards enables the *Convention* definition to evolve in a contextually sensitive way. By embracing the interconnection between international refugee law and the increasingly sophisticated body of international human rights law, decision-makers are provided with an external point of reference that allows for the progressive development of international refugee law through the medium of the *Convention*. This in turn allows the *Convention* to respond to circumstances that may not have been apparent to its drafters. For example, the recognition of the relationship between the *Convention* and the broader framework of international human rights law has been critical in advancing claims involving gender-related persecution, persecution related to sexual orientation, and social and economic deprivation. So too, international human rights law, in particular the *CRC*, now has a vital role to play in advancing the protection of refugee children.

1.3.3 The CRC as an Independent Source of Status

The *CRC* may also give rise to an independent source of protection outside the international refugee protection regime. It is generally accepted that the *CRC* contains a complementary source of protection via the principle of *non-refoulement* implicit in, at the very minimum, arts 6 and 37. In that regard, the UNCRC has underlined that a state shall not return a child to her country of origin where there are 'substantial grounds for believing that there is a real risk of irreparable harm to the child'.[130] The UNCRC has not provided an exhaustive definition of irreparable harm but has indicated that it includes, though is 'by no means

---

Kelsen's Pure Theory and Related Problems in International Law (1953) 59, 76–7, cited in Goodwin-Gill, 'The Search for the One, True Meaning' (2010) *supra* n 94, 208.

[127] *R v SSHD; Ex parte Adan* [2001] 2 AC 477, 515–17; *R v SSHD; Ex parte Adan* [1999] 3 WLR 1274, 1296; *Al-Sirri v SSHD* [2013] 1 AC 745, [36]; *Applicant A v MIEA* (1997) 190 CLR 225; *X v RSAA* [2009] NZCA 488.

[128] Hathaway (1998) *supra* n 117.   [129] See, e.g., *CRC*, art 24(3).   [130] UNCRC, *GC6*, [27].

limited to', those harms contemplated under arts 6 and 37 of the *CRC*.[131] The Committee goes on to suggest that underage military recruitment and participation in armed conflict 'entails a high risk of irreparable harm involving fundamental human rights, including the right to life'.[132] Accordingly, the Committee takes the view that the obligations in art 38 of the *CRC*, along with arts 3 and 4 of the *OPAC*, 'entail extraterritorial effects' and that 'States [are obliged to] refrain from returning a child in any manner whatsoever to the borders of a State where there is a real risk of underage recruitment'.[133]

Article 3 of the *CRC*, which specifies that the best interests of the child shall be a primary consideration in all actions concerning her, provides a critical additional safeguard for children seeking international protection. Article 3(1) mandates not only that decision-makers consider the best interests of the child but, more specifically, that those interests are a *primary consideration* in any actions concerning the child. The obligation under art 3 attaches to all children falling within a state's jurisdiction,[134] and a state cannot limit the application of the provision on the basis of a child's citizenship or immigration status. Although it is now generally accepted that art 3 is relevant to children seeking international protection, this recognition has tended to focus on the influence of the obligation on the procedural guarantees afforded to at-risk children and the treatment of children during and subsequent to any status determination process. But while art 3 is plainly relevant to the procedures and treatment afforded children seeking international protection, the best interests principle may also be engaged as an independent basis for protection outside the traditional refugee protection regime. In particular, an assessment of the best interests of the child may preclude the return of a child to her home country notwithstanding the fact that the child is not eligible for protection under the *Convention* or the more traditional *non-refoulement* obligations noted above.

1.4 A Systemic Approach to Interpreting the *Refugee Convention*

A number of arguments can be called upon to promote greater recourse to the *CRC* and its associated jurisprudence in claims involving refugee children. As outlined above, the *CRC* provides a comprehensive, state-generated framework of rules of undisputed legal author-ity. This authority is underscored by the treaty's near-universal ratification. In addition, the *CRC* is complemented by a sophisticated and fast-evolving body of international jurispru-dence, principally in the form of General Comments, Concluding Observations and Discussion Days. Notwithstanding this normative appeal, there is clear value in outlining a legal basis to justify reliance on the *CRC* in refugee claims involving children. As the England and Wales Court of Appeal has cautioned, '[h]owever wide the canvas facing the judge's brush, the image he makes has to be firmly based on some conception of objective principle which is recognised as a legitimate source of law'.[135]

The legal basis for invoking the *CRC* as a procedural guarantee (the first mode of interaction) or an independent source of status (the third mode of interaction) is straight-forward. In both contexts the *CRC* is being relied on as a *direct* source of obligation. Hence, in the absence of any reservation limiting the application of the *CRC* to non-citizen children,[136] the rule of *pacta sunt servanda* applies and the obligations contained in the

---

[131] *Ibid.*, [27].   [132] *Ibid.*, [28].   [133] *Ibid.*, [28].   [134] *CRC*, art 2(1).
[135] *Sepet v SSHD* [2001] EWCA Civ 681, [66].   [136] See *supra* n 10.

CRC must be performed in good faith.[137] There is no suggestion that the *Convention* operates as a form of *lex specialis* that has the effect of excluding from refugee children the benefit of the simultaneously applicable framework of the *CRC*. Indeed, such an argument is expressly forbidden by the *Convention*, which provides that '[n]othing in [the] Convention shall ... impair any rights and benefits granted by a Contracting State to refugees apart from this Convention'.[138] A review of the drafting history of the *Convention* makes clear that art 5 applies to pre-existing rights as well as to any rights that might accrue in the future.[139]

The legal basis for invoking the *CRC* as an interpretative tool to inform the interpretation of the *Convention* (the second mode of interaction) is more involved. The discussion above outlines a number of normative bases that support this integrative approach. A further, principled basis can be located in the international rules of treaty interpretation, which provide a critical source of support for greater interaction between international refugee law and international law on the rights of the child and, in particular, for drawing on the *CRC* as an interpretative aid when interpreting the open-textured provisions of the *Convention*.

The *VCLT* provides the authoritative set of rules to guide the interpretation of treaties (the 'Vienna rules'). The ICJ has pronounced that the Vienna rules constitute customary international law and therefore apply to the interpretation of any treaty, irrespective of whether the states parties involved are parties to the *VCLT*.[140] This is significant as the *VCLT* does not apply retroactively,[141] and both the *1951 Convention* and the *1967 Protocol* predate it. The applicability of the Vienna rules is widely accepted in international courts and tribunals[142] and has received widespread endorsement at a national level. The discussion that follows considers how the Vienna rules might be used to promote what is termed here a *systemic approach* to interpreting the *Convention*.[143]

1.4.1 The Interpretation of an International Treaty in Domestic Fora

Before turning to the Vienna rules, it is necessary to outline why the discussion is grounded in international rules of treaty interpretation rather than domestic rules of statutory interpretation. In circumstances where many jurisdictions have codified the *Convention* definition in a domestic statutory instrument, it is certainly arguable that the latter is more appropriate. Indeed, these domestic principles may in certain jurisdictions provide a more straightforward route for invoking the *CRC*.

---

[137] *VCLT*, arts 26–7.   [138] Art 5.   [139] Hathaway (2005) *supra* n 96, 110.
[140] *Territorial Dispute (Libyan Arab Jamahiriya/Chad) (Judgment)* [1994] ICJ Rep 6, 21.
[141] *VCLT*, art 4.   [142] R Gardiner, *Treaty Interpretation* (2nd edn, 2015) 13–20.
[143] The terminology adopted here derives from M Koskenniemi, ILC, *Fragmentation of International Law: Difficulties Arising from the Diversification and Expansion of International Law – Report of the Study Group of the International Law Commission*, A/CN.4/L.682 (2006), [57]. See *infra* text accompanying n 172–187. The approach outlined here has been influenced by Hathaway's 'interactive understanding' of treaty interpretation set out in Hathaway (2005) *supra* n 96, 48–74. However, the inquiry here is narrower, focusing specifically on the elements of the *VCLT* that have the capacity to support an interpretation of the *Refugee Convention* that promotes its systemic integration into the broader international human rights framework. In contrast, Hathaway seeks to outline a more general theory of treaty interpretation. As a result of this book's more tailored inquiry, greater emphasis is placed here on the interpretative rule codified in art 31(3)(c) of the *VCLT*.

There are three principal reasons why this chapter focuses on the Vienna rules rather than principles of domestic statutory interpretation. First, the Vienna rules are specifically tailored to the interpretation of international treaties and therefore provide the appropriate analytical framework wherever domestic legislation incorporates an international treaty. The application of domestic principles of statutory interpretation may produce a different result than that which would follow the application of the Vienna rules which, by requiring a decision-maker to take into account the treaty's object and purpose, ensures that human rights treaties are not given a narrow or restricted interpretation.[144] Second, an interpretation grounded in the Vienna rules is more likely to lead to uniformity in the interpretation of the *Convention*.[145] By contrast, there is a danger that relying on domestic principles of statutory interpretation – which vary from state to state – may give rise to conflicting interpretations and the corresponding risk of fragmentation. Third, the approach adopted in this chapter is consistent with that of senior courts, particularly in the common law world, where there has been increased engagement with the Vienna rules in national courts, coupled with a recognition that in interpreting the *Convention* 'the rules applicable to the interpretation of treaties must be applied to the transposed text and rules generally applicable to the interpretation of domestic statutes give way'.[146]

1.4.2 A General 'Rule' of Treaty Interpretation

Article 31 of the *VCLT* codifies what is often referred to as the general 'rule' of treaty interpretation. Article 31(1) requires a decision-maker to interpret a treaty 'in good faith in accordance with the ordinary meaning to be given to the terms of the treaty in their context and in the light of its object and purpose'. Article 31(2) sets out the permissible sources that

---

[144] 'Inevitably the final text will have been the product of a long period of negotiation and compromise. One cannot expect to find the same precision of language as one does in an Act of Parliament drafted by parliamentary counsel . . . It follows that one is more likely to arrive at the true construction of article 1A (2) by seeking a meaning which makes sense in the light of the Convention as a whole, and the purposes which the framers of the Convention were seeking to achieve, rather than by concentrating exclusively on the language. A broad approach is what is needed, rather than a narrow linguistic approach': *Adan v SSHD* [1999] 1 AC 293, 305. See also *Applicant A v MIEA* (1997) 190 CLR 225, 255 (McHugh J); Gardiner (2015) *supra* n 142, 51–4.

[145] See *supra* text accompanying n 121–7.

[146] *Applicant A v MIEA* (1997) 190 CLR 225, 230–1. In the United Kingdom see, e.g., *R (ST) v SSHD* [2012] 2 AC 135, [30] ('[The *Refugee Convention*] must be interpreted as an international instrument, not a domestic statute'); *R v Asfaw* [2008] 1 AC 1061, [125] ('The starting point for the interpretation of an international treaty such as the Geneva Convention is the [*VCLT*]'); *Januzi v SSHD* [2006] 2 AC 426, [4] ('[The *Refugee Convention*] must be interpreted as an international instrument, not a domestic statute, in accordance with the rules prescribed in the [*VCLT*]'); *R v SSHD; Ex parte Adan* [2001] 2 AC 477, 513–15 (observing that 'a treaty should be interpreted "unconstrained by technical principles of English law, or by English legal precedent, but on broad principles of general application"', citing *James Buchanan & Co Ltd v Babco Forwarding and Shipping (UK) Ltd* [1978] AC 141); *R v SSHD; Ex parte Adan* [1999] 3 WLR 1274, 1295 ('[The *VCLT's*] provisions imply that every treaty falling within its scope has to be interpreted in accordance with objective cannons of construction'); *Sepet v SSHD* [2003] 1 WLR 856, [6]–[7] (Lord Bingham) ('In interpreting the [*Refugee Convention*] the House must respect articles 31 and 32 of the [*VCLT*]'); *Fornah v SSHD* [2007] 1 AC 412, [10] ('Since the Convention is an international instrument which no supra-national court has the ultimate authority to interpret, the construction put upon it by other states, while not determinative . . . is of importance, and in cases of doubt articles 31–33 of the [*VCLT*] may be invoked to aid the process of interpretation')).

may comprise the context of a treaty, centred on material relating to the conclusion of the treaty. Article 31(3) is forward-focused, and requires that an understanding of the treaty's context be supplemented by a number of extrinsic sources, including subsequent interpretative agreement between the parties, subsequent practice in the application of the treaty relevant to its interpretation, and any relevant rules of international law applicable in the relations between the parties to the treaty.

The use of the singular noun, *'General rule* of interpretation', suggests that the article comprises a single holistic 'rule' of interpretation.[147] As Aust explains, 'the three paragraphs represent a logical progression, nothing more. One naturally begins with the text, followed by the context, and then other matters, in particular subsequent material'.[148] The adoption of a 'single, closely integrated rule'[149] underscores the need to look beyond a literal construction of the text and to consider the terms of the treaty in light of their object and purpose, in their context and taking into account subsequent extrinsic sources.[150] This rejection of strict literalism has found favour in domestic refugee jurisprudence, where senior courts have repeatedly emphasised the importance of interpreting the *Convention* in a manner 'which makes sense in the light of the Convention as a whole', while at the same time respecting the expressed intention of the parties.[151]

The discussion that follows considers the extent to which the constituent elements of art 31 support a *systemic approach* to interpreting the *Convention*.[152] At the outset it is important to acknowledge that treaty interpretation is an inexact science.[153] Although framed as a 'rule', the general rule codified in art 31 is not intended to act as a straightjacket limiting other interpretative devices that may assist a decision-maker in ascertaining the meaning of a treaty provision.[154] In this sense, the Vienna rules are perhaps

---

[147] This was the ILC's explicit intention: ILC, 'Reports of the Commission to the General Assembly' [1966] (2) *Yearbook of the International Law Commission* 169, 219–20.

[148] A Aust, *Modern Treaty Law and Practice* (3rd edn, 2013) 208. See generally McAdam (2011) *supra* n 71, 83.

[149] ILC, 1966 *Reports, supra* n 147, 220.

[150] As the ILC noted in its Commentaries on the Draft Articles: 'the application of the means of interpretation in the article would be a single combined operation. All the various elements as they were present in any given case would be thrown in the crucible and their interaction would give the legally relevant interpretation': ILC, 1966 *Reports, supra* n 147, 219–20.

[151] *Applicant A v MIEA* (1997) 190 CLR 225, 252–3 (McHugh J), 231 (Brennan CJ); *Adan v SSHD* [1999] 1 AC 293, 305; *R v Asfaw* [2008] 1 AC 1061, [11]; *Januzi v SSHD* [2006] 2 AC 426, [4]; *R (European Roma Rights Centre) v Immigration Officer at Prague Airport* [2005] 2 AC 1, [18].

[152] The following discussion focuses on the requirement to interpret a provision 'in light of its object and purpose' (art 31(1)), taking into account 'any relevant rules of international law applicable in the relations between the parties' (art 31(3)(c)), on the basis that these elements most strongly support a *systemic approach* to interpreting the *Convention*. For reasons noted at *supra* n 69, the obligation to take into account '[a]ny subsequent agreement between the parties' (art 31(3)(a)) is of limited utility in the *Convention* context. As to 'subsequent practice' (art 31(3)(b)), although the book draws strongly on national case-law (see Introduction, 'Methodology and Research Design'), this domestic practice lacks the consensus required to 'establish[] the agreement of the parties' about the *Convention*'s interpretation.

[153] ILC, 'Law of Treaties' [1964] (2) *Yearbook of the International Law Commission* 5, 54. See generally M Waibel, 'Demystifying the Art of Interpretation' (2010) 22 *European Journal of International Law* 571.

[154] See generally J Tobin, 'Seeking to Persuade: A Constructive Approach to Human Rights Treaty Interpretation' (2010) 23 *Harvard Human Rights Journal* 1. Gardiner underlines that the Vienna rules do not provide a 'step-by-step formula for producing an irrebuttable interpretation': Gardiner (2015) *supra* n 142, 10.

more appropriately characterised as guidelines or principles.[155] As Tobin observes, 'the VCLT's general rule may frame the interpretative process, but it is ultimately unable to resolve the question of how to choose *a* meaning from the text of a treaty from among the inevitable range of potential meanings'.[156] But while it is important to acknowledge the limits of the *VCLT*, it is nonetheless clear that the interpretative principles codified in art 31 provide an objective and principled source of guidance for decision-makers and, insofar as that guidance promotes an interpretation of the *Convention* that takes into account the broader international human rights framework, art 31 provides a persuasive source of support for a *systemic approach* to interpreting the *Convention*.

1.4.3 A Human Rights Object and Purpose

The object and purpose of the *Refugee Convention* might be used in two complementary ways to support recourse to the broader framework of international human rights law when interpreting the *Convention* definition. First, the widely,[157] although not universally,[158] held view that the *Convention* has a human rights object and purpose might be used to support an interpretation of the *Convention* that imports the human rights standards subsequently agreed by states. As UNHCR has explained,[159]

> the aim of the drafters [was] to incorporate human rights values in the identification and treatment of refugees, thereby providing helpful guidance for the interpretation, in harmony with the Vienna Treaty Convention, of the provisions of the 1951 Convention ... Human rights principles, not least because of this background, should inform the interpretation of the definition of who is owed [refugee] protection.

As a matter of principle, the argument finds support in the preamble to the *1951 Convention*, which makes express reference to the *UDHR* and affirms the principle that 'human beings shall enjoy fundamental rights and freedoms without discrimination' and observes a need to 'assure refugees the widest possible exercise of these fundamental rights and freedoms'.[160] Further support can be taken from the text and drafting history of art 5 of the *Convention*, which signals that the drafters envisaged that the *Convention* – at the time one of only two international human rights treaties – would one day need to be reconciled with subsequent international human rights accords.[161]

The humanitarian object and purpose of the *Convention* has been repeatedly relied on by senior appellate courts to justify recourse to the wider remit of international human rights law to interpret the definitional elements of the *Convention*. In *Canada (Attorney General) v Ward*, the Supreme Court of Canada drew on the *Convention*'s underlying 'commitment

---

[155] See, e.g., Gardiner (2015) *supra* n 142, 38–41.

[156] Tobin (2010) *supra* n 154, 3 (emphasis in original).

[157] For an excellent discussion see Foster (2007) *supra* n 71, 40–9. See, e.g., *R v Immigration Appeal Tribunal; Ex parte Shah* [1999] 2 AC 629, 639.

[158] Foster (2007) *supra* n 71, 44–5.

[159] UNHCR, *Interpreting Article 1 of the 1951 Convention Relating to the Status of Refugees* (2001), [4]–[5].

[160] *1951 Convention*, Preamble paras 1–2. See also the Preamble to the *1967 Protocol*. Recourse to the Preamble finds further support in the requirement, in *VCLT*, art 31(1), to interpret the terms of the treaty 'in their context'. Article 31(2) includes in 'context' a treaty's 'text including its *preamble and annexes*' (emphasis added).

[161] See Hathaway (2005) *supra* n, 96, 100.

to the assurance of basic human rights without discrimination'[162] to conclude that '[t]he meaning assigned to a "particular social group" in the [*Convention*] should take into account the general underlying themes of the defence of human rights and anti-discrimination that form the basis of the international refugee protection initiative'.[163] In *Pushpanathan v Canada (MCI)* the same court held that '[the] overarching and clear human rights object and purpose [of the *Convention*] is the background against which interpretation of individual provisions must take place'.[164] Senior courts in the United Kingdom have made similar observations. In *Fornah v SSHD*, the House of Lords noted that it is well established that the *Convention* 'must be interpreted in accordance with its broad humanitarian objective and having regard to the principles, expressed in the preamble, that human beings should enjoy fundamental rights and freedoms without discrimination'.[165] More recently, in *HJ (Iran) v SSHD*, the UK Supreme Court drew attention to the reference to the *UDHR* in the preamble to the *Convention*, noting that '[t]he guarantees in the Universal Declaration are fundamental to a proper understanding of the Convention'.[166]

The language of object and purpose has also been construed to embody a principle of 'effectiveness'.[167] Hathaway has developed this idea in the context of the *Convention*, arguing that 'the obligation to interpret the text of a treaty in the light of its object and purpose should be conceived as incorporating the overarching duty to interpret a treaty in a way that ensures its effectiveness'.[168] He takes the view that in order to be effective a treaty must be interpreted in a way that reconciles it with its 'contemporary international legal context'.[169] Hathaway's argument finds support in decisions of senior courts, which, although not always tied to an explication of the Vienna rules, have underlined the need to treat the *Convention* as a living instrument to ensure its continued effective application.

---

[162] *Canada (Attorney General) v Ward* [1993] 2 SCR 689, 733.

[163] *Ibid.*, 739. This approach was subsequently approved by the House of Lords in *R v Immigration Appeal Tribunal; Ex parte Shah* [1999] 2 AC 629, 651 (Lord Hoffmann): 'In my opinion, the concept of discrimination in matters affecting fundamental rights and freedoms is central to an understanding of the Convention . . . The obvious examples, based on the experiences of the persecutions in Europe which would have been in the minds of the delegates in 1951, were race, religion, nationality and political opinion. But the inclusion of "particular social group" recognised that there might be different criteria for discrimination, in *parie materiae* with discrimination on other grounds, which would be equally offensive to human rights . . . In choosing to use the general term "particular social group" rather than an enumeration of specific social groups, the framers of the Convention were in my opinion intending to include whatever groups might be regarded as coming within the anti-discriminatory objectives of the Convention.'

[164] *Pushpanathan v Canada (MCI)* [1998] 1 SCR 982, 1024.   [165] *Fornah v SSHD* [2007] 1 AC 412, [10].

[166] *HJ (Iran) v SSHD* [2011] 1 AC 596, [14]. See also *RT (Zimbabwe)* [2013] 1 AC 152, [29]–[31].

[167] Although the ILC did not expressly include a principle of 'effective interpretation' in the *VCLT*, it indicated that regard to a treaty's effects was relevant to the 'object and purpose' inquiry. 'When a treaty is open to two interpretations one of which does not enable the treaty to have appropriate effects, good faith and the objects and purposes of the treaty demand that the former interpretation should be adopted': ILC, 1966 *Reports, supra* n 147, 219. See generally Waibel (2010) *supra* n 153, 581–3; E Bjorge, *The Evolutionary Interpretation of Treaties* (2014) 8–9.

[168] Hathaway (2005) *supra* n 96, 62.

[169] Hathaway (2005) *supra* n 96, 64; see also at 67–8: '[A]n interpretative approach that synthesizes foundational insights from analysis of the historical normative legal context and practical landscape within which treaty duties are now to be implemented is the most objective and legally credible means of identifying how best to make the treaty effective. It is an approach fully in line with the basic obligation of *pacta sunt servanda*, since it honors the original goals which prompted elaboration of the treaty even as it refuses to allow those commitments to atrophy through passage of time.'

For example, in *R v Immigration Appeal Tribunal; Ex parte Shah*, the England and Wales High Court cautioned that 'unless [the *Convention*] is seen as a living thing, adopted by civilised countries for a humanitarian end which is constant in motive but mutable in form, the Convention will eventually become an anachronism'.[170] Similarly, in *R v SSHD; Ex parte Adan* the House of Lords considered it clear that, as 'the signatory states intended that the Convention should afford continuing protection for refugees in the changing circumstances of the present and future world[,] ... the Convention has to be read as a living instrument'.[171]

1.4.4 *The* CRC *as a* Relevant Rule of International Law

A systemic approach to interpreting the *Convention* is premised on the principle that international treaties are to be interpreted 'by reference to their normative environment ("system")'.[172] As the ILC has noted:[173]

> The rationale for such a principle is understandable. All treaty provisions receive their force and validity from general law, and set up rights and obligations that exist alongside rights and obligations established by other treaty provisions and rules of customary international law. None of such rights or obligations has any *intrinsic* priority amongst the others. The question of their relationship can only be approached through a process of reasoning that makes them appear as parts of some coherent and meaningful whole.

This principle of 'systemic integration' finds its clearest exposition in art 31(3)(c) of the *VCLT*,[174] which sets out the circumstances in which external rules of international law must be taken into account in interpreting the text of a treaty. The provision requires a decision-maker to take into account, together with context, 'any relevant rules of international law applicable in the relations between the parties'. It has been suggested that art 31(3)(c) provides the 'master key' to the house of international law.[175] Indeed, as both McLachlan and Sands have observed, in some instances it may provide the only key.[176]

Despite its potential scope as an interpretative mechanism,[177] until recently the provision was rarely invoked by decision-makers at an international or domestic level, either in the refugee context or in international law more generally.[178] Relative to the other elements of

---

[170] *R v Immigration Appeal Tribunal; Ex parte Shah* [1997] Imm AR 145, 152, approved by the House of Lords in *Sepet v SSHD* [2003] 1 WLR 856, [6].

[171] *R v SSHD; Ex parte Adan* [2001] 2 AC 477, 500.

[172] ILC (2006) *Fragmentation Report, supra* n 143, [413].   [173] *Ibid.*, [414].

[174] The ILC has noted the 'systemic nature of international law has received clearest formal expression in [art 31(3)(c)]': *Ibid.*, [420].

[175] The analogy can be attributed to Xue Hanquin, Ambassador of China to the Netherlands and member of the ILC: see C McLachlan, 'The Principle of Systemic Integration and Article 31(3)(c) of the Vienna Convention' (2005) 54 *International and Comparative Law Quarterly* 279, 281, citing Xue Hanquin.

[176] See P Sands, 'Treaty, Custom and the Cross-Fertilization of International Law' (1998) 1 *Yale Human Rights and Development Law Journal* 85; McLachlan (2005) *supra* n 175. See also D French, 'Treaty Interpretation and the Incorporation of Extraneous Legal Rules' (2005) 55 *International and Comparative Law Quarterly* 281, 301.

[177] Sands (1998) *supra* n 176, 85, notes that art 31(3)(c) 'appears to the only tool available under international law to construct a general international law by reconciling norms arising in treaty and custom across different subject matter areas'.

[178] Foster (2007) *supra* n 71, 52.

art 31, the provision has also attracted very little academic attention. One commentator remarked that the instruction in art 31(3)(c) appeared for a long time to be a 'dead letter';[179] another described the provision as 'languished in ... obscurity'.[180] This did not mean that decision-makers were not referring to the wider remit of international law when interpreting at treaty;[181] there was, however, a reluctance to operationalise such recourse by reference to art 31(3)(c). This general reluctance might be attributed to at least two interdependent factors. The first derives from the laconic nature of the provision itself. A member of the ICJ, in considering the principle of contemporaneity in the application of environmental norms, noted that '[t]he provision in [art 31(3)(c)] ... scarcely covers this aspect with the degree of clarity requisite to so important a matter'.[182] The second relates to the availability of other interpretative mechanisms that might yield the same result.[183] For instance, in the context of the *Convention*, the requirement to interpret a treaty in light of its object and purpose, discussed above, is often relied on to legitimise recourse to international human rights instruments. Neither of these explanations necessarily renders art 31(3)(c) a dead letter. They do, however, demonstrate the need for a more detailed consideration of how art 31(3)(c) might apply in a given context and the extent to which the provision might benefit from judicial or legislative development.[184]

More recently there has been greater judicial engagement with art 31(3)(c), suggesting that the provision 'has a capacity to become applicable in a greater variety of circumstances than its origins would suggest'.[185] The provision has also been the subject of a thorough analysis by the ILC as part of its wider work on the fragmentation of international law,[186] and more sustained academic engagement, particularly within the context of broader debates surrounding 'systemic integration'.[187]

In the refugee context, academic attention on art 31(3)(c) has been more limited. The one exception is Foster, who has undertaken a detailed examination of the application of art

---

[179] Gardiner (2015) *supra* n 142, 304.   [180] McLachlan (2005) *supra* n 175, 279.   [181] *Ibid.*, 280.

[182] *Gabčíkovo-Nagymaros Project (Hungary/Slovakia) (Judgment)* [1997] ICJ Rep 7, 114 (Separate Opinion of Vice-President Weeramantry). See also Sands (1998) *supra* n 176, 100–1.

[183] ILC (2006) *Fragmentation Report, supra* n 143, [421].

[184] See generally Sands (1998) *supra* n 176, who considers (at 102) how art 31(3)(c) might 'be developed into an operationally useful tool'.

[185] Gardiner (2015) *supra* n 142, 290. See especially decisions of the ECtHR (*Loizidou v Turkey (Merits)* (1996) 23 EHRR 513, [43]; *Al-Adsani v UK* (2002) 23 EHRR 11, [55]; *Fogarty v UK* (2002) 34 EHRR 12, [35]; *McElhinney v Ireland* (2002) 34 EHRR 13, [36]; *Demir v Turkey* (2009) 48 EHRR 54, [146]; *Neulinger v Switzerland* (2012) 54 EHRR 31, [131]; *National Union of Rail, Maritime and Transport Workers v UK* (2015) 60 EHRR 10, [76]), the WTO (Panel Reports, *European Communities – Measures Affecting the Approval and Marketing of Biotech Products*, WT/DS291–3/R, WT/DS332–4/R (29 September 2006)) and the ICJ (*Oil Platforms (Iran/US) (Merits)* [2003] ICJ Rep 161). In the domestic context, see, e.g., *R (SG and others) v Secretary of State for Work and Pensions* [2015] 1 WLR 1449, [116]; *ZH (Tanzania) v SSHD* [2011] 2 AC 166, [21]; *Moohan and another v Lord Advocate* [2015] AC 901, [99]–[100]; *R (Al-Saadoon) v Secretary of State for Defence* [2015] 3 WLR 503, [276].

[186] For the study group's consolidated report see ILC (2006) *Fragmentation Report, supra* n 143. A further report of the same title summarises the group's conclusions: ILC, *Fragmentation of International Law: Difficulties Arising from the Diversification and Expansion of International Law – Report of the Study Group of the International Law Commission*, A/CN.4/L.702 (2006). See also *Report of the International Law Commission – Fifty-Eighth Session*, A/61/10 (2006) ch XII. Broader issues surrounding the fragmentation of international law are beyond the scope of this book.

[187] See McLachlan (2005) *supra* n 175; French (2005) *supra* n 176; J Pauwelyn, *Conflict of Norms in Public International Law: How WTO Law Relates to Other Rules of International Law* (2003) 243–74; Gardiner (2015) *supra* n 142, 289–343.

31(3)(c) to a decision-maker's consideration of the interpretation of the *Refugee Convention*. In support of a broader argument promoting the alignment of the *Convention* with developments in economic and social rights, Foster argues that art 31(3)(c) provides the 'clear[est] justification' for interpreting the *Convention* in a manner 'consistent with international human rights law'.[188] The argument advanced by Foster has clear merit, speaking with particular force when viewed in the context of the broader goals of 'systemic integration'. Although art 31(3)(c) requires a decision-maker to establish that a rule of international law is *relevant* to the treaty being interpreted, it is not necessary to explicitly link the rule, for example, with the object and purpose of the treaty.[189] So in the refugee context, while art 31(1) has previously been used to justify recourse to international human rights law in the interpretation of the *Convention*, art 31(3)(c) might be used to support reliance on a wider province of international law – for example, international humanitarian law.[190]

Article 31(3)(c) forms parts of the holistic 'general rule of interpretation' – it is neither a 'discretionary add-on'[191] nor a supplementary means of interpretation.[192] As French has noted, 'whatever flexibility and discretion the rules themselves may provide, ignoring them is not part of this'.[193] The failure of practitioners to raise the provision in legal argument, and the corresponding lack of judicial engagement with art 31(3)(c), is in many ways a symptom of the lack of awareness of the obligatory character of art 31(3)(c). This is not to understate the deficiencies of the provision and, in particular, the limited guidance as to when and how it is to be applied. However, the issue then is 'not whether the rule found in Article 31(3)(c) *exists*',[194] but, rather, how the rule can be *operationalised*.[195] With this in mind, the discussion that follows considers four specific issues concerning the scope and application of art 31(3)(c). Although some of the discussion is necessarily general, at its core the discussion is grounded in a consideration of the manner in which art 31(3)(c) might be used to promote greater interaction between international refugee law and international law on the rights of the child.

1.4.4 1 *'Take into Account'*

International law provides no general definition of the phrase 'take into account'. Sands suggests that the phrase reflects a stronger interpretative obligation than 'take into consideration' and a weaker obligation than 'apply', and that the burden should 'be on the party opposing the interpretation compatible with the customary rule to explain why it should not be applied'.[196] This approach is broadly consistent with domestic principles of statutory interpretation, which will assume that the legislature has adopted laws consistent with

---

[188] Foster (2007) *supra* n 71, 52.
[189] There are, however, other limiting elements, such as the requirement that the rule is 'applicable between the parties'. See *infra* text accompanying n 208–19.
[190] Which may be relevant, for example, to *Convention*, art 1F.
[191] French (2005) *supra* n 176, 301. Article 31(3) provides: 'There *shall* be taken into account' (emphasis added).
[192] *Contra* art 32 of the *VCLT*.   [193] French (2005) *supra* n 176, 301.
[194] McLachlan (2005) *supra* n 175, 281 (emphasis added).
[195] *Ibid.*, 281. Here McLachlan adopts the language of Sands (1998) *supra* n 176, 88.
[196] Sands (1998) *supra* n 176, 104. Although Sands' argument is made in the context of the relationship between the primary treaty and customary international law, it speaks with equal force to other 'rules of international law'.

international obligations.[197] It is important to underline, however, that the requirement 'to take into account' is an interpretative obligation, rather than a duty to apply the relevant rule of international law. As Orakhelashvili observes, 'the purpose of interpreting by reference to "relevant rules" is, normally, not to defer the provisions being interpreted to the scope and effect of those "relevant rules", but to clarify the content of the former by referring to the later'.[198] In other words, art 31(3)(c) codifies an interpretative obligation, rather than a duty to achieve a particular result.

1.4.4 2 'Rules of International Law'

The second issue can be dealt with briefly, in part because of the limited remit of the argument advanced in this chapter.[199] The key question here is whether an international treaty is a 'rule of international law' for the purposes of art 31(3)(c). A logical reference point is art 38(1) of the *Statute of the International Court of Justice*, which serves as a catalogue of the sources of international law: international treaties, international custom, general principles of law and, as subsidiary sources, judicial decisions and academic commentary. This interpretation is consistent with the approach adopted by the ILC.[200] That art 31(3)(c) is sufficiently broad to capture international treaties has also been confirmed by the WTO Panel in the Panel Reports, *European Communities – Measures Affecting the Approval and Marketing of Biotech Products* decision.[201]

1.4.4 3 'Relevant' Rules of International Law

The third parameter requires that a rule of international law be *relevant* to the treaty being interpreted. This instruction has two dimensions. The first relates to the question of intertemporal law – in the context of the *Convention*, are decision-makers restricted to a consideration of international rules in existence at the time of the conclusion of the *Convention* or able to look to those in force at the moment the interpretative exercise is taking place? The answer depends on the nature of the particular treaty being interpreted and, specifically, whether the treaty in question evinces an intention to allow for an evolutionary approach to interpretation.[202] Adopting this interpretation, art 31(3)(c) may on its face appear more restrictive than the approach laid down by the ICJ in *Legal Consequences for States of the Continued Presence of South Africa in Namibia (South West Africa) Notwithstanding Security Council Resolution 276 (1970) (Advisory Opinion).*[203]

---

[197] Sands (1998) *supra* n 176, 104–5.

[198] A Orakhelashvili, 'Restrictive Interpretation of Human Rights Treaties in the Recent Jurisprudence of the European Court of Human Rights' (2003) 14 *European Journal of International Law* 529, 537.

[199] This book articulates a legal basis for recourse to an extrinsic international *treaty*, and does not consider the extent to which art 31(3)(c) might allow recourse to customary international law and/or 'soft law' in interpreting the *Convention*.

[200] *ILC Report* (2006) *supra* n 186, [251(18)].

[201] Panel Reports, *European Communities – Measures Affecting the Approval and Marketing of Biotech Products*, WT/DS291–3/R, WT/DS332–4/R (29 September 2006) 332.

[202] The *VCLT*'s drafting history supports this interpretation. See Gardiner (2015) *supra* n 142, 295–8, 317–20; Bjorge (2014) *supra* n 167, 142–67; I Sinclair, *The Vienna Convention on the Law of Treaties* (1984) 138–40; ILC, *Fragmentation Report* (2006) *supra* n 143, [475]–[478]; *ILC Report* (2006) *supra* n 186, [251(22)].

[203] '[A]n international instrument has to be interpreted and applied within the framework of the entire legal system prevailing at the time of the interpretation': *Legal Consequences for States of the Continued*

However, as Gardiner has observed, that decision was itself circumscribed by the provisions of the treaty in question and influenced by the fact that the relevant concepts being interpreted 'were not static, but were by definition evolutionary'.[204] Here we find ourselves in a similar position. The discussion in Section 1.3 provided support for the proposition that the *Convention* was drafted in a sufficiently ambiguous manner to allow it to evolve to meet the 'changing circumstances of the present and future world'.[205] Hence, the *Convention* evinces an intention to allow for an evolutionary interpretation, and in the context of art 31(3)(c) a decision-maker will therefore be required to look beyond the rules in force at the time of the conclusion of the *Convention* and to take into account subsequent developments in international law. As recognised by Lauterpacht and Bethlehem:[206]

> the law on human rights which has emerged since the conclusion of the 1951 Convention is an essential part of the framework of the legal system that must, by reference to the ICJ's observations in the *Legal Consequences for States of the Continued Presence of South Africa in Namibia (South West Africa) Notwithstanding Security Council Resolution 276 (1970) (Advisory Opinion)* case, be taken into account for the purposes of interpretation.

The second dimension relates to the *content* of the relevant 'rules of international law'. It is clear that not every treaty in force at any moment in time will be relevant to the interpretation of the *Convention*. As Foster has noted, there is a need for caution in accepting without reservation the relevance of a treaty from one area of international law to the interpretation of a treaty from another area.[207] Here, however, we find a clear parallel between international refugee law and international law on the rights of the child. It seems that one would have little difficulty in establishing that the *CRC, OPAC* and *OPSC* are appropriate tools of reference for interpreting provisions of the *Convention*, particularly where the latter is applied to children seeking international protection.

1.4.4.4 Relevant Rules of International Law 'Applicable in the Relations Between the Parties'

Article 31(3)(c) is limited to rules of international law that are 'applicable in the relations between the parties'. In the context of international treaties, the provision raises the following rather intractable problem: is it necessary that *all* of the parties to the treaty being interpreted are also party to the second treaty being relied upon as a 'rule of international law'? This of course raises an issue for the *Convention* given that, if such co-existence were required, no other international treaty would satisfy the requisite threshold. In the context of children seeking international protection, the failure of the United States

---

Presence of South Africa in Namibia (South West Africa) Notwithstanding Security Council Resolution 276 (1970) (Advisory Opinion) [1971] ICJ Rep 16, 31.

[204] Gardiner (2015) *supra* n 142, 295–6; *Legal Consequences for States of the Continued Presence of South Africa in Namibia (South West Africa) Notwithstanding Security Council Resolution 276 (1970) (Advisory Opinion)* [1971] ICJ Rep 16.

[205] *R v SSHD; Ex parte Adan* [1999] 3 WLR 1274, 1296.

[206] E Lauterpacht and D Bethlehem, 'The Scope and Content of the Principle of Non-Refoulement' in E Feller, V Türk and F Nicholson (eds), *Refugee Protection in International Law: UNHCR's Global Consultations on International Protection* (2003) 87, 113.

[207] Foster (2007) *supra* n 71, 57.

to ratify the *CRC* would limit the capacity of art 31(3)(c) to function as a legal basis for comparative treaty interpretation.

Three dominant approaches to the phrase 'applicable in the relations between the parties' have emerged from judicial and academic analysis; however, the 'correct' interpretation of the phrase remains unclear.

The first and narrowest approach is that adopted by the WTO Panel in the Panel Reports, *European Communities – Measures Affecting the Approval and Marketing of Biotech Products* decision, which requires co-extensive membership between the two relevant treaties.[208] As noted above, this interpretation would severely curtail the scope of art 31(3)(c) in the context of multilateral treaties. As the ILC Study Group has recognised, '[t]his would have the ironic effect that the more the membership of a multilateral treaty . . . expanded, the more those treaties would be cut off from the rest of international law'.[209] As a matter of practice, this would result in 'the isolation of multilateral agreements as "islands" permitting no references *inter se* in their application . . . This would seem contrary to the legislative ethos behind most . . . multilateral treaty-making and, presumably . . . the intent of most treaty-makers.'[210]

A second approach has been to interpret 'between the parties' to mean the states that are party to the dispute, thereby 'permit[ing] reference to another treaty provided that the *parties in dispute* are also parties to that other treaty'.[211] This approach is consistent with the objectives of art 31(3)(c) to integrate a treaty into the wider system of international law.[212] Although this approach will allow a greater range of treaties to be taken into account, it also creates the possibility of divergent interpretations dependent on which states parties are parties to a dispute.[213] For example, a decision-maker in Australia would, where relevant, be required to take into account the provisions of the *CRC* when interpreting a definitional element of the *Convention*, whereas a decision-maker in the United States would not. This in turn creates the possibility of conflicting interpretations, which, as discussed above, is undesirable in an international refugee protection regime.[214]

A third approach is to take into account those rules that 'can be said to be at least *implicitly* accepted or tolerated . . . in the sense that [the rule] can reasonably be considered to express the common intentions or understandings of all members as to the meaning of the . . . term concerned'.[215] This approach may provide a sensible compromise between the two more extreme positions. It is reflected, at least in part, in the final, slightly ambiguous guidance offered by the ILC:[216]

> Article 31(3)(c) also requires the interpreter to consider other treaty-based rules so as to arrive at a consistent meaning. Such other rules are of particular relevance where parties

---

[208] Panel Reports (2006) supra n 201, 333.
[209] ILC, *Fragmentation Report* (2006) *supra* n 143, [471] (citations omitted).   [210] *Ibid.*
[211] *Ibid.*, [472] (emphasis in original).   [212] Gardiner (2015) *supra* n 142, 312.
[213] The difficulties are particularly acute in the refugee context: Foster (2007) *supra* n 71, 56.
[214] See *supra* Section 1.3.
[215] J Pauwelyn, 'The Role of Public International Law in the WTO: How Far Can We Go?' (2001) 95 *American Journal of International Law* 535, 576 (emphasis added). See also Pauwelyn (2003) *supra* n 187. Although not expressed in these terms, this approach is consistent with Hathaway's reference to the International Bill of Rights as a tool for ascertaining the meaning of 'being persecuted' and is also consistent with his later concession that other treaties that have gained the acceptance of a 'super-majority of parties' to the *Refugee Convention* might be instructive for its interpretation: see Hathaway (1998) *supra* n 117.
[216] *ILC Report* (2006) *supra* n 186, [251(21)].

to the treaty under interpretation are also parties to the other treaty, where the treaty rule has passed into or expresses customary international law or where they provide evidence of the common understanding of the parties as to the object and purpose of the treaty under interpretation or as to the meaning of a particular term.

In the context of the *Convention* and the *CRC* it is arguable that the signature of the *CRC* by the United States may be sufficient to constitute interpretative agreement for the purposes of art 31(3)(c),[217] thereby legitimising recourse to the *CRC* as a relevant rule of international law when interpreting the terms of the *Convention*.[218]

Conclusions

International law has long played an important role in securing special protection for refugee children. As Simmons has argued, international law provides a 'rights based framework to supplement the protective framework that has a much longer history in many societies' and a 'lever to give . . . would-be advocates influence over policies likely to have an important impact on the well-being of those who are not able to organize and speak for themselves'.[219] Within the international human rights legal framework, the *CRC* provides the most comprehensive and exacting set of standards on the treatment of children, including refugee children. Rather than simply asserting a need for greater interaction between international refugee law and international law on the rights of the child, this chapter has attempted to map out the substantive contours of the relationship between the *Convention* and the *CRC* and to anchor that relationship in the international rules of treaty interpretation. The chapter outlined three modes of interaction where the *CRC* might be engaged in the refugee status determination process: the *CRC* as a procedural guarantee, the *CRC* as an *interpretative aid* and the *CRC* as an *independent source of status*. These three modes of interaction – together, a child-rights framework for assessing the status of refugee child – provide the foundation for the five chapters that follow.

---

[217] This position finds some support in art 18 of the *VCLT*, which provides that a state 'is obliged to refrain from acts which would defeat the object and purpose of a treaty' when it has signed (but not ratified) that treaty. The United States has also, in official refugee manuals, accepted that aspects of the *CRC* may be drawn upon in interpreting the *Refugee Convention*: see, e.g., INS, *Guidelines*, 2 ('[b]ecause the United States has signed but not ratified the CRC, its provisions, as noted above, provide guidance only and are not binding on adjudicators. Having signed the CRC, however, the United States is obliged under international treaty law to refrain from acts which would defeat the object and purpose of the Convention'); USCIS Asylum Division, 'Asylum Officer Basic Training Course: Guidelines for Children's Asylum Claims' (21 March 2009) 8–9. The US government has also relied on the provisions of the *CRC* in cases involving child refugees: see, e.g., United States Attorney, 'Brief', filed in *Gonzalez v Reno* (24 April 2000), discussed in Chapter 2, text accompanying n 101–113. The United States has ratified the *OPSC* and *OPAC*.

[218] A similar argument might be advanced in respect of the International Bill of Rights. See also Foster (2007) *supra* n 71, 56–7.

[219] B A Simmons, *Mobilizing for Human Rights* (2009) 307.

2

The Child and the Refugee Status Determination Process

Introduction

One of the dominant features of the international refugee legal framework is the level of control that states retain in the design and implementation of the refugee status determination process. Indeed, the *Refugee Convention* is altogether silent on the procedural aspects of the international refugee protection regime, allowing states a high degree of discretion in the design and implementation of their domestic refugee status determination procedures. The *Convention* provides no guidance, for instance, on the procedures that should be put in place to assess the claim of an at-risk child, whether the child constitutes part of a family unit or is unaccompanied or separated. The *Convention* says nothing about whether a child's status should be independently assessed or should simply flow from the successful or unsuccessful determination of a parent's or guardian's claim.[1] And the *Convention* provides no direction on the circumstances in which a child (or her parent) may be derivatively eligible for protection in order to avoid breaking up a family unit.

There is, however, an outer limit to the procedural discretion afforded states, set both by the *Convention* itself and also by the broader international human rights framework. This chapter considers the relevance of the *CRC* to the procedural dimension of the refugee protection regime and the extent to which its provisions inform and strengthen the procedural guarantees afforded children throughout the refugee status determination process. The focus here is on the first mode of interaction identified in Chapter 1: the *CRC* as a procedural guarantee.

Section 2.1 sets the scene for the chapter, outlining the various ways in which children have been rendered invisible within domestic refugee status determination processes. There are a number of scenarios in which a child's claim may (or may not) come before a decision-maker. A child's claim for refugee status is most likely to be overlooked where a family member accompanies the child. In this scenario, the child's claim is generally treated as inseparable from the claims of the family member, despite the fact that there may be

---

[1] This chapter focuses on the child–parent relationship. Although the UNCRC has not expressly addressed the definition of 'parent', it has acknowledged that it is 'hard to argue for a single notion of the family': UNCRC, *Report on the Seventh Session*, CRC/C/34 (1994) ch IV pt F (summary of Day of General Discussion on 'The Role of the Family in the Promotion of the Rights of the Child'), [190]. Tobin argues that the diversity of contemporary society invites an interpretation 'whereby neither biology nor a heterosexual union should be the sole determinants of parenthood' and suggests that a child may have a number of different parents, including birth parents, biological parents and social parents: J Tobin, 'Parents and Children's Rights under the Convention on the Rights of the Child: Finding Reconciliation in a Misunderstood Relationship' (2005) 7(2) *Australian Journal of Professional and Applied Ethics* 31, 34. For support of an expansive understanding of who may constitute a parent, see *CRC*, art 5; UNCRC, *GC7*, [15]; HRC, *GC17*, [6]; HRC, *GC19*, [2].

evidence that the child faces an autonomous risk of harm. There is a greater chance that the child's claim will be independently assessed where the child is unaccompanied or separated, although in a limited range of circumstances states have suggested that an unaccompanied child lacks the capacity independently to claim refugee status.[2]

Section 2.2 considers the circumstances in which a state is required to individually assess a child's eligibility for refugee status. It argues that the removal of a child without a review of the child's independent claim for refugee status may give rise to a risk of a violation of the duty of *non-refoulement* protected under art 33 of the *Convention*[3] and a violation of the *CRC*'s procedural requirement that the child have an opportunity to express views freely in matters affecting them and be heard in judicial and administrative proceedings.[4] This argument has been endorsed by UNHCR and is reflected in the state practice of a number of jurisdictions. The section commences with a consideration of the relevant international legal obligations. This is followed by a review of state practice to provide a contextualised account of the various procedural mechanisms that might be implemented in order to ensure that a child is not removed without an independent assessment of refugee status. The discussion on state practice should not be read as an exhaustive treatment of the refugee status determination procedures in any individual state, but rather as an illustration of the range of mechanisms that have been adopted that may or may not comply with a state's obligations under international law.

Finally, Section 2.3 considers the application of family unity obligations to the refugee status determination process, with a focus on the duty of *non-separation* contained in art 9 of the *CRC*. The duty of non-separation requires a state party to 'ensure that a child shall not be separated from his or her parents against their will'.[5] That obligation falls away only where 'separation is necessary for the best interests of the child'.[6] If separation is not in the best interests of the child a state will be under a duty to take positive measures to ensure that the child and her parents can remain together, irrespective of the fact that only one member of the family may be eligible for refugee protection. Although host states will almost uniformly afford a form of derivative protection to a child where her parents are eligible for refugee status, a number of states will deny a refugee child the right to extend protection to her parents. In these jurisdictions there is an assumption that the 'children's immigration status must derive from their parents rather than vice versa'.[7] This asymmetrical approach provides an explanation for the reluctance of families to advance a child's claim separately, notwithstanding the legislative entitlement to do so.[8] The approach runs counter to the near-absolute obligation codified in art 9, which provides a robust and principled safety net to prevent the separation of families.

---

[2] A related issue, addressed in Chapter 6, is the attempt by states to side-step the refugee protection regime by granting a lesser form of humanitarian protection deriving from the child's minority status. Although in some circumstances this may be desirable, it is important to appreciate the potential shortcomings of circumventing the *Refugee Convention* in this way. See Chapter 6, Section 6.3.5.

[3] Although this chapter focuses on *non-refoulement* under the *Convention*, a failure to consider a child's claim separately will also enhance the likelihood that a decision-maker will fail to identify eligibility for protection under the broader international human rights framework: see Chapter 6.

[4] *CRC*, art 12.   [5] *CRC*, art 9(1).   [6] *CRC*, art 9(1).

[7] J Bhabha, 'The "Mere Fortuity" of Birth? Are Children Citizens?' (2004) 15(2) *Differences: A Journal of Feminist Cultural Studies* 91, 96.

[8] See *infra* text accompanying n 45.

At the outset it is important to acknowledge that the invisibility of children is not simply the product of a decision-maker's failure to turn their mind to a child's independent refugee claim. Additional procedural safeguards will be necessary to ensure that a child can effectively navigate the refugee status determination process. As Crock observes, '[d]ecision-makers need to consider the *procedural* concessions that are necessary if children are to be able to tell their stories and to articulate the dangers that they do (or should) fear'.[9] In a single chapter it is not possible to fully explore the application of the *CRC* to the refugee determination process. The chapter does not, for instance, consider age-assessment procedures, guardianship and care arrangements, the provision of legal assistance, interview and courtroom concessions, or the detention of children throughout the determination process,[10] although there can be little doubt that the *CRC* is relevant to each of these important procedural issues.[11] The chapter's more focused analysis on arts 9 and 12 does, however, demonstrate the capacity of the *CRC* to secure procedural guarantees not otherwise provided under the *Refugee Convention*. It is hoped that this analysis can serve as an illustrative platform to facilitate more sustained engagement with the *CRC* in the design and implementation of the procedural dimension of the international refugee protection regime more generally.

2.1 The Invisibility of Refugee Children

The reluctance of states to treat children as refugees in their own right has been well documented. Bhabha has for some time observed that children rarely benefit from refugee protection and 'have simply not been thought of as appropriate subjects of asylum applications or refugee status grants'.[12] Tuitt has suggested that 'children are ascribed an essentially "passive" role in refugee-like situations – a role which significantly posits the view that something or someone other than the child was the real focus of the harm'.[13] Accordingly,

---

[9] M Crock, 'Re-Thinking the Paradigms of Protection: Children as Convention Refugees in Australia' in J McAdam (ed), *Forced Migration, Human Rights and Security* (2008) 155, 158. See also J Bhabha, 'Independent Children, Inconsistent Adults: Child Migration and the Legal Framework' (Innocenti Discussion Paper No IDP-2008–02, UNICEF, May 2008) 7 ('[S]ecuring a valid legal status is dependent on the child having access to effective mentorship and legal representation, which is frequently not the case').

[10] Each of these issues has received a considerable degree of attention, both from academics and non-governmental organisations. For recent examples, see ILPA, *Working with Refugee Children: Current Issues in Best Practice* (2012); S Mullally, 'Separated Children in Ireland: Responding to "Terrible Wrongs"' (2011) 23(4) *International Journal of Refugee Law* 632; European Migration Network, *Policies on Reception, Return and Integration arrangements for, and Numbers of, Unaccompanied Minors – An EU Comparative Study* (2010); C Watters, *Refugee Children: Toward the Next Horizon* (2008); J Bhabha and M Crock, *Seeking Asylum Alone: A Comparative Study* (2007); H Crawley, 'Child First, Migrant Second: Ensuring That *Every* Child Matters' (Policy Paper, ILPA, February 2006); H E Andersson et al. (eds), *The Asylum-Seeking Child in Europe* (2005).

[11] See, e.g., arts 3 (best interests), 16 (private and family life), 20 (special assistance for children deprived of a family environment), 21 (adoption), 22 (special protection measures for refugee children), 37 (arbitrary detention), 39 (rehabilitation). See generally J Pobjoy, 'Article 22' in P Alston and J Tobin (eds), *The UN Convention on the Rights of the Child: A Commentary* (2017) (forthcoming).

[12] J Bhabha, '"More Than Their Share of Sorrows": International Migration Law and the Rights of Children' (2003) 22 *Saint Louis University Public Law Review* 253, 266; J Bhabha, 'Un "Vide Juridique"? – Migrant Children: The Rights and Wrongs' in C Bellamy et al. (eds), *Realizing the Rights of the Child* (2007) 206.

[13] P Tuitt, 'The State, the Family and the Child Refugee' in D Fottrell (ed), *Revisiting Children's Rights: 10 Years of the UN Convention on the Rights of the Child* (2000) 149, 153.

for Tuitt, the status of child refugees in legal discourse has become 'largely inseparable from their status as family members'[14] and this has 'adversely affected the nature and scope of protection afforded to them'.[15] In a similar vein, Thronson has argued that the '[denial of] agency throughout the principal frameworks of immigration law' has resulted in the systemic devaluation of children's interests.[16] UNHCR has also identified *invisibility* as one of the key challenges that children face in establishing entitlement to refugee status, observing that children may be 'perceived as part of a family unit rather than as individuals with their own rights and interests', explicable by 'the subordinate roles, positions and status children still hold in many societies worldwide'.[17]

The invisibility of children in domestic asylum-seeking processes reinforces discredited conceptions of children as 'passive subjects of social structures and processes'.[18] In the case of an accompanied child, the child finds herself 'passively advanced through the [refugee status determination] process by successful parents or held back by unsuccessful parents'.[19] This construction is at odds with a vision of children as social agents with their own 'concerns, interests and points of view';[20] a vision to which the global community has institutionally committed itself via the CRC. As the South African Constitutional Court has elegantly observed, '[if] a child is to be constitutionally imagined as an individual with a distinctive personality, and not merely as a miniature adult waiting to reach full size, he or she cannot be treated as a mere extension of his or her parents, umbilically destined to sink or swim with them.'[21]

2.1.1 Unaccompanied or Separated Children

The arrival of unaccompanied and separated refugee children has compelled decision-makers to shift away from a parent-centred paradigm, resulting in the enhanced visibility

---

[14] *Ibid.*, 150.

[15] *Ibid.*, 150. See also Crock (2008) *supra* n 9, 178 (emphasis added): 'It is important to note that the norm among both legal advisers and government decision-makers has not been to insist on the articulation of separate refugee claims by children embedded in a family group. *Until this occurs, it is difficult to see how the refugee claims of children will be given the attention they deserve.*'

[16] D Thronson, 'You Can't Get Here from Here: Toward a More Child-Centered Immigration Law' (2006) 14 *Virginia Journal of Social Policy and the Law* 58, 67. Thronson has elsewhere argued that '[b]roader debates about children's rights have largely bypassed immigration law and efforts to develop workable, child-centered approaches in immigration law have gained little footing': D Thronson, 'Kids Will Be Kids? Reconsidering Conceptions of Children's Rights Underlying Immigration Law' (2002) 63(3) *Ohio State Law Journal* 979, 980. See also D Thronson, 'Choiceless Choices: Deportation and the Parent-Child Relationship' (2006) 6 *Nevada Law Journal* 1165; D Thronson, 'Clashing Values and Cross Purposes: Immigration Law's Marginalization of Children and Families' in J Bhabha (ed), *Children without a State: The Scope of Child Statelessness in the 21st Century* (2011) 237.

[17] UNHCR, 2009 *Guidelines*, [2]. See also UNHCR, 'Progress Report on Refugee Children and Adolescents, including UNHCR's Strategy for Follow-Up to the Report of the Impact of Armed Conflict on Children', EC/47/SC/CRP.19 (9 April 1997), [6]–[10] ('the "invisibility" of refugee children and adolescents . . . is a problem that affects all aspects of policy making and operations').

[18] A James and A Prout, *Constructing and Reconstructing Childhood* (1990) 8. See also *Kim v Canada (MCI)* [2011] 2 FCR 448, [50] ('In the eyes of the law, children have long been voiceless citizens. Even after all of the progress that has been made in empowering groups that used to be voiceless, such as women and ethnic and religious minorities, children remain largely silenced').

[19] Thronson, 'Choiceless Choices' (2006) *supra* n 16, 1181.   [20] UNCRC, *GC7*, [5].

[21] *M v State* [2007] ZACC 18, [18].

of children in the refugee status determination process.[22] Moreover, as demonstrated in Chapters 3 to 5, the arrival of unaccompanied children has given rise to the development of a contemporary jurisprudence addressing the child in international refugee law. Tuitt cogently makes the point:[23]

> In positive terms [the arrival of unaccompanied children] has [enriched] refugee discourse, which now embraces dimensions brought about through the acknowledgement of the particular suffering of refugee children. It is undoubtedly the case that child refugees only acquired real visibility within the legal regime once they had become separated not only from their State of origin but from their families too. Thus, although child refugeehood as a sociological phenomenon was known to the world, the child refugee as denoting an identifiable legal category owes its presence within contemporary legal discourse to the existence of the unaccompanied refugee child.

This is not to suggest that unaccompanied children do not face significant challenges in establishing eligibility for refugee status.[24] The point is simply that it is more difficult for a state to overlook a child's claim for protection where the child arrives alone.

The majority of jurisdictions do afford unaccompanied children the right to apply for refugee status, although in a limited range of circumstances states have attempted to restrict the capacity of a child to exercise that right. One of the most public examples is the case of Elián González, a six-year-old Cuban boy rescued at sea after his mother had attempted to take him to the United States without the knowledge of his father. His mother, and several others, had drowned during the voyage. González, with the assistance of a great-uncle, subsequently claimed refugee status on the basis that the Castro government had persecuted his family and he feared that he 'would be subjected to involuntary indoctrination in the tenets of communism'.[25] His father disagreed and requested that his child be returned to him in Cuba.[26] The INS refused to adjudicate González's claim on the basis that a six-year-old child 'lack[ed] the capacity to file personally for asylum against the wishes of their parent'.[27] At no stage did the INS speak with González about his views.[28]

The INS's decision in the case of González was grounded on two core policy decisions: first, that 'six-year-old children lack the capacity to sign and to submit personally an

---

[22] 'The accounts of children are more likely to be examined individually when the children are unaccompanied than when they are accompanied by their families': UNHCR, 2009 *Guidelines*, [2].

[23] Tuitt (2000) *supra* n 13, 154. See also J Bhabha, *Child Migration and Human Rights in a Global Age* (2014) 206–7; D Anker, N Kelly, J Willshire Carrera and S Ardalan, 'Mejilla-Romero: A New Era for Child Asylum', 12–09 *Immigration Briefings* (September 2012) 1, 1.

[24] For a comprehensive review of the obstacles that an unaccompanied child may face in a host state, see the comparative research of Jacqueline Bhabha and Mary Crock, collated in *Seeking Asylum Alone: A Comparative Study*: (2007) *supra* n 10. Bhabha and Crock suggest that, '[o]nce an unaccompanied or separated child has managed to flee danger and home and reach the territory of a safe state, he or she faces other daunting journeys – less arduous in terms of geographic distance, but complex, tortuous and often dangerous, both physically and emotionally': at 105.

[25] *Gonzalez v Reno*, 212 F 3d 1338, 1345 (11th Cir, 2000). See also *Gonzalez v Reno*, 86 F Supp 2d 1167 (SD Fla, 2000).

[26] *Gonzalez v Reno*, 212 F 3d 1338, 1345 (11th Cir, 2000).

[27] *Ibid*. See also Memorandum from Bo Cooper, General Counsel, INS to Doris Meissner, Commissioner of INS, 3 January 2000 (on file with author): 'The INS need not . . . process such applications if they reflect that the purported applicants are so young that they necessarily lack the capacity to understand what they are applying for or, failing that, that the applicants do not present an objective basis for ignoring the parents' wishes'.

[28] *Gonzalez v Reno*, 212 F 3d 1338, 1355 (11th Cir, 2000).

application for asylum';[29] second, that, 'absent special circumstances, the *only* proper adult to represent a six-year-old child is the child's parent'.[30] The Court of Appeals for the Eleventh Circuit considered that both policy decisions were reasonable and therefore entitled to judicial deference.[31] In relation to the decision-making capacity of a six-year-old child, the Court stated:[32]

> we do not think that the [INS], as a matter of law, must individually assess each child's mental capacity; we cannot say that looking at capacity instead of age for young children is required. Instead, we recognize that absolute line drawing – although necessarily sacrificing accuracy and flexibility for certainty and efficiency – is an acceptable approach.

The Court also considered that it was reasonable for the INS to determine that, absent special circumstances, only a parent can act for his six-year-old child in immigration matters.[33] In this case the Court accepted the INS's decision that there were no special circumstances to justify interference with his father's wishes.[34] Elián González was subsequently removed to Cuba.

2.1.2 Accompanied Children

A child's independent refugee claim is most likely to be overlooked where the child arrives accompanied by a family member.[35] In these cases it is common practice for the child's claim to be subsumed into the claim of one of her parents, with the child's status flowing directly from the status granted to her parent.[36] In cases where the parent is granted refugee status, this derivative procedure presents few difficulties. More problematic is the converse scenario: where the parent's claim is rejected and the child's claim automatically denied

---

[29] *Gonzalez v Reno*, 212 F 3d 1338, 1349–50 (11th Cir, 2000). The INS relied on *Polovchak v Meese*, 774 F 2d 731, 736 (7th Cir, 1985), which determined that a 12-year-old child was entitled independently to claim refugee status while suggesting, however, that 12 years 'was presumably near the lower end of an age range in which a minor may be mature enough to assert certain individual rights that equal or override those of his parents'.

[30] *Gonzalez v Reno*, 212 F 3d 1338, 1350 (11th Cir, 2000) (emphasis added). Both policy decisions are important because, in addition to González filing his own application, his great-uncle had separately filed an application on the child's behalf.

[31] *Ibid.*, 1351.   [32] *Ibid.*

[33] *Ibid.*, 1351–2. In making this finding, the Court noted that the policy allowed for a non-parental representative where special circumstances, such as a substantial conflict of interest between the parent and child, render it inappropriate for the parent to act for the child.

[34] *Ibid.*, 1353.

[35] Issues facing accompanied refugee children have received less scholarly attention than unaccompanied children, although there are some notable exceptions: Tuitt (2000) *supra* n 13; Bhabha (2003) *supra* n 12; Bhabha (2007) *supra* n 12, 206; Thronson, 'Choiceless Choices' (2006) *supra* n 16; Thronson (2002) *supra* n 16; L Melo, 'When Children Suffer: The Failure of US Immigration Law to Provide Practical Protection for Persecuted Children' (2010) 40 *Golden Gate University Law Review* 263.

[36] 'In this way, children are passively advanced through the process by successful parents and are held back by unsuccessful parents': Thronson (2011) *supra* n 16, 238. For an empirical illustration, see, e.g., UNHCR, 'Quality Integration Project: Considering the Best Interests of a Child within a Family Seeking Asylum' (December 2013): '[A] strong overall finding was that current [UK] Home Office policy and processes do not provide for the participation of children who are dependants in a family asylum claim and this was reflected wholly in the practice' (at 23).

without any separate consideration. This may occur despite the fact that the child has a stronger independent claim for refugee status, for example because she faces a risk of being persecuted that would not be faced by her parents. A child may, for instance, be at risk of a child-specific form of persecutory harm, such as pre-puberty FGC, deprivation of an education, parental abuse, involuntary gang or military recruitment, or discrimination on account of being born in circumstances considered illegitimate.[37] This derivative procedure may also give rise to a protection gap where a child's parent is excluded under art 1F of the *Refugee Convention*, where there are doubts regarding the credibility of a claim advanced by a family member[38] or where there is a conflict of interest between a child and parent.[39] In each of these scenarios, in the absence of an independent assessment of the child's claim, there is a possibility that a child will be returned to her country of origin in circumstances where there is a real chance that she will be persecuted.[40]

The invisibility of accompanied children is compounded by the fact that a number of states, including the United States, the United Kingdom and Canada, deny children the right to extend derivative protection to their parents. As Thronson notes, '[t]he system is geared to assimilate children's status to that of their parents, not the other way around'.[41] Bhabha suggests that '[t]his asymmetry reflects an anachronistic set of assumptions about the nature of family life in a globalized era … assum[ing] the absolute primacy of parental rather than child migration considerations'.[42] The US Court of Appeals for the Ninth Circuit outlined the procedural difficulties of this asymmetrical approach in *Tchoukhrova v Gonzales*, a case involving a Russian mother and her disabled son:[43]

> The procedural issue arises as a consequence of the limited scope of derivative asylum applications … Although the statute provides that minor children may obtain asylum derivatively through their parents, there is no comparable provision permitting parents to obtain that relief derivatively through their minor children. Accordingly, if a minor child is granted asylum as a derivative applicant of his parent's principal application, both parents and child can stay in the United States. However, if the child is the principal

---

[37] See Chapter 4.

[38] *Newton v Canada (MCI)* (2000) 182 FTR 294, [1]; *Richards v Canada (MCI)* 2011 FC 1391, [12]–[13]. A related issue may arise where a family member is found to be incredible where advancing a claim on behalf of a child. In *SBAH of 2001 v MIMIA* [2002] FCAFC 426, [4], Madgwick J, in a compelling dissent, took the view that where a mother is found to be an 'irresponsible liar or … at best … confused and unable to articulate a coherent and consistent story' the mother is revealed to be an inappropriate person 'to have the carriage of the child's case'. See also *AZAEF v MIBP* [2016] FCAFC 3, [79], [87]–[98], [107] (Griffiths J), [112]–[131] (White J).

[39] *Polovchak v Meese*, 774 F 2d 731 (7th Cir, 1985); *Houareau v Canada (MCI)* (1996) 108 FTR 71.

[40] For example, in *Barry v Gonzales*, 445 F 3d 741, 747 (4th Cir, 2006), the mother, the principal applicant, claimed that the family was at risk of political persecution; however, this claim was rejected. It subsequently came to light that the daughter was at risk of FGC. The Court of Appeals acknowledged that the applicant's daughter 'would likely be subjected to FGM if she returned to Guinea' but refused to reopen the claim on the basis that this evidence was not provided earlier.

[41] Thronson, 'Choiceless Choices' (2006) *supra* n 16, 1181.   [42] Bhabha (2004) *supra* n 7, 96.

[43] *Tchoukhrova v Gonzales*, 404 F 3d 1181, 1191 (9th Cir, 2005); see also at 1184–7. The 14-year-old boy was born with cerebral palsy. The child received 'wretched treatment' from both the Russian government and from private individuals on account of his disability. At birth, he was discarded into a disposal bin, on the basis that medical staff 'didn't see the reason why he needed to live'. He was banned from receiving any medical support for his condition and denied access to public school. Country reports confirmed that this was common practice in Russia.

applicant and is granted asylum, the child can legally stay in this country, but his parents will be removed.

The consequence of the adoption of this approach in this case was that a '[d]isabled child[] would be able to live either in a country free from persecution or with a care-giving parent, but not both'.[44]

This procedural context provides an explanation as to why, in certain jurisdictions, a family will often list the parent as the principal applicant, notwithstanding the fact that the child may be entitled to apply separately for refugee status and may, in reality, be the real victim of persecutory harm. A review of case-law involving accompanied children in the United States indicates that this occurs in a significant number of cases.[45] The same review reveals a variety of legal strategies that have emerged to draw attention to the risk faced by the child in the context of the parent's refugee application. Courts have, for instance, held that a mother is eligible for refugee status on the basis that she will suffer physical harm if she attempts to shield her daughter from persecution[46] or, alternatively, psychological harm if forced to witness such persecution.[47] Courts have similarly recognised that a parent may be a refugee where a child is targeted in order to harm the parent.[48] The Court of Appeals for

---

[44] *Ibid.*, 1192.

[45] See, e.g., *Benyamin v Holder*, 579 F 3d 970 (9th Cir, 2009) (daughter at risk of FGC, father the principal applicant); *Tchoukhrova v Gonzales*, 404 F 3d 1181 (9th Cir, 2005) (son at risk of ongoing discrimination on account of disability, mother the principal applicant); *Barry v Gonzales*, 445 F 3d 741 (4th Cir, 2006) (daughter at risk of female genital cutting, mother the principal applicant). Cases involving migrant families comprising US-citizen children, where the parent must establish refugee status independently because the US-citizen child is not legislatively entitled to sponsor her parent, evidence a similar trend: see, e.g., *Dieng v Holder*, 698 F 3d 866 (6th Cir, 2012); *Seck v Attorney General*, 663 F 3d 1356 (11th Cir, 2011); *Kone v Holder*, 620 F 3d 760 (7th Cir, 2010); *Kone v Holder*, 596 F 3d 141 (2nd Cir, 2010); *Kane v Holder*, 581 F 3d 231 (5th Cir, 2009); *Gumaneh v Mukasey*, 535 F 3d 785 (8th Cir, 2008); *Re A-K-*, 24 I & N Dec 275 (BIA, 2007); *Hassan v Gonzales*, 484 F 3d 513 (8th Cir, 2007); *Niang v Gonzales*, 492 F 3d 505 (4th Cir, 2007); *Abebe v Gonzales*, 432 F 3d 1037 (9th Cir, 2005); *Mansour v Ashcroft*, 390 F 3d 667 (7th Cir, 2004); *Abebe v Ashcroft*, 379 F 3d 755 (9th Cir, 2004); *Olowo v Ashcroft*, 368 F 3d 692 (7th Cir, 2004); *Oforji v Ashcroft*, 354 F 3d 609 (7th Cir, 2003); *Nwaokolo v INS*, 314 F 3d 303 (7th Cir, 2002).

[46] Melo (2010) *supra* n 35, 278–9, discussing *Abebe v Gonzales*, 432 F 3d 1037 (9th Cir, 2005).

[47] *Abay v Ashcroft*, 368 F 3d 634, 642 (6th Cir, 2004): '[There is] . . . a governing principle in favor of refugee status in cases where a parent and protector is faced with exposing her child to the clear risk of being subjected against her will to a practice that is a form of physical torture causing grave and permanent harm . . . [W]e conclude that Abay's fear of taking her daughter into the lion's den of female genital mutilation in Ethiopia and being forced to witness the pain and suffering of her daughter is well-founded. Accordingly, we find that Abay is also a "refugee" within the meaning of the Act.' However, the First and Fourth Circuits have expressly rejected this approach, making the unqualified assertion that '"persecution" cannot be based on a fear of psychological harm alone': *Niang v Gonzales*, 492 F 3d 505 (4th Cir, 2007), 512, approved in *Kechichian v Mukasey*, 535 F 3d 15, 22 (1st Cir, 2008). See also *Re A-K-*, 24 I & N Dec 275, 278 (BIA, 2007). Similar reasoning can be found in the United Kingdom: see, e.g., *CA v SSHD* [2004] EWCA Civ 1165, [26] ('[i]t seems to be obvious simply as a matter of humanity that for a mother to witness the collapse of her newborn child's health and perhaps its death may be a kind of suffering far greater than might arise by the mother's confronting the self-same fate herself'). For a general discussion on the emerging support for the view that psychological harm is appropriately understood to be persecutory under the *Refugee Convention*, see J C Hathaway and J Pobjoy, 'Queer Cases Make Bad Law' (2012) 44(2) *New York University Journal of International Law and Politics* 315, 364–71.

[48] 'If . . . your child [is] killed . . . in order to harm you, the fact that you are not touched does not mean that those acts cannot constitute persecution of you': *Gatimi v Holder*, 578 F 3d 611, 617 (7th Cir, 2009), approved in *Ni v Holder*, 635 F 3d 1014, 1018 (7th Cir, 2011).

the Ninth Circuit has taken a particularly robust approach, suggesting that a decision-maker should assess harms inflicted on family members cumulatively,[49] and that '[i]mputing the disabled child's harms to the parent ... renders the law consonant with both common sense and ... family values'.[50] The Ninth Circuit has also developed a theory of 'constructive deportation', which suggests that a parent may be eligible for refugee status on the basis that the denial of status would result in the constructive deportation of, and accompanying risk of harm to, the child.[51] These strategies – while representing creative attempts to protect children and their families – provide clear evidence of the practical and conceptual difficulties generated by a parent-centred approach to refugee status determination. In order to keep a family together, a parent finds themselves compelled to construct an independent (and at times tenuous) claim rather than simply advance the more solid and straightforward refugee claim of their child.

2.2 The Individual Assessment of Status

As the above discussion makes clear, there has been a general reluctance amongst states to assess individually the protection claims of children, particularly where the child arrives as part of a family. This is despite the fact that as a matter of principle a child, irrespective of age, and irrespective of whether accompanied or unaccompanied, is entitled to have her claim for refugee status adjudicated prior to removal.[52] As the ECRE has observed, 'the [*Convention*] does not discriminate in terms of age as to whether applications are admissible'.[53] The UNCRC has similarly underlined that '[a]sylum-seeking children,

---

[49] *Tchoukhrova v Gonzales*, 404 F 3d 1181, 1192 (9th Cir, 2005).

[50] *Ibid.* The decision was subsequently vacated, on other grounds, by the US Supreme Court: *Gonzales v Tchoukhrova*, 549 US 801 (2006). Nevertheless, the decision has subsequently been cited with approval: *Gatimi v Holder*, 578 F 3d 611, 617 (7th Cir, 2009); *Bustami v Holder*, 385 Fed Appx 719, 721 (9th Cir, 2010).

[51] In *Benyamin v Holder*, 579 F 3d 970 (9th Cir, 2009), the principal applicant was the father (with his wife and three daughters listed as derivative beneficiaries of his claim). The primary decision-maker held that she could only consider whether the father himself was at risk of being persecuted. The Court of Appeals for the Ninth Circuit considered that it was necessary to consider the effect that the denial of the father's claim would have on his minor children. The Court, at 974, cited its earlier decision in *Abebe v Gonzales*, 1049, for the proposition that 'when addressing the parent['s] application for asylum, it is proper to consider not only the potential persecution the child may face, but also any hardship to the alien child due to the deportation of her parent[]'. The concept of constructive deportation was first raised in the case of *Salameda v INS*, 70 F.3d 447, 451: 'Since [the child] will have to follow his parents into exile, having no legal right to remain in the United States, he is constructively deported and should therefore, one might suppose, be entitled to ask ... for suspension.' The Seventh Circuit has since held that the 'constructive deportation' theory is applicable only where the child has no legal right to remain in the United States (for example, the theory is inapplicable where the child is a US citizen): see *Oforji v Ashcroft*, 354 F 3d 609, 618 (7th Cir, 2003), 614–18; *Olowo v Ashcroft*, 368 F 3d 692 (7th Cir, 2004), 701; *contra Mansour v Ashcroft*, 390 F 3d 667 (7th Cir, 2004), 682–4 (Pregerson J dissenting); *Nwaokolo v INS*, 314 F 3d 303 (7th Cir, 2002), 307–10. In *Kone v Holder*, 620 F 3d 760 (7th Cir, 2010), 764–5, it was suggested that the decisions in *Oforji v Ashcroft* and *Olowo v Ashcroft* might be distinguished in cases where both parents are going to be removed, as in both *Oforji v Ashcroft* and *Olowo v Ashcroft* one of the parents was eligible to remain in the United States with the US-citizen child. On this point, see also *Re A-K-*, 24 I & N Dec 275 (BIA, 2007), 276; *Hassan v Gonzales*, 484 F 3d 513 (8th Cir, 2007), 519. For further discussion, see generally D E Anker, *Law of Asylum in the United States* (2015) 255–99, 472–3.

[52] The *Convention* applies to 'any person': art 1A(2). See also *CRC*, art 22(1).

[53] ECRE, 'Position on Refugee Children' (Policy Statement, November 1996), [23].

including those who are accompanied or separated, shall enjoy access to asylum procedures and other complementary mechanisms providing international protection, *irrespective of their age*.[54] At a domestic level, the position has been affirmed by the Australian High Court in a case involving a three-and-a-half-year-old boy:[55]

> The [*Refugee Convention*] applies, in terms, to a 'person' ... By Australian law, as well as by international law, a child is a person. It could hardly be otherwise. Indeed for the purposes of international refugee law, children are often amongst the most vulnerable groups of refugees in special need of the protection of the Convention ... [U]nder Australian law, the child was entitled to have his own rights determined as that law provides. He is not for all purposes subsumed to the identity and legal rights of his parents.

It is important to acknowledge that in many cases the apparent disinclination to individually assess a child's refugee claim has translated into positive protection outcomes for children. As noted above, in a number of jurisdictions there is a long-established practice of automatically conferring protection on an entire family if the parent is found to be a refugee. But while there may be a principled basis for assimilating the status of a child with the status of her parent in cases involving the *conferral* of protection, the same cannot be said for cases involving the *denial* of protection. The point is forcefully made by UNHCR in its *Handbook*:[56]

> if the head of the family is not a refugee, there is nothing to prevent any one of his dependants, if they can invoke reasons on their own, from applying for recognition as refugees under the 1951 Convention or the 1967 Protocol. *In other words, the principle of family unity operates in favour of dependants and not against them.*

The position has been repeatedly affirmed by UNHCR, which has stressed the importance of 'providing each family member with the possibility of separately submitting any refugee claims that he or she may have'.[57] The denial of refugee status to a child's parent does not

---

[54] UNCRC, *GC6*, [66] (emphasis added). See also UNHCR, 'Submission from the United Nations High Commissioner for Refugees (UNHCR) to the legal representatives in case numbers XXX, XXX and XXX before the Danish Refugee Appeal Board' (2015), [18]–[23].

[55] *Chen Shi Hai v MIMA* (2000) 201 CLR 293, [77]–[78]. *Contra* finding of the majority of the Full Federal Court in *MIMA v Chen Shi Hai* (1999) 92 FCR 333, [28]: 'In this particular case, both parents sought, but were refused, refugee status. Hence, it must follow as a matter of logic, that if the parents cannot claim refugee status, then their child (who, in this particular case, is dependent upon their fears for his status) cannot succeed in a claim for refugee status.' In the EU context, see art 7(3) of the *Asylum Procedures Directive*.

[56] UNHCR, *Handbook*, [185] (emphasis added). The drafters of the *Convention* made a similar observation, noting that family members can be regarded as refugees 'even if the head of the family is not a refugee': *Report of the Ad Hoc Committee on Statelessness and Related Problems*, E/AC.32/5 (1950) 40. Shortly after the adoption of the *Convention*, Grahl-Madsen, observed: 'There is no basis today for assimilating the status of family members to that of the head of the family in cases where the latter's claim to refugee status has been rejected. If a person qualifies as a refugee in his or her own right, the fact that his or her spouse or parent does not qualify cannot operate against him or her': A Grahl-Madsen, *The Status of Refugees in International Law* (1966) vol 1, 418.

[57] UNHCR ExCom, *Conclusion on the Protection of the Refugee's Family*, No 88 (L) (1999), [(b)]. See also *infra* text accompanying n 71. A similar point is made in INS, *Guidelines*, 15: 'The UNHCR believes that "invisibility" is a common problem for refugee children. In recognition of this problem, Asylum Officers should not assume that a child cannot have an asylum claim independent of the parents. When a parent or parents do not appear to have an approvable claim, an Asylum Officer should routinely make an

obviate the need to independently assess whether the child is eligible for protection as a refugee in her own right. Indeed, the removal of a child without an individual assessment of refugee status may give rise to a risk of *refoulement* contrary to art 33 of the *Convention* and almost certainly a violation of the *CRC*'s procedural requirement that the child have an opportunity to express views freely in matters affecting them and be heard in judicial and administrative proceedings. The argument applies with equal force to an accompanied child as to an unaccompanied or separated child.[58]

2.2.1 The Duty of Non-Refoulement

The duty of *non-refoulement* prohibits the return of a refugee 'in any manner whatsoever to the frontiers of territories where his life or freedom would be threatened'.[59] As with each of the rights protected under the *Refugee Convention*, the obligation of *non-refoulement* is not qualified by an applicant's age. The effective implementation of the *non-refoulement* duty requires an individual examination of risk prior to removal.[60]

The view that 'a fair refugee status determination is [an] essential component of the ... prohibition on *refoulement*'[61] finds support in the principle of *pacta sunt servanda*, which requires that a treaty be performed in good faith.[62] It is difficult to conceive how this standard will be satisfied in circumstances where a child is removed without first ascertaining whether that child meets the refugee definition. The argument also finds support in the work of the UNHCR ExCom, which has since 1977 reiterated the central importance of

inquiry into the child's case even though the child may be listed merely as a derivative on a parent's application and may not have filed a separate ... asylum application'.

[58] 'Each child has the right to make an independent refugee claim, regardless of whether s/he is accompanied or unaccompanied': UNHCR, 2009 *Guidelines*, [6]. Neither the *Refugee Convention* nor the *CRC* draws any distinction between the protection to be afforded to accompanied children as compared to unaccompanied or separated children. To the contrary, art 22 of the *CRC* expressly provides that states parties shall take appropriate measures to ensure that 'a child who is seeking refugee status or who is considered a refugee in accordance with applicable international or domestic law and procedures shall, *whether unaccompanied or accompanied by his or her parents or by any other person*, receive appropriate protection and humanitarian assistance in the enjoyment of applicable rights set forth in the present Covenant' (emphasis added).

[59] *Convention*, art 33(1). It is clear from the language of art 33(1) that the duty inheres irrespective of whether or not an individual has been formally granted refugee status, and that the obligation is binding from the moment that a refugee is subject to a state's jurisdiction up until the moment of expulsion.

[60] E Lauterpacht and D Bethlehem, 'The Scope and Content of the Principle of Non-Refoulement' in E Feller, V Türk and F Nicholson (eds), *Refugee Protection in International Law: UNHCR's Global Consultations on International Protection* (2003) 87, 118 ('[i]n particular a *denial* of protection in the absence of a review of individual circumstances would be inconsistent with the prohibition of *refoulement*'); J C Hathaway, *The Rights of Refugees under International Law* (2005) 319–20 ('[t]he duty of *non-refoulement* can also be infringed by the refusal to consider a claim to refugee status, knowing that such a refusal leaves the refugee exposed to removal on general immigration grounds ... There is [thus] no basis for a bar on considering the refugee claims made by children of the kind often applied in Europe, and advocated as a general standard by Australia'); G S Goodwin-Gill, 'Part II: Final Report and Draft Declaration on Minimum International Standards for Refugee Procedures' in International Law Association, *Delhi Conference – Committee on Refugee Procedures* (2002) 18, 20.

[61] S H Legomsky, 'Second Refugee Movements and the Return of Asylum Seekers to Third Countries: The Meaning of Effective Protection' (2003) 15 *International Journal of Refugee Law* 567, 654.

[62] *VCLT*, art 26.

procedures for determining refugee status in order to identify those eligible for protection under the *Convention*.[63] In particular, the ExCom has emphasised that such procedures must be 'adequate to ensure in practice that persons in need of international protection are identified and that refugees are not subject to *refoulement*'.[64]

2.2.2 A Child's Right to Be Heard

Article 12 of the *CRC* is recognised by the UNCRC as one of the four guiding principles underpinning the interpretation and application of the instrument.[65] The provision provides:

(1) States Parties shall assure to the child who is capable of forming his or her own views the right to express those views freely in all matters affecting the child, the views of the child being given due weight in accordance with the age and maturity of the child.

(2) For this purpose, the child shall in particular be provided the opportunity to be heard in any judicial and administrative proceedings affecting the child, either directly, or through a representative or an appropriate body, in a manner consistent with the procedural rules of national law.

In affording children the right to express views freely in matters affecting them, and to be heard in judicial and administrative proceedings, art 12 'recognises the dangers of wrapping [children] in silence'.[66] Article 12 emphasises the importance of addressing the 'needs of a child as a true legal person, and not just as an object of protection'.[67] The provision thus both reflects and reinforces the paradigm shift away from thinking about children as passive objects, and promotes the participation[68] of children in decision-making processes. Article 12 codifies a vision of children as autonomous social actors with 'real hopes, fears, hurts and joys',[69] and imposes a procedural responsibility on states to ensure that such hopes, fears,

---

[63] UNHCR ExCom, *Determination of Refugee Status*, No 8 (XVIII) (1977), [(a)]; UNHCR ExCom, *Follow-Up on Earlier Conclusions of the Sub-Committee of the Whole on International Protection on the Determination of Refugee Status, Inter Alia, with Reference to the Role of UNHCR in National Refugee Status Determination Procedures*, No 28 (XXXIII) (1982), [(c)]; UNHCR ExCom, *The Problem of Manifestly Unfounded or Abusive Applications for Refugee Status or Asylum*, No 30 (XXXIV) (1983), [(e)]; UNHCR ExCom, *General*, No 71 (XLIV) (1993), [(i)]; UNHCR ExCom, *General*, No 74 (XLV) (1994), [(i)]; UNHCR ExCom, *General*, No 81 (XLVII) (1997), [(h)].

[64] UNHCR ExCom, *General*, No 71 (XLIV) (1993), [(l)].

[65] UNCRC, *GC12*, [2] ('[t]he right of all children to be heard and taken seriously constitutes one of the fundamental values of the Convention'); UNCRC, *GC5*, [12].

[66] M Freeman, 'The Human Rights of Children' (2010) 63 *Current Legal Problems* 1, 20. This is also reflected in the inclusion of traditional civil and political rights in the *CRC*, including freedom of expression (art 13), freedom of religion (art 14) and freedom of association and assembly (art 15).

[67] *Juridical Status and Human Rights of the Child*, Advisory Opinion OC-17/02, 28 August 2002, IACHR (Ser A) No 17, [28].

[68] Article 12 is often referred to as codifying a 'right to participation', although that term is not actually used in the *CRC*: see UNCRC, *GC12*, [3]. As Krappmann has noted, '[p]articipation is a very good term for that which results from expressing views, listening and giving due weight to the views, interests and goals of the child': L Krappmann, 'The Weight of the Child's Views (Article 12 of the Convention on the Rights of the Child)' (2010) 18 *International Journal of Children's Rights* 501, 502.

[69] M Minow, 'Children's Rights: Where We've Been and Where We're Going' (1995) 68 *Temple Law Review* 1573, 1583.

hurts and joys are taken into account in any matter affecting them. A decision to return a child to a country where she may be at risk of harm almost certainly triggers that responsibility.

Both UNHCR and the UNCRC have called attention to the significance of art 12 in determining the status of a refugee child.[70] In its 2009 *Guidelines*, UNHCR states that, '[e]ven at a young age, a child may still be considered the principal asylum applicant'[71] and that 'the right of children to express their views in all matters affecting them, including to be heard in all judicial and administrative proceedings[,] ... needs to be taken into account'.[72] Similarly, in *GC6* the UNCRC employs art 12 to promote measures that ensure 'the child's views and wishes [are] elicited and taken into account'.[73] Of particular significance, in *GC12* the UNCRC emphasises that 'it is urgent to fully implement [a child's] right to express their views on all aspects of the immigration and asylum proceedings' and that 'the child must ... have the opportunity to present her or his reasons leading to the asylum claim.[74] Article 12 has also increasingly found favour at the national level, with domestic legislation,[75] guidelines[76]

---

[70] A number of commentators have also highlighted the relevance of art 12 in this context. See, e.g., J Bhabha and W Young, 'Not Adults in Miniature: Unaccompanied Child Asylum Seekers and the New US Guidelines' (1999) 11(1) *International Journal of Refugee Law* 84, 96; E Nykanen, 'Protecting Children? The European Convention on Human Rights and Child Asylum Seekers' (2001) 3 *European Journal of Migration and Law* 315, 320–3; H Lidén and H Rusten, 'Asylum, Participation and the Best Interests of the Child: New Lessons from Norway' (2007) 21 *Children and Society* 273; E Feller, 'Statement by Erika Feller' (2004) 23(2) *Refugee Survey Quarterly* 329; D O'Donnell, 'The Rights of Children to Be Heard: Children's Right to Have Their Views Taken into Account and to Participate in Legal and Administrative Proceedings' (Innocenti Working Paper No IWP-2009-04, UNICEF, April 2009) 29–31; S Bolton et al., 'Vulnerable Persons Working Group' (Workshop Discussion Paper, International Association of Refugee Law Judges, World Conference, Slovenia, 2011) 13–18.

[71] UNHCR, 2009 *Guidelines*, [5].

[72] *Ibid.*, [8]. The 2009 *Guidelines* further note (at [70]) that '[t]he right of children to express their views and to participate in a meaningful way is ... important in the context of asylum procedures. A child's own account of his/her experience is often essential for the identification of his/her individual protection requirements and, in many cases, the child will be the only source of this information.' The 2009 *Guidelines* (at [70] n 136) appropriately recognise that '[t]he CRC does not set any lower age limit on children's right to express their views freely as it is clear that children can and do form views from a very early age'. UNHCR's earlier policies also noted the importance of allowing children to participate in decisions affecting them: see, e.g., UNHCR ExCom, *UNHCR Policy on Refugee Children*, EC/SCP/82 (1993), [24] ('[children] are people in their own right, with suggestions, opinions and abilities to participate in decisions and activities that affect their lives. Efforts on behalf of refugee children fall short if they are perceived only as individuals to be fed, immunized or sheltered, rather than treated as participating members of their community'). See, more recently, UNHCR, *Quality Integration Project* (2013) *supra* n 36, 21–2.

[73] UNCRC, *GC6*, [25].   [74] UNCRC, *GC12*, [123].

[75] See, e.g., ch 1 s 11 of the Swedish *Aliens Act* (2005:716) ('In assessing questions of permits under this Act when a child will be affected by a decision in the case, the child must be heard, unless this is inappropriate. Account must be taken of what the child has said to the extent warranted by the age and maturity of the child').

[76] By way of example, in Canada, the relevant domestic guidelines explicitly refer to art 12 as affording children the 'right to be heard in regard to his or her refugee claim' and outline seven principles for eliciting the evidence of a child: IRB, *Guidelines*, 4–6. In New Zealand, the applicable guidelines provide that, '[i]n any claim by the minor to be recognised as a refugee or protected person, as far as practicable, the minor must be given an opportunity to express their views on the matter, whether personally or through a responsible adult' and that '[t]he refugee and protection officer must give due weight to those views, taking into account the minor's age and level of maturity and understanding': Immigration New

and judicial decisions[77] explicitly engaging with the participatory obligations contained in the *CRC*.

The interpretation and application of art 12 is best understood by unpacking the constituent elements of the provision. This interpretative exercise has been undertaken by the UNCRC in its *GC12*,[78] and has been the subject of detailed academic commentary.[79] The discussion that follows focuses on those elements particularly salient to the application of art 12 to the refugee status determination process.

Article 12(1) provides that states parties 'shall assure to the child who is capable of forming his or her own views the right to express those views freely in all matters affecting the child'. The deliberate adoption of the phrase 'shall assure' signifies that there is no scope for discretion and that states are under a strict obligation to undertake all appropriate measures for the implementation of the right.[80] The UNCRC has noted that the phrase 'capable of forming his or her own views' should not be viewed as a limitation, but rather an obligation for states parties to assess the child's capacity to form an autonomous opinion: 'States parties should presume that a child has the capacity to form her or his own views and recognize that she or he has the right to express them; it is not up to the child to first prove her or his capacity'.[81] There is no lower age limit imposed on the right to participate, with the UNCRC emphasising that art 12 'applies both to younger and to older children'.[82] There is thus no principled basis in the *CRC* to support the imposition of a minimum age on the right to participate in the refugee status determination process.

Zealand, *Immigration New Zealand Operational Manual: Refugees and Protection* (2011), [C7.1.15]. In Sweden, the Migration Board's official internal handbook instructs officers to interview very young children as 'they can be understood as skilled story tellers from the age of four': Migration Board, *Utlänningshandboken* [Handbook on Foreigners] (undated), cited in A Lundberg, 'The Best Interests of the Child Principle in Swedish Asylum Cases: The Marginalization of Children's Rights' (2011) 3(1) *Journal of Human Rights Practice* 49, 56–7.

[77] See, e.g., *ZH (Tanzania) v SSHD* [2011] 2 AC 166, [34], [37] ('Acknowledging that the best interests of the child must be a primary consideration in these cases immediately raises the question of how these are to be discovered. An important part of this is discovering the child's own views … [T]he immigration authorities must be prepared at least to consider hearing directly from a child who wishes to express a view and is old enough to do so. While their interest may be the same as their parents' this should not be taken for granted in every case … Children can sometimes surprise one'); *H (H) v Deputy Prosecutor of the Italian Republic, Genoa* [2013] 1 AC 338, [85]; *Baker v Canada (MCI)* [1999] 2 SCR 817, [7]; *X v MIMA* (1999) 92 FCR 524, [39]; *Ye v Minister of Immigration* [2009] NZSC 76, [51]–[53].

[78] See also the precursor to *GC12*: UNCRC, *Report on the Forty-Third Session*, CRC/C/43/3 (2006) pt VII (summary of Day of General Discussion on 'The Child's Right to Be Heard') [988].

[79] See especially A MacDonald, *The Rights of the Child: Law and Practice* (2011) 297–391; J Tobin, 'Justifying Children's Rights' (2013) 21 *International Journal of Children's Rights* 395; UNICEF, *Implementation Handbook for the Convention on the Rights of the Child* (3rd edn, 2007) 149–75; O'Donnell (2009) *supra* n 70; S Detrick, *A Commentary on the United Nations Convention on the Rights of the Child* (1999), 213–30.

[80] *CRC*, art 4; UNCRC, *GC12*, [19]. Art 12(2) similarly provides that states 'shall' afford the child an opportunity to be heard in any judicial and administrative proceedings affecting him.

[81] UNCRC, *GC12*, [20]. The right applies to children capable of *forming* their own views, not *expressing* their own views, and accordingly the 'full implementation of article 12 requires recognition of, and respect for, non-verbal forms of communication including play, body language, facial expressions, and drawing and painting, through which very young children demonstrate understanding, choices and preferences': at [21]. For a summary of research on child and adolescent developmental capacity for decision-making, see J Fortin, *Children's Rights and the Developing Law* (2009) 82–9.

[82] UNCRC, *GC7*, [14]; *GC6*, [66]. *Contra* J Griffin, *On Human Rights* (2008) 83–94 (arguing that children acquire rights and agency, in stages).

Article 12(1) provides children with the right to express their views 'freely' but imposes no obligation on them to do so.[83] As discussed below, there may be scenarios where it will be in a child's interests to remain silent and seek to assimilate her status with that of her parent or guardian.

Article 12(1) imposes a positive obligation on states not simply to listen to the views of a child but also to take those views seriously.[84] However, the obligation is not absolute. The *CRC* does not require a child's views to be treated as dispositive,[85] but that their views be given 'due weight according to the age and maturity of the child'.[86] This qualification illustrates the misconceived nature of suggestions that the participatory model codified under the *CRC* requires children to be abandoned to their autonomy[87] and devalues the authority and role of parents.[88] Article 12 is to be read in conformity, and is entirely reconcilable with, the requirement under art 5 that states 'respect the responsibilities, rights and duties of parents or . . . other persons legally responsible for the child, to provide, in a manner consistent with the evolving capacities of the child, appropriate direction and guidance in the exercise by the child of the rights recognized in the present Convention'.[89] Read together, arts 12 and 5 afford children a right to direction and guidance to compensate for their lack of knowledge and experience while ensuring that, as a child acquires capacities,

---

[83] UNCRC, *GC12*, [16] ('The child . . . has the right not to exercise this right. Expressing views is a choice for the child, not an obligation').

[84] UNCRC, *GC12*, [28] ('Article 12 stipulates that simply listening to the child is insufficient; the views of the child have to be seriously considered when the child is capable of forming her or his own views').

[85] Tobin (2005) *supra* n 1, 40–1. See also Nykanen (2001) *supra* n 70, 321 ('[t]he right to express one's view and the obligation to take them into account should not be confused with the child's absolute right to decide. The weight given to the views of the child depends on the child and her personal capacities: as the capacities evolve, the weight should increase. The child's wishes are not necessarily a determining factor but in any case they should be taken seriously'); UNICEF (2007) *supra* n 79, 150 ('[t]he rights of the child set out in [art 12] do not provide a right to self-determination but concern involvement in decision-making'); J Eekelaar, 'The Interests of the Child and the Child's Wishes: The Role of Dynamic Self-Determinism' in P Alston (ed), *The Best Interest of the Child: Reconciling Culture and Human Rights* (1994) 42.

[86] The reference to the twin criteria – age and maturity – reaffirms that there is no basis under the *CRC* for an age barrier to the participation of children. The UNCRC observes that '[c]hildren's levels of understanding are not uniformly linked to their biological age. Research has shown that information, experience, environment, social and cultural expectations, and levels of support all contribute to the development of a child's capacities to form a view. For this reason, the views of the child have to be assessed on a case-by-case basis': UNCRC, *GC12*, [29].

[87] B Hafen and J Hafen, 'Abandoning Children to Their Autonomy: The United Nations Convention on the Rights of the Child' (1996) 37 *Harvard International Law Journal* 449.

[88] M Guggenheim, *What's Wrong with Children's Rights* (2005).

[89] While not considering the *CRC* directly, in the case of *Re S (a minor) (Independent Representation)* [1993] Fam 263, 279–80, Sir Thomas Bingham MR of the England and Wales Court of Appeal explained the importance of striking a 'judicious balance' between the principles that underpin arts 12 and 5: 'First is the principle . . . that children are human beings in their own right with individual minds and wills, views and emotions, which should command serious attention. A child's wishes are not to be discounted or dismissed simply because he is a child. He should be free to express them and decision-makers should listen. Second is the fact that a child is, after all, a child . . . Everything of course depends on the individual child in his actual situation . . . a babe in arms and a sturdy teenager on the verge of adulthood are both children, but their positions are quite different: for one the second consideration will be dominant, for the other the first principle will come into its own. The process of growing up is . . . a continuous one. The judge has to do his best, on the evidence before him, to assess the understanding of the individual child in the context of the proceedings in which he seeks to participate.'

'they are entitled to an increasing level of responsibility for the regulation of matters affecting them'.[90]

In the context of the refugee status determination process, an assessment of the age and maturity of the child is most likely to be relevant in two specific contexts. First, where the interests of a child do not align with the interests of her parent or guardian; for example, where the child applies for protection in a host state and the parent seeks to return to their country of origin. Second, and more commonly, the age and maturity of a child will be relevant when assessing the cogency of a child's evidence.[91]

Article 12(2) has particular consequence in the context of the refugee status determination process, stipulating that children have a right to be heard in 'any judicial and administrative proceedings affecting the child'.[92] In the refugee context, the language is wide enough to cover both the original administrative decision-making process as well as any subsequent judicial review.[93] The antecedent clause '[f]or this purpose' indicates that the components of art 12(1) carry through to art 12(2) – namely, that there can be no age barrier to the right to be heard, and that decision-makers in courts or other administrative proceedings have a duty not just to hear the child's views but also to afford them due weight, having regard to age and maturity. If the child decides to be heard, she can be heard 'either directly, or through a representative or appropriate body', although the UNCRC has recommended that, 'wherever possible, the child must be given the opportunity to be directly heard'.[94]

The emphasis on a child's right to be heard in judicial and administrative proceedings should not be underestimated. Article 12(2) accords with the basic requirement of procedural fairness that any individual affected by a judicial or administrative decision should have an opportunity to be heard in respect of that decision. One commentator suggests that the provision may have been intended as a partial substitute for the right to equal protection of law,[95] one of a small number of international human rights that was not explicitly reaffirmed in the CRC.[96] Irrespective of whether that was the intention, a child remains eligible to benefit from any additional protection that the general human rights treaties may provide,[97] including the requirement that '[a]ll persons shall be equal before the courts and tribunals'.[98]

---

[90] UNCRC, GC12, [84]–[85]. See generally S Brennan and R Noggle, 'The Moral Status of Children: Children's Rights, Parents' Rights, and Family Justice' (1997) 23 Social Theory and Practice 1, 11–12; Tobin (2005) supra n 1, 41.

[91] See Chapter 3, Section 3.3.4.

[92] Article 12(2) is bolstered by art 22 of the CRC, which provides that all children seeking refugee status must 'receive appropriate protection and humanitarian assistance in the enjoyment of applicable rights'. In a limited subset of cases, the participatory right under art 9(2) might also be relevant; specifically, where the expulsion of a family member – the child or the parent or guardian – will result in their separation. Article 9(2) provides that in this situation 'all interested parties shall be given an opportunity to participate in the proceedings and make their views known'. Although beyond the scope of this book, art 37(d) of the CRC recognises the right of a child deprived of his liberty to challenge the legality of that measure before a court or other competent, independent and impartial authority.

[93] UNCRC, GC12, [32], [123].

[94] UNCRC, GC12, [35]–[37]. See generally A Nolan, Children's Socio-Economic Rights, Democracy and the Courts (2011) 226–7.

[95] UDHR, art 7; ICCPR, art 14.   [96] O'Donnell (2009) supra n 70, 3.   [97] CRC, art 41.

[98] ICCPR, art 14(1). This has been confirmed by the HRC, which has noted that 'as individuals, children benefit from all of the civil rights enunciated in the [ICCPR]' (HRC, CG17, [2]) and, in the context of art 14 specifically, that '[j]uveniles are to enjoy at least the same guarantees and protection as are accorded to adults under article 14' (HRC, GC13, [16]).

2.2.3 Implementing a Child-Centred Framework

The requirement that a child have an opportunity to express views freely in matters affecting her, and be heard in any judicial and administrative proceedings, coupled with the heightened risk of *refoulement* where a child is not afforded such an opportunity, provides a compelling and principled basis for the proposition that the removal of a child without an independent assessment of refugee status amounts to a violation of international law. The discussion that follows draws on state practice to provide a contextualised account of the various procedural mechanisms that might be implemented in order to ensure that a child is not removed without an independent assessment of refugee status. As will be apparent, there are a number of ways in which the international obligations that a state owes to an at-risk child may be implemented, and states ultimately retain control as to the specific procedures adopted. The outer contours of that discretion are however circumscribed by both art 12 of the *CRC* and the duty of *non-refoulement*.

2.2.3.1 Unaccompanied or Separated Children

As noted earlier, the majority of host states afford unaccompanied children the right to apply for refugee status. A separate question has arisen in relation to the *capacity* of unaccompanied children to apply for refugee status, with decision-makers drawing a distinction between the right to apply for refugee status and the capacity to exercise that right. This distinction is difficult to reconcile with the duty of *non-refoulement* and the child's right to be heard under art 12. Although factors such as a child's age and whether she has arrived with her family or not will be relevant to determining any procedural or evidential concessions that may be required in order to ensure the child's rights are effectively protected,[99] these factors are immaterial to the question of whether the child can advance an independent claim for refugee status.[100]

The difficulties generated by failing to independently assess the refugee claim of a child can be illustrated by revisiting the case of Elián González, the six-year-old Cuban boy rescued at sea after the death of his mother.[101] In that case the INS refused to adjudicate González's refugee claim, taking the view that a six-year-old child lacked the capacity to file a refugee claim against the wishes of his parents. As the above discussion makes clear, the duty of *non-refoulement* is not qualified by age; it protects a six-year-old boy in precisely the same manner as it does a 40-year-old adult. It is difficult to appreciate how a decision-maker can effectively assess the risk of *refoulement* without an individual assessment of the child's eligibility for refugee status.[102] The INS's policy also disregarded the UNCRC's guidance

---

[99] See, e.g., UNHCR, 2009 *Guidelines*, [65]–[77].

[100] By way of illustration, in the context of claims involving a risk of female genital cutting, see UNHCR, *Guidance Note on Refugee Claims Relating to Female Genital Mutilation* (2009), [11]: 'Where a family seeks asylum based on a fear that a female child of the family will be subjected to FGM, the child will normally be the principal applicant, even where accompanied by her parents . . . Even when very young, the child may still be considered the principal applicant. In such cases, the evolving capacities of the child need to be taken into account and the parent, caregiver or other person representing the child will have to assume a greater role in making sure that all relevant aspects of the child's claim are presented.'

[101] See *supra* text accompanying n 25–34.

[102] Indeed, the Court of Appeals suggested that if González's claim had been 'accepted and fully adjudicated' he may have established eligibility for refugee status: *Gonzalez v Reno*, 212 F 3d 1338, 1356 (11th Cir, 2000).

that there can be no minimum age prescribed to limit a child's right to be heard in any judicial or administrative proceeding in which the child's interests are affected.[103]

Although the INS's policy was upheld by the Court of Appeals for the Eleventh Circuit, it is clear the Court had some misgivings about the decision. In a telling passage, the Court stated:[104]

> Although the INS is not required to let six-year-old children speak for themselves about asylum, neither is the INS required to ignore the expressed statements of young children. Even young children can be capable of having an accurate impression of the facts about which they might speak. To obtain asylum, we doubt that it is essential for a child to be able to debate the merits of Marxism-Leninism against the merits of Western-style democracy. Some reasonable people could conclude that it should be sufficient for a child to be able to speak about his fears and to recount the facts that support his fears about returning to another country. Not infrequently, the law does permit six-year-old children (and even younger children) to speak and, in fact, does give their words great effect.

The Court was also troubled 'by the degree of obedience that the INS policy appears to give to the wishes of parents',[105] recognising that such deference 'might hinder some six-year-olds with non-frivolous asylum claims and prevent them from invoking their statutory right to seek asylum'.[106]

The case of Elián González provides an illustration of the delicate interplay between protecting the interests of a child and respecting the role and authority of the parent. The *CRC* is designed to strike a balance between these interests. In its submission to the Court,[107] the US Attorney General expressly relied on the *CRC* for the proposition that states are required to 'tak[e] into account the rights and duties of his or her parents',[108] 'respect the responsibilities, rights and duties of parents ... in a manner consistent with the evolving capacities of the child'[109] and recognise that 'parents ... have the primary responsibility for the upbringing and development of the child'.[110] The Attorney General's selective reading overlooked the *CRC*'s requirement that parents are legally responsible for providing 'appropriate direction and guidance *in the exercise by the child of the rights recognized in the [CRC]*'[111] and that '[t]he best interests of the child will be their basic concern'.[112] A parent's refusal to allow a child to apply for refugee status, in circumstances where there is a real chance that the child will be persecuted if returned, may well be contrary to the child's best interests. Indeed, the point was explicitly acknowledged by the Court of Appeals, which suggested that '[a] parent's unwillingness to seek asylum on [a] child's behalf may indicate ... that the parent is not representing adequately the child's interests'.[113] Unfortunately, the Court did not engage in any detail with the provisions of the *CRC*, notwithstanding the fact that the *CRC* provides a principled framework for mediating precisely the conflict that was before the Court.

Australian courts have adopted an approach that is more easily reconcilable with art 12 of the *CRC* and the duty of *non-refoulement*. In *X v MIMA*, the Australian government argued

[103] The Court of Appeals explicitly noted its concern that 'the INS, in making a preliminary assessment of the strength of [González's] asylum claim, never interviewed [González]'. *Gonzalez v Reno*, 212 F 3d 1338, 1355 n 25 (11th Cir, 2000).

[104] *Gonzalez v Reno*, 212 F 3d 1338, 1351 n 18 (11th Cir, 2000). See also the earlier interlocutory decision: *Gonzalez v Reno*, 2000 US App LEXIS 7025, [15] (11th Cir, 2000).

[105] *Gonzalez v Reno*, 212 F 3d 1338, 1352 (11th Cir, 2000). [106] *Ibid.*, 1353.

[107] United States Attorney, 'Brief', filed in *Gonzalez v Reno* (24 April 2000) 57. [108] *CRC*, art 3.

[109] *Ibid.*, art 5. [110] *Ibid.*, art 18(1). [111] *Ibid.*, art 18(1) (emphasis added). [112] *Ibid.*, art 18(1).

[113] *Gonzalez v Reno*, 212 F 3d 1338, 1352 (11th Cir, 2000).

that two Kenyan boys (aged sixteen and seventeen) lacked the legal capacity to independently bring an action for judicial review in the context of a guardianship application.[114]
The argument was rejected by the Federal Court. The Court drew expressly on art 12 of the
CRC, noting that 'the [CRC] recognises that children must be able to put forward their
claims against the denial of . . . rights in administrative and legal proceedings' and that 'they
must be given a direct voice if they are capable of making it heard'.[115] In the Court's view it
logically followed that the two Kenyan children had the capacity to bring the action on their
own behalf.[116] A similar approach was adopted in *Jaffari v MIMA*,[117] where the Federal
Court was called upon to determine whether an Afghan teenager could, absent an adult
representative, bring review proceedings challenging a negative refugee decision. The Court
underlined the fact that 'questions of Australia's protection obligations under the Refugee
Convention . . . are serious ones and the outcomes, if they are not honoured, may be most
serious for the person wrongly returned to a place in which he or she may be persecuted'.[118]
The Court considered that '[t]he fact that a person is a minor should not be seen, of itself, as
imposing any procedural barrier to invoking the legal processes necessary to establish that
the person is a refugee and entitled to protection'.[119]

2.2.3.1 Accompanied Children

As discussed in Section 2.1, an accompanied child's claim is often subsumed within the
application of her parent, with the child's status automatically flowing from the status
granted to the parent. The removal of a child in these circumstances, without an individual
assessment of the child's eligibility for refugee status, may give rise to a risk of a violation of
the duty of *non-refoulement* and will almost certainly constitute a violation of art 12 of the
CRC. In order to safeguard against these risks, several jurisdictions have implemented
domestic procedures that require decision-makers to undertake a separate refugee status
determination for each individual child irrespective of whether the child is part of a family
unit. This approach – adopted in Canada,[120] New Zealand[121] and several European
jurisdictions[122] – finds some support in guidance issued by UNHCR.

[114] The case arose in extraordinary circumstances. The two unaccompanied children applied for refugee
status, but this was rejected both at first instance and by the RRT. The children were subsequently placed
on an aircraft and removed to Singapore, notwithstanding the fact that the children intended to appeal
the decision of the RRT (and the time period for doing so had not yet expired) and despite the fact that
orders had been made by the Federal Court preventing the return of the children. X v MIMA (1999) 92
FCR 524 concerned the capacity of the children to personally bring an application to both review the
decisions made by the RRT that refused their refugee claims and file a motion for contempt in
connection with the circumstance of their removal. Following this decision, the Federal Court determined that the RRT had erred in its assessment and remitted the cases for further consideration: X v
MIMA [2000] FCA 702; Y v MIMA [2000] FCA 703.

[115] X v MIMA (1999) 92 FCR 524, [41]; see also at [39] (explicitly referring to art 12 of the CRC).

[116] Ibid., [75]. The decision was approved by the Full Court of the Federal Court of Australia in Odhiambo
v MIMA [2002] FCAFC 194, [106] and SFTB v MIMIA [2003] FCAFC 108, [7].

[117] Jaffari v MIMA [2001] FCA 985.   [118] Ibid., [18] (French J).   [119] Ibid.

[120] The Canadian system is discussed in detail below.

[121] In New Zealand, every individual who seeks recognition as a refugee must have their claim separately
determined: Immigration Act 2009 (NZ) ss 125, 133.

[122] For instance, in Sweden the decision-maker must undertake a separate status determination for every
child and has a statutory obligation to have regard to 'the child's health and development and the best
interests of the child in general': Swedish Aliens Act (2005: 716), ch 1 s 10. However, a study conducted
by Lundberg (2011) supra n 76, 63–4, suggests that, as a matter of practice, the individual claims of

Although UNHCR has consistently affirmed the principle that family members of a refugee should also be afforded protection,[123] its position on whether family members should first be subject to an independent assessment of status to ascertain the *basis* of that protection is less than clear. UNHCR's internal procedural standards for refugee status determination suggest that children 'who are determined to fall within the criteria for refugee status in their own right should be granted refugee status rather than derivative refugee status' and that 'persons who may have grounds to make an independent refugee claim should not be discouraged from doing so solely because they may be eligible for derivative status under the right to family unity'.[124] In its *Handbook*, UNHCR states that '[i]t is obvious ... that formal refugee status should not be granted to a dependant if this is incompatible with his personal legal status'.[125] Of more recent vintage, UNHCR's 2009 *Guidelines* provides:[126]

> Where the parents or the caregiver seek asylum based on a fear of persecution for their child, the child normally will be the principal applicant even when accompanied by his/her parents. In such cases, just as a child can derive refugee status from the recognition of a parent as a refugee, a parent can, *mutatis mutandis*, be granted derivative refugee

---

children are generally afforded little weight: 'In many of the decisions, it seemed as if no child existed, even though each person in the family, including the children, formally got an individual decision. It can also be noted that in 70 per cent of the [102] cases in the study, the child appeared to have his or her own individual asylum claim, that is a claim directly related to his or her identity or situation.' A similar conclusion was reached in a 2005 study by E Nillson, 'A Child Perspective in the Swedish Process: Rhetoric and Practice' in H E Anderson et al. (eds), *The Asylum-Seeking Child in Europe* (2005) 73, 80: 'The children are not the real focus of this process; even if children are subjects of an investigation, when it comes to the decision they are quite beside the point. [Even] with good intentions and a legislation which allows for assessing the circumstances in each case, the main problem thus seems to be our frame of thought: we simply do not move beyond the "add and stir approach".' For further discussion on the Swedish experience with refugee children, see M Eastmond and H Ascher, 'In the Best Interest of the Child? The Politics of Vulnerability and Negotiations for Asylum in Sweden' (2011) 37(8) *Journal of Ethnic and Migration Studies* 1185. For further European case studies, including a critique of the implementation of child 'conversations' in Norway, see K Vitus and H Lidén, 'The Status of the Asylum-Seeking Child in Norway and Denmark: Comparing Discourses, Politics and Practices' (2010) 23(1) *Journal of Refugee Studies* 62; Lidén and Rusten (2007) *supra* n 70.

[123] See *infra* text accompanying n 176–9.

[124] UNHCR, *Procedural Standards for Refugee Status Determination under UNHCR's Mandate* (2003), [5.1.1].

[125] UNHCR, *Handbook*, [184]. *Contra* the more opaque statement (at [213]) that, '[i]f a minor is accompanied by one (or both) of his parents, or another family member on whom he is dependent, who requests refugee status, the minor's own refugee status will be determined according to the principle of family unity'. Standing Committee of the UNHCR ExCom, *Family Protection Issues*, EC/49/SC/CRP.14 (1999), [9], elaborates upon the position set out in the *Handbook*: 'It is generally agreed that applicants for refugee status must normally show good reasons why, individually, they fear persecution. However, it follows from the principle of family unity that, if the head of a family meets the criteria for recognition of refugee status, the dependent members of his or her family should normally be recognized as refugees. Such recognition would not, of course, be appropriate if it is incompatible with the personal legal status of the member of the family in question. For instance, recognition of refugee status would not be appropriate if the member of the family is a national of the country of asylum, or has another nationality and enjoys the protection of the country of that nationality. Equally, recognition of refugee status would not be warranted where the dependent member of the family falls within the scope of the exclusion clauses.'

[126] UNHCR, 2009 *Guidelines*, [9].

status. In situations where both the parent(s) and the child have their own claims to refugee status, it is preferable that each claim be assessed separately.

These statements support the adoption of a procedure that separately considers the claim of each family member in order to ascertain whether the family member is eligible for refugee status under the *Convention* or to a derivative form of protection on family-unity grounds. However, this position is difficult to reconcile with a number of UNHCR ExCom Conclusions, which recommend that, where the principal applicant is recognised as a refugee, the other family members should automatically be recognised as refugees, irrespective of whether they independently qualify for refugee status.[127]

The Canadian system requires all applicants to file an individual claim for refugee status irrespective of whether the applicant is accompanied by a family member, and decision-makers are statutorily obliged to make a separate refugee status determination for each individual applicant.[128] The obligation applies equally to all children regardless of age, with a number of procedural concessions in place to assist children to navigate the asylum process.[129] The requirement for a separate determination does not require the claims to be heard individually, and in most cases a child's claim will be heard jointly with the claims of the other family members.[130] However, the Canadian courts have made clear that, where a child's claim is heard jointly with the family, a failure to consider the separate nature and basis of the child's claim will give rise to a reviewable error.[131] The Federal Court of Canada has held that a decision-maker 'must be alert

---

[127] UNHCR ExCom, *Refugee Children*, No 47 (XXXVIII) (1987), [(h)] ('*recommend*[*ing*] that children who are accompanied by their parents should be treated as refugees if either of the parents is determined to be a refugee'); UNHCR ExCom, *Conclusion on the Protection of the Refugee's Family*, No 88 (L) (1999) [(b)] ('[*u*]*nderlin*[*ing*] the need for the unity of the refugee's family to be protected, *inter alia* by . . . provisions and/or practice allowing that when the principal applicant is recognized as a refugee, other members of the family unit should normally also be recognized as refugees').

[128] IRB, *Guidelines*, 1.

[129] For instance, a designated representative is appointed for all children under the age of 18: see, e.g., *Immigration and Refugee Protection Act*, SC 2001, c 27, s 167(2). That representative must be over the age of 18, appreciate the nature of the proceedings, not be in a conflict of interest situation with the child, and must be willing and able to fulfill the duties of a representative and act in the 'best interests of the child': IRB, *Guidelines*, 2–3. In cases where a child is accompanied, a parent is generally appointed as the designated representative of the child applicant; however, the court has recognised that in some cases such designation will be inappropriate: see, e.g., *Espinoza v Canada (MCI)* [1999] 3 FC 73, [27]. *Contra Coomaraswamy v Canada (MCI)* 2002 FC 501, [36]. For discussion of similar issues in the Australian context, see *WZAOT v Minister for Immigration [No 3]* [2011] FMCA 967.

[130] Indeed, the *Refugee Protection Division Rules* provide that the Division '*must* join the claim of a claimant to a claim made by the claimant's spouse or common law-partner, child, parent, brother, sister, grand-child or grandparent': *Refugee Protection Division Rules*, SOR/2012-256, r 55 (emphasis added). Rule 56 permits an applicant to make separate claims; however, Canadian courts have generally proven reluctant to hear claims separately unless there is a clear conflict between the claims of a parent and child: see, e.g., *Lu v Canada (MCI)* 2004 FC 1517, [8]–[9].

[131] 'Though the claims [are] heard jointly, it is recognized that each claim must be considered and determined individually': *Csonka v Canada (MEI)* 2001 FCT 915, [7]. In *Seevaratnam v Canada (MCI)* (1999) 167 FTR 130, [18], the Federal Court held that a decision-maker has 'a duty to assess the child's risk of persecution', and that 'failing to do so and focusing exclusively on the principal applicant [constitutes] a reviewable error'. See also *Kaniz v Canada (MCI)* [2013] FCJ No 63, [16]–[19]; *SRH v Canada (MCI)* [2012] FCJ No 1372, [32]–[34]; *Cruz v Canada (MCI)* [2012] FCJ No 650, [54]–[57]; *Mohacsi v Canada (MCI)* [2003] 4 FC 772, [13]–[16]; *Zakar v Canada (MCI)* 2005 FC 1016, [17]; *Chehar v Canada (MCI)* [1997] FTR LEXIS 3234, [5].

and alive to the specific interests of the child, especially where there is some distinction between the claims of the parent and the child (or children)'.[132] On this basis, the Federal Court has remitted cases where the initial decision-maker failed to take into account a child's distinct risk of child abuse,[133] sexual violence,[134] discrimination,[135] schoolyard beatings,[136] forced military recruitment[137] and use as a human shield in civil conflict.[138] The Federal Court has, however, indicated that if the child does face a distinctive risk of harm it is necessary for the applicant, or her designated representative, to identify that risk.[139] A decision-maker is thus unlikely to commit a reviewable error if the decision-maker was not put on notice that the child faced a distinct risk of harm. This does not mean that the child's independent claim needs to be advanced formally or particularised, but rather that, for practical reasons, evidence of such risk should be made available to the decision-maker.[140]

---

[132] *Zakar v Canada (MCI)* 2005 FC 1016, [17].

[133] *Ibid.*, [14] ('[t]he critical element of fear was not identical as between the mother and daughter. The daughter had a different basis for her claim of domestic abuse, that of fear of injury from her father. As a child, she stood in a more vulnerable position to that of her mother'); *Akhter v Canada (MCI)* [2000] FTR LEXIS 561. Contra *Garcia v Canada (MCI)* 2011 FC 1080, [20]–[23]; *Gilbert v Canada (MCI)* 2010 FC 1186, [20]–[27]; *Nam v Canada (MCI)* 2010 FC 783, [25]–[29].

[134] *Seevaratnam v Canada (MCI)* (1999) 167 FTR 130, [17] ('[t]here was documentary evidence . . . stating that young Tamil girls are being raped and that Tamil girls and boys as young as ten years of age are being recruited by the LTTE and used as human shields').

[135] *Cheung v Canada (MEI)* [1993] 2 FC 314, 325 ('if [the applicant] were sent back to China, she would, in her own right, experience such concerted and severe discrimination, including deprivation of medical care, education and employment opportunities and even food, so as to amount to persecution').

[136] *Mohacsi v Canada (MCI)* [2003] 4 FC 772, [13] ('[u]nless express reasons are provided . . . the Court cannot simply infer that the particular treatment received in Hungary by the principal applicant means that his . . . minor children, who also allege other acts of persecution – such as the fear of being beaten at school, or of being killed by skinheads like the principal applicant's nephew – cannot reasonably justify a claim of a well-founded fear of persecution').

[137] *Mulaja v Canada (MCI)* 2004 FC 1296, [7] ('[a] totally separate claim was advanced for the minor applicant based on forced recruitment and sexual abuse. It is the duty of the Board to address each major claim advanced by an Applicant; failure to do so amounts to a reversible error'); *Manoharan v Canada (MCI)* 2003 FC 871, [5]–[6]; *Gengeswaran v Canada (MCI)* (1999) 169 FTR 148, [10]; *Selvarajah v Canada (MCI)* (1997) 138 FTR 237. Contra *AMC v Canada (MCI)* 2011 FC 1012.

[138] *Al Asali v Canada (MPSEP)* 2007 FC 991, [24] ('There was . . . evidence on file which showed the nature of the risks faced by Palestinian children living in the West Bank. The record contained evidence that Palestinian children risked being shot and killed by Israeli Defense Forces and were being used as human shields'); *Gonsalves v Canada (MCI)* 2008 FC 844, [27]–[29]; *Csonka v Canada (MEI)* 2001 FCT 915, [28]; *Iruthayathas v Canada (MCI)* (1994) 82 FTR 154, [10].

[139] *Suppiah v Canada (MCI)* 2008 FC 1170, [15] ('[The decision-maker] is required to assess only those risks which are raised by the applicants. In the case at bar, no risks were raised as being faced by the children separate from those faced by their parents. It was therefore not an error to address all claims simultaneously'); *Garcia v Canada (MCI)* 2011 FC 1080, [20]–[23]; *Gilbert v Canada (MCI)* 2010 FC 1186, [20]–[27]; *Nam v Canada (MCI)* 2010 FC 783, [25]–[29]; *Mikiani v Canada (MCI)* 2005 FC 1285, [10]–[11]; *Neethinesan v Canada (MCI)* 2004 FC 138, [13]–[14]; *Nikolov v Canada (MCI)* 2003 FCT 231, [13]; *Kamalraj v Canada (MCI)* [2000] Fed Ct Trial LEXIS 932, [9]; *Ganji v Canada (MCI)* (1997) 135 FTR 283, [23].

[140] Contra *Ganji v Canada (MCI)* (1997) 135 FTR 283, [23], where the Federal Court held that a decision-maker was not required to examine a possible claim based upon interference with the child's right to education where the distinct claim, although raised in evidence, was not formally advanced. But see Chapter 3, Section 3.3.1.

The Canadian system requires a decision-maker to turn their mind to the individual circumstances of the child and ensure that a child's claim is not refused on account of the fact that her parents have failed to establish refugee status.[141] This approach does, however, give rise to a number of concerns. First, there is a practical concern that requiring decision-makers to undertake a separate refugee status determination for accompanied children is procedurally cumbersome. Based on this criterion alone, it is clear that an approach such as that adopted in the United States, where the child's status flows directly from the status granted to their parents, will generally be more efficient. However, it is important to acknowledge that the Canadian system draws a distinction between individual *determination* and individual *proceedings*.[142] As noted above, unless there is a good reason for separating the claims, a child's claim will be heard jointly with the claims of other family members. Although all children are required to submit an individual application, there is no obligation to advance a claim distinct from the parent's. Indeed, in the vast majority of cases the child's claim will be indistinguishable from the parent's claim, either because the claim is based on the same *Convention* ground,[143] or because the claim is based on the family as a particular social group. The point is nicely made by Grahl-Madsen:[144]

> in cases where it has been established that one member of a family has well-founded fear of being persecuted for one of the reasons set forth in the Refugee Convention ... one may often presume that the other members of the same family are in an identical position. It would seem that persons who are presumed to have well-founded fear, and who satisfy the other criteria of refugeehood ... [,] are refugees in their own right. Their

---

[141] Although the United Kingdom does not require a separate refugee status determination for each individual child, decision-makers have affirmed the need to consider whether a child has an individual claim. In *RA v SSHD* [2015] UKUT 00242, the Upper Tribunal stressed that 'notwithstanding that no separate claim may be expressly advanced on behalf of a child, the circumstances may be such as to warrant independent investigation' (at [73]). In that case, the Office of the Children's Commissioner had made submissions on 'the invisibility of accompanied children', emphasising the fact that a child's claim may be 'overlooked and treated as inseparable from that of an accompanying family member', 'despite the fact that a child may have a stronger independent asylum or human rights claim than an adult' (at [72]).

[142] The same distinction has been drawn by the UK House of Lords in a related context in *EM (Lebanon) v SSHD* [2009] 1 AC 1198, [49]: 'Separate consideration and separate representation are, however, two different things. Questions may have to be asked about the situation of other family members, especially children, and about their views. It cannot be assumed that the interests of all the family members are identical. In particular, a child is not to be held responsible for the moral failures of either of his parents ... But in most immigration situations ... the interests of different family members are unlikely to be in conflict with one another. Separate legal (or other) representation will rarely be called for.'

[143] For instance race, religion or nationality: Grahl-Madsen (1966) *supra* n 56, vol 1, 413. In some instances, it may be that evidence provided by a child strengthens the claim advanced by the parent. McAdam refers to the example of a six-year-old girl whose exposure and subsequent reaction to the rape and abuse of her mother was held to strengthen the mother's refugee claim: J McAdam, *Complementary Protection in International Refugee Law* (2007) 185. In the case of *Morgan v Mukasey*, 529 F 3d 1202 (9th Cir, 2008), the Court held that the primary decision-maker had committed an error by denying the principal applicant's two children the ability to testify, when they were in a position to corroborate the mother's claim. See also INS, *Guidelines*, 15, acknowledging that 'the fears and experiences of the child may help to enhance the strength of the parents' claim'.

[144] Grahl-Madsen (1966) *supra* n 56, 423.

status as such is not derived from that of the first-recognized family member. It is only the eligibility procedure which is simplified in their case.

In such cases it is common practice for the child to advance their claim simply by explicit reference to their mother or father's application.[145] In these cases, although the decision-maker is required to deliver a separate determination for the child, unless a distinct risk of harm becomes apparent during the course of the proceeding,[146] the task is no more onerous than it would be in a jurisdiction that makes a single determination per family unit.

Second, there is a concern that the separate assessment of an accompanied child's eligibility for refugee status may have the unintended consequence of breaking up the family unit, if some members of the family are determined to be ineligible for refugee status.[147] By contrast, a single determination for the family ensures that all members of the family are granted (or denied) the same protection status, thereby avoiding the potential fragmentation of the family unit. The concern is not a hypothetical one, as the Canadian experience illustrates. Canadian courts have, on various occasions, determined that: a parent is eligible for refugee status but the child is not;[148] a child is eligible, but a parent is not;[149] and a child is eligible, but a sibling is not.[150] A similar set of examples can be found in New Zealand, which, as noted above, also requires a separate claim to be advanced for each family member.[151] These examples do not, however, provide a principled basis for diluting a child's participatory rights, nor a child's right to be protected against the risk of *refoulement*. Rather, the examples illustrate the need to ensure the effective implementation of the principle of family unity, and in particular the duty of non-separation protected under art 9 of the *CRC*.[152] In both Canada and New Zealand, eligibility for refugee status and the

---

[145] For instance 'see my father's story', as in *Kukunov v Canada (MCI)* 2001 FCT 1377, [11].

[146] See, e.g., *Ganji v Canada (MCI)* (1997) 135 FTR 283.

[147] See, e.g., K Jastram and K Newland, 'Family Unity and Refugee Protection' in E Feller, V Türk and F Nicholson (eds), *Refugee Protection in International Law: UNHCR's Global Consultations on International Protection* (2003) 555, 571–2.

[148] See, e.g., *MA3–08450 and MA3–08451* (IRB, 4 April 2004); *VA3–01886, VA3–01887, VA3–01887, VA3–01888 and VA3–01889* (IRB, 5 February 2004); *AA0–00661, AA0–00662, AA0–00663, AA0–00664 and AA0–00665* (IRB, 11 January 2001); *M99–04586, M99–04587, M99–04588 and M99–04589* (IRB, 21 December 1999); *U97–00946 and U97–00947* (IRB, 21 January 1998); *T95–01010, T95–01011 and T95–01012* (IRB, 30 July 1996); *Casetellanos v Canada (Solicitor General)* [1995] 2 FC 190; *Rafizade v Canada (MCI)* (1995) 92 FTR 55.

[149] *Bueckert v Canada (MCI)* 2011 FC 1042; *VA1–03231, VA1–03232 and VA1–03233* (IRB, 12 March 2003); *VA1–02828, VA1–02826, VA1–02827 and VA1–02829* (IRB, 27 February 2003); *T97–00096, T97–00097 and T97–00098* (IRB, 22 January 1998).

[150] *MA0–10045 and MA0–10446* (IRB, 7 December 2001); *A99–00575, A99–00576 and A99–00577* (IRB, 29 December 2000).

[151] See, e.g., *Refugee Appeal Nos 74580, 74579 and 74578* (RSAA, 13 October 2003); *Refugee Appeal Nos 74862, 74863, 74864 and 74865* (RSAA, 19 February 2004); *Refugee Appeal Nos 75045, 75046 and 75047* (RSAA, 6 September 2004); *Refugee Appeal Nos 73931, 73932 and 73933* (RSAA, 21 February 2005); *Refugee Appeal Nos 74122, 74123, 74124 and 74125* (RSAA, 23 June 2005); *Refugee Appeal Nos 76478, 76479, 76480 and 76481* (RSAA, 11 June 2010); *Refugee Appeal Nos 76485, 76486 and 76487* (RSAA, 17 June 2010); *Refugee Appeal Nos 76380, 76381, 76382 and 76383* (RSAA, 30 June 2010); *AH (Iran)* [2011] NZIPT 500395; *BL (Iran)* [2012] NZIPT 500963; *BP (Iran)* [2012] NZIPT 500965; *AD (Czech Republic)* [2012] NZIPT 500876.

[152] See *infra* Section 2.3.

protection of the family unit are treated as *distinct* inquiries. As the Canadian Federal Court observed, the *Convention* 'does not incorporate the concept of family unity . . . [and] [t]here is no justification for doing so'.[153] The principle is, however, incorporated in Canadian legislation which 'embraces the principle of family unity [by] allow[ing] a person who has been determined to be a Convention refugee to apply to an immigration officer for the landing of that person and any dependants'.[154]

Although separating out the assessment of refugee status from the application of family unity principles is a conceptually more principled basis for assessing the protection needs of families, it is important to acknowledge that requiring decision-makers to undertake a separate refugee status determination for each child is not the only procedural device that would safeguard against a violation of art 12 and/or a risk of *refoulement*. It is entirely within the prerogative of a state to adopt a more generous policy of affording every member of a family a derivative protection status if a single member of the family is granted refugee status, without considering the separate claims of the remaining family members. Although at first blush this procedural shortcut may seem to be at odds with the individualistic nature of the refugee definition, it is explicable on at least two bases. First, it reflects and reinforces the reality that refugee status determination is a declaratory rather than constitutive process, and that the primary concern is about providing the protection that is owed, and not the formality of granting refugee status.[155] As the Canadian Federal Court of Appeal has observed, a refugee 'does not become a refugee because he is recognized, but is recognized because he is a refugee; there is first a situation of fact which gives rise to a condition, then recognition of a right which is expressed by a status'.[156] Hence, so long as a child receives the protection to which she is entitled as a refugee, the fact that it was the child's parent who was the formally recognised applicant is immaterial. Second, even if on the declaratory theory the child were not eligible for refugee status, as discussed below it is likely that the child would be eligible for a derivative form of protection on family unity grounds, thereby achieving the same result.[157]

---

[153] *Casetellanos v Canada (Solicitor General)* [1995] 2 FC 190, 200–1.

[154] *Ibid.*, 207–8. A similar point was made in *Pour-Shariati v Canada (MEI)* [1995] 1 FC 767, [13]–[15], affirmed by the Federal Court of Appeal in *Pour-Shariati v Canada (MEI)* (1997) 215 NR 174. *Contra Cheung v Canada (MEI)* [1993] 2 FC 314, 325. The IRB has also explicitly pointed to the fact that other provisions within the domestic *Immigration and Refugee Protection Act*, SC 2001, c 27 provided an avenue to ensure that the family is not separated. For instance, in *AA0–00661, AA0–00662, AA0–00663, AA0–00664 and AA0–00665* (IRB, 11 January 2001) 2, the IRB reassured the applicant that while '[t]he principle of family unity does not operate in refugee law', 'other aspects of the *Immigration Act* are there to provide that your family can stay together here in Canada'. See also *A99–00575, A99–00576 and A99–00577* (IRB, 29 December 2000), 3; *T95–01010, T95–01011 and T95–01012* (IRB, 30 July 1996), [22]. Similar statements of principle can be found in the New Zealand context: see, e.g., *Refugee Appeal Nos 75045, 75046 and 75047* (RSAA, 6 September 2004), [64].

[155] 'A person is a refugee within the meaning of the 1951 Convention as soon as he fulfills the criteria contained in the definition. This would necessarily occur prior to the time at which his refugee status is formally determined. Recognition of his refugee status does not therefore make him a refugee but declares him to be one. He does not become a refugee because of recognition, but is recognized because he is a refugee': UNHCR, *Handbook*, [28]. Conversely, simply because an individual is granted refugee rights as a family member of a refugee, this does not automatically mean that that a family member is a refugee for the purposes the *Refugee Convention*: see *MS (Somalia) v SSHD* [2010] EWCA Civ 1236, [22]–[24].

[156] *Mileva v Canada (MEI)* [1991] 3 FC 398, 411.

[157] See *infra* Section 2.3. See, e.g., UNHCR, *2003 Procedural Standards, supra* n 124, [5.1.1].

There are two important caveats. First, where a child is automatically conferred protection without a determination as to whether she is a refugee in her own right, it will be necessary for a state to ensure that the child receives the protection to which she would be entitled *as a refugee*. The absence of a formal determination provides no basis for affording a more limited set of rights than that which is owed under the *Convention*.[158] Second, and in contrast to the approach currently adopted in a number of jurisdictions, it is critical for the decision-maker to look beyond the claim of the first principal applicant if that initial claim fails. Jastram and Newland suggest that a decision-maker should continue to address the claims of each family member, but 'as soon as one member of the family has been found to have a valid claim, the others should be granted derivative refugee status'.[159] The derivative protection therefore flows from the first-recognised family member, rather than necessarily from the 'head of the family' – now a largely antiquated notion.[160]

2.3 Family Unity Procedures

As noted in Section 2.2, one of the key arguments advanced against the individual assessment of a child's status is that it may have the unintended consequence of separating the family unit if the family were to end up with mixed protection statuses. Indeed, family unity concerns are often used to rationalise domestic policies that assimilate the status of family members in cases involving the denial of protection, the logic being that it will be in the best interests of a child to remain with her parents, whether that be in the country of origin or the host country. As Thronson observes, 'although this version of family integrity does, in most instances, tend to keep children together with parents, it has no concern for where the family ends up or for children whose parents are unable to or choose not to assist them'.[161] This logic – referred to by one commentator as family unity with 'a vengeance'[162] – misappropriates the principle of family unity. In particular, the reasoning fails to appreciate that the individual recognition of a child's protection claim and the preservation of the

---

[158] This is the position adopted by UNHCR in its internal procedural guidelines for UNHCR mandate refugees: UNHCR, *2003 Procedural Standards, supra* n 124, [5.1.1].

[159] Jastram and Newland (2003) *supra* n 147, 572.

[160] 'On the whole the very concept of "head of the family" appears to have lost in significance. We have no basis for laying down strict rules as to who are to be considered heads of families ... we must use common sense. The emphasis is on the factual unity of a family group': Grahl-Madsen (1966) *supra* n 56, 418. By way of illustration, in Australia all family members are encouraged, although not required, to advance separately any independent claim for protection: see DIAC, 'Application for a Protection (Class XA) Visa' (Form 866, July 2013) 2. If one of the family members (generally referred to as the 'main applicant') is eligible for refugee status, the other members of the same family unit are automatically granted derivative protection without an individual assessment of refugee status. Critically – and in contrast to the position in the United Kingdom and the United States – in Australia the 'main applicant' can be a child, and the child can extend derivative protection to her parents. See generally Refugee and Humanitarian Division, 'Protecting the Refugee's Family (The Final Act of the 1951 United Nations Conference of Plenipotentiaries): An Australian Perspective' in DIMIA, *Interpreting the Refugees Convention: An Australian Contribution* (2002) 175, 177–85.

[161] Thronson, 'Choiceless Choices' (2006) *supra* n 16, 1181. See also discussion in *AN (Nwole) v Minister for Justice, Equality and Law Reform* [2007] IESC 44, [36]–[38].

[162] Hathaway (2005) *supra* n 60, 541.

family unit are not mutually exclusive. Rather, the two objectives are inextricably related and can collectively provide a principled basis to afford protection to an *entire* family where the child alone is eligible for refugee status.

International law recognises the family as the 'natural and fundamental group unit of society' entitled to 'protection by society and the State'.[163] Although the drafters of the *Convention* acknowledged the importance of ensuring the unity of the family, and issued a non-binding declaration to that effect, the *Convention* itself contains no right to family unity. In contrast, both international humanitarian law and international human rights law have long committed states to take measures to protect and facilitate family unity.[164] The strongest exposition is now enshrined in art 9 of the *CRC*, which, in near-absolute terms, provides that states '*shall* ensure that a child shall not be separated from his or her parents against their will, except when ... such separation is necessary for the best interests of the child'.[165] In the refugee context, the principle of non-separation codified in art 9 relates to a narrowly defined beneficiary class: parents and children who are already together within the borders of a host state.[166] However, for that beneficiary class the principle affords an unprecedented level of protection, reflecting the fact that '[d]eportation of a person from the country in which he or she has been residing with other family members is a direct attack by the state on family life'.[167] In contrast to earlier human rights accords, which prohibited only arbitrary and unlawful interference with the family unit,[168] the unambiguous limitation in art 9 makes plain that *no* public interest, including immigration control measures, can be invoked to justify the separation of a parent and child.

---

[163] *UDHR*, art 16(3); *ICCPR*, art 23(1); *ICESCR*, art 10; *CRC*, Preamble.

[164] '[I]t is clear in the [*CRC*], or for that matter the [*ICCPR*] or other international instruments, that the parent child relationship is fundamental to the human community, so much so that it is recognized that such a relationship can only be severed by action of law in a state of where the rule of law prevails under very, very particular and limited conditions': *A99–00918 and A99–00919* (IRB, 28 February 2000) 6. As regards international humanitarian law, the *Geneva Convention Relative to the Protection of Civilian Persons in Time of War*, opened for signature 21 April 1949, 75 UNTS 287 (entered into force 21 October 2000) prohibits the separation of families by an occupying power. Goodwin-Gill has noted that '[b]oth the Geneva Conventions and the Additional Protocols repeatedly link the protection of the child to the maintenance of *family life*': G S Goodwin-Gill, 'Unaccompanied Refugee Minors: The Role and Place of International Law in the Pursuit of Durable Solutions' 3 *International Journal of Children's Rights* (1995) 405, 414 (emphasis in original).

[165] *CRC*, art 9(1) (emphasis added).

[166] It is to be contrasted to the principle of family *reunification*, which concerns the situation where a family has been separated and then seeks to be reunited. The latter scenario is addressed in art 10 of the *CRC*, which provides that '[i]n accordance with the obligation of States Parties under article 9, paragraph 1, applications by a child or his or her parents to enter or leave a State Party for the purpose of family reunification shall be dealt with by States Parties in a positive, humane and expeditious manner'. The distinction is neatly outlined in the case of *Casetellanos v Canada (Solicitor General)* [1995] 2 FC 190, 198: 'Family unity only applies when all claiming family members are already on Canadian soil whereas the policy of family reunification does not have this requirement.' See also *De Guzman v Canada (MCI)* [2006] 3 FCR 655, [96]. A consideration of international family reunification is beyond the scope of this book. See generally E F Abram, 'The Child's Right to Family Unity in International Immigration Law' (1995) 17 *Law and Policy* 397, 421–6; Jastram and Newland (2003) *supra* n 147, 576–82; J Pobjoy and J Tobin, 'Article 10' in P Alston and J Tobin (eds), *The UN Convention on the Rights of the Child: A Commentary* (2017) (forthcoming).

[167] *De Guzman v Canada (MCI)* [2006] 3 FCR 655, [96].   [168] See *infra* text accompanying n 185–6.

2.3.1 Recommendation B

The drafting history of the *Convention* suggests that the delegates had assumed that, if the 'head of the family' was considered to be a refugee, immediate family members would benefit from the *Convention* even if they were not themselves able to establish an independent claim.[169] Notwithstanding that view, this position was never the subject of any formal debate, with the result that the *Convention* contains no express provision on the issue of family unity. The delegates did, however, insert a declaration (in the form of Recommendation B) into the *Final Act of the United Nations Conference of Plenipotentiaries on the Status of Refugees and Stateless Persons*, which recommends that governments take 'the necessary measures for the protection of the refugee's family, especially with a view to . . . [e]nsuring that the unity of the refugee's family is maintained particularly in cases where the head of the family has fulfilled the necessary conditions for admission to a particular country'.[170] The declaration was recommended by the Holy See, which took the view that, while the proposition that '[a]ssistance to refugees automatically implied help for their families . . . was an obvious one', it was nonetheless 'wise to include explicit reference to the families'.[171] The initiative was well received, with the US and Italian representatives 'wholeheartedly support[ing]' the recommendation[172] and the UK representative considering it 'both useful and desirable'.[173]

While the drafters of the *Convention* showed foresight in emphasising the responsibility of states to preserve the unity of the family, they made clear that that responsibility was 'naturally not of a contractual nature'.[174] Moreover, although Recommendation B provides a compelling affirmation of the then long-established practice of automatically granting protection to an entire family where the parent is found to be a refugee, it provides a less secure legal basis for the principle of non-separation more generally.[175] In particular, the

---

[169] In comments annexed to an early draft of the *Convention*, the Ad Hoc Committee on Statelessness and Related Problems stated that '[m]embers of the immediate family of a refugee should, in general, be considered as refugees if the head of the family is a refugee as here defined': E/AC.32/5 (1950) *supra* n 56, 40. Although the Ad Hoc Committee acknowledged that family members are to be regarded as refugees 'even if the head of the family is not a refugee', it did not address the application of family unity principles in that scenario. The view of the Committee was referred to with approval by the delegates to the Conference of Plenipotentiaries on the Status of Refugees and Stateless Persons and subsequently 'not[ed] with satisfaction' in a declaration inserted into the *Final Act of the United Nations Conference of Plenipotentiaries on the Status of Refugees and Stateless Persons*, A/CONF.2/108/Rev.1 (1952): *Summary Record of the Thirty-Fourth Meeting*, E/CONF.2/SR.34 (1951) 4–9. The position accorded with the approach taken under earlier accords, including the *IRO Constitution*.

[170] *Final Act of the United Nations Conference of Plenipotentiaries on the Status of Refugees and Stateless Persons*, A/CONF.2/108/Rev.1 (1952).

[171] E/CONF.2/SR.34 (1951) *supra* n 169, 4. [172] *Ibid.*, 6–7. [173] *Ibid.*, 7. [174] *Ibid.*, 4.

[175] Both the drafting history (see *supra* n 169) and the language of the declaration itself ('particularly in cases where') place emphasis on the need to protect the unity of the family *where the head of the family is found to be a refugee*. A similar emphasis is evident in UNHCR, *Handbook*, [181]–[188]. There is a plausible argument that the original draft of Recommendation B would have afforded greater protection for the principle of non-separation more generally. The original draft contained a separate recommendation that states should 'exten[d] the rights granted to the refugee to cover all the members of his family': *Holy See: Draft Recommendations for Inclusion in the Final Act of the Conference*, E/CONF.2/103 (1951). This more inclusive recommendation was subsequently transposed into the opening statements, where it was expressly linked to views of the Ad Hoc Committee, which had focused on the application of family unity principles where the head of the family is found to be a refugee.

declaration does not address the situation where the principal applicant is the child and it is her parents that are seeking derivative protection on family unity grounds.

The comparatively bare bones of Recommendation B have since been supplemented by a myriad of resolutions of the UNHCR ExCom which explicate a more inclusive position on the application of family unity principles.[176] Of particular relevance, the ExCom has:[177]

> Underline[d] the need for the unity of the refugee's family to be protected, *inter alia* by ... provisions and/or practice allowing that when the principal applicant is recognized as a refugee, other members of the family unit should normally also be recognized as refugees, and by providing each family member with the possibility of separately submitting any refugee claims that he or she may have.

The ExCom's systematic affirmation and expansion of Recommendation B provides an authoritative, if non-binding, endorsement for the principle that a state is required to take all possible measures to prevent the separation of the family unit.[178] That endorsement has now been supplemented by art 9 of the *CRC*, which captures the principle of non-separation in unambiguous and largely unqualified terms.[179]

2.3.2 *The Duty of Non-Separation*

Article 9(1) of the *CRC* provides:

> States Parties shall ensure that a child shall not be separated from his or her parents against their will, except when competent authorities subject to judicial review determine, in accordance with applicable law and procedures, that such separation is necessary for the best interests of the child. Such determination may be necessary in

---

[176] UNHCR ExCom, *Refugee Children*, No 47 (XXXVIII) (1987) 127 [(d)] ('*stress*[ing] that all action taken on behalf of refugee children must be guided by the principle of the best interests of the child as well as by the principle of family unity'), [(h)] ('*recommend*[ing] that children who are accompanied by their parents should be treated as refugees if either of the parents is determined to be a refugee'); UNHCR ExCom, *Conclusion on Refugee Children and Adolescents*, No 84 (XLVIII) (1997), [(b)] ('*urg*[ing] States and concerned parties to take all possible measures to protect child and adolescent refugees ... by ... preventing separation of children and adolescent refugees from their families'); UNHCR ExCom, *Conclusion on International Protection*, No 85 (XLIX) (1998), [(v)] ('*recommend*[ing] that Governments take appropriate measures to ensure that the unity of the family is maintained, particularly in cases where the head of the family has been admitted as a refugee to a particular company'), [(x)] ('*encourag*[ing] States, which have not already done so, to consider developing the legal framework to give effect at the national level to a right to family unity for all refugees, taking into account the human rights of the refugees and their families'); UNHCR ExCom, *Conclusion on the Protection of the Refugee's Family*, No 88 (L) (1999) [(b)]; UNHCR ExCom, *Conclusion on Children at Risk*, No 107 (LVIII) (2007), [(b)] ('*recogniz*[ing] that ... [d]ue consideration should be given to the importance of the family and family support structures for the protection of children'), [(h)] ('*recommend*[ing] that States ... [f]acilitate children's enjoyment of family unity through putting in place procedures to prevent separation').

[177] UNHCR ExCom, *Conclusion on the Protection of the Refugee's Family*, No 88 (L) (1999), [(b)].

[178] The UN General Assembly has also endorsed the fundamental importance of family unity in the refugee context, in resolutions under the title *Assistance to Unaccompanied Refugee Minors*: see, e.g., A/RES/58/150 (2004), [4]; A/RES/56/136 (2002), [5]; A/RES/54/145 (2000), [5]; A/RES/52/105 (1998), [4]; A/RES/51/73 (1997), [4].

[179] The UNHCR ExCom has expressly acknowledged the relevance of the *CRC* to the issue of family unity: UNHCR ExCom, *General*, No 81 (XLVII) (1997) Preamble paras 3–4.

a particular case such as one involving abuse or neglect of the child by the parents, or one where the parents are living separately and a decision must be made as to the child's place of residence.

In any proceedings that engage art 9(1), all interested parties, including the child, 'shall be given an opportunity to participate in the proceedings and make their view known'.[180] Where a child is separated from one or more of her parents, states must 'respect the right of the child ... to maintain personal relations and direct contact with both parents on a regular basis, except if it is contrary to the child's best interests'.[181] And where such separation results from any action initiated by the state, such as the 'detention, imprisonment, exile, deportation or death ... of one of the parents', the state shall provide the child (or her family) with 'the essential information concerning the whereabouts of the absent member(s) of the family unless the provision of the information would be detrimental to the well-being of the child'.[182]

The application of art 9 is limited in two significant respects. First, the duty specifically concerns the separation of children and parents, rather than the separation of the family unit more generally. Second, and of particular significance in the asylum context, the provision only relates to parents and children who are already together within a state's jurisdiction. But where a child and parent satisfy these preconditions, art 9(1) affords an unprecedented level of protection. This is achieved primarily by the narrowly circumscribed limitation clause which provides that the *only* scenario in which a child and parent may be involuntarily separated is where 'separation is *necessary for the best interests of the child*'.[183] The 'best interests of the child' is not a primary or paramount consideration, but rather the exclusive basis on which a state can justify the involuntary separation of child and parent.[184] This represents a significant departure from the approach taken in earlier human rights accords, which allow interference with the family unit in a wider, although still tightly circumscribed, range of circumstances. For instance, art 17(1) of the *ICCPR* is limited to the prohibition of 'arbitrary or unlawful interference with ... [the] family'.[185] In this context, the HRC has confirmed that 'the separation of a person from his family ... could be regarded as an arbitrary interference' but only if the 'separation ... and its effects ... were disproportionate to the objectives of the removal'.[186] A child's interests in remaining with

---

[180] *CRC*, art 9(2).   [181] *Ibid.*, art 9(3).   [182] *Ibid.*, art 9(4).   [183] Emphasis added.

[184] *Contra CRC*, art 3, which provides that 'the best interests of the child shall be a primary consideration'. As one commentator notes, '[the] flexible and relativistic formula [in article 3] is transformed by article 9 into a standard that makes the child's best interests the single overriding factor determining whether a child may be separated from parents against their will': Abram (1995) *supra* n 166, 419.

[185] A comparable provision can be found in *CRC*, art 16. See also *ECHR*, art 8, which protects against interference, 'except such as is in accordance with the law and is necessary in a democratic society in the interests of national security, public safety or the economic well-being of the country, for the prevention of disorder or crime, for the protection of health or morals, or for the protection of the rights and freedoms of others'.

[186] HRC, *Views: Communication No 1557/2007*, CCPR/C/102/D/1557/2007 (2011) ('*Nystrom v Australia*') [7.7]. Notwithstanding this qualification, art 17 remains an important protection for children in the immigration context, particularly where the relevant separation does not involve a parent and child (for example, brother/sister) or where a state is not party to the *CRC* (for example, the United States). It is thus significant that the HRC has on a number of occasions demonstrated a willingness to treat the involuntary separation of family members in the immigration context as constituting an arbitrary interference with the family: see HRC, *Views: Communication No 1069/2002*, CCPR/C/79/D/1069/ 2002 (2003) ('*Bakhtiyari v Australia*'); HRC, *Views: Communication No 930/2000*, CCPR/C/72/D/930/ 2000 (2001) ('*Winata v Australia*').

her parent(s) will thus find itself squared off against a state's interest in enforcing its immigration regime. In contrast, the language of art 9(1) makes plain that no countervailing interests, including the enforcement of immigration control measures, can be invoked to justify the separation of a parent and child.[187]

Article 9 has far-reaching, although still largely unexplored, implications for children seeking international protection.[188] It is perhaps unsurprising therefore that attempts have been made by states to limit its application in the immigration context. Specifically, it has been suggested that art 9 was never intended to encumber a state's ability to establish and regulate immigration laws.[189] In support of this proposition, attention has been drawn to a declaration by the Chairman of the Working Group drafting the CRC that:[190]

> It is the understanding of the Working Group that article 6 [now art 9] of the Convention is intended to apply to separations that arise in domestic situations, whereas article 6 *bis* [now art 10] is intended to apply to separations involving different countries and relating to cases of family reunification. Article 6 *bis* is not intended to affect the general right of States to establish and regulate their respective immigration laws in accordance with their international obligations.

This declaration – not legally binding, in any event[191] – simply affirms the point made earlier: that art 9 relates to a narrowly defined beneficiary class, being parents and children *already within* the jurisdiction of a host state.[192] In this sense, it is entirely appropriate to describe art 9 as applying only 'to separations that arise in domestic situations'. Moreover, the drafters' statement regarding the establishment and regulation of immigration laws was explicitly referable to the separate family reunification provision, now contained in art 10 of the CRC.[193]

It has also been suggested that art 9(4) in some way qualifies the art 9(1) obligation. In *ZH (Tanzania) v SSHD*, the UK Supreme Court suggested that art 9 draws a distinction between 'the compulsory separation of a child from her parents, which must be necessary in her best interests' and 'the separation of a parent from his child, for example, by detention, imprisonment, exile, deportation or even death'.[194] The Supreme Court took the view that in the latter scenario the best interests of the child must be a primary, but not the

---

[187] 'No public interest can justify the negation of family unity, only private interest of a child. Under the CRC, a country's economic absorptive capacity or domestic unemployment cannot justify the separation of a child from parents. The principle of progressive implementation of rights subject to available national resources is applied by article 4 of the Convention to "economic, social and cultural rights." The child's right to live with the parents is not economic, social or cultural; it is an individual human right, which may be denied only for the child's best interests': Abram (1995) *supra* n 166, 418.

[188] Although the scope of art 9 in the immigration context has been addressed by a number of commentators, it has received limited attention in domestic courts: see generally Jastram and Newland (2003) *supra* n 147, 575; Bhabha (2003) *supra* n 12, 262–3; Abram (1995) *supra* n 166, 417–21.

[189] For example, the position was advanced by Canada in one of its oral sessions with the UNCRC: *Summary Record of the 216th Meeting*, CRC/C/SR.216 (1995), [55] (Ms Rodney, Canada). See discussion in *Liu v Chief Executive, Department of Labour* [2012] NZHC 2753, [23]–[53].

[190] *Report of the Working Group on a Draft Convention on the Rights of the Child*, E/CN.4/1989/48 (1989), [203].

[191] *Ibid.*, annex.   [192] See *supra* text accompanying n 166.

[193] See, e.g., *Liu v Chief Executive, Department of Labour* [2012] NZHC 2753, [42]–[53].

[194] *ZH (Tanzania) v SSHD* [2011] 2 AC 166, [25] (Baroness Hale). This list derives from art 9(4) (see *supra* text accompanying n 182).

determinative, consideration.[195] This distinction is at odds with the express language of the provision, which makes clear that art 9(4) entails a cumulative obligation, rather than a qualification to art 9(1). The critical language is the opening phrase '[w]here *such* separation', which indicates that separation in the context of art 9(4) is to be understood as subject to the general principle set out in art 9(1). The sole purpose of art 9(4) is to ensure that 'adequate information . . . concerning the whereabouts of the absent parent or child' was provided where the separation has been occasioned by state-initiated actions.[196] The *additional* right was never intended to derogate from the general duty of non-separation codified under art 9(1), and it was certainly not intended to suggest that state-initiated actions were *prima facie* legitimate.[197] Indeed, such an interpretation would lead to the absurd result that art 9(1) would not apply to any separation initiated by a state party,[198] thereby rendering the provision largely nugatory.

What, then, does art 9(1) mean for a child at risk of being separated from her parents, either because the child is found to be a refugee and her parents are not, or a parent is found to be a refugee and the child is not? If separation is not in the best interests of the child, a state will be under a duty to take positive measures to ensure that the child and her parents can remain together, irrespective of the fact that only one member of the family may be eligible for refugee protection. Critically, the protection against *refoulement* and the preservation of the family unit are not mutually exclusive, but cumulative obligations.[199] This means that a state cannot satisfy its duty of non-separation under art 9(1) by determining that a refugee (whether the child or the parent) can return to their country of origin with the remaining family members and thereby preserve the unity of the family. Outside the refugee context, there may be cases where the deportation of one family member will not result in the separation of a parent and child because the other family members can voluntarily follow without a risk of persecutory harm.[200] But this cannot be the case where the parent or child is a refugee. In these circumstances, both the duty of *non-refoulement* and the duty of non-separation must be simultaneously protected within the jurisdiction of the host state or, in limited circumstances, a third country.

---

[195] *ZH (Tanzania) v SSHD* [2011] 2 AC 166, [25]. This finding is *obiter* only, as art 9 was not in fact relevant to the claim before the Supreme Court: it was open to the children to return to Tanzania with their mother without a risk of harm. The Court was therefore correct to apply the art 3 best interests standard, rather than art 9(1). Courts in New Zealand (*Chief Executive, Ministry of Business, Innovation and Employment v Liu* [2014] NZCA 37, [18]–[28]; *Ye v Minister of Immigration* [2008] NZCA 291, [69]; *Zanzoul v Removal Review Authority* [2009] NZHC 687, [143]–[147]; contra *Liu v Chief Executive, Department of Labour* [2012] NZHC 2753; *Huang v Minister of Immigration* [2008] NZCA 377, [29]; *A v Chief Executive, Department of Labour* [2001] NZAR 981, [31]; *Tavita v Minister of Immigration* [1994] 2 NZLR 257), Canada (*Simoes v Canada (MCI)* 2000 FTR LEXIS 948, [15]) and the United States (*Cabrera-Alvarez v Gonzales*, 423 F 3d 1006, 1011 (9th Cir, 2005); contra *Abebe v Ashcroft*, 379 F 3d 755, 764 (9th Cir, 2004) (Judge Ferguson, dissenting)) have interpreted art 9 in a similar way.

[196] S Detrick, *The United Nations Convention on the Rights of the Child: A Guide to the 'Travaux Préparatoires'* (1992) 172.

[197] *Ibid.*

[198] Article 9(4) is engaged wherever 'such separation results from any action initiated by a State Party' and the list of examples is expressly non-exhaustive.

[199] See GC6, [81]–[82].

[200] Article 9 will not be triggered in these cases, although the obligations under arts 12 and 3 will apply: see, e.g., *Baker v Canada (MCI)* [1999] 2 SCR 817; *ZH (Tanzania) v SSHD* [2011] 2 AC 166. See generally Chapter 6.

There are two scenarios where art 9 will be triggered in the refugee status determination context. The first is where a parent is eligible for refugee status but the child is not. For example, in a Canadian case,[201] the IRB determined that a Jamaican mother was eligible for refugee status arising from a risk of domestic violence at the hands of her violent husband, but held that her two young sons were ineligible because there was no evidence that they were at risk of harm. In another Canadian case,[202] the IRB determined that a young Somali mother was eligible for refugee status arising from a risk of rape and other physical abuse; however, her son was ineligible because he was a US citizen and could obtain protection there. In situations such as these a host state will generally afford a derivative form of protection to the child to prevent the separation of the family. This will be done either by automatically conferring protection on a child where a parent or guardian is found to be a refugee, without any individual assessment of the child's status or, alternatively, in states that require an individual assessment of a child's claim irrespective of the status of the child's parent, by way of a separate administrative procedure.[203] Although both procedural mechanisms satisfy the art 9 obligation, the latter approach – separating out the assessment of refugee status from the application of family unity principles – is a conceptually more principled basis for ascertaining protection needs.

The second scenario arises where a child is eligible for protection as a refugee but the parent is not. For example, in *Bueckert v Canada (MCI)*, a seven-year-old child had been physically and sexually abused by his mother; the child's claim was accepted, but his father's claim was rejected on the basis that he had not demonstrated that he will face a risk of serious harm.[204] This scenario has given rise to a range of domestic responses. In Australia, a child has the ability to extend protection to a parent in precisely the same manner that a parent may extend protection to a child.[205] By contrast, in the United States the applicable legislation expressly precludes a child from extending protection to a parent.[206] Similarly, in the United Kingdom, the relevant guidelines provide that '[p]arents of a child applying for

---

[201] *T95–01010, T95–01011 and T95–01012* (IRB, 30 July 1996).

[202] *MA3–08450 and MA3–08451* (IRB, 4 April 2004).

[203] For example, in Canada s 176(1) of the *Immigration and Refugee Protection Regulations*, SOR/2002–227, provides that if an individual is recognised as a refugee, they may 'include in their application to remain in Canada as a permanent resident any of their family members'. The definition of 'family members' includes '(a) the spouse or common-law partner of the person; (b) the dependent child of the person or of the person's spouse or common-law partner; and (c) the dependent child of a dependent child referred to in paragraph (b)': s 1. In New Zealand a child in this scenario may be eligible for a humanitarian protection status under ss 206–7 of the *Immigration Act 2009* (NZ): see, e.g., *BL (Iran)* [2012] NZIPT 500963; *BP (Iran)* [2012] NZIPT 500965; *AD (Czech Republic)* [2012] NZIPT 500876.

[204] For further examples, see *supra* n 149.

[205] DIAC, *Procedures Advice Manual 3 – Policy and Procedural Instructions for Officers Administering Migration Law* (1 January 2015), Protection Visa Procedures Advice Manual pts 34–7. See, e.g., *1209930* [2012] RRTA 802; *0903733* [2009] RRTA 1067; *060741183* [2006] RRTA 185. Statistics provided by the RRT indicate that there are a number of cases where the child has arrived with family members and is listed as the main applicant. Between 1 July 2005 and 31 March 2012 there were 80 applications where the child was the main applicant with derivative dependents (these figures include cases involving unaccompanied children where the child lists a sibling, or her own child, as a dependent family member): Email from T Bridge, Publications Team, RRT, 7 May 2012 (on file with author). See further *supra* n 160.

[206] 8 CFR §207.7(b)(6).

asylum cannot be considered as dependent on their child's claim'.[207] In Canada, the administrative procedure that allows a parent to extend protection to their child does not allow a child to extend protection to her parent.[208] In each of the United States, the United Kingdom, Canada and New Zealand, a parent must look to other, generally discretionary forms of relief in order to remain with her child.[209] Failing that, the family is saddled with the Hobson's choice of separating or returning together to the country of origin notwithstanding the risk of harm to the child.[210] Whatever option is taken,[211] the result will be difficult to reconcile with a state's international legal obligations.

In sum, there is no principled basis under international law for denying children the agency to extend protection to their parents where the child is a refugee. There is no basis for limiting the application of family unity principles and, in particular, the obligation of non-separation in art 9, to the scenario where it is the parent that is the recognised refugee. *Mutatis mutandis*, the same obligations apply to the scenario where the child is the recognised refugee.[212]

---

[207] UKBA, *Asylum Process Guidance*, [3.2]. See also Home Office, *Family reunion: for refugees and those with humanitarian protection* (ver 2.0, 29 July 2016) 18. *Contra* the position adopted in the recast *EU Qualification Directive*, art 2(j), which added the following clause to the incumbent definition of 'family member': 'the father, mother or another adult responsible for the beneficiary of international protection whether by law or by the practice of the Member State concerned, when that beneficiary is a minor and unmarried'.

[208] The definition of 'family member' in the *Immigration and Refugee Protection Regulations*, SOR/ 2002–227 does not include the parents of a recognised refugee: see *supra* n 203.

[209] For instance, in Canada, the parent may apply for permanent resident status on humanitarian and compassionate grounds: *Immigration and Refugee Protection Regulations*, SOR/2002–227, ss 66–9. In New Zealand a parent in this scenario may be eligible for a humanitarian protection status under ss 206–7 of the *Immigration Act 2009* (NZ).

[210] 'Congress has foreseen such difficult choices [and] has opted to leave the choice with the illegal immigrant, not the courts': *Oforji v Ashcroft*, 354 F 3d 609, 618 (7th Cir, 2003). See also *Niang v Gonzales*, 492 F 3d 505, 514, 519–20 (4th Cir, 2007). *Contra Abebe v Ashcroft*, 379 F 3d 755, 764 (9th Cir, 2004) (Judge Ferguson, dissenting), expressly citing art 9 of the *CRC*: 'I do not believe that Congress intended any parent to face that choice. If Congress failed to clarify, in so many words, that a parent may claim asylum on the basis of a threat to her child, that omission is attributable only to a failure to imagine that so many young children would be independently targeted for persecution … Surely, Congress did not intend parents to choose between exposing their children to such threats and abandoning them halfway around the world.'

[211] In fact, a state may not even give the family this choice. In the case of *Olowo v Ashcroft*, 368 F 3d 692 (7th Cir, 2004), a mother sought refugee status on the basis that her US-citizen daughters would be subjected to female genital cutting if returned to Nigeria. The Court of Appeals for the Seventh Circuit rejected the mother's claim but went further, noting that the 'notion that Ms Olowo's daughters will be removed to Nigeria and subjected to this brutal procedure offends our sense of decency, and allowing Ms Olowo to make this decision unilaterally disregards the legal rights of the children' (at 703). The Court continued: 'At oral argument, we asked counsel for the [Department of Homeland Security] if the Department had alerted state authorities that Ms Olowo had expressed the intent to expose her daughters to the threat of FGM. Counsel replied that, to her knowledge, the [Department] had not, but she undertook to relay our concerns to the Department.'

[212] An argument for symmetry finds support in non-discrimination principles. In the Canadian context, this argument was raised by the applicants in the case of *KH v Canada (MCI)*, Court File No IMM 1485. The applicant argued that the definition of 'family member' in s 1(3) of the *Immigration and Refugee Protection Regulations*, SOR/2002–227, which excludes the parents of a refugee (*supra* n 203), amounted to a violation of his equality rights under s 15 of the *Canada Act 1982* (UK) c 11, sch B pt I (*Canadian Charter of Rights and Freedoms*). See G Sadoway, 'Applicants' Further Memorandum of Argument', filed in *KH v Canada (MCI)* (9 January 2008). The state granted humanitarian protection to the parent before the decision was handed down.

Article 9 is blind to the circumstances giving rise to the child–parent separation, with the only relevant consideration being whether the separation is 'necessary for the best interests of the child'. If it is not, the state is under a duty to take positive measures to ensure that the child and her parents can remain together in the country of origin or, in limited circumstances, a third country where no member of the family is at risk of being persecuted. Article 9 thus both reflects and reinforces the international community's long-held recognition that the 'family is the natural and fundamental group unit of society and is entitled to protection by society and State'.[213]

Conclusions

Although it remains the case that states are afforded discretion in the procedural dimension of the international refugee legal regime, the analysis in this chapter has demonstrated that in claims involving children the discretion is limited in several important respects. The removal of a child – whether that child is accompanied or unaccompanied – without a separate consideration of the child's eligibility for refugee status may give rise to a risk of a violation of the *non-refoulement* obligation that lies at the core of the international refugee protection regime, and will almost certainly infringe art 12 of the *CRC*. In circumstances where a child is eligible for refugee status but a parent is not, art 9 of the *CRC* affords a robust and largely unqualified safeguard to protect the unity of the family. The individual recognition of a child's protection claim, coupled with a state's duty to avoid the separation of a parent and child, provides a principled basis to afford protection to an entire family where the child alone is eligible for refugee status.

The effective implementation of the obligations contained in both art 12 and art 9 has the capacity to significantly enhance the visibility of the child in the refugee status determination process. As noted in the Introduction, the visibility of children in the refugee status determination process will not guarantee that a child will enjoy effective protection. Indeed, there is a real risk that shining a spotlight on the claims of refugee children will give rise to a distinct set of procedural and doctrinal challenges. The three chapters that follow test the capacity of the *Convention* definition to respond to the specific needs and circumstances of refugee children.

---

[213] *UDHR*, art 16(3).

3

An Age-Sensitive Assessment of Risk

Introduction

The previous chapter considered the relevance of the *CRC* to the procedural dimension of the international refugee protection regime. It concluded that the obligations enshrined in the *CRC* – in particular, the right to be heard and the duty of non-separation – have the capacity to enhance the visibility of children throughout the refugee status determination process. The book turns now to consider the manner in which the *Convention* definition is interpreted and applied in assessing the refugee status of children. UNHCR has suggested that in cases where a child's claim is assessed independently, the claim is often *incorrectly assessed* because decision-makers fail to interpret the *Convention* in a manner that takes into account the fact that the applicant is a child.[1] This chapter and the two that follow examine the key doctrinal challenges that children face in demonstrating eligibility for refugee status and test the capacity of the *Convention* to respond to those challenges.

The chapter opens with a number of preliminary observations relating to the relationship between the *Convention* definition and the *CRC*, reintroducing the second mode of interaction identified in Chapter 1. Section 3.2 marks the beginning of the book's examination of the constituent elements of the *Convention* definition. The 'well-founded fear' criterion requires an applicant to demonstrate that a risk of cognisable harm is genuine, in the sense that there is a real chance that the risk of being persecuted will materialise if the applicant is sent home. This requirement has given rise to a number of challenges for children, with decision-makers often failing to engage in an age-sensitive assessment of risk. In particular, Section 3.2 focuses on the challenges presented by the bipartite understanding of 'well-founded fear', which requires a child to demonstrate subjective fear in addition to an objective risk of prospective harm. Section 3.3 considers the evidential challenges that children may encounter in demonstrating that they face a forward-looking risk of actual harm if returned to their country of origin.

3.1 The Refugee Definition and the *CRC*

In order to be recognised as a refugee, a child needs to satisfy each element of the refugee definition.[2] A child will thus be a refugee, and entitled to the protections afforded under the

---

[1] UNHCR, 2009 *Guidelines*, [1].

[2] UNHCR, 2009 *Guidelines*, [4] ('Adopting a child-sensitive interpretation of the 1951 Convention does not mean, of course, that child asylum-seekers are automatically entitled to refugee status. The child applicant must establish that s/he has a well-founded fear of being persecuted for reasons of race, religion, nationality, membership of a particular social group or political opinion'). See also UNHCR, *Handbook*, [213] ('The same definition of a refugee applies to all individuals, regardless of their age').

Convention, only if the child is outside her country of origin, and there is a genuine risk of the child 'being persecuted' that is causally connected to one of the five enumerated forms of civil or political status.[3] Refugee status will not be warranted where a child either has or can re-avail herself of protection in her home state,[4] has secured durable protection elsewhere,[5] or has committed a crime that renounces her entitlement to refugee protection.[6]

As discussed in the preceding chapters, the refugee definition has traditionally been interpreted through an 'adult-focused lens',[7] which has, in turn, given rise to a jurisprudence centred on the experiences of adult refugee claimants. It is only in recent years that the arrival of unaccompanied refugee children has compelled decision-makers to shift away from this adult-centred optic and to revisit the *Convention* definition and to consider how it might be interpreted and applied to accommodate the special protection needs of children. A number of commentators have suggested that the *Convention* is simply not up to the task. Goodwin-Gill has for some time called 'for a total re-alignment of protection, away from the formalities of 1951-style refugee status towards a complete welfare approach'.[8] More recently, he has suggested that no 'useful purpose is served by forcing the child asylum seeker through the process of refugee status determination, or by requiring the child ... to show that he or she has a well-founded fear of persecution'.[9] Goodwin-Gill considers that the 'best interests principle' codified in art 3 of the *CRC* provides a more appropriate basis for assessing the protection needs of at-risk children.

But while there is clear value in emphasising the capacity of art 3 of the *CRC* to provide an independent source of protection – an argument developed in Chapter 6 – it is less clear why this requires the dismantling of a regime that has clear protection-inducing value and may in certain circumstances provide a greater level of protection than the *CRC*. To the extent that the *Convention* definition can be interpreted to accommodate the claims of refugee children, what, if any, downside is there in seeking to protect at-risk children by invoking the protection afforded by international refugee law *in addition to* international law on the rights of the child?

This chapter and the two that follow draw on contemporary developments in the interpretation of the *Convention* definition, informed where appropriate by the legal framework of the *CRC*, to test the capacity of the *Convention* to respond to the special protection needs of children. The focus here is on the second mode of interaction identified in Chapter 1: the *CRC* as an interpretative aid. As discussed in detail in Chapter 1, recourse to the *CRC* as a tool to inform the interpretation of the *Convention* definition finds support in guidance provided by UNHCR and UNCRC and is consistent with principles of treaty interpretation. As the discussion in the following chapters will demonstrate, it now also finds support in the fast-evolving, though still nascent, jurisprudence of national courts, particularly in the common law world.

At the outset it is helpful to set out two caveats regarding the interaction between the *Convention* definition and the *CRC*. First, while the provisions of the *CRC* may inform the content of the respective limbs of the *Convention* definition, it cannot displace the

---

[3] *Convention*, art 1A(2).   [4] *Ibid.*, art 1C.   [5] *Ibid.*, art 1C(3).   [6] *Ibid.*, art 1F.

[7] M Crock, *Seeking Asylum Alone: Australia* (2006) 244.

[8] G S Goodwin-Gill, 'Who to Protect, How ..., and the Future?' (1997) 9 *International Journal of Refugee Law* 1, 6.

[9] G S Goodwin-Gill, 'The United Nations Convention on the Rights of the Child and Its Application to Child Refugee Status Determination and Asylum Processes: Introduction' (2012) 26 *Journal of Immigration, Asylum and Nationality Law* 226, 228.

definitional criterion. There is no legal basis, for instance, for the recognition of *refugee status* simply on the basis that such a finding would be in the best interests of the child and therefore compatible with art 3 of the *CRC*.[10] While the best interests principle may call for an inclusive and age-sensitive interpretation of the *Convention* definition, and will almost certainly require that a child not be returned to her country of origin where the child is eligible for refugee status, it does not provide an alternative route to satisfying the *Convention* definition. Second, the role of the *CRC* as an interpretative aid should not be over-emphasised. As the discussion on the bipartite understanding of well-founded fear in Section 3.2 illustrates, in some circumstances an age-sensitive interpretation can be achieved by way of a principled interpretation of the *Convention* definition without recourse to the framework of the *CRC*.

The following three chapters address distinct elements of the *Convention* definition that have proven particularly pertinent to claims involving children. The separate treatment of the constituent elements accords with the prevailing view that 'adjudicators and tribunals give better reasoned and more lucid decisions if they go step-by step rather than follow a recital of the facts and arguments with a single laconic assessment which others'then have to unpick'.[11] The following chapters address the requirement that a child demonstrate a 'well-founded fear' of harm (Chapter 3); the requirement that a child be at risk of 'being persecuted', meaning that the child is at risk of serious harm that cannot or will not be rectified by the applicant's own country (Chapter 4); and the requirement that the risk be causally connected to one of the five enumerated forms of civil or political status (Chapter 5). Each of the three chapters adopts a broadly similar structure, beginning with an overview of current practice and the challenges faced by child applicants followed by an examination of how these challenges might be overcome, drawing on contemporary under-standings of the *Convention* definition and, where appropriate, the broader framework of the *CRC*. Although international law provides the starting point for the discussion, the chapters also draw extensively on domestic case-law in order to provide a contextually grounded understanding of the *Convention* definition.

In three chapters it is not possible to address every aspect of the *Convention* definition, and the case-law review has been used to identify the key doctrinal challenges that children have faced to date in demonstrating eligibility for refugee status. As the above outline suggests, the book focuses primarily on the criteria for *inclusion* set out under art 1A(2), with limited attention given to interpretation of the cessation and exclusion provisions.[12] Although relevant to the inclusion criterion, the book does not separately address the requirement that the individual be outside their country of origin or the issues relating to the availability of an internal protection alternative. This is not to suggest, however, that the *CRC* is not relevant to each of these areas, a point returned to in the final chapter.

3.2 The Well-Founded Fear Requirement

A refugee must have a '*well-founded fear* of being persecuted' if returned to their country of origin. The well-founded fear requirement has traditionally been interpreted as entailing two separate elements: first, demonstration of genuine subjective trepidation; and, second, evidence of an objective, forward-looking risk of being persecuted.

---

[10] See Chapter 6, Section 6.2.   [11] *Svazas v SSHD* [2002] 1 WLR 1891, [30].
[12] *Convention*, arts 1C–1F.

The subjective element has raised a number of issues for children, who, for various reasons, are often unable to conceive or to articulate a future apprehension of harm. The consequence of insisting that a child prove subjective fear is that the child's claim may get rejected even though she is, as a matter of objective evidence, actually at risk of harm. For the most part, this result has been avoided by decision-makers adopting a number of strategies to circumvent the subjective requirement. Unfortunately, these strategies present their own challenges for children. In truth, the practical difficulties that children face in proving subjective apprehension bespeak a broader issue concerning the relevance of subjective fear to the refugee definition. In the discussion that follows it is suggested that an applicant's internal fear has nothing to do with being a refugee, and that the well-founded fear requirement should be interpreted – consistent with both the *Convention*'s plain text and its humanitarian object and purpose – as comprising an entirely objective standard.

3.2.1 The Bipartite Understanding of Well-Founded Fear

The bipartite understanding of well-founded fear – requiring evidence of both objective risk and subjective apprehension – is widely accepted as standard doctrine. The interpretation finds support in jurisprudence of all senior courts in the common law world[13] and has been repeatedly affirmed by UNHCR.[14] It is also universally accepted that the term 'fear' mandates a forward-looking assessment of risk.[15] This prospective examination has caused difficulties for adult applicants seeking to rely exclusively on harms that they suffered as children.[16] For example, in *Katwaru v Canada (MCI)*,[17] a 21-year-old applicant relied on incidents of bullying as a child, including an incident where a schoolyard bully stabbed the applicant in the eye. The Federal Court of Canada held that, although evidence of past persecution may support a well-founded fear of future persecution, '[t]he test for Convention refugee status is prospective not retrospective' and 'it is a finding that there is a well-founded fear of persecution in the future that is critical'.[18] Hence, although evidence that an adult suffered harm as a child may provide critical support for a finding that the applicant faces a well-founded fear of future harm, it alone will generally be insufficient.[19]

---

[13] See, e.g., *INS v Cardoza-Fonseca*, 480 US 421, 431 (1987) ('that the fear must be 'well-founded' does not alter the obvious focus on the individual's subjective beliefs'); *MIAC v SZJGV* (2009) 238 CLR 642, [53] ('the Convention definition of refugee has been held to encompass both subjective and objective elements. The subjective question is whether the applicant ... has a fear of persecution. If that question is answered in the affirmative, the following question, whether that fear is well-founded, is an objective one').

[14] See, e.g., UNHCR, *Handbook*, [38].

[15] See, e.g., *MIMA v Respondents S152/2003* (2004) 222 CLR 1, [74] (McHugh J). See J C Hathaway, *The Law of Refugee Status* (1991) 66–9, for an overview of the historical foundation of the prospective risk requirement.

[16] See UNHCR, 2009 *Guidelines*, [65], which makes clear that the age of the applicant at the time of the decision is relevant given the prospective nature of the well-founded fear inquiry.

[17] *Katwaru v Canada (MCI)* 2010 FC 196.

[18] *Ibid.*, [29], citing *Pour-Shariati v Canada (MEI)* [1995] 1 FC 767, [17].

[19] In the United States, domestic legislation provides for a remedy beyond that contemplated by the *Convention*, allowing for a grant of refugee status to persons who are unable to return home 'because of persecution or a well-founded fear of persecution': 8 USC §1101(a)(42)(A). However, as a matter of practice, a finding of past persecution simply creates an evidential presumption that there is a risk of future persecution, and the government can then rebut that presumption (see 8 CFR §208.13(b)(1)).

While there can be no dispute that the refugee definition entails a forward-looking assessment of actual risk, the requirement that an applicant demonstrate, in addition, a subjective fear has given rise to a number of challenges in cases involving children.

First, a child may lack the ability to understand or appreciate any risk of future harm. The child may, for instance, not be aware of the dangers that she fled because her parents sent her abroad without providing any explanation or reason. In the case of a very young child, the child may lack the cognitive ability to experience fear or at least to connect it to a risk of prospective harm. This is not to suggest that a child is incapable of feeling fear. Indeed, in many cases a child will have a very clear conception of the perils that she will face in her country of origin. As the UNCRC has recognised, '[y]oung children are acutely sensitive to their surroundings and very rapidly acquire understandings of the people, places and routines in their lives' – it is important 'to take account of individual variations in the capacities of children of the same age and of their ways of reacting to situations'.[20] In this regard, Goodwin-Gill and McAdam[21] are appropriately critical of the position taken by UNHCR in its *Handbook*, which suggests that 'a person of 16 or over may be regarded as sufficiently mature to have a well-founded fear of persecution', but that '[m]inors under 16 years of age may normally be assumed not to be sufficiently mature'.[22] This arbitrary line-drawing obscures the fact that even a very young child may be able to experience a subjective fear of harm, just as an older child may not be able to.[23]

Second, in cases where a child is aware of and appreciates the nature of the risk, she may nonetheless have difficulty in articulating her emotional state to a decision-maker.[24] Psychology studies suggest that 'children's memories for trauma have less sensory detail and are less coherent than memories for positive events' and that 'the validity of trauma

Thus, notwithstanding the statutory language, the focus remains on the forward-looking risk. See, e.g., *Ixtlilco-Morales v Keisler*, 507 F 3d 651, 655 (8th Cir, 2007). See also *Re A-T-*, 24 I & N Dec 296 (BIA, 2007), vacated and remanded, 24 I & N Dec 617 (Attorney General, 2008), which suggested that FGC was a one-time act that could not repeated, and thereby rebutted any presumption of future risk (this interpretation has since been discredited: see, e.g., *Mohammed v Gonzales*, 400 F 3d 785 (9th Cir, 2005); *Bah v Mukasey*, 529 F 3d 99 (2nd Cir, 2008)). In certain circumstances US regulations allow for a discretionary grant of asylum arising out of the severity of the past persecution, or the possibility of other serious harm in the applicant's country of origin (unconnected to a Convention ground): 8 CFR §208.13(b)(1)(iii). See, e.g., *Chen*, 20 I & N Dec 16 (BIA, 1989), where a 31-year-old applicant relied on harm he suffered at the hands of the Red Guards as a young child in China during the so-called Cultural Revolution. The BIA considered that the severity of the past persecution warranted a discretionary grant of asylum, notwithstanding that the applicant had 'not established a well-founded fear of present or future persecution': at 21. Similarly, in *S-A-K & H-A-H*, 24 I & N Dec 464 (BIA, 2008) the BIA granted discretionary asylum to a mother and daughter on the basis that they had both undergone the most severe form of female genital cutting. See also *Timnit Daniel* (BIA, 2002). In Canada the *Immigration and Refugee Protection Act*, SC 2001, c 27, s 108(4), provides that past persecution may be sufficient in circumstances where there are 'compelling reasons'. See, e.g., *VA2-03015* (IRB, 6 August 2003).

[20] UNCRC, *GC7*, [14], [17]. See also *CRC*, art 5.

[21] G S Goodwin-Gill and J McAdam, *The Refugee in International Law* (3rd edn, 2007) 130.

[22] UNHCR, *Handbook*, [215].

[23] E Nykanen, 'Protecting Children? The European Convention on Human Rights and Child Asylum Seekers' (2001) 3 *European Journal of Migration and Law* 315, 318. The invocation of 16 years as a developmental sign-post has not been restated in any of the key material on refugee children subsequently published by UNHCR.

[24] J E B Myers et al., 'Psychological Research on Children as Witnesses: Practical Implications for Forensic Interviews and Courtroom Testimony' (1996) 28 *Pacific Law Journal* 3.

experiences should [therefore] not be judged on the basis of vividness or coherence'.[25] The difficulty will be particularly acute where a child is suffering from a psychological condition, such as PTSD.[26]

The implications of these challenges should not be underestimated. Because both objective risk and subjective fear are preconditions to satisfying the well-founded fear standard, a strict application of the bipartite test will warrant – indeed, mandate – the denial of refugee status to children unable to conceive or articulate a subjective fear. The 'absurd result' is that 'children would be routinely rejected as Convention refugees even where the risk to the child has been clearly established'.[27]

3.2.2 Why Require a Child to Establish Subjective Fear?

The reality that children are likely to face obstacles in conceiving and articulating a fear of future harm has not gone unnoticed. UNHCR's 2009 *Guidelines* recognise that a child 'may be too young or immature to be able to evaluate what information is important or to interpret what they have witnessed or experienced in a manner that is easily understandable to an adult' and that '[c]hildren cannot be expected to provide adult-like accounts of their experiences'.[28] Domestic guidelines similarly acknowledge that 'child[ren] may have little or no concept of fear'[29] and 'may be unable . . . to provide evidence about the circumstances surrounding their past experiences or their fear of future persecution'.[30]

In *Yusuf v Canada (MEI)*[31] the Canadian Federal Court of Appeal held that a refugee claim could not be rejected 'solely on the ground that as the claimant is a young child . . . he or she was incapable of experiencing fear, the reasons for which clearly exist in objective terms'.[32] The decision was affirmed in *Canada (MCI) v Patel*, with the Federal Court rebuking the Minister's suggestion that the refugee claim of a 13-year-old orphan should

---

[25] L Berliner et al., 'Children's Memory for Trauma and Positive Experiences' (2003) 16 *Journal of Traumatic Stress* 229, 234.

[26] B A van der Kolk, 'The Complexity of Adaptation to Trauma: Self-Regulation Stimulus Discrimination, and Characterological Development' in B A van der Kolk et al. (eds), *Traumatic Stress: The Effects of Overwhelming Experience on Mind, Body, and Society* (1996) 182, 193. Recent studies suggest that 19–54% of refugee children suffer from PTSD: I Bronstein and P Montgomery, 'Psychological Distress in Refugee Children: A Systematic Review' (2011) 14 *Clinical Child and Family Psychology Review* 44, 48. See further W D'Andrea et al., 'Understanding Interpersonal Trauma in Children: Why We Need a Developmentally Appropriate Trauma Diagnosis' (2012) 82(2) *American Journal of Orthopsychiatry* 187; J Herlihy and S W Turner, 'The Psychology of Seeking Protection' (2009) 21(2) *International Journal of Refugee Law* 171.

[27] *Canada (MCI) v Patel* 2008 FC 747, [33]–[34]. As the Federal Court explained, this will be the case 'even if their older family members had been accepted on the same facts': at [34].

[28] UNHCR, 2009 *Guidelines*, [72]. See also UNHCR, *Handbook*, [213]–[215]; UNHCR, *Note on Refugee Children*, EC/SCP/46 (1987), [15]; UNHCR, *Guidelines on Policies and Procedures in Dealing with Unaccompanied Children Seeking Asylum* (1997), [8.6].

[29] UKBA, *Asylum Process Guidance*, [16.5.1]; Home Office, *Processing Children's Asylum Claims*, 40.

[30] IRB, *Guidelines*, 4–5. As a result, children 'may not be able to express a subjective fear of persecution in the same manner as an adult': at 6. See also IRB, *Interpretation of the Convention Refugee Definition in the Case Law* (31 December 2010), [5.3.1]: 'children or persons suffering from mental disability may be incapable of experiencing fear . . . age or disability may cause a claimant to be incapable of articulating his or her subjective fear in a rational manner'. In the United States, see INS, *Guidelines*, 5, 13, 19.

[31] *Yusuf v Canada (MEI)* [1992] 1 FC 629.   [32] *Ibid.*, 632.

be rejected because the child had provided 'no evidence of subjective fear of persecution'.[33] In *Abay v Ashcroft* the US Court of Appeals stressed the importance of 'keeping in mind [the fact] that very young children may be incapable of expressing fear to the same degree or with the same level of detail as an adult'.[34] Similarly, in *MIMA v Chen Shi Hai* the Full Court of the Federal Court of Australia noted that a three-year-old Chinese national 'would have no knowledge of, or comprehension of *"the one child policy"*' and suggested that 'limit[ing] oneself to the fears of the individual child would ... deny children of tender years the benefits of the [Refugee] Convention'.[35]

Faced with the *Convention*'s purported insistence on evidence of subjective fear, how, then, does one address the reality that, in many instances, a child will be unable to identify or communicate such emotional response? In order to avoid denying protection to children in this scenario, decision-makers have developed a variety of strategies to circumvent a strict application of the bipartite test. The first strategy is to impute fear from the parent to the child. The High Court of Australia is among the senior courts that have held that '[the child applicant's] parents' fears on his behalf are sufficient'.[36] Support for this view can be found in UNHCR's 2009 *Guidelines*, which provide that '[w]hen the parent or caregiver of a child has a well-founded fear of persecution for their child, it may be assumed that the child has such a fear, even if s/he does not express or feel that fear'.[37] Although this is more likely to occur where a child is accompanied by a parent or guardian,[38] courts have also been willing

---

[33] *Canada (MCI) v Patel* 2008 FC 747, [21]. See also at [28], [30] ('The upshot of the [Minister's] submission is that all persons who are incompetent will, by reason of that incompetence, be unable to qualify as Convention refugees. This will include most children and anyone who is incompetent by reason of mental disability (including those whose mental disability was due to trauma caused by persecution) ... In the context of persecution it may be contrary to the child's interests and health to inform the child of the risks the child faces upon return to his home country. It may also be injurious to the child to require the child to anticipate the harms that could be visited upon the child should he/she return to their home country'). See further *Voskova v Canada (MCI)* [2011] FCJ No 1682, [36]; *Uthayakumar v Canada (MCI)* [1999] FCJ No 1013, [23]–[28]. Contra *Jabari v Canada (MCI)* [2008] FCJ No 295, [15]–[18].

[34] *Abay v Ashcroft*, 368 F 3d 634, 640 (6th Cir, 2004). The IJ had denied the claim of the nine-year old Ethiopian applicant at risk of female genital cutting because he considered that she had 'no imminent fear [of female genital cutting], but rather a general ambiguous fear'. See also *Mejilla-Romero v Holder*, 600 F 3d 63, 83 (1st Cir, 2010), where Judge Stahl (in dissent) noted that 'a child experiences traumatic events in ways that are different from an adult, and a child is less likely to understand and to be able to explain the reasons that violence has been inflicted upon him'. The dissent of Judge Stahl was largely vindicated in *Mejilla-Romero v Holder*, 614 F 3d 572 (1st Cir, 2010). See also UNHCR, 'Brief *Amicus Curiae* of the United Nations High Commissioner for Refugees in Support of Petitioner's Petition for Rehearing En Banc', filed in *Mejilla-Romero* (18 June 2010) (copy on file with author) 12–13; and D Anker, N Kelly, J Willshire Carrera and S Ardalan, 'Mejilla-Romero: A New Era for Child Asylum', 12-09 *Immigration Briefings* (September 2012) 1.

[35] *MIMA v Chen Shi Hai* (1999) 92 FCR 333, [27].

[36] *Chen Shi Hai v MIMA* (2000) 201 CLR 293, [4], affirming the view of the Full Court of the Federal Court of Australia in *MIMA v Chen Shi Hai* (1999) 92 FCR 333, [27] ('a [child] could have the necessary subjective fear by virtue of the subjective fear of one or other of his parents') and the Federal Court of Australia in *Chen Shi Hai v MIMA* [1998] FCA 622, 14 ('[a]lthough a well founded fear in a subjective sense is necessary, it can, in the case of a child, in my opinion, be derived from the fear held for the child by his or her parents').

[37] UNHCR, 2009 *Guidelines*, [11].

[38] *Ibid.*, [11] refers to a 'parent or caregiver'. Courts have also been willing to derive the child's fear from a child's guardian or designated representative: see, e.g., *Canada (MCI) v Patel* 2008 FC 747, [32]–[33]; *T95-00479* (IRB, 5 July 1996).

to adduce evidence of the fears of parents remaining in the country of origin,[39] or to assume parental fear by reason of the fact that the child was sent away.[40]

Although in many cases attributing the fears of a parent to the child will lead to positive protection outcomes, there are a number of dangers associated with this approach. In the case of *MIMA v Chen Shi Hai* both the RRT and the Full Court of the Federal Court of Australia rejected the claim of a three-year-old boy, the Court reasoning that 'it must follow as a matter of logic, that if the parents cannot claim refugee status, then their child (*who, in this particular case, is dependent upon their fears for his status*) cannot succeed in a claim for refugee status.'[41] While the reasoning is plainly fraught – conflating the parents' own fear of being persecuted for violating China's one-child policy with the parents' fear that the child will be the subject of ongoing discrimination – the decision demonstrates the possibility that decision-makers may consider it appropriate to reject a child's claim simply because her parents' claims have failed.[42] The decision was over-turned by the High Court of Australia, with Kirby J emphasising that a child 'is not for all purposes subsumed to the identity and legal rights of his parents' and that '[s]eparate and different considerations might arise in a child's case'.[43] Although the High Court made plain that a child can be recognised as a refugee notwithstanding the fact that her parents lack a subjective fear of being persecuted, the Court did not address how a decision-maker should deal with the subjective element of the well-founded inquiry where it cannot be imputed from the parent. In a subsequent decision concerning a 12-month-old child born to Libyan parents, the Full Court of the Federal Court of Australia noted that this question had indeed been left open.[44]

In addition to cases where parents are unable to demonstrate subjective fear, the imputed parental model also presents challenges where a parent is *unwilling* to demonstrate subjective fear. This would arise, for instance, where a child claims refugee status against the wishes of a parent and the parent denies holding any fear for the welfare of the child.[45]

A second strategy has been to dispense with the subjective requirement altogether in cases involving children. UNHCR's 2009 *Guidelines* provide that '[where] a child is unable to express fear when this would be expected or, conversely, exaggerates the fear . . . decision

---

[39] See, e.g., *T98-09801* (IRB, 11 March 1999), where the IRB accepted the evidence of a ten-year-old child's aunt that the applicant's mother, who remained in Sri Lanka, had indicated that she feared that the Liberation Tigers of Tamil Eelam would forcibly recruit her son.

[40] UNHCR, *Handbook*, [218] ('If there is reason to believe that the parents wish their child to be outside the country of origin on grounds of well-founded fear of persecution, the child himself may be presumed to have that fear'); INS, *Guidelines*, 20 ('If the child was sent abroad by his or her parents or family members, the circumstances of that departure are also relevant to the child's asylum application').

[41] *MIMA v Chen Shi Hai* (1999) 92 FCR 333, [28] (emphasis added).

[42] See, e.g., *Voskova v Canada (MCI)* [2011] FCJ No 1682; *TA6-06827* (IRB, 7 February 2007); *Al Raied v MIMA* [2001] FCA 313; *Al Raied v MIMA* [2000] FCA 1357; *C95-00441* (IRB, 17 December 1996).

[43] *Chen Shi Hai v MIMA* (2000) 201 CLR 293, [78].   [44] *Al Raied v MIMA* [2001] FCA 313, [43].

[45] See, e.g., the case of Elián González discussed in Chapter 2, text accompanying n 25–34, and the decision in *VA0-02635* (IRB, 22 March 2001) 10, where a 19-year-old unaccompanied youth testified that his parents' will was in conflict with his own. This difficulty is acknowledged by UNHCR in the *Handbook*, which provides that '[i]f the will of the parents cannot be ascertained or if such will is in doubt or in conflict with the will of the child, then the examiner, in cooperation with the experts assisting him, will have to come to a decision as to the well-foundedness of the minor's fear on the basis of all the known circumstances, which may cause for a liberal application of the benefit of the doubt' (at [219]).

makers must make an objective assessment of the risk that the child would face'.[46] In the United Kingdom, the *Immigration Rules* expressly require that a child's refugee application 'should not be refused only because the child is too young to understand the situation or have formed a well-founded fear of persecution' and that 'more weight should be given to objective indications of risk than to the child's state of mind and understanding of his situation'.[47]

While less objectionable than the attribution of parental fear, there is little guidance on how and when this approach should be adopted. For example, how are decision-makers to ascertain whether a child has the ability to understand or express a subjective fear? UNHCR has provisionally suggested that children under the age of 16 'may normally be assumed' not to be mature enough to establish subjective fear;[48] however, as noted above, calendar age will often be an inaccurate indicator of a child's ability to experience or communicate fearfulness.[49] Conversely, the *Handbook*'s suggestion that the decision-maker also take into account the child's 'personal, family and cultural background'[50] introduces an extraordinary degree of subjectivity into the decision-making process, which may lead to unwarranted denials of protection. As Hathaway and Hicks note, 'the absence of any principled method of determining which minors should be exempted ... injects a degree of arbitrariness into the refugee status determination that is unacceptable given the extraordinary cost of error'.[51]

Although there are pragmatic justifications for eliminating the subjective fear requirement in cases involving children, it is unclear how, as a matter of principle, this can be reconciled with the bipartite approach. If proof of subjective trepidation truly is an essential element of the well-founded fear standard, how can it so easily be dispensed with? One answer is to view the practical difficulties that children face in satisfying the subjective fear requirement as a symptom of a broader diagnosis highlighting the frailties of the bipartite understanding of well-founded fear. The conceptual and practical shortcomings of the compound standard have been identified by a number of scholars who have suggested that the well-founded fear standard should be understood as exclusively objective.[52] In 1966

---

[46] UNHCR, 2009 *Guidelines*, [11]. See also UNHCR, *Handbook*, [217] ('[w]here the minor has not reached a sufficient degree of maturity to make it possible to establish well-founded fear in the same way as for an adult, it may be necessary to have greater regard to certain objective factors'). The UNCRC has similarly recognised that a child may have a well-founded fear of being persecuted 'even if unable to explicitly articulate a concrete fear': UNCRC, *GC6*, [66]. In the context of large-scale refugee movements, the UNCRC suggests that 'all unaccompanied or separated children are entitled to be granted the same status as other members of the particular group': at [73].

[47] United Kingdom, *Immigration Rules*, para 351. See also *R (Osmani) v Immigration Adjudicator* [2001] EWHC 1087 (Admin), [4].

[48] UNHCR, *Handbook*, [215].   [49] See *supra* text accompanying n 20–3.

[50] UNHCR, *Handbook*, [216].

[51] Hathaway, *The Law of Refugee Status* (1991) *supra* n 15, 65–75; J C Hathaway and W S Hicks, 'Is There a Subjective Element in the Refugee Convention's Requirement of "Well-Founded Fear"?' (2004) 26 *Michigan Journal of International Law* 505.

[52] See, e.g., Michigan Guidelines on the International Protection of Refugees, 'The Michigan Guidelines on Well-Founded Fear' (2004), [3]; A Grahl-Madsen, *The Status of Refugees in International Law* (1966) vol 1, 173–4; Hathaway and Hicks (2004) *supra* n 51; M Bossin and L Demiradache, 'A Canadian Perspective on the Subjective Component of the Bipartite Test for "Persecution": Time for Re-Evaluation' (2004) 22 (1) *Refuge* 108; G Noll, 'Evidentiary Assessment under the Refugee Convention: Risk, Pain and the Intersubjectivity of Fear' in G Noll (ed), *Proof, Evidentiary Assessment and Credibility in Asylum Procedures* (2005) 141; B Carr, 'We Don't Need to See Them Cry: Eliminating the Subjective

Grahl-Madsen opined that '[t]he frame of mind of the individual hardly matters at all'[53] and that an individual will be a refugee 'irrespective of whether he jitters at the very thought of his return to his home country, is prepared to brave all hazards, or is simply apathetic or even unconscious of the possible dangers'.[54] According to Grahl-Madsen, '[j]ust as the nervous, the brave, and the foolhardy should be subject to the same gauge, "well-founded fear" may exist, irrespective of whether the individual in question is a babe-in-arms, a lunatic, ignorant or well-informed, naïve or cunning'.[55]

More recently, Hathaway and Hicks have advanced a compelling argument that the subjective fear requirement is 'unjustified as a matter of principle and almost impossible practically to implement in a fair and consistent manner'.[56] In particular, the authors are concerned that the absence of any principled way to evaluate an applicant's subjective state of mind has necessitated reliance on 'largely artificial, surrogate indicators of trepidation'.[57] For example, decision-makers often draw inferences from pre-application conduct[58] and routinely equate lack of credibility with an absence of subjective fear.[59] These mechanisms are artificial and often unreliable, and may result in the unwarranted denial of refugee status to persons who face an actual risk of being persecuted.[60] Hathaway and Hicks suggest that the willingness of decision-makers to dispense with the subjective inquiry in a number of common scenarios – including in cases involving children – raises the question of whether subjective fear can truly be understood as an essential element of the well-founded fear standard.[61] The authors conclude that '[w]hether a person is, or is not, subjectively fearful of return to actual risk should be recognized as legally immaterial'[62] and propose that it is time to 'move beyond routinized deference to tradition in order to ... [allow] the Refugee Convention to serve its core purpose of protecting at-risk persons from being persecuted'.[63]

An exclusively objective understanding of well-founded fear is consistent with both the plain language of art 1A(2) – in addition to an emotional response, 'fear' can also refer to a prospective expectation of risk[64] – and with the humanitarian object and purpose of the *Convention*. It accords with the long-held view that '[t]he Convention aims at the protection of those whose human dignity is imperilled',[65] while respecting the fact that human rights

---

Apprehension Element of the Well-Founded Fear Analysis for Child Refugee Applicants' (2006) 33 *Pepperdine Law Review* 535; A Zimmerman (ed), *The 1951 Convention Relating to the Status of Refugees and Its 1967 Protocol: A Commentary* (2011) 338–40.

[53] Grahl-Madsen (1966) *supra* n 52, 174.   [54] *Ibid.*   [55] *Ibid.*

[56] Hathaway and Hicks (2004) *supra* n 51, 509. See also Hathaway, *The Law of Refugee Status* (1991) *supra* n 15, 70–5; J C Hathaway and M Foster, *The Law of Refugee Status* (2nd ed, 2014) 93–108.

[57] Hathaway and Hicks (2004) *supra* n 51, 509.

[58] *Ibid.*, 525–31. For example, in the case of *Taj v Canada (MCI)* [2004] FCJ No 880, the Federal Court drew inferences from the fact that the applicant had delayed leaving Pakistan (at the age of 13) and had delayed applying for protection in the United States (between the ages of 13 and 16). But see *Basak v Canada (MCI)* [2005] FCJ No 1839, [12] ('it was ... patently unreasonable for the [IRB] to conclude that a delay on the part of others in advancing [the applicant's] refugee claim was indicative of a lack of subjective fear of persecution on her part'); *Ruiz v Canada (MCI)* 2012 FC 258, [52]–[61]. Decision-makers have also drawn inferences from the action (or inaction) of an adult applicant when they were children. For example, in *Lorne v Canada (MCI)* 2006 FC 384, the IJ had held that an applicant had no subjective fear of harm by reason of the fact that she had not reported that her uncle raped her, once or twice a week, between the ages of 12 and 18. That decision was appropriately vacated by the Federal Court.

[59] Hathaway and Hicks (2004) *supra* n 51, 531–4. See, e.g., *ZJ (Afghanistan) v SSHD* [2008] EWCA Civ 799, [8].

[60] Hathaway and Hicks (2004) *supra* n 51, 514, 534.   [61] *Ibid.*, 524.   [62] *Ibid.*, 562.   [63] *Ibid.*, 562.

[64] *Ibid.*, 535.   [65] *Win v MIMA* [2001] FCA 132, [20].

standards are common to all 'and do not vary as a function of particularised perceptions or conditions'.[66] The point has not been lost on courts, which have recognised that the *Convention* 'is not designed to exclude brave or simply stupid persons in favour of those who are more timid or intelligent'[67] but rather to provide surrogate protection to 'the timorous as well as the bold, the inarticulate as well as the outspoken . . . the ordinary person as well as the extraordinary one'.[68]

The application of the well-founded fear standard to children provides a clear illustration of the normative and practical challenges of the traditional bipartite test. Although decision-makers have attempted to compensate for these challenges by sidestepping the subjective inquiry in certain circumstances, these strategies have given rise to a host of new problems. As a matter of principle, it is difficult to explain courts' routine dispensation with what is otherwise regarded an essential element of the *Convention* definition. In these circumstances it is hardly surprising that there is increasing support for the view that the well-founded fear standard 'requires only evidence of a forward-looking expectation of actual risk'.[69] This interpretation – consistent with the plain language of the *Convention* and with the *Convention*'s underlying humanitarian goals – provides a principled guarantee to ensure that a child – or, indeed, any applicant – is not refused protection simply because she is unable to conceive or articulate a fear of harm that plainly exists as a matter of objective evidence.

3.3 Assessing the Objective Risk

Irrespective of the child's emotional state, it will always be necessary for the child applicant to demonstrate a forward-looking risk of actual harm. While courts have framed the relevant objective standard in various ways – insisting that there be a 'reasonable possibility',[70] a 'reasonable degree of likelihood'[71] or a 'real chance'[72] that the risk will accrue, while requiring that the risk not be one that is 'remote',[73] 'insubstantial'[74] or a 'far-fetched possibility'[75] – the upshot of each of these tests is essentially the same. Refugee status is to be recognised only where there is credible evidence – though it need not rise to the level of probability – that the harm said to be persecutory may well occur. In assessing the forward-looking risk of harm it is necessary to have regard to the applicant's age, in addition to other identity-based characteristics of the child, which may enhance the likelihood of harm.[76] A child with a disability is, for instance, more likely to be denied medical treatment or to be the subject of widespread societal discrimination. Similarly, a young girl who is

---

[66] Hathaway, *The Law of Refugee Status* (1991) *supra* n 15, 70.

[67] *Yusuf v Canada (MEI)* [1992] 1 FC 629, 632.

[68] *Win v MIMA* [2001] FCA 132, [20]. See also the position in New Zealand, where the courts have repeatedly affirmed that the well-founded fear standard is exclusively objective. See, e.g., *Refugee Appeal No 72668* (RSAA, 5 April 2002), [133]; *Refugee Appeal No 77074* (RSAA, 17 September 1996), [25]–[42].

[69] Hathaway and Hicks (2004) *supra* n 51, 561.   [70] *INS v Cardoza-Fonseca*, 480 US 421, 440 (1987).

[71] *R v SSHD; ex parte Sivakumaran* [1988] AC 958, 994 (Lord Keith), 1000 (Lord Goff).

[72] *Chan Yee Kin v MIEA* (1989) 169 CLR 379, 388 (Mason CJ).   [73] *Ibid.*, 389 (Mason CJ).

[74] *Ibid.*, 398 (Dawson J).   [75] *Ibid.*, 429 (McHugh J).

[76] 'Alongside age, other identity-based, economic and social characteristics of the child, such as family background, class, caste, health, education and income level, may increase the risk of harm, influence the type of persecutory conduct inflicted on the child and exacerbate the effect of the harm on the child': UNHCR, 2009 *Guidelines*, [12].

homeless and living on the street is more likely to be at risk of sexual exploitation or trafficking.[77]

A comprehensive review of the evidential challenges that children may encounter in demonstrating a prospective risk of harm (or indeed, any of the other elements of the *Convention* definition) is beyond the scope of this book. The following discussion addresses four evidential issues that have proven particularly salient in cases involving children.

3.3.1 A Shared Duty of Fact-Finding

It is a fundamental principle that in claims for refugee protection 'the duty to ascertain and evaluate all the relevant facts is *shared* between the applicant and the examiner'.[78] Thus, 'while the burden of proof in principle rests on the applicant', 'it may be for the examiner to use all the means at his disposal to produce the necessary evidence in support of the application'.[79] This flexibility accounts for the 'vulnerability of the individual in this context'[80] and the 'difficulty of proof inherent in the special situation in which an applicant for refugee status finds himself'.[81] In the case of children these difficulties will often be amplified. In recognition of this, UNHCR's 2009 *Guidelines* provide that, '[a]lthough the burden of proof usually is shared between the examiner and the applicant in adult claims, it may be necessary for an examiner to assume a greater burden of proof in children's claims, especially if the child concerned is unaccompanied'.[82]

A decision-maker is thus required to take an active role in ascertaining and evaluating the relevant objective facts in order to properly assess whether a child is genuinely at risk of future harm. The responsibility is cogently set out in domestic guidance issued in the United Kingdom, which provides that '[t]here needs to be an awareness of the increased burden on case owners to ascertain and evaluate the facts of a child's asylum claim, including the need to be proactive in obtaining relevant objective information and evidence relevant to the children's claim'.[83] In addition to facilitating a child's effective participation in the determination process, this shared responsibility of fact-finding also flows directly from the principle of *non-refoulement*, which requires that the fact-finding process be conducted in

---

[77] For further examples, see *ibid.*   [78] UNHCR, *Handbook*, [196] (emphasis added).

[79] *Ibid.* This will include, but will not necessarily be limited to, the decision-maker 'being familiar with the objective situation in the country of origin concerned, being aware of relevant matters of common knowledge, guiding the applicant in providing the relevant information and adequately verifying facts alleged which can be substantiated': UNHCR, 'Note on Burden and Standard of Proof in Refugee Claims' (16 December 1998), [6]. In Sweden the shared responsibility of fact-finding has been codified in domestic legislation: see A Lundberg, 'The Best Interests of the Child Principle in Swedish Asylum Cases: The Marginalization of Children's Rights' (2011) 3(1) *Journal of Human Rights Practice* 49, 55.

[80] UNHCR, 'Background Note on the Application of the Exclusion Clauses: Article 1F of the 1951 Convention Relating to the Status of Refugees' (4 September 2003), [105].

[81] UNHCR, *Handbook*, [197]. As the United States Court of Appeals has recognised, '[a]sylum cases differ from ordinary civil cases in that the events happened in foreign countries, and the expense and difficulty of obtaining corroboration can be overwhelming': *Singh v Holder*, 638 F 3d 1264, 1270 (9th Cir, 2011).

[82] UNHCR, 2009 *Guidelines*, [73].

[83] UKBA, *Asylum Process Guidance*, [16.4]; Home Office, *Processing Children's Asylum Claims*, 34. See also USCIS Asylum Division, 'Asylum Officer Basic Training Course: Guidelines for Children's Asylum Claims' (21 March 2009) 35: 'While the onus is on the child, through his or her advocate or support person, to produce relevant supporting material, asylum officers should also supplement the record as necessary to ensure a full analysis of the claim.' See also INS, *Guidelines*, 26–7.

a way that allows for the effective identification of individuals in need of international protection.

Significantly, the shared responsibility extends beyond the collation of relevant objective evidence. As the Federal Court of Canada has noted, a decision-maker must be 'alert and alive to the specific interests of the child'.[84] This may require evaluating a claim not formally articulated by the child, for example because the child has failed to identify the nature of the harm that is likely to accrue or failed to identify the *Convention* ground giving rise to the risk of harm.[85] As the Supreme Court of Canada has noted, the ultimate question for the decision-maker is 'whether the Convention definition is met',[86] and the decision-maker is required to deal with any evidence that may be relevant to that question.

As a matter of practice the shared duty of fact-finding is not always respected. For example, in *Ganji v Canada (MCI)* it became apparent during the hearing that the children of the adult applicant may have a distinct claim to refugee status based on interference with their right to education. The Federal Court refused to deal with the evidence on the basis that it considered it inappropriate to place an onus on a decision-maker to 'recognize and examine claims that have not been asserted where evidence comes before it that might support a claim'.[87] Equally troubling is *Yaabe v Canada (MCI)*,[88] where the Federal Court refused to examine the risk that a nine-year-old boy would face by reason of his physical disability on the basis that the refugee claim was based on clan affiliation, rather than physical handicap.[89] These decisions are difficult to reconcile with both the pragmatic and the principled justifications underpinning the shared duty of fact-finding.

3.3.2 Country of Origin Information

The appropriate starting point for the assessment of prospective risk will generally be an examination of independent and credible information detailing the human rights conditions in the applicant's country of origin.[90] The assessment of country of origin information will often be particularly important in cases involving children, as the child 'may have limited knowledge of conditions in the country of origin or may be unable to explain the reasons for their persecution'.[91] In these circumstances, and in recognition of the shared responsibility of fact-finding, it has been suggested that decision-makers make 'special

---

[84] *Zakar v Canada (MCI)* 2005 FC 1016, [17].

[85] See, e.g., *Ganji v Canada (MCI)* (1997) 135 FTR 283; UKBA, *Asylum Process Guidance*, [16.5]; Home Office, *Processing Children's Asylum Claims*, 34, 38.

[86] *Canada (Attorney General) v Ward* [1993] 2 SCR 689, 693. Here the Supreme Court considered a *Convention* ground (political opinion) even though it had not been initially raised by the applicant, opining that the 'claimant is not required to identify the reasons for persecution'.

[87] *Ganji v Canada (MCI)* (1997) 135 FTR 283, [23]. The applicant relied on the Supreme Court of Canada's decision in *Canada (Attorney General) v Ward* [1993] 2 SCR 689. The Federal Court rejected this analogy, drawing an unprincipled distinction between a decision-maker being required to evaluate all relevant Convention grounds and being required to evaluate all relevant persecutory harm.

[88] *Yaabe v Canada (MCI)* [1997] FCJ No 1633.　　[89] *Ibid.*, [6]–[7].

[90] Hathaway, *The Law of Refugee Status* (1991) *supra* n 15, 80–3. See also Goodwin-Gill and McAdam (2007) *supra* n 21, 545–7.

[91] UNHCR, 2009 *Guidelines*, [74]. UKBA, *Asylum Process Guidance*, [16.5.2] similarly acknowledges that '[a] child may be less able to produce objective evidence to corroborate their claim, and may in fact have very limited life experience'. See also Home Office, *Processing Children's Asylum Claims*, 41.

efforts' to obtain up-to-date country of origin information relevant to the child's claim.[92] States have developed a number of tools to assist decision-makers in the fact-finding process, including the preparation and dissemination of country reports on human rights practices and the establishment of country guidance services.

One of the concerns that has arisen regarding the use of country of origin information in cases involving children is that the information may not sufficiently identify the distinct risks faced by children. As the 2009 *Guidelines* note, '[j]ust as country of origin information may be gender-biased to the extent that it is more likely to reflect male as opposed to female experiences, the experiences of children may also be ignored'.[93] To provide an example, in 2008 the UK Home Office commissioned a study to consider the coverage of issues relating to children in its country of information reports.[94] The final report suggested that the risks faced by children were strongly presented in some reports and weakly presented in others.[95] The Afghanistan report was cited as a good practice example, on the basis that it gave prominence to the *CRC* and provided child-specific information relating to education, child care, health, child labour, child kidnapping, child marriage and child soldiers.[96] In contrast, the Sudan report dedicated less than 3 per cent of the report (comprising approximately 850 words) to issues concerning children and contained no reference to the *CRC*.[97] The study recommended that the Home Office adopt a reporting structure modelled on the *CRC*, on the basis that it provided 'the basic internationally agreed humanitarian rights based framework within which children's lives and circumstances are understood'.[98] The Home Office accepted the recommendation, acknowledging that '[t]he UNCRC [provides] a good starting point in developing a more comprehensive template' and proposing to use the *CRC* 'as the foundation on which [it] will build a new framework'.[99]

There are several pragmatic advantages to using the *CRC* as a point of departure when preparing or acquiring country of origin information. First, it aligns neatly with the proposition, advanced in Chapter 4, that a decision-maker should be guided by the rights contained in the *CRC* when assessing whether the prospective harms faced by a child are sufficiently serious to satisfy the 'serious harm' limb of the 'being persecuted' inquiry. Second, there is a wealth of independent and credible information specifically addressing state compliance with the *CRC*, prepared by the UNCRC, the UN Special Representative of the Secretary-General for Children and Armed Conflict and UNICEF. These sources provide a sound and appropriately tailored basis for assessing the status of children's rights in an applicant's country of origin.[100]

---

[92] UNHCR, 2009 *Guidelines*, [74].   [93] *Ibid.*

[94] R K S Kohli and F Mitchell, 'An Analysis of the Coverage of Issues Related to Children in COI Reports Produced by the Home Office' (Paper prepared for the Advisory Panel on Country Information, April 2008). See also R K S Kohli, F Mitchell, and H Connolly, 'An Analysis of the Coverage of Issues Related to *Children* in Country of Origin Reports Produced by the Home Office' (Paper prepared for the Independent Advisory Group on Country Information, October 2012).

[95] Kohli and Mitchell (2008) *supra* n 94, 1.   [96] *Ibid.*, 18–24.   [97] *Ibid.*, 106–12.   [98] *Ibid.*, 4.

[99] *Ibid.*, 15. This is now reflected in UK national guidelines: UKBA, *Asylum Process Guidance*, [16.1].

[100] This was a key recommendation in the aforementioned study, and was accepted by the Home Office: Kohli and Mitchell (2008) *supra* n 94, 9. For a good illustration of the use of child-specific country of origin information see, e.g., *AK (Brazil)* [2016] NZIPT 800834-35, [63]–[84]; *Refugee Appeal Nos 76305, 76306, 76307 and 76308* (RSAA, 30 June 2010), [132]–[140]; *Refugee Appeal Nos 75940, 75941, 75942 and 75943* (RSAA, 15 October 2007), [87]–[88]; *AA (unattended children) Afghanistan CG* [2012] UKUT 00016.

3.3.3 Similarly Situated Persons

In cases involving children, and particularly unaccompanied children, it is common for decision-makers to look at the situation of any family members remaining in the applicant's country of origin to assess whether there is an objective risk of future harm to the child. This common practice finds support in the UNHCR *Handbook*[101] and has been affirmed in guidance issued in a number of domestic jurisdictions.[102] But while it is well established that evidence of risk to similarly situated persons is an appropriate reference point for decision-makers,[103] some care needs to be taken in cases involving children to ensure that the comparator is an appropriate one. As the High Court of Australia has emphasised, 'the critical question is how similar are the cases that are being compared'.[104] There is little utility in considering the situation of a parent remaining in the country of origin if the applicant's claim is based on a child-specific form of harm or a *Convention* ground only applicable to the child.[105] Similarly, an assessment of the risk faced by a parent will not take into account the particular susceptibilities of a child. As the UK IAT has observed, 'the same matrix of facts for an adult claimant do not necessarily lead to the same conclusions as they would for a minor'.[106] Thus, while in many cases the experience of remaining family members will provide a reliable gauge of risk,[107] this will only be the case when those family members can truly be described as comparably situated to the child applicant.[108]

3.3.4 A Liberal Benefit of the Doubt

The assessment of credibility is a central issue in a significant proportion of decisions involving child applicants. Although particularly salient to the well-founded fear inquiry, the issue of credibility permeates the entire refugee status determination process. In this regard, decision-makers have denied refugee status to children not only on the basis of adverse credibility findings as to the existence of an objective risk of harm, but also on the basis of adverse credibility findings as to the child's country of origin[109] or a child's religion,

---

[101] UNHCR, *Handbook*, [218] ('The circumstances of the parents and other family members, including their situation in the minor's country of origin, will have to be taken into account').

[102] See, e.g., INS, *Guidelines*, 20.   [103] See, e.g., *Voskova v Canada* (MCI) [2011] FCJ No 1682, [26]–[34].

[104] *Appellant S395/2002 v MIMA* (2003) 216 CLR 473, [75].

[105] For example, in *Lusingo v Gonzales*, 420 F 3d 193 (3rd Cir, 2005), the BIA attached weight to the fact that the Tanzanian government had not retaliated against the family of a 16-year-old boy who absconded while attending an International Boy Scout Jamboree in the United States. The Court of Appeals was 'at a loss to understand the significance the [BIA] attached to [that] fact', as there was nothing to suggest that the Tanzanian government suspected that the parents were complicit in their child's unauthorised stay in the United States. In these circumstances it was inappropriate to suggest that 'the government's failure to retaliate against Lusingo's parents should undermine the objective reasonableness of Lusingo's fear of retaliation': at 200.

[106] *Jakitay v SSHD* (IAT, Appeal No 12658, 15 November 1995) 5.

[107] See, e.g., *Firempong v INS*, 766 F 2d 621, 626 (1st Cir, 1985).

[108] 'The Board erred by limiting the comparison of the Applicant to only one other similarly situated person, that is, his father. The fault was not in looking for a comparator . . . but in defining the comparator group too narrowly': *Pacificador v Canada (MCI)* [2003] FCJ No 1864, [76]. Similarly, in *Voskova v Canada (MCI)* [2011] FCJ No 1682, [37], the Court held that the primary decision-maker had 'limit[ed] the . . . comparator group too narrowly' by focusing on the situation of the applicant children's mother.

[109] For instance, in Australia interviews with children have been recorded and sent to a language laboratory in Sweden to assess the applicant's country of origin. This evidence – which has been criticised on

political opinion or membership in a particular social group.[110] In recent years the 'culture of disbelief'[111] has proven particularly pernicious in the context of age assessments; that is, the assessment of whether a child is in fact a child.[112] A comprehensive review of the challenges inherent in assessing the credibility of a child is beyond the scope of this chapter.[113] Rather, the focus here is on a specific safeguard developed at both the international and domestic levels to guard against unwarranted denials of refugee status based on credibility findings: the principle that a child be afforded a liberal benefit of the doubt throughout the refugee status determination process.

The 'benefit of the doubt' principle was first endorsed by UNHCR in its *Handbook*, which advises that, 'if the applicant's account appears credible, he should, unless there are good reasons to the contrary, be given the benefit of the doubt'.[114] The principle,[115] which applies

---

methodological grounds – has been accepted to impugn the credibility of a child: see, e.g., *Odhiambo v MIMA* (2002) 122 FCR 29; *WAEF v MIMIA* [2002] FCA 1121. See generally M Crock, 'Lonely Refuge: Judicial Responses to Separated Children Seeking Refugee Protection in Australia' (2005) 22(2) *Law in Context* 120.

[110] See, e.g., *Qiu v Canada (MCI)* [2009] FCJ 790 (IRB found that an eight-year-old boy was not a genuine practising Christian; overturned by the Federal Court). Adverse credibility findings can be particularly problematic in claims involving sexual orientation. For example, in *Kimumwe v Gonzales*, 431 F 3d 319, 322–3 (8th Cir, 2005), the Court of Appeals accepted the decision of the IJ that the applicant did not establish that he was gay because he had 'presented no objective evidence to confirm his homosexuality': at 321. This was notwithstanding the fact that the applicant had produced proof of his expulsion from school at the age of 12 for having sex with another boy and evidence that he was arrested and detained for two months at the age of 16 for having sex with another male student while at college. The point was taken up by Judge Heaney in a strong dissent (at 323–4): 'I take issue with the IJ's statement that Kimumwe presented no objective evidence to confirm his homosexuality. It is unclear what type of evidence would satisfy the IJ. Kimumwe testified he was openly gay. He stated that he realized he was gay when he was seven years old. He presented a letter from a Kenyan orphanage administrator ... indicating that Kimumwe was gay. After carefully perusing the record, I have found no evidence whatsoever that would contradict Kimumwe's claimed sexual orientation and accept that he is openly gay.' See generally S Hazeldean, 'Confounding Identities: The Paradox of LGBT Children under Asylum Law' (2011) 45 *UC Davis Law Review* 373, 383–4, 411–13.

[111] J Bhabha and M Crock, *Seeking Asylum Alone: A Comparative Study* (2007) 204.

[112] See UNHCR, 2009 *Guidelines*, [75]–[76]. For a discussion on the debate surrounding age assessments, with a focus on the practices in the United Kingdom, see S Shin Luh, 'Best Practice in Age Dispute Challenges' in ILPA, *Working with Refugee Children: Current Issues in Best Practice* (2012) 65; H Crawley, ILPA, *When Is a Child Not a Child? Asylum, Age Disputes and the Process of Age Assessment* (2007).

[113] For an excellent overview, see UNHCR, *The Heart of the Matter: Assessing Credibility when Children Apply for Asylum in the European Union* (2014). See also Noll (2005) *supra* n 52, 141; M Kagan, 'Refugee Credibility Assessment and the "Religious Imposter" Problem: A Case Study of Eritrean Pentecostal Claims in Egypt' (2010) 43(5) *Vanderbilt Journal of Transnational Law* 1179; J A Sweeney, 'Credibility, Proof and Refugee Law' (2009) 21(4) *International Journal of Refugee Law* 700; M Kagan, 'Is Truth in the Eye of the Beholder? Objective Credibility Assessment in Refugee Status Determination' (2003) 17 *Georgetown Immigration Law Journal* 367; J Cohen, 'Questions of Credibility: Omissions, Discrepancies and Errors of Recall in the Testimony of Asylum Seekers' (2001) 13(3) *International Journal of Refugee Law* 293.

[114] UNHCR, *Handbook*, [204]. The *Handbook* acknowledges that it is 'hardly possible for a refugee to "prove" every part of his case' and that if this were a requirement 'the majority of refugees would not be recognized': at [203].

[115] It is appropriate to refer to the benefit of the doubt as a principle or notion, rather than a rule of law: see *KS (benefit of the doubt)* [2014] UKUT 00552, [61]–[62].

to all applicants (not just children), is elaborated on in UNHCR's *Note on Proof*.[116] The general principle is reinforced in the context of child applicants, with the *Handbook* suggesting that the assessment of a child's refugee status 'may call for a *liberal* application of the benefit of the doubt'.[117] Although the UNHCR *Handbook* suggests that the 'benefit of the doubt should ... only be given ... when the examiner is satisfied as to the applicant's general credibility',[118] both UNHCR and the UNCRC have made clear that the principle also has a role to play in assessing the child's credibility.[119] UNHCR's 2009 *Guidelines* advise that 'child[ren] should be given the benefit of the doubt should there be some concern regarding the credibility of part of his/her claim'.[120] Similarly, the UNCRC has noted that 'the child should be given the "benefit of the doubt", should there be credibility concerns relating to his or her story'.[121]

The principle that the benefit of the doubt should be applied liberally in cases involving children has been explicitly endorsed in guidelines published in the United States[122] and the United Kingdom,[123] with the latter providing that '[t]he benefit of the doubt will need to be applied more generously when dealing with a child, particularly where a child is unable to

---

[116] UNHCR, *Note on Proof* (1998) *supra* n 79, [12].

[117] UNHCR, *Handbook*, [219] (emphasis added). UNHCR has emphasised that this principle applies to the assessment of age: UNHCR, *Unaccompanied Children Guidelines* (1997) *supra* n 28, [5.11]; UNHCR ExCom, *Conclusion on Children at Risk*, No 107 (LVIII) (2007), [(g)(ix)]; UNHCR, 2009 *Guidelines*, [75]. Again, although not a rule of law, the phrase 'liberal application of the benefit of doubt' 'points to an approach which in some cases it may be very useful to have in mind': *MD (Guinea) v SSHD* [2009] EWCA Civ 733, [12].

[118] UNHCR, *Handbook*, [204].

[119] See also *KS (benefit of the doubt)* [2014] UKUT 00552, [57], [64]–[77]. *Contra* Hathaway and Foster, *supra* n 56, 120–1. Hathaway and Foster observe that '[w]hile it is sometimes said that the claimant is entitled to the "benefit of the doubt" if there is an insufficiency of evidence, this principle in substance adds little to the intentionally low threshold of the well-founded fear'. Although there is some force to this observation, there is clear benefit in adopting the principle as a signpost in order to make clear the lower standard of proof that is inbuilt into the well-founded fear test. In claims involving children, 'the notion of a liberal application of [the benefit of the doubt] is best understood simply as an expression of how the lower standard of proof is to be applied in making such an assessment. Application of that standard when the subject-matter is the evidence of a child must take account of the fact that the applicant is a child and that children in general are vulnerable in a way most adults are not': *KS (benefit of the doubt)* [2014] UKUT 00552, [90].

[120] UNHCR, 2009 Guidelines, [73], citing International Committee of the Red Cross, *Inter-Agency Guiding Principles on Unaccompanied and Separated Children* (2004) 61. See also UNHCR, *Refugee Children: Guidelines on Protection and Care* (1994) 101 ('The problem of "proof" is great in every refugee status determination. It is compounded in the case of children. For this reason, the decision on a child's refugee status calls for a liberal application of the principle of the benefit of the doubt. This means that should there be some hesitation regarding the credibility of the child's story, the burden is not on the child to provide proof, but the child should be given the benefit of the doubt'); UNHCR, UNICEF and Save the Children, Separated Children in Europe Programme, *Statement of Good Practice* (4th revised edn) (2009) 36.

[121] UNCRC, *GC6*, [71]. It has been argued that the benefit of doubt principle is bolstered by the *CRC*'s requirement that the 'best interests of the child' be a primary consideration (see, generally, Chapter 6). Bhabha and Young suggest that a combination of these principles 'mandate[s] a generous approach to child persecution cases that affirms applications rather than dismisses them when the evidence is unreliable or inadequate': J Bhabha and W Young, 'Not Adults in Miniature: Unaccompanied Child Asylum Seekers and the New US Guidelines' (1999) 11(1) *International Journal of Refugee Law* 84, 114.

[122] INS, *Guidelines*, 26; USCIS Asylum Division (2009) *supra* n 83, 34–5, 42.

[123] UKBA, *Asylum Process Guidance*, [16.4]; Home Office, *Processing Children's Asylum Claims*, 38.

provide detail on a particular element of their claim'.[124] The principle has also been accepted, to varying degrees, by national decision-makers in the United Kingdom,[125] the United States[126] and Canada.[127]

But while there is clear international and domestic support for the general principle, it is less clear what a 'liberal benefit of the doubt' rule might mean as a matter of practice. Although there is no definitive guidance on the application of the principle, domestic practice provides some insight into the minimum standards that may be required. At the very least it is clear that a child should be afforded evidential concessions consistent with the individual child's age and evolving developmental capacities.[128] The Federal Court of Canada has described the need for an evidential continuum: '[c]learly a twelve-year-old claimant must be given more latitude than a fifteen-year-old. The child's degree of maturity, as well as their age, must be taken into account in assessing their evidence.'[129]

If a child presents a cognisable claim that is, taking into account the child's age and developmental capacities, 'on balance, capable of being believed',[130] this should be sufficient for the purposes of establishing refugee status.[131] This standard may be satisfied by the applicant's written or oral testimony,[132] by testimony from lay or expert witnesses (such as a parent),[133] by reference to independent and reliable country of origin information, or by

---

[124] UKBA, *Asylum Process Guidance*, [16.4]. The guidance further provides that '[i]n young or less mature children a different degree in their knowledge and information is to be expected and the benefit of the doubt must be applied more liberally': at [16.2]. See also Home Office, *Processing Children's Asylum Claims*, 38–39.

[125] *AA (unattended children) Afghanistan CG* [2012] UKUT 00016, [117] ('[i]n assessing the appellant's evidence we have borne in mind that ... [the] benefit of the doubt should be applied liberally in his favour'); *TN (Afghanistan) v SSHD* [2014] 1 WLR 2095, [21]; *HK (Afghanistan) v SSHD* [2012] EWCA Civ 315, [34]; *DS (Afghanistan) v SSHD* [2011] EWCA Civ 305, [14]; *ZJ (Afghanistan) v SSHD* [2008] EWCA Civ 799, [16].

[126] *Abay v Ashcroft*, 368 F 3d 634 (6th Cir, 2004).

[127] *Canada (MCI) v Patel* 2008 FC 747, [11]; *T93-02403* (IRB, 15 March 1994) 4.

[128] IRB, *Guidelines*, 4–6; INS, *Guidelines*, 26–7; MRT and RRT, *Guidance on the Assessment of Credibility* (March 2012), [4.7]; UKBA, *Asylum Process Guidance*, [16.2]–[16.4]; Home Office, *Processing Children's Asylum Claims*, 38–9.

[129] *Ni v Canada (MCI)* [2001] FCJ No 1711, [10]. See also *Nahimana v Canada (MCI)* [2006] FCJ No 219, [24], [29] ('In making its decision, the Board should have been more sensitive to the fact that Ms. Nahimana was a minor at the time of the relevant events, including at the time of the hearing, and that she comes from a society where women are told very little ... This is supported by article 3(1) of the [CRC] ... [a]s well, article 22(1) of the [CRC] deals specifically with refugee matters, stating that states must ensure children refugees or refugee claimants receive adequate protection'). Conversely, in *KS (benefit of the doubt)* [2014] UKUT 00552 it is suggested that a liberal application of the benefit of the doubt 'may not necessarily be given if the applicant has equivalent maturity to an adult' (at [96]).

[130] UNHCR, *Note on Proof* (1998) *supra* n 79, [11].

[131] 'What is capable of being believed is not to be determined according to the [decision-maker's] subjective belief or gut feeling about whether an [a]pplicant is telling the truth or not. A [decision-maker] should focus on what is objectively or reasonably believable in the circumstances': MRT and RRT, *Guidance on the Assessment of Credibility* (March 2012), [2.4].

[132] 'A child, like an adult, is not required to provide corroborating evidence in all cases, and may rely solely on testimony when that testimony is credible, consistent, and sufficiently detailed to provide a plausible and coherent account of the basis of the child's alleged fear': INS, *Guidelines*, 26.

[133] The testimony of a parent, designated representative or other lay witness may be particularly significant in cases where a child is too young to provide her own testimony. The fact that an adult may be testifying

a combination of these sources. In limited circumstances it may be necessary to require a child to provide additional corroborating evidence, but only where it is reasonable to expect such evidence to take into account the individual circumstances of the child.[134]

In circumstances where a child provides written or oral testimony, allowances should be made for inconsistencies or gaps in a child's story.[135] It has been suggested that decision-makers should take into account the 'developmental or cultural reasons for a child's vagueness or inconsistency, and not assume that it is an indicator of unreliability'.[136] As UNHCR has pointed out, 'what might constitute a lie in the case of an adult might not necessarily be a lie in the case of a child'.[137] It will therefore generally be inappropriate to impugn the credibility of a child on the basis that her evidence is contradictory[138] or deemed implausible,[139] or because she has been unable

does not, however, obviate the liberal benefit of the doubt owed to the child applicant. As the Federal Court of Canada has held, '[the] analysis cannot end with the determination of the credibility of the witness; instead it must examine the balance of the evidence before it': *Voskova v Canada (MCI)* [2011] FCJ No 1682, [26] (in this case the IRB had rejected the claim of two minor applicants because their mother was not credible). But see *Richards v Canada (MCI)* [2011] FC 1391 (rejecting the claim of two minor applicants because of negative credibility findings made against their designated representative, despite the fact that the applicants insisted 'that they [were] capable of expressing themselves and negative inferences should not have been made from their lack of fulsome testimony' (at [12])).

[134] INS, *Guidelines*, 27. See, e.g., *MFD v Canada (MCI)* [2001] FCJ No 771, [11]–[13] (it was unreasonable for the IRB to draw adverse influences from the fact that a 17-year-old girl had failed to produce photos of the family member that had raped her); *Kalu v Canada (MCI)* [2008] FCJ No 488, [12].

[135] 'In general, children are not able to present evidence with the same degree of precision as adults with respect to context, timing, importance and details ... [T]he [decision-maker] should consider the opportunity the child had for observation, the capacity of the child to observe accurately and to express what he or she has observed, and the ability of the child to remember the facts as observed. These factors may be influenced by the age, gender and cultural background of the child as well as other factors such as fear, memory difficulties, post-traumatic stress disorder and the child's perception of the [determination] process': IRB, *Guidelines*, 4, 6. See, e.g., *Mejilla-Romero v Holder*, 600 F 3d 63, 83–5 (1st Cir, 2010) (Judge Stahl, dissenting), acknowledging that the applicant's testimony was undermined by three factors: the fact that it recounted events that occurred when he was between the ages of 5 and 11; the fact that he gave his oral testimony when he was 13; and the fact that he had been diagnosed with post-traumatic stress disorder. Judge Stahl suggests that the transcript of oral testimony is 'exactly what one would expect from a thirteen-year-old discussing events that occurred when he was five to eleven years old. His description of multiple incidents of violence is simplistic; he can only offer basic explanations for why such violence was inflicted upon him and his family; and he shows only a very basic, one might say "child-like," understanding of the political context of the trauma that engulfed his young life': at 85. See also, e.g., *Ngani v Canada (MCI)* 2016 FC 167, [6].

[136] INS, *Guidelines*, 15.

[137] UNHCR, 2009 *Guidelines*, [72]. The *Guidelines* further note: '[Children] may be too young or immature to be able to evaluate what information is important or to interpret what they have witnessed or experienced in a manner that is easily understandable to an adult. Some children may omit or distort vital information or be unable to differentiate the imagined from reality. They may experience difficulty relating to abstract notions, such as time or distance.'

[138] See, e.g., IRB, *Guidelines*, 4. See also *T99-11706, T99-11707 and T99-11707 and T99-11708* (IRB, 26 January 2001). But contra *SI v Canada (MCI)* [2004] FCJ No 2015, [3]; *Feng Chai Li v Canada (MCI)* [2001] FCJ No 1710, [16].

[139] See, e.g., *MFD v Canada (MCI)* [2001] FCJ No 771, [11]–[13] (finding that the IRB had displayed a lack of 'sensitivity and contextualization' in finding it implausible that a young teenage girl would have remained in the family home despite being subjected to ongoing sexual assault and rape by a family member over the course of several years).

to present evidence on every fact in support of her claim.[140] In circumstances where a child is unlikely to have a full understanding of immigration processes, it will generally be inappropriate to treat the timing of a refugee claim as an indicator of her credibility.[141]

In the context of oral testimony, it is also generally accepted that little, if any, weight should be given to a child's demeanour.[142] It has been suggested that decision-makers should avoid drawing adverse inferences from the fact that a child's testimony appears 'evasive',[143] 'ambiguous'[144] or 'uncooperative'.[145]

Critically, even where a child, or her parent or designated representative, is disbelieved, the requirement that the child be given a liberal benefit of the doubt does not fall away. As the High Court of Australia has underlined, 'the fact that an applicant for refugee status may yield to temptation to embroider an account of his or her history is hardly surprising. It is necessary always to bear in mind that an applicant for refugee status is, on one view of events, engaged in an often desperate battle for freedom, if not life itself'.[146] The refugee status determination process should accordingly be viewed as a process for 'arriving at the best possible understanding of the facts in an inherently imperfect environment. It is not to punish or disadvantage vulnerable people because they have made false or inconsistent statements, or are believed to have done so'.[147] These statements speak with particular force in the context of children, who are more likely to be overwhelmed or confused by the determination process and to feel a need to exaggerate or omit certain details of their claim. However, as Hathaway has observed, '[e]ven clear evidence of a lack of candour does not necessarily negate a claimant's need for protection'.[148] In this regard, a child's testimony is simply a means to address the ultimate question of whether the child is eligible for international refugee protection.[149] If other evidence is available that supports

---

[140] 'A [decision-maker] must not draw an adverse credibility inference from omissions in the child's knowledge or account if it is likely that their age or maturity is [a] factor or if there are logical or other reasons for those omissions': UKBA, *Asylum Process Guidance*, [16.4]; Home Office, *Processing Children's Asylum Claims*, 39. In these situations, the decision-maker 'should consider whether it is able to infer the details of the claim from the evidence presented': IRB, *Guidelines*, 6. See, e.g., *Uthayakumar v Canada (MCI)* [1999] FCJ No 1013, [28] ('The panel clearly did not take into consideration the fact that the applicants were ten and twelve years of age when they travelled to Canada and that these two children clearly did not have to keep a log throughout their travels. Furthermore, it was quite possible, and perhaps even likely realistic, that both of the applicants could not precisely remember all of the circumstances of the journey, which must certainly have been very stressful under the circumstances'); *Mendoza-Pablo v Holder*, 667 F 3d 1308, 1313 (9th Cir, 2012) ('[I]t is clear from our case law that an infant can be the victim of persecution, even though he has no present recollection of the events that constituted his persecution').

[141] See, e.g., *R (AN) (a child) v SSHD* [2012] EWCA Civ 1636, [113]–[114].   [142] INS, *Guidelines*, 13–15.

[143] *Uthayakumar v Canada (MCI)* [1999] FCJ No 1013, [11], [24]–[28]. Contra *Feng Chai Li v Canada (MCI)* [2001] FCJ No 1710, [18].

[144] *Abay v Ashcroft*, 368 F 3d 634, 640 (6th Cir, 2004).   [145] INS, *Guidelines*, 14.

[146] *Abebe v Commonwealth* (1999) 197 CLR 510, [191] (Gummow and Hayne JJ).

[147] *MIMIA v SGLB* (2004) 207 ALR 12, [73] (Kirby J).

[148] Hathaway, *The Law of Refugee Status* (1991) supra n 15, 86.

[149] See, e.g., *TA2-00795* (IRB, 2 December 2002) (IRB finding that the 15-year-old applicant was at risk of domestic violence, despite the fact that it considered that the applicant's evidence was 'internally and externally inconsistent' and was 'exaggerated to boost her claim'). Contra *TA6-06827* (IRB, 7 February 2007), 6 (IRB rejecting the claim of a seven-year-old girl on credibility grounds, notwithstanding 'persuasive evidence that young girls continue to be forced to undergo FGM').

a conclusion that the child is genuinely at risk of being persecuted – for instance, country of origin information[150] – then refugee status ought to be recognised irrespective of any credibility finding.[151]

Conclusions

The analysis in this chapter has demonstrated the challenges that children face in establishing a *genuine risk* of being persecuted for a *Convention* reason in their home country. The first challenge is doctrinal and derives from the bipartite approach to interpreting the 'well-founded fear' requirement. Although decision-makers have attempted to modify this approach in cases involving children, such modification has given rise to a host of new problems. A more principled approach, consistent with principles of treaty interpretation, is to recognise that the well-founded fear standard is inherently objective and does not require an applicant to demonstrate subjective fear. The second sets of challenges relate to the difficulties that a child may encounter in establishing that there is evidence of an objective risk of prospective harm. A number of principles have developed to assist a child in navigating these evidential obstacles. The shared duty of fact-finding underscores that decision-makers are required to evaluate all relevant risks that a child may face, irrespective of the fact that the child may not have formally articulated those risks. Recourse to child-specific country of origin information, and evidence of the risks faced by individuals who truly are similarly situated to a child applicant, assists in ensuring that the assessment of risk takes into account the distinct risks faced by children. And the liberal benefit of the doubt rule provides a shorthand way of signifying that evidential concessions may be required to safeguard against the risk that, for reasons unconnected to the likelihood of

---

[150] Hence the focus on objective factors and information in claims involving children: see INS, *Guidelines*, 26–27; UKBA, *Asylum Process Guidance*, [2], [13.1], [16.2]; Home Office, *Processing Children's Asylum Claims*, 34, 38. The UK legislation, for instance, appropriately recognises that '[m]ore weight should be given to objective indicators of risk that to the child's state of mind and understanding of the situation': United Kingdom, *Immigration Rules*, para 351. See also UKBA, *Asylum Process Guidance*, [2]; Home Office, *Processing Children's Asylum Claims*, 38.

[151] '[E]ven if an applicant is disbelieved, the primary decision-maker . . . must still consider whether, on any other basis asserted, a fear of persecution exists which is well founded so as to ground the protection claimed': *Abebe v Commonwealth* (1999) 197 CLR 510, [211] (Kirby J). INS, *Guidelines*, 15, similarly provides that where a child tells a fabricated story it remains incumbent on the decision-maker to 'undertake a careful and searching examination of the underlying merits of the child's case'. See, e.g., *Mejilla-Romero v Holder*, 600 F 3d 63, 77 (1st Cir, 2010) (Judge Stahl, dissenting), criticising the majority for 'limiting its analysis to the oral testimony of a child, diagnosed with post traumatic stress disorder (PTSD), and testifying about events that occurred when he was very young', where '[a] review of the record as a whole compels the conclusion that [the applicant] is entitled to the protections afforded to refugees'. In an amicus brief in support of the applicant's petition for a re-hearing, UNHCR stressed the importance of considering 'all evidence in the record': 'Although testimony alone can be sufficient to support a claim for asylum, where corroborating evidence is submitted, the claim must be assessed on the entirety of the record. This is especially critical in the context of a child applicant. Children may have limited knowledge of country conditions or family circumstances, may be unable to fully explain the reasons for the persecution or may not fully comprehend their vulnerability.' UNHCR, 'Brief *Amicus Curiae*' (2010) *supra* n 34, 13–14. See also Center for Gender and Refugee Studies et al., 'Brief of *Amici Curiae* in support of Petitioner's Petition for Rehearing or Rehearing *En Banc*', filed in *Mejilla-Romero* (21 June 2010) (copy on file with author) 9–12.

prospective harm, a child may be returned to a risk of being persecuted. Although these principles do not displace or modify the requirement that a child must demonstrate a genuine risk of prospective harm, they provide appropriate recognition of the need for greater care when assessing the likelihood that a child will be at risk of harm if returned to her home country.

4

A Child-Rights Framework for Identifying Persecutory Harm

Introduction

At the core of the refugee definition is the requirement that an applicant demonstrate that they are at risk of 'being persecuted'. Despite its importance, the phrase is left undefined in the *Refugee Convention*. This opacity is perhaps deliberate, 'given that it must apply to the great variety of acts of oppression, despotism, fanaticism, cruelty and intolerance of which humanity is capable'.[1] Despite the term's malleability, the 'being persecuted' standard has traditionally been interpreted in a way that fails to take into account the distinct ways in which children can be persecuted. The point is elegantly made by the Canadian IRB:[2]

> Was his school experience persecutory? From the lordly perch of an adult, one could say it was not. The reason for such a view is, of course, that the Convention refugee definition and its evolving law is mostly about adults. 'Persecution' – the single most important concept in refugee law[–]takes adult situations into account ... The regime of rights that adults have developed is in response to adult needs, the unjust denial of which is tantamount to persecution.

An adult-centred understanding of 'being persecuted' is largely unsurprising given that the majority of refugee jurisprudence has developed in the context of claims generated by adults. But as Judge Pregerson of the Ninth Circuit Court of Appeals has cautioned, the '[a]pplication of a singular definition of persecution to both adult- and child-based claims fails to address adequately the fact that suffering or harm inflicted on children is far more "offensive" than identical suffering or harm inflicted on adults'.[3]

This chapter commences with an overview of the dominant approach to understanding the 'being persecuted' standard – the human rights framework – which draws upon human rights standards to identify persecutory harm. This overview is pertinent to the balance of the chapter, which examines the application of the framework to claims involving children. Section 4.2 begins by identifying the distinct ways in which children may be subject to a risk of 'being persecuted'. Drawing on the core precepts of the human rights framework, the remainder of the section develops an argument for greater interaction between the 'being persecuted' standard and the provisions of the *CRC*. This is referred to as a child-rights

---

[1] *Chen Shi Hai v MIMA* (2000) 201 CLR 293, [46] (Kirby J). See also A Grahl-Madsen, *The Status of Refugees in International Law* (1966) vol 1, 193 ('[i]t seems as if the drafters ... wanted to introduce a flexible concept which might be applied to circumstances as they might arise; or in other words, that they capitulated before the inventiveness of humanity to think up new ways of persecuting fellow men').

[2] *TA1-03656, TA1-03657 and TA1-03658* (IRB, 19 December 2002), [7]–[8].

[3] *Mansour v Ashcroft*, 390 F 3d 667, 681 (7th Cir, 2004) (Judge Pregerson, dissenting).

framework for understanding persecutory harm. Section 4.3 examines the application of the child-rights framework in a series of individual case studies.

4.1 The Definition of 'Being Persecuted'

As noted above, the phrase 'being persecuted' is left undefined in the *Convention*, with a number of scholars suggesting that this was a deliberate omission.[4] But while there are clear benefits in adopting a malleable standard, a commitment to fair and consistent decision-making signals a need to establish some objective basis to guide the assessment of when an applicant apprehends a form of harm that amounts to 'being persecuted'.[5] This is particularly critical in circumstances where the outcome may 'be [a] life or death decision ... for an applicant'.[6] As the High Court of Australia has explained, '[a] plethora of tests, indeed what may amount to the same test though expressed in a variety of ways, can only lead to uncertainty and, all too likely, confusion in an area where the future of individuals is at stake'.[7] In these circumstances it is unsurprising that decision-makers have considered it necessary 'to understand what is encompassed by the notion of persecution'.[8]

The challenge, then, has been to ascertain a standard that both promotes objective and consistent decision-making and that respects the drafters' desire to adopt a standard that is sufficiently flexible to allow the *Convention* to adapt to contemporary realities. In 1991, Hathaway suggested that this challenge might be overcome by linking the 'being persecuted' standard to the emerging corpus of international human rights law.[9] The adoption of a human rights framework for understanding the 'being persecuted' definition now reflects

---

[4] P Weis, 'The Concept of the Refugee in International Law' (1960) 87 *Journal du droit international* 928, 970; J C Hathaway, *The Law of Refugee Status* (1991) 102.

[5] Hart argues that a 'central element in the idea of justice' is rooted in the legal adage 'treat like cases alike and different cases differently': H L A Hart, *The Concept of Law* (3rd edn, 2012) 164.

[6] *MIAC v SZLSP* (2010) 187 FCR 362, [98].   [7] *Chan v MIEA* (1989) 169 CLR 379, 407 (Toohey J).

[8] *Horvath v SSHD* [2000] INLR 15, 36. Some jurisdictions, most strikingly the United States, have preferred to retain a subjective, case-by-case approach. This has resulted in 'inconsistent, result-oriented analysis', ultimately 'confus[ing] the development of a meaningful framework for analyzing persecution': D E Anker, *Law of Asylum in the United States* (2015) 221. In *Mansour v Ashcroft*, 390 F 3d 667, 681 (7th Cir, 2004), Judge Pregerson (dissenting) acknowledges that '[t]he definition of persecution that our court applies is a creature of purely our own case law'.

[9] Hathaway, *The Law of Refugee Status* (1991), *supra* n 4, 101–5. Although the widespread adoption of the human rights framework is appropriately attributed to Hathaway, it is important to acknowledge that the relationship between international human rights law and the definition of 'being persecuted' had been recognised for some time. As early as 1953, Jacques Vernant had equated the concept of persecution with 'severe measures and sanctions of an arbitrary nature, incompatible with the principles set forth in the Universal Declaration of Human Rights': J Vernant, *The Refugee in the Post-War World* (1953) 8. Guy Goodwin-Gill later observed that 'comprehensive analysis requires the general notion [of being perse-cuted] to be related to developments within the broad field of human rights': G S Goodwin-Gill, *The Refugee in International Law* (1983) 38. Equally, it is important to acknowledge that this interpretative approach it is not universally accepted, either by decision-makers or scholars: see, e.g., D Martin, 'The Refugee Concept: On Definitions, Politics, and the Careful Use of a Scarce Resource' in H Adelman (ed), *Refugee Policy: Canada and the United States* (1991) 30; D Martin, 'Review of Hathaway, *The Law of Refugee Status*' (1993) 87 *American Journal of International Law* 348; M E Price, 'Persecution Complex: Justifying Asylum Law's Preference for Persecuted People' (2006) 47(2) *Harvard International Law Journal* 413.

the dominant approach to this task. This section provides an overview of that approach, focusing on two specific issues relating to its application: first, which human rights obligations are relevant to the inquiry and in what circumstances a human rights violation will amount to persecutory harm; and, second, what the role of state protection is within the human rights framework.

4.1.1 A Human Rights Framework

At the core of the human rights framework is an understanding that the drafters of the *Convention* were concerned with 'identify[ing] forms of harm demonstrative of breach by a state of its basic obligations of protection'.[10] Hathaway suggests that international human rights law, and in particular the International Bill of Rights, provides the appropriate standard against which to assess the minimum duties that a state owes its citizens.[11] Two core ideas – that the *Convention* was conceived to provide back-up protection where a state has failed in its protection duties and that international human rights law provides the appropriate benchmark to assess whether these duties have been met – underpinned Hathaway's now broadly accepted definition of 'being persecuted' as 'the sustained or systemic violation of basic human rights demonstrative of a failure of state protection'.[12]

As discussed in Chapter 1, the recognition of a link between the 'being persecuted' definition and international human rights law sits comfortably with the rules of treaty interpretation. In addition to ensuring consistency with the *VCLT*, the human rights framework offers a number of clear advantages.[13] Reliance on external standards provides decision-makers with an objective benchmark which can assist in promoting fair and consistent decision-making, while also accommodating an interpretation of the *Refugee Convention* that is sensitive to the reality that states can only be bound by what they have agreed. At the same time, international human rights law provides an increasingly sophisticated and continuously developing external point of reference to ensure that the definition of 'being persecuted' does not stagnate, but can evolve to respond to contemporary refugee flows. As Verdirame has observed, 'the open texture of the Refugee Convention [is] enriched and deepened through the link with human rights'.[14]

At the outset, it is important to acknowledge that international human rights standards are being invoked in order to obtain objective and principled guidance on what might properly be regarded as 'being persecuted'. In no sense is international refugee law concerned with adjudicating the responsibility of a state under an international human rights treaty. The relevant question in any refugee status determination is whether an applicant is at risk of 'being persecuted' and international human rights standards are being drawn upon as a benchmark to assist in that assessment. The human rights framework, consistent with the rules of treaty interpretation, provides an interpretative tool to assist decision-makers in

---

[10] Hathaway, *The Law of Refugee Status* (1991) *supra* n 4, 104. See more recently J C Hathaway and M Foster, *The Law of Refugee Status* (2nd edn, 2014) 193–208.

[11] Hathaway, *The Law of Refugee Status* (1991) *supra* n 4, 106.

[12] *Ibid.*, 104–5.

[13] See generally Hathaway and Foster (2014) *supra* n 10, 193–208; and Chapter 1, Section 1.4.

[14] G Verdirame, 'A Friendly Act of Socio-Cultural Contestation: Asylum and the Big Cultural Divide' (2012) 44 *New York University Journal of International Law and Politics* 559, 559.

identifying those standards of harm that have been deemed sufficiently serious to warrant the intervention of the international community.[15]

The human rights framework for identifying persecutory harm has received widespread approval, particularly in the common law world.[16] It also increasingly finds favour in civil law jurisdictions.[17] The human rights framework has also been repeatedly endorsed by UNHCR,[18] and has been adopted by a significant number of scholars.[19] Although reference is most often made to the *UDHR, ICCPR* and *ICESCR*, decision-makers are also beginning to engage with the specialist human rights treaties including *CEDAW, CERD* and, as the discussion below demonstrates, the *CRC*.

But while there is general agreement that international human rights norms are relevant to the identification of persecutory harm, there is marked divergence in the manner in which the human rights framework is understood and applied.[20] This divergent practice risks undermining the value of the human rights framework and its ability to provide an objective basis to guide the assessment of 'being persecuted'.[21] This section focuses on two related questions that have arisen in applying the human rights framework, with the objective of providing an analytical framework that goes beyond simply invoking the link between international human rights law and the 'being persecuted' standard. First: is a risk to any international agreed human rights obligation sufficient to constitute a risk of 'being persecuted' for the purposes of the *Convention*? Second: what is the role of state protection in the human rights framework and, specifically, what is the relevant standard against which to assess whether a country of origin has failed in its duty to protect its citizens?

---

[15] Hathaway and Foster (2014) *supra* n 10, 200.

[16] The human rights framework was first endorsed by the Supreme Court of Canada in *Canada (Attorney General) v Ward* [1993] 2 SCR 689, 723–4. It has since been formally embraced by the UK House of Lords and Supreme Court in a series of cases: *Horvath v SSHD* [2001] 1 AC 489, 495 (Lord Hope); *Sepet v SSHD* [2003] 1 WLR 856, [7] (Lord Bingham); *R (Ullah) v Special Adjudicator* [2004] 2 AC 323, 355 [32] (Lord Steyn); *HJ (Iran) v SSHD* [2011] 1 AC 596, 621 [13] (Lord Hope). Although not uniformly embraced in Australia, this approach was endorsed expressly by Kirby J and implicitly by Gleeson CJ of the Australian High Court in *MIMA v Khawar* (2002) 210 CLR 1, [70], [111]. In the United States, although the interpretation of 'being persecuted' is not grounded in any particular framework, in *Stenaj v Gonzalez*, 227 Fed Appx 429, 433 (6th Cir, 2007), the US Court of Appeals for the Sixth Circuit observed that '[w]hether the treatment feared by a claimant violates recognized standards of basic human rights can determine whether persecution exists' (citing *Abay v Ashcroft*, 368 F 3d 634, 638–9 (6th Cir, 2004)). See also *Mansour v Ashcroft*, 390 F 3d 667, 681 (7th Cir, 2004). See, further, Hathaway and Foster (2014) *supra* n 10, 185, 196–7.

[17] See generally A Zimmermann and C Mahler, 'Article 1A, Para 2' in A Zimmermann (ed), *The 1951 Convention Relating to the Status of Refugees and Its 1967 Protocol: A Commentary* (2011) 281, 351–8.

[18] This is reflected, e.g., in UNHCR, 2009 *Guidelines*, and in amicus submissions of UNHCR: see, e.g., UNHCR, 'Case for the First Intervener', filed in *HJ* (undated), [21] ('[p]ersecution comprises human rights abuses or other serious harm, often, but not always, with a systematic or repetitive element'); UNHCR, 'Brief *Amicus Curiae* of the United Nations High Commissioner for Refugees in Support of Petitioner's Petition for Rehearing En Banc', filed in *Mejilla-Romero* (18 June 2010) (copy on file with author) 6 ('[persecution] has long been recognized to encompass serious human rights violations, including a threat to life or freedom, as well as other kinds of serious harm or intolerable situations').

[19] For a précis, see M Foster, *International Refugee Law and Socio-Economic Rights: Refuge from Deprivation* (2007) 33. For a particularly erudite endorsement, see D Anker, 'Refugee Law, Gender, and the Human Rights Paradigm' (2002) 15 *Harvard Human Rights Journal* 133.

[20] For an excellent critique, see Foster (2007) *supra* n 19, 36–86.   [21] Foster (2007) *supra* n 19, 74.

4.1.2 Taking Human Rights on Their Own Terms

In addition to the *UDHR* and the nine international human rights treaties, there are a large number of non-binding declarations, principles, guidelines, standard rules and recommendations that relate to human rights and are thus potentially relevant to the identification of persecutory harm.[22] How, then, should one go about identifying which of these instruments is legally relevant to the identification of persecutory harm? Hathaway suggests that the human rights framework should be circumscribed in two respects. First, he suggests that recourse should be limited to legal standards, primarily treaties, rather than non-binding 'soft law' standards.[23] This is not to suggest that 'soft law' is not relevant to the inquiry, but that there is a critical distinction between the identification of relevant human rights standards and the interpretation of the content of those standards. As Foster has sought to illustrate, 'soft law' may play a critical role in explicating or amplifying existing obligations.[24] Reliance on 'soft law' has thus 'proven extremely helpful to refugee decision-makers in understanding the scope and parameters of international human rights treaty provisions, their application to specific groups and circumstances, and evolving notions of rights and corresponding obligations'.[25]

As a second limitation, Hathaway suggests that the 'being persecuted' standard ought to be interpreted only by reference to international legal standards that enjoy the widespread support of states.[26] Hathaway initially restricted himself to the standards set out in the International Bill of Rights, citing the 'extraordinary consensus achieved on the soundness of its standards, its regular invocation by states and its role as the progenitor for the many more specific human rights accords'.[27] More recently, and with the benefit of significant developments in international human rights law, Hathaway has appropriately

---

[22] The focus here is on international human rights law rather than regional human rights law. However, it is important to acknowledge that decision-makers are increasingly taking into account regional human rights norms in assessing the 'being persecuted' standard. This is particularly evident in EU member states, with the *EU Qualification Directive* explicitly linking the definition of 'persecution' to the obligations contained in the *ECHR*. Although regional jurisprudence may provide insight into the interpretation of international human rights standards, care should be taken where standards in the regional instrument differ substantively from those in the cognate international instrument. See Foster (2007) *supra* n 19, 67–70; *AB (Germany)* [2012] NZIPT 800107, [144]–[149].

[23] 'At a minimum ... it seems ... that a commitment to legal positivism requires, first, that we focus on legal standards – primarily treaties – not on so-called "soft law", which simply doesn't yet bespeak a sufficient normative consensus. While we can logically resort to these evolving standards as a means to contextualize and elaborate the substantive content of genuine legal standards, they should not, in my view, be treated as authoritative in and of themselves': J C Hathaway, 'The Relationship between Human Rights and Refugee Law: What Refugee Judges Can Contribute' in International Association of Refugee Law Judges, *The Realities of Refugee Determination on the Eve of a New Millennium: The Role of the Judiciary* (1998) 80, 86.

[24] Foster (2007) *supra* n 19, 72. Lowe describes 'soft law' as 'norms that are not binding but which colour the application of norms that are legally binding': V Lowe, *International Law* (2007) 95–6. The 'soft law' instruments thus 'form part of the broader normative context within which expectations of what is reasonable or proper State behaviour are formed': *ibid*. See also A Boyle, 'Some Reflections on the Relationship of Treaties and Soft Law' (1999) 48 *International & Comparative Law Quarterly* 901.

[25] Foster (2007) *supra* n 19, 74. See also G Noll, 'Asylum Claims and the Translation of Culture into Politics' (2006) 41 *Texas International Law Journal* 491, 494–5.

[26] 'Until and unless we are able honestly to say that a given treaty enjoys general support it ought not to be used to interpret a term in what is meant to be a *universal* treaty on refugee protection': Hathaway (1998) *supra* n 23, 86.

[27] Hathaway, *The Law of Refugee Status* (1991) *supra* n 4, 106–7.

acknowledged that other widely ratified international human rights treaties may provide insight on international standards of acceptable behaviour and thereby inform the definition of 'being persecuted'.[28] Specifically, he has suggested that a given treaty may be relied on if it has been ratified by a super-majority of the UN member states, including some support from each of the major geopolitical groupings.[29] As a matter of principle, this approach finds support in art 31(3)(c) of the *VCLT*. As discussed in Chapter 1, it has been argued that that provision requires a decision-maker to take into account relevant rules of international law that 'can reasonably be considered to express the common intentions or understandings of all members of the treaty'.[30] There is a compelling argument that an international human rights treaty that has been ratified by a super-majority of parties to the *Convention* satisfies this threshold.[31] In addition to the *ICCPR* and *ICESCR*, this would include the *CRC*, its two Optional Protocols (the *OPAC* and *OPSC*), *CERD* and *CEDAW*.

Having identified the relevant human rights instruments, it is then necessary to consider the method that should be adopted to distinguish between human rights violations that constitute persecutory harm and human rights violations that do not. A number of approaches have developed to attempt to limit the circumstances in which a risk of a violation of an international human right obligation will satisfy the 'being persecuted' standard. The first has been to categorise rights according to a scale of normative value or importance.[32] This hierarchical approach invariably ranks civil and political rights on a higher plane than economic, social and cultural rights, with the consequence that a violation of the former is more likely to meet the standard of 'being persecuted'.[33] A second approach has been to require an applicant to demonstrate something more than a violation of a human right in order to satisfy the 'being persecuted' standard – for instance, that a violation is particularly 'serious' or 'severe',[34] or that the violation touches the 'core' or 'essence'[35] of the human right in question.

---

[28] Hathaway (1998) *supra* n 23, 86; Hathaway and Foster (2014) *supra* n 10, 201. See generally *Refugee Appeal No 74665/03* [2005] INLR 68.

[29] Hathaway (1998) *supra* n 23, 86. Hathaway suggests that the standard of assent required within the UN for votes on 'important questions' – two-thirds of the UN membership – might provide an appropriate litmus test for ascertaining when a treaty enjoys general support. Rather than looking at the ratification rate amongst all UN member states, it may be more appropriate to assess whether a super-majority of states that are party to the *Convention* have ratified the relevant treaty (although the result is likely to be the same).

[30] J Pauwelyn, 'The Role of Public International Law in the WTO: How Far Can We Go?' (2001) 95 *American Journal of International Law* 535, 576.

[31] The argument has been made by Foster (2007) *supra* n 19, 56–7.

[32] For a comprehensive discussion on the adoption of hierarchies in international refugee law, see Foster (2007) *supra* n 19, 113–201. This hierarchical approach is often attributed to Hathaway, who proposed a model that categorised human rights according to four distinct types of obligations: Hathaway, *The Law of Refugee Status* (1991) *supra* n 4, 109–11. Although the language of 'hierarchy' was perhaps unfortunate, and notwithstanding the manner in which the 'hierarchy' has often been misappropriated by decision-makers, it is important to acknowledge that Hathaway's model was based on the nature of the obligation, rather than the normative value of the rights. See Foster (2007) *supra* n 19, 168–81.

[33] Foster (2007), *supra* n 19, 123–54. K Jastram, 'Economic Harm as a Basis for Refugee Status and the Application of Human Rights Law to the Interpretation of Economic Persecution' in J Simeon (ed), *Critical Issues in International Refugee Law* (2010) 143.

[34] *EU Qualification Directive*, art 9.

[35] See, e.g., Zimmermann and Mahler (2011) *supra* n 17, 354–8, particularly relating to German jurisprudence which has developed a differentiation between so-called *forum externum* and *forum internum*. The adoption of the core/margin approach is also often attributed to the decision of Rodger Haines QC of

Both approaches are difficult to reconcile with contemporary understandings of international human rights law. The adoption of a hierarchy of rights bespeaks a failure to appreciate the entrenched notion that '[a]ll human rights are universal, indivisible and interdependent and interrelated' and that '[t]he international community must treat human rights globally in a fair and equal manner, on the same footing, and with the same emphasis'.[36] Similarly, there is no basis for grafting additional qualifiers onto human rights standards in order to somehow distinguish between those rights that are important and those that are not. The superimposition of qualifiers that are largely foreign to international human rights law threatens to undermine the cogency of the link between international human rights law and the definition of 'being persecuted'.

A more principled and coherent approach is simply to take international human rights law on its own terms.[37] If international human rights law is accepted as the most authoritative benchmark against which to assess whether a country of origin will provide the requisite level of protection to an individual seeking international protection, it is difficult to conceive a principled justification for imposing an extra requirement that a right be sufficiently 'fundamental' or a violation particularly 'egregious'. As Hathaway and Foster explain, '[t]here is, in truth, no convincing conceptual framework that is capable of distinguishing on an absolute basis between those rights that are "basic", "fundamental" or "important" and those that are not'.[38] A state has either failed to satisfy its international human rights obligations or it has not. As Sedley LJ noted, '[t]o say that particular ill-treatment falls toward the bottom end of the scale of what amounts to persecution is not . . . to say anything that matters legally'.[39] In order to ascertain whether an individual is at risk of persecutory harm a decision-maker must assess whether an applicant is at risk of a violation of a human right protected under an international human rights treaty that has the general support of the international community. This assessment will require the decision-maker to consider the relevant human rights obligation on its own terms.

This approach raises legitimate concerns about over-inclusivity. Martin has, for instance, argued that the definition of 'being persecuted' should not be understood as implicating the

---

the RSAA in *Refugee Appeal No 74665/03* [2005] INLR 68. Haines suggests that the focus must be on 'the minimum core entitlement conferred by the relevant right': at [90]. The difficulty with this approach is evident in his attempt to identify what is at the 'core' and what is at 'margin' of the right to privacy. The two examples of 'marginal' activities – adoption by unmarried persons and same-sex marriage – are in fact not at the margin of the right but, at least as presently understood, outside the scope of the right altogether. The idea that it is possible to identify a minimum core obligation has found some traction in the context of social, economic and cultural rights, yet even here the idea remains deeply contested: see Foster (2007) *supra* n 19; K Young, 'The Minimum Core of Economic and Social Rights: A Concept in Search of Content' (2008) 33 *Yale Journal of International Law* 113.

[36] *Vienna Declaration and Programme of Action*, A/CONF.157/23 (1993), [5]. A core goal of the HRC's Universal Periodic Review Mechanism is to '[p]romote the universality, interdependence, indivisibility and interrelatedness of all human rights': HRC, *Report of the Human Rights Council: Report of the Third Committee*, A/62/434 (2011), [3]. The interdependence and indivisibility of human rights is most clearly illustrated in the CRC, which 'entrenches the human rights of children from both categories of so-called "civil and political" and "economic, social and cultural rights" in a way that does not segregate them, nor, indeed, even indicate whether a given right falls into one category or the other': C Scott and P Alston, 'Adjudicating Constitutional Priorities in a Transnational Context: A Comment on Soobramoney's Legacy and Grootboom's Promise' (2000) 16 *South African Journal on Human Rights* 206, 227. See also HRC, *GC5*, [6].

[37] See Hathaway and Foster (2014) *supra* n 10, 204– 7.

[38] *Ibid.*

[39] *Svazas v SSHD* [2002] 1 WLR 1891, [39].

full range of rights enshrined in International Bill of Rights, let alone the specialist treaties.[40] Martin's argument is principally a pragmatic one, driven by the concern that refugee protection remains a 'scarce resource' and the continued viability of the regime relies on legal doctrine that recognises the political constraints of refugee protection.[41] Quite apart from the problems associated with '[i]nterpreting the Convention in light of desired policy outcomes',[42] arguments based on over-inclusivity often fail to take into account the in-built circumscriptions of the human rights framework and the *Convention*, and the fact that the human rights framework is being engaged as an interpretative tool to guide decision-makers in ascertaining the meaning of 'being persecuted', rather than a dispositive straightjacket that mandates a particular outcome.

The first limitation is inherent in the structure of international human rights law. The vast majority of international human rights are not absolute, but are subject to restrictions that may reduce their scope or application.[43] A number of human rights are expressly defined to be subject to limitations that limit the scope of the right. For instance, arts 12(1)–(2) of the *ICCPR* may be limited as is 'necessary to protect national security, public order (*ordre public*), public health or morals or the rights and freedoms of others'.[44] Articles 21 and 22 of the *ICCPR* permit restrictions 'which are necessary in a democratic society'.[45] The *ICESCR* contains a general limitation clause that allows for limitations 'only in so far as this may be compatible with the nature of these rights and solely for the purpose of promoting the general welfare in a democratic society'.[46] International human rights may also be subject to derogation clauses which may allow a state to suspend its human rights obligations in certain (generally tightly circumscribed) circumstances, for example '[i]n time of public emergency which threatens the life of the nation'.[47] The adoption of an approach that embraces international human rights law on its own terms necessarily imports each of these limitations and derogation provisions, thereby limiting the range of harms that can appropriately be characterised as persecutory.[48] As Hathaway and Foster note, '[d]rawing on these express limitations and authorized forms of flexibility, international human rights law positions refugee decision-makers to take a non-absolutist yet principled approach to the identification of serious harm'.[49]

The second limitation is the *Convention*'s nexus criterion. As Jastram explains, 'it is well established that not all violations of civil and political rights, much less of economic, social and cultural rights, will merit recognition as a refugee'.[50] In addition to a risk of being persecuted, an applicant must demonstrate that the risk accrues '*for reasons of* race, religion, nationality, membership of a particular social group or political opinion'. The additional requirement, essentially one of social disenfranchisement, undermines Martin's argument that the refugee definition ought to be narrowly interpreted to encourage individuals to stay in their country of origin and fight for better human rights protection.[51] The *Convention*

---

[40] Martin (1993) *supra* n 9, 350. See also M Fullerton, 'The Law of Refugee Status by James C. Hathaway and Michelle Foster' (2015) 109(4) *American Journal of International Law* 908, 915–17.

[41] Martin (1991) *supra* n 9, 64.   [42] Jastram (2010) *supra* n 33, 162.

[43] See, generally, F Mégret, 'Nature of Obligations' in D Moeckli, S Shah and S Sivakumaran, *International Human Rights Law* (2nd edn, 2014) 96, 110–14.

[44] *ICCPR*, art 12(3). See also arts 18(3), 19(3); *UDHR*, art 29; *CRC*, arts 13(2), 14(2).

[45] *ICCPR*, arts 21, 22(2). See also *CRC*, art 15(2).   [46] *ICESCR*, art 4.   [47] *ICCPR*, art 4.

[48] See, e.g., *Applicant NABD of 2002 v MIMIA* (2005) 216 ALR 1, [113] (Kirby J).

[49] Hathaway and Foster (2014) *supra* n 10, 205.   [50] Jastram (2010) *supra* n 33, 160.

[51] Martin (1991) *supra* n 9, 64.

definition makes clear that the refugee protection regime is, by operation of the nexus clause, limited to persons who are unable 'to work within or even to restructure the national community of which they are nominally a part'.[52]

Notwithstanding these limitations, there will be cases where there is a risk of a violation of an international human rights standard but where the putative harm is so far at the outer-margins of the right that it would not be appropriate for a decision-maker to treat that harm as falling within the concept of 'being persecuted'. In other words, there may be cases where there will be imperfect alignment between international human rights norms and the 'being persecuted' standard. Hathaway and Foster have argued that in such cases there must be a 'clear and convincing basis' to find that the 'risk of denial of a broadly subscribed international human right is truly *de minimis* in the circumstances of a particular case, recalling ... that a risk of being persecuted may be founded on an agglomeration of harms that, taken individually, might not rise to the level of persecution'.[53] Although the recognition of such an exception does introduce a risk of subjectivity and arbitrariness – which the human rights framework was introduced to guard against – the assessment as to whether the rights violation is truly *de minimis* for the purposes of the 'being persecuted' standard must still be undertaken within the framework of the authoritative human rights standards. Hence, it will not be sufficient for a decision-maker to simply state that a putative harm falls on the outer-margins of a right, but the burden rests on a decision-maker to positively engage with the right in question and justify why that is the case.[54]

4.1.3 The Role of State Protection

The availability of state protection in the applicant's country of origin has long been accepted as a central component of the *Convention* definition.[55] This is again premised on the idea that international refugee law was 'formulated to serve as a back-up to the protection one expects from the state'[56] and 'to enable the person who no longer has the benefit of protection against persecution for a Convention reason in his own country to turn for protection to the international community'.[57] The idea that refugee law was intended as a 'forum of second resort'[58] is reflected in Hathaway's formulation of 'being persecuted' as the 'the sustained or systemic violation of basic human rights *demonstrative of a failure of state protection*'.[59]

---

[52] Hathaway, *The Law of Refugee Status* (1991) *supra* n 4, 135.

[53] Hathaway and Foster (2014) *supra* n 10, 206.   [54] *Ibid.*

[55] 'It is the absence of state protection which constitutes the full and complete negation of society and the basis of refugeehood': A Shacknove, 'Who Is a Refugee' (1985) 95 *Ethics* 274, 277.

[56] 'At the outset, it is useful to explore the rationale underlying the international refugee protection regime, for this permeates the interpretation of the various terms requiring examination. International refugee law was formulated to serve as a back-up to the protection one expects from the state of which an individual is a national. It was meant to come into play only in situations when that protection is unavailable, and then only in certain situations': *Canada (Attorney General) v Ward* [1993] 2 SCR 689, 709.

[57] *Horvath v SSHD* [2001] 1 AC 489, 495.

[58] *Canada (Attorney General) v Ward* [1993] 2 SCR 689, 716.

[59] Hathaway, *The Law of Refugee Status* (1991) *supra* n 4, 104–5 (emphasis added). Similarly, at 112, Hathaway states that 'persecution is most appropriately defined as the sustained or systemic failure of state protection in relation to one of the core entitlements which has been recognized by the international community'.

The formulation of 'being persecuted' advanced by Hathaway is often described as a 'bifurcated model', requiring an applicant to demonstrate both an underlying risk of serious harm and a failure of the state to protect against that harm. The UK House of Lords made clear its view that 'being persecuted' is a construct of two separate elements endorsing the following, now oft-cited equation: 'persecution = serious harm + failure of state protection'.[60] This bifurcated understanding of 'being persecuted' has been critical to the development of jurisprudence responsive to risks emanating from non-state actors:[61]

> in the context of an allegation of persecution by non-state agents, the word 'persecution' implies a failure by the state to make protection available against the ill-treatment or violence which the person suffers at the hands of the persecutors. In a case where the allegation is of persecution by the state or its own agents the problem does not, of course, arise. There is a clear case for the surrogate protection by the international community. But in the case of an allegation of persecution by non-state agents, the failure to provide the protection is nevertheless an essential element. It provides the bridge between persecution by the state and persecution by non-state agents which is necessary in the interest of the consistency of the whole scheme.

The understanding of 'being persecuted' as incorporating two constitutive elements has been central to the recognition that for the purposes of satisfying the 'for reasons of' clause of art 1A(2), the causal link can be provided *either* by the non-state actor that perpetrates the harm *or* the state that fails to protect the applicant.[62]

But while it is generally accepted that the 'being persecuted' standard incorporates a consideration of the availability of state protection,[63] it is less than clear what 'protection' actually means. That is, what is the relevant *level* or *standard* of protection that a state owes to its citizens? This question has proven particularly critical in cases involving private actors where the state has not instigated, tolerated or otherwise sponsored the persecutory acts but is unable to prevent the acts occurring. There are conflicting views as to the standard of protection required in these circumstances which, broadly speaking, reflect two distinct conceptual approaches.[64] The first, often referred to as the 'protection theory', draws on international human rights law to define the scope of a state's duty to protect. The second

---

[60] *R v Immigration Appeal Tribunal; Ex parte Shah* [1999] 2 AC 629, 653. This equation, initially derived from the Refugee Women's Legal Group, *Gender Guidelines for the Determination of Asylum Claims in the UK* (1998), has since been widely endorsed. See, e.g., *Horvath v SSHD* [2001] 1 AC 489, 515–16 (Lord Clyde); *MIMA v Khawar* (2002) 210 CLR 1, [118] (Kirby J); *Refugee Appeal No 71427/99* (RSAA, 16 August 2000), [12].

[61] *Horvath v SSHD* [2001] 1 AC 489, 497–8.

[62] 'The necessary discriminatory element may be supplied either by the non-State agents who perpetrate the maltreatment or it may be supplied by the state which fails to protect the victims': *Horvath v SSHD* [2000] INLR 15, 56. See also *Horvath v SSHD* [2001] 1 AC 489, 497–8; *R v Immigration Appeal Tribunal; Ex parte Shah* [1999] 2 AC 629, 653–4; *MIMA v Khawar* (2002) 210 CLR 1, [119]–[121]; *Refugee Appeal No 71427/99* (RSAA, 16 August 2000), [112]. See generally J C Hathaway and M Foster, 'The Causal Connection ("Nexus" to a Convention Ground)' (2003) *International Journal of Refugee Law* 462, 464–5.

[63] This is not universally accepted, with some decision-makers preferring to situate consideration of state protection within different parts of art 1A(2). See, e.g., dissenting judgment of Lord Lloyd in *Horvath v SSHD* [2001] 1 AC 489. See generally P Mathew, J C Hathaway and M Foster, 'The Role of State Protection in Refugee Analysis' (2003) 15 *International Journal of Refugee Law* 444.

[64] A third approach, often referred to as the 'accountability theory', is not considered here on the basis that it has been widely discredited: see *Adan v SSHD* [1999] 1 AC 293; *MIMA v Respondents S152/ 2003* (2004) 222 CLR 1.

approach, defined here as the 'alleviation of risk theory', focuses on whether a state is able to offer a level of protection that will reduce the underlying risk of harm to the point where it can no longer be said to be well-founded. The two approaches are addressed in turn below.

The protection theory proceeds from the idea that international refugee law was conceived to provide surrogate or substitute protection in circumstances where such protection is lacking in the applicant's country of origin. As outlined above, it is widely accepted that international human rights law provides the appropriate standard against which to assess whether a country has failed in its duty to protect its citizens. Hathaway is a leading proponent of the theory:[65]

> Because international human rights law is conceived as the means of defining the basic duties of states to their citizens, including both freedoms from interference and entitlements to resources, individuals ought not to be required to endure life in societies which fail to meet its standards ... Thus, the state which ignores or is unable to respond to legitimate expectations as defined in international human rights law fails to comply with its most basic duty, thereby giving rise to the prospect of legitimate disengagement from that community in favour of surrogate protection elsewhere.

Anker has similarly noted that 'protection is not provided against all breaches of rights, but only those violations that states have a duty to prevent'.[66] Goodwin-Gill and McAdam have also emphasised the link between international human rights law and the concept of state protection, observing that '[t]he notion of lack of protection ... invites attention to the general issue of a State's duty to protect and promote human rights'.[67]

Senior courts in the United Kingdom, Canada and Australia have endorsed the protection theory, including the invocation of international human rights standards to assess the scope of a state's protection obligations.[68] In *MIMA v Respondents S152/2003*, the majority of the High Court of Australia defined a 'failure of state protection' as 'a failure to meet the standards of protection required by international standards'.[69] In a separate concurring opinion, Kirby J justified such endorsement in the following terms:[70]

> The ultimate purpose of the Convention is to shift a very important obligation of external protection from the country of nationality to the international community. On the face of things, this may suggest that there is some good reason for doing so – either the active participation or collusion of that country, its agencies and officials in the

---

[65] J C Hathaway, 'Reconceiving Refugee Law as Human Rights Protection' (1991) 4 *Journal of Refugee Studies* 113, 122–3.

[66] Anker (2015) *supra* n 8, 239–40. See also D Anker, 'Refugee Status and Violence against Women in the "Domestic" Sphere: The Non-State Actor Question' (2001) 15 *Georgetown Immigration Law Journal* 391, 400.

[67] G S Goodwin-Gill and J McAdam, *The Refugee in International Law* (3rd edn, 2007) 133.

[68] See, e.g., *Canada (Attorney General) v Ward* [1993] 2 SCR 689, 709; *Horvath v SSHD* [2001] 1 AC 489, 495 (Lord Hope); *MIMA v Respondents S152/2003* (2004) 222 CLR 1, [20], [27] (Gleeson CJ, Hayne and Heydon JJ), [110]–[111] (Kirby J).

[69] *MIMA v Respondents S152/2003* (2004) 222 CLR 1, [27].

[70] *Ibid.*, [110]. See also the majority decision of Gleeson CJ, Hayne and Heydon JJ at [20] ('The wider context is that of an instrument which provides an important, but defined and limited, form of international responsibility towards a person whose fundamental human rights and freedoms have been violated in a certain respect in the person's country of nationality. Because it is the primary responsibility of the country of nationality to safeguard those rights and freedoms, the international responsibility has been described a form of "surrogate protection"').

persecutory acts, or the failure of that country to afford protection where ordinarily, by international standards, that could be expected.

In a similar vein, Lord Hope in *Horvath v SSHD* ('*Horvath (House of Lords)*') apprised that, '[i]f the principle of surrogacy is applied, the criterion must be whether the alleged lack of protection is such as to indicate that the home state is unable or unwilling to discharge its duty to establish and operate a system for the protection against persecution of its own nationals'.[71]

The protection theory represents a fundamental aspect of the human rights framework for understanding 'being persecuted'. In international human rights law a violation of a human right can by definition only occur where a state has failed in its duty to protect an individual.[72] A consideration of the availability of state protection is thus an integral – indeed, essential – element in the assessment of whether there has been a violation of a human right.[73] It follows, then, that – although the bifurcated approach provides a convenient means to underline the need to consider both the underlying harm and the state's involvement in or response to that harm[74] – at a strictly conceptual level the protection theory suggests that the 'being persecuted' standard comprises a *single* question:[75] is the applicant at risk of a violation of a broadly accepted human right? If the answer is 'yes', it will generally follow that there is a failure of state protection and the applicant will satisfy the 'being persecuted' criterion. That is, the failure of state protection is not an independent requirement, but, rather, an integrated feature of the human rights understanding of 'being persecuted', with recourse to international human rights standards necessarily importing a consideration of state protection. To return to the initial formulation conceived by Hathaway, the failure of state protection is '*demonstrated through* the denial of core, international recognized rights'.[76]

Linking the standard of protection to international human rights standards does not detract from the well-established principle that the *Convention* protects against risks of harm deriving from non-state actors.[77] International human rights law recognises that states are under a duty to protect individuals from infringements of their human rights by non-state actors.[78] This obligation derives from the obligation on states not simply to

---

[71] *Horvath v SSHD* [2001] 1 AC 489, 495. Lord Clyde similarly noted that '[w]hat [the *Convention*] seeks to achieve is the preservation of those rights and freedoms for individuals where they are denied them in their own state': at 508–9.

[72] J Tobin, 'Assessing GLBTI Refugee Claims: Using Human Rights Law to Shift the Narrative of Persecution within Refugee Law' (2012) 44 *New York University Journal of International Law and Politics* 447, 452.

[73] *Ibid.*, 452.

[74] *MIMA v Khawar* (2002) 210 CLR 1, [119] (Kirby J) ('When this concise formula is kept in mind it becomes easier to approach with legal accuracy the "nexus issue" presented by the Convention definition's requirement that the persecution be (relevantly) "for reasons of . . . membership of a particular social group"').

[75] Tobin, 'Assessing GLBTI Refugee Claims' (2012) *supra* n 72, 452.

[76] Hathaway, 'Reconceiving Refugee Law' (1991) *supra* n 65, 122 (emphasis added).

[77] D Anker, 'Boundaries in the Field of Human Rights: Refugee Law, Gender and the Human Rights Paradigm' (2002) 15 *Harvard Human Rights Journal* 133, 146–9.

[78] 'The role of the state in responding to human rights violations committed by non-state actors has been described as 'one of the most dramatic developments within international human rights law over the past two decades': P Alston and R Goodman, *International Human Rights in Context: Law Politics Morals* (4th edn, 2013) 1461. For an excellent discussion of these developments, see A Reinisch, 'The Changing International Legal Framework for Dealing with Non-State Actors' in P Alston (ed), *Non-State Actors*

'respect' human rights but also to take positive steps to 'ensure',[79] 'guarantee'[80] and 'secure'[81] them.[82] The HRC has thus stressed that[83]

> the positive obligations on States parties to ensure [ICCPR] rights will only be fully discharged if individuals are protected by the State, not just against violations of Covenant rights by its agents, but also against acts committed by private persons or entities that would impair the enjoyment of Covenant rights insofar as they are amenable to application between private persons or entities.

The UNCESCR has similarly emphasised the need to protect individuals from infringements by non-state actors, including in the context of gender equality,[84] the right to food and water,[85] the right to health[86] and the right to work.[87] The UNCEDAW has also been particularly instrumental in making clear that states have positive duties to protect individuals from harm committed by non-state actors.[88] Finally, as will be examined in detail in Section 4.3, the CRC is particularly explicit in setting out a state's duty to protect against the infringement of human rights by non-state actors.[89]

The obligations[90] set out in each of the human rights treaties and elaborated on by the supervising treaty bodies provide refugee decision-makers with an external, continuously evolving benchmark to assess the scope of a state's duty to protect against threats by non-state actors. Critically, there is no single standard for assessing the scope of a state's duty, and it will therefore be necessary to examine the specific human rights treaties and obligations that have been engaged.[91]

---

and Human Rights (2005) 37, 78–82. See also R McCorquodale (ed), International Law Beyond the State: Essays on Sovereignty, Non-State Actors and Human Rights (2011); R McCorquodale, 'Non-State Actors and International Human Rights Law' in S Joseph and A McBeth (eds), International Human Rights Law (2009) 97; A Clapham, Human Rights Obligations of Non-State Actors (2006) 317–46; P Alston (ed), Non-State Actors and Human Rights (2005) 3; A Clapham, Human Rights in the Private Sphere (1993).

[79] ICCPR, art 2(1); CRC, art 2(1).   [80] ICESCR, art 2(2).   [81] ECHR, art 1.

[82] Reinisch (2005) supra n 78, 79.

[83] HRC, GC31, [8]. The HRC has also suggested that, in addition to the general obligation enshrined in art 2, a number of substantive provisions also contain additional positive obligations (at [8]): 'The Covenant itself envisages in some articles certain areas where there are positive obligations on States Parties to address the activities of private persons or entities. For example, the privacy-related guarantees of article 17 must be protected by law. It is also implicit in article 7 that States Parties have to take positive measures to ensure that private persons or entities do not inflict torture or cruel, inhuman or degrading treatment or punishment on others within their power. In fields affecting basic aspects of ordinary life such as work or housing, individuals are to be protected from discrimination within the meaning of article 26.'

[84] UNCESCR, GC16.   [85] UNCESCR, GC12; UNCESCR, GC15.   [86] UNCESCR, GC14.

[87] UNCESCR, GC18.

[88] UNCEDAW, General Recommendation No 19: Violence against Women, HRI/GEN/1/Rev.8 (1992). See generally Clapham (2006) supra n 78, 333–4.

[89] See infra Section 4.3.1. See especially CRC, arts 3, 19, 20, 24(3), 39, and UNCRC, GC5.

[90] Variously characterised as 'responsibilities for "omissions", "positive obligations", "duties to protect" and "duties of due diligence"': Clapham (2006) supra n 78, 318. Clapham notes the need to 'examine specific human rights to gauge the extent of the obligation to protect the beneficiaries of the treaty from non-state actors': ibid.

[91] It would thus be inappropriate to resolve the question of state protection exclusively by reference to the ILC's Articles on Responsibility of States for Internationally Wrongful Acts reproduced in Report of the International Law Commission – Fifty-Third Session, A/56/10 (2001), [76]. Indeed, as Clapham notes, art 55 of the Articles expressly highlights that human rights treaties may diverge from the rules set out in the Articles: Clapham (2006) supra n 78, 317. See also Goodwin-Gill and McAdam (2007) supra n 67, 99–100.

In recent years, a number of scholars and decision-makers have expressed concern that the protection theory is insufficiently inclusive, and may result in an applicant being returned in circumstances where there is a genuine risk of violence or some other form of serious harm from a non-state actor.[92] This concern may, at least in part, be attributed to discomfort with decisions that have misapplied the protection theory and set a standard of protection unmoored to developments in international human rights law. For instance, the 'due diligence' standard explicated in *Horvath (House of Lords)* is often referred to as an example of the shortfalls of the 'protection theory'; however, it is by no means clear that the standard applied in *Horvath (House of Lords)* is consistent with international human rights norms.[93] Indeed, the England and Wales Court of Appeal has since distanced itself from the standard set by the House of Lords, while still embracing the protection theory.[94] But putting that to one side, it remains true that there may conceivably be instances where a state has satisfied its international human rights obligations, but there is nonetheless a real chance that an applicant will be harmed if returned.

A second conceptual approach has been developed to deal with the potential under-inclusivity of the protection theory. The 'alleviation of risk theory' focuses on whether the protection afforded by the state alleviates the risk of harm such that the applicant's fear is no longer well-founded. This theory was advanced by the Refugee Legal Centre in *Horvath (House of Lords)*,[95] but was explicitly rejected by the House of Lords.[96] It was subsequently adopted by the New Zealand RSAA, which considered that, '[i]f the net result of a state's "reasonable willingness" to operate a system for the protection of the citizen is that it is incapable of preventing a real chance of persecution of a particular individual, refugee status cannot be denied that individual'.[97] The alleviation of risk theory was also endorsed (and the protection theory expressly rejected) in the separate, concurring opinion of McHugh J in *MIMA v Respondents S152/2003*.[98]

The alleviation of risk theory appears to provide more a liberal standard against which to assess the availability of state protection, which may, in turn, expand the scope of protection afforded to applicants in cases involving risks emanating from non-state actors. It is necessary, however, to acknowledge the broader implications of this approach, and in particular the extent to which it can be reconciled with the human rights framework for understanding 'being persecuted'.

Most significantly, the alleviation of risk theory removes the assessment of state protection from the 'being persecuted' limb of art 1A(2). As recognised by Kirby J in *MIMA v Respondents S152/2003*, '[t]he new theory of "persecution" would confine the consideration of responses, if any, of State agencies and officials to the question whether the "fear" is

---

[92] *Kovac v SSHD* (IAT, 15 February 2000), cited in *Horvath v SSHD* [2001] 1 AC 489, 516. See further P Mathew, J C Hathaway and M Foster, 'The Role of State Protection in Refugee Analysis' (2003) 15 *International Journal of Refugee Law*, 448–53; Hathaway and Foster (2014) *supra* n 10, 308–13; *MIMA v Respondents S152/2003* (2004) 222 CLR 1, [59]–[65] (McHugh J); *Refugee Appeal No 71427/99* (RSAA, 16 August 2000), [62]–[67].

[93] See, e.g., H Lambert, 'The Conceptualisation of "Persecution" by the House of Lords: *Horvath v SSHD*' (2001) 13 *International Journal of Refugee Law* 16, 26–9, citing *Osman v UK* (2000) 29 EHRR 245.

[94] See, e.g., *Noune v SSHD* [2000] EWCA Civ 306; *Atkinson v SSHD* [2004] EWCA Civ 846; *DK v SSHD* [2006] EWCA Civ 682.

[95] *Horvath v SSHD* [2001] 1 AC 489, 493.   [96] *Ibid.*, 516.

[97] *Refugee Appeal No 71427/99* (RSAA, 16 August 2000), [63]

[98] *MIMA v Respondents S152/2003* (2004) 222 CLR 1, [59]–[65] (McHugh J). For academic support see, e.g., Hathaway and Foster (2014) *supra* n 10, 314–19.

"well-founded". The consideration would not be relevant to whether the impugned conduct was "persecution".[99] Although it has been suggested that the alleviation of risk theory is reconcilable with the bifurcated understanding of 'being persecuted',[100] it is difficult to conceive how this can be correct given that the decision-maker is confined to considering whether or not there is a real chance of serious harm. Indeed, in adopting this theory McHugh J made clear his view that his approach excised the assessment of state protection from the 'being persecuted' inquiry.[101]

A wholesale adoption of the alleviation of risk theory therefore requires a reconceptualisation of the alignment between international human rights law and the definition of 'being persecuted'. If the availability of state protection no longer constitutes an element of the 'being persecuted' standard, it would be inaccurate, at least from the perspective of a human rights jurist, to speak of 'being persecuted' as comprising a violation of a human right.[102] As noted above, in international human rights law a violation of a human right can only occur where a state has failed in its duty to protect an individual. This is not to say that human rights norms will not still be relevant to the assessment of persecutory harm;[103] the point is simply that the alleviation of risk theory envisages the grant of protection in circumstances where there has been no violation of a human right. In other words, the alleviation of risk theory requires a contracting state to step in and provide surrogate protection in circumstances where the applicant's country of origin has satisfied, at least as adjudged by international human rights standards, its human rights obligations. This entails a departure from the *Convention*'s underlying rationale to provide 'an important, but defined and limited, form of international responsibility towards a person whose fundamental human rights and freedoms have been violated in a certain respect in the person's country of nationality'.[104]

The protection theory and alleviation of risk theory raise a number of fundamental questions that go to the heart of the international refugee protection regime. Does the *Convention* permit the return of an applicant to a country of origin where there is a real chance that she will be subject to serious harm at the hands of non-state actors (as the protection theory may require)? Or can the *Convention* be interpreted so as to require contracting states to provide surrogate protection in circumstances where the applicant's country of origin guarantees a standard of protection that satisfies international human rights standards (as the alleviation of risk theory appears to entail)? A full examination of both questions is beyond the more focused remit of this book, but they are identified here to illustrate that there are legitimate concerns with the protection theory. It may be that over time those concerns will fall away, particularly if the development of international human rights law continues on its current trajectory towards ensuring *effective* protection against

---

[99] *MIMA v Respondents S152/2003* (2004) 222 CLR 1, [106]; see also at [107].

[100] See, e.g., *Refugee Appeal No 71427/99* (RSAA, 16 August 2000).

[101] 'In neither its ordinary nor its Convention meaning does the term "persecution" require proof that the State has breached a duty that is owed to the applicant for refugee status': *MIMA v Respondents S152/ 2003* (2004) 222 CLR 1, [65].

[102] See Tobin, 'Assessing GLBTI Refugee Claims' (2012) *supra* n 72, 452 ('[I]t makes no sense to speak of a human rights violation *and* a failure of state protection').

[103] Tobin suggests that, in this context, it may be more accurate to speak of an 'interference' with a human right: Tobin, 'Assessing GLBTI Refugee Claims' (2012) *supra* n 72, 453.

[104] *MIMA v Respondents S152/2003* (2004) 222 CLR 1, [20] (Gleeson CJ, Hayne and Heydon JJ).

threats emanating from non-state actors.[105] Indeed, as demonstrated below, that trajectory is most clearly reflected in the *CRC* and its associated jurisprudence.[106]

In light of the widespread acceptance of the protection theory, and the capacity, as illustrated below, of the *CRC* to provide robust protection against threats emanating from non-state actors, the discussion that follows adopts the protection theory to assess the applicable standard of protection owed by a state to its citizens. Section 4.2 and 4.3 of the chapter examine the application of the protection theory to children and, in doing so, offer a contextually grounded account of the relationship between international human rights standards and the availability of state protection.

This section has outlined a conceptual framework for understanding the definition of 'being persecuted'. It has suggested that the 'being persecuted' standard will be satisfied where there is a risk of a violation of a human right that is protected under an international human rights law treaty that enjoys the general support of the international community. This requires an assessment of the scope of the right or rights that have been engaged, including, invariably, a consideration of the scope of a state's duty of protection. The remainder of the chapter examines the application of this human rights framework to claims involving children.

4.2 The Definition of 'Being Persecuted' in Claims Involving Children

Domestic jurisprudence on the definition of 'being persecuted' has largely developed in the context of claims brought by adults. It has only been in recent years that decision-makers have made efforts to engage with the concept from the perspective of the child. Although decision-makers are increasingly acknowledging the need to assess the 'being persecuted' standard in view of the applicant's age,[107] there has been a general reluctance to assess the standard by reference to international human rights law. This reluctance is surprising given the availability of an instrument that provides a comprehensive and state-generated framework identifying the distinct rights and protection needs of children. As the Federal Court of Canada has recently noted, the *CRC* 'adds nuances' to the understanding of being persecuted 'based on an appreciation that children have distinct rights, are in need of special protection, and can be persecuted in ways that would not amount to persecution of an adult'.[108]

This section begins by identifying the various ways in which persecutory harm can manifest itself in the context of children. The discussion evinces a range of scenarios where a child may be at risk of being persecuted notwithstanding the fact that a comparably placed adult would not be. The remainder of the section draws on the core precepts of the human rights framework to develop an argument for greater interaction between the 'being persecuted' definition and the rights enshrined in the *CRC*.

4.2.1 The Persecution of Children

The discussion that follows draws on existing refugee jurisprudence to identify the particular ways that children can suffer persecution. At the outset, it is important to acknowledge

---

[105] See *supra* text accompanying n 77–91.   [106] See, e.g., *infra* Section 4.3.1.
[107] '[A]ge can be a critical factor in the adjudication of asylum claims and may bear heavily on the question of whether an applicant was persecuted': *Liu v Ashcroft*, 380 F 3d 307, 314 (7th Cir, 2004).
[108] *Kim v Canada (MCI)* [2011] 2 FCR 448, [61].

that in a significant proportion of cases children will be threatened with a form of harm that is similar or identical to that faced by adults.[109] A child may, for instance, be at risk of death,[110] torture or cruel, inhuman or degrading treatment,[111] involuntary confinement,[112] kidnapping[113] or sexual assault.[114] In these cases a failure to take into account the applicant's age in assessing the nature of the prospective harm is likely to be of limited consequence. However, in other cases a child's minority status will be critical to understanding whether or not the child apprehends a form of harm that amounts to persecution. These cases can be arranged by reference to two scenarios. First, a child may be at risk of a form of harm that can only be inflicted on children. Second, a child may apprehend a level or degree of physical or psychological harm that will not qualify as persecution in the case of an adult but which may amount to persecution when considered from the perspective of a child.

The first scenario is reasonably straightforward, capturing situations where the nature of the prospective harm is such that it can only be inflicted on children.[115] Only a child can be at risk of infanticide, underage military recruitment, forced child labour, forced underage marriage, child prostitution, child pornography, domestic child abuse, corporal punishment or pre-puberty FGC. Similarly, only a child can be denied a primary education, separated from a parent because of discriminatory custody laws or discriminated against because of her status as an illegitimate child. A failure to take into account a child's minority status in each of these scenarios may result in a decision-maker failing to identify the relevant harm or neglecting to appreciate its specific consequences in the context of childhood. For example, in a number of these situations, conduct which may not be harmful to a consenting adult will be considered exploitative in the context of a child because of the child's inability to provide informed consent.[116]

A number of commentators have suggested that the traditional adult-focused understanding of 'being persecuted' has often failed adequately to address situations of child-specific harm, in the same way that, until recently, the male-dominated understanding of 'being persecuted' hindered the recognition of gender-related claims of women.[117] Although the jurisprudence is still in its infancy, there are signs that this is beginning to change, with the case-law review evincing a greater awareness of the need to take into account the specific types of harm that may befall children.[118] This is supplemented by domestic legislation and guidelines emphasising the need to take into account child-specific

---

[109] J Bhabha and M Crock, *Seeking Asylum Alone: A Comparative Study* (2007) 158.

[110] *HS (Homosexuals: Minors, Risk on Return) Iran* [2005] UKAIT 00120.

[111] *Mashiri v Ashcroft*, 2004 US App LEXIS 22714, 17: '[The applicant's] young sons were humiliated, terrorized, and left with permanent physical scars'.

[112] *Tchoukhrova v Gonzales*, 404 F 3d 1181, 1193 (9th Cir, 2005): a disabled child confined in an *internaty* in inhumane conditions for two months against his parents' will.

[113] *Malchikov v Canada (MCI)* 120 FTR 138.

[114] *Hernandez-Montiel v Immigration and Naturalization Service*, (2000) 225 F 3d 1084, 1098 (9th Cir, 2000), appropriately recognising that '[t]here is no reason to believe that the trauma for male victims of rape is any less severe than for female victims.' But see *Calle v US Attorney General*, 264 Fed Appx 882, 884 (11th Cir, 2008); *Joaquin-Porras v Gonzales*, 435 F 3d 172, 174 (2nd Cir, 2006).

[115] See generally UNHCR, *2009 Guidelines*, [18]; UNCRC, *GC6*, [74].

[116] J Bhabha and S Schmidt, *Seeking Asylum Alone: United States* (2006) 20.

[117] J Bhabha and W Young, 'Not Adults in Miniature: Unaccompanied Child Asylum Seekers and the New US Guidelines' (1999) 11 *International Journal of Refugee Law* 84, 103.

[118] See *infra* Section 4.3.

harms. The *EU Qualification Directive*, for instance, explicitly requires decision-makers to take into account acts of a child-specific nature.[119] Similar direction is provided in national guidelines published in Australia,[120] Canada,[121] the United Kingdom[122] and the United States.[123]

This is not to suggest that applicants at risk of child-specific harms have not faced difficulty in satisfying the being persecuted criterion. By way of illustration, in the case of *Benyamin v Holder*, the Court of Appeals for the Ninth Circuit appropriately overturned a decision of an IJ who had rejected an application on the basis that the physical harm inflicted on a five-day-old infant subjected to FGC appeared to be 'minimal'.[124] In *Fornah v SSHD*, the England and Wales Court of Appeal took the view that FGC 'however repulsive to most societies outside Sierra Leone, is, on the objective evidence . . . clearly accepted and/ or regarded by the majority of the population of that country . . . as traditional and part of the cultural life of its society as a whole'.[125] In *Johnson v SSHD*,[126] the Outer House of the Scottish Court of Session suggested that a risk of FGC would only be persecutory if the *parents* of the intended victim objected.[127] In *VA1-00781* the Canadian IRB accepted that corporal punishment was not persecutory given that it was 'part of the culture of a country that is in transition and still believes in using the "rod"'.[128] And in *Canada (MCI) v Lin* the Canadian Federal Court of Appeal rejected the primary decision-maker's finding that subjecting a 17-year-old boy to servitude in the United States to pay off a trafficking debt to snakeheads and to provide support to his family amounted to persecution, on the basis that the Court could not comprehend 'why supporting one's family members amount[ed] to persecution'.[129]

The second scenario arises where the objective underlying risk is similar or identical for an adult and a child but by reason of a child's heightened sensitivity and developmental needs the child will suffer a greater degree of harm.[130] The applicable standard remains the same ('being persecuted'); however the standard will generally be more easily satisfied in claims involving children. The importance of understanding persecution as a relative concept has been emphasised on a number of occasions by UNHCR, including in its 2009 *Guidelines:*[131]

---

[119] 'Acts of persecution . . . can take the form of . . . acts of a gender-specific or child-specific nature': *EU Qualification Directive*, art 9(2). This provision has, for example, been expressly codified in domestic legislation in Norway: *Act of 15 May 2008 on the Entry of Foreign Nationals into the Kingdom of Norway and Their Stay in the Realm (Immigration Act)*, s 29.

[120] DIAC, 'Refugee Law Guidelines' (March 2010), [9.5], [9.7].   [121] IRB, *Guidelines*, 8.

[122] UKBA, *Asylum Process Guidance*, [16.5]; Home Office, *Processing Children's Asylum Claims*, 40.

[123] INS, *Guidelines*, 18–20; USCIS Asylum Division, 'Asylum Officer Basic Training Course: Guidelines for Children's Asylum Claims' (21 March 2009) 36–40.

[124] *Benyamin v Holder*, 579 F 3d 970, 975–7 (9th Cir, 2009).

[125] *Fornah v SSHD* [2005] 1 WLR 3773, 3787. The decision was overturned by the House of Lords in *Fornah v SSHD* [2007] 1 AC 412.

[126] *Johnson v SSHD* 2005 SLT 393.   [127] *Ibid.*, [17].   [128] *VA1-00781* (IRB, 22 February 2002) 7.

[129] *Canada (MCI) v Lin* [2001] FCJ No 1574, [18].

[130] Bhabha and Young (1999) *supra* n 117, 102. See also G Sadoway, 'Refugee Children before the Immigration and Refugee Board' (1996) 15(5) *Refuge* 17, 17–18.

[131] UNHCR, 2009 *Guidelines*, [15]. This builds on the recognition in UNHCR, *Handbook*, [52], that '[d]ue to variations in the psychological make-up of individuals . . . interpretations of what amounts to persecution are bound to vary'. See also UNHCR, *Guidelines on Policies and Procedures in Dealing with Unaccompanied Children Seeking Asylum* (1997), [8.7]; UNHCR, 'Brief *Amicus Curiae*' *supra* n 18, 6–9.

While children may face similar or identical forms of harm as adults, they may experi-ence them differently. Actions or threats that might not reach the threshold of persecu-tion in the case of an adult may amount to persecution in the case of a child because of the mere fact that s/he is a child. Immaturity, vulnerability, undeveloped coping mechanisms and dependency as well as the differing stages of development and hindered capacities may be directly related to how a child experiences or fears harm ... To assess accurately the severity of the acts and their impact on a child, it is necessary to examine the details of each case and to adapt the threshold for persecution to that particular child.

This age-sensitive construction of 'being persecuted' requires a decision-maker to assess the relative impact that the apprehended harm will have on a child, taking into account the child's evolving capacities and developmental needs. This includes a consideration of the longer-term physical and emotional implications of the maltreatment. The point is illustrated by Senior Immigration Judge Jarvis of the UK Upper Tribunal:[132]

[C]hildren are more egregiously affected by death and injury than adults. A child loses a greater part of his or her life, a greater part of his or her good health and ability to develop to full potential and enjoy all the rights and freedoms to which a child is entitled, for example those rights from the CRC ... simply by reason of the fact that he or she is a child. A forty four year old man who steps on a landmine and loses a leg has to a considerable degree lived a life already ... whereas a child, born in Afghanistan ... is less likely to survive such an attack, or if he or she survives, to recover from it.

This age-sensitive approach has been particularly influential in US jurisprudence.[133] In 1998 the Department of Justice published guidelines which provide that '[t]he harm a child fears or has suffered ... may be relatively less than that of an adult and still qualify as persecution'.[134] More recently, this has been elaborated on in the USCIS's Asylum Officer training manual, which explains that such an approach is necessary 'because children, dependent on others for their care, are prone to be more severely and potentially perma-nently affected by trauma than adults, particularly when their caretaker is harmed'.[135] The First,[136] Second,[137] Sixth,[138] Seventh[139] and Ninth[140] Circuit Court of Appeals and the BIA[141] have since adopted this age-sensitive construction of being persecuted,

---

[132] *FM (Afghanistan) v SSHD* (Upper Tribunal, AA/01079/2010, 10 March 2011), [132].

[133] For an excellent discussion on the jurisprudence, see Center for Gender and Refugee Studies *et al.*, 'Brief of *Amici Curiae* in support of Petitioner's Petition for Rehearing or Rehearing *En Banc*', filed in *Mejilla-Romero* (21 June 2010) (copy on file with author) 12–15.

[134] INS, *Guidelines*, 19.

[135] USCIS Asylum Division, *Children's Claim Guidelines* (2009) *supra* n 123, 37.

[136] *Civil v INS*, 140 F 3d 52, 62 (Judge Bownes, dissenting) (1st Cir, 1998); *Mejilla-Romero v Holder*, 600 F 3d 63, 83–4 (1st Cir, 2010) (Judge Stahl, dissenting); *Mejilla-Romero v Holder*, 614 F 3d 572, 573 (1st Cir, 2010); *Ordonez-Quino v Holder*, 760 F 3d 80, 91 (1st Cir, 2014).

[137] *Jorge-Tzoc v Gonzales*, 435 F 3d 146, 150 (2nd Cir, 2006); *Poplavskiy v Mukasey*, 271 Fed Appx 130, 133 (2nd Cir, 2008).

[138] *Nabhani v Holder*, 382 Fed Appx 487, 492 (6th Cir, 2010).

[139] *Liu v Ashcroft*, 380 F 3d 307, 314 (7th Cir, 2004); *Kholyavskiy v Mukassey*, 540 F 3d 555, 571 (7th Cir, 2008).

[140] *Mansour v Ashcroft*, 390 F 3d 667, 680–2 (7th Cir, 2004) (Judge Pregerson, dissenting); *Hernandez-Ortiz v Gonzales*, 496 F 3d 1042, 1045–6 (9th Cir, 2007); *Winata v Holder*, 2011 US App LEXIS 16962, [3]–[7] (9th Cir, 2011); *Mendoza-Pablo v Holder*, 667 F 3d 1308 (9th Cir, 2012).

[141] *Timnit Daniel* (BIA, 2002).

acknowledging that '[t]here may be situations where children should be considered victims of persecution though they have suffered less harm than would be required for an adult'.[142] Although less developed, domestic guidelines and case-law in other common law jurisdictions have similarly acknowledged the fact that children may experience harm differently from adults.[143] In the European context, the *EU Qualification Directive* expressly requires a decision-maker to take into account 'the individual position and personal circumstances of the applicant, including factors such as background, gender and *age*, so as to assess whether . . . the acts to which the applicant has been or could be exposed would amount to persecution'.[144]

Although equally applicable to physical harm,[145] the age-sensitive approach has played a particularly significant role in claims involving psychological harm.[146] As Judge Stahl recognised in *Mejilla-Romero v Holder*, 'behaviors that an adult may not typically associate with persecution or serious harm may produce lasting damage or psychological trauma in a child and thus constitute persecution'.[147] A child is, for instance, likely to be more sensitive to injuries that are inflicted on other family members. As UNHCR has observed, 'a child who has witnessed violence against, or experienced the disappearance or killing of a parent or other person on whom the child depends, may have a well-founded fear of persecution even if the act was not targeted directly against him/her'.[148] In *Kahssai v INS* the Ninth Circuit Court of Appeals recognised that 'when a young girl loses her father, mother and brother – sees her family effectively destroyed – she plainly suffers severe emotional and developmental injury'.[149] The Court considered that to return the applicant in these circumstances 'might only compound that injury'.[150] In *Hernandez-Ortiz v Gonzales* the same Court suggested that '[it] is surely a matter of common sense [that] a child's reaction to injuries to his family is different from an

---

[142] *Liu v Ashcroft*, 380 F 3d 307, 314 (7th Cir, 2004).

[143] See, e.g., *1106185* [2011] RRTA 844, [92]–[93] ('an analysis of potential harm in the case of a child must take into account the particular vulnerabilities of children, and that a threat of harm which might not constitute persecution in the case of an adult might take on this character when inflicted on a child'); *1304507* [2013] RRTA 342, [11]–[16]; *1211431* [2012] RRTA 975, [112]–[113]; *FM (Afghanistan) v SSHD* (Upper Tribunal, AA/01079/2010, 10 March 2011), [132]; UKBA, *Asylum Process Guidance*, [16.5.3]; Home Office, *Processing Children's Asylum Claims*, 40. See further Foster (2007) *supra* n 19, 208–10.

[144] *EU Qualification Directive*, art 4(3)(c) (emphasis added).

[145] In the context of physical harm, the level of maltreatment required to meet the persecutory threshold will be lower in the case of a child than in the context of an adult. So, for example, '[a]ggressive police questioning, handcuffing, slapping or rough handling that may not constitute "serious harm" for an adult . . . may produce lasting damage, physical or psychological trauma in a child that amounts to persecution': Bhabha and Young (1999) *supra* n 117, 104. See, e.g., *Tchoukhrova v Gonzales*, 404 F 3d 1181, 1193 (9th Cir, 2005), where the Court of Appeals for the Ninth Circuit considered that the fact that the applicant was of 'tender years' when detained in an *internaty* and subjected to harsh conditions 'strengthen[ed] his claim': 'The time he spent suffering, without any stimulus or love, were two developmentally crucial months of his life'. Contra *Shanmuganathan v Canada (MCI)* 2000 FTR LEXIS 1699, where the Canadian Federal Court upheld a decision of the IRB that the two-day detention and rough interrogation of a nine-year-old child was not persecutory.

[146] 'Children are more likely to be distressed by hostile situations, to believe improbable threats, or to be emotionally affected by unfamiliar circumstances': UNHCR, 2009 *Guidelines*, [16].

[147] *Mejilla-Romero v Holder*, 600 F 3d 63, 68 (1st Cir, 2010) (Judge Stahl, dissenting).

[148] UNHCR, 2009 *Guidelines*, [17].   [149] *Kahssai v INS* 16 F 3d 323, 329 (9th Cir, 1994).   [150] *Ibid.*

adult's. The child is part of the family, the wound to the family is personal, the trauma apt to be lasting'.[151]

A critical factor in assessing the impact that the injury or death of a family member may have on a child is the child's dependence on family members for care and subsistence. In *Mendoza-Pablo v Holder* the applicant was born several weeks premature during civil conflict in Guatemala, and for the first three months of his life he was severely malnourished because of his mother's flight to Mexico. The Court of Appeals for the Ninth Circuit held:[152]

> While the precise long-term effect of these circumstances on Mendoza-Pablo's physical and mental development may well be impossible to determine, it would fly in the face of common experience not to recognize the likelihood that these deprivations would have some deleterious and long-lasting effects ... Accordingly ... we conclude that where a pregnant mother is persecuted in a manner that materially impedes her ability to provide for the basic needs of her child, where that child's family has undisputedly suffered severe persecution, and where the newborn child suffers serious deprivations directly attributable not only to those facts, but also to the material ongoing threat of continued persecution of the child and the child's family, that child may be said to have suffered persecution and therefore be eligible for asylum.

In a case involving a similar set of facts, the Court of Appeals for the Second Circuit placed emphasis on the fact that the applicant 'was a child at the time of the massacres and thus necessarily dependent on both his family and his community ... This combination of circumstances [displacement, economic hardship, and viewing the bullet-ridden body of his cousin] could well constitute persecution to a small child totally dependent on his family and community'.[153]

Although the jurisprudence is less developed, decision-makers have also acknowledged that the denial of certain social, economic or cultural rights will have a greater impact on children than adults.[154] The point has been emphasised by UNHCR, which has noted that '[c]hildren's socio-economic needs are often more compelling than those of adults, particularly due to their dependency on adults and unique developmental needs'.[155] This is recognised in the decision of the Court of Appeals in *Mendoza-Pablo v Holder*, mentioned immediately above, where the Court took into account the deleterious and long-lasting effects of malnourishment on a newborn infant.[156] Similarly, in *MIMA v Chen Shi Hai*, the Full Court of the Australian Federal Court considered that the applicant – a three-year-old child born in contravention of China's 'one-child policy' – would be denied access to

---

[151] *Hernandez-Ortiz v Gonzales*, 496 F 3d 1042, 1045 (9th Cir, 2007). See also *Rusak v Holder*, 734 F 3d 894, 897 (9th Cir, 2013); *SSPM v Canada (MCI)* [2013] FCJ No 1391, [16]–[20].

[152] *Mendoza-Pablo v Holder*, 667 F 3d 1308, 1314–15 (9th Cir, 2012).

[153] *Jorge-Tzoc v Gonzales*, 435 F 3d 146, 150 (2nd Cir, 2006). See also *T93-12579 and T93-12586* (IRB, 25 July 1995) 22 (finding that the child applicant's claim must be assessed 'keeping in mind her vulnerability which results partly from her dependence on adults. Given her tender years she is unable to provide for her own needs or to protect herself from harm'); *T98-03163, T98-03164 and T98-03165* (IRB, 7 May 2001).

[154] 'Children are developing. They grow in developmental sequences, like a tower of bricks, each layer depending on the one below it. Serious delays interrupting these sequences can severely disrupt development': UNHCR, *Refugee Children: Guidelines on Protection and Care* (1994) preface. See generally Foster (2007) *supra* n 19, 207–12; Bhabha and Young (1999) *supra* n 117, 104–5.

[155] UNHCR, 2009 *Guidelines*, [14].

[156] *Mendoza-Pablo v Holder*, 667 F 3d 1308, 1314–15 (9th Cir, 2012).

subsidised food, health and education and all other welfare benefits, which would have a 'serious continuing perhaps life-long effect on the child'.[157] Decision-makers have been particularly attentive to the impact that the denial of education may have on a child's future.[158]

The adoption of the age-sensitive construction of 'being persecuted' provides a clear illustration of the way in which creative advocacy and progressive decision-making can generate positive protection outcomes for refugee children. However, this approach has also given rise to a number of challenges. In particular, the case-law review revealed a striking lack of consistency in the manner and extent to which decision-makers apply the persecutory threshold to account for a child's age. This is perhaps unsurprising given the absence of any principled framework to guide decision-makers in the application of this approach.[159]

By way of illustration, the cases discussed above might be compared to the decision of the Seventh Circuit Court of Appeals in *Liu v Ashcroft*. In that case a 16-year-old Chinese girl was arrested because of suspected involvement for selling books associated with Falun Gong. She was interrogated, beaten, detained for two days and subsequently expelled from school because of the arrest. The Court accepted that the applicant's age was a critical fact in the adjudication of asylum claims but suggested that '[the] *slight calibration* this may warrant ... is insufficient to transform [the applicant's] experiences with the Chinese authorities from harassment to persecution'.[160] Similarly, in *Mejilla-Romero v Holder* the IJ and Court of Appeals for the First Circuit explicitly acknowledged the need to take into account the differential impact of harm inflicted on a child, but considered that witnessing the machete-wounded corpse of an uncle, being hung on a barbed wire fence and cut with a machete, having snakes thrown at one's face and experiencing death threats and attempted rapes between the ages of 5 and 11 did not rise to the level of being persecuted.[161]

---

[157] *MIMA v Chen Shi Hai* (1999) 92 FCR 333, [47]. See also *Chen Shi Hai v MIMA* (2000) 201 CLR 293, [29]; *1004814* [2010] RRTA 862, [122]–[124]; *1004817* [2010] RRTA 862, [122]–[124].

[158] '[B]earing in mind the fundamental importance of education and the significant impact a denial of this right may have for the future of a child, serious harm could arise if a child is denied access to education on a systematic basis': UNHCR, 2009 *Guidelines*, [36]. 'In developing countries it is difficult to conclude that a lack of provision of education would not have an impact on a person's capacity to subsist as at the very least it provides a basic denial of access to an essential service namely an education, or involves significant economic hardship threatening the person's capacity to subsist by denial of that education': *M93 of 2004 v Minister for Immigration* [2006] FMCA 252, [42]. See further *infra* Section 4.3.2.

[159] In the US context, this lack of consistent reasoning mirrors the approach taken to the 'being persecuted' definition generally, which is often characterised as result-oriented and inconsistent: see Anker (2015) *supra* n 8, 221. In the Australian context, domestic guidelines acknowledge that '[t]here is no authority relating to what extent an applicant's particular vulnerability may be taken into account': DIAC, *Guidelines, supra* n 120, [9.5].

[160] *Liu v Ashcroft*, 380 F 3d 307, 314 (7th Cir, 2004) (emphasis added).

[161] *Mejilla-Romero v Holder*, 600 F 3d 63, 70–1 (1st Cir, 2010). See also *Razzak v Attorney General*, 287 Fed Appx 208 (3rd Cir, 2008); *Poplavskiy v Mukasey*, 271 Fed Appx 130 (2nd Cir, 2008); *Khachaturyan v Ashcroft*, 86 Fed Appx 207 (7th Cir, 2004); *Kimumwe v Gonzales*, 431 F 3d 319 (9th Cir, 2005); *Mansour v Ashcroft*, 390 F 3d 667 (7th Cir, 2004) (majority decision); *Shanmuganathan v Canada (MCI)* 2000 FTR LEXIS 1699. For further examples in the context of LGBT children, see S Hazeldean, 'Confounding Identities: The Paradox of LGBT Children under Asylum Law' (2011) 45 *UC Davis Law Review* 373, 382, 393–4, 434.

4.2.2 The CRC as a Benchmark

The above discussion demonstrates an increased awareness of the distinct and various ways that children can experience harm. In particular, the case-law review evinces a willingness on the part of decision-makers to assess the 'being persecuted' criterion by reference to an applicant's age and provides support for the 'unremarkable proposition that age is a factor to be considered in determining whether persecution has occurred'.[162] But while acknowledging the need to assess the 'being persecuted' standard in light of an applicant's age is a critical first step, it is important that this is accompanied by the identification and development of a framework to guide decision-makers in performing that task. Although there are notable exceptions, in cases involving children decision-makers have generally preferred to adapt the 'being persecuted' standard on a case-by-case basis with limited recourse to objective indicators or benchmarks. So, for instance, while the *EU Qualification Directive* explicitly requires decision-makers to take into account 'acts of a child-specific nature', the *Directive* provides no guidance on the range or distinct characteristics of child-specific forms of harm. Similarly, although the age-sensitive approach requires decision-makers to apply the persecutory threshold in light of an applicant's age, there is no guidance on the manner and extent to which the threshold should be adjusted in light of the applicant's age. As noted earlier, the absence of a principled analytical framework heightens the risk of inconsistent and incoherent decision-making.

The current approach to identifying persecutory harm in cases involving children is surprising given the existence of a ready-made framework – the product of more than 20 years of negotiation and endorsed by more states than any other international human rights treaty – that comprehensively sets out the range of behaviour that states themselves have defined as unacceptable in the context of children. In circumstances where there is general agreement that international human rights law is relevant to the identification of persecutory harm, and where an overwhelming majority of states have acknowledged that children have a distinct set of human rights, it becomes difficult to justify the present disinclination to fully engage with the corpus of rights enshrined in the *CRC* when applying the 'being persecuted' standard to children. As the Federal Court of Canada has lucidly apprised, '[i]f the CRC recognizes that children have human rights and that "persecution" amounts to the denial of basic human rights, then if a child's rights under the CRC are violated in a sustained or systematic manner demonstrative of a failure of state protection, that child may qualify for refugee status'.[163]

The rights protected under the *CRC* are tailored to take into account the fact that children experience harms in different ways to adults. The treaty thus provides an automatic and principled means for adapting the persecutory threshold to take into account a child's heightened sensitivities and distinct developmental needs. In this respect the child-rights framework for understanding 'being persecuted' performs a similar function to the age-sensitive construction discussed above, although avoiding reliance on subjective percep-tions of what impact a child's age may have in any given case. By drawing on the *CRC* as a benchmark to identify persecutory harm, a decision-maker automatically incorporates the pre-determined 'modifications' built into the *CRC* framework.

---

[162] *Mendoza-Pablo v Holder*, 667 F 3d 1308, 1318 (9th Cir, 2012).
[163] *Kim v Canada (MCI)* [2011] 2 FCR 448, [51].

An approach that promotes greater interaction between the definition of being persecuted and the rights enshrined in the *CRC* sits comfortably with the human rights framework set out in Section 4.1 of this chapter. As explained above, the *CRC* can plainly be
characterised as a treaty that enjoys the general support of the international community.
Indeed, there is no human rights treaty that enjoys *greater* international support.

In addition to the aforementioned arguments drawing on principles of treaty interpretation, the use of the *CRC* to inform the definition of 'being persecuted' might also be justified
by reference to the best interests principle enshrined in its art 3. UNHCR has, for instance,
suggested that '[t]he best interests of the child requires that the harm be assessed from the
child's perspective'[164] and that '[t]his may include an analysis as to how the child's rights or
interests are, or will be, affected by the harm'.[165]

The argument for greater interaction between the being persecuted standard and the
framework of rights enshrined in the *CRC* finds further support in art 22 of the *CRC*, which
entails a duty to ensure that a child seeking refugee protection receive 'appropriate protection and humanitarian assistance in the enjoyment of applicable rights set forth in this
Convention and in other international human rights or humanitarian instruments'.[166]
Although art 22 does not amend the refugee definition set out under art 1 of the *Refugee
Convention*, there is a compelling argument that the duty to ensure that a child seeking
refugee status receives '*appropriate* protection' requires a state to give consideration to the
fact that the beneficiary of protection is a child, which in turn requires that the art 1
definition be interpreted in such a way that takes into account the distinct rights and
interests of the child applicant. By way of illustration, a state's duty to afford a child
'*appropriate* protection' may require a consideration of the extent to which the child's rights
under the *CRC* will be threatened if she were to be returned to her country of origin. Indeed,
it is difficult to appreciate how 'protection' could be characterised as '*appropriate*' if any
decision as to protection failed to take into account the specificity of the intended beneficiary and the distinct subset of rights that a state owes to a child.[167]

Both UNHCR and the UNCRC have issued guidance that promotes interaction between
the 'being persecuted' definition and the *CRC*. In its 1997 *Unaccompanied Children
Guidelines*, UNHCR underlined that in identifying persecutory harm in cases involving
children '[i]t should be . . . borne in mind that, under the [*CRC*], children are recognized [to
have] certain specific human rights, and that the manner in which those rights may be
violated as well as the nature of such violations may be different from those that may occur
in the case of adults'.[168] The point is re-articulated in UNHCR's 2009 *Guidelines*:[169]

---

[164]   UNHCR, 2009 *Guidelines*, [10]. See also UNCRC, *GC14*, [6], which underlines the role of art 3 as an
        interpretative legal principle, noting that '[i]f a legal provision is open to more than one interpretation,
        the interpretation which most effectively serves the child's best interests should be chosen'.

[165]   UNHCR, 2009 *Guidelines*, [10]. See also UNHCR, 'Submission from the United Nations High
        Commissioner for Refugees (UNHCR) to the legal representatives in case numbers XXX, XXX and
        XXX before the Danish Refugee Appeal Board' (2015), [23].

[166]   *CRC*, art 22(1). The reference to 'other international human rights or humanitarian instruments' must
        include the *Refugee Convention*.

[167]   See generally J Pobjoy, 'Article 22' in P Alston and J Tobin (eds), *The UN Convention on the Rights of the
        Child: A Commentary* (2017) (forthcoming).

[168]   UNHCR, *Unaccompanied Children Guidelines* (1997) *supra* n 131, [8.7].

[169]   UNHCR, 2009 *Guidelines*, [13]. At [19]–[36] the *Guidelines* provide an overview of a number of forms of
        child-specific persecution, drawing heavily on the provisions of the *CRC*. The *Guidelines* suggest that in
        the context of Africa, the *African Charter on the Rights and Welfare of the Child*, opened for signature

A contemporary and child-sensitive understanding of persecution encompasses many types of human rights violations, including violations of child-specific rights. In determining the persecutory character of an act inflicted against a child, it is essential to analyse the standards of the CRC and other relevant international human rights instruments applicable to children. Children are entitled to a range of child-specific rights set forth in the CRC which recognize their young age and dependency and are fundamental to their protection, development and survival.

The UNCRC has similarly emphasised the need to 'take into account the development of, and formative relationship between, international human rights and refugee law' when assessing the 'being persecuted' definition.[170] The link between the CRC and the 'being persecuted' criterion has also been recognised by a number of scholars, each supporting the general proposition that the 'child-centered and rights-based approach to children contained in [the CRC] should inform the application of the concept of persecution to children'.[171]

The relationship between the 'being persecuted' definition and the CRC has also been acknowledged at the domestic level, both in guidelines produced by governments[172] and in the jurisprudence of national courts and tribunals.[173] The clearest endorsement is found in Canadian jurisprudence. In *Kim v Canada (MCI)* the Canadian Federal Court was called upon to consider the impact of the CRC on the definition of 'being persecuted'. Although the Court agreed with the argument put forward by the government that '[t]he [CRC] does not change the definition ... by which a child can be found to be a Convention refugee',[174] it considered that the government had failed to appreciate the 'nuances' that the CRC added to the 'being persecuted' criterion:[175]

---

1 July 1990, OAU Doc CAB/LEG/24.9/49 (entered into force 29 November 1999) should also be taken into account in interpreting 'being persecuted' standard. On the use of regional law as an interpretative aid see *supra* n 22. See also UNHCR ExCom, *Conclusion on Children at Risk*, No 107 (LVIII) (2007), [(b)(x)], [(g)(viii)].

[170] UNCRC, *GC6*, [74]. According to the UNCRC, 'the refugee definition ... must be interpreted in an age and gender-sensitive manner, taking into account the particular motives for, and forms and manifestations of, persecution experienced by children'. See also at [59].

[171] Bhabha and Young (1999) *supra* n 117, 103. For further support see Foster (2007) *supra* n 19, 64–6, 207–12; Bhabha and Crock (2007) *supra* n 109, 158–62; M Crock, 'Re-Thinking the Paradigms of Protection: Children as Convention Refugees in Australia' in J McAdam (ed), *Forced Migration, Human Rights and Security* (2008) 155, 166–71; T Löhr, *Die kinderspezifische Auslegung des völkerrechtlichen Flüchtlingsbegriffs* (2009) 180–268; T Löhr, 'Der Flüchtlingsbegriff im Lichte der Kinderrechtskonvention' in K Barwig, S Beichel-Benedetti and G Brinkmann (eds), *Hohenheimer Tage zum Ausländerrecht* (2010) 300; Sadoway (1996) *supra* n 130, 17–18.

[172] For example, in Canada the relevant guidelines provide that, '[i]n determining the child's fear of persecution, the international human rights instruments, such as the [CRC] ... should be considered in determining whether the harm which the child fears amounts to persecution': IRB, *Guidelines*, 8. In the United States, the training manual for asylum officers provides that 'fundamental rights of children listed in the CRC that may rise to the level of persecution if violated include the rights to be registered with authorities upon birth and acquire a nationality (Art 7.1), to remain with one's family (Art 9.1), to receive an education (Art 28), and to be protected from economic exploitation (Art 32)': USCIS Asylum Division, *Children's Claim Guidelines* (2009) *supra* n 123, 39–40. In Australia, the domestic guidelines state that the denial of a human right may constitute persecution and expressly cite the CRC as a relevant international treaty: DIAC, *Guidelines* (2010) *supra* n 120, [9.7].

[173] In addition to the examples cited below, see the case-law review in *infra* Section 4.3.

[174] *Kim v Canada (MCI)* [2011] 2 FCR 448, [61].   [175] *Ibid.*, [57], [74].

To acknowledge that children have distinctive rights is not to graft additional rights onto the [*Convention* definition], but is instead to interpret the definition of 'persecution' in accordance with the distinctive rights that children possess, as recognized in the CRC ...

[T]herefore, when determining whether a child claiming refugee status fits the definition ... decision makers must inform themselves of the rights recognized in the CRC. It is the denial of these rights which may determine whether or not a child has a well-founded fear of persecution if returned to his or her country of origin.

This approach has since been approved in a series of Federal Court decisions involving child applicants.[176] In the United Kingdom, the Upper Tribunal has expressly accepted that 'the UN Convention on the Rights of the Child and other child-based instruments, have relevance for the assessment of whether the harm that a child might face in the country of origin is serious enough to engage protection or whether any well-founded fear of persecution is for a Refugee Convention reason'.[177] Decision-makers in New Zealand[178] and the United States[179] have also on occasion demonstrated a willingness to draw on the framework of the *CRC* to identify persecutory harms.

4.2.3 What Does the CRC Add?

Before turning to the examination of selected case studies, it is necessary to say something about why it is important that decision-makers adopt a *child*-rights framework for understanding the 'being persecuted' definition. In particular, it is necessary to identify what the *CRC* substantively adds to the interpretation of 'being persecuted' above and beyond the

---

[176] See, e.g., *Ruiz v Canada (MCI)* 2012 FC 258, [60]; *Voskova v Canada* (MCI) [2011] FCJ No 1682, [43]; *Bueckert v Canada (MCI)* 2011 FC 1042, [17]. For earlier endorsements of the use of the *CRC* in defining the 'being persecuted' standard in Canada, see, e.g., *MA1-11675, MA1-11676 and MA1-11677* (IRB, 16 June 2003); *VA1-02828, VA1-02826, VA1-02827 and VA1-02829* (IRB, 27 February 2003); *Zhu v Canada (MCI)* 2001 FCT 884, [10]–[18]; *M99-07094, M99-07096 and M99-07098* (IRB, 31 May 2001); *VA0-02635* (IRB, 22 March 2001); *V99-02926 and V99-02950* (IRB, 9 May 2000); *V99-02929* (IRB, 21 February 2000); *V97-01419, V97-01420, V97-01421, V98-02335, V98-02345 and V98-02346* (IRB, 9 August 1999); *V97-03500* (IRB, 31 May 1999); *T91-01497 and T91-01498* (IRB, 9 August 1994); *Khadra Hassan Farah* (10 May 1994); *T93-09636, T93-09638 and T93-09639* (IRB, 26 January 1994).

[177] *ST (Child Asylum Seekers: Sri Lanka)* [2014] INLR 332, [21]. See also *Fornah v SSHD* [2007] 1 AC 412, [94] (Baroness Hale): '[FGC] is a human rights issue, not only because of the unequal treatment of men and women, but also because the procedure will almost inevitably amount either to torture or to other cruel, inhuman or degrading treatment within the meaning of ... article 37(a) of the [*CRC*]'; *FM (Afghanistan) v SSHD* (Upper Tribunal, AA/01079/2010, 10 March 2011) [108], [119]; and *JA (child – risk of persecution) Nigeria* [2016] UKUT 00560, [15]–[21].

[178] The RSAA and the recently established NZIPT regularly refer to the *CRC* in interpreting the 'being persecuted' standard: see, e.g., *DQ (Iran)* [2015] NZIPT 800868, [38]–[40], [47]; *Refugee Appeal Nos 76494 and 76495* (RSAA, 23 November 2010); *Refugee Appeal Nos 76226 and 76227* (RSAA, 12 January 2009), [111]–[115]; *Refugee Appeal Nos 75301, 75302 and 75303* (RSAA, 24 January 2006), [43]–[47]; *Refugee Appeal Nos 76380, 76381, 76382 and 76383* (RSAA, 30 June 2010). But see *Refugee Appeal Nos 72072/2000 and 72073/2000* (RSAA, 7 December 2000), [43].

[179] See, e.g., *Mansour v Ashcroft*, 390 F 3d 667, 681 (7th Cir, 2004), (Judge Pregerson, dissenting) ('impositions rise to the level of persecution if directed at a child because they implicate a child's fundamental human rights ... [T]he [CRC] articulates a wide range of children's rights and substantive obligations imposed on states to protect children ... Among other obligations, the CRC requires states to protect children from physical or mental abuse, maltreatment and exploitation'); *Abebe v Ashcroft*, 379 F 3d 755, 764 (9th Cir, 2004).

rights codified in the International Bill of Rights. Hathaway has argued that 'the rights guaranteed in the specialized human rights treaties of recent years merely contextualize and add "meat" to the "bones" of the . . . human rights already declared in the International Bill of Rights'.[180] While acknowledging the value of the specialist treaties as interpretative aids, Hathaway suggests that he has 'yet to see a single decision that grounds its understanding of unacceptably serious harm in one of the specialized treaties, that could not equally have invoked the International Bill of Rights to achieve the same outcome'.[181] Hathaway's reluctance to fully embrace the specialist treaties, including the *CRC*, is unfortunate and arguably misconceived. Although it is true that the *CRC* reaffirms many of the core rights contained in the *ICCPR* and the *ICESCR*, the value of the *CRC* goes significantly beyond that, strengthening many of those rights and introducing a number of distinct rights and obligations specifically tailored to the needs and vulnerabilities of children. In this regard, Hathaway's claim that he has not seen a single decision grounded in the *CRC* that could not have been reached by invoking the International Bill of Rights should perhaps not be read as a reflection on the nature of the rights themselves, but rather a failure on the part of decision-makers to fully appreciate and engage with the vision of children codified in the *CRC*.

This is not to suggest that the International Bill of Rights is not relevant to the identification of persecutory harm in claims involving children. It is trite to say that children retain the benefits of the rights codified in the *ICCPR* and the *ICESCR*. As art 41 makes clear, '[n]othing in the [*CRC*] shall affect any provisions which are more conducive to the realization of the rights of the child'. It is thus imperative that the treaties are read together to ensure children are guaranteed maximum protection.[182] For example, in a number of areas the *ICCPR* and the *ICESCR* offer greater protection to children.[183] In other situations the comprehensive guidance produced by the HRC and the UNCESCR will assist decision-makers in the interpretation of similar provisions under the *CRC*. But while these treaties remain relevant, it is clear that the *CRC* provides the most appropriate focal point for a consideration of whether a child is at risk of a form of harm that can be characterised as persecutory.

There are four distinctive features of the *CRC* that may have bearing on a decision-maker's assessment of the 'being persecuted' standard.

First, the *CRC* contains express provisions addressing various child-specific forms of harm. For example, the *CRC* contains express provisions on the abduction and trafficking of children,[184] harmful traditional practices,[185] the right to engage in play and recreational activities,[186] child labour,[187] sexual and other forms of exploitation,[188] the recruitment of children into armed forces[189] and the separation of children from their parents.[190] While it may be true that each of these situations could be recognised as persecutory by reference to

---

[180] Hathaway (1998) *supra* n 23, 89.   [181] *Ibid.*

[182] 'For the advocate, what is important is to ensure that, while the fullest attention be given to the [*CRC*], other paths to the higher level of protection are not ignored': I Cohn, 'The Convention on the Rights of the Child: What It Means for Children in War' (1991) 3(1) *International Journal of Refugee Law* 100, 109.

[183] For example, the *CRC* does not contain a number of rights covered in the *ICCPR* and *ICESCR* (e.g., arts 2(3), 12, 13, 16, 23 and 26 of the *ICCPR*). Further, in certain circumstances the rights as formulated under the *ICCPR* and *ICESCR* may afford greater protection (compare, e.g., *CRC*, art 15 with *ICCPR*, art 18).

[184] *CRC*, arts 11, 35.   [185] *Ibid.*, art 24(3).   [186] *Ibid.*, art 30.   [187] *Ibid.*, art 32.   [188] *Ibid.*, art 34.

[189] *Ibid.*, art 38.   [190] *Ibid.*, art 9.

rights contained in the *ICCPR* or the *ICESCR*, the *CRC*'s explicit signposting of these child-specific forms of harm enhances the likelihood that a decision-maker will correctly identify and assess the distinct risks that a child may face if returned home.

The signposting of child-specific rights in the *CRC* may for instance assist decision-makers in identifying the persecutory nature of certain acts which may not be considered harmful if imposed on a consenting adult but are inherently exploitative in the context of children. As Judge Pregerson of the US Court of Appeals for the Ninth Circuit has recognised, certain actions such as conscription as a soldier, short-term forced labour or arranged marriage, 'while unfortunate and deplorable, may not constitute persecution if imposed on an adult. Under international law, however, such impositions rise to the level of persecution if directed at a child because they implicate a child's fundamental human rights'.[191] This issue has arisen in cases involving children at risk of trafficking.[192] For example, in *Li v Canada (MCI)* the Canadian Federal Court, drawing on the provisions of the *CRC*, accepted a child applicant 'could not "consent" to being "trafficked", whether or not they were of "tender years"'.[193]

By explicitly setting out the specific rights that children enjoy, the *CRC* also provides a principled mechanism for responding to arguments based on cultural customs and norms. As UNHCR has acknowledged, 'harmful practices in breach of international human rights law and standards cannot be justified on the basis of historical, traditional, religious or cultural grounds'.[194] As discussed in Section 4.3, this may be especially relevant in claims involving a risk of domestic violence.[195]

Second, the *CRC* strengthens many of the existing rights in the *ICCPR* and the *ICESCR*. Most significantly, the *CRC* does not permit derogation from any of its provisions at any time, including in wartime situations.[196] In the context of social, economic and cultural rights, the *CRC* does not allow developing states to limit the circumstances in which economic rights will be guaranteed to non-nationals.[197] Moreover, the *CRC* accommodates the greater developmental needs of children by strengthening a number of the social, economic and cultural rights codified in the *ICESCR*.[198] Although a number of the rights in the *CRC* do contain in-built limitations, these are often more narrowly framed than the cognate provisions in the *ICCPR* or the *ICESCR*. For example, art 37 of the *CRC* mandates an absolute prohibition on the imposition of capital punishment or life imprisonment

---

[191] *Mansour v Ashcroft*, 390 F 3d 667, 680 (7th Cir, 2004) (dissenting).

[192] See generally *CRC*, art 35; *OPSC*; UNHCR, *Guidelines on International Protection: The Application of Article 1A(2) of the 1951 Convention and/or 1967 Protocol Relating to the Status of Refugees to Victims of Trafficking and Persons at Risk of Being Trafficked*, HCR/GIP/06/07 (2006), [11]; UNHCR, 2009 *Guidelines*, [25].

[193] *Li v Canada (MCI)* (2000) 198 FTR 81, [23]. Similarly, in *Zhu v Canada (MCI)* 2001 FCT 884, the applicants argued that 'it would be contradictory to suggest that children could forgo all such special protections and care [guaranteed by the *CRC*] if they were perceived to have consented to such exploitations' (at [16]) and criticised the IRB for failing to 'meaningfully examine the provisions of the [*CRC*]' (at [17]).

[194] UNHCR, *Guidelines on International Protection: Gender-Related Persecution within the Context of Article 1A(2) of the 1951 Convention and/or Its 1967 Protocol Relating to the Status of Refugees*, HCR/GIP/02/01 (2002), [5].

[195] See *infra* Section 4.3.1.   [196] Contra *ICCPR*, art 4.

[197] Contra *ICESCR*, art 2(3). See, e.g., UNCRC, GC6, [16], expressly recognising that art 2(3) of *ICESCR* would not apply to unaccompanied refugee children.

[198] See, e.g., *CRC*, arts 6, 24, 27–9.

without the possibility of release for offences committed by persons under 18 years of age.[199] The provision goes on to provide that 'no child shall be deprived of his or her liberty unlawfully or arbitrarily' and that the arrest, detention or imprisonment of a child 'shall be in conformity with the law and shall be used only as a measure of last resort and for the shortest appropriate period of time'.[200] By contrast, the equivalent provision in art 9 of the *ICCPR* provides that '[n]o one shall be deprived of his liberty except on such grounds and in accordance with such procedures as are established by law'.

The enhanced protection under art 37, read alongside art 40, of the *CRC* will be particularly significant where a refugee decision-maker is required to consider whether the prosecution or punishment of a child will constitute persecutory treatment. The provisions make clear that there will be situations where a child is at risk of prosecution or punishment that may be considered legitimate if applied to an adult but will be disproportionate or otherwise illegitimate if imposed on a child.[201] To take an extreme example, while in a very limited range of circumstances the death penalty might be considered an appropriate response to adult criminal behaviour, it will never be legitimate in the context of a child.[202] Other less severe instances of prosecution or punishment may similarly lack a legitimate justification if applied to children. This has arisen, for example, where a child is at risk of being punished because of their illegal exit from their home country. In *V99-02943* the Canadian IRB recognised the need to consider 'whether the penalty meted out to persons such as the claimant, a minor girl who has left illegally, will be so severe and out of proportion with the offence as to amount to persecution'.[203] This approach can be contrasted to the decision of the IRB in *V99-03528*, where the Board expressly rejected the proposition that 'a 17-year-old who leaves illegally ought to be found to be a Convention refugee because she faces the same treatment as an 18-year-old adult'.[204] This issue has also arisen in the context of children at risk of being deprived of basic social services because they were born in contravention of China's family planning programmes. As Justice Kirby of the High Court of Australia has noted, '[w]hat may possibly be viewed as

---

[199] *Ibid.*, art 37(a).

[200] *Ibid.*, art 37(b). Article 37(c) goes on to provide that 'every child deprived of liberty shall be treated with humanity and respect for the inherent dignity of the human person, and in a manner which takes into account the needs of persons of his or her age. In particular, every child deprived of liberty shall be separated from adults unless it is considered in the child's best interests not to do so and shall have the right to maintain contact with his or her family through correspondence and visits, save in exceptional circumstances'. Article 37 of the *CRC* thus goes considerably further than art 9 of the *ICCPR*.

[201] '[F]or example, imprisonment of street children or child beggars, solitary confinement, and life imprisonment without the possibility of release. Similarly, some punishments may be acceptable for older children but unacceptable for younger ones': Bhabha and Young (1991), *supra* n 117, 105. See also M Crock, *Seeking Asylum Alone: Australia* (2006) 173.

[202] W Schabas, *The Abolition of the Death Penalty in International Law* (3rd edn, 2002) 84–6, 187–97.

[203] (IRB, 12 May 2000) 8, applying the decision of the Canadian Federal Court of Appeal in *Cheung v Canada (MEI)* [1993] 2 FC 314. In this case the court considered that the risk of a fine and detention for 'a few days or weeks for identification purposes' did not amount to persecution, even taking into account the applicant's youth: at 8–9. In *V99-03532* (IRB, 12 October 2001) 17–18, the Board acknowledged the need to take into account the differential impact of punishment on a minor, but considered the risk of 'a significant fine and a possible detention of up to one year ... [was not] so out of proportion to the offence [of illegal exit] that it should constitute persecution ... even considering the youth of the claimant'.

[204] *V99-03528* (IRB, 27 January 2000) 14.

acceptable enforcement of laws and programmes of general application in the case of the parents may nonetheless be persecution in the case of a child'.[205]

Third, and related, in certain situations the CRC requires a state to afford a higher standard of protection than would otherwise be required under the ICCPR or the ICESCR.[206] The UNCRC has underlined that:[207]

> young children require particular consideration because of the rapid developmental changes they are experiencing; they are more vulnerable to disease, trauma, and distorted or disturbed development, and they are relatively powerless to avoid or resist difficulties and are dependent on others to offer protection and promote their best interests.

The point has been recognised by the Canadian IRB:[208]

> The panel finds that for children, who are unable to care for themselves ... a higher level [of] protection must be provided than would be necessary for adults. Because children are more vulnerable, less experienced and less able to defend themselves, as well as being less mobile, they require more constant and direct protection than do adults who have some ability to fend for themselves.

This higher standard of protection may be particularly relevant in cases where a child is at risk of domestic violence or is deprived of parental care because she has been neglected or abandoned by her parents or because of the illness or death of a primary caregiver.[209] In these situations it will be necessary for a state to provide alternative care and protection.[210]

The higher standard of protection may also be relevant in cases involving discrimination. Although it may be the case that discrimination would not satisfy the persecutory standard in a case involving in an adult, it is more likely to satisfy the requisite threshold in a case involving children.[211] Discrimination against children is a matter of considerable gravity. The UNCRC has emphasised that art 2 of the CRC 'requires States actively to identify individual children and groups of children the recognition and realization of whose rights may demand special measures'.[212] The UNCRC has recognised that young children are especially at risk of discrimination, because they are relatively powerless and depend on

---

[205] *Chen Shi Hai v MIMA* (2000) 201 CLR 293, [79].

[206] See, e.g., *CRC*, arts 19, 20, 24(3), 39. See generally Crock (2008) *supra* n 171, 171; Foster (2007) *supra* n 19, 209–10. In certain situations, e.g., in the case of children with a disability, the obligation may be even higher: *CRC*, art 23. In *Tchoukhrova v Gonzales*, 404 F 3d 1181, 1191 (9th Cir, 2005), the Court of Appeals for the Ninth Circuit noted that, '[a]lthough all children are dependent and vulnerable, disabled children are particularly so. Children with disabilities have unique needs, their treatment frequently requires specialized knowledge, and their care often involves heightened levels of compassion and patience that parents are particularly suited, and motivated, to give.' As stated during the Day of General Discussion on 'Children without Parental Care', other groups of children in need of special protection measures include 'children associated with drug abuse, street children, refugee children or asylum-seeking children and children infected with or affected by HIV/AIDS': UNCRC, *Report on the Fortieth Session*, CRC/C/153 (2006), [670].

[207] UNCRC, *GC7*, [36].

[208] *T96-02166 and T96-02168* (IRB, 14 May 1997) 3. Contra *VA8-04301 and VA8-04302* (IRB, 28 July 2009), [33] (emphasis added), a case involving two Korean minors who has been abandoned by their mother, where the IRB stressed 'that minor claimants *do not* possess more substantive rights than adult claimants'. This decision was overturned in *Kim v Canada (MCI)* [2011] 2 FCR 448.

[209] See *CRC*, arts 18–20.   [210] See *infra* Section 4.3.3.   [211] Foster (2007) *supra* n 19, 208–9.

[212] UNCRC, *GC5*, [12].

others to realise their rights.[213] According to the Committee, '[d]iscrimination . . . excludes children from full participation in society' and 'affects children's opportunities and self-esteem as well as encouraging resentment and conflict among children and adults'.[214] Articles 6 (survival and development) and 27 (adequate standard of living) will also be important in assessing whether discriminatory treatment satisfies the 'being persecuted' threshold.[215]

Finally, one must not underestimate the symbolic function of the *CRC*. As Van Bueren has noted, the *CRC* 'provides a necessary focus which the scattering of law among so many treaties and standards has so far failed to provide'.[216] In this way, the invocation of the *CRC* enhances the likelihood that the *Convention* will be interpreted and applied with the child's distinct interests at the forefront of the decision-maker's mind.

In sum, a child-rights framework for understanding being persecuted requires a decision-maker to assess whether a child is at risk of a violation of a right protected under the *CRC*. This approach is the logical extension of the traditional human rights framework for understanding being persecuted, both reflecting and reinforcing the international community's near-universal acceptance of children as individual rights-bearers. Indeed, in circumstances where the *CRC* provides a comprehensive and state-generated framework setting out a child's distinct and especially tailored set of human rights, it is difficult to conceive any principled justification for failing to engage with the treaty in the assessment of the being persecuted standard. The final section of this chapter examines the application of the child-rights framework in a series of individual case studies.

4.3 Four Case Studies

This final section turns to more detailed consideration of the application of a child-rights framework for identifying persecutory harm. It does this by looking at four case studies: children at risk of domestic violence; children at risk of being deprived of a primary or secondary education; children at risk of being separated from the family; and children at risk of psychological harm. The discussion is not intended to provide a comprehensive account of the specific risks that children may face in their country of origin. Rather, the four case studies have been selected to provide an illustrative platform to examine the application of the child-rights framework set out in Section 4.2. This section does not, for instance, individually consider harmful traditional practices, child trafficking, underage military recruitment, forced gang recruitment, socio-economic deprivation on account of being born outside family planning policies, child labour or other forms of economic exploitation, or children exposed to generalised violence in civil conflict zones, though the *CRC* is plainly relevant to each of these forms of harm. In cases where more than one human right

---

[213] UNCRC, *GC7*, [11].   [214] *Ibid.*

[215] See, e.g., *Refugee Appeal Nos 76226 and 76227* (RSAA, 12 January 2009), which involved a three-year old girl at risk of being persecuted if returned to Iran on account of being the child of a divorced woman. The RSAA held that '[t]he daughter is also at risk of being persecuted on return to Iran. Given the likely social and economic situation of the appellant as a divorced woman with a child, there is a real chance that the daughter too will be subject to social discrimination and harassment . . . the daughter [will be exposed] to financial deprivation on the grounds of gender and social status discrimination, a breach of Articles 26 and 27 of the [*CRC*]' (at [111]).

[216] G Van Bueren, *The International Law on the Rights of the Child* (1998) xx.

is engaged, the decision-maker must take into account the cumulative impact of the persecutory harm.[217]

4.3.1 Domestic Child Abuse

The past decade has seen the emergence of a particularly important body of refugee jurisprudence concerning family violence. This has corresponded with the recognition that violence committed in the home falls within the purview of international human rights law.[218] Although developments both in international human rights law and refugee law initially focused on the protection of women at risk of domestic violence,[219] in recent years there has been greater emphasis on domestic abuse perpetrated against children.[220] A seminal report completed in 2006 at the behest of the UN Secretary-General illustrated the prevalence of violence against children by parents and other family members and emphasised that 'children's rights to life, survival, development, dignity and physical integrity do not stop at the door of the family home, nor do States' obligations to ensure these rights for children'.[221] The report underlined that '[c]hildren have suffered adult violence unseen and unheard for centuries' and that '[n]ow that the scale and impact of all forms of violence against children is becoming better known, children must be provided with the effective prevention and protection to which they have an unqualified right'.[222]

In refugee claims based on a risk of domestic child abuse, decision-makers have had little difficulty identifying the underlying risk of harm. In the domestic sphere a child may be at risk of physical violence,[223] psychological harm,[224] neglect or negligent

---

[217] See, e.g., *Canada (MCI) v Patel* 2008 FC 747, [45] ('[A] tribunal is required to assess the cumulative impact of the hardships faced by the claimant. Therefore, even if none of the individual harms feared by the applicant are persecutory when viewed individually, the combined or cumulative effect of these harms may be persecutory'); *R (Hoxha) v Special Adjudicator* [2005] 1 WLR 1063, [36].

[218] See generally A Edwards, *Violence against Women under International Human Rights Law* (2010).

[219] See, e.g., Anker (2002) *supra* n 77, 146–9; T Spijkerboer, *Gender and Refugee Status* (2000);

[220] See, e.g., UNHCR, 2009 *Guidelines*, [32]–[33]; UNHCR, *UNHCR Handbook for the Protection of Women and Girls* (2008) 142–4.

[221] *Report of the Independent Expert for the United Nations Study on Violence against Children*, A/61/299 (2006), [38].

[222] *Ibid.*, [6].

[223] See, e.g., *JNJ v Canada (MPSEP)* 2010 FC 1088, [5] ('[s]ome of the incidents highlighted as examples of the abuse include being beaten and stabbed with a broken bottle, being burned by her mother and being beaten with a cricket bat while tied to a tree'); *Aguirre-Cervantes v INS*, 242 F 3d 1169, 1172 (9th Cir, 2001) ('[the applicant] testified that from the time she was about three years old, her father beat her frequently and severely, sometimes daily and sometimes weekly. In administering these beatings, he employed a horsewhip, tree branches, a hose and his fists'); *Re S-A-*, 22 I & N Dec 1328, 1329 (BIA, 2000) ('her father verbally reprimanded her, heated a straight razor, and burned those portions of her thighs that had been exposed while wearing the skirt. He told her that he was taking this action to scar her thighs so that, in the future, she would not be tempted to wear what he considered improper attire'); *Matter of Juan Carlos Martinez-Mejia* (BIA, 1999) ('[the] abuse consisted of beatings with an electrical cord, kneeling on corn with the sun directly overhead for long periods of time, hanging upside down from the ceiling for extended periods of time, and beatings for falling down while standing on his hands with his feet against the wall'); *SA v Canada (MCI)* 2010 FC 344, [11]; *Re John Doe*, 23 Immigration Reporter B1-159 (BIA, 2001).

[224] See, e.g., *SSPM v Canada (MCI)* [2013] FCJ No 1391, [16]–[20]; *VA0-02635* (IRB, 22 March 2001); *TA0-03535* (IRB, 1 May 2001).

treatment,[225] traditional harmful practices including FGC[226] and forced marriage,[227] sexual abuse including incest,[228] and various forms of exploitation including child prostitution and pornography, debt bondage, child labour and child trafficking.[229] Each of these child-specific manifestations of harm is explicitly set out in the *CRC*[230] or the *OPSC*,[231] which are supplemented by guidance published by the UNCRC.[232]

The greater challenge for decision-makers in claims involving children at risk of domestic violence is the issue of state protection and, specifically, the assessment of whether the country of origin is willing and able to respond to the risk of domestic child abuse. As discussed above, there is long-standing acceptance that international refugee law is capable of responding to risks emanating from non-state actors, including family members.[233] As Mary Robinson has acknowledged, a child's human rights will be violated 'not only when violence [is] exerted by agents of the State, but also when States fail[] to live up to their obligation to protect children from violence at the hands of others'.[234] A host state's protection obligations under the *Convention* may thus be engaged notwithstanding the fact that the harm will occur behind closed doors in the 'private sphere' of the family home. It is also accepted that for the purposes of satisfying the nexus criterion in art 1A(2) of the *Convention*, the causal link can be provided either by the non-state actor responsible for the underlying risk of harm or the state for failing to protect the child against that harm.[235]

As discussed in Section 4.1, there will only be a violation of a human right, and therefore cognisable persecutory harm, where the country of origin has failed in its duty to protect its citizens. In cases where domestic violence is expressly condoned or otherwise tolerated by

---

[225] See, e.g., *T98-09341 and T98-09342* (IRB, 16 September 1999) 2 ('[the applicants] alleged that they beat them, deprived them of food and exposed them to witnessing their drug abuse and trafficking in their home').

[226] *Fornah v SSHD* [2007] 1 AC 412; *Kourouma v Holder*, 588 F 3d 234 (4th Cir, 2009); *Abay v Ashcroft*, 368 F 3d 634 (6th Cir, 2004); *MA2-10373* (IRB, 12 June 2003); *MA1-00356, MA1-00357 and MA1-00358* (IRB, 18 December 2001); *Re Fauziya Kasinga*, 21 I & N Dec 357 (BIA, 1996); *Khadra Hassan Farah* (10 May 1994). See generally UNHCR, *Guidance Note on Refugee Claims Relating to Female Genital Mutilation* (2009); UNHCR, 2009 *Guidelines*, [31].

[227] See, e.g., *RG (Ethiopia) v SSHD* [2006] EWCA Civ 339; *Canada (MCI) v Lin* [2001] FCJ No 609; *MA1-07929* (IRB, 13 March 2002); *T99-14088* (IRB, 17 July 2000).

[228] See, e.g., *Lorne v Canada (MCI)* 2006 FC 384 (applicant sexually molested by step-father on a weekly basis between the ages of six and 12); *Fladjoe v Attorney General (US)*, 411 F 3d 135 (3rd Cir, 2005) (applicant held by her father as a slave from the age of seven and subjected to physical beatings and frequent rape pursuant to tenets of the Trokosi religion); *Canada (MCI) v Smith* [1999] 1 FC 310 (applicant sexually abused by father); *1009355* [2011] RRTA 120 (applicant sold into sexual servitude by her step-father when she was 12 years old).

[229] *Zhu v Canada (MCI)* 2001 FCT 884; *Li v Canada (MCI)* (2000) 198 FTR 81; *V99-02926 and V99-02950* (IRB, 9 May 2000); *V99-02929* (IRB, 21 February 2000). See generally, UNHCR, 2009 *Guidelines*, [24]–[30]; UNHCR, *Victims of Trafficking Guidelines* (2006) supra n 192.

[230] *CRC*, arts 3, 6, 19, 24, 24(3), 32, 34, 35, 36, 37(a).   [231] *OPSC*, art 1.

[232] UNCRC, *GC13*, [20]–[32]; UNCRC, *GC7*, [36]; UNCRC, *GC8*, [11].

[233] 'The non-state actor doctrine is based on the principle of international law that a state's obligations to protect include a duty to defend and secure the enjoyment of basic human rights, both by refraining from violations and by engaging in positive intervention and enforcement. This doctrine has particular salience for children, because of their dependence and vulnerability, the power disparity vis-à-vis their adult caretakers, and their lack of easy access to non-familial sources of protection': Bhabha and Young (1999) supra n 117, 106. See supra Section 4.1.3.

[234] UNCRC, *Report of the Twenty-Eighth Session*, CRC/C/111 (2001), [685] (pt V contains a summary of the Day of General Discussion on 'Violence against Children, within the Family and in Schools').

[235] See supra Section 4.1.3.

a state, the assessment of state protection will be reasonably straightforward.[236] More common, however, is a scenario where the state is willing to provide protection against child abuse, but the applicant claims that the state is unable to provide effective protection. In this situation it will be necessary to assess the standard or level of protection required by the applicant's country of origin.

The *Convention* requires 'a reasonable level of protection, not a perfect one'.[237] As the Australian High Court has observed, 'no country can guarantee that its citizens will at all times, and in all circumstances, be safe from violence'.[238] International human rights law provides a principled framework that ascribes what the international community has defined as a reasonable standard of protection. It is here that the import of the *CRC* comes to the fore, with art 19 of the treaty explicitly identifying the measures that a state must take in order to protect children from domestic violence.[239] Article 19[240] provides as follows:

> (1) States Parties shall take all appropriate legislative, administrative, social and educational measures to protect the child from all forms of physical or mental violence, injury or abuse, neglect or negligent treatment, maltreatment or exploitation, including sexual abuse, while in the care of parent(s), legal guardian(s) or any other person who has the care of the child.
>
> (2) Such protective measures should, as appropriate, include effective procedures for the establishment of social programmes to provide necessary support for the child and for those who have the care of the child, as well as for other forms of prevention and for identification, reporting, referral, investigation, treatment and follow-up of instances of child maltreatment described heretofore, and, as appropriate, for judicial involvement.

The obligations set out in art 19 have since been explicated by the UNCRC in *GC13*.

Critically, the express terms of art 19 and the associated guidance provided in the UNCRC's *GC13* make clear that states owe children a *higher* standard of protection than adults in situations of domestic violence.[241] This strikes one as intuitively right. Children are

---

[236] See, e.g., *Tchoukhrova v Gonzales*, 404 F 3d 1181, 1193 (9th Cir, 2005).

[237] *MIMA v Respondents S152/2003* (2004) 222 CLR 1, [117] (Kirby J).

[238] *Ibid.*, [26] (Gleeson CJ, Hayne and Heydon JJ).

[239] '[Article 19] is a bold and ambitious outcome, the significance of which should not go underestimated given the historical failure of international law to tackle the issue of violence against children within the home': J Tobin, 'Parents and Children's Rights under the Convention on the Rights of the Child: Finding Reconciliation in a Misunderstood Relationship' (2005) 7(2) *Australian Journal of Professional and Applied Ethics* 31, 37.

[240] Article 19 is a civil right and therefore places an immediate and unqualified obligation on states irrespective of any economic constraints: see *CRC*, art 4; UNCRC, *GC13*, [65]; UNCRC, *GC8*, [22]. This is made clear by the mandatory language of art 19(1) ('shall take').

[241] 'There can be no compromise in challenging violence against children. Children's uniqueness – their potential and vulnerability, their dependence on adults – makes it imperative that they have more, not less, protection from violence': UNCRC, *Violence Against Children Report* (2006) *supra* n 221, [2]. At a regional level, this is reflected in the ECtHR's jurisprudence on art 3 of the *ECHR*: see, e.g., *A v UK* (1999) 27 EHRR 611; *Z v UK* (2002) 34 EHRR 97; *E v UK* (2003) 36 EHRR 519. In *Re E (a child)* [2009] 1 AC 536, [8]–[9], the House of Lords suggested that the special vulnerability of children is relevant to a consideration of art 3 of the *ECHR* in two ways: 'First, it is a factor in assessing whether the treatment to which they have been subjected reaches the "minimum level of severity" ... needed to attract the protection of article 3. ... The special vulnerability of children is also relevant to the scope of the obligations of the state to protect them from such treatment.'

'least able to avoid or resist, least able to comprehend what is happening and least able to seek the protection of others'.[242] As the UNCRC has explained, '[t]he distinct nature of children, their initial dependent and developmental state, their unique human potential as well as their vulnerability, all demand *the need for more, rather than less*, legal and other protection from all forms of violence'.[243]

Hence, where a child is accompanied by a parent who is also at risk of domestic violence, it may be necessary for a decision-maker separately to assess the availability of state protection for the child and the adult. By way of illustration, in *Zakar v Canada (MCI)* the Canadian Federal Court recognised that '[t]he daughter had a different basis for her claim of domestic abuse, that of fear of injury from her father', and that, '[a]s a child, she stood in a more vulnerable position to that of her mother'.[244] The Court considered that the IRB had erred by 'integrally mix[ing]' the assessment of state protection for the daughter and the mother: '[T]he Panel failed to adequately consider the separate nature and basis of the child's own claim for protection. The Panel must be alert and alive to the specific interests of the child, especially where there is some distinction between the claims of the parent and the child.'[245]

Although the question of whether a state has taken appropriate measures to protect a child from domestic violence will ultimately need to be evaluated on a case-by-case basis,[246] a number of general observations can be made based on the guidance and direction provided in art 19 and GC13.[247] First and most significantly, the concept of 'protection' should not be narrowly construed; art 19 requires a state to undertake a broad range of measures to protect children against domestic child abuse that extend considerably beyond the mere criminalisation thereof.[248] Thus, while the enactment of legislation prohibiting domestic violence will be an important consideration, it alone is insufficient to establish that effective protection is available in an applicant's country of origin.[249] Similarly, the fact that

---

[242] UNCRC, *GC7*, [36].

[243] UNCRC, *GC8*, [21] (emphasis added). See, e.g., *Bueckert v Canada (MCI)* 2011 FC 1042, [17] (separately considering the state's protective obligations to the father and the son because of the need to take into account the child's 'special vulnerabilities').

[244] *Zakar v Canada (MCI)* 2005 FC 1016, [14].   [245] *Ibid.*, [15], [17].

[246] UNHCR, 2009 *Guidelines*, [37].

[247] Notwithstanding its recognition as the 'core provision' relating to violence perpetrated against children (UNCRC, *GC13*, [7]), art 19 has received limited attention in refugee case-law involving children at risk of domestic child abuse. Even UNHCR has only afforded the provision a cursory reference in its 2009 *Guidelines*. For case-law that has engaged with art 19, see *Khadra Hassan Farah* (IRB, 10 May 1994); *Mansour v Ashcroft*, 390 F 3d 667, 681 (7th Cir, 2004) (Judge Pregerson, dissenting); *FM (Afghanistan) v SSHD* (Upper Tribunal, AA/01079, 10 March 2011), [108]; *T91-01497 and T91-01498* (IRB, 9 August 1994); *V97-03500* (IRB, 31 May 1999).

[248] The inadequacy of existing domestic legislative frameworks is underlined in UNCRC, *GC13*, [12]: 'Legal frameworks in a majority of States still fail to prohibit all forms of violence against children, and where laws are in place, their enforcement is often inadequate. Widespread social and cultural attitudes and practices condone violence. The impact of measures taken is limited by lack of knowledge, data and understanding of violence against children and its root causes, by reactive efforts focusing on symptoms and consequences rather than causes, and by strategies which are fragmented rather than integrated. Resources allocated to address the problem are inadequate.'

[249] Having said that, the *absence* of a legislative framework criminalising violence against children would generally suggest that state protection is inadequate: see, e.g., *Refugee Appeal Nos 75805 and 75806* (IRB, 30 November 2007), [56]–[58] (no specific provisions outlawing domestic violence in Mali); *Aguirre-Cervantes v INS*, 242 F 3d 1169, 1178–9 (9th Cir, 2001) (in the majority of Mexico's 32 states it was legal for husbands to use 'correction' discipline to handle wives and children).

the applicant's home country has signed and ratified the *CRC* is a relevant though not dispositive consideration.[250] The UNCRC has indicated 'in the strongest terms' that 'child protection must begin with proactive prevention of all forms of violence as well as explicitly prohibit[ing] all forms of violence'.[251] Article 19 thus places an obligation on states 'to adopt all measures necessary to ensure that adults responsible for the care, guidance and upbringing of children will respect and protect children's rights'.[252]

In its *GC13* the UNCRC outlines the range of measures – legislative, administrative, social and educational – which 'must be used *and be effective* in order to respond to all forms of violence'.[253] The Committee underlines that '[a]uthorities at all levels of the State responsible for the protection of children ... may directly and indirectly cause harm by lacking *effective means of implementation* of obligations under the Convention'.[254] According to the Committee, '[s]uch omissions include the failure to adopt or revise legislation and other provisions, inadequate implementation of laws and other regulations and insufficient provision of material, technical and human resources and capacities to identify, prevent and react to violence against children'.[255] By adopting the language of 'effectiveness' the UNCRC makes clear that art 19 requires more than the mere existence of 'a system of domestic protection and machinery for the detection, prosecution and punishment [of domestic child abuse]' and 'an ability and a readiness to operate that machinery'.[256]

Article 19(2) sets out a non-exhaustive list of protective measures that a state should take to safeguard children against violence. The provision expressly identifies, for instance, the importance of social conditions and cultural attitudes to the protection of children against domestic violence. In *GC13* the UNCRC emphasises that 'prevention must remain paramount at all times in the development and implementation of child protection systems'.[257] This may include 'public health and other measures to positively promote respectful child-rearing ... and [target] the root causes of violence at the levels of the child, family, perpetrator, community, institution and society'.[258] The UNCRC also underlines the need for accessible and child-friendly reporting mechanisms,[259] rigorous and child-sensitive investigation procedures,[260] medical treatment and longer-term follow-up services[261] and, where necessary, procedures for judicial involvement.[262]

Adopting a child-rights framework, the 'being persecuted' standard will be satisfied where a child is at risk of domestic child abuse and the country of origin has failed to satisfy its protective obligations mandated under art 19 of the *CRC*. In assessing the availability of state protection, a decision-maker might usefully draw on country of origin information that addresses state compliance with obligations under the *CRC*. A paucity of information on how a government deals with domestic child abuse may in itself be suggestive of insufficient protection mechanisms.[263]

---

[250] See, e.g., *TA0-05472* (IRB, 30 May 2001) 12.

[251] UNCRC, *GC13*, [46]. This finds support in the *CRC*'s *travaux préparatoires*, which demonstrate that the drafters felt that emphasis should be placed on the need for preventative measures: see, e.g., *Report of the Working Group on a Draft Convention on the Rights of the Child*, E/CN.4/1984/71 (1984).

[252] UNCRC, *GC13*, [46].   [253] *Ibid.*, [39] (emphasis added). See also at [38]–[44].

[254] *Ibid.*, [31] (emphasis added). GC13 further provides that the protective measures 'must be used *and be effective* in order to prevent and respond to' violence against children: at [39] (emphasis added). Article 19(2) of the *CRC* also refers to the need for '*effective* procedures' (emphasis added). See further UNCRC, *GC13*, [57]–[58].

[255] UNCRC, *GC13*, [31].   [256] *Horvath v SSHD* [2001] 1 AC 489, 510.   [257] UNCRC, *GC13*, [46].

[258] *Ibid.*   [259] *Ibid.*, [48]–[49].   [260] *Ibid.*, [51].   [261] *Ibid.*, [52]–[53].   [262] *Ibid.*, [54].

[263] *Refugee Appeal Nos 75301, 75302 and 75303* (RSAA, 24 January 2006), [43].

In assessing the availability of state protection, a decision-maker must look beyond the mere existence of formal legal mechanisms and take into account the wider institutional and cultural context.[264] For instance, evidence that authorities regard domestic child abuse as a private family matter will generally be demonstrative of a failure of state protection.[265] The adequacy of state protection must be assessed at the operational level.[266] As the Federal Court of Canada has held, '[decision-makers] are required to take a bottom line approach and assess evidence of state protection not on the intention and initiatives of the state, but on its implementation and effectiveness'.[267] In other words, there must be 'effective and meaningful protection'.[268] To provide an example, in a case involving a 14-year-old Polish boy at risk of child abuse, the IRB acknowledged the fact that Poland had ratified the CRC, criminalised domestic child abuse and introduced legislation providing for the appointment of an Ombudsman for children's rights; however, it considered that these efforts were countered by evidence suggesting that child abuse was infrequently reported and that convictions for child abuse were rare. The IRB considered that this evidence demonstrated that 'protective measures [were] not effectively in place' and that state protection was therefore not available to the applicant.[269] In another case, involving a 16-year-old Chinese boy at risk of being sent into debt bondage overseas by his father, the IRB placed emphasis on the fact that the criminal laws prohibiting violence against children were 'seldom invoked' and thus afforded limited protection to children at risk of domestic child abuse.[270]

Article 19(1) prohibits 'all forms of ... violence' against children, and the UNCRC has made clear that the provision leaves no room for exceptions that might be invoked to justify the infliction of child abuse.[271] Accordingly, there is no support for the view that the

---

[264] *Refugee Appeal Nos 76410 and 76411* (RSAA, 14 December 2009), [70].

[265] For example, in *Charles v Canada (MCI)* 2007 FC 103, [4], the applicant was the victim of child abuse since the age of nine, and when she was 17 years old went to the police only to be told that the matter 'should be dealt with at home as it was a domestic dispute'. In *V99-02929* (IRB, 21 February 2000) 7, the evidence suggested that 'domestic abuse is regarded by the police as a family matter and that the husband/father is regarded as head of the family and thus its chief decision-maker'. In *Re S-A-*, 22 I & N Dec 1328, 1330 (BIA, 2000), the applicant gave evidence that 'in Morocco, a father's power over his daughter is unfettered'. See also *V97-00156 and V97-00962* (IRB, 23 July 1998), [22]; *A99-00789, A99-00790, A99-00791, A99-00792 and A99-00793* (IRB, 8 April 2002); *MA1-00356, MA1-00357 and MA1-00358* (IRB, 18 December 2001).

[266] *Katwaru v Canada (MCI)* 2007 FC 612, [21] ('Democracy alone does not guarantee effective state protection ... The [decision-]maker is required to do more than determine whether a country has a democratic political system and must assess the quality of the institutions that provide state protection').

[267] *JNJ v Canada (MPSEP)* 2010 FC 1088, [26]. Similarly, in *JB v Canada (MCI)* 2011 FC 210, [47] (emphasis added), the Federal Court emphasised that 'the mere willingness of a state to ensure the protection of its citizens is not sufficient in itself to establish its ability. *Protection must have a certain degree of effectiveness.*'

[268] *Cho v Canada (MCI)* 2009 FC 70, [44]. In that case the Court emphasised the importance of 'ascertain-[ing] the *actual effectiveness* of state protection in Korea': at [42] (emphasis added). See also *AK (Brazil)* [2016] NZIPT 800834-35, [85]–[90], applying the alleviation of risk theory.

[269] *TA0-05472* (IRB, 30 May 2001) 13.

[270] *V99-02929* (IRB, 21 February 2000). See also *TA2-00795* (IRB, 2 December 2002).

[271] UNCRC, GC13, [17]. The UNCRC has noted that the word 'appropriate' in art 19(1) 'cannot be interpreted to mean acceptance of some forms of violence': at [39]. In UNCRC, GC8, [13]–[14], the Committee draws a distinction between physical actions and interventions designed to protect children and 'the deliberate and punitive use of force to cause some degree of pain, discomfort or humiliation'.

standard of state protection should be moderated to take into account a country of origin's cultural customs and norms.[272] The Canadian IRB helpfully develops the point in a case involving a young child subjected to severe physical and psychological abuse from his father designed to instil unquestioning obedience:[273]

> The States parties to the [CRC] took a stand against violence towards children, and by doing so clearly held that the international community should not tolerate certain patterns of behaviour, whether or not they are culturally-specific. Using children as soldiers, selling them into prostitution, and beating them into submission are all acts enjoined by the [CRC], wrong wherever they are practiced, in China or in Canada. Thus, when 'filial piety' and 'patrilineal authority' result in the psychological disabling of a child's normal functioning, 'cultural' values must take a back seat to the child's best interests. It is persecution to be beaten in this cruel and systematic way, whatever arguments we advance to justify it.

As the Board made clear, any argument that the international community should turn a blind-eye to cases of domestic violence because of a country's values such as 'filial piety' or 'patrilineal authority' is rendered irrelevant when assessed against arts 19 and 37(a) of the CRC. The UK House of Lords has made similar findings in assessing the claim of a child at risk of FGC, noting that the fact that the practice is 'widespread and widely accepted in Sierra Leonean society' is immaterial given that '[t]here is no doubt that [FGC] is in breach of international human rights law and standards'.[274]

Finally, it will generally be inappropriate for a decision-maker to draw any inferences about the availability of state protection from the fact that a child has not previously sought protection from state authorities.[275] A child cannot be expected to approach the state for protection if it would be impractical, futile or otherwise unreasonable for them to do so.[276] As the Canadian Federal Court has observed,[277] '[t]he reasonableness of the applicants' willingness to seek protection … must be assessed in light of their status as minors. As children, the applicants may be less inclined to seek the protection of the state, particularly where this would require them going against their parents' directions.' The point is illustrated in *Bueckert v Canada (MCI)*, a case involving a seven-year-old

---

[272] Contra the position taken by the UKIAT in *SSHD v Fatemah Firouz Ranjbar* (IAT, 28 June 1994): 'we do not read the [*Refugee Convention*] as extending … to ill-treatment within a family unit by the head of the family, whose social and legal responsibilities towards his children neither we nor an adjudicator could, as a rule fully or properly assess'. See *supra* text accompanying n 194–5.

[273] *VA0-02635* (IRB, 22 March 2001) 9.

[274] *Fornah v SSHD* [2007] 1 AC 412, 466. See generally *CRC*, art 24(3); J Tobin, *The Right to Health in International Law* (2012) 303–24; UNHCR, *Female Genital Mutilation Guidance Note* (2009) *supra* n 226.

[275] UNHCR, 2009 *Guidelines*, [39]. See also INS, *Guidelines*, 26, which provide that '[t]he fact that a child did not specifically seek protection does not necessarily undermine his or her case, but instead the adjudicator must explore what, if any, means the child had of seeking protection'. Conversely, evidence demonstrating that a child attempted to seek protection from the state but it was not provided will be particularly relevant to the assessment of state protection: see, e.g., *IECC v Canada (MCI)* [2006] FCJ No 409, [2]–[7]; *MA0-10528 and MA0-10529* (IRB, 29 October 2001).

[276] Consider the following observation of the Canadian IRB in *V99-02929* (IRB, 21 February 2000) 7: '[T]he [applicant child] has testified that attempting to invoke [state protection] puts him in a difficult position. If unsuccessful, he could be subject to even worse abuse. If successful, he might send to jail the sole breadwinner of the family. Under these circumstances, he worried how the family would survive. Seeing his way out of what appeared to be a no-win situation is probably not possible for a child as young as he is.'

[277] *Zhu v Canada (MCI)* 2001 FCT 884, [28], approved in *Lorne v Canada (MCI)* 2006 FC 384, [18].

child from Belize who was physically and emotionally abused by his mother from the time he was one-year-old. In its initial decision the IRB placed significant weight on the fact that the applicant and his father had never tested state protection in Belize. The Federal Court held that 'this finding completing ignored the fact that [the applicant] was never in a position ... to test the adequacy of state protection' as he was only three years old at the time.[278] As the Court recognised, '[it] is not immediately apparent how anyone that age could ever personally test the adequacy of state protection'.[279]

Similar concessions may also be appropriate in cases involving older children. In *Charles v Canada (MCI)*[280] the applicant was abused by her cousin between the ages of nine and 17. At various times the child attempted to tell her mother and great aunt but was disbelieved. At one stage the applicant went to the police, only to be told that it was a domestic dispute that should be dealt with at home. The IRB considered that 'it was unreasonable for the claimant not to have made a greater effort to seek protection' and that she ought to have 'exhausted other avenues of protection'.[281] This finding was firmly rebuked by the Canadian Federal Court on the basis that such reasoning 'not only untenable, [but also] patently unreasonable'.[282] The Court considered that the reasoning demonstrated 'a surprising and unacceptable lack of consideration for the vulnerability and trauma suffered by abused children'.[283]

4.3.2 Education

The right to an education has been characterised as one of the most important human rights that a child possesses.[284] The UNCESCR has underlined the fact that '[e]ducation is both a human right in itself and an indispensable means of realising other human rights'.[285] The denial of the right to an education may irreparably curtail a child's ability to develop their 'personality, talent and mental and physical abilities to their fullest potential'.[286] This in turn may inhibit a child's ability to 'grow up and play their part in the adult world'.[287] In the refugee context, decision-makers have appropriately recognised that the denial of

---

[278] *Bueckert v Canada (MCI)* 2011 FC 1042, [18].

[279] *Ibid.* See also *Bringas-Rodriguez v Lynch*, 805 F 3d 1171, 1192–3 (9th Cir, 2015) (Judge Fletcher, dissenting).

[280] *Charles v Canada (MCI)* 2007 FC 103.   [281] *Ibid.*, [5].   [282] *Ibid.*, [6].

[283] *Ibid.* See also *Lorne v Canada (MCI)* 2006 FC 384, [16]–[20] (accepting that 'it is unreasonable to expect a scared child of twelve who is being raped twice weekly to do more than report the matter to her teacher'); *T99-11540 and T99-11541* (IRB, 31 May 2001) 5 (finding it 'unlikely given [the applicants'] ages and emotional condition that they would ever venture to seek state protection'); *V97-03500* (IRB, 31 May 1999) 4 (finding a 16-year-old applicant 'vulnerable and incapable of accessing state protection on his own').

[284] J Fortin, *Children's Rights and the Developing Law* (2009) 189.   [285] UNCESCR, *GC13*, [1].

[286] *CRC*, art 29(1)(a).

[287] *Ali v Head Teacher and Governors of Lord Grey School* [2006] 2 AC 363, [81] (Baroness Hale). See also Warren CJ in *Brown v Board of Education of Topeka*, 347 US 483, 493 (1954): '[Education] is the very foundation of good citizenship. Today it is a principal instrument in awakening the child to cultural values, in preparing him for later professional training, and in helping him to adjust normally to his environment. In these days, it is doubtful that any child may reasonably be expected to succeed in life if he is denied the opportunity of an education. Such an opportunity, where the state has undertaken to provide it, is a right which must be made available to all on equal terms.'

education may amount to persecutory harm.[288] The discussion below examines the scope of the right and addresses a number of scenarios where the right may be engaged.

A child's right to education is protected under art 13 of the *ICESCR* and art 28 of the *CRC*.[289] These provisions provide that primary education must be 'compulsory and available free to all'[290] and that secondary education, including general and vocational education, must be 'generally available and accessible to all by every appropriate means, and in particular by the progressive introduction of free education'.[291] Article 29 of the *CRC* adds a qualitative dimension, establishing the right to a 'specific quality of education'.[292] The UNCRC has explained that the provision is intended to emphasise the importance of child-centred education: 'that the key goal of education is the development of the individual child's personality, talents and abilities, in recognition of the fact that every child has unique characteristics, interests, abilities, and learning needs'.[293]

Although both the *ICESCR* and *CRC* acknowledge the constraints of limited available resources and allow for the progressive realisation of the right to an education, a number of obligations are immediately binding. Most significantly in the refugee context, states are required to ensure that the right will be protected 'without discrimination of any kind'[294] and 'on the basis of equal opportunity'.[295] As the UNCESCR has underlined, the prohibition against discrimination is 'subject to neither progressive realization nor the availability of resources; it applies fully and immediately to all aspects of education'.[296] In the context of primary education, the UNCESCR has stated that the obligation 'to provide primary education for all' is an immediately binding obligation and forms part of the 'minimum core obligation' required to satisfy the right to education.[297] States are also under an immediate obligation to take 'deliberate, concrete and targeted' measures towards the full realisation of the right to a secondary education.[298]

---

[288] For an excellent discussion on the right to education in the refugee context, see Foster (2007) *supra* n 19, 214–26.

[289] See also *UDHR*, art 26; *Declaration of the Rights of the Child*, UNGA Res 1386 (XIV) (1959), Principle 7. In the context of the *CRC*, the denial of the right to education may also engage a number of related provisions, including, in particular, arts 3, 5, 6, 12, 14, 17, 18, 23, 24 and 30: see generally UNCRC, *GC1*, [6].

[290] *CRC*, art 28(1)(a); *ICESCR*, art 13(2)(a).

[291] *ICESCR*, art 13(2)(b); *CRC*, art 28(1)(b). The discussion here focuses on primary and secondary education. For a discussion on the availability of higher education in the refugee context, see Foster (2007) *supra* n 19, 221–6.

[292] UNCRC, *GC1*, [9].   [293] *Ibid.*   [294] *CRC*, art 2(1); *ICESCR*, art 2(2).

[295] *CRC*, art 28(1). The 'equal opportunity' formulation is significant, underlining that in certain circumstances it may be necessary to take preferential treatment for a disadvantaged group (for example, young girls, children in rural communities, children with a disability). See generally S Fredman, *Discrimination Law* (2nd edn, 2011) 18–19.

[296] UNCESCR, *GC13*, [31].

[297] *Ibid.*, [57]; see also at [59]; *ICESCR*, art 14; UNCESCR, *GC11*. See also *A World Fit for Children*, A/RES/S-27/2 (2002), [7]: 'All girls and boys must have access to and complete primary education that is free, compulsory and of good quality as a cornerstone of an inclusive basic education.'

[298] *ICESCR*, art 2(1); *CRC*, art 4. See generally UNCESCR, *GC13*, [43]–[46], [59]; UNCESCR, *GC3*, [8]–[10]; UNCRC, *GC5*, [6]–[8]. The UNCESCR has also stated that '[t]here is a strong presumption of impermissibility of any retrogressive measures taken in relation to the right to education': UNCESCR, *GC13*, [45]. Thus, there may be a violation of the right to an education 'where a state removes educational opportunities from a particular region or section of the population': Foster (2007), *supra* n 19, 221. For example, in *Bucur v INS*, 109 F 3d 399, 405 (7th Cir, 1997) the Court of Appeals for the Seventh Circuit suggested that, '[i]f a government as part of an official campaign against some religious

A child will most clearly be at risk of a violation of the right to an education – and thus at risk of 'being persecuted' – where there is a real chance that the state will deny the child access to primary or secondary education because of a *Convention* reason: for example, because of the child's race, religion, political opinion, gender, sexuality, disability or status as an 'illegitimate child'. In this scenario the persecutory act is the *discriminatory* denial of education, which is prohibited irrespective of any resource constraints that the state may have. The point is clearly made by the US Court of Appeals for the Ninth Circuit:[299]

> claims of financial difficulties cannot be used to justify the deprivation of services essential to human survival and development, if the deprivation is based on the recipient's membership in a statutorily protected group. The government's refusal to provide medical care and an elementary education to 'disabled children' . . . cannot be excused on the basis of the need to limit expenditures. If medical or educational resources are to be limited, the allocation of funds must be based on other, less invidious, grounds.

Thus, a child's right to education will be infringed where a state adopts policies or enacts legislation that discriminate against certain groups of children.[300] In *Chen Shi Hai v MIMA* the High Court of Australia accepted the refugee claim of a three-year-old infant because, among other things, the home government would deny the child subsidised education because he was born in contravention of China's 'one-child' policy. The Court considered that denying a child 'an opportunity to obtain an education involve[s] such a significant departure from the standards of the civilized world as to constitute persecution'.[301]

The expulsion or indefinite suspension of a child may also violate the right to be educated where this occurs for a *Convention* reason. For example, in a case before the Canadian IRB, two Chinese boys were suspended from school indefinitely because of their father's political activities.[302] The Board stated that the concept of 'being persecuted' must be interpreted in a manner consistent with international human rights instruments, including the *CRC*, and explicitly engaged with art 28 thereof. The Board determined that 'the extended suspension of these two children and the uncertainty about whether they will be able to return to school are inconsistent with the principle set out in the [*CRC*], and have resulted in serious and sustained harm to these children'.[303]

In addition to situations where a child is directly deprived of an education, a child may also be at risk of a violation of the right where there is an *effective* or *de facto* denial of the right.[304] This may occur where a third party, typically a parent or guardian, prevents a child from going to school. The UNCESCR has made clear that states are required 'to take

sect closed all the sect's schools (but no other private schools) and forced their pupils to attend public school, this would be . . . a form of religious persecution.'

[299] *Tchoukhrova v Gonzales*, 404 F 3d 1181, 1194 (9th Cir, 2005).   [300] UNCESCR, *GC13*, [59].

[301] *Chen Shi Hai v MIMA* (2000) 201 CLR 293, [29]. See also *D (a minor) v Refugee Appeals Tribunal & Anor* [2011] IEHC 431, [25] ('it . . . seems impossible to avoid the conclusion that the denial of even basic education amounts to a severe violation of basic human rights'); *0906142* [2009] RRTA 955, [67] ('[t]he Tribunal . . . considers that denial of access to a basic education may threaten the capacity of the [applicant] to find employment and to subsist, especially given the baby's status not only as a black child, but also as an illegitimate child who is likely to suffer further social discrimination for this reason'); *1004339* [2010] RRTA 816, [113]; *1000003* [2010] RRTA 400, [60]; *0906198* [2009] RRTA 891, [60].

[302] *VA1-03231, VA1-03232 and VA1-03233* (IRB, 12 March 2003).

[303] *Ibid.*, 4. The right is not unlimited, and does not extend, e.g., 'to the right to attend elite schools or to be accepted for enrolment by the school of your choice': *Refugee Appeal Nos 76352, 76353 and 76354* (RSAA, 26 January 2010), [97].

[304] Foster (2007) *supra* n 19, 216–19.

measures that prevent third parties from interfering with the enjoyment of the right to education'.[305] Thus, the Federal Magistrates Court of Australia was entirely correct to accept the refugee claim of a 13-year-old Thai girl who had been abandoned by her parents and sent to live with her extended family, who required her to work on their farm rather than attend school:[306]

> It is difficult to conceive that a child returned to Thailand to work on a farm, denied the opportunity of education, could be regarded as not suffering serious harm. The serious harm ... need not be overt physical ill treatment, significant economic hardship or denial of access to basic services but rather may be constituted by the simple denial of education to a child which at the very least would appear to be a fundamental right.

A child may also effectively be deprived of an education where she is too scared or traumatised to attend school because of sustained harassment or bullying from other students,[307] discrimination or corporal punishment from teachers,[308] or a general atmosphere of violence in the community.[309] It may be that these risks will themselves amount to persecutory treatment; for example, the UNCRC has made clear that corporal punishment is a violation of art 37 of the CRC.[310] The Canadian Federal Court has made clear that it is inappropriate to suggest that a child can avoid these forms of persecution by refusing to attend school.[311] That is, 'where the only way a child can avoid persecution is to cease attending school, asking the child to do so violates his or her right to an education and the child should therefore be found a refugee'.[312] By way of illustration, in *Refugee Appeal Nos 76305, 76306, 76307 and 76308* two young Afghan boys were unable to attend school because of a risk of 'violence by anti-government insurgents at school', together with a risk of being 'harassed, physically harmed or kidnapped while travelling to and from school'.[313] The New Zealand RSAA underlined that 'to provide a primary education for all is an immediate duty of all States parties'[314] and determined that '[t]he fact that [the

---

[305] UNCESCR, *GC13*, [47]. See also *CRC*, art 28(1)(e).

[306] *M93 of 2004 v Minister for Immigration* [2006] FMCA 252, [42].

[307] See, e.g., *TA1-03656, TA1-03657 and TA1-03658* (IRB, 19 December 2002); *Kholyavskiy v Mukassey*, 540 F 3d 555, 570 (7th Cir, 2008).

[308] See, e.g., *VA1-02828, VA1-02826, VA1-02827 and VA1-02829* (IRB, 27 February 2003); *T95-01828 and T95-01829* (IRB, 1 October 1996); *SBAS v MIMIA* [2003] FCA 528.

[309] See, e.g., *Mashiri v Ashcroft*, 2004 US App LEXIS 22714 (9th Cir, 2004); *Refugee Appeal Nos 76305, 76306, 76307 and 76308* (RSAA, 30 June 2010).

[310] See *CRC*, arts 28(2), 37(1); UNCRC, *GC8*; UNCRC, *GC13*, [24]. In these situations there may also be a risk of psychological harm: see *infra* Section 4.3.4. See also UNHCR, 2009 *Guidelines*, fn 88, noting that case-law in both Canada and Australia has accepted that '*bullying and harassment of school children may amount to persecution*': see *VA1-02828, VA1-02826, VA1-02827 and VA1-02829* (IRB, 27 February 2003) 9, and *N03/46545* [2003] RRTA 670.

[311] 'I do not agree with this reasoning since it means if [the applicant] is returned to Afghanistan, the only way she can avoid being persecuted is to refuse to go to school. Education is a basic human right and I direct the Board to find that she should be found to be a Convention refugee': *Ali v Canada (MCI)* (1996) 119 FTR 258, [4]. In this case the Tribunal had held that only *educated* women were at risk of violence in Afghanistan, and that the child applicant could avoid that risk by remaining *uneducated*: at [3].

[312] *SBG v Canada (MCI)* 2001 FC 648, [21]. The Federal Court here suggested that, '[i]n order for leaving school to be determinative, the [decision-maker] must first find that the ill treatment the child faces at school is persecution': at [22].

[313] *Refugee Appeal Nos 76305, 76306, 76307 and 76308* (RSAA, 30 June 2010), [142].   [314] *Ibid.*, [144].

applicants'] non-attendance would be directly attributable to the inability of the State to provide access and attendance at school amounts to a violation of their right to education'.[315]

Although the de jure or de facto denial of an education is itself sufficient to satisfy the 'being persecuted' standard, the forward-looking nature of the refugee inquiry suggests that in certain circumstances it may also be appropriate to look at the longer-term consequences that such denial will have on a child.[316] In this regard, the UNCESCR has recognised that a 'lack of educational opportunities for children often reinforces [a child's] subjection to various other human rights violations'.[317]

In addition to access to an education, art 29 of the *CRC* makes clear that children are entitled to a specific *quality* of education.[318] In particular, art 29(1) provides that[319]

> the education of the child shall be directed to ... [t]he development of the child's personality, talents and mental and physical abilities to their fullest potential ... [and] the development of respect for the child's parents, his or her own cultural identity, language and values, for the national values of the country in which the child is living, the country from which he or she may originate, and for civilizations different from his or her own.

Article 29 was expressly invoked by the Canadian IRB in a case involving two Peruvian children who were ostracised by students and teachers because of their Chinese ethnicity.[320] The teachers at the school spoke negatively about Chinese people and culture, teaching the students that they should not travel to China because 'if they believe in Jesus Christ they will be killed'.[321] The parents made repeated complaints to the teachers and school authorities, but no corrective action was taken. The parents were also unable to find another school where their children would receive better treatment. In reaching its decision the IRB engaged with arts 28, 29 and 30 of the *CRC* and determined that 'the sustained and repeated acts faced by these children at their school were inconsistent with the principles set out in the [*CRC*] and resulted in serious and sustained harm to these children'.[322] The Board considered that the children 'did not receive equal opportunity to education in Peru, their cultural identity and values were not respected, nor were they allowed to enjoy the culture'[323] and that '[t]he state was complicit in this persecution as the school authorities were aware of the problem and did nothing to correct it'.[324]

A child's right to a specific quality of education may also be relevant where a child is at risk of being afforded inferior education on the basis of a *Convention* reason – for example, because she belongs to a particular racial or ethnic group or suffers from a mental or physical disability. For instance, refugee decision-makers in Canada[325] and

---

[315] *Ibid.* The RSAA relied on art 13 of the *ICESCR* rather than art 28 of the *CRC*.

[316] As Grahl-Madsen has observed, '[w]ith respect to education, it seems clear that if a person will be excluded from institutions of learning in his home country for political reasons, this will affect his whole life much more profoundly than a relatively short term of imprisonment': Grahl-Madsen (1966) *supra* n 4, vol 1, 215. See, e.g., *M93 of 2004 v Minister for Immigration* [2006] FMCA 252, [42] ('it is difficult to conclude that a lack of provision of education would not have an impact on a person's capacity to subsist').

[317] UNCESCR, *GC11*, [4].   [318] See also UNCRC, *GC1*, [6]–[14].   [319] *CRC*, art 29(1).

[320] *VA1-02828, VA1-02826, VA1-02827 and VA1-02829* (IRB, 27 February 2003).   [321] *Ibid.*, 2.

[322] *Ibid.*, 9.   [323] *Ibid.*   [324] *Ibid.*

[325] See, e.g., *JB v Canada (MCI)* 2011 FC 210; *T97-00096, T97-00097 and T97-00098* (IRB, 22 January 1998). Contra the approach taken in *Jaroslav v Canada (MCI)* 2011 FC 634, [72], where the Court considered

New Zealand[326] have recognised the refugee status of Roma children at risk of being segregated in ordinary schools, or sent to 'special schools' for children with mental disabilities solely on account of their Roma ethnicity.[327] Similarly, decision-makers have recognised that a disabled child will be at risk of persecutory harm where the state does not provide educational facilities tailored to meet the child's distinct needs,[328] as required by arts 23, 28 and 29 of the *CRC*[329] and art 24 of the *Disability Convention*.

4.3.3 Separation from the Family

The separation of a child from her primary caregiver can have debilitating effects on a child's physical and emotional well-being and may seriously impede a child's development.[330] As Baroness Hale of the UK House of Lords has recognised, '[c]hildren need to be brought up in a stable and loving home, preferably by parents who are committed to their interests. Disrupting such a home risks causing lasting damage to their development, damage which is different in kind from the damage done to a parent by the removal of her child, terrible though that can be.'[331] As discussed in Chapter 2, international human rights law recognises the family as the 'natural and fundamental group unit of society' and requires states to adopt

that there was adequate state protection available because '[t]he European Court of Human Rights has shown a willingness to deal with discrimination against Roma children in the Czech education system'. It is difficult to conceive how a decision of the ECtHR, finding that Roma children were being discriminated against in the Czech Republic, demonstrates that the state is providing sufficient protection to Roma children.

[326] See, e.g., *AE (Hungary)* [2012] NZIPT 800325-327, [110]–[141] (citing arts 28 and 29 of the *CRC*) ('The son has been limited to education of an inferior standard by being unable to participate, at all in certain classes and activities such as art and sport, competitions and school outings. In the classes that he is permitted to attend, he has been prevented from actively participating in them. He sits to the side of the classroom and is not permitted to ask any questions, or otherwise interact with the teachers and other non-Roma students ... The son has been distinguished, excluded, ill-treated and subject to limitations of a discriminatory character in his education because he is a Roma and not for any objective or reasonable purpose. This discrimination strikes at the heart of the rights to education and to be free from discrimination', at [139]–[140]); *Refugee Appeal Nos 76380, 76381, 76382 and 76383* (RSAA, 30 June 2010), [144]–[157] (citing arts 2 and 28 of the *CRC*); *Refugee Appeal Nos 75829, 75830, 75831, 75832 and 75833* (RSAA, 7 March 2007), [158].

[327] See generally UNCERD, *General Recommendation XXVII on Discrimination against Roma*, HRI/GEN/1/Rev.8 (2000).

[328] See, e.g., *Hernandez v Canada (MCI)* 2010 FC 179; *Tchoukhrova v Gonzales*, 404 F 3d 1181, 1194 (9th Cir, 2005); UNHCR ExCom, *Conclusion on Refugees with Disabilities and Other Persons with Disabilities Protected and Assisted by UNHCR*, No 110 (LXI) (2010) (reproduced in *Report of the Sixty-First Session of the Executive Committee of the High Commissioner's Programme*, A/AC.96/1095 (2010), [13]), Preamble para 7 ('[r]ecognizing that children with disabilities are at greater risk of ... denial of the right to education').

[329] See generally UNCRC, *GC9*, [62]–[69]; UNCRC, *GC1*, [10].

[330] UNCRC, *GC7*, [18] ('Young children are especially vulnerable to adverse consequences of separations because of their physical dependence on and emotional attachment to their parents/primary caregivers. They are also less able to comprehend the circumstances of any separation').

[331] *EM (Lebanon) v SSHD* [2009] 1 AC 1198, [46]. See also *TA1-03656, TA1-03657 and TA1-03658* (IRB, 19 December 2002), [7]–[8] ('[t]he greatest fear of a child of five ... is of losing the mother. Thus for a child of five, the prospect of going to jail is of little consequence; it is the prospect of losing the mother that matters'); *V91-00998* (IRB, 15 November 1991) 3 ('ever since Moses was hidden in an ark of bulrushes to escape the Pharaoh's edict that all sons of the Israelites be killed at birth, it has been clear that a child must depend upon others to escape acts of persecution when that child is of tender years').

measures to protect and facilitate family unity.[332] The Preamble to the *CRC* provides that 'the child, for the full and harmonious development of his or her personality, should grow up in a family environment, in an atmosphere of happiness, love and understanding'. This statement finds formal expression in arts 7 (identity), 9 (non-separation), 10 (family reunification), 16 (privacy and family life), 18 (parental responsibilities) and 20 (alternative parental care) of the *CRC*.

For the purposes of art 1A(2) of the *Convention*, the separation of a child from her parent(s) or guardian(s) may give rise to a predicament of 'being persecuted' in two related contexts. First, the separation itself may amount to a violation of *CRC* and constitute persecutory harm. Second, and irrespective of whether the separation itself is persecutory, the resulting consequence of the separation – for instance, leaving a child destitute and living alone on the street – may satisfy the 'being persecuted' threshold.

Turning to the first context, it has been suggested that the '[r]emoval of children from their parents without justification is one of the gravest violations of rights the State can perpetrate against children'.[333] Article 9 of the *CRC* provides that a child may only be separated from her parents where competent authorities determine that 'separation is *necessary for the best interests of the child*'.[334] That determination must be made according to applicable laws and procedures and must be subject to judicial review.[335] All interested parties, including the child, must be given an opportunity to participate in the proceedings and make their view known.[336] Decision-makers in several jurisdictions have recognised that a child may be at risk of 'being persecuted' where there is a real chance that she will be separated from a parent in circumstances that contravene art 9.[337]

By way of illustration, a child may be at risk of being forcibly separated from her mother because of discriminatory custodial laws that arbitrarily favour the interests of the child's father or (where the father is deceased) the father's extended family. Although art 9(1) explicitly acknowledges the reality that separation from a parent will be inevitable where the child's parents are living separately, it is clear that the determination as to the child's place of residence must be made according to the child's best interests rather than by any cultural bias towards the father (or the mother). The RSAA has held on a number of occasions that the arbitrary deprivation of maternal care as a result of 'demonstrably discriminatory custody laws' in place in Iran constitutes persecutory treatment under the *Convention*.[338] The Authority has emphasised that the decision by a government to award custody to one

---

[332] *UDHR*, art 16(3).

[333] UNICEF, *Implementation Handbook for the Convention on the Rights of the Child* (3rd edn, 2007) 265.

[334] Art 9(1) (emphasis added).   [335] *CRC*, art 9(1).   [336] *CRC*, arts 9(2), 12.

[337] For refugee decisions that have engaged explicitly with art 9, see *Khadra Hassan Farah* (IRB, 10 May 1994); *T93-09636, T93-09638 and T93-09639* (IRB, 26 January 1994); *M99-07094, M99-07096 and M99-07098* (IRB, 31 May 2001); *V97-01419, V97-01420, V97-01421, V98-02335, V98-02345 and V98-02346* (IRB, 9 August 1999); *A99-00215, A99-00256 and A99-00258* (IRB, 30 September 1999). In the United States, the training manual for asylum officers expressly provides that a violation of art 9(1) may satisfy the 'being persecuted' threshold: USCIS Asylum Division, *Children's Claim Guidelines* (2009) *supra* n 123, 39–40. For academic support, see Foster (2007) *supra* n 19, 209; Bhabha and Young (1999) *supra* n 117, 105; Crock (2008) *supra* n 171, 171.

[338] *Refugee Appeal Nos 75301, 75302 and 75303* (RSAA, 24 January 2006), [43]–[47]. See also *Refugee Appeal Nos 76226 and 76227* (RSAA, 12 January 2009), [111]–[115]; *Refugee Appeal Nos 76494 and 76495* (RSAA, 23 November 2010). In identifying the persecutory harm the RSAA has focused on art 3 (best interests) and art 7 (the right to know and be cared for by his or her parents) of the *CRC*, rather than art 9.

parent or the other is not itself persecutory, but that such a determination takes on a persecutory character if the government does 'not take appropriate account of the "best interests of the child"'.[339] In these cases the Authority considered that the best interests of the child were subverted by the patriarchal and discriminatory privileges afforded to males in Iranian society.[340]

Canadian decision-makers have expressly relied on art 9 to find that the implementation of discriminatory custody laws may constitute persecutory harm. In *Khadra Hassan Farah* a ten-year-old girl and seven-year-old boy from Somalia were at risk of being returned to their abusive father. The IRB expressly engaged with arts 3, 9 and 12 of the *CRC* and made the following determination:[341]

> Based on the evidence before us, the panel is not satisfied that the best interest of this minor applicant would be considered at all in Somalia because his father's right to custody is automatic. There is no evidence to suggest that the claimant's own wishes would be take into account; that he would be permitted to maintain contact with his mother; or that his father's violent behaviour would be a factor in the decision. Thus, the minor claimant would not have the benefit of his internationally protected human rights in any decision regarding which parent is to have custody of him.

Similarly, in *T93-09636, T93-09638 and T93-09639* two young girls from the United Arab Emirates had been physically abused by their father but, owing to Sharia law, were likely to be returned to his custody. The IRB considered that such a result did not conform to 'internationally accepted standards for protection of children', explicitly engaging with arts 3, 9 and 12 of the *CRC*.[342]

A child may be separated from her primary caregiver in a range of other situations that may similarly amount to persecutory conduct. For example, the separation of a parent and child in the following scenarios may satisfy the 'being persecuted' threshold: the incarceration of a parent;[343] the kidnapping or parental abduction of a child;[344] the removal of an

---

[339] *Refugee Appeal Nos 75301, 75302 and 75303* (RSAA, 24 January 2006), [47].

[340] *Ibid.* Contra the decision of the NZIPT in *DQ (Iran)* [2015] NZIPT 800868, [42]–[43], [55].

[341] *Khadra Hassan Farah* (10 May 1994) 7.

[342] *T93-09636, T93-09638 and T93-09639* (IRB, 26 January 1994) 6. See also *M99-07094, M99-07096 and M99-07098* (IRB, 31 May 2001) 16 ('[d]espite the fact that [the father] had been granted custody of the children in France, the evidence shows that the plan was not motivated by the children's "best interests"'); *V97-01419, V97-01420, V97-01421, V98-02335, V98-02345 and V98-02346* (IRB, 9 August 1999) 14 ('the children have a fundamental human right to be with the surviving parent, their mother. If they were to be placed in the custody and under the guardianship of their paternal father, *in these particular circumstances*, their fundamental human rights as children would be violated' (emphasis in original)); *T99-11540 and T99-11541* (IRB, 31 May 2001); *V96-02102 and V96-02103* (IRB, 28 May 1999); *MA1-00356, MA1-00357 and MA1-00358* (IRB, 18 December 2001). The issue has also arisen in the United Kingdom in the context of claims based on art 8 of the *ECHR*: see especially *EM (Lebanon) v SSHD* [2009] 1 AC 1198, [46] ('[i]f [the applicant] were obliged to return to a country where he would inevitably be removed from [his mother's] care, with only the possibility of supervised visits, then the very essence of his right to respect for his family life would be destroyed. And it would be destroyed for reasons which could never be justified . . . because they are purely arbitrary and pay no regard to his interests'); *KA (domestic violence – risk on return) Pakistan CG* [2010] UKUT 216, [213].

[343] See, e.g., *KA (domestic violence – risk on return) Pakistan CG* [2010] UKUT 216; *Refugee Appeal Nos 74957 and 74958* (RSAA, 12 May 2004).

[344] See, e.g., *M99-07094, M99-07096 and M99-07098* (IRB, 31 May 2001).

illegitimate child from a parent for 'honour' reasons;[345] the institutionalisation of a parent or child;[346] the separation of a mixed-sect family;[347] and the extrajudicial killing of a parent.[348] In each of these scenarios the determinative inquiry is whether the anticipated separation is in the child's best interests.[349]

Of course, a state cannot guarantee every child a family. In many – perhaps the majority – of cases, the separation of a child from her parents occurs in circumstances outside the control of the state.[350] In other cases it will be in the best interests of a child to be separated from her parents, for example because of abuse or neglect.[351] In these situations, though the separation of child and parent is itself unlikely to be persecutory, the child may be placed in circumstances that give rise to a risk of 'being persecuted' given a child's dependence on family for care and subsistence. The UNCRC has stressed that '[c]hildren's rights to development are at serious risk when they are orphaned, abandoned or deprived of family care or when they suffer long-term disruptions to relationships or separations'.[352] According to the Committee, '[t]hese adversities will impact on children differently depending on their personal resilience, their age and their circumstances, as well as the availability of wider sources of support and alternative care'.[353]

Decision-makers have accepted the refugee claims of children at risk of living on the street in order to escape violence in the home. In *V97-03500*, a 16-year-old child argued

---

[345] See, e.g., *AC (Czech Republic)* [2012] NZIPT 800183-186, [60]–[61]; *Refugee Appeal Nos 75186 and 75187* (RSAA, 30 November 2005), [130]–[131]; *AM and BM (Trafficked Women) Albania CG* [2010] UKUT 80, [171].

[346] See, e.g., *Tchoukhrova v Gonzales*, 404 F 3d 1181, 1193 (9th Cir, 2005).

[347] *AK (Iraq)* [2015] NZIPT 800716-720, [95]–[101].

[348] See, e.g., *A99-00918 and A99-00919* (IRB, 20 March 2000). In this case the mother was at risk of being detained and raped by rebel forces. The Board noted that, according to the *CRC*, the parent/child relationship 'can only be severed by action of law in a state of where the rule of law prevails under very, very particular and limited conditions': at 6. The Board considered that the risk that the mother faced could result in the child being separated from her mother and could thus have 'a direct consequence for the child ... [such] that she is a Convention refugee as well': at *ibid.*

[349] A child may also be separated from her parents where a *host* state grants a parent but not a child refugee status, and the child will be returned without her family. In this situation the host state may have directly violated art 9 of the *CRC*. See, e.g., *A99-00215, A99-00256 and A99-00258* (IRB, 30 September 1999) 5–6 (finding that a three-year-old child will face a real chance of being persecuted in Djibouti if forced to return there alone, with no close family members available to take care of her and, further, that 'it would be persecutory in itself to separate such a young child from her mother' (citing arts 9 and 16 of the *CRC*)); *U94-04870, U94-04871, U94-04872 and U94-04873* (IRB, 19 July 1996), [46] (relying on the best interests principle to reach the same result). See further Chapter 2, Section 2.3.2.

[350] For example, due to the illness or death of a family member.

[351] See, e.g., *Maerschalack v Gonzales*, 159 Fed Appx 29 (10th Cir, 2005). In certain circumstances separation may be required by *CRC*, art 19. However, '[r]emoval of a child from the care of the family should be seen as a measure of last resort and should, whenever possible, be temporary and for the shortest possible duration': *Guidelines for the Alternative Care of Children*, A/RES/64/142 (2010), [14]. Critically, '[f]inancial and material poverty, or conditions directly and uniquely imputable to such poverty, should never be the only justification for the removal of a child from parental care': at [15]. Rather, this should be seen as 'a signal for the need to provide appropriate support to the family', for example, pursuant to arts 18(2), 26(2) and 27(3) of the *CRC*.

[352] UNCRC, *GC7*, [36]. See also UNHCR, 2009 *Guidelines*, [36] ('[c]hildren who lack adult care and support, are orphaned, abandoned or rejected by their parents, and are escaping violence in their homes may be particularly affected by ... forms of discrimination').

[353] UNCRC, *GC7*, [36].

that if returned he would be forced to live on the streets in order to escape his abusive mother. The IRB determined that the applicant could 'very easily be victimized by drug dealers, pimps and other predators on the street and that the State [was] unwilling – or, by the sheer numbers of street children in need – unable, to protect the claimant'.[354] Similar reasoning applies where a child has no remaining family members in the country of origin or has lost contact with any remaining family members. Consider, for example, the following passage from the opinion of Judge Stahl of the US Court of Appeals for the First Circuit:[355]

> Celvyn is still a child. If he returns to Honduras he has only two family members with whom he could conceivably live, his grandmother and his father. It is unreasonable to expect Celvyn to relocate with his father because . . . he has never cared for Celvyn, and there is no reason to believe he would today. It is equally unreasonable to expect his elderly ill grandmother to relocate with Celvyn to another part of the country. Given that he has no other means, if Celvyn cannot live with either of these adults it is almost a foregone conclusion that he would live on the street somewhere in Honduras. Further, the record is clear about the tremendous problems facing street children in Honduras, including persecution by the police.

In *FM (Afghanistan) v SSHD* the Upper Tribunal similarly held that to return a 16-year-old child to Afghanistan in circumstances where all contact with family had been lost would give rise to a risk of 'being persecuted'. The Tribunal considered that the applicant 'would be vulnerable to sexual exploitation, exposing him to rape, other sexual abuse and forced prostitution. His vulnerability to these risks would be exacerbated by the lack of the basics of safe shelter, food and clothing and of medical treatment'.[356]

In cases involving children that are deprived of a family environment, art 20 of the *CRC* provides a principled point of reference to guide a decision-maker in assessing whether the country of origin provides effective state protection.[357] Article 20(1) states that 'a child temporarily or permanently deprived of his or her family environment, or in whose own best interests cannot be allowed to remain in that environment, shall be entitled to special

---

[354] *V97-03500* (IRB, 31 May 1999) 4–5. See also *Matthews v Canada (MCI)* 2008 FC 770, [9]–[13]; *Matter of Juan Carlos Martinez-Mejia* (BIA, 1999) 3.

[355] *Mejilla-Romero v Holder*, 600 F 3d 63, 91 (1st Cir, 2010).

[356] *FM (Afghanistan) v SSHD* (Upper Tribunal, AA/01079/2010, 10 March 2011), [146]. This issue has arisen in a series of recent decisions in the United Kingdom involving unaccompanied children from Afghanistan: see *LQ (Age: immutable characteristic) Afghanistan* [2008] UKAIT 0005; *DS (Afghanistan) v SSHD* [2011] EWCA Civ 305; *AA (unattended children) Afghanistan CG* [2012] UKUT 00016, [133]; *HK (Afghanistan) v SSHD* [2012] EWCA Civ 315; *KA (Afghanistan) v SSHD* [2013] 1WLR 615. In this context the England and Wales Court of Appeal has determined that the government is under a duty to undertake tracing inquiries in order to assess a child's refugee claims. In *HK (Afghanistan) v SSHD* [2012] EWCA Civ 315, [54], the Court emphasised that this duty 'is not distinct from the asylum application', but is 'intimately connected with the determination of that application'. See also *Council Directive 2013/33/EU of the European Parliament and of the Council of 26 June 2013 laying down standards for the reception of applicants for international protection* [2013] OJ L 180, art 24(3).

[357] A number of other provisions of the *CRC* may also be engaged, including, in particular, the obligation on a state under art 6(2) to 'ensure to the maximum extent possible the survival and development of the child'. See generally UNCRC, *Discussion Day: State Violence against Children* (2000), [21]; UNCRC, *Report on the Fortieth Session* (2006) *supra* n 206, pt VI (summarising the Day of General Discussion on 'Children without Parental Care'); *Guidelines for the Alternative Care of Children* (2010), *supra* n 351; UNCRC, *GC7*, [36]. On children orphaned by HIV/AIDS, see UNCRC, *GC3*, [31]–[35].

protection and assistance provided by the State'.[358] Articles 20(2)–(3) further provide that states must 'ensure alternative care for such a child', which might, for example, involve 'foster placement, kafalah of Islamic law, adoption or . . . placement' in a state-run institution. The need to assess the availability of alternative care arrangements for children without parental care has been explicitly acknowledged in the *EU Qualification Directive*, which provides that '[w]hen the applicant is an unaccompanied minor, the availability of appropriate care and custodial arrangements, which are in the best interests of the unaccompanied minor, should form part of the assessment as to whether that protection is effectively available'.[359]

A child is unlikely to satisfy the 'being persecuted' standard on the basis that she is or will be deprived of a family environment and will, for example, be exposed to the perils of living as a street child, if there is evidence that the state provides protection to children in these circumstances. By way of illustration, in a case involving two young girls from Grenada, the Canadian IRB concluded that the state provided alternative care arrangements for children abused or neglected by their parents.[360] By contrast, in *Canada (MCI) v Patel*, the Federal Court of Canada held that a 13-year-old Indian boy, abandoned by both of his mother and father, would be at risk of 'being persecuted' if returned because 'he would have no caregiver, no emotional support and no access to the necessities of life'.[361] In reaching that decision the Court examined documentary evidence which indicated that there were more than 100,000 children living as street children in India and demonstrated that there was 'a general malaise in India towards its treatment of the most vulnerable in its society, its children'.[362]

4.3.4 Psychological Harm

An especially interesting area of refugee jurisprudence in recent years has been the recognition that psychological harm may satisfy the 'being persecuted' standard.[363] The view that psychological harm constitutes persecutory harm sits comfortably with international human rights jurisprudence and the absolute prohibition on the infliction of 'cruel, inhuman or degrading treatment or punishment'.[364] In the context of child applicants, art 37(a)

---

[358] The obligation on a state to afford children deprived of a family environment special protection has long been recognised by the international community. For example, the *1924 Declaration*, second para, explicitly provided that 'the orphan and the waif must be sheltered and succored'.

[359] Recital 27.

[360] *T98-09341* and *T98-09342* (IRB, 16 September 1999) 3 ('The Social Welfare Division within the Ministry of Labour provides probationary and rehabilitation services to youths, day care services and social work programs to families, assistance to families wishing to adopt or foster children, and financial assistance to the three children's homes run by private organizations. Abused children are either placed in a government-run home or in private foster homes. Although not necessarily perfect, it is adequate protection for these abandoned minors').

[361] *Canada (MCI) v Patel* 2008 FC 747, [41].   [362] *Ibid.*

[363] For a detailed discussion on this jurisprudence, see J C Hathaway and J Pobjoy, 'Queer Cases Make Bad Law' (2012) 44 *New York University Journal of International Law and Politics* 315, 358–71. This section draws in part on that analysis.

[364] 'No one shall be subjected to torture or to cruel, inhuman or degrading treatment or punishment. In particular, no one shall be subjected without his free consent to medical or scientific experimentation': *ICCPR*, art 7. *ECHR*, art 3, and the *American Convention on Human Rights*, opened for signature 22 November 1969, 1144 UNTS 123 (entered into force 18 July 1978), art 5, contain similar provisions. Article 16 of the *CAT* provides that each state party 'shall undertake to prevent in any territory under its

of the *CRC* provides that 'no child shall be subjected to torture or other cruel, inhuman or degrading treatment or punishment'. This is complemented and expanded by art 19(1), which requires states to 'protect the child from all forms of *physical or mental* violence, injury or abuse, neglect or negligent treatment, maltreatment or exploitation, including sexual abuse, while in the care of parent(s), legal guardian(s) or any other person who has the care of the child'.[365]

It has been suggested that the range of actions encompassed by the notion of cruel, inhuman or degrading treatment is as 'extensive as the ingenuity of perpetrators'.[366] Although the UNCRC has issued limited guidance on art 37(a),[367] the HRC has made clear that the cognate provision under the *ICCPR* encompasses both physical *and* psychological harm. In its *GC20*, the HRC has signalled that the prohibition relates 'not only to acts that cause physical pain, but also to acts that cause mental suffering to the victim'.[368] This proposition finds support in the jurisprudence of the HRC.[369] For example, in *Quinteros Almeida v Uruguay* the Committee determined that the mental anguish caused to a mother following the disappearance of her daughter amounted to a violation of art 7.[370] Similarly, in *C v Australia* the Committee determined that a violation of art 7 had occurred where immigration detention under Australia's mandatory detention policy for unauthorised 'asylum-seekers' had resulted in the development of a serious mental illness.[371]

---

jurisdiction any other acts of cruel, inhuman or degrading treatment or punishment which do not amount to torture as defined in article 1'. See generally S Joseph, J Schultz and M Castan, *The International Covenant on Civil and Political Rights: Cases, Materials, and Commentary* (2nd edn, 2004) 218–23; M Nowak and E McArthur, *The United Nations Convention Against Torture: A Commentary* (2008) 538–76; N Jayawickrama, *The Judicial Application of Human Rights Law: National, Regional and International Jurisprudence* (2002) 296–352.

[365] Emphasis added. For further discussion on art 19, see *supra* Section 4.3.1. In its *GC13*, the UNCRC has explained that 'mental violence' can include '[s]caring, terrorizing and threatening; exploiting and corrupting; spurning and rejecting; isolating, ignoring and favouritism' ([21(b)]), '[e]xposure to domestic violence' ([21(e)], '[i]nsults, name-calling, humiliation, belittling, ridiculing and hurting a child's feelings' ([21(g)], and '[p]sychological bullying ... by adults or other children' ([21(g)]). Other *CRC* rights may be relevant here, including arts 6(2) (survival and development), 24 (highest attainable standard of health) and 39 (rehabilitation).

[366] N Rodley, *The Treatment of Prisoners under International Law* (2009) 140.

[367] See also UNCRC, *GC8*, but that is focused on corporal punishment: see especially at [11], which recognises that 'non-physical forms of punishment' may be 'cruel and degrading'. See also definition of mental violence in UNCRC, *GC13*, [21]. See generally G Van Bueren, 'Opening Pandora's Box: Protecting Children against Torture or Cruel, Inhuman and Degrading Treatment or Punishment' (1995) 17 *Law and Policy* 378.

[368] HRC, *GC20*, [5].

[369] See Joseph, Schultz and Castan, *supra* n 364, 218–23. See also J C Hathaway and W S Hicks, 'Is There a Subjective Element in the Refugee Convention's Requirement of "Well-Founded Fear"?' (2004) 26 *Michigan Journal of International Law* 505, 556–60.

[370] '[There was] anguish and stress caused to the mother by the disappearance of her daughter and by the continuing uncertainty concerning her fate and whereabouts. The author has the right to know what has happened to her daughter. In these respects, she too is a victim of the violation of the Covenant suffered by her daughter in particular, of article 7': HRC, *Views: Communication No 107/1981*, CCPR/C/19/D/107/1981 (1983), [14] ('*Quinteros Almeida v Uruguay*'). A similar conclusion was reached in HRC, *Communication No 886/1999*, CCPR/C/77/D/886/1999 (2003), [10.2] ('*Schedko v Belarus*') and HRC, *Views: Communication No 887/1999*, CCPR/C/77/D/887/1999 (2003), [9.2] ('*Staselovich v Belarus*'). For further examples of jurisprudence from the HRC and the Committee against Torture, see Hathaway and Pobjoy (2012) *supra* n 363, 362–3.

[371] HRC, *Views: Communication No 900/1999*, CCPR/C/76/D/900/1999 (2002), [8.5] ('*C v Australia*').

In assessing whether the substantive harm feared satisfies the requisite threshold, the HRC has made clear the need to take into account the individual circumstances and vulnerabilities of the applicant, including the applicant's age.[372] The point is nicely illustrated in the case of *Mayeka and Mitunga v Belgium*,[373] which concerned the application of the equivalent regional provision in the *ECHR*. The case involved a five-year-old unaccompanied Congolese girl who had been detained in a centre designed for adults, with no one assigned to look after her. The ECtHR considered that her position 'was characterised by her very young age, the fact that she was an illegal immigrant in a foreign land and the fact that she was unaccompanied by her family from whom she had become separated'.[374] The Court held that the detention of the child reflected a lack of 'awarene[ss] of the serious psychological effects it would have on her' and 'demonstrated a lack of humanity to such a degree that it amounted to inhuman treatment'.[375]

These insights from international and regional human rights law align neatly with the growing number of refugee decisions, noted above and elaborated on immediately below, that have recognised psychological harm as persecutory in claims involving children. Although the jurisprudence often fails to identify explicitly the cruel, inhuman or degrading standard, the case-law demonstrates that the proposition advanced here – that psychological harm is appropriately understood to be persecutory, particularly when assessed from the perspective of a child – is by no means novel.

A child may be at risk of psychological harm in a range of contexts. The first involves situations where the child is not at risk of physical violence but someone related to the child is at risk of an exogenous form of harm. As noted earlier, decision-makers have appropriately recognised that a child's response to an injury inflicted on a family member is likely to be more acute than the response of a similarly placed adult.[376] It is thus necessary to 'look at the event from [the child's] perspective, [and] measure the degree of ... injur[y] by [the] impact on children of [that] age'.[377] Adopting this approach, decision-makers in the

---

[372] 'While the *standards* of international human rights law are of, of course, universal, this does not mean that their application is in any sense insensitive to the specific vulnerabilities of particular persons. To the contrary, the prohibition of cruel, inhuman or degrading treatment focuses on the nature of the harm experienced by each individual, requiring attention to be paid not just to what harm is threatened, but also to how that harm would impact the applicant himself': Hathaway and Pobjoy (2012) *supra* n 363, 363 (emphasis in original). In HRC, *Views: Communication No 265/1987*, CCPR/C/35/D/265/ 1987 (1989), [9.2] ('*Vuolanne v Finland*'), the HRC expressly affirmed that the application of art 7 of the *ICCPR* depends on 'all the circumstances of the case, such as the duration and manner of the treatment, its physical or mental effects as well as the sex, age and state of health of the victim'. In interpreting the regional cognate right, the ECtHR has similarly acknowledged the need to consider 'the age, sex, and health condition of the person exposed to [the treatment]': *Ireland v UK* (1979–80) 2 EHRR 25, 109.

[373] *Mayeka and Mitunga v Belgium* (2008) 46 EHRR 23.

[374] *Ibid.*, [55]. This reasoning was affirmed in *E v Chief Constable of the Royal Ulster Constabulary* [2009] 1 AC 536, [7]–[9]; and *SQ (Pakistan) v Upper Tribunal Immigration and Asylum Chamber* [2013] EWCA Civ 1251, [17]–[19]. See also *Güveç v Turkey* (ECtHR, Application No 70337/01, 20 January 2009), [90].

[375] *Mayeka and Mitunga v Belgium* (2008) 46 EHRR 23, [58].

[376] See *supra* text accompanying n 147–53 UNHCR has also suggested that '[w]itnessing the violent destruction of [a] child's home is another form of traumatic event that could give rise to fear of persecution': UNHCR, 'Brief *Amicus Curiae*' filed in *Mejilla-Romero* (18 June 2010) *supra* n 18, 9.

[377] *Hernandez-Ortiz v Gonzales*, 496 F 3d 1042, 1045 (9th Cir, 2007), cited with approval in *Winata v Holder*, 2011 US App LEXIS 16962.

United States[378] and Canada[379] have determined that psychological trauma to a child triggered by the infliction of violence on a family member may amount to persecutory harm.[380] This might arise, for instance, where a child is at risk of exposure to domestic spousal abuse,[381] to the death or disappearance of a family member[382] or to witnessing the infliction of other forms of violence on a family member.[383] An illustrative example is provided in a case involving a nine-year-old Bulgarian girl who witnessed her mother being physically beaten by her father on multiple occasions.[384] In assessing the degree of harm suffered by the applicant, the Canadian IRB drew on the framework of the CRC, and in particular arts 19(1), 24 and 37(a), determining that '[t]he mental and psychological duress suffered by the minor claimant due to her father's violence is a form of harm from which the state is expected to protect its children'.[385]

A further group of cases that recognises the plausibility of endogenous forms of persecutory harm involves claims where the child has suffered psychological harm as a consequence of threats of violence. New Zealand decision-makers have accepted that 'children are less equipped to deal with stress and ... the corrosive effect of an incessant subjective concern

---

[378] See, e.g., *Winata v Holder*, 2011 US App LEXIS 16962; *Hernandez-Ortiz v Gonzales*, 496 F 3d 1042, 1045-6 (9th Cir, 2007); *Jorge-Tzoc v Gonzales*, 435 F 3d 146, 150-1 (2nd Cir, 2006); *Argueta-Rodriguez v INS*, 1997 US App LEXIS 29864, 12 (4th Cir, 1997); *Kahssai v INS*, 16 F 3d 323 (9th Cir, 1994).

[379] See, e.g., *MA1-11675, MA1-11676 and MA1-11677* (IRB, 16 June 2003); *V98-00787* (IRB, 4 June 1999); *V97-00708, V97-00709 and V97-00710* (IRB, 8 July 1998); *T95-05227 and T95-05228* (IRB, 2 July 1996); *T94-00416, T94-00418 and T94-00419* (IRB, 25 August 1994); *T91-01497 and T91-01498* (IRB, 9 August 1994).

[380] This comports with the approach taken by the HRC: see *supra* text accompanying n 370. It is important to acknowledge this approach is not boundless and there must be evidence that the child is at risk of psychological harm rather than invoking what would otherwise amount to a purely derivative harm. In this context descriptors such as 'derivative harm' and 'indirect persecution' are largely unhelpful as they are apt to lead to confusion.

[381] In *V97-00708, V97-00709, V97-00710 and V97-00711* (IRB, 11 August 1998), [37], the IRB considered that 'the panel cannot ignore the psychological impact on these children of repeatedly witnessing the physical abuse of their mother ... It appears to the panel that the circumstances they have witnessed constitute direct abuse by their father of their still fragile psyches, the trauma they have suffered as the result of family strife is as real as if they had been directly physically targeted'. Similarly, in *MA1-11675, MA1-11676 and MA1-11677* (IRB, 16 June 2003) 6, it was not suggested that the children were the subject of physical violence from their father, but the IRB considered that 'they suffered psychological abuse in witnessing the mistreatment inflicted by their father on their mother'. The IRB further considered that '[s]ince young children, who are much more emotionally fragile than adults, are involved ... the treatment imposed on their mother and the fact that young children are powerless in such circumstances ... could have a persecutory effect on them'. See also *T95-05227 and T95-05228* (IRB, 2 July 1996) 10–12; *T94-00416, T94-00418 and T94-00419* (IRB, 25 August 1994) 5.

[382] '[I]t is hard to imagine a more direct, atrocious, and final persecution than to have both of one's parents, all five siblings, sundry other relatives, and just about everyone one grew up knowing all brutally murdered and then incinerated': *Argueta-Rodriguez v INS*, 1997 US App LEXIS 29864, 12 (4th Cir, 1997), 12. See also *Jorge-Tzoc v Gonzales*, 435 F 3d 146, 150 (2nd Cir, 2006): a seven-year-old boy experienced the murder of his sister and witnessed the bullet-ridden body of one of his cousins.

[383] 'The claimant was thirteen years old when he lost his twelve-year-old brother and watched him die. His father died in his arms of gunshot wounds. No thirteen-year-old child should be subjected to such appalling circumstances': *V98-00787* (IRB, 4 June 1999) 6. Contra *Rodriguez-Ramirez v Ashcroft*, 398 F 3d 120, 124 (1st Cir, 2005): 'We acknowledge that watching one's father beaten may be a horrific experience for a young child – but not all horrific experiences translate into persecution.'

[384] *T92-01497 and T91-01498* (IRB, 9 August 1994).

[385] *Ibid.*, 6. For further discussion on domestic violence, and in particular the state's protection duties in this context, see *supra* Section 4.3.1.

about crime and personal safety can have a detrimental effect on a child's mental and emotional well-being'.[386] To similar effect, the Australian RRT has recognised '[the] capacity to cope with these threats in practice and with the psychological harm caused by attempting to do so will place [the child] under enormous pressure and at risk of serious harm'.[387] These decisions accord with the view of UNHCR that '[i]n the case of a child applicant, psychological harm may be a particularly relevant factor to consider', given that '[c]hildren are more likely to be distressed by hostile situations, to believe improbable threats, or to be emotionally affected by unfamiliar circumstances'.[388]

Decision-makers have also recognised that children may be at risk of psychological harm when exposed to ongoing discrimination and/or ostracism.[389] In *Kholyavskiy v Mukasey*[390] the applicant was subjected to regular discrimination and harassment between the ages of eight and 13 because of his Jewish ethnicity and religion.[391] On one occasion he was forced into a school bathroom, where his fellow students pulled down his pants to expose his penis and laughed at his circumcision.[392] His teachers required him 'on a quarterly basis, to stand up and identify himself as a Jew', 'children regularly mocked him and urinated on him' and 'school officials not only sat silently by, but they also told his parents that the "jewish child [wa]s just making things up"'.[393] As a result the applicant 'became afraid both to attend school and to go outside' and 'took to hiding in the attic of his family's apartment'.[394] Both the IJ and BIA considered that the mistreatment of the applicant did not rise to the level of persecutory harm.[395] This finding was firmly rebuked by the Court of Appeals for the Seventh Circuit, which emphasised the importance of evaluating 'the impact of these actions on a child between the ages of eight and thirteen', given that the applicant's age at the time the events occurred 'may bear heavily on the question of whether an applicant was persecuted'.[396] In another case, *TA1-03656*, a 16-year-old Costa Rican boy was repeatedly harassed and rejected by his school peers because of his Chinese ethnicity. The IRB considered that 'peer rejection had, in his particular circumstances, caused him *intense* pain' which 'cannot be dismissed as trivial' and 'ought not to be devalued simply because it is not traceable to an adult cause'.[397] The IRB concluded that the minor claimant 'suffered persecution at school by reason of his ethnicity'.[398]

---

[386] *AI (South Africa)* [2011] NZIPT 800050–53, [56]. In Australia see, to similar effect, *1211431* [2012] RRTA 975 (19 October 2012), [113] ('[the] capacity to cope with these threats in practice and with the psychological harm caused by attempting to do so will place [the child] under enormous pressure and at risk of serious harm').

[387] *1211431* [2012] RRTA 975 (19 October 2012), [113].   [388] UNHCR, 2009 *Guidelines*, [16].

[389] See generally Hathaway and Pobjoy, *supra* n 363, 368–9.   [390] 540 F 3d 555 (7th Cir, 2008).

[391] See also 'Initial Brief Filed by the Appellant-Petitioner', filed in *Kholyavskiy v Mukasey* (15 June 2007) (copy on file with author).

[392] *Kholyavskiy v Mukasey* 540 F 3d 555 (7th Cir, 2008) (15 June 2007), 570.   [393] *Ibid.*, 571.   [394] *Ibid.*

[395] *Ibid.*, 570.

[396] *Ibid.*, 571. For a similar, equally disturbing set of facts, see *Re O-Z and I-Z*, 22 I & N Dec 23 (BIA, 1998).

[397] *TA1-03656, TA1-03657 and TA1-03658* (IRB, 19 December 2002) 4 (emphasis in original). See also *SZDAG v MIMIA* [2006] FMCA 987 (applicant argued (at [44]) that '[t]o be branded a child without "hukou" is in fact [a] statement by the authorities and the Chinese community alike that the child is [to] be singled out and look[ed] down upon as one who is not socially recognised by the community . . . and [is] to be treated as a sub[-]standard class of person'; the Court allowed the appeal (at [45]–[47]) on the basis that the RRT had failed to consider the psychological implications of being denied 'hukou'); *Mansour v Ashcroft*, 390 F 3d 667, 677–8 (7th Cir, 2004), 677–82 (Judge Pregerson, dissenting); *T95-01828 and T95-01829* (IRB, 1 October 1996).

[398] *TA1-03656, TA1-03657 and TA1-03658* (IRB, 19 December 2002) 5.

Children may also be at risk of psychological harm where they will be required to modify their behaviour in a fundamental way when returned to their home country. This may arise, for example, where a child would be compelled to conceal her sexual orientation, or desist from activities connected to her sexuality identity, in order to avoid exogenous harm.[399] There is ample evidence that such self-repression may have damaging implications on the psyche,[400] a reality attested to in a number of refugee decisions involving adult gay applicants at risk of enforced concealment on return.[401]

One of the most far-reaching developments in refugee jurisprudence relating to psychological harm has been the recognition that a child's exposure to physical or psychological trauma *in the past* may have enduring implications that place an applicant at a heightened risk of psychological harm in the future.[402] A child may already be suffering from a psychological condition,[403] or such a condition might be triggered by being required to return to the place where the initial persecutory acts occurred. Consider, for example, the testimony of a young Eritrean woman who had been detained for 6 days at the age of 15:[404]

> Memories of those days still haunt us. We have endured so many sleepless nights thinking about the cruelty that was inflicted upon us. When people mention Eritrea or Ethiopia, all that comes to mind is the filth and stench of the prison cell crowded with innocent citizens ... Being beaten and kicked by soldiers and being spat on by them broke our dignity and made us feel subhuman. The present government of Eritrea in no way guarantees our safety in a way that can alleviate those feelings. We still remember vividly the cruelty, the crowded jail, not having enough to eat, and watching others being terrorized as we imagined what would happen to us in turn. All during my childhood we had seen people being taken off to prison, people disappearing and never being heard from again. It is hard to forget those things. To us, returning would mean a return to our awful childhood there.

---

[399] This argument is developed in Hathaway and Pobjoy (2012) *supra* n 363.

[400] See, e.g., M King *et al.*, 'A Systematic Review of Mental Disorder, Suicide, and Deliberate Self Harm in Lesbian, Gay and Bisexual People' (2008) 8 *PMC Psychiatry* 70. For further sources relating to children, see Tobin, 'Assessing GLBTI Refugee Claims' (2012), *supra* n 72, 463–4.

[401] In *MK (Lesbians) v SSHD* [2009] UKAIT 0036, [67]: the UK AIT heard evidence from a psychiatrist that a lesbian's attempt to suppress her sexual identity would be a 'very potent factor contributing further to her deterioration'. The psychiatrist considered that 'suppressing sexual identity meant living as someone whom you were not, which resulted in an anxiety increase, paranoia and disassociation': at [68]. See also *SW (Lesbians) v SSHD* [2011] UKUT 00251.

[402] UNHCR, 2009 *Guidelines*, [16] ('[m]emories of traumatic events may linger in a child and put him/her at heightened risk of future harm'). These developments sit comfortably with the exemption clause in art 1C(5) of the *Refugee Convention*, which provides for an exemption from cessation for refugees who establish that they are unable to return home due to 'compelling reasons arising out of previous persecution'. The drafting history suggests that this exemption was intended, in part, to 'recognise the legitimacy of the psychological hardship that would be faced by the victims of persecution were they to be returned to the country responsible for their maltreatment': Hathaway, *The Law of Refugee Status* (1991) *supra* n 4, 203–4.

[403] Consider, for example, the case of *Mejilla-Romero v Holder*, 600 F 3d 63, 83 (1st Cir, 2010), where the applicant, still a child, was diagnosed with PTSD 'caused by "exposure to traumatic events" in Honduras, including being "hung on a barb wire fence," being "cut with a machete," and experiencing "death threats, attempted rapes and other forms of violence where he feared for his life."' For a further example, see *Applicant SBAP of 2001 v MIMIA* [2003] FCAFC 79.

[404] *Timnit Daniel* (BIA, 2002) n 3.

This case involved two Eritrean sisters (aged 14 and 15) who were targeted because of a political opinion imputed to them.[405] They were spat upon, interrogated, repeatedly slapped, beaten with a 'big stick', and in constant fear that they would be victims of sexual assault. The IJ held that the respondents' single six-day detention was insufficiently severe to constitute persecution. The BIA disagreed on the basis that the applicants had suffered persecutory treatment as young girls, that these past experiences continued to haunt them and that the Eritrean government could do nothing to alleviate those feelings.[406]

The continuing effects of trauma were similarly acknowledged by the US Court of Appeals for the First Circuit in *Civil v INS*,[407] a case involving a young woman whose home was stoned by militia overnight when she was 14 years old. In a strong dissent Judge Bownes emphasised that '[p]hysical harm is not the touchtone for establishing persecution'[408] and that the 'terror that [the applicant] experienced probably had a far greater and more long-lasting impact on someone of her age than it would have had on a full-grown adult'.[409] The Judge stressed that the relevant question 'is not what an administrative law judge sitting in the safety of the United States can choose to believe; the question is what a young person, who has been forced to hide under the bed in the middle of the night, in terror of being killed, would think about her safety if she were to return home'.[410]

Canadian decision-makers have adopted a similar approach, as illustrated by a case involving a 14-year-old boy who had experienced significant physical abuse at the hands of his uncle.[411] Although there was no risk that the boy would be returned to live with the uncle, the IRB accepted that the applicant was suffering from psychological distress as a result of the abuse he had suffered, and there was a risk that this would increase if he were to return to Iran.[412] In claims based on the enduring psychological effects of past exposure to trauma it will often be necessary for the decision-makers to assess whether the country of origin is willing and able to provide adequate medical treatment to aid the child's recovery.[413] In this context, decision-makers should be guided by art 39 of the *CRC*, which provides that states 'shall take

---

[405] *Ibid.*, 4.   [406] *Ibid.*, 3.   [407] *Civil v INS* 140 F 3d 52, 62–3 (Judge Bownes, dissenting) (1st Cir, 1998).

[408] *Ibid.*, 62.   [409] *Ibid.*

[410] *Ibid.* See also *Kahssai v INS* 16 F 3d 323, 329 (9th Cir, 1994): 'To take [the applicant] from her remaining family members in the United States and force her to return to the place where her family was persecuted might only compound [her emotional and developmental] injury'.

[411] *VA2-03015* (IRB, 6 August 2003). In this case the decision-maker invoked the 'compelling reasons' exception set out in s 108(4) of the *Immigration and Refugee Protection Act*, SC 2001, c 27. See Chapter 3, *supra* n 19.

[412] *VA2-03015* (IRB, 6 August 2003) 5–6. See also *V93-02093* (IRB, 4 May 1994) 6 ('[a]ll these psychosomatic reactions are reflections of psychological trauma resulting from the assault and the injury sustained from it. We believe that, in this case, the perception of threat can be the basis for a well-founded fear of persecution in a child'); *V98-00787* (IRB, 4 June 1999) 10 ('[o]ne must consider the negative or psychological effect of past persecution. Evidence in the form of a medical report or psychological assessment as we have here, which shows present psychological and emotional suffering [,] can be used to demonstrate that the claimant continues to suffer the effects of past persecution'. In New Zealand, decision-makers have suggested that parents may have a role to play in alleviating the risk of psychological harm occasioned by exposure to traumatic events. Specifically, the NZIPT has held that there is an expectation 'that parents will do their best to shield their children from the effects of such incidents and any fear or anxiety that they experience as a result': *BI (Fiji)* [2012] NZIPT 800082–85, [22]. See also *AI (South Africa)* [2011] NZIPT 800050-53, [57]; *AF (South Africa)* [2011] NZIPT 800100–102, [49]–[65].

[413] See, e.g., *AJ (Liberia) v SSHD* [2006] EWCA Civ 1736, a case involving the application of art 3 of the *ECHR*.

all appropriate measures to promote physical and psychological recovery and social reintegration of a child victim of: any form of neglect, exploitation, or abuse; torture or any other form of cruel, inhuman or degrading treatment or punishment; or armed conflicts'.[414] Critically, if the initial action that gave rise to the psychological harm was linked to a *Refugee Convention* ground,[415] the nexus requirement will still be satisfied even if the state's unwillingness or inability to provide adequate rehabilitation services is not linked to a *Convention* ground. This is because the only reason that the child now faces the enduring risk of psychological harm is because of past persecution that was connected to a *Convention* ground.[416] There is thus no principled basis for the New Zealand RSAA's rejection of the refugee claim of a 15-year-old girl on the basis that although '[t]he mental illness [the applicant] now suffers may be the result of her past persecution but any failure to treat it does not of itself conduct persecutory conduct and would not be protected by the Convention unless it was motivated by a Convention reason'.[417]

Conclusions

In circumstances where children are becoming increasingly visible in the refugee status determination process, the concept of 'being persecuted' must be recalibrated to take into account the particular ways that persecution can manifest itself in the context of children. The human rights framework provides a principled analytical framework for identifying persecutory harm relevant to children. As outlined in Section 4.2 and demonstrated in Section 4.3, recourse to the *CRC* to identify persecutory harm in refugee claims involving children is the logical and necessary extension of the traditional human rights framework. The point is elegantly made by the Federal Court of Canada: '[i]f the CRC recognizes that children have human rights and that "persecution" amounts to the denial of basic human rights, then if a child's rights under the CRC are violated in a sustained or systematic manner demonstrative of a failure of state protection, that child may qualify for refugee status'.[418] That must be right. A *child*-rights framework – which requires a decision-maker to assess whether a child is at risk of a violation protected under the *CRC* – provides decision-makers with a bespoke framework specifically adapted to take into account a child's heightened sensitivities and distinct developmental needs; a framework that ensures 'that the term "persecution" [is] made relevant to the world of the child as well'.[419]

---

[414] Article 39 further provides that '[s]uch recovery and reintegration shall take place in an environment which fosters the health, self-respect and dignity of the child'. Similar obligations are contained in *OPAC*, art 7, and *OPSC*, art 9(3). See further UNCRC, Discussion Day: State Violence against Children (2000), [27]–[28]; UNCRC, *GC13*, [52]. Article 39 of the *CRC* is broader in scope than the only other similar international human rights law provision, art 14 of the *CAT*, which applies solely to victims of torture.

[415] See Chapter 5.

[416] The *Convention* ground 'need only be a contributing factor to the risk of being persecuted': Michigan Guidelines on the International Protection of Refugees, 'The Michigan Guidelines on Well-Founded Fear' (2004), [14].

[417] *Refugee Appeal Nos 74632 and 74633* (RSAA, 27 June 2003), [41]. The Authority went so far as to admit that it '[did] not know whether adequate treatment facilities would be available', but considered that this was irrelevant as it was clear that the applicant would not be denied treatment for a *Convention* ground.

[418] *Kim v Canada (MCI)* [2011] 2 FCR 448, [51].

[419] *TA1-03656, TA1-03657 and TA1-03658* (IRB, 19 December 2002), [9].

5

Nexus to a *Convention* Ground

Introduction

In addition to establishing a risk of being persecuted, the *Refugee Convention* requires an applicant to demonstrate that the risk arises 'for reasons of' one of the five enumerated forms of civil or political status: 'race, religion, nationality, membership of a particular social group or political opinion'. The requirement that the risk be causally connected to one of the *Convention* grounds provides a critical delimitation for refugee status: if a child is unable to demonstrate a link between a *Convention* ground and the risk of being persecuted, she will not be a refugee. At the core of the nexus criterion is the principle of non-discrimination – a core human rights value in the international system and one of the general principles underpinning the *CRC*[1] – which provides a principled reference point for establishing the interests protected by the *Convention*'s nexus grounds, while also informing the interpretation of the 'for reasons of' clause. As the UK House of Lords has observed, 'the Convention is concerned not with all cases of persecution but with persecution which is based on discrimination, the making of distinctions which principles of fundamental human rights regard as inconsistent with the right of every human being'.[2]

The requirement that an applicant demonstrate a nexus to a *Convention* ground has given rise to a number of difficulties in claims involving children. This chapter identifies those difficulties and examines the extent to which they may be resolved by way of a principled interpretation of the *Convention*, informed, where appropriate, by the broader child-rights framework set out under the *CRC*. Section 5.1 considers the causal requirement, focusing, in particular, on whether the 'for reasons of' clause requires an applicant to demonstrate persecutory intent. Section 5.2 examines the three *Convention* grounds that have given rise to specific issues for child applicants: 'political opinion', 'religion' and 'membership of a particular social group'.

5.1 The Causal Link – The Predicament of Childhood

In order to be a refugee an applicant must establish a causal link between the risk of being persecuted and one of the five *Convention* grounds. The nexus requirement – which finds expression in the 'for reasons of' clause in art 1A(2) – has given rise to a variety of interpretative challenges and generated a substantial body of case-law. The first interpretative challenge concerns the *nature* of the causal link. An issue that has proven particularly salient in claims involving children is whether the 'for reasons of' clause incorporates an element of intention. Specifically, is it necessary for an applicant to establish that the

---

[1] UNCRC, *GC5*, [12]; *CRC*, art 2.   [2] *Fornah v SSHD* [2007] 1 AC 412, [13] (Lord Bingham).

perpetrator intends to inflict persecution for a *Convention* reason, or is it sufficient to demonstrate a causal link between the *Convention* ground and the predicament that the applicant has found herself in? This section examines the two dominant approaches that emerge from the case-law[3] – the 'intention-based approach' and the 'predicament approach' – and evaluates the implications of each for claims involving children.

A second interpretative challenge, not considered in detail here, is the appropriate *standard* of causation required to satisfy the nexus clause. The issue arose in *Fornah v SSHD*, a case involving an Iranian mother and her young son who were at risk because of activities of the father, and a separate claim involving a 15-year-old girl from Sierra Leone at risk of FGC. Lord Bingham observed that the 'ground on which the claimant relies need not be the only or even the primary reason for the apprehended persecution. It is enough that the ground relied on is an effective reason'.[4] According to Lord Bingham, '[i]n deciding whether the causal link is established, a simple "but for" test of causation is inappropriate: the Convention calls for a more sophisticated approach, appropriate to the context and taking account of all the facts and circumstances relevant to the particular case.' Although a variety of expressions are adopted, there is now widespread authority for the proposition that the *Convention* ground need only be an operative reason for the risk of being persecuted.[5]

5.1.1 An Intention Requirement

In many cases it will be clear that a persecutor intends to harm an applicant for a *Convention* reason. In a claim involving a homosexual teenager at risk of criminal prosecution under anti-sodomy laws, it is clear that the state is motivated by the child's sexual orientation. Similarly, a young girl at risk of harm from her community because of her refusal to conform to particular religious codes is plainly targeted by her persecutor(s) because of her religious belief. In these cases, a focus on the persecutor's intention provides the most straightforward method by which to demonstrate the requisite causal link. The issue, however, is not whether persecutory intent provides a *sufficient* means to satisfy the 'for reasons of' clause – it plainly does – but whether persecutory intent provides the *exclusive* means by which the causal link can be established. A number of leading courts have adopted the latter view, insisting that the nexus criterion can only be satisfied where a *Convention* ground is connected either to the intention of an individual persecutor or the intention of the state in failing to protect the applicant.[6]

---

[3] See, e.g., J C Hathaway and M Foster, 'The Causal Connection ("Nexus") to a Convention Ground' 15 (2003) *International Journal of Refugee Law* 461, 463–7; M Foster, *International Refugee Law and Socio-Economic Rights: Refuge from Deprivation* (2007) 263–86.

[4] *Fornah v SSHD* [2007] 1 AC 412, [17].

[5] See, e.g., J C Hathaway and M Foster, *The Law of Refugee Status* (2nd edn, 2014) 389–390; Michigan Guidelines on International Protection of Refugees, 'The Michigan Guidelines on Nexus to a Convention Ground' (2002), [13]; *Chen Shi Hai v MIMA* (2000) 201 CLR 293, [66]–[74] (Kirby J).

[6] The reference to the intention of an individual persecutor (or persecutors) or of the state derives from the fact that only one of the 'serious harm' or the 'failure of state protection' needs to be causally connected to the protected interest. Hence '[t]he necessary discriminatory element may be supplied either by the non-state agents who perpetrate the maltreatment or it may be supplied by the state which fails to protect the victims': *Horvath v SSHD* [2000] INLR 15, 56. Although the recognition that the requisite intention can derive from either the individual persecutor(s) *or* the state is a welcome development, both approaches treat intention as an essential element and give rise to similar limitations.

The incorporation of an intention requirement into the nexus clause has generated difficulties for child applicants in a range of contexts. The first and most significant challenge derives from the fact that children are often at risk of being persecuted by non-state agents whose intentions are generally presumed to be personal and thus not causally connected to a *Convention* ground.[7] Refugee decision-makers have thus held that: a child at risk of domestic abuse is not targeted for a *Convention* reason but simply because of 'exposure to a violent, unstable person';[8] a child at risk of trafficking is not a refugee because her traffickers are motivated not by any *Convention* ground but by 'profit, if not callous greed';[9] a child at risk of gang-related violence does not satisfy the nexus criterion because gang members do not commit violent acts for 'reasons other than gaining more influence and power, and recruiting young males to fill their ranks';[10] a child at risk of harm because his father had acted as a witness against a violent criminal fails to satisfy the nexus criterion because the persecutor's motives are 'quintessentially personal';[11] and a child at risk of being abducted by the Lord's Resistance Army is not targeted for any *Convention* reason but simply 'due to its need for labor'.[12] In each of these cases, the decision-maker treated the persecutor's motive as a critical ingredient, and the absence of

---

[7] Foster (2007) *supra* n 3, 265 makes a similar observation in relation to claims advanced by women.

[8] *Gomez-Romero v Holder*, 2012 US App LEXIS 7521, [7] (6th Cir, 2012). See also *Re R-A-*, 22 I & N Dec 906, 920 (BIA, 2001) (finding that the applicant was not abused for reasons of a *Convention* ground, but because of '[o]ther factors, ranging from jealousy to growing frustration with his own life to simple unchecked violence tied to the inherent meanness of [her husband's] personality' (at 926)).

[9] *Xiao v Canada (MCI)* [2001] FCJ No 349, [26] ('[n]o evidence was presented to the Board that the snakeheads targeted the applicant because of her status as a minor, or because of any Convention ground. The evidence demonstrated that the snakeheads smuggle for profit, if not callous greed'). See also *Zhu v Canada (MCI)* 2001 FCT 884, [39] ('[i]t is the intent of the persecutor which is relevant in determining whether the harm which an individual fears is related to a Convention ground ... There was no evidence before the Tribunal that the snakeheads or the applicants' parents smuggled or trafficked the applicants because [of] their status as minors from Fujian province, or because [of] any other Convention ground. There was clear evidence that the snakeheads smuggled or trafficked the applicants for profit'); *Hong v Attorney General*, 165 Fed Appx 995, 997 (3rd Cir, 2006) (IJ had held that a young boy who was at risk of serious harm because he testified against the smugglers in the United States was not at risk by reason of any *Convention* ground 'but rather for retribution for his actions in testifying against four smugglers ... [and] retribution over personal matters do not qualify for asylum'). See generally Foster (2007) *supra* n 3, 265–7.

[10] *S-E-G-*, 24 I & N Dec 579, 588 (BIA, 2008), rejecting the refugee claim of three siblings (a girl and two boys), who were beaten and threatened with death and rape for refusing to join the MS-13 gang. See also *Rivera-Barrientos v Holder*, 666 F 3d 641, 647 (10th Cir, 2012) ('[the applicant] must ... show that her attack was motivated by more than anger at her unwillingness to join MS-13 and a desire to coerce her into joining'); *Bueso-Avila v Holder*, 663 F 3d 934, 939 (7th Cir, 2011) ('there is substantial evidence in the record to support the finding that the gang threatened and harmed Bueso-Avila simply because he was a youth who refused to join their street gang'); *Barrios v Holder*, 581 F 3d 849, 856 (9th Cir, 2009) ('[t]he evidence instead supports the conclusion that the gang victimized him for economic and personal reasons').

[11] *Demiraj v Holder*, 631 F 3d 194, 199 (5th Cir, 2011) ('[t]he crucial finding here is that the record discloses no evidence that Mrs Demiraj would be targeted for her membership in the Demiraj family *as such*. Rather, the evidence strongly suggests that Mrs Demiraj, her son, and Mr Demiraj's nieces were targeted because they are people who are important to Mr Demiraj – that is, because hurting them would hurt Mr Demiraj' (emphasis in original)).

[12] *Lukwago v Ashcroft*, 329 F 3d 157, 173 (3rd Cir, 2003) ('[b]ased on the evidence on record, the BIA's finding that the LRA did not target Lukwago for persecution based on his age is supported by substantial evidence. The BIA found that the LRA abducted Lukwago due to its need for labour, not on account of his membership in any "particular social group."'). See also *Cruz-Diaz v INS*, 86 F 3d 330, 331–2 (4th Cir, 1996).

any evidence connecting such motivation to a *Convention* reason proved fatal to the child's refugee claim.

The second, now largely historical, difficulty relates to the importation of a requirement that the persecutor display some form of enmity or malignity towards the applicant.[13] This additional animus requirement, a clear by-product of the intention-based approach, has caused particular difficulties in cases involving children, who are often placed 'at the mercy of adults who may inflict harm without viewing it as such'.[14] A child's parent may, for instance, genuinely believe that they are doing what is best for a child by taking steps to 'cure' or 'treat' a particular characteristic, such as the child's sexual orientation,[15] or by subjecting the child to a traditional cultural practice such as FGC.[16] Although the animus requirement is now widely discredited,[17] its evolution highlights – in rather stark terms – the conceptual problems with the intention requirement.

The final difficulty is a practical one: in many cases it is exceptionally difficult – if not impossible – to establish the intention of the persecutor. As the High Court of Australia has sensibly recognised, '[b]y definition, the Convention will ordinarily be invoked in a foreign country where an inquiry into the motives and feelings of the alleged "persecutors" will be extremely difficult or impossible to perform'.[18] These difficulties are amplified in the context of a child applicant, who, by reason of her age, may not fully understand the reasons why she is at risk of being persecuted or may otherwise find the requirement to demonstrate what is in the minds of her persecutors an impossible burden.[19]

5.1.2 The Predicament Approach

In response to the challenges occasioned by importing an intention requirement into the nexus criterion, an alternative approach has begun to emerge in the jurisprudence that focuses on whether there is a causal link between a *Convention* ground and the applicant's predicament.[20] This approach shifts the focus away from the intention of the persecutor and/or state and focuses attention on the protected characteristic of the applicant.[21] If the applicant's protected characteristic – race, religion, political opinion, religion or social

---

[13] See, e.g., the initial decision of the RRT cited in *Chen Shi Hai v MIMA* (2000) 201 CLR 293, [7], denying refugee status to a three-and-a-half-year-old child on the basis that the consequences which he was likely to suffer in China would not 'result from any malignity, enmity or other adverse intention toward him'.

[14] INS, *Guidelines*, 21. See also *Chen Shi Hai v MIMA* (2000) 201 CLR 293, [35] (Gleeson CJ, Gaudron, Gummow and Hayne JJ), [63] (Kirby J).

[15] INS, *Guidelines*, 21.

[16] In *Re Fauziya Kasinga*, 21 I & N Dec 357 (BIA, 1996), the government's reply brief stated that the elders or midwives 'did not have an intent to punish for a Convention reason; to the contrary, "presumably most of . . . [them] believe that they are simply performing an important cultural rite that bonds the individual to society"' (cited in A Gupta, 'The New Nexus' (2014) 85 *University of Colorado Law Review* 377, 394). See also, e.g., *Ezedunor v Canada (MCI)* 2015 FC 783, [14].

[17] See, e.g., *Chen Shi Hai v MIMA* (2000) 201 CLR 293, [7]; *Fornah v SSHD* [2007] 1 AC 412, [17]; *Re Fauziya Kasinga*, 21 I & N Dec 357, 365 (BIA, 1996).

[18] *Chen Shi Hai v MIMA* (2000) 201 CLR 293, [64].   [19] INS, *Guidelines*, 21.

[20] For a comprehensive discussion on the predicament approach see Hathaway and Foster, (2003) *supra* n 3, 465–9; Foster (2007) *supra* n 3, 270–86; Hathaway and Foster (2014) *supra* n 5, 376–82.

[21] '[The] predicament approach . . . focuses on the reason for the applicant's fear, rather than the reason for the persecutor's decision to harm the applicant': Foster (2007) *supra* n 3, 271.

group – explains why the applicant will be exposed to a risk of being persecuted, the applicant will be at risk 'for reasons of' a *Convention* ground.

As a matter of treaty interpretation, the predicament approach is consistent with the language of art 1A(2), which contains no reference to the intention of the persecutor. Rather, the use of the passive voice – requiring a well-founded fear of *being persecuted* for reasons of a *Convention* ground, rather than a well-founded fear of *persecution* for reasons of a *Convention* ground – suggests that attention should be directed 'more to the basis for the applicant's predicament than exclusively to the intention of either the persecutor or of a state which withholds its protection'.[22] The predicament approach also aligns comfortably with the non-discrimination norms that underpin the nexus requirement.[23] As the Federal Court of Australia has recognised, discrimination law 'treats as uncontroversial the proposition that discrimination may be legally established where *either the intent or the effect of conduct is discriminatory*'.[24] Senior UK courts have been particularly explicit in underlining the clear link between discrimination principles and the 'for reasons of' clause.[25] In *Sepet v SSHD* the Court of Appeal accepted that an element of conscious discrimination is not a necessary ingredient of the *Convention* definition, emphasising that '[t]he question is always whether the asylum claimant faces discrimination on a Convention ground'.[26] In line with domestic and international principles of discrimination law,[27] there will be cases where discrimination can be established by reference to the persecutor's motives; equally there will be cases where a persecutor's motives are irrelevant and the discrimination is established by looking to the substantive result of particular conduct or treatment.[28]

The predicament approach has been endorsed by UNHCR, which affirms that '[t]he intent of the persecutor can be a relevant factor to establishing the "causal" link but it is not a prerequisite'[29] and 'when analysing the causal connection between a Convention ground and the applicant's well-founded fear, the focus should be on the reasons for the applicant's predicament'.[30] The approach has also been approved in domestic guidelines, with Australian guidance underlining that '[t]he terms of the Convention only require that the

---

[22] Hathaway and Foster (2003) *supra* n 3, 468. See also *Refugee Appeal No 72635/01* (RSAA, 6 September 2002), [168]; *Chen Shi Hai v MIMA* (2000) 201 CLR 293, [65].

[23] Foster (2007) *supra* n 3, 276–9.   [24] *NACM v MIMIA* [2003] FCA 1554, [59] (emphasis added).

[25] See I Macdonald and R Toal, *Immigration Law and Practice in the United Kingdom* (9th ed, 2014) vol 1, 1014–15.

[26] *Sepet v SSHD* [2001] EWCA Civ 681, [93]. Although more equivocal, the House of Lords agreed: *Sepet v SSHD* [2003] 1 WLR 856, [23] (Lord Bingham), [54] (Lord Hoffmann). See also *R (Sivakumar) v SSHD* [2003] 2 All ER 1097, [41]; *Fornah v SSHD* [2007] 1 AC 412, [17].

[27] See, e.g., HRC, *GC18*, [7] (emphasis added): 'which has the purpose *or effect* of nullifying or impairing the recognition, enjoyment or exercise by all persons, on an equal footing, of all rights and freedoms'.

[28] See S Fredman, *Discrimination Law* (2nd edn, 2011) 177–90.

[29] UNHCR, *Guidelines on International Protection No 9: Claims to Refugee Status Based on Sexual Orientation and/or Gender Identity within the Context of Article 1A(2) of the 1951 Convention and/or Its 1967 Protocol Relating to the Status of Refugees*, HCR/GIP/12/09 (2012), [39]. See also UNHCR, *UNHCR Guidance Note on Refugee Claims Relating to Sexual Orientation and Gender Identity* (2008), [28]; UNHCR, *Guidelines on International Protection: The Application of Article 1A(2) of the 1951 Convention and/or 1967 Protocol Relating to the Status of Refugees to Victims of Trafficking and Persons at Risk of Being Trafficked*, HCR/GIP/06/07 (2006), [31]–[32].

[30] UNHCR, 'Brief of the United Nations High Commissioner for Refugees as Amicus Curiae in Support of the Petitioner', filed in *Bueso-Avila* (9 November 2010) 10.

harm alleged arise "for reasons of" a Convention ground ... The Convention does not specify that a persecutor must have a particular motivation'.[31]

Although many jurisdictions continue to require an applicant to demonstrate a causal link between a *Convention* ground and the intent of the individual persecutor or of the state in failing to protect the applicant, there are signs that this is beginning to change, with an expanding body of case-law focusing on the predicament of the applicant rather than the motives of the persecutor or the state.[32] New Zealand decision-makers have been robust advocates for this approach, with the RSAA determining that the language of art 1A(2) 'draws attention to the fact of exposure to harm, rather than to the act of inflicting harm' and that '[t]he focus is on the reasons for the claimant's predicament rather than on the mindset of the persecutor'.[33] This gradual trend is particularly noticeable in claims involving children, where decision-makers have evidently struggled with the consequences of a strict application of the intention requirement. This can be illustrated by looking at three categories of claims: children deprived of a family environment; children at risk of domestic violence; and children at risk of being trafficked.

Although decision-makers have had little difficulty in finding that a child deprived of her family environment will be at a heighted risk of various forms of persecutory harm, these claims may nonetheless fail because of the difficulty in demonstrating persecutory intent. This is demonstrated in a case involving a 13-year-old Thai girl who was abandoned by her family and feared that she would be subjected to ongoing physical and emotional abuse from her extended family, including a risk of sexual abuse and sale into child prostitution.[34] At first instance, the RRT held that 'any harm or threat of harm that would emanate from the applicant's relatives or others would be motivated by financial reasons or personal gratification' rather than because of her 'race, religion, nationality or political opinion, [or] because of her membership of any particular social group ... such as "abandoned young girls."'[35] The decision was overturned on appeal, with the Federal Magistrates Court accepting the applicant's submissions that a decision-maker is required to look beyond the motivation of the persecutors and examine the reasons why the applicant is exposed to the risk of persecutory harm.[36] In this case, the young girl's predicament and correlative risk of persecutory harm was engendered by her status as an abandoned young girl.

A similar departure from the intention-based approach can be seen in a decision of the BIA in a case involving a young girl abandoned by her parents:[37]

> In this case, the respondent has shown that the acts of persecution occurred because of her membership in a group of children who have been abandoned by their parents and

---

[31] DIAC, 'Refugee Law Guidelines' (March 2010), [9.19]. The predicament approach has also received widespread academic support: see, e.g., Hathaway and Foster (2003) *supra* n 3, 465–9; Foster (2007) *supra* n 3, 270–86; *The Michigan Guidelines* (2002) *supra* n 5, [6]–[10]; G S Goodwin-Gill and J McAdam, *The Refugee in International Law* (3rd edn, 2007) 100–2; Hathaway and Foster (2014) *supra* n 5, 376–83.

[32] Foster (2007) *supra* n 3, 280–6; Hathaway and Foster (2014) *supra* n 5, 380–1.

[33] *Refugee Appeal No 72635/01* (RSAA, 6 September 2002), [168].

[34] *M93 of 2004 v Minister for Immigration* [2006] FMCA 252.   [35] *Ibid.*, [63].

[36] 'It was submitted that persecution for reasons of financial reward can nonetheless be for reasons of the applicant's particular social group. In this instance the claim was based upon the applicant's status as "an abandoned young girl" who was vulnerable and at risk of commercial exploitation in the form of child prostitution. That risk it was submitted was real because of the Government's inability to protect her and because child prostitution was a significant problem partly due to the country's extreme poverty': *Ibid.*, [64].

[37] Unnamed File (BIA, 2003) 6, cited in Foster (2007) *supra* n 3, 280, 283–4.

who have not received a surrogate form of protection. Because the respondent was not protected by her parents or surrogate protector, she lived in an extreme state of vulnerability. In such a state, dangerous actors persecuted her because they could do so without any negative repercussions. The respondent, a powerless child with no one looking after her, was an easy target over which they could assert their power . . . But for her extreme vulnerability caused by her parents' abandonment and lack of a surrogate protector, the respondent would not have fallen prey to the act of persecution described above.

Similar reasoning can be seen in a decision of the IRB involving a 16-year-old boy who feared that he would be forced to live on the streets of Mexico if he was returned.[38] The Board considered that the applicant was 'a child who could very easily be victimized by drug dealers, pimps and other predators on the street'[39] and that these risks were causally linked to the applicant's status as an 'abandoned child in Mexico'.[40]

The predicament approach has also been applied in cases involving children at risk of domestic child abuse. As noted above, a strict application of the intention-based approach can prove fatal to these claims, as the persecutor's intention is generally presumed to be personal and not causally connected to a *Convention* ground. This neglects the reality that a child's vulnerability, particularly in a familial context, is very often the reason why the child is exposed to a risk of harm.[41] The predicament approach shifts the decision-maker's focus away from the motivation of the persecutor and allows for a more inclusive assessment of the reasons why the child is exposed to a risk of domestic violence. This is illustrated in *Refugee Appeal Nos 76494 and 76495*, a case involving a mother and her son who fled Iran to escape domestic violence and the discriminatory effect of Iran's custodial laws. The New Zealand RSAA accepted that, if returned, the child was likely to find himself in the custody of his father and would again be subject to abuse. Notwithstanding the absence of any evidence regarding the motivation for the abuse, the Authority concluded that '[the child's] predicament arises by virtue of his membership of a particular social group, namely "children"'.[42] The IRB applied similar reasoning in a case involving a Chinese boy subjected to violent beatings and debt bondage by his father. The Board held that the child 'has a [causal] link as a member of a particular social

---

[38] *V97-03500* (IRB, 31 May 1999).   [39] *Ibid.*, 4.

[40] *Ibid.* The predicament approach has also been applied in claims involving socio-economic deprivation. In a particularly liberal application of the predicament approach, the Canadian IRB held that the potential harm that a child may suffer if returned to Zaire, including a lack of education, medical attention, food and secure protection, was causally connected to government policies (or a lack thereof): *A95-00633* (IRB, 28 January 1998), [12]–[13]. Although no government policy specifically targeted impoverished children, the Board considered that 'the potential deprivations the claimants would face are the direct result of government policies', including, in particular, the fact that civil servants, including teachers, were not being paid, and the absence of funding for medical services or other services to assist the poor, particularly youth: at [12].

[41] See, e.g., *V97-00156 and V97-00962* (IRB, 28 May 1998) 5, where the IRB paraphrased the wording of the IRB's Gender Guidelines: 'A subgroup of . . . [children] may be identified by reference to their exposure or vulnerability for physical, cultural or other reasons to violence, including domestic violence, in an environment that denies them protection. These . . . [children] face violence amounting to persecution because of their particular vulnerability as . . . [children] in their societies and because they are so unprotected'.

[42] *Refugee Appeal Nos 76494 and 76495* (RSAA, 23 November 2010), [76]. See also *Refugee Appeal Nos 76226 and 76227* (RSAA, 12 January 2009), [114]; *Refugee Appeal Nos 75301, 75302 and 75303* (RSAA, 24 January 2006), [46].

group – namely, minors' and that '[t]he child's vulnerability arises as a result of his status as a minor'.[43]

Finally, the predicament approach has proven critical in cases involving children at risk of trafficking for labour or sexual exploitation.[44] For example, in a claim involving a young woman who was trafficked into domestic servitude from Ethiopia when she was 14, the IRB concluded that, '[c]onsidering the claimant's gender, age, educational level and the fact that [she] has no family or ties to any persons in Ethiopia to assist and guide her', the applicant 'faces a serious possibility of persecution *based on her profile*'.[45] The predicament approach has similarly been applied in cases involving applicants who have been trafficked in the past and now fear that they will be at risk of being harmed by their former traffickers if they were to return to their country of origin. For example, in *SB v SSHD*[46] a young Moldovan woman, trafficked to the United Kingdom for the purpose of sexual exploitation, feared that she would be harmed by her traffickers because she had given evidence against a member of the trafficking network. The UK AIT held that 'anyone who is at a heightened risk of ill-treatment ... which is shown to be at least *related* to the individual's past experience of having been trafficked constitutes harm for a [*Convention*] reason'.[47] The approach adopted in these cases echoes the position taken by UNHCR in its guidance on trafficking-related claims, which affirms (in understated terms) that a trafficker's 'overriding economic motive does not ... exclude the possibility of Convention-related grounds in the targeting and selection of victims of trafficking'.[48]

In each of the cases discussed above the decision-maker has focused on the reasons why the child is susceptible to the risk of persecutory harm, rather than the reasons why the persecutor is seeking to harm the child or the state has failed to protect the child. As a result, decision-makers have sensibly recognised that a child's heightened vulnerability is in many cases the reason why the child is exposed to a risk of persecutory harm. Although still embryonic, the gradual shift from a focus on the intention of the persecutor to a focus on the status and predicament of the child applicant is to be welcomed. Such an approach is faithful to both the text and object and purpose of art 1A(2), and the non-discrimination principles underpinning the nexus criterion. The predicament approach also avoids the evidential difficulties that a child would otherwise face if required to establish the motivations of her persecutor.

---

[43] *V99-02929* (IRB, 21 February 2000) 6. See also *T93-09636, T93-09638 and T93-09639* (IRB, 26 January 1994); *T94-00416, T94-00418 and T94-00419* (IRB, 25 August 1994); *T91-01497 and T91-01498* (IRB, 9 August 1994).

[44] See generally A Dorevitch and M Foster, 'Obstacles on the Road to Protection: Assessing the Treatment of Sex-Trafficking Victims under Australia's Migration and Refugee Law' (2008) 9(1) *Melbourne Journal of International Law* 1.

[45] *TA4-16915* (IRB, 16 March 2006) 7 (emphasis added). See also the decisions discussed in Foster, (2007) *supra* n 3, 283–4. Similar reasoning could logically be applied in cases involving children at risk of involuntary gang recruitment, a point recognised in UNHCR, 'Brief of the United Nations High Commissioner for Refugees as Amicus Curiae in Support of the Petitioners and Reversal of the BIA's Decision', filed in *Orellana-Monson v Holder* (7 May 2009) 18: 'Young people may, precisely because of the characteristics that set them apart in society, such as their young age, impressionability and dependency, be more susceptible to recruitment attempts or other clandestine approaches by gangs. Indeed, recent studies have found that the recruitment policies of Central American gangs are often age-driven and frequently target young people.'

[46] *SB v SSHD* [2008] UKAIT 00002.

[47] *Ibid.,* [79] (emphasis in original). See also *Hong v Attorney General*, 165 Fed Appx 995 (3rd Cir, 2006).

[48] UNHCR, *Victims of Trafficking Guidelines, supra* n 29, [31].

5.2 The *Convention* Grounds

Although all five *Convention* grounds may potentially apply in claims involving children, this chapter focuses on the interpretation and application of the 'political opinion', 'religion' and 'membership of a particular social group' grounds on the basis that these grounds have given rise to specific issues for child applicants. Although it is only necessary to establish a causal connection to a single *Convention* ground, in many cases the risk of being persecuted will be causally linked to several grounds.[49] For instance, a Chinese boy born in violation of China's one-child policy may be at risk of systemic discrimination because of his imputed political opinion, membership in the particular social group of family or membership in the *hei haizi* particular social group. Similarly, a young Sudanese girl may be at risk of FGC for reason of her race, nationality, gender or age. As discussed in Chapter 3, consistent with the shared duty of fact-finding, a decision-maker must consider a *Convention* ground even where the applicant has not identified the ground expressly.[50] This duty has particular salience in claims involving children, where the child may not fully appreciate the reason that she is at risk of being targeted.

There are two further foundational principles that can be addressed briefly. The first is the now firmly entrenched principle that an individual need not actually possess the relevant racial, religious, national, political or social characteristic; it is sufficient that the characteristic is attributed to the individual by the potential persecutor. In other words, risk for reasons of *imputed identity* satisfies the nexus criterion as much as risk that follows from *actual identity*.[51] This principle arises in claims involving children due to the reality that children are very often targeted because of the particular affiliations or activities of the child's family members. Second, the nexus requirement will be satisfied where the risk of harm accrues by reason of the applicant's identity *or* where the risk accrues in response to activity or behaviour that is connected to that protected identity. This reflects the reality that an affiliation with some *Convention* grounds, such as religion, political opinion and particular social groups based on sexual orientation, is less immediately visible than an affiliation with other *Convention* grounds, such as race or nationality. Senior courts have appropriately insisted that, save for a limited range of circumstances where a limitation on behaviour is permissible under international human rights law, a person cannot be expected to modify their conduct in order to avoid the risk of being persecuted.[52]

---

[49] UNHCR, *Handbook*, [66].

[50] *Canada (Attorney General) v Ward* [1993] 2 SCR 689, 693. See also *SHBB v Minister for Immigration* [2003] FMCA 82, [22]. Contra the position taken in *Yaabe v Canada (MCI)* [1997] FCJ No 1633, where the Federal Court of Canada refused to examine the risk that a nine-year-old boy would face by reason of his physical disability on the ground that the refugee claim was based on clan affiliation rather than physical handicap. To similar effect, in *Cruz-Diaz v INS*, 86 F 3d 330 (4th Cir, 1996), the Court of Appeals for the Fourth Circuit dismissed the claim of a 15-year-old former child soldier from El Salvador on the basis that the applicant had not demonstrated that he faced a risk of being persecuted because of his political opinion. The Court failed, however, to consider whether the child was at risk by reason of his status as a former child soldier.

[51] *HJ (Iran) v SSHD* [2011] 1 AC 596, [32].

[52] See generally J C Hathaway and J Pobjoy, 'Queer Cases Make Bad Law' (2012) 44 *New York University Journal of International Law and Politics* 315.

5.2.1 Political Opinion

The *Convention* ground 'political opinion' arises in two principal contexts in claims involving children. The first and more common context is where a child is at risk because of the political views or activities of the child's parent or other family member.[53] It is widely accepted that the political opinion of a family member may be imputed to a child by the authorities or by non-state actors, thereby giving rise to a risk of the child being persecuted for reasons of political opinion.[54] As the US Court of Appeals for the Ninth Circuit has explained, 'government suspicion of one family member is easily generalized into suspicion, and persecution, of the rest.'[55] A paradigm example is the case of a child at risk of persecutory harm because her family's resistance to China's coercive family planning laws has been imputed to her. In the case of *Shi Chen v Holder*[56] the applicant, a child born in contravention of China's one-child policy, was denied many of the rights of full citizenship, including access to state-funded elementary schooling, higher education, health care and other basic government services. In the future he was also likely to be excluded from many jobs and denied the right to own property and to marry and have children. The US Court of Appeals for the Seventh Circuit sensibly determined that the child's claim fell comfortably within the imputed political opinion theory.[57] A child may also be targeted for political reasons where a persecutor seeks to extract information relating to a politically active family member[58] or where the child is used as a tool to punish a family member.[59] Critically, in cases involving children it is accepted that a political opinion can be imputed to a child even where the child is unable to identify the political views or activities of the parent – for

---

[53] These cases may engage both the political opinion ground and the membership of a particular social group ground ('the family'). See *infra* Section 5.2.3.3. As to the scope of what is properly understood to constitute a 'political opinion' see *RT (Zimbabwe) v SSHD* [2013] 1 AC 152, [42]–[52].

[54] See, e.g., *Mema v Gonzales*, 474 F 3d 412, 419 (7th Cir, 2007), where the Court of Appeals for the Seventh Circuit allowed a petition for review because the IJ had failed to give sufficient weight to the fact that the applicant had been abducted, detained and beaten because the authorities had mistaken him for his identical twin brother 'and thus they imputed [the brother's] political opinions and activities to [him]'. Similarly, in *Mejilla-Romero v Holder*, 600 F 3d 63, 89 (1st Cir, 2010), Judge Stahl, in a strong dissent, held that, as a child, the applicant 'found himself living with the family's elderly matriarch, who was an active and visible political activist, and as a result [the applicant] suffered the same persecution that his many family members had, merely because of a political opinion imputed to him'. See also *Mukendi v SSHD* [2002] UKIAT 06741 (son will be at risk of harm from authorities because of his father's involvement as an organiser of a student demonstration); *U95-03968 and U95-03969* (IRB, 28 August 1996) (there was a real chance that the son of an escaped perceived counter-revolutionary in China would be subjected to persecution by authorities by reason of his imputed political opinion); *FM (Afghanistan) v SSHD* (Upper Tribunal, AA/01079/2010, 10 March 2011), [151]. Contra the more restrictive approach taken in *Vicente v Holder*, 451 Fed Appx 738, 742–3 (10th Cir, 2011). For further discussion, see UNHCR, 2009 *Guidelines*, [46].

[55] *Kahssai v INS* 16 F 3d 323, 329 (9th Cir, 1994).   [56] 604 F 3d 324 (7th Cir, 2010).

[57] *Shi Chen v Holder*, 604 F 3d 324, 333 (7th Cir, 2010). See also *Zhang v Gonzales*, 408 F 3d 1239, 1247 (9th Cir, 2005); *Lin v Ashcroft*, 377 F 3d 1014, 1031 (9th Cir, 2004).

[58] UKBA, *Asylum Process Guidance*, [16.9]; Home Office, *Processing Children's Asylum Claims*, 42.

[59] 'Oft time persecutors target children of political dissidents not because they have imputed the parents' political opinion to the children, but as a means of harassing, intimidating, and influencing the behavior of the parent': *Mema v Gonzales*, 474 F 3d 412, 417 (7th Cir, 2007). For instance, in *Gjerazi v Gonzales*, 435 F 3d 800, 803 (7th Cir, 2006) the child of an anti-socialist activist was abducted and his release conditioned on the Socialist Party winning the vote in the town where the activist worked at the polling station.

example, because the parent has deliberately withheld this information from the child to protect her.[60]

The second context arises where a child is at risk of harm because of an independently held political opinion or imputed political opinion. The case-law demonstrates that these claims have presented a number of challenges for child applicants. The first derives from a tendency of decision-makers to treat children as apolitical: incapable of expressing political views or engaging in political activity.[61] As Crawley explains, '[the] evidence suggests that what children do – and what is done to them – is not viewed as "political" … [and] [a]s a result, applications for asylum made by separated children are often dismissed.'[62] This is illustrated in a case before the UK AIT involving a young Kurdish boy from Iran who feared that he would be targeted by authorities because of his involvement in destroying a statue of an important Islamic leader. The Tribunal Member considered that the applicant 'shared no serious interest or real knowledge of politics, as of course would be expected of most boys of the age he was then', and that the applicant's age made it 'unlikely that [he was] politically active as claimed'.[63]

The second related challenge is that the concept of 'political activity' is often defined in an adult-centric way. As a result, decision-makers have failed to afford adequate weight to political acts that are, in certain societies, more likely to be carried out by children: preparing or distributing pamphlets, acting as couriers and participating in school strikes or protests. These activities tend to be 'discounted as not being really political, because prevailing judicial conceptions of political activism revolve around an adult norm'.[64]

The third challenge stems from a perception that children are less likely to be taken seriously by a persecuting state regime or non-state actor. Hence, even where it is accepted that a child will be politically active in the country of origin, decision-makers have determined that because the child will not be viewed as a threat she is unlikely to be targeted for reasons of her political opinion. Thus, an IJ rejected the claim of a 15-year-old boy on the basis that 'it is almost inconceivable to believe that the Ton Ton Macoutes [a paramilitary organisation] could be fearful of the conversation of 15-year-old children'.[65] The Court of Appeals for the First Circuit was appropriately critical of this aspect of the IJ's decision, noting that the evidence presented by the applicant 'casts serious doubt on

---

[60] See, e.g., *Singh v Gonzales*, 406 F 3d 191, 197 (3rd Cir, 2005), where the Court criticised the BIA for its apparent view that the applicant's 'lack of knowledge about his father's political and other affiliations' was relevant to the applicant's imputed political opinion claim: 'There is nothing in the case law that suggests that an asylum applicant claiming imputed political opinion is required to have any knowledge about the political belief that is being imputed to him. The focus is instead on whether this attribution has in fact occurred, and that is what we look at here'. See also UNHCR, 2009 *Guidelines*, [46]; IRB, *Guidelines*, 6.

[61] 'For many the very essence of childhood, at least in contemporary western terms, prohibits political participation such that the "political child" is seen as the "unchild", a counter-stereotypical image of children that does not fit with the way we commonly view childhood': M Wyness, L Harrison and I Buchanan, 'Childhood, Politics and Ambiguity: Towards an Agenda for Children's Political Inclusion' (2004) 38(1) *Sociology* 81, 82.

[62] H Crawley, '"Asexual, Apolitical Beings": The Interpretation of Children's Identities and Experiences in the UK Asylum System' (2011) 37 *Journal of Ethnic and Migration Studies* 1171, 1177.

[63] Cited in *ibid.*, 1177.

[64] J Bhabha, 'Minors or Aliens? Inconsistent State Intervention and Separated Child Asylum-Seekers' (2001) 3 *European Journal of Migration and Law* 283, 311.

[65] Cited in *Civil v INS*, 140 F 3d 52, 55 (1st Cir, 1998).

the IJ's contention that "15-year-old children" are unlikely targets of political violence in Haiti'.[66]

The assumption that political identity and activity are the exclusive province of adults is difficult to reconcile with the reality that children can be politically active and targeted because of that activity.[67] Indeed, both arts 12 and 15 of the *CRC* imply that children have a right to express political opinions and to engage in political activity. This reality is now acknowledged in UNHCR's 2009 *Guidelines*, which underline that 'children can be politically active and hold particular political opinions independently of adults . . . for which they may fear being persecuted'[68] and that '[d]ismissing a child's claim based on the assumption that perpetrators would not take a child's views seriously or consider them a real threat could be erroneous'.[69] The 2009 *Guidelines* sensibly apprise that '[w]hether or not a child is capable of holding a political opinion is a question of fact and is to be determined by assessing the child's level of maturity and development, level of education, and his/her ability to articulate those views'.[70] Domestic guidelines published in the United States and the United Kingdom have similarly affirmed that decision-makers 'should not assume that age alone prevents a child from holding political opinions for which he or she may have been or will be persecuted'.[71]

This guidance is complemented by a small body of case-law which recognises that a child may be risk of being persecuted because of an independently held political opinion. One of the earliest decisions is *Polovchak v Meese*, which involved a 12-year-old boy who, along with his 17-year-old brother, had refused to move back to the Soviet Union with his parents. The Court of Appeals for the Seventh Circuit considered that:[72] 'The ability of a young person to decide to which political system he professes allegiance necessarily increases with age. We do not suggest that every twelve year old entertains serious political views (although some may); we would, however, suggest that many seventeen year olds do.' In the case of *Canjura-Flores v INS*, the Court of Appeals for the Ninth Circuit rejected the findings of the IJ and BIA that it 'was unlikely that the government would seek out [the applicant] because of his youth' on the basis that this conflicted with the testimony of the applicant and country of origin information.[73] Similar reasoning can be seen in *Salaam v INS*,[74] where the Court of

---

[66] *Ibid.*, 56. See also the case of a Chilean child whose claim was rejected by the Canadian Refugee Status Advisory Committee on the basis that a 12- or 13-year-old child would not have been perceived as a threat to the Chilean regime: cited in G Sadoway, 'Refugee Children before the Immigration and Refugee Board' (1996) 15(5) *Refuge* 17, 18.

[67] See, e.g., *Civil v INS*, 140 F 3d 52, 61 (1st Cir, 1998) (Judge Bownes, dissenting).

[68] UNHCR, 2009 *Guidelines*, [45].

[69] *Ibid.*, [11]. The 2009 *Guidelines* go on to note that '[m]any national liberation or protest movements are driven by student activists, including schoolchildren' and that 'children may be involved in distributing pamphlets, participating in demonstrations, acting as couriers or engaging in subversive activities': at [45].

[70] *Ibid.*, [45].

[71] INS, *Guidelines*, 22. See also UKBA, *Asylum Process Guidance*, [16.9] ('[a] child can be politically active and/or hold particular political opinions independently of adults for which he or she may fear being persecuted. For example, children may be involved in the distribution of pamphlets, participation in demonstrations, acting as couriers, or engagement in subversive activities. These activities may be considered politically active in other countries but not in the UK'); Home Office, *Processing Children's Asylum Claims*, 42.

[72] *Polovchak v Meese*, 774 F 2d 731, 737 (7th Cir, 1985).

[73] *Canjura-Flores v INS*, 784 F 2d 885, 887 (9th Cir, 1985).

[74] *Salaam v INS*, 229 F 3d 1234 (9th Cir, 2000).

Appeals for the Ninth Circuit criticised the BIA for its conclusion that it was implausible that the applicant was a leading member of the Free Nigeria Movement at the age of 18. The Court granted the applicant's petition for review on the basis that this finding was 'based entirely on an unsupported assumption ... that "important" organizations do not have young leaders'.[75] More recently, in *AA (unattended children) Afghanistan CG* the UK Upper Tribunal allowed the appeal of a 17-year-old Afghan boy who feared that the Taliban would target him because as a young teenager he had sung an anti-Taliban song at a public gathering.[76]

An interesting recent development in the United States has been the increased reliance on the 'political opinion' ground in claims brought by children who have resisted gang recruitment in their home country.[77] Although traditionally characterised as 'particular social group' claims, the difficulties created by the introduction of the 'social visibility' and 'particularity' tests[78] have seen applicants argue that the fear of being persecuted is linked to the applicant's anti-gang political opinion. This argument finds implicit support in *S-E-G-*, where the BIA appeared to leave open the possibility that an applicant could have a well-founded fear of being persecuted for reasons of their political opinion if they were 'politically active or made any anti-gang political statements'.[79] There is a compelling argument that in certain contexts rejecting a recruitment effort may itself convey a political opinion. As UNHCR has observed, such an action 'may convey anti-gang sentiments as clearly as an opinion expressed in a more traditional political manner by, for instance, vocalizing criticism of gangs in public meetings or campaigns'.[80]

5.2.2 Religion

Similar to the 'political opinion' *Convention* ground, claims based on a risk of being persecuted for reasons of religion arise in two principal contexts in claims involving children. The first is where a child is perceived to hold a particular religious belief or to belong to a particular religious group, generally because of the religious beliefs and/or

---

[75] *Ibid.*, 1238.

[76] *AA (unattended children) Afghanistan CG* [2012] UKUT 00016, [121]–[122] (the tribunal disagreed with the Secretary of State's original conclusion that the applicant's account of the public gathering 'lack[ed] credibility' and that, 'even if it were true, it had not been shown how the Taliban would have become aware of him singing a song about them'). See also *Refugee Appeal No 76344* (RSAA, 24 July 2009) (applicant at risk of being persecuted if returned to Iran because as a teenager he had refused to comply with state-imposed dress and social codes); *Timnit Daniel* (BIA, 2002) (Eritrean military targeted 14- and 15-year-old girls on account of a political opinion imputed to them); *0909848* [2010] RRTA 216 (17-year-old boy engaged in activities after arriving in Australia that would be perceived as separatist by the Chinese authorities).

[77] See, e.g., Harvard Immigration Refugee Clinical Program, 'Brief of *Amici Curiae* Harvard Immigration and Refugee Clinical Program and Other Immigration Rights Advocates in Support of Petitioner', filed in *José Fuentes-Colocho v United States Attorney General* (19 November 2013); D Anker, N Kelly, J Willshire Carrera and S Ardalan, 'Mejilla-Romero: A New Era for Child Asylum', 12-09 *Immigration Briefings* (September 2012) 1, 9.

[78] See *infra* text accompanying n 183–201.

[79] *S-E-G-*, 24 I & N Dec 579, 589 (BIA, 2008). See also *Lukwago v Ashcroft*, 329 F 3d 157, 181–2 (3rd Cir, 2003).

[80] UNHCR, *Guidance Note on Refugee Claims Relating to Victims of Organized Gangs* (2010), [50].

affiliations of a family member.[81] It is widely accepted that 'a person may qualify as a refugee if that person has a well-founded fear of persecution for imputed or perceived religious beliefs'.[82] Such a scenario is sharply illustrated in *Matter of Chen*,[83] where the applicant, as a young child, was beaten, detained and 're-educated' by the Red Guards because of his father's activities as a Christian minister. The applicant considered that, as the son of a Christian minister, he could 'never outlive [his] status as a pariah, an outcast, an "unrepentant" element'.[84]

The second context is where a child is at risk of being persecuted because of the child's own religious belief and/or affiliation.[85] For instance, the New Zealand RSAA upheld the refugee claim of a ten-year-old national of Iran on the basis that he was likely to expose himself and his family as Christian converts. In a discerning decision, the Authority observed that the applicant was 'a devout and forceful advocate of the Christian faith' and, '[p]robably as a result of his age, he accepts his belief in absolute terms' and 'will [not] shrink back from persuading others to listen to his beliefs and adopt them, even in the face of conflict [or] resistance'.[86] The Authority took the view that 'this expression of strident belief and intolerance of other religions will inevitably lead him into conflict' and thus gave rise to a risk of being persecuted.[87]

In assessing whether or not a child holds a particular religious belief, a decision-maker must take account of a child's age and maturity. The Canadian Federal Court thus appropriately allowed the appeal of an eight-year-old Christian boy on the basis that the IRB had contradicted itself by acknowledging that the applicant's knowledge of Christianity 'reflects both his minimal experience and his young age' and then, without any explanation, concluding that the applicant was not a genuine practising Christian.[88]

A child's religion need not be the same as the religion observed by a parent or other family member. As the NZIPT has explained, '[c]hildren are not excluded from the fundamental right to have or to adopt a religion or belief, even one that differs from the religion in which their parents seek to instruct them'.[89] Hence, although states should 'not prevent parents giving religious instruction to the child', the state must also not 'collude with parents who seek to deny the child access to information about other religions or beliefs'.[90] This would

---

[81] The reference to 'religious belief' captures a theistic, non-theistic or atheistic belief.

[82] *WALT v MIMIA* [2007] FCAFC 2, [37]. See also UNHCR, 2009 *Guidelines*, [42] (citations omitted): 'It is sufficient that the child simply be perceived as holding a certain religious belief or belonging to a sect or religious group, for example, because of the religious beliefs of his/her parents.'

[83] *Matter of Chen* (BIA, 1989).

[84] *Ibid.*, 20. See also *071687786* [2007] RRTA 318 ('even if [the children] themselves have not developed a genuine commitment to Christianity . . . there is a real chance that they will accompany their parents to an underground Catholic church if they return to China').

[85] Article 14(1) of the *CRC* provides that states parties shall respect the right of the child to 'freedom of thought, conscience and religion'. See generally S Langlaude, *The Right of the Child to Religious Freedom in International Law* (2007).

[86] *Refugee Appeal Nos 76083, 76084 and 76085* (RSAA, 27 June 2008), [85].

[87] *Ibid.*, [86]. See also discussion in *DF (Iran)* [2014] NZIPT 800646-7, [78]–[81]; *Mansour v Ashcroft*, 390 F 3d 667, 677-8 (7th Cir, 2004) (Judge Pregerson, dissenting).

[88] *Qiu v Canada (MCI)* [2009] FCJ No 790, [22]–[23].   [89] *AB (Germany)* [2012] NZIPT 800107, [102].

[90] *Ibid.*, [103].

amount to 'a clear interference with the child's Article 14(1) right to have freedom of thought, conscience and religion'.[91]

In line with the broad scope of religious freedom under international human rights law,[92] a child may be at risk of being persecuted not only because of what the child does believe, but also because of what the child does *not* believe. This *Convention* ground may thus be engaged where a child refuses to hold a particular religious belief or fails to conform to a particular role or abide by a particular religious code.[93] A child may, for instance, refuse to engage in mandated religious education,[94] to undergo a traditional religious practice[95] or to submit to other religion-inspired restrictions or demands.[96] By way of illustration, in *SBAS v MIMIA*[97] an Iranian family with two young daughters claimed that they would be at risk of being persecuted by reason of their Mandean religion. The Federal Court of Australia allowed an appeal on the basis that the RRT gave insufficient regard to the official policy of the Iranian government, which was to force children to study Islam at school and to deny children access to further education or employment opportunities where they refused to embrace the Islamic faith.[98] The Court considered that 'the policy was implemented in a way that denigrated and scared young children and discouraged or hindered them in the obtaining of a school education in contradistinction to that which was made available to Muslim children'.[99]

In the context of female children, a refusal to conform to prescribed gender roles may also give rise to a risk of being persecuted for reasons of religion.[100] In the case of *Re S-A-*, the applicant was beaten by her father, and forbidden from leaving the home and attending school on account of his view that 'a girl should stay at home and should be covered or veiled

---

[91] *Ibid.* This is reflected in art 14(2) of the *CRC* which provides that 'States Parties shall respect the rights and duties of the parents and, when applicable, legal guardians, to provide direction to the child in the exercise of his or her right *in a manner consistent with the evolving capacities of the child*' (emphasis added). This represents a marked improvement on art 18(4) of the *ICCPR*, which excludes any consideration of the educational wishes of the child. Contra *DQ (Iran)* [2015] NZIPT 800868, [45]–[49].

[92] See, e.g., *RT (Zimbabwe) v SSHD* [2013] 1 AC 152, [38]–[39].   [93] UNHCR, 2009 *Guidelines*, [44].

[94] UNHCR, *Guidelines on International Protection: Religion-Based Refugee Claims under Article 1A(2) of the 1951 Convention and/or the 1967 Protocol Relating to the Status of Refugees*, HCR/GIP/04/06 (2004), [21]. This may also be incompatible with art 14(2) of the *CRC*, which provides that states shall respect the rights and duties of parents 'to provide direction to the child in the exercise of his or her right in a manner consistent with the evolving capacities of the child', and art 18(4) of the *ICCPR*, which provides that states shall 'have respect for the liberty of parents and, when applicable, legal guardians to ensure the religious and moral education of their children in conformity with their own convictions'. For an excellent discussion on the relationship between education and religious freedom, see *AB (Germany)* [2012] NZIPT 800107, which concerned a Christian German family who wanted to home-school their children because they did not wish their children to be taught subjects which they perceived to be in conflict with their religious beliefs.

[95] UNHCR, 2009 *Guidelines*, [44]; UNHCR, *Religion-Based Claims Guidelines* (2004) *supra* n 94, [24].

[96] *Re S-A-*, 22 I & N Dec 1328, 1336 (BIA, 2000).   [97] *SBAS v MIMIA* [2003] FCA 528.   [98] *Ibid.*, [63].

[99] *Ibid.*, [63].

[100] See generally UNHCR, *Religion-Based Claims Guidelines* (2004) *supra* n 94, [24]. This may also engage the 'political opinion' *Convention* ground, particularly where the particular role ascribed to women can be traced back to the state and the 'failure to conform could be interpreted as holding an unacceptable political opinion that threatens fundamental power structures': UNHCR, 2009 *Guidelines*, [47]. See also UKBA, *Asylum Process Guidance*, [16.8]; Home Office, *Processing Children's Asylum Claims*, 42. Similar considerations may apply where a male child fails to conform to state-imposed social codes: see, e.g., *Refugee Appeal No 76344* (RSAA, 24 July 2009).

all the time'.[101] The BIA correctly determined that the harm suffered by the applicant 'was on account of her religious beliefs, as they differed from those of her father concerning the proper role of women in Moroccan society.'[102]

5.2.3 Membership of a Particular Social Group

The 'membership of a particular social group' ground is the most critical but also the most challenging *Convention* ground for children seeking to establish entitlement to refugee status. Added to the art 1A(2) definition as an afterthought,[103] the final *Convention* ground has been variously described as 'elusive',[104] 'the ground with the least clarity'[105] and 'a promising yet highly controversial element of the refugee definition'.[106] Although its precise boundaries remain unclear,[107] two dominant approaches have emerged in the jurisprudence, which attempt to provide a framework to guide the interpretation of 'particular social group': the *ejusdem generis* approach and the social perception approach. After a brief overview of the two conceptual approaches, the remainder of this section examines the application of the two approaches to the categories of 'particular social group' most relevant in claims involving children: social groups defined by a child's age – either age alone or age in combination with some other characteristic (such as a 'street child', 'abandoned child' or 'trafficked child') – and by their family.[108]

5.2.3.1 Conceptual Approaches
The *ejusdem generis* approach remains the dominant approach among common law countries. In *Re Acosta* the BIA invoked the principle of *ejusdem generis* to insist that the particular social group ground be understood 'to mean persecution that is directed toward an individual who is a member of a group of persons all of whom share a common, immutable characteristic'.[109] That construction derives from the fact that each of the

---

[101] *Re S-A-*, 22 I & N Dec 1328, 1329 (BIA, 2000).
[102] *Ibid.* See also *Fatin v INS*, 12 F 3d 1233 (3rd Cir, 1993).
[103] A Grahl-Madsen, *The Status of Refugees in International Law* (1966) vol 1, 219.
[104] *Castellano-Chacon v INS*, 341 F 3d 533, 546 (6th Cir, 2003).   [105] UNHCR, *MPSG Guidelines*, [1].
[106] M Foster, 'The "Ground with the Least Clarity": A Comparative Study of Jurisprudential Developments Relating to "Membership of a Particular Social Group"' (UNHCR Legal and Protection Policy Series Paper, August 2012) 2.
[107] Although there were some early attempts to define the 'particular social group' as a residual catch-all, this approach has now been categorically rejected on the basis that it would render the other *Convention* grounds superfluous: see, e.g., *Applicant A v MIEA* (1997) 190 CLR 225, 260 (McHugh J) ('if [the drafters] had intended to provide a "catch all ... ", it is more likely than not that they would have amended the draft treaty by eliminating the specific grounds of persecution'). Similarly, senior courts have rejected an entirely subjective understanding of 'particular social group', underlining the need for clear and objective standards 'by which administrative decisions may determine the fate of individuals': at 277 (Gummow J).
[108] It is important to acknowledge that in some cases it may be appropriate to define a particular social group without any reference to the child's age or family relationship. For example, a gay child living in a society that criminalises homosexuality may be at risk for reasons of his homosexuality alone.
[109] *Re Acosta* 19 I & N Dec 211, 233 (BIA, 1985). The *ejusdem generis* principle is applied where a phrase beginning with genus-describing terms is concluded by a wider, more general term. The effect of the principle is 'to curtail the literal meaning of the residuary words so as to confine it to the genus implicitly described': F Bennion, *Bennion on Statutory Interpretation* (5th edn, 2008) 1239. As Lord Campbell

other *Convention* grounds – race, religion, nationality and political opinion – is referable to an immutable characteristic 'that either is beyond the power of an individual to change or is so fundamental to individual identity or conscience that it ought not be required to be changed'.[110]

In *Canada (Attorney General) v Ward* the Canadian Supreme Court drew on the reasoning in *Re Acosta* – which it considered reflected a 'classic discrimination analysis'[111] – to determine that the meaning assigned to particular social group should 'find inspiration in discrimination concepts'[112] and 'take into account the general underlying themes of the defence of human rights and anti-discrimination that form the basis for the international refugee protection initiative'.[113] The Court considered that in circumstances where non-discrimination principles underpin each of the other four *Convention* grounds,[114] it follows that the particular social group *Convention* ground must also be interpreted in consonance with those same principles.[115] The approach adopted in *Re Acosta* and *Canada (Attorney General) v Ward* was approved by the House of Lords in *R v Immigration Appeal Tribunal; Ex parte Shah*, where Lord Hoffmann observed that 'the inclusion of "particular social group" recognised that there might be different criteria for discrimination, in pari materiae with discrimination on other grounds, which would be equally offensive to human rights'[116] and that '[i]n choosing to use the general term "particular social group" rather than an enumeration of specific social groups, the framers of the Convention were . . . intending to include whatever groups might be regarded as coming within the anti-discriminatory objectives of the Convention'.[117]

The *ejusdem generis* approach does not capture every imaginable group, but is limited to those groups that share some form of immutable or fundamental characteristic. Hence, the approach excludes those groups 'defined by a characteristic which is changeable or from which disassociation is possible, as long as neither option requires renunciation of basic human rights'.[118] The *ejusdem generis* approach is thus consistent with the international rules of treaty interpretation in that it respects the language of art 1A(2), which plainly evinces that the final *Convention* ground is not intended to act as a residual catch-all category, while also providing a principled means for establishing the beneficiary class captured by the ground that is consistent with the

---

observed in *R v Edmundson* (1859) 28 LJ MC 213, 215: 'where there are general words following particular and specific words, the general words must be confined to things of the same kind as those specified'.

[110] *Re Acosta*, 19 I & N Dec 211, 233 (BIA, 1985).

[111] *Canada (Attorney General) v Ward* [1993] 2 SCR 689, 736.   [112] *Ibid.*, 734.   [113] *Ibid.*, 739.

[114] The link between the particular social group ground and non-discrimination principles had previously been identified by a number of scholars, including Hathaway and Goodwin-Gill, both of whom were cited with approval by the Supreme Court in *Canada (Attorney General) v Ward* [1993] 2 SCR 689. In the first edition of G S Goodwin-Gill, *The Refugee in International Law* (1983) 26–7, Goodwin-Gill notes that '[t]he Convention identifies five relevant grounds of persecution, all of which, in varying degrees, have been correspondingly developed in the field of non-discrimination'. See also J C Hathaway, *The Law of Refugee Status* (1991) 160–1.

[115] *Canada (Attorney General) v Ward* [1993] 2 SCR 689, 734.

[116] *R v Immigration Appeal Tribunal; Ex parte Shah* [1999] 2 AC 629, 651.

[117] *Ibid.* See also *Fornah v SSHD* [2007] 1 AC 412, [11]–[16].

[118] *Canada (Attorney General) v Ward* [1993] 2 SCR 689, 737–8, citing Hathaway, *The Law of Refugee Status* (1991) *supra* n 114, 161.

Convention's underlying commitment to the 'assurance of basic human rights without discrimination'.[119]

The second dominant approach – the social perception approach – shifts attention away from the internal characteristics of a putative group and focuses on the external or outward perception of a group. This approach originates from *Applicant A v MIEA*, where the High Court of Australia expressly rejected the *ejusdem generis* approach in favour of a more literal construction of art 1A(2). Brennan CJ considered that neither the text of art 1A(2) nor the *travaux préparatoires* suggests that a particular social group must necessarily exhibit 'an inherent characteristic such as an ethnic or national identity or an ideological characteristic such as adherence to a particular religion or the holding of a political opinion'.[120] Rather, '[b]y the ordinary meaning of the words used, a "particular group" is a group identifiable by any characteristic common to the members of the group and a "social group" is a group the members of which possess some characteristic which distinguishes them from society at large.'[121] In the subsequent decision of *Applicant S v MIMA*,[122] the High Court suggested that a putative group must be shown to possess three features in order to be considered a particular social group: first, the group 'must be identifiable by a characteristic or attribute common to all members of the group'; second, the 'characteristic or attribute common to all members of the group cannot be the shared fear of persecution'; and, third, 'the possession of that characteristic or attribute must distinguish the group from society at large'.[123] In *Applicant S v MIMA*, the High Court made clear that, although highly relevant, it is not necessary for the society to perceive there to be a particular social group; it is sufficient that the group is objectively cognisable or otherwise set apart from society in some way.[124]

In an attempt to resolve the impasse between the two approaches, UNHCR, in 2002, issued the *MPSG Guidelines*, recommending the adoption of a single standard that incorporated both dominant approaches.[125] UNHCR's formulation makes clear that the *ejusdem generis* approach lies at the core of any consideration of particular social group, while also endorsing recourse to the social perception approach where the *ejusdem generis* test is not satisfied. This is made clear in UNHCR's more recent articulations of the formulation, with the organisation underlining that 'the only requirements to establish a "particular social group" are those recited in the "protected characteristics" approach or, *only in the event these are not met*, those in the "social perception" approach.'[126]

---

[119] *Canada (Attorney General) v Ward* [1993] 2 SCR 689, 733. See also *Fornah v SSHD* [2007] 1 AC 412, [13].

[120] *Applicant A v MIEA* (1997) 190 CLR 225, 234: see also at 241 (Dawson J), 294–5 (Kirby J).

[121] *Ibid.*, 234.   [122] *Applicant S v MIMA* (2004) 217 CLR 387.

[123] *Ibid.*, 400 (Gleeson CJ, Gummow and Kirby JJ).   [124] *Ibid.*, 410 (McHugh J).

[125] UNHCR, *MPSG Guidelines*, [10]–[13]. These are affirmed in UNHCR, 2009 *Guidelines*, [48].

[126] UNHCR, 'The United Nations High Commissioner for Refugees' Amicus Curiae Brief in Support of Petitioner', filed in *Henrique-Rivas v Attorney General* (23 February 2012) 16 (emphasis in original). See also UNHCR, 'Brief of the United Nations High Commissioner for Refugees as Amicus Curiae in Support of Petitioner', filed in *Rivera-Barrientos* (18 August 2010) 12–13 (emphasis added) ('In UNHCR's view, and as articulated in the *[MPSG] Guidelines*, the first step in any social group analysis is to determine whether the group in question is based on an immutable or fundamental characteristic. If, at the end of this assessment, the group is found *not* to share a characteristic that can be defined as either innate or fundamental "further analysis should be undertaken to determine whether the group is nonetheless perceived as a cognizable group in that society" ... *This second inquiry is an alternative to be considered only if it is determined that the group characteristic is neither immutable or fundamental*').

UNHCR's *MPSG Guidelines* have been widely misapplied as sanctioning a cumulative test that requires an applicant to satisfy *both* the *ejusdem generis* and the social perception tests. The clearest example of this is art 10(d) of the *EU Qualification Directive*. The cumulative approach has also been adopted in the United States, with the BIA relying on the UNHCR *MPSG Guidelines* to introduce what is now commonly referred to as a 'social visibility' requirement into the *ejusdem generis* test.[127] The cumulative approach is impossible to reconcile with the rules of treaty interpretation and, in particular, the object and purpose of the *Convention*, a point repeatedly made by UNHCR in its attempts to clarify the formulation set out in original 2002 *MPSG Guidelines*.[128] In addition to being based on an erroneous interpretation of UNHCR guidance, a 'social visibility' requirement is also inconsistent with the social perception approach itself, which is focused on whether the social group is *objectively* cognisable. Although, as noted above, being socially visible may help to identify the group, social visibility is not a prerequisite under the social perception approach.[129] In UNHCR's view, there are no additional requirements to establishing a particular social group 'other than those in the "protected characteristics" or "social perception" approaches',[130] and to require any more 'is likely to lead to erroneous decisions and a failure of protection to refugees in contravention of the [*1951 Convention*] and its [*1967 Protocol*]'.[131]

The discussion below adopts the approach advanced by UNHCR, focusing principally on the application of the *ejusdem generis* approach to claims involving children, while also considering, where relevant, the capacity of the social perception approach to provide a supplementary basis for establishing a protected social group where the *ejusdem generis* test is not satisfied.

5.2.3.2 *Children as a Particular Social Group*
Both the *ejusdem generis* approach and social perception approach support the recognition of particular social groups defined in whole or in part by a child's age. For the purposes of the particular social group analysis a child is generally defined, consistent with art 1 of the *CRC*, as a human being below the age of 18 years. Decision-makers have, however, appropriately acknowledged the dangers of drawing inflexible distinctions when delineating an age-based social group. From a practical perspective, adopting a rigid approach fails to have regard to the fact that 'in many areas of the world even today exact ages and dates of birth are

---

[127] *Re CA*, 23 I & N Dec 951, 956 (BIA, 2006). The 'social visibility' requirement has now been adopted by the majority of Circuit Courts of Appeal, save for the Seventh (*Gatimi v Holder*, 578 F 3d 611, 615 (7th Cir, 2009)) and Third Circuits (*Valdiviezo-Galdamez v Attorney General*, 663 F 3d 582, 608–9 (3rd Cir, 2011)). See generally Foster (2012) *supra* n 106, 27–34, and *infra* text accompanying n 183–201.

[128] See, e.g., UNHCR, *Brief in Henrique-Rivas* (2012) *supra* n 126, 10–21; UNHCR, *Brief in Rivera-Barrientos* (2010) *supra* n 126, 9–16; UNHCR, 'Brief *Amicus Curiae* of the Office of the United Nations High Commissioner for Refugees in Support of Respondent X', filed in *Matter of X* (17 August 2010) 5–14; UNHCR, 'Brief of the United Nations High Commissioner for Refugees as Amicus Curiae in Support of Petitioner', filed in *Gaitan v Attorney General* (13 June 2010) 9–16; UNHCR, 'Brief *Amicus Curiae* of The United Nations High Commissioner for Refugees in Support of Respondent Francis Gatimi', filed in *Matter of Gatimi* (25 March 2010); UNHCR, *Brief in Orellana-Monson* (2009) *supra* n 45, 7–16; UNHCR, 'Brief of the United Nations High Commissioner for Refugees as *Amicus Curiae* in Support of the Petitioner', filed in *Valdiviezo-Galdamez* (14 April 2009) 7–13.

[129] See *supra* text accompanying n 124.   [130] UNHCR, *Brief in Orellana-Monson* (2009) *supra* n 45, 16.

[131] *Ibid*.

imprecise'.[132] Moreover, there is something inherently artificial in the suggestion that a risk can subsist up until the eve of a child's eighteenth birthday and then cease the following day.[133] As the England and Wales Court of Appeal has acknowledged, 'persecution is not respectful of birthdays' and 'there is no temporal bright line across which the risks to and the needs of the child suddenly disappear'.[134] In circumstances where it is the applicant's youth and/or vulnerability that underpins the risk of persecutory harm, an applicant's 'apparent or assumed age is more important than chronological age'.[135]

As the discussion below evinces, in claims involving children there are two principal techniques that have been adopted for defining an age-based particular social group: first, to define the social group exclusively by reference to the child's age; second, to define the social group by reference to the child's age plus some other characteristic or factor. The second approach is appropriate where it is the combination of age and the other characteristic or factor that explains why the applicant will be exposed to a risk of being persecuted. For example, it may be that in the destination country only children of a particular status – for instance, girl children or *hei haizi* – will be at risk of being persecuted. In such cases, a wider characterisation of the particular social group may give rise to difficulties in satisfying the nexus criterion.

The first and more straightforward route is to define the putative group exclusively by reference to the child's age. In Canada, for instance, decision-makers have recognised 'children',[136] 'minors'[137] and 'minor children'[138] as particular social groups. A similar approach can be seen in New Zealand, where decision-makers have had little difficulty in finding that an applicant's risk of being persecuted arises 'by virtue of his membership of a particular social group, namely "children"'.[139] Although less common, decision-makers in Australia and the United Kingdom have also been willing to recognise children as a particular social group.[140]

---

[132] *Jakitay v SSHD* (IAT, Appeal No 12658, 15 November 1995).

[133] 'Does membership cease on the day of the person's eighteenth birthday? It is not easy to see that risks of the relevant kind to a person who is a child would continue until the eve of that birthday, and cease at once the next day': *DS (Afghanistan) v SSHD* [2011] EWCA Civ 305, [54].

[134] *KA (Afghanistan) v SSHD* [2013] 1WLR 615, [18].

[135] *Ibid.* See also *VA0-02635* (IRB, 22 March 2001) 11 (acknowledging that while the applicant was chronologically an adult, he was, because of sustained abuse as a child, 'a psychological child'); *V97-00156 and V97-00962* (IRB, 28 May 1998) 6 ('[t]he fact that he is now over the age of 18 does not have the effect of nullifying his claim on the basis of child abuse'). The UNHCR, 2009 *Guidelines*, [7] (citations omitted), adopts a similar position, acknowledging that '[t]here may be exceptional cases for which these guidelines are relevant even if the applicant is 18 years of age or slightly older. This may be particularly the case where persecution has hindered the applicant's development and his/her psychological maturity remains comparable to that of a child.'

[136] See, e.g., *V99-03532* (IRB, 12 October 2001); *Canada (MCI) v Li* [2001] FCJ No 620, [11]; *Xiao v Canada (MCI)* [2001] FCJ No 349, [14]; *Li v Canada (MCI)* (2000) 198 FTR 81, [22]; *VA0-02635* (IRB, 22 March 2001) 10; *A95-00633* (28 January 1998) 2; *V97-00156 and V97-00962* (IRB, 28 May 1998) 5.

[137] *V99-02929* (IRB, 21 February 2000) 6; *T93-12579 and T93-12586* (IRB, 25 July 1995) 22; *T91-01497 and T91-01498* (IRB, 9 August 1994) 7; *T94-00416, T94-00418 and T94-00419* (IRB, 25 August 1994) 5; *Khadra Hassan Farah* (10 May 1994).

[138] *T93-09636, T93-09638 and T93-09639* (IRB, 26 January 1994) 9.

[139] *Refugee Appeal Nos 76494 and 76495* (RSAA, 23 November 2010), [76]. See also *Refugee Appeal Nos 75301, 75302 and 75303* (RSAA, 24 January 2006), [46]; *Refugee Appeal Nos 76226 and 76227* (RSAA, 12 January 2009), [114]; *Refugee Appeal Nos 76305, 76306, 76307 and 76308* (RSAA, 30 June 2010), [147].

[140] In Australia, see, e.g., *VFAY v Minister for Immigration* [2003] FMCA 35, [25]; *0803919* [2008] RRTA 333, [75]; *060741183* [2006] RRTA 185. In the United Kingdom, see, e.g., *LQ (Age: immutable characteristic) Afghanistan* [2008] UKAIT 0005, [6]–[7]; *DS (Afghanistan) v SSHD* [2011] EWCA Civ 305, [4]; *FM (Afghanistan) v SSHD* (Upper Tribunal, AA/01079/2010, 10 March 2011), [151]; UKBA,

Recognition that a particular social group can be defined exclusively by reference to a child's age sits comfortably with the *ejusdem generis* approach, on the basis that, at any given point in time, children share a common and immutable characteristic.[141] This finds support in non-discrimination principles and the recognition in international law that age is a protected category for discrimination purposes.[142] Although it has been suggested that age is not an immutable characteristic because 'unlike innate characteristics, such as sex or color, age changes over time',[143] that analysis has been sensibly rebuffed at both an international and domestic level. As UNHCR has observed, '[a]lthough age, in strict terms, is neither innate nor permanent as it changes continuously, being a child is in effect an immutable characteristic *at any given point in time*'.[144] To similar effect, a UK tribunal held that '[a]t the date when the appellant's status has to be assessed he is a child and although, assuming he survives, he will in due course cease to be a child, he is immutably a child at the time of assessment.'[145] The reality that a child may at some point in time in the future fall outside the scope of the proposed social group is immaterial in assessing the present risk of persecutory harm. Applying the *ejusdem generis* approach, the relevant

---

Asylum Process Guidance, [16.10] ('[a]ge groupings such as "children" or "young men", or "young girls" may constitute a particular social group; depending on the specific country context and the treatment of this group and how they are perceived within that society and the laws of the relevant country. Case owners should bear in mind that at any given point, a child's age may be considered an immutable characteristic (for example, notwithstanding the fact that the child will ultimately grow out of his/her present age grouping)'); Home Office, *Processing Children's Asylum Claims*, 42.

[141] The broader categorisation is also consistent with the well-established principle that the size of the group is not a relevant consideration to whether a social group exists. This is self-evidently correct, given that each of the other *Convention* grounds (race, religion, nationality and political opinion) are shared by large numbers of people. See, e.g., UNHCR, *MPSG Guidelines*, [18]; *MIMA v Khawar* (2002) 210 CLR 1, [127] (Kirby J); *Perdomo v Holder*, 611 F 3d 662, 669 (9th Cir, 2010).

[142] The HRC has recognised 'age' within the 'other status' criterion of art 2 and art 26 of the *ICCPR*: see S Joseph and M Castan, *The International Covenant on Civil and Political Rights* (3rd edn, 2013) 792–3 (citing, e.g., HRC, Views: Communication No 983/2001, CCPR/C/77/D/983/2001 (2003) ('*Love v Australia*')). On the protection of children against discrimination generally, see *CRC*, art 2; *ICCPR*, art 24; HRC, *GC17*, [5]; UNCESCR, *GC20*, [29]; UNCRC, *GC5*, [12]; UNCRC, *GC6*, [18]; UNCRC, *GC14*, [41].

[143] *Lukwago v Ashcroft*, 329 F 3d 157, 171 (3rd Cir, 2003). See also *Escobar v Gonzales*, 417 F 3d 363, 367 (3rd Cir, 2005); *LQ (Age: immutable characteristic) Afghanistan* [2008] UKAIT 0005, [5]; *Jean v Canada (MCI)* [2010] FCJ No 769, [43].

[144] UNHCR, 2009 *Guidelines*, [49] (emphasis added). See also UNHCR, *Brief in Orellana-Monso* (2009) *supra* n 45, 17 ('"[y]outh" can be considered an immutable characteristic as one cannot change one's age, except by waiting and letting time pass; thus, the immutable character of "age" or "youth" is gradual, yet, in effect, unchangeable at any given point in time'); UNHCR, *Victims of Trafficking Guidelines* (2006) *supra* n 29, [38].

[145] *LQ (Age: immutable characteristic) Afghanistan* [2008] UKAIT 0005, [6]. See also *V99-02929* (IRB, 21 February 2000) 6–7 ('[t]he child's vulnerability arises as a result of his status as a minor. His vulnerability as a minor is an innate and unchangeable characteristic, notwithstanding the child will grow into an adult'); *S-E-G-*, 24 I & N Dec 579, 583 (BIA, 2008) ('we acknowledge that the mutability of age is not within one's control, and that if an individual has been persecuted in the past on account of an age-described particular social group, a claim for asylum may still be cognizable'); *T91-01497 and T91-01498* (IRB, 9 August 1994) 7 ('[f]ollowing the Supreme Court decision in *Ward*, the panel finds that the minor claimant is a member of a particular social group, namely minors, based on the "innate and unchangeable characteristic" of being under the age of majority – a fact she cannot change for the foreseeable future'); *T93-09636, T93-09638 and T93-09639* (IRB, 26 January 1994) 9.

inquiry is whether the child can, at the time of assessment, disassociate herself from her age in order to avoid the risk of being persecuted.[146]

A particular social group defined exclusively by age will also satisfy the social perception approach, given that children possess age-based characteristics which distinguish them from society and are generally readily identifiable as a discrete group within any given community.[147] This is illustrated by the fact that many domestic laws and policies are circumscribed by reference to age, including policies relating to criminal responsibility, the right to vote, sexual activity, military conscription and mandatory education.[148] In *VFAY v Minister for Immigration* the Australian Federal Magistrates Court applied the social perception approach to conclude that 'children are a particular social group for the purposes of the Convention and ... a subset of children can, in particular circumstances, also constitute a particular social group'.[149] According to the Court, '[c]hildren as a whole plainly do share characteristics which make them recognisable or cognisable as a social group set apart from the rest of the community' and it is 'self[-]evident that children are readily identifiable as a particular social group in any society'.[150]

The second, more common method for defining a social group in claims involving children is to do so by reference to the child's age plus some other characteristic. As noted above, this approach may be more appropriate where it is an intersection of factors, including the child's age, which provides the operative reason why the child will be exposed to a risk of being persecuted if returned to her country of origin.[151] In these cases, decision-makers must be careful not to define the proposed social group so narrowly as to violate the well-established rule that, in order to avoid circularity, a particular social group cannot be defined exclusively by a shared risk of being persecuted;[152] for example, 'children at risk of FGC' or 'children at risk of domestic child abuse' are not cognisable social groups.

---

[146] 'The fact that the child eventually will grow older is irrelevant to the identification of a particular social group, as this is based on the facts as presented in the asylum claim': UNHCR, 2009 *Guidelines*, [49]. See also Foster (2007) *supra* n 3, 329–33. There is debate as to whether the transition from childhood to adulthood will engage the cessation provision under art 1C of the *Convention*. Hathaway and Foster mount a convincing argument that the cessation provision was not intended to authorise cessation for purely personal reasons but was limited to changes to the objective situation in the applicant's home country. According to the authors, 'contemplating cessation because a refugee has matured provides an especially stark example of precisely the sort of unduly intrusive disruption of a recognized refugee's legitimate interest in a secure future that the [cessation] clauses were designed to avert': Hathaway and Foster (2014) *supra* n 5, 481–2. Contra *Ixtlilco-Morales v Keisler*, 507 F 3d 651 (8th Cir, 2007); *Valcu v Attorney General*, 394 Fed Appx 884 (3rd Cir, 2010).

[147] As UNHCR has observed, children 'share many general characteristics, such as innocence, relative immaturity, impressionability and evolving capacities' and, in most societies, 'are set apart from adults as they are understood to require special attention or care': UNHCR, 2009 *Guidelines*, [49].

[148] *Ibid.*

[149] *VFAY v Minister for Immigration* [2003] FMCA 35, [25]. In so finding, the Court referred extensively to the *CRC* and criticised the primary decision-maker for failing to refer to the *CRC* in considering whether children or separated children constitute a particular social group in Afghanistan: at [22]. The Court considered that '[t]he significance of these international instruments is that they demonstrate that children have been recognised internationally as an identifiable group meriting consideration as asylum seekers': at [23]. The decision was overturned on appeal on other grounds: see *MIMIA v VFAY* [2003] FCAFC 191, [62].

[150] *VFAY v Minister for Immigration* [2003] FMCA 35, [25].

[151] 'A range of child groupings, thus, can be the basis of a claim to refugee status under the "membership of a particular social group" ground': UNHCR, 2009 *Guidelines*, [50].

[152] UNHCR, *MPSG Guidelines*, [14].

In practice, however, it is relatively straightforward to identify the additional identifying element, with courts appropriately recognising that 'the actions of the persecutors may serve to identify or even cause the creation of a particular social group in society'.[153]

Adopting this second 'age-plus' approach to defining a social group, decision-makers have accepted the following subsets of children as particular social groups: 'unaccompanied children';[154] 'orphaned children';[155] 'abandoned children';[156] 'impoverished children';[157] 'street children';[158] 'girl children';[159] 'children of widowed mothers';[160] 'children of inter-clan marriages';[161] 'children with a disability';[162] 'children diagnosed with a medical condition';[163] 'children with parents with a medical illness';[164] 'young males';[165] 'black children' or 'hei haizi';[166] '"out of wedlock" children';[167] 'children who are sold into prostitution';[168] 'children of women who are victims of spousal abuse';[169] 'gay, bisexual and transgender children';[170] 'westernised children';[171] and 'children resistant to gang-recruitment'.[172] Decision-makers have also appropriately recognised that a child's *former*

---

[153] *Applicant A v MIEA* (1997) 190 CLR 225, 264.

[154] *SGBB v MIMIA* [2003] FCA 709, [23]; *VFAY v Minister for Immigration* [2003] FMCA 35, [24]–[31]. See generally C Seugling, 'Toward a Comprehensive Response to the Transnational Migration of Unaccompanied Minors in the United States' (2004) 37 *Vanderbilt Journal of Transnational Law* 861, 890–2.

[155] *V98-00787* (IRB, 4 June 1999) 10; *LQ (Age: immutable characteristic) Afghanistan* [2008] UKAIT 0005, [7]; *DS (Afghanistan) v SSHD* [2011] EWCA Civ 305, [4]; *0903098* [2009] RRTA 113, [156].

[156] *M93 of 2004 v Minister for Immigration* [2006] FMCA 252, [61]–[70]; *V97-03500* (IRB, 31 May 1999) 4.

[157] *A95-00633* (28 January 1998) 3; *1106185* [2011] RRTA 844, [85].

[158] *A95-00633* (28 January 1998). See also *Re Brus Funetes Ortega* (BIA, 2001). In the United States, a number of IJs have also recognised street children as a particular social group: see D Anker, *Law of Asylum in the United States* (2015) 508–9; contra *Escobar v Gonzales*, 417 F 3d 363, 367 (3rd Cir, 2005).

[159] *1103242* [2011] RRTA 517, [73]; *0806954* [2009] RRTA 264, [90]. On the relationship between gender and age more generally see, *Fornah v SSHD* [2007] 1 AC 412, [31] (Lord Bingham), [69]–[81] (Baroness Hale); *Re Fauziya Kasinga*, 21 I & N Dec 357 (BIA, 1996) 375–8; see Foster (2007) *supra* n 3, 324–8, 334.

[160] *V97-01419, V97-01420, V97-01421, V98-02335, V98-02345 and V98-02346* (IRB, 9 August 1999) 15.

[161] *T96-06291 and T96-06292* (IRB, 2 September 1997) 6; *T96-04645* (IRB, 25 August 1997) 5.

[162] *Tchoukhrova v Gonzales*, 404 F 3d 1181, 1188 (9th Cir, 2005); *TA0-05472* (IRB, 30 May 2001) 6; *071775230* [2007] RRTA 343. Similar reasoning may apply in cases involving children with other medical illnesses. For example, UNHCR has suggested that 'children affected by HIV/AIDS' – either because the child is HIV-positive or has an HIV-positive parent or guardian – may constitute a particular social group: UNHCR, 2009 *Guidelines*, [52]. This has been acknowledged in national guidelines in the United Kingdom: UKBA, *Asylum Process Guidance*, [16.10]; Home Office, *Processing Children's Asylum Claims*, 42.

[163] *071775230* [2007] RRTA 343.   [164] *Canada (MCI) v Oh* [2009] FCJ No 640, [10].

[165] *Applicant S v MIMA* (2004) 217 CLR 387, 411; *Paramananthan v MIMA* (1998) 94 FCR 28, 61, 69. For further examples, see Foster (2007) *supra* n 3, 334.

[166] *Chen Shi Hai v MIMA* (2000) 201 CLR 293, [2]; *Cheung v Canada (MEI)* [1993] 2 FC 314, 325; *Shi Chen v Holder*, 604 F 3d 324, 335 (7th Cir, 2010). These cases are also often dealt with under the political opinion ground: see *supra* text accompanying n 56–7.

[167] *0900423* [2009] RRTA 191, [37].

[168] *SSHD v Nigerian Minor* (IAT, Appeal No HX/27501/03, 26 January 2005).

[169] *V97-00708, V97-00709, V97-00710 and V97-00711* (IRB, 11 August 1998).

[170] UKBA, *Asylum Process Guidance*, [16.10]; Home Office, *Processing Children's Asylum Claims*, 43; *1007384* [2010] RRTA 1050, [71].

[171] *0800288* [2008] RRTA 133.

[172] This proffered group has given rise to a considerable body of jurisprudence in the United States. Although the BIA has acknowledged that 'youth who have been targeted for recruitment by, and resisted criminal gangs, may have a shared past experience, which, by definition, cannot be changed' (*S-E-G-*, 24

status may give rise to a cognisable social group, including where the applicant is no longer a child.[173] For instance, 'former child soldiers'[174] and 'former victims of trafficking or prostitution'[175] have been recognised as social groups.

These age-plus social groups will generally satisfy both the *ejusdem generis* and social perception approaches. As to the *ejusdem generis* approach, it is self-evident that the majority of the groups share some form of immutable or fundamental characteristic. There can be no doubt, for instance, that being an orphaned child is an 'innate and unchangeable characteristic';[176] that a child born in contravention of China's family planning laws is 'persecuted for what they are (the circumstances of their parentage, birth and status) and not by reason of anything they themselves have done';[177] and that a child's status as a former child soldier 'is a characteristic that he cannot change and one that is now, unfortunately, fundamental to his identity'.[178]

It has been suggested that the 'street children' social group fails to satisfy the *ejusdem generis* approach on the basis the child's circumstances may change.[179] For example, in *LQ (Age: immutable characteristic) Afghanistan v SSHD*, the government argued that the child's status as a 'street child' is not an immutable characteristic because the child 'might at any moment be adopted or receive some other form of care'.[180] This argument has no regard to the reality that the child's *situation* may be immutable, in that the child may be unable to remove herself from her circumstances.[181] The argument was appropriately dismissed by the UK AIT as 'pure speculation', with the tribunal affirming that the applicant in that case

I & N Dec 579, 584 (BIA, 2008)), US courts have proven reluctant to accept that children targeted for recruitment by gangs constitute a particular social group. UNHCR has strongly argued that these children may fall within a cognisable social group: see, e.g., UNHCR, 2009 *Guidelines*, [52]; UNHCR, *Organized Gangs Guidance Note* (2010) *supra* n 80, [34]–[42]; UNHCR, *Brief in Orellana-Monson* (2009) *supra* n 45. See further J Bhabha, *Child Migration & Human Rights in a Global Age* (2014) 233–6.

[173] 'The applicant's membership in a child-based social group does not necessarily cease to exist merely because his/her childhood ends. The consequences of having previously belonged to such a group might not end even if the key factor of that identity (that is, the applicant's young age) is no longer applicable': UNHCR, 2009 *Guidelines*, [51].

[174] In *Lukwago v Ashcroft*, 329 F 3d 157, 178–9 (3rd Cir, 2003) the Court of Appeals for the Third Circuit accepted 'former child soldiers who have escaped' as a particular social group. The Court considered that the fact that the applicant is no longer a child 'is not to the point because [the applicant] does not assert . . . a social group based on age. He asserts that he is a member of the group of *former* child soldiers who have escaped': at 178 (emphasis in original). Contra the approach taken to 'former gang members': see discussion in Anker (2015) *supra* n 158, 497–501.

[175] *SSHD v Nigerian Minor* (IAT, Appeal No HX/27501/03, 26 January 2005), [11]; *SB v SSHD* [2008] UKAIT 00002, [56]; *Hong v Attorney General*, 165 Fed Appx 995 (3rd Cir, 2006). See also UNHCR, *Victims of Trafficking Guidelines*, *supra* n 29, [37]–[39]; Foster (2007) *supra* n 3, 339.

[176] *V98-00787* (IRB, 4 June 1999) 10.   [177] *Chen Shi Hai v MIMA* (2000) 201 CLR 293, [18].

[178] *Lukwago v Ashcroft*, 329 F 3d 157, 178 (3rd Cir, 2003).

[179] An identical argument has been advanced in relation to 'unaccompanied children': see, e.g., *T96-02166 and T96-02168* (IRB, 14 May 1997).

[180] *LQ (Age: immutable characteristic) Afghanistan* [2008] UKAIT 0005, [7]. More generally, see *Escobar v Gonzales*, 417 F 3d 363, 367 (3rd Cir, 2005); M Muller, D Anker and L Rosenberg, '*Escobar v Gonzales*: A Backwards Step for Child Asylum Seekers and the Rule of Law in Particular Social Group Asylum Claims' (2006) 10(1) *UC Davis Journal of Juvenile Law and Policy* 243.

[181] 'Especially for children who have grown up in such situations, their way of life is fundamental to their identity and often difficult to change': UNHCR, 2009 *Guidelines*, [52]. See also Foster (2007) *supra* n 3, 335; Anker (2015) *supra* n 158, 506.

belonged to a group that 'shar[ed] an immutable characteristic and constitute[ed], for the purposes of the Refugee Convention, a particular social group'.[182]

The age-plus social groups will also satisfy the social perception approach, given that the groups are objectively identifiable by a common characteristic. Indeed, in many cases the identification of the particular social group may be assisted by the fact that, in addition to age, the child shares a further distinguishing social characteristic (such as being an orphan, disabled or a 'black child').[183]

The introduction of the 'particularity' and 'social visibility' requirements in the United States have presented challenges to the recognition of particular groups based on age,[184] although the 'social visibility' requirement has been appropriately diluted in recent decisions of the US BIA. The particularity criterion imposes a requirement that the proposed group be capable of being 'accurately ... described in a manner sufficiently distinct that the group would be recognized in the society in question, as a discrete class of persons'.[185] It has been suggested that 'the size of the proposed group may be an important factor in determining whether the group can be so recognized'.[186] This has led the US Court of Appeals for the Sixth Circuit to reject the social group 'Guatemalan children under age fourteen' – clearly a group that satisfies both the *ejusdem generis* and social perception approach – on the basis that it lacked sufficient particularity. The Court observed that the 'proposed group would include, at some point, Guatemala's entire population'.[187] To similar effect, in *Díaz Ruano v Holder* the First Circuit rejected the social group 'young males' – which would again satisfy both the *ejusdem generis* and social perception approach – on the basis that 'the age parameters ('young males') are ... lacking in precision', given that '[o]ne who is "young" in the eyes of one observer may not be 'young in the eyes of another observer'.[188] These decisions are difficult to reconcile with the reality that 'the characteristics of gender and age are ... susceptible to easy definition'.[189] The apparent focus on the size of a putative group is also inconsistent with the well-established principle that the size of a social group is not a relevant criterion in determining whether a particular social group exists.[190]

The 'social visibility' criterion also proved particularly pernicious in claims involving children. Although age-based social groups are capable of satisfying the social perception approach,[191] the introduction of this additional hurdle, which originally appeared to require that a group be literally visually identifiable to the naked eye, caused particular difficulties for particular social groups based on age. The central problem with requiring *actual* visibility is that, in some cases, the protected characteristic will not be socially visible, either

---

[182] *LQ (Age: immutable characteristic) Afghanistan* [2008] UKAIT 0005, [7].

[183] UNHCR, 2009 *Guidelines*, [49]; UNHCR, *Brief in Orellana-Monson, supra* n 45, 21–2.

[184] Both requirements have been widely criticised by UNHCR, some federal courts in the United States, and commentators. See, e.g., *supra* n 127–128; Foster (2012) *supra* n 106, 27–34; Hathaway and Foster (2014) *supra* n 5, 430–6; Anker (2015) *supra* n 158, 442–56.

[185] *S-E-G-*, 24 I & N Dec 579, 584 (BIA, 2008).

[186] *Ibid*. But see *Valdiviezo-Galdamez v Attorney General*, 663 F 3d 582, 608 (3rd Cir, 2011).

[187] *Gomez-Guzman v Holder*, 485 Fed Appx 64, 67 (6th Cir, 2012).

[188] *Díaz Ruano v Holder* 420 Fed Appx 19, 21 (1st Cir, 2011). See also *Escobar-Batres v Holder*, 385 Fed Appx 445, 447 (11th Cir, 2010); decision of the BIA cited in *Valdiviezo-Galdamez v Attorney General*, 663 F 3d 582, 589 (3rd Cir, 2011); *Flores-Cruz v Holder*, 325 Fed Appx 512, 514 (9th Cir, 2009); *S-E-G-*, 24 I & N Dec 579, 584–5 (BIA, 2008); *Velasquez v US Attorney General*, 490 Fed Appx 266, 268 (11th Cir, 2012).

[189] *Rivera-Barrientos v Holder*, 666 F 3d 641, 650 (10th Cir, 2012).   [190] See *supra* n 141.

[191] See *supra* text accompanying n 147–150.

because of the nature of the characteristic (for example, a child who has not been subject to FGC,[192] a child who resists gang membership,[193] or a former child soldier[194] or victim of trafficking[195]), or because the applicant is compelled to hide the characteristic in order to avoid persecution (for example, her homosexuality[196]). Justice Posner of the Seventh Circuit has observed that the 'social visibility' requirement 'makes no sense'[197] for this very reason:[198]

> If you are a member of a group that has been targeted for assassination or torture or some other mode of persecution, you will take pains to avoid being socially visible; and to the extent that the members of the target group are successful in remaining invisible, they will not be 'seen' by other people in the society 'as a segment of the population'.

The Third and Seventh Circuit Courts of Appeal appropriately rejected the social visibility requirement as an 'unreasonable addition to the requirements for establishing refugee status'.[199] This is consistent with the position adopted by UNHCR, which has repeatedly underlined that there is nothing in the *Refugee Convention* or the *MPSG Guidelines* that support the imposition or continued use of the 'social visibility' requirement.[200] In 2014, the US BIA published two decisions that expressly shifted away from a 'social visibility' requirement – rejecting a requirement for actual 'ocularity' – to a 'social distinction' approach that more comfortably aligns with the social perception approach discussed above.[201]

5.2.3.3 *Family as a Particular Social Group*

Senior appellate courts have had no difficulty in finding that the family constitutes a particular social group for the purposes of art 1A(2).[202] Indeed, the family has been described as 'a prototypical example of a "particular social group"'[203] and as a 'social group *par excellence*'.[204] This accords with the long-standing recognition under international law that the family is the 'fundamental group of society and the natural environment for the growth and well-being of all its members and particularly children' and should thus 'be afforded the necessary protection and assistance so that it can fully assume its

---

[192] *Gatimi v Holder*, 578 F 3d 611, 615 (7th Cir, 2009).

[193] See, e.g., *S-E-G-*, 24 I & N Dec 579, 587 (BIA, 2008).

[194] E Rossi, 'A "Special Track" for Former Child Soldiers: Enacting a "Child Soldier Visa" as an Alternative to Asylum Protection' (2013) 31 *Berkeley Journal of International Law* 392, 406–12.

[195] F Marouf, 'The Emerging Importance of "Social Visibility" in Defining a "Particular Social Group" and Its Potential Impact on Asylum Claims Related to Sexual Orientation and Gender' (2008) 27 *Yale Law and Policy Review* 47, 98–102.

[196] *Gatimi v Holder*, 578 F 3d 611, 615 (7th Cir, 2009); Marouf (2008) *supra* n 195, 79–88.

[197] *Gatimi v Holder*, 578 F 3d 611, 615 (7th Cir, 2009).   [198] *Ibid.*

[199] *Valdiviezo-Galdamez v Attorney General*, 663 F 3d 582, 604 (3rd Cir, 2011). See further *supra* n 127.

[200] See *supra* n 128.

[201] *Matter of M-E-V-G-*, 26 I & N Dec 388 (BIA, 2014) and *W-G-R-*, 26 I & N 208 (BIA, 2014), discussed in Anker (2015) *supra* n 158, 448–56.

[202] As to the definition of family, see: *MIMA v Sarrazola (No 2)* (2001) 107 FCR 184, 193; Chapter 2, n 1.

[203] *Sanchez-Trujillo v INS*, 801 F 2d 1571, 1576 (9th Cir, 1986), cited with approval in INS, *Guidelines*, 24.

[204] Macdonald and Toal (2014) *supra* n 25, vol 1, 1034. See also *Casetellanos v Canada* [1995] 2 FC 190, 204 ('one cannot imagine a closer-knit or easier to confirm unit than the family. This is especially true with respect to immediate family, being a person's sons, daughters, parents and any other blood relative they permanently reside with. There can be absolutely no doubt that the family forms a social group which is protected against persecution').

responsibilities within the community'.[205] The identification of the family as a particular social group sits most securely with the *ejusdem generis* approach.[206] As the First Circuit Court of Appeals has recognised, 'there can, in fact, be no plainer example of a social group based on common, identifiable and immutable characteristics than that of the nuclear family'.[207] In the context of children this view finds clear support in art 2(2) of the *CRC*, which expressly recognises familial membership as a protected status for the purposes of discrimination law, providing that a state must take all appropriate measures to ensure that a child is 'protected against all forms of discrimination or punishment on the basis of the status, activities, expressed opinions, or beliefs of the child's parents, legal guardians or family members'. The particular social group of family also satisfies the social perception approach, with the family being both objectively cognisable and distinguishable from society at large.[208]

A child will most commonly be at risk of persecutory harm for reasons of her family where the family is at risk of being targeted by external forces because of the status or activities of a family member.[209] That risk may, for instance, derive from a family member's race,[210] political affiliation,[211] disability or illness,[212] or a family's general wealth or

---

[205] *CRC*, Preamble. See also UDHR, art 16(3); *ICCPR*, art 23(1); *ICESCR*, art 10.

[206] Indeed, in *Re Acosta*, 19 I & N Dec 211 (BIA, 1985), the BIA decision credited for the *ejusdem generis* approach, the tribunal described 'kinship ties' as a clear example of an innate shared characteristic (at 233).

[207] *Gebremichael v INS*, 10 F 3d 28, 36 (1st Cir, 1983), cited with approval in INS, *Guidelines*, 24. See also *Fornah v SSHD* [2007] 1 AC 412, [45] ('[t]he ties that bind members of a family together, whether by blood or by marriage, define the group. It is those ties that set it apart from the rest of society'); *Crespin-Valladares v Holder*, 632 F 3d 117, 124–5 (4th Cir, 2011) (affirming that kinship ties are 'paradigmatically immutable', 'that family bonds are innate and unchangeable' and that every US circuit that has considered the question 'has held that family ties can provide a basis for asylum'); *Aguirre-Cervantes v INS*, 242 F 3d 1169, 1177 (9th Cir, 2001) ('[f]amily membership is clearly an immutable characteristic, fundamental to one's identity'); *Demiraj v Holder*, 631 F 3d 194, 203 (5th Cir, 2011) (Judge Dennis, dissenting) ('[f]amily membership is a characteristic that a person either cannot change (if he or she is related by blood) or should not be required to change (if he or she is related by marriage). The purpose of asylum law is to honor a moral obligation to protect people who are threatened with persecution because of characteristics like these'); *AN (Pakistan)* [2013] NZIPT 800422-426, [62] ('[m]embership of the family is an immutable and innate characteristic ... [i]t is beyond their power to change'); *Refugee Appeal Nos 76485, 76486 and 76487* (RSAA, 17 June 2010), [79] ('[m]embership of a family is undoubtedly an immutable characteristic'); UNHCR, 2009 *Guidelines*, [50]; UNHCR, 'Position on Claims for Refugee Status under the 1951 Convention Relating to the Status of Refugees Based on a Fear of Persecution due to an Individual's Membership of a Family or Clan Engaged in a Blood Feud' (17 March 2006), [16]–[20].

[208] See, e.g., *Fornah v SSHD* [2007] 1 AC 412, [45] ('It is universally accepted that the family is a socially cognisable group in society'); *Sarrazola v MIMA* [1999] FCA 101, [36] ('[m]embership of a family is a characteristic which distinguishes members of that family from society at large'); *C and S v MIMA* [1999] FCA 1430, [33]; *MIMA v Sarrazola (No 2)* (2001) 107 FCR 184, 192–6; UNHCR, *Blood Feud Position Paper, supra* n 207, [16]–[20].

[209] Hathaway and Foster (2014) *supra* n 5, 446.

[210] See, e.g., *Refugee Appeal Nos 74046, 74047, 74048 and 74049* (RSAA, 30 June 2005), [91].

[211] See, e.g., *Lin v Ashcroft*, 377 F 3d 1014, 1039–41 (9th Cir, 2004) (parent's resistance to family planning policies); *Macias v Canada (MCI)* 2004 FC 1749, [10] (political activities of father); *AA0-00661, AA0-00662, AA0-00663, AA0-00664 and AA0-00665* (IRB, 11 January 2001) 6 (political activities of father); *Gutierrez v Canada (MCI)* [2000] FCJ No 636, [33]–[45] (family of 'reactionaries'); *Refugee Appeal Nos 73898 and 73899* (RSAA, 9 November 2004), [92]–[94] (imputed political opinion of mother).

[212] See, e.g., *T98-03163, T98-03164 and T98-03165* (IRB, 7 May 2001) 14 (family led by a single parent female with serious mental health problems); *V95/03256* [1995] RRTA 263, [46] (family members of HIV sufferers).

prominence in the community.[213] A child may also be at risk as a member of a family where her family is targeted for retribution, for instance where a parent or sibling has acted as an informant,[214] committed a criminal act[215] or refused to join or co-operate with a criminal organisation.[216]

More recently, there have been an increasing number of cases where the particular social group of family has been invoked where the risk derives from *inside* the family unit. The paradigm case is where a child is at risk of domestic violence at the hands of her parents. Although these cases can typically be analysed by way of an age-based social group,[217] in certain cases the particular social group of family may more accurately explain an operative reason why the child will be exposed to a risk of being persecuted. By way of illustration, in *Aguirre-Cervantes v INS* the Ninth Circuit Court of Appeals reached the 'inescapable' conclusion that a young Mexican woman had been beaten by her father for reasons of her family membership in circumstances where there was undisputed evidence demonstrating that the father's 'goal was to dominate and persecute members of his immediate family'.[218] Similar reasoning was adopted in *VA0-00091*,[219] where the IRB held that a 17-year-old Chinese boy smuggled to New York by his family to work in order to send money back to China was at risk of persecutory harm because of his status as a child in a Chinese family expected to provide support for other family members. The IRB underlined that '[t]he fact that the agents of persecution, the parents, are also members of the same family does not detract from the claimant being a *bona fide* member of a particular social group'.[220]

A category of claims that has given rise to difficulties for child applicants is where the principal family member is at risk for a non-*Convention* reason – for example, for reasons of revenge or retaliation.[221] In these cases, a number of jurisdictions have taken the unfortunate position that a child (or other family member) genuinely at risk for reasons of their family membership will not qualify as a refugee unless the principal target is also at risk for reasons of a *Convention* ground.[222] This approach, which finds no support in the language

---

[213] See, e.g., *0807174* [2009] RRTA 1060, [76] (upper middle class family in Colombia).

[214] See, e.g., *Demiraj v Holder*, 631 F 3d 194, 201–3 (5th Cir, 2011) (father acting as a material witness in a prosecution against a human smuggler); *C and S v MIMA* [1999] FCA 1430, [30]–[34] (father reported criminal activities of former employer).

[215] See, e.g., *Thomas v Gonzales*, 409 F 3d 1177, 1184–9 (9th Cir, 2005) (criminal activities of father-in-law).

[216] See, e.g., *FM (Afghanistan) v SSHD* (Upper Tribunal, AA/01079/2010, 10 March 2011), [115] (father's disloyalty to the Taliban); *Lopez-Soto v Ashcroft*, 383 F 3d 228, 235, 244 (4th Cir, 2004) (older brother's refusal to join Mara 18 gang); *Refugee Appeal Nos 76485, 76486 and 76487* (RSAA, 17 June 2010), [79]–[84] (mother refused to comply with demands of paramilitary groups); *Giraldo v MIMA* [2001] FCA 113, [42]–[68] (members of extended family refused to comply with demands of the FARC); *Badran v Canada (MCI)* (1996) 111 FTR 211, [7] (father's status as police officer); *U94-04870, U94-04871, U94-04872 and U94-04873* (IRB, 19 July 1996), [43]–[44] (parents threatened by LTTE, including veiled threats against the children).

[217] See Foster (2007) *supra* n 3, 336–7, and *supra* text accompanying n 132–201.

[218] *Aguirre-Cervantes v INS*, 242 F 3d 1169, 1178 (9th Cir, 2001).   [219] *VA0-00091* (IRB, 29 May 2000).

[220] *VA0-00091* (IRB, 29 May 2000) 7. See also *Refugee Appeal Nos 75805 and 75806* (RSAA, 30 November 2007), [77]–[78]; *MA1-11675, MA1-11676 and MA1-11677* (IRB, 16 June 2003) 6; *M99-07094, M99-07096 and M99-07098* (IRB, 31 May 2001) 8, 17; *T94-00001, T94-00002, T94-00003 and T94-00004* (IRB, 17 May 1994) 4.

[221] See generally Hathaway and Foster (2014) *supra* n 5, 447–9; Foster (2012) *supra* n 106, 56–7.

[222] For an overview of the jurisprudence see Hathaway and Foster (2014) *supra* n 5, 447–9; Foster (2012) *supra* n 106, 56–7.

of art 1A(2) and undermines entirely the near-universal recognition that the family constitutes a cognisable social group, has been categorically rejected in the United States, the United Kingdom and New Zealand.[223] In *Fornah v SSHD*, the House of Lords rejected the argument on the basis that it implies that 'membership of a particular social group is . . . to be regarded as merely adjectival to or parasitic upon the other reasons'.[224] This was considered to be inconsistent with both the language of art 1A(2), which 'treats membership of a particular social group as being in pari materia with the other "Convention reasons" for persecution', and with the reality that the persecution of a person 'simply because he is a member of the same family as someone else is as arbitrary and capricious and just as pernicious, as persecution for reasons of race and religion'.[225]

Conclusions

The *Refugee Convention* requires that an applicant demonstrate a causal link between a *Convention* ground and the risk of being persecuted. If a child is unable to demonstrate that she is at risk of harm because of who she is or what she believes in then she will not be a refugee. At the core of the nexus criterion is the principle of non-discrimination, one of the general principles identified by the UNCRC as underpinning the effective implementation of the *CRC*.[226] As the analysis in this chapter has demonstrated, the non-discrimination norm has provided a critical source of support for the predicament approach, which is premised on the proposition, uncontroversial in domestic and international discrimination law, that discrimination may be legally established where either the intent or the substantive result of particular conduct or treatment is discriminatory.

The development of the predicament approach has played an important role in shifting focus away from the intention of the persecutor and/or state and focusing attention on the *reasons for* the applicant's predicament. This has proven particularly significant in claims involving children, because children are often at risk of harm at the hands of a non-state agent whose intentions will generally be presumed to be personal and thus not causally connected to a *Convention* ground. Adopting the predicament approach, if a child's protected characteristic explains why the applicant is exposed to a risk of being persecuted – bearing in mind that there may be more than one contributing reason – then she will be at risk 'for reason of' that *Convention* ground irrespective of the motivation of her persecutor. Non-discrimination principles have also provided the conceptual basis for the *ejusdem generis* approach to identifying the categories of 'particular social group'. Adopting this approach, courts have appropriately recognised groups defined by age – either age alone ('children', 'minors', 'minor children') or age plus some other characteristic ('street child', 'abandoned child', 'trafficked child') – and the family unit as cognisable social groups for the purpose of the *Convention*.

---

[223] Hathaway and Foster (2014) *supra* n 5, 447–9; Foster (2012) *supra* n 106, 56-7.

[224] *Fornah v SSHD* [2007] 1 AC 412, [20] (Lord Bingham). See further [39]–[52] (Lord Hope), [67] (Lord Rodger) [105] (Lady Hale).

[225] *Fornah v SSHD* [2007] 1 AC 412, [45]. See also *Thomas v Gonzales*, 409 F 3d 1177, 1188 (9th Cir, 2005); *Refugee Appeal Nos 76485, 76486 and 76487* (RSAA, 17 June 2010), [79]–[83].

[226] UNCRC, *GC5*, [12]; *CRC*, art 2.

6

The *Convention on the Rights of the Child* as a Complementary Source of Protection

Introduction

The concept of complementary protection has been the subject of considerable scholarly debate over the past decade. There has, however, been reasonably limited engagement with how the doctrine applies to children.[1] The term 'complementary protection' is generally used to refer to international protection for persons who fall outside the scope of the protection provided under the *Refugee Convention* but who otherwise have a claim for protection based on obligations under international human rights law.[2] The doctrine is thus founded on the international protection obligations owed by a state to an individual that are *complementary* to the protection obligations assumed under the *Convention*. This final chapter examines the complementary protection obligations enshrined in the *CRC* and assesses the extent to which those obligations may give rise to an independent source of protection for children seeking international protection.[3]

This chapter examines two forms of complementary protection available to children. It begins by examining the more traditional source of complementary protection: the obligation of *non-refoulement* implicit in, at the very minimum, arts 6 and 37 of the *CRC*. Section 6.1 seeks to demonstrate that these child-specific duties of *non-refoulement* cast a wider and more tailored net than the generic *non-refoulement* obligations under the *CAT* and the *ICCPR*. In the same way that art 1 of the *Refugee Convention* must be interpreted to take into account the specific needs and vulnerabilities of children, so too must a state's *non-refoulement* obligations be interpreted in a way that takes account of the fact that a child may

---

[1] There are two exceptions: the scholarship of Jane McAdam: 'Seeking Asylum under the Convention on the Rights of the Child: A Case for Complementary Protection' (2006) 14 *International Journal of Children's Rights* 251; and Guy Goodwin-Gill: 'Unaccompanied Refugee Minors: The Role and Place of International Law in the Pursuit of Durable Solutions' (1995) 3 *International Journal of Children's Rights* 405; and 'The United Nations Convention on the Rights of the Child and Its Application to Child Refugee Status Determination and Asylum Processes: Introduction' (2012) 26 *Journal of Immigration, Asylum and Nationality Law* 226.

[2] It has been suggested that the concept of complementary protection should be defined more broadly to include temporary protection, protection in accordance with the expanded definitions in the *OAU Convention Governing the Specific Aspects of Refugee Problems in Africa*, opened for signature 10 September 1969, 1001 UNTS 45 (entered into force 20 June 1974) and the *Cartagena Declaration on Refugees* (in Inter-American Commission on Human Rights, *Annual Report of the Inter-American Commission on Human Rights*, OEA/Ser.L/V/II.66/doc.10, Rev.1 (1984–85)), and protection for purely humanitarian reasons. In this sense, 'complementary protection' has been used to describe *any* protection that falls outside the *Convention*. Although by no means seeking to devalue the needs of individuals captured by these broader notions of protection, this chapter focuses on those humanitarian concerns that are grounded in international treaty-based obligations.

[3] This is the third mode of interaction identified in Chapter 1.

be eligible for complementary protection in a wider range of circumstances than a comparably placed adult.

The balance of the chapter considers a more embryonic form of complementary protection:[4] the best interests principle enshrined in art 3 of the *CRC*, which mandates that 'in all actions concerning children ... the best interests of the child shall be a primary consideration'. Section 6.2 develops an argument that art 3 provides an independent basis for complementary protection which may, in certain circumstances, prohibit the removal of a child notwithstanding the fact that the child is not eligible for protection as a refugee or protection under the *non-refoulement* obligations discussed above. In addition to a brief exposition of the argument, this section provides an overview of support for the argument from academic commentators, the UNCRC and UNHCR. Section 6.3 examines the manner in which the best interests principle has been employed in a range of migration-related contexts. An examination of the application of the best interests principle in each of these contexts illustrates that the thesis advanced here is neither fanciful nor purely aspirational, with the best interests principle being engaged in migration contexts on a regular basis. Section 6.4 outlines a two-stage framework for assessing what is in the best interests of a child and the circumstances in which those interests will preclude the removal of a child from a host state.

There are three reasons why it is important to consider these child-specific complementary protection obligations. First, participation in the *CRC* is greater than participation in the *Refugee Convention*.[5] For host states that have not yet ratified the *Convention*, the *CRC* may provide the strongest – indeed, in some cases, the only – treaty-based entitlement capable of preventing the removal of an at-risk child from a host state. Second, there will be children who are at risk of some form of harm but who do not satisfy the *Convention* refugee definition. In these cases the *CRC* has the capacity to provide a critical additional layer of protection.[6] Third, and finally, there is a greater level of international oversight of state compliance with the *CRC*, predominately through the UNCRC. This level of oversight is generally lacking in the context of the *Convention*, which has no interstate supervisory body to hold states accountable for non-compliance with the treaty-based obligations.[7] This oversight is reinforced by the *OPCP*, which provides children with a direct mechanism to bring complaints against a state for a failure to meet the protection obligations under the *CRC*.

---

[4] Although adopted here to refer to the various forms of protection falling outside the scope of the protection provided under *Convention*, the term 'complementary protection' is arguably inappropriate in the context of art 3 of the *CRC*. There is a compelling argument, given the scope and legal standing of the best interests principle, that where a state is party to both the *CRC* and the *Convention*, art 3 should provide the *principal* basis for international protection in claims involving protection, and should therefore not be understood as providing protection that is *complementary* to the *Convention*: Goodwin-Gill (2012) *supra* n 1, 228–9; Conclusions, text accompanying n 10–19.

[5] As at March 2016 there are 145 parties to the *1951 Convention* and 146 parties to the *1967 Protocol*, as against 196 parties to the *CRC*.

[6] The UNCRC has emphasised the need to consider complementary forms of protection in claims involving children. In its *GC6*, the UNCRC states that, in cases where 'the requirements for granting refugee status under the 1951 Refugee Convention are not met, unaccompanied and separated children shall benefit from available forms of complementary protection to the extent determined by their protection needs': at [77]. See also at [66].

[7] See J C Hathaway, A M North and J Pobjoy, 'Supervising the Refugee Convention: Introduction' (2013) 26 *Journal of Refugee Studies* 323.

6.1 *Non-Refoulement* Under the CRC

The principle of *non-refoulement* prohibits a state from returning an individual to her country of origin in certain defined circumstances.[8] Although the most widely cited exposition of the principle is found in art 33 of the *Convention*, which prohibits the return of a person who satisfies the refugee definition set out under art 1 of the *Convention*, the evolution of international human rights law has given rise to the development of additional explicit and implicit duties of non-return.[9] The clearest example is found in art 3 of the *CAT*, which contains an express and absolute prohibition on returning an individual to a country 'where there are substantial grounds for believing that he would be in danger of being subjected to torture'.[10] Although the *ICCPR* does not expressly proscribe *refoulement*, the HRC has stated that art 2 of the *ICCPR* contains an obligation not to remove a person where there are substantial grounds for believing there is a 'real risk of irreparable harm', such as that contemplated by arts 6 or 7 of the *ICCPR*.[11]

In the context of an at-risk child, the UNCRC has underlined that a state must not return a child to her country of origin where there are 'substantial grounds for believing that there is a real risk of irreparable harm to the child'.[12] Although, like the HRC, the UNCRC does not provide an exhaustive definition of irreparable harm, it has stated that the concept includes (although is 'by no means limited to') those harms contemplated under arts 6 (right to life, survival and development) and 37 (right to liberty and freedom from torture and

---

[8] See generally E Lauterpacht and D Bethlehem, 'The Scope and Content of the Principle of Non-Refoulement' in E Feller, V Türk and F Nicholson (eds), *Refugee Protection in International Law: UNHCR's Global Consultations on International Protection* (2003) 87; G S Goodwin-Gill and J McAdam, *The Refugee in International Law* (3rd edn, 2007) 201–84; J C Hathaway, 'Leveraging Asylum' (2010) 45 *Texas International Law Journal* 503; J Pobjoy, 'Treating Like Alike: The Principle of Non-Discrimination as a Tool to Mandate the Equal Protection of Refugees and Beneficiaries of Complementary Protection' (2010) 34 *Melbourne University Law Review* 181; F Messineo, 'Non-Refoulement Obligations in Public International Law: Towards a New Protection Status?' in S Juss (ed), *Research Companion to Migration Theory and Policy* (2012) 129; K Wouters, *International Legal Standards for the Protection from Refoulement* (2009); UNHCR, 'Advisory Opinion on the Extraterritorial Application of *Non-Refoulement* Obligations under the 1951 Convention relating to the Status of Refugees and its 1967 Protocol' (Opinion, 26 January 2007).

[9] The discussion below focuses on treaty-based obligations under international human rights law. This chapter does not consider art 3 of the *ECHR*, nor does it consider the argument that common art 3 of the *Geneva Conventions* can give rise to *non-refoulement* obligations. There is also no engagement with the long-standing debate as to whether *non-refoulement* might amount to a principle of customary international law. This argument has been advanced by Lauterpacht and Bethlehem (2003) *supra* n 8. For a response, see Hathaway (2010) *supra* n 8.

[10] Article 16(1) of the *International Covenant for the Protection of All Persons from Enforced Disappearance*, opened for signature 6 February 2007, A/RES/61/177, entered into force 12 December 2010 also expressly prohibits the *refoulement* of an individual 'where there are substantial grounds for believing that he or she would be in danger of being subjected to enforced disappearance'. At the European level see *ECHR*, art 3.

[11] HRC, *GC31*, [12]. See also HRC, *GC20*, [9]. Although the majority of the non-return jurisprudence before the HRC relates to communications brought under arts 6 and 7 (see, e.g., HRC, *Views: Communication No 900/1999*, CCPR/C/76/D/900/1999 (2002) ('*C v Australia*')), the Committee seems to have left open the possibility that a real risk of a violation of any *ICCPR* right could trigger a state's non-refoulement obligations. This is evident from the language of HRC, *GC31*, [12]. See also HRC, *GC15*, which considers the position of aliens under the *ICCPR*.

[12] UNCRC, *GC6*, [27]. Similar to the *ICCPR*, this derives from a state's obligation to 'respect and ensure the rights set forth in the [CRC]': *CRC*, art 2(1).

cruel, inhuman or degrading treatment) of the *CRC*.[13] The UNCRC explains that a *non-refoulement* obligation may arise 'irrespective of whether serious violations of [*CRC*] rights ... originate from non-State actors or whether such violations are directly intended or are the indirect consequence of action or inaction' and that:[14]

> The assessment of the risk of such serious violations should be conducted in an age and gender-sensitive manner and should, for example, take into account the particularly serious consequence for children of the insufficient provision of food or health services.

Consistent with its assertion that the *non-refoulement* obligation is not limited to arts 6 and 37, the UNCRC has indicated that underage military recruitment and participation in armed conflict 'entails a high risk of irreparable harm involving fundamental human rights, including the right to life'.[15] Accordingly, the Committee has observed that art 38 of the *CRC*, read alongside arts 3 and 4 of the *OPAC*, has extraterritorial effect.[16] States must therefore 'refrain from returning a child in any manner whatsoever to the borders of a State where there is a real risk of underage recruitment'.[17]

The *non-refoulement* obligations under each of the *CAT*, the *ICCPR* and the *CRC* share a number of common features.[18] First, under each of the treaties the requisite standard of proof required to engage the *non-refoulement* obligation is that there are 'substantial grounds for believing' that the relevant risk will accrue. This phrase has been subject to conflicting interpretations, which has led to divergent state practice.[19] In the United Kingdom, decision-makers have taken the view that 'substantial grounds for believing' requires the same standard as the 'well-founded fear' inquiry under the *Convention*.[20] In contrast, in the United States and Canada a higher 'more likely than not' test has been applied.[21] McAdam has argued that the former approach is to be preferred: it sits comfortably with international jurisprudence while at the same time avoiding the mental gymnastics that the adoption of different standards of proof would require.[22] Second, in contrast to the *Convention*, the prohibition on *non-refoulement* under international human rights law is absolute and allows for no exceptions.[23] Finally, under the three human rights accords, the *non-refoulement* obligation will be triggered irrespective of whether the risk is causally connected to a person's race, religion, political opinion, nationality or membership of a particular social group.[24]

The *non-refoulement* obligations under the *CAT*, the *ICCPR* and the *CRC* are thus both narrower than the protection afforded under art 33 of the *Refugee Convention* – which

---

[13] UNCRC, *GC6*, [27]. [14] *Ibid.* [15] *Ibid.*, [28]. [16] *Ibid.*

[17] *Ibid.* The implied *non-refoulment* obligation under the *CRC* has also been endorsed by UNHCR: UNHCR, 'Advisory Opinion' (2007) *supra* n 8, [19].

[18] See generally Pobjoy (2010) *supra* n 8, 188–92.

[19] J McAdam, 'Australian Complementary Protection: A Step-By-Step Approach' (2011) 33 *Sydney Law Review* 687, 716–22.

[20] *Ibid.*, 717–19. As the UK AIT stated in *Kacaj v SSHD* [2001] INLR 354, [10], '[a]part from the undesirable result of such a difference of approach when the effect on the individual who resists return is the same, and may involve inhuman treatment or torture or even death, an adjudicator and the tribunal would need to indulge in mental gymnastics. Their task is difficult enough without such refinements'. See also J McAdam, 'Individual Risk, Armed Conflict and the Standard of Proof in Complementary Protection Claims: The European Union and Canada Compared' in J C Simeon (ed), *Critical Issues in International Refugee Law: Strategies for Interpretative Harmony* (2010) 59, 78–83.

[21] McAdam (2011) *supra* n 19, 719–20. [22] *Ibid.*, 716–22. [23] Contra *Convention*, arts 1F, 33(2).

[24] Contra *Convention*, art 1A(2).

protects against a broader range of risks through the concept of 'being persecuted' – and wider in allowing for no exceptions and mandating protection irrespective of the reason for the apprehended harm.

Academic attention on the expanded duty of *non-refoulement* has focused primarily on the explicit obligation under art 3 of the *CAT* and the implicit obligations under arts 6 and 7 of the *ICCPR*. Far more limited attention has been given to the implied obligations under the *CRC*, despite the clear direction provided by the UNCRC in its *GC6*.[25] The *CRC* has also been overlooked in the development of regional and domestic complementary protection regimes. The *EU Qualification Directive* – the first supranational instrument to codify a system of complementary protection – makes no reference to the *non-refoulement* obligations under the *CRC*.[26] Similarly, domestic statutory mechanisms in the United States,[27] Canada,[28] New Zealand[29] and Australia[30] focus exclusively on the *non-refoulement* obligations protected under the *CAT* and/or the *ICCPR*.[31] In the same way that children are often overlooked in the refugee determination process, there has been a tendency to treat children as invisible in the context of complementary protection regimes.

To take a recent example, in 2011 the Australian government introduced a statutory complementary protection regime.[32] Throughout the consultation process the Australian government was criticised for its failure to incorporate the *non-refoulement* obligations under the *CRC* into the proposed regime.[33] This was despite the fact that the express

---

[25] But see M Foster, 'Non-Refoulement on the Basis of Socio-Economic Deprivation: The Scope of Complementary Protection in International Human Rights Law' (2009) *New Zealand Law Review* 257; A Farmer, 'A Commentary on the Committee on the Rights of the Child's Definition of Non-Refoulement for Children: Broad Protection for Fundamental Rights' (2011) 80 *Fordham Law Review Res Gestae* 39; G Noll, 'Seeking Asylum at Embassies: A Right to Entry under International Law?' (2005) 27 *International Journal of Refugee Law* 542, 570–1.

[26] See *EU Qualification Directive*, art 15. This was criticised during the drafting process of the original *Council Directive 2004/83/EC of 29 April 2004 on Minimum Standards for the Qualification and Status of Third Country Nationals or Stateless Persons as Refugees or as Persons Who Otherwise Need International Protection and the Content of the Protection Granted* [2004] OJ L 304/12 by G S Goodwin-Gill and A Hurwitz, 'Memorandum' reproduced in House of Lords Select Committee on the European Union, *Defining Refugee Status and Those in Need of International Protection*, House of Lords Paper No 156, Session 2001-02 (2002) ('Minutes of Evidence Taken before the European Union Committee (Sub-Committee E)' (10 April 2002) 1–3), [10], [23]. McAdam has argued that the scope of 'complementary protection' under the *Directive* is '[t]he result of a political compromise, based on international and regional human rights standards, but nonetheless conservative in its scope', and that '[i]t cannot be regarded as an innovative blueprint applying human rights law to the protection context': J McAdam, *Complementary Protection in International Refugee Law* (2007), 64. The *2004 Qualification Directive*, recital 12, did, however, acknowledge that the 'best interests of the child shall be a primary consideration of Member States when implementing the Directive'. This is expanded upon in the recast 2011 *EU Qualification Directive*, which provides that, '[i]n assessing the best interests of the child, Member States should in particular take due account of the principle of family unity, the minor's well-being and social development, safety and security considerations and the views of the minor in accordance with his or her age and maturity': recital 18. This finds operative expression in art 20(5).

[27] 8 CFR §208.16-208.18 (*CAT* protection).

[28] *Immigration and Refugee Protection Act*, SC 2001, c 27, s 97 (*CAT* and *ICCPR* protection).

[29] *Immigration Act 2009* (NZ) ss 130–1 (*CAT* and *ICCPR* protection).

[30] *Migration Act 1958* (Cth) s 36(2A) (*CAT* and *ICCPR* protection).

[31] For further examples, see McAdam, (2011) *supra* n 19, 688.

[32] *Migration Amendment (Complementary Protection) Act 2011* (Cth).

[33] See, e.g., Human Rights Law Resource Centre, Submission No 5 to Senate Legal and Constitutional Affairs Legislation Committee, Parliament of Australia, *Inquiry into the Migration Amendment*

purpose of the legislation was to 'introduce greater fairness, integrity and efficiency into Australia's arrangements for adhering to its *non-refoulement* obligations under the [*ICCPR*], the [*CRC*] and the [*CAT*]'.[34] Notwithstanding that criticism, the final version of the legislation refers only to the obligations contained under the *CAT* and *ICCPR*.

The failure to take into account the specific *non-refoulement* obligations under the *CRC* may reflect a view that arts 6 and 7 of the *ICCPR* are wide enough in scope to subsume the obligations under the *CRC*.[35] The Explanatory Memorandum to the *Migration Amendment (Complementary Protection) Act 2011* (Cth) provides a clear illustration of that misconception, suggesting that the obligations contained under the *ICCPR* may also be implied under the *CRC* 'to the extent that the [*CRC*] contains obligations in the same terms as the [*ICCPR*]'.[36] However, conflating the obligations in this way fails to appreciate that the *CRC*'s *non-refoulement* obligations are wider in scope in a number of significant respects. This more expansive scope is unsurprising given the long-standing recognition that children may experience harm in different ways to adults and that a child may suffer a more acute form of harm than an adult subject to the same objective risk.[37] An exclusive focus on general *non-refoulement* obligations, without regard to child-specific obligations, gives rise to a danger that a child will be returned to a risk of harm in direct violation of a state's obligations under the *CRC*.

The remainder of this section examines the provisions that the UNCRC has explicitly identified as giving rise to a *non-refoulement* obligation: the right to life, survival and development (art 6); the right to liberty and freedom from torture and cruel, inhuman or degrading treatment (art 37); and the right to protection against underage military recruitment (art 38 and the *OPAC*). Although the Committee has made clear that a *non-refoulement* obligation may arise in the context of other rights – the overarching inquiry being whether there 'is a real risk of irreparable harm to the child' – these particular rights provide a sensible point of departure from which to examine the distinct nature of the *non-refoulement* obligations under the *CRC*. It is important to note that the discussion that follows is not intended to provide an exhaustive account of the circumstances in which the *CRC* obligation may give rise to a *non-refoulement* duty. No attempt is made, for instance, to identify the range of circumstances in which a risk of an art 6 violation may give rise to real risk of irreparable harm to a child. Rather, the central thesis advanced here is simply that the obligations under the *CRC* are distinct from, and in several important respects wider than,

---

(Complementary Protection) Bill 2009 (September 2009) [20]–[22]; M Foster and J Pobjoy, Submission No 9 to Senate Legal and Constitutional Affairs Legislation Committee, Parliament of Australia, *Inquiry into the Migration Amendment (Complementary Protection) Bill 2009* (28 September 2009) 16–18.

[34] Parliament of Australia, Explanatory Memorandum, Migration Amendment (Complementary Protection) Bill 2011 (Cth) 1.

[35] This may be a symptom of a broader tendency to conflate *non-refoulement* obligations. But, as Messineo explains, there is no single overarching 'principle of *non-refoulement*' and, although '[c]onflating all obligations in one single overarching concept may please one's sense of legal aesthetics, [it] runs the risk of undermining international protection rather than enhancing it': Messineo (2012) *supra* n 8, 132. On the risks of conflation, see Hathaway (2010) *supra* n 8, 509–10.

[36] Parliament of Australia, Explanatory Memorandum, Migration Amendment (Complementary Protection) Bill 2011 (Cth) 13.

[37] Chapter 4, Section 4.2. See, e.g., *Mayeka and Mitunga v Belgium* (2008) 46 EHRR 23, [55]; *E v Chief Constable of the Royal Ulster Constabulary* [2009] 1 AC 536, [7]–[9]; *R (SQ) (Pakistan) v Upper Tribunal Immigration and Asylum Chamber* [2013] EWCA Civ 1251, [17]–[19]; *GS v SSHD* [2012] UKUT 00397, [85(7)].

the more general obligations under the *CAT* and the *ICCPR*, and therefore warrant separate consideration in claims involving children.

6.1.1 Right to Life, Survival and Development

Article 6 of the *CRC* protects a child's inherent right to life[38] and places an obligation on states to ensure to the maximum extent possible the survival and development of the child.[39] The right has been characterised as 'the most fundamental of all human rights of the child'[40] and has been identified by the UNCRC as one of the four guiding principles underpinning the interpretation and application of the *CRC*.[41] The Committee has expressly stated that a violation of art 6 may constitute irreparable harm and engage a state's *non-refoulement* obligations under the *CRC*.[42]

Article 6(1) encompasses both an obligation to respect the right to life by refraining from state interference and an obligation to protect the right to life by taking measures to protect against undue interference by non-state parties.[43] Article 6(1) may thus be engaged where the risk derives from a state actor (for instance, through the imposition of the death penalty[44] or via direct or indirect involvement in armed conflict[45]) or a non-state actor (for instance, where a child is at risk of infanticide, harmful traditional practices[46] or other forms of violence or exploitation that may endanger a child's life[47]). The *CRC* prohibits a state from returning a child to her country of origin where there are substantial grounds for believing that a child will be at risk of any of these self-evidently irreparable forms of harm.

Article 6(2) extends the scope of art 6 substantially beyond traditional conceptions of the right to life.[48] It achieves this by combining the right to life with a positive duty to ensure the survival and development of the child. Article 6 thus recognises that the right to life extends beyond a negative duty to respect and protect life and encompasses a positive obligation to ensure the survival and development of the child. Although the right to life under art 6 of the *ICCPR* has been progressively interpreted to entail positive duties,[49] the language of art 6(2) of the *CRC*[50]

---

[38] *CRC*, art 6(1).   [39] *CRC*, art 6(2).

[40] M Nowak, *Article 6: The Right to Life, Survival and Development* (2005) 1. Article 6 was deliberately 'listed as a priority before other rights of the child': *Report of the Working Group on a Draft Convention on the Rights of the Child*, E/CN.4/1988/28 (1988), [21].

[41] UNCRC, *GC5*, [12].   [42] See *supra* text accompanying n 12–13.

[43] Nowak (2005) *supra* n 40, 18–36.

[44] See also *CRC*, art 37(a). More generally, see W Schabas, *The Abolition of the Death Penalty in International Law* (3rd edn, 2002) 84–6, 187–97.

[45] See also *CRC*, art 38; Nowak (2005) *supra* n 40, 20–3; *infra* Section 6.1.3.

[46] For example, honour killings, FGC, forced marriage. See *CRC*, art 24(3).

[47] For example: physical or mental violence (*CRC*, art 19); economic exploitation (art 32); illicit use of narcotics (art 33); sexual exploitation (art 34); trafficking (art 35); or other forms of exploitation (art 36). See generally Nowak (2005) *supra* n 40, 35–6.

[48] The framers of the *CRC* took the view that '[t]he approach to the right to life in the [*ICCPR*] was rather negative, while that of the [*CRC*] should be positive and should take into account economic, social and cultural conditions': *Report of the Working Group on a Draft Convention on the Rights of the Child*, E/CN.4/1988/28 (1988), [21].

[49] See, e.g., HRC, *GC6*, [5].

[50] Nowak (2005) *supra* n 40, 37. The UNCRC has noted that states are expected to 'interpret "development" in its broadest sense as a holistic concept, embracing the child's physical, mental, spiritual, moral,

leave[s] no doubt that the right to life, survival and development obliges States Parties to adopt a holistic approach to the child's development and to take comprehensive positive measures to fulfil, to the maximum extent possible, the survival and healthy development of the child.

These measures may include 'growth monitoring, oral rehydration and disease control, breast-feeding, immunization, child spacing, food, and female literacy'.[51] Additional specific measures may be required for particular groups of children, such as unaccompanied children,[52] children with HIV/AIDS[53] or children with disabilities.[54] In defining the scope of art 6(2) it has been suggested that reference should be made to other rights in the CRC, including the rights to education (art 28), the highest attainable standard of health (art 24) and an adequate standard of living (art 27).[55]

Although the extent to which art 6(2) might give rise to a *non-refoulement* obligation remains largely untested,[56] there is a good argument that it is broader in scope than the cognate non-return duty under art 6 of the ICCPR. This is particularly so in respect of risks relating to the deprivation of social and economic rights.[57] Indeed, in its GC6 the UNCRC emphasised that in considering the scope of the *non-refoulement* obligation states should 'take into account the particularly serious consequences for children of the insufficient provision of food or health services'.[58] Although not every violation of art 6(2) will automatically engage a state's *non-refoulement* obligations – the overarching test remains that there be substantial grounds for believing that a child is at risk of irreparable harm – it is conceivable that the obligation may be triggered where a child is at risk of being returned to a country which, for instance, has failed to take any measures to combat malnutrition or disease or reduce infant mortality rates,[59] or has failed to meet the basic health[60] or educational needs of children.[61]

6.1.2 Right to Liberty and Freedom from Torture and Cruel, Inhuman or Degrading Treatment or Punishment

Article 37(a) of the CRC protects a child against 'torture or other cruel, inhuman or degrading treatment or punishment' in similar terms to art 7 of the ICCPR. The jurisprudence of the HRC thus serves as a useful benchmark in defining the scope of art 37(a). Of particular salience is the direction that the application of art 7 of the ICCPR

psychological and social development' and that implementation measures 'should be aimed at achieving the optimal development for all children': UNCRC, GC5, [12].

[51] Observation made by the World Health Organization during the drafting of the CRC: *Report of the Working Group on a Draft Convention on the Rights of the Child*, E/CN.4/1989/48 (1989), [88].

[52] UNCRC, GC9, [31].   [53] UNCRC, GC3, [11].   [54] UNCRC, GC6, [23].

[55] See G Van Bueren, *The International Law on the Rights of the Child* (1998) 293; J Tobin, 'Beyond the Supermarket Shelf: Using a Rights Based Approach to Address Children's Health Needs' (2006) 14 *International Journal of Children's Rights* 275; Nowak (2005) *supra* n 40, 36–49.

[56] Shortly prior to the publication of the UNCRC's GC6, Christoph Bierwirth drew attention to the potential extraterritorial effects of art 6(2) and suggested that future efforts might usefully focus on the extent to which the provision may give rise to distinct *non-refoulement* obligations: C Bierwirth, 'The Protection of Refugee and Asylum-Seeking Children, the Convention on the Rights of the Child and the Work of the Committee on the Rights of the Child' (2005) 24(2) *Refugee Survey Quarterly* 98, 114.

[57] See Foster (2009) *supra* n 25, 278–85.   [58] UNCRC, GC6, [27].

[59] See CRC, art 24(2)(a), (c); J Tobin, *The Right to Health in International Law* (2012) 255–61, 267–85.

[60] See CRC, art 24; Tobin (2012) *supra* n 59, 261–7.   [61] See CRC, art 28.

depends on 'all the circumstances of the case, such as the duration and manner of the treatment, its physical or mental effects as well as the sex, *age* and state of health of the victim'.[62]

The UNCRC has similarly underscored the importance of taking into account the individual circumstances and vulnerabilities of the applicant in assessing whether the risk of harm is sufficient to give rise to a *non-refoulement* obligation.[63] An age-sensitive application of art 37(a) thus opens up the possibility that specific treatment may be acceptable if inflicted on an older child but unacceptable if inflicted on a younger child.[64] Although the UNCRC's guidance on the interpretation of art 37(a) remains comparatively limited,[65] the Committee has made clear that corporal punishment, including that which takes place in domestic, educational or penal settings, may constitute cruel, inhuman or degrading treatment.[66]

Article 37 of the *CRC* extends beyond the prohibition of torture or other cruel, inhuman or degrading treatment or punishment, thus raising the possibility that a *non-refoulement* obligation will be engaged in a broader range of circumstances than would be the case under art 7 of the *ICCPR*. For instance, art 37(a) contains an absolute prohibition on the imposition of capital punishment or life imprisonment without the possibility of release for offences committed by persons below 18 years of age; the first time an international treaty has prohibited the life imprisonment of a child. In addition, art 37(b) protects a child against unlawful or arbitrary deprivation of liberty. Although the provision is based on art 9 of the *ICCPR*, it is wider in scope, providing that the arrest, detention or imprisonment of a child 'shall be in conformity with the law and shall be used only as a measure of last resort and for the shortest appropriate period of time'.[67] This suggests that even where the deprivation of a child's liberty is lawful and not arbitrary, it should be viewed as an exceptional measure. The UNCRC has thus suggested that states are under an obligation to develop and implement alternative measures, particularly in response to juvenile delinquency.[68] Article 37(c) details the requisite conditions of detention or imprisonment, providing that every child 'shall be treated with humanity and respect for the inherent dignity of the human person, and in a manner which takes into account the needs of persons of his or her age', and that children deprived of liberty shall be separated from adults unless it is considered in the child's best interest not to do so. Finally, art 37(d) provides that any child deprived of her

---

[62] HRC, *Views: Communication No 265/1987*, CCPR/C/35/D/265/1987 (1989) ('*Vuolanne v Finland*'), [9.2] (emphasis added).

[63] UNCRC, *GC6*, [27] ('[t]he assessment of the risk of such serious violations should be conducted in an age [-] and gender-sensitive manner').

[64] G Van Bueren, 'Opening Pandora's Box: Protecting Children against Torture or Cruel, Inhuman and Degrading Treatment or Punishment' (1995) 17 *Law and Policy* 378, 385.

[65] *Ibid.*, 385.

[66] UNCRC, *GC8*; UNCRC, *GC13*, [24]; UNCRC, *Report of the Twenty-Eighth Session*, CRC/C/111 (2001) pt V (summary of Day of General Discussion on 'Violence against Children, within the Family and in Schools') [689], [699]. Article 37(a) is complemented by art 19 of the *CRC*. See further, Chapter 4, Section 4.3.1.

[67] Contra *ICCPR*, art 9. This is based on Rules 13, 17 and 19 of the 1985 *United Nations Standard Minimum Rules for the Administration of Juvenile Justice ("The Beijing Rules")*, A/RES/30/33 (1985) Annex, and Rules 1, 2 and 17 (amongst others) of the 1990 *United Nations Rules for the Protection of Juveniles Deprived of their Liberty*, A/RES/45/113 (1990) Annex.

[68] See UNCRC, *GC10*; *CRC*, art 40(4).

liberty shall have a right to 'prompt access to legal and other appropriate assistance, as well as the right to challenge the legality of the deprivation'.[69]

6.1.3 Freedom from Underage Military Recruitment

The UNCRC has recognised that underage military recruitment and direct and indirect participation in armed conflict entails a high risk of 'irreparable harm involving fundamental human rights'.[70] According to the Committee:[71]

> States shall refrain from returning a child in any manner whatsoever to the borders of a State where there is a real risk of underage recruitment, including recruitment not only as a combatant but also to provide sexual services for the military or where there is a real risk of direct or indirect participation in hostilities, either as a combatant or through carrying out other military duties.

Article 38 places a duty on states to take measures to ensure that children under the age of 15 do not take a direct part in armed conflict,[72] and prohibits the recruitment of children under 15 years of age.[73] Critically, art 38 deals with voluntary recruitment only; under *no* circumstances may a child be forcibly conscripted into the armed forces, whatever her age.[74] The *CRC* must now be read in conjunction with the *OPAC*, which provides that states 'shall take all feasible measures to ensure that members of their armed forces who have not attained the age of 18 years do not take a direct part in hostilities'. The *OPAC* raises the minimum age of recruitment for non-government military groups to 18 years,[75] and provides that states must raise the minimum age for recruitment to government controlled armed forces, though it does not specify an age.[76]

Notwithstanding the various age permutations permitted by art 38 of the *CRC*, the *OPAC* and international humanitarian law, it arguable that a *non-refoulement* obligation may be engaged wherever any child is at risk of underage recruitment or direct or indirect involvement in hostilities (including, for example, sexual servitude) on the basis that that

---

[69] See generally UNCRC, *GC10*; UNICEF, *Implementation Handbook for the Convention on the Rights of the Child* (3rd edn, 2007) 556–67.

[70] UNCRC, *GC6*, [28]. See generally G Machel, *Impact of Armed Conflict on Children*, A/51/306 (1996), [34]–[62]; G S Goodwin-Gill, 'The Challenge of the Child Soldier' in H Strachan and S Scheipers (eds), *The Changing Character of War* (2011) 410; I Cohn and G S Goodwin-Gill, *Child Soldiers: The Role of Children in Armed Conflict* (1994); M Happold, *Child Soldiers in International Law* (2005).

[71] UNCRC, *GC6*, [28].   [72] *CRC*, art 38(2).

[73] *CRC*, art 38(3). See also *Rome Statute of the International Criminal Court*, opened for signature 17 July 1998, 2187 UNTS 3 (entered into force 1 July 2002), art 8(2)(b)(xxvi), (e)(vii); *Protocol Additional to the Geneva Conventions of 12 August 1949, and Relating to the Protection of Victims of International Armed Conflicts (Protocol I)*, opened for signature 8 June 1977, 1125 UNTS 3 (entered into force 7 December 1978), art 77(2).

[74] This is confirmed by *OPAC*, art 2. In 1999, art 3(a) of the *Convention Concerning the Prohibition and Immediate Action for the Elimination of the Worst Forms of Child Labor (ILO No 182)*, opened for signature 17 June 1999, 2133 UNTS 161 (entered into force 19 November 2000) identified the forced or compulsory recruitment of children for use in armed conflict as one of 'the worst forms of child labour'.

[75] *OPAC*, art 4.

[76] *OPAC*, art 3(1). Goodwin-Gill suggests that in principle states are required to raise the minimum age from 15 to 18 for voluntary recruitment: Goodwin-Gill (2011) *supra* n 70, 416. Where a state continues to allow for underage recruitment, art 3 of the *OPAC* provides a number of minimum safeguards to be adopted to ensure that that such recruitment is truly voluntary.

involvement will give rise to a real risk of irreparable harm. That argument – which can be bolstered by reference to a child's right to life, survival and development under art 6 of the *CRC* – finds support in the UNCRC's discussion on the scope of the *non-refoulement* obligation in its *GC6*.[77]

The above discussion makes clear that in the context of children the *CRC* casts a wider and more tailored net than the general *refoulement* provisions under the *ICCPR* and the *CAT*. In the same way that the *Convention* definition needs to be interpreted to take account of the specific needs and vulnerabilities of children, so too must a state's *non-refoulement* obligations be construed in a manner that takes account of the fact that a child will be at risk of irreparable harm in a wider range of circumstances than a comparably placed adult. This reality has been acknowledged by the UNCRC, which in its *GC6* provides useful, though non-exhaustive, guidance on the circumstances that may trigger a *non-refoulement* duty under the *CRC*. A failure to take into account the distinct nature of these obligations may give rise to a situation where a child is returned despite a risk of irreparable harm in direct violation of a state's obligations under the *CRC*.

6.2 Article 3 as an Independent Source of Protection

Article 3 of the *CRC* provides a critical additional safeguard for children seeking international protection.[78] Article 3 is an umbrella provision that mandates that the best interests of the child shall be a primary consideration in all actions concerning children.[79] This includes actions undertaken by 'public or private social welfare institutions, courts of law, administrative authorities or legislative bodies'.[80] Article 3 thus requires '[e]very legislative, administrative and judicial body or institution … to apply the best interests principle by systematically considering how children's rights and interests are or will be affected by their decisions or actions'.[81] The express language of the provision, which captures all actions *concerning* children, makes clear that the best interests principle is engaged not only where a decision directly affects a child, for example where a child independently claims international protection, but also when a child is indirectly affected by a decision, for example where a child's parent is at risk of being removed.

The UNCRC has in its recent *GC14* underlined that art 3(1) operates as a three-fold concept: as a substantive right, an interpretative legal principle and a rule of procedure.[82]

---

[77] See *supra* n 17.
[78] The 'best interests' language appears on several occasions in the *CRC* (arts 9, 18, 20, 21, 37, 40), though art 3 is the core provision. That provision is based on Principle 2 of the *Declaration of the Rights of the Child*, UNGA Res 1386 (XIV) (1959). It is also reflected in two provisions of *CEDAW* (arts 5(b) and 16(1)(d)); the *Disability Convention* (art 7(2)); the *African Charter on the Rights and Welfare of the Child*, opened for signature 1 July 1990, OAU Doc CAB/LEG/24.9/49 (entered into force 29 November 1999) (art IV) and the Charter of Fundamental Rights of the European Union [2000] OJ C 361/1 (art 24(2)). Further to art 3(1) of the *CRC*, art 3(2) places an obligation on states 'to ensure the child such protection and care as is necessary for his or her well-being, taking into account the rights and duties of his or her parents, legal guardians, or other individuals legally responsible for him or her, and, to this end, [to] take all appropriate legislative and administrative measures'. On the argument advanced in this section see, generally, J Pobjoy, 'The Best Interests of the Child Principle as an Independent Source of Protection' (2015) 64(2) *International Comparative Law Quarterly* 327.
[79] *CRC*, art 3(1).   [80] *Ibid.*   [81] UNCRC, *GC5*, [12].
[82] UNCRC, *GC14*, [6], affirmed, e.g., in *Mathieson v Secretary of State for Work and Pensions* [2015] 1 WLR 3250, [39]; *R (SG and others) v Secretary of State for Work and Pensions* [2015] 1 WLR 1449, [106] (Lord

As regards the first aspect (substantive right), the Committee observed that art 3(1) incorporates '[t]he right of the child to have his or her best interests assessed and taken as a primary consideration when different interests are being considered . . . *and* the guarantee that this right will be implemented whenever a decision is to be made concerning a child'.[83] According to the Committee, art 3(1) 'creates an intrinsic obligation for States, is directly applicable (self-executing) and can be invoked before a Court'.[84] As regards the second aspect (interpretative legal principle), the Committee explained that art 3(1) entails 'a fundamental, interpretative legal principle', such that '[i]f a legal provision is open to more than one interpretation, the interpretation which most effectively serves the child's best interests should be chosen'.[85] As regards the third aspect (rule of procedure), the Committee observed that '[a]ssessing and determining the best interests of the child requires procedural guarantees' and that '[w]henever a decision is to be made that will affect a specific child, an identified group of children or children in general, the decision-making process must include an evaluation of the possible impact (positive or negative) of the decision on the child or children concerned'.[86]

The obligation under art 3(1) attaches to all children within a state's jurisdiction.[87] A state cannot limit the application of the provision on the basis of a child's citizenship or immigration status. This is made clear by the non-discrimination guarantee in art 2(1) of the *CRC* as well as art 22, which provides that unaccompanied or accompanied children seeking refugee status are entitled to enjoy all applicable rights in the *CRC* on a non-discriminatory basis. Although it is now generally accepted that art 3 is relevant to children seeking international protection, such recognition has tended to focus on procedural guarantees and the treatment of children during and subsequent to any status determination process.[88] But while art 3 is plainly relevant to both the procedures and treatment applicable to children seeking international protection, the best interests principle may also be relevant to the substantive determination as to whether a child is in fact eligible for international protection. This aspect of the obligation is often overlooked by states,[89] despite the fact that the best interests principle applies to '*all* actions concerning children'[90] and must therefore 'be respected during all stages of the displacement cycle'.[91]

Carnwath). In the latter case, Lord Carnwath describes *GC14* as 'the most authoritative guidance now available on the effect of article 3.1': *ibid.*, [105]. See also UNHCR and UNICEF, *Safe & Sound: What States Can Do to Ensure Respect for the Best Interests of Unaccompanied and Separated Children in Europe* (2014) 19.

[83] *Ibid.* (emphasis added).

[84] *Ibid.* The suggestion that art 3(1) is self-executing is obviously problematic, given that the question as to whether a treaty or treaty provision is 'self-executing' is determined by the municipal system in question, not *ex cathedra* by a treaty-supervising body.

[85] *Ibid.*

[86] *Ibid.* There is clear overlap between the first aspect (substantive right) and third aspect (rule of procedure).

[87] *CRC*, art 2(1).

[88] See, e.g., UNHCR, *UNHCR Guidelines on Determining the Best Interests of the Child* (2008). At a domestic level, see, e.g., IRB, *Guidelines*, 2; INS, *Guidelines*, 3.

[89] UNCRC, '2012 Day of General Discussion: The Rights of All Children in the Context of International Migration' (Background Paper, August 2012) 20.

[90] *CRC*, art 3(1) (emphasis added).

[91] UNCRC, *GC6*, [19]. As guidelines published by the UK Home Office have acknowledged, the best interests principle requires 'a continuous assessment that starts from the moment the child is encountered and continues until such time as a durable solution has been reached': UKBA, *Asylum Process*

Article 3 of the *CRC* may be relevant in adjudicating the status of an at-risk child in two distinct ways. First, as touched upon in earlier chapters, the best interests principle may inform the interpretation of a state's protection obligations under the *Convention* or the *non-refoulement* obligations discussed in Section 6.1 above.[92] In particular, the best interests principle demands an age-sensitive and inclusive interpretation of the respective obligations. This is consistent with the UNCRC's affirmation that, where a legal provision is open to more than one interpretation, the decision-maker should favour the interpretation that most accommodates the child's best interests.[93] This is not to suggest that the best interests principle in any way amends or displaces the definitional criterion set out under the *Convention* (or, indeed, the broader *non-refoulement* obligations under international human rights law). In this respect, states are entirely correct to caution that the 'best interests principle ... does not replace or change the refugee definition in determining substantive eligibility'.[94] But accepting that circumscription does not render the best interests principle otiose to the interpretation of the *Convention* definition.[95] In the context of interpreting the constituent elements of the refugee definition the principle must simply be understood as norm-shaping rather than norm-producing.[96]

By way of illustration, in the context of the 'being persecuted' definition, UNHCR has recognised that '[t]he best interests of the child requires that the harm be assessed from the child's perspective' and that '[t]his may include an analysis as to how the child's rights or interests are, or will be, affected by the harm'.[97] National decision-makers have similarly drawn upon the best interests principle in assessing the suitability of an internal protection

---

Guidance, [1.3]. In the United Kingdom this is now reflected in s 55 of the *Borders, Citizenship and Immigration Act 2009*, c 11.

[92] UNCRC, *GC14*, [6].

[93] *Ibid.*

[94] 'While the Authority is conscious of article 3(1) of the [*CRC*] ... the requirement to consider the best interests of the child, whom it is accepted is more vulnerable than an adult, cannot somehow elevate the child ... to refugee status where there is no real chance of that child ... suffering persecution if returned to their country of origin. Whether or not these people are refugees depends on the application of the definition of refugee in the Refugee Convention to each of them and not on the application of article 3(1) of the Convention on the Rights of the Child': *Refugee Appeal No 70695/97* (RSAA, 30 April 1998) 23. See also INS, *Guidelines*, 18 (although this must be read taking into account the fact that the United States has not ratified the *CRC*).

[95] Contra INS, *Guidelines*, 3, which provide that the best interests principle 'does not play a role in determining substantive eligibility under the ... refugee definition'. Bhabha and Young have identified that this statement was a late-minute addition, with an earlier version of the guidelines emphasising that '[t]he need for sensitive treatment of child asylum-seekers extends not only to interviewing techniques *but also to the legal analysis of the child's claims*': J Bhabha and W Young, 'Not Adults in Miniature: Unaccompanied Child Asylum Seekers and the New US Guidelines' (1999) 11 *International Journal of Refugee Law* 84, 97 (emphasis added). Contra also the position taken by the Federal Court of Canada in *Kim v Canada (MCI)* [2007] FCJ No 1399, [6]: 'It is clear that the best interests of the child cannot substantively influence the answer with regard to whether a child is a refugee, but the best interests of the child are central to the procedure by which to reach a decision'. This characterisation is incorrect. For a more principled treatment of the best interests principle by the Federal Court of Canada, see *Patel v Canada (MCI)* [2005] FCJ No 1305, [61]–[63]. See also the approach taken in the recent guidance in UKBA, *Asylum Process Guidance*, [1.3].

[96] The author thanks Professor James Hathaway for this characterisation.

[97] UNHCR, *2009 Guidelines*, [10].

alternative,[98] the appropriateness of removing a child to a 'safe third-country' for processing[99] and the scope of the *Convention*'s exclusion provisions.[100] In each of these examples the best interests principle has been drawn upon to inform the interpretation of a particular element of the *Convention* definition, rather than being invoked as an alternative or replacement to the *Convention* criterion.

The second context in which art 3 may be engaged is as an independent basis for international protection. In particular, an assessment of the best interests of the child may preclude the removal of a child to her home country notwithstanding the fact that the child is not eligible for protection under the *Convention* or the more traditional *non-refoulement* obligations noted above. Article 3 thus creates a new category of protected persons whose claims will need be assessed and evaluated by domestic decision-makers.[101] The relevant inquiry in these cases is whether the removal of the child is in the child's best interests. If removal is contrary to those interests, there will be a strong presumption against removing the child, subject only to a tightly circumscribed range of countervailing considerations that may in certain circumstances override the child's best interests.

The argument that art 3 provides an independent basis for international protection has both academic and institutional support. Goodwin-Gill has for some time emphasised the relevance of the best interests principle in determining whether or not a state owes a child international protection.[102] More than 15 years ago, Goodwin-Gill contemplated that the *CRC* may provide for a 'total realignment of protection' for child refugee applicants.[103]

---

[98] See, e.g., *RA (AP) v SSHD* [2011] CSOH 68, [25]; *EU Qualification Directive*, Recital 27; UNHCR, 2009 *Guidelines*, [56].

[99] Although states may in certain circumstances send a refugee to a non-persecutory state (including, for instance, the state of first arrival), domestic and regional courts have appropriately recognised that any removal decision must be guided by the best interests principle in art 3 of the *CRC*. See, e.g., *R (TS) v SSHD* [2010] EWHC 2614 (Admin); *R (BT) v SSHD* [2011] EWCA Civ 1446; *ALJ and A, B and C's Application for Judicial Review* [2013] NIQB 88; *R (MA) v SSHD*, C-648/11, EU:C:2013:367 (6 June 2013); 'Opinion of Advocate General Cruz Villalón', Opinion in *R (MA) v SSHD*, C-648/11, EU: C:2013:367 (21 February 2013); *SSHD v ZAT and ors* [2016] EWCA Civ 810; *R (ZAT and ors) v SSHD* [2016] UKUT 61. In the European context, this is codified in art 6(1) of *Dublin III*, which states that '[t] he best interests of the child shall be a primary consideration for Member States with respect to all procedures provided for in [the] Regulation'. This is complemented by recital 13, which provides that 'the best interests of the child should be a primary consideration of Member States when applying this Regulation. In assessing the best interests of the child, Member States should, in particular, take due account of the minor's well-being and social development, safety and security considerations and the views of the minor in accordance with his or her age and maturity, including his or her background. In addition, specific procedural guarantees for unaccompanied minors should be laid down on account of their particular vulnerability'. Art 8(1) of *Dublin III* further provides that '[w]here the applicant is an unaccompanied minor, the Member State responsible shall be that where a family member or a sibling of the unaccompanied minor is legally present, provided that it is in the best interests of the minor': see too art 8(2) and recitals 16, 24, 35 and 39. Although less secure, *Dublin II* contains similar provisions to arts 6(1) and 8(1) of *Dublin III*: see arts 6 and 15(3).

[100] See, e.g., *R (ABC) (a minor) (Afghanistan) v SSHD* [2011] EWHC 2937 (Admin).

[101] N Blake, 'Current Problems in Asylum and Protection Law: The UK Judicial Perspective' (Paper presented at the Ninth World Conference of the International Association of Refugee Law Judges, Slovenia, 7 September 2011) 10.

[102] G S Goodwin-Gill, 'Unaccompanied Refugee Minors: The Role and Place of International Law in the Pursuit of Durable Solutions' (1995) 3 *International Journal of Children's Rights* 405; G S Goodwin-Gill, 'Who to Protect, How . . ., and the Future?' (1997) 9 *International Journal of Refugee Law* 1, 7; Goodwin-Gill (2012) *supra* n 1.

[103] Goodwin-Gill (1997) *supra* n 102, 7.

In a subsequent submission to the UK House of Lords Select Committee on the European Union, Goodwin-Gill, writing with Agnès Hurwitz, criticised the draft *2004 Qualification Directive* for its failure to engage sufficiently with the *CRC* and, in particular, the best interests principle. They submitted that '[i]n every decision affecting the child, the best interests of the child shall be a primary consideration, and where children are concerned (particularly the unaccompanied), a duty to protect may arise, absent any well-founded fear of persecution or possibility of serious harm'.[104] This argument has since been taken up and developed by McAdam:[105]

> the best interests of the child, reflecting an absolute principle of international law, are highly relevant in determining whether or not a child needs international protection. The principle applies to any protection claim concerning children, irrespective of whether they are unaccompanied, accompanied by family members (even where the child is not the primary applicant), or seeking family reunion ... [B]est interests are also relevant to removal cases which will personally affect a child, such as where the State seeks to deport a parent.

McAdam argues that the best interests principle adds an additional layer of consideration to the interpretation and application of the *Convention*, in addition to 'constitut[ing] a complementary ground of protection in its own right'.[106]

Both the UNCRC and UNHCR have also endorsed the argument that art 3 creates a new category of protected persons. The clearest affirmation is found in the UNCRC's *GC6*, which provides that '[r]eturn to the country of origin shall in principle only be arranged if such return is in the best interests of the child'.[107] Notwithstanding this unqualified formulation, the Committee later acknowledges that other considerations may override the best interests of the child; it stresses, however, that such considerations must be rights-based and that '[n]on-rights-based arguments such as those relating to general migration control, cannot override best interests considerations'.[108] According to the Committee, this determination should take into account: the views of the child; the safety, security and socio-economic conditions awaiting the child upon return; the availability of care arrangements for the child; the child's level of integration in the host country; the child's right to preserve her identity, including her nationality, name and family relationship; and the desirability of continuity in a child's upbringing.[109]

In recent years, the UNCRC has underlined the need for states to 'conduct individual assessments and evaluations of the best interests of the child at all stages of ... any migration

---

[104] Goodwin-Gill and Hurwitz (2002) *supra* n 26, [10].

[105] McAdam (2007) *supra* n 26, 173. See also McAdam (2006) *supra* n 1.

[106] McAdam (2007) *supra* n 26, 173–4. For further endorsement see S Bolton, 'Promoting the Best Interests of the Child in UK Asylum Law and Procedures' (2012) 26 *Journal of Immigration, Asylum and Nationality Law* 232; A Lundberg, 'The Best Interests of the Child Principle in Swedish Asylum Cases: The Marginalization of Children's Rights' (2011) 3 *Journal of Human Rights Practice* 49; B Carr, 'Incorporating a "Best Interests of the Child" Approach into Immigration Law and Procedure' (2009) 12 *Yale Human Rights and Development Law Journal* 120; J K Dalrymple, 'Seeking Asylum Alone: Using the Best Interests of the Child Principle to Protect Unaccompanied Minors' (2006) 26 *Boston College Third World Law Journal* 131.

[107] UNCRC, *GC6*, [84].

[108] UNCRC, *GC6*, [86]. See also at [20]. For a discussion on what may be meant by 'rights-based', see *infra* text accompanying n 354–6.

[109] UNCRC, *GC6*, [84].

process affecting children'.[110] In particular, the Committee has explained that 'primary consideration should be given to the best interests of the child in any proceeding resulting in the child's or their parents' detention, return or deportation'.[111] For example, in its most recent observations on Australia, the Committee counselled Australia to ensure that 'its migration and asylum legislation and procedures have the best interests of the child as the primary consideration in all immigration and asylum processes' and that 'determinations of the best interests are consistently conducted by professionals who have been adequately trained in best interests determination procedures'.[112] Further support for the approach taken by the Committee can be found in the reports of the Special Rapporteur on the Human Rights of Migrants, who has stressed that 'children should be repatriated only if it is in their best interests, namely, for the purpose of family reunification and after due process of law'.[113] This view also finds support in the work of the Office of the UN High Commissioner for Human Rights, which has acknowledged that 'the ability of States to return children in the context of migration is constrained by a number of factors' and that '[t]he principle of the best interest of the child ... should be a primary consideration in any decision to return, and in decisions on the deportation of their parents'.[114]

UNHCR has similarly acknowledged the importance of art 3 in determining the eligibility of a child for international protection. In its *Unaccompanied Children Guidelines*, UNHCR states that, where a child is found not to qualify for refugee status, 'an assessment of the solution that is in the best interests of the child should follow as soon as practicable after the negative result'.[115] The UNHCR ExCom has also recognised that '[t]he principle of the best interests of the child shall be a primary consideration in regard to all actions concerning children',[116] and recommended that states adopt 'appropriate procedures for the determination of the child's best interests which facilitate adequate child participation without discrimination'.[117] To assist decision-makers in that determination process, UNHCR and UNICEF have published a set of guidelines outlining a formal mechanism for determining the best interests of children.[118]

Although the role of the best interests principle is well established as a matter of international obligation, there has, at a domestic level, traditionally been a general lack of enthusiasm with the idea that the best interests principle may provide an independent basis for international protection. There are, however, signs that this is beginning to change.

---

[110] UNCRC, 2012 *Discussion Day Report*, [72].

[111] *Ibid.*, [72].

[112] UNCRC, *Consideration of Reports Submitted by States Parties under Article 44 of the Convention – Concluding Observations: Australia*, CRC/C/AUS/CO/4 (2012), [80].

[113] J Bustamante, *Report of the Special Rapporteur on the Human Rights of Migrants*, A/64/213 (2009), [85]. See also at [97]; J Bustamante, *Report of the Special Rapporteur on the Human Rights of Migrants*, A/HRC/11/7 (2009), [57], [123].

[114] *Study of the Office of the United Nations High Commissioner for Human Rights on Challenges and Best Practices in the Implementation of the International Framework for the Protection of the Rights of the Child in the Context of Migration*, A/HRC/15/29 (2010), [46]–[47].

[115] UNHCR, *Guidelines on Policies and Procedures in Dealing with Unaccompanied Children Seeking Asylum* (1997), [9.2].

[116] UNHCR ExCom, *Conclusion on Children at Risk*, No 107 (LVIII) (2007), [(b)].

[117] *Ibid.*, [(g)]. See also UNHCR ExCom, *Conclusions on the Provision of International Protection Including through Complementary Forms of Protection*, No 103 (LVI) (2005), [(n)].

[118] UNHCR, *Child's BID Guidelines* (2008) *supra* n 88; UNHCR, *Field Handbook for the Implementation of UNHCR BID Guidelines* (2011); UNHCR and UNICEF, *Safe & Sound* (2014) *supra* n 82.

The experience in the United Kingdom provides a clear example. Following the United Kingdom's withdrawal of its reservation to the CRC – which had reserved the right to limit the application of the CRC, including the best interests principle, to non-citizen children – the Parliament enacted legislation requiring the state to 'make arrangements for ensuring that [the Secretary of State's] functions are discharged having regard to the need to safeguard and promote the welfare of children who are in the United Kingdom'.[119] The withdrawal of the reservation and the subsequent passage of domestic legislation provided an impetus for a series of decisions considering the application of art 3 to migration-related decisions involving children. As Bolton explains, 'it was this withdrawal … that began to level the playing field … to create conditions for more substantive progress to be made in the arena of immigration and asylum law and policy, nearly two decades after the [CRC] was ratified by the UK.'[120]

A recent decision of the UK Upper Tribunal provides a good illustration of the operation of the principle in practice. In RA v SSHD[121] a mentally ill Nigerian mother and her five-year-old son were removed to Nigeria without any independent consideration of the child's best interests (or refugee claim). The Upper Tribunal held that the decision-maker had failed to take into account the implications of the mother's mental health for the child, and the risk of the mother's health degenerating in Nigeria.[122] The Secretary of State had therefore failed to have regard to the child's best interests as a primary consideration.[123] The Upper Tribunal ordered the Secretary of State to return the mother and child to the United Kingdom so that a best interests assessment could be undertaken.[124] The decision was upheld by the Court of Appeal in RA v SSHD [2015] EWCA Civ 679.

Although the United Kingdom is at the forefront of recent developments, a number of jurisdictions have for some time engaged with the best interests principle in determining whether a child is entitled to an international protection status. Senior courts in Canada, Australia and New Zealand have, for instance, long recognised that a decision involving the deportation or extradition of a child's parent must necessarily entail a consideration of the best interests of the child. The US government has drawn on the best interests principle to develop a specific protection status for unaccompanied children. And a number of jurisdictions, including Canada, Australia, New Zealand and several European states, have also implemented discretionary humanitarian protection schemes that require decision-makers

---

[119] Borders, Citizenship and Immigration Act 2009, c 11, s 55. This duty is explicated in statutory guidance, which provides that the 'the best interests of the child will be a primary consideration (although not necessarily the only consideration) when making decisions affecting children': UKBA, Every Child Matters: Statutory Guidance to the UK Border Agency on Making Arrangements to Safeguard and Promote the Welfare of Children (November 2009), [2.7].

[120] Bolton (2012) supra n 106, 235 (citations omitted). In the UK, s 55 of the Borders, Citizenship and Immigration Act 2009, c 11, is strengthened by art 24 of the Charter of Fundamental Rights of the European Union [2000] OJ C 361/1. The Explanations to the EU Charter makes clear that art 24 is based on the CRC, and 'particularly Articles 3, 9, 12 and 13 thereof': Explanations Relating to the Charter of Fundamental Rights [2007] OJ C 303/17. A point recently acknowledged by the UK Supreme Court, observing that art 24(2) is 'clearly modelled on [art 3(1)] of the [CRC]': In the matter of N (Children) [2016] UKSC 15, [42]). Given its constitutional footing, art 24 may provide a powerful freestanding right for children seeking international protection: see, e.g., Abdul v SHHD [2016] UKUT 00106 [27]–[32] and, more generally, S Peers et al., The EU Charter of Fundamental Rights: A Commentary (2014) 661–91.

[121] RA v SSHD [2015] UKUT 00242.   [122] Ibid., [86].   [123] Ibid.

[124] RA v SSHD [2015] UKUT 00292.

to take into account the best interests of any child affected by a decision to remove a child and/or the child's parent or guardian. The following section examines the manner and extent to which the best interests principle has been applied in each of these contexts.

6.3 An Overview of State Practice

This section examines the manner in which the best interests principle has been employed in a range of migration contexts involving children.[125] This largely expository discussion serves two related purposes. First, it demonstrates that the argument advanced in this chapter is neither unfamiliar nor entirely aspirational. To the contrary, a review of state practice reveals that the best interests principle is regularly employed by states in migration-related contexts. Second, the developing jurisprudence in each of these related areas offers a critical source of guidance to inform the application of art 3 to children seeking international protection: the focus of Section 6.4. In circumstances where the best interests principle is often criticised for its lack of precision, the jurisprudence provides a platform from which to develop a framework for assessing the scope of art 3 and identifying the circumstances in which the provision may preclude the removal of a child from a host state.

6.3.1 International Models

Although the *CRC* would not be formally adopted until more than 40 years after the Second World War, the best interests principle was central to the work of the IRO in addressing the needs of the large number of children who became separated from their families during that War.[126] As noted in Chapter 1, the *IRO Constitution* established a priority obligation to render all possible assistance to unaccompanied children. There were, however, divergent views as to who was ultimately responsible for making a determination regarding the repatriation or resettlement of unaccompanied children and how that determination should be carried out. For instance, did responsibility reside with the IRO, the child's parents or guardians (where they could be located), the government of the country of origin or the government of the host country? And to what extent, if at all, should any determination take into account the wishes of the individual children who, in many cases, had strong views of their own?[127]

A number of governments, including the USSR, Byelorussia and Poland, took the view that all children should be repatriated regardless of whether their parents could be located and that the country of nationality should be responsible for these children.[128] It was

---

[125] The discussion that follows is illustrative only. It does not provide an exhaustive account of all migration contexts in which the best interests principle has been applied, nor does it present a comprehensive overview of any particular domestic system.

[126] The UN Department of Social Affairs estimated that approximately 60 million children needed help during the Second World War and that approximately 13 million children were orphaned by the conflict: E D Pask, 'Unaccompanied Refugee and Displaced Children: Jurisdiction, Decision-Making and Representation' (1989) 1(2) *International Journal of Refugee Law* 199, 202, citing *Children Deprived of a Normal Home Life*, E/CN.5/271 (1952) 7-8.

[127] L W Holborn, *The International Refugee Organization: A Specialized Agency of the United Nations – Its History and Work, 1946-1952* (1956) 495.

[128] *Ibid.*, 496.

suggested that it would be a violation of international law to take into account the views of a minor.[129] By contrast, the British and US governments took the view that the best interests of the child should be the guiding consideration and that the removal of a child to its country of origin would thus not be appropriate 'if the paramount consideration, the welfare of the child, seemed to oppose repatriation and call for resettlement or local settlement'.[130]

In 1948, the Preparatory Commission of the IRO submitted a report to ECOSOC. It provided an account of the situation of children removed from their country of origin and set out the measures taken by the IRO on their behalf and recommendations for future action.[131] The discussions in ECOSOC that followed illustrated the divergent views regarding the treatment of unaccompanied children.[132] The delegates for the Soviet Union and Byelorussia considered that the reference to the 'best interests of the individual child' should be deleted from the draft resolution under consideration, expressing a concern for children who had not been returned even where their parents had been identified and had requested their return. The delegate for the United States considered that the phrase was particularly important: 'The competent authorities would be dealing with defenceless and feeble human beings, and in the settlement of their fate the best interest of the children should be constantly born in mind'.[133] The final resolution adopted by ECOSOC set out the policy in the following terms:[134]

(1)   to unite children with their parents wherever the latter may be; and
(2)   in the case of orphans or unaccompanied children whose nationality has been established beyond doubt to return them to their country, always providing that the best interests of the individual child shall be the determining factor.

The first provision emphasised that the primary task of the IRO was to reunite children with their families wherever possible. In the context of orphans or unaccompanied children, the IRO was to promote repatriation where it was considered in the best interests of the child and, where it was not, to facilitate arrangements for resettlement.[135]

Within the US-occupied zone in Germany, decisions regarding a child's best interests were initially made through administrative channels; however, that role was later delegated to the HICOG courts. As Holborn reports, this established 'a more normal legal machinery for determination of the best interests of the children'.[136] Article 14 of the governing law sets out a range of factors that must be considered in determining a child's best interests.[137] The British authorities adopted a less formal approach, setting up a Child Welfare Board in coordination with the IRO, which made recommendations, on humanitarian grounds, for the future placement of each child.[138] In total, in the period 1 July 1947 to

---

[129]   *Ibid.*, 496.   [130]   *Ibid.*, 497.   [131]   *Ibid.*, 498.   [132]   The below account draws from *ibid.*, 499.
[133]   *Ibid.*, 499.
[134]   *Progress and Prospect of Repatriation, Resettlement and Immigration of Refugees and Displaced Persons – Resolution of 24 August 1948*, ECOSOC Res 157 (VII), E/1027 (1948).
[135]   Holborn (1956) *supra* n 127, 499.
[136]   *Ibid.*, 500, citing *Report to US HICOG on IRO, US Zone of Germany* (22 October 1951) (reproduced in Holborn (1956) *supra* n 127, 500) 10.
[137]   *Ibid.*, 501, citing HICOG, *Law No 11* (reproduced in Holborn (1956) *supra* n 127, 501).
[138]   *Ibid.*, 501–2.

31 December 1951, the IRO was involved in the repatriation of 1,898 unaccompanied children and the resettlement of a further 4,053 children.[139]

A similar emphasis on the best interests principle – this time expressly inspired by art 3 of the CRC – can be seen in the *Comprehensive Plan of Action for Indo-Chinese Refugees* ('*CPA*') adopted by the International Conference on Indo-Chinese Refugees held in Geneva on 13 and 14 June 1989.[140] In response to a concern that a significant number of new arrivals from Vietnam were 'economic migrants' rather than refugees, the *CPA* introduced screening procedures to identify genuine refugees who were eligible for resettlement. A special procedure was established for unaccompanied children, referable not only to the *Convention* definition, but also to a state's obligations under the *CRC*. This special procedure recognised that it was 'inappropriate for unaccompanied children to be treated in the same way as adults'[141] and provided that decisions involving unaccompanied children 'should not be based exclusively on the child's eligibility to refugee status under the standard definition set forth in the [*Refugee Convention*], but should also take into account the principles of family unity and the best interests of the child'.[142]

In consultation with national authorities, UNHCR developed a set of guidelines to assist in the application of the *CPA* to unaccompanied children.[143] Children that were over 15 years of age were subject to a two-stage process, commencing with an assessment of refugee status pursuant to the *Convention*. If refugee status was established the child would be referred for resettlement. If the child was found to be ineligible for refugee status, she was then referred to a Special Committee, composed of representatives of governments and UNHCR, including experts in child welfare. That Committee was charged with determining, on a case-by-case basis, 'which solution is in the best interest of each unaccompanied minor'.[144] If repatriation was found to be in the child's best interests, it 'would be implemented only on condition that certain arrangements (including assessment of willingness by the minor's family in the country of origin to accept the return of the minor) were made prior to the return'.[145] Children under the age of 15 were presumed to be too immature to hold a well-founded fear of being persecuted[146] and were thus referred directly to the Special Committees without any consideration of refugee status.

---

[139] *Ibid.*, 513–14.

[140] International Conference on Indo-Chinese Refugees, Office of the UNHCR, *Report of the Secretary General*, A/44/523 (1989) Annex pt II. The *CPA* replaced the earlier ad hoc international plan adopted at the Meeting on Refugees and Displaced Persons in July 1979. Under that plan the more proximate states of South-East Asia agreed to provide temporary protection to boat people arriving from Vietnam (who were presumptively considered to be genuine refugees) on the condition that they would subsequently be resettled to an industrialised state: see generally D O'Donnell, 'Resettlement or Repatriation: Screened out Vietnamese Child Asylum Seekers and the Convention on the Rights of the Child' (1989) 6(3) *International Journal of Refugee Law* 382, 383. See also J M Freeman and N D Huu, *Voices from the Camps: Vietnamese Children Seeking Asylum* (2003); J Crisp, 'Meeting the Needs and Realizing the Rights of Refugee Children and Adolescents: From Policy to Practice' (1996) 15(3) *Refugee Survey Quarterly* 1, 20–2; McAdam (2007) *supra* n 26, 188–9.

[141] Crisp (1996) *supra* n 140, 20.   [142] O'Donnell (1989) *supra* n 140, 391.

[143] See discussion in *ibid.*, 391–2. See also UNHCR, *Note on International Protection (Submitted by the High Commissioner)*, A/AC.96/728 (1989), [58].

[144] UNHCR, *Note on International Protection* (1989) *supra* n 143, [58].   [145] *Ibid.*

[146] This misconception derived from an unfortunate passage of UNHCR, *Handbook*. See Chapter 3, text accompanying n 21–23.

In the majority of cases where a child was found not to be a refugee and had family remaining in Vietnam, the Special Committee recommended, on family unity principles, that the child be repatriated.[147] The Committee made clear, however, that the principle of family unity did not provide an automatic trump card. This is consistent with art 9 of the CRC,[148] which provides that the separation from a child and parent can be justified where such separation is necessary for the best interests of the child.[149] Thus, in a limited range of cases – for example, where a child required medical care or treatment unavailable in Vietnam or where there was evidence of domestic child abuse in Vietnam – the Committee determined that repatriation was inappropriate.[150]

The two historical case studies discussed above demonstrate a willingness on the part of the international community to draw on the best interests principle as a means of assessing the protection status of at-risk children. Although both case studies must be understood in light of their specific historical context, aspects of these protection models may provide instruction to national decision-makers seeking to apply the best interests principle on a more routine basis.

6.3.2 Article 8 of the ECHR

Article 8 of the ECHR has begun to play an increasingly significant role in immigration cases involving children. Article 8(1) provides that '[e]veryone has the right to respect for his private and family life, his home and his correspondence'. The obligation is not an absolute one and allows for interference that is[151]

> in accordance with law and is necessary in a democratic society in the interests of national security, public safety or the economic well-being of the country, for the prevention of disorder or crime, for the protection of health or morals, or for the protection of the rights and freedoms of others.

Article 8 is most likely to be engaged in cases involving the removal or deportation of an individual where this will result in the disruption of her family or private life (for instance, the deportation of a parent where this will result in separation from her children)[152] or cases involving the admission of an individual seeking entry for family reunification purposes (for instance, the admission of a child to join her other family

---

[147] By the first quarter of 1995, decisions had been made for approximately 6,000 children: Crisp (1996) *supra* n 140, 22. Of these, 4,700 had been returned to Vietnam and 1,000 had been resettled in third countries.

[148] CRC, art 9(1).   [149] See the detailed discussion in Chapter 2, Section 2.3.2; and *infra* Section 6.4.1.

[150] O'Donnell (1989) *supra* n 140, 391, 396.   [151] ECHR, art 8(2).

[152] A comprehensive examination of the application of art 8 in the immigration context is beyond the scope of this book. See generally H Storey, 'The Right to Family Life and Immigration Case Law at Strasbourg' (1990) 39 *International & Comparative Law Quarterly* 328; H Lambert, 'The European Court of Human Rights and the Rights of Refugees and Other Persons in Need of Protection to Family Reunion' (1999) 11 (3) *International Journal of Refugee Law* 427; N Blake and R Husain, *Immigration, Asylum and Human Rights* (2003) 165–210; I MacDonald and R Toal, *MacDonald's Immigration Law and Practice* (9th edn, 2014) vol 1, 602–36; C Costello, *The Human Rights of Migrants and Refugees in European Law* (2016) 112–30.

members).[153] Although geographically restricted,[154] an examination of the manner in which regional and domestic courts have drawn on the best interests principle in interpreting art 8 may prove instructive in considering the interpretation and application of the best interests principle more generally.

Although art 8 of the *ECHR* does not guarantee the right of an individual to enter or reside in a particular country,[155] the obligation to respect an individual's family and private life will, in certain circumstances, circumscribe a state's discretion to refuse entry to, or to remove or deport, a non-citizen.[156] In assessing whether there is a violation of art 8, it is first necessary to establish the existence of an interference with an individual's family or private life. If the impugned decision will result in the separation of family members there will generally be no difficulty establishing an interference with family life. The deportation of a child may also amount to an interference with a child's private life,[157] particularly if the individual has spent most, if not all, of her childhood in the host country.[158] After the interference has been established, it is then necessary to consider whether that interference can be justified pursuant to art 8(2). The qualifying provision requires a decision-maker to answer three questions: first, whether the interference is in accordance with law; second, whether the interference pursues one of the eight legitimate aims listed in art 8(2); and, finally, whether the interference is necessary in a democratic society. The third question requires a decision-maker to balance the rights of the individuals affected with the interests of the community and to assess whether the interference is proportionate to the legitimate

---

[153] See, e.g., *Şen v Netherlands* (2003) 36 EHRR 81; *Tuaquabo-Tekle v Netherlands* (Application No. 60665/00, 1 December 2005). Contra the earlier approach taken in *Gül v Switzerland* (1996) 22 EHRR 93. See also *Singh v Entry Clearance Officer, New Delhi* [2005] QB 608.

[154] Both the *ICCPR* (art 17) and *CRC* (art 16) contain a similar provision to *ECHR*, art 8; however, these provisions have received more limited judicial consideration, thus the focus on the regional instrument here. There are, however, a number of Views of the HRC that have considered the applicability of art 17 of the *ICCPR* in immigration cases involving children: see, e.g., HRC, *Views: Communication No 930/2000*, CCPR/C/72/D/930/2000 (2001) ('*Winata v Australia*'); HRC, *Views: Communication No 893/1999*, CCPR/C/77/D/893/1999 (2003) ('*Sahid v New Zealand*'); HRC, *Decision: Communication No 820/1998*, CCPR/C/78/D/820/1998 (2003) ('*Rajan v New Zealand*'); HRC, *Views: Communication No 1069/2002*, CCPR/C/79/D/1069/2002 (2003) ('*Bakhtiyari v Australia*'); HRC, *Views: Communication No 1011/2001*, CCPR/C/81/D/1011/2001 (2004) ('*Madafferi v Australia*'); HRC, *Views: Communication No 1222/2003*, CCPR/C/82/D/1222/2003 (2004) ('*Byahuranga v Denmark*'); HRC, *Views: Communication No 1557/2007*, CCPR/C/102/D/1557/2007 (2011) ('*Nystrom v Australia*').

[155] *Üner v Netherlands* (2007) 45 EHRR 14, [55].

[156] In the EU context, additional protection may be provided by general principles of EU law, particularly where the child concerned is a citizen of an EU member state: see, e.g., *Zambrano v Office national de l'emploi*, C-34/09, EU:C:2011:124 (8 March 2011).

[157] *Üner v Netherlands* (2007) 45 EHRR 14, [59]. See also *Maslov v Austria* [2009] INLR 47, [63].

[158] 'Whether the child is British or not, the longer a child spends in the United Kingdom, the stronger and more extensive their network of psychological, personal and social ties[,] i.e. their private life, will become. There will come a point at which it becomes simply unreasonable to expect that child to be uprooted and start a new life in a different country': Appellant, 'Case for the Appellant', filed in *ZH (Tanzania) v SSHD* (undated) (copy on file with author), [72]. In *SS (India) v SSHD* [2010] EWCA Civ 388, [49], the England and Wales Court of Appeal held that the tribunal had erred by failing to conduct an 'analysis of the social effect on the children of being wrenched from their social milieu in the UK'. See also *R (Cheung Yew Mine) v SSHD* [2011] EWHC 2337 (Admin), [36]–[46]; *E-A v SSHD* [2011] UKUT 00315, [26]; *FM (Afghanistan) v SSHD* (Upper Tribunal, AA/01079/2010, 10 March 2011), [159]–[161]; *R (B) v SSHD* [2010] EWHC 2571 (Admin), [21]–[26].

aim pursued. In order for interference to be justifiable, all three questions must be answered in the affirmative.

It is in the context of the art 8(2) proportionality assessment that the ECtHR has emphasised the importance of taking into account the best interests of any child affected by an immigration decision. In *Üner v Netherlands*, a case involving the expulsion of a father of three children following his conviction for manslaughter, the ECtHR explicitly identified 'the best interests and well-being of the children' as a criterion to assess whether deportation was necessary in a democratic society and proportionate to the legitimate public aim sought to be achieved.[159] The Court held that, in cases involving the deportation of a parent, particular attention should be placed on 'the seriousness of the difficulties which any children of the applicant are likely to encounter in the country to which the applicant is to be expelled'.[160]

The principle was elaborated on in the case of *Neulinger v Switzerland*,[161] which considered the applicability of art 8 in the context of a challenge to the return of a child pursuant to the *Convention on the Civil Aspects of International Child Abduction*.[162] The Court observed that 'the [ECHR] cannot be interpreted in a vacuum but must be interpreted in harmony with the general principles of international law' including, pursuant to art 31(3)(c) of the *VCLT*, 'any relevant rules of international law applicable in the relations between the parties'.[163] In these circumstances, it was appropriate for the Court to pay particular regard to the fact that 'there is currently a broad consensus – including in international law – in support of the idea that in all decisions concerning children, their best interests must be paramount'.[164] The Court went on to state:[165]

> In this area the decisive issue is whether a fair balance between the competing interests at stake – those of the child, of the two parents, and of public order – has been struck . . . bearing in mind, however, that the child's best interests must be the primary consideration . . .
>
> The child's best interests, from a personal development perspective, will depend on a variety of individual circumstances, in particular his age and level of maturity, the presence or absence of his parents and his environment and experiences . . . For that reason, those best interests must be assessed in an individual case.

The decisions in *Üner v Netherlands* and *Neulinger v Switzerland* evince a clear acknowledgement of the need to pay special attention to the interests of any child that may be affected by an immigration decision. The Court made clear that the *ECHR* should be read in conformity with the *CRC* and that, in any case where the rights of a child are involved, the

---

[159] *Üner v Netherlands* (2007) 45 EHRR 14, [58]. This principle is reflected in earlier decisions of the ECtHR: see, e.g., *Rodrigues da Silva v Netherlands* (2007) 44 EHRR 34, [44]; *Tuaquabo-Tekle v Netherlands* (Application No. 60665/00, 1 December 2005), [47]; *Şen v Netherlands* (2003) 36 EHRR 81, [40].

[160] *Üner v Netherlands* (2007) 45 EHRR 14, [58].   [161] *Neulinger v Switzerland* (2012) 54 EHRR 31.

[162] *Convention on the Civil Aspects of International Child Abduction*, opened for signature 25 October 1980, 1343 UNTS 89 (entered into force 1 December 1983). The first applicant was a mother who had removed her child (the second applicant) from Israel to Switzerland: *Neulinger v Switzerland* (2012) 54 EHRR 31, [28]. The second applicant's father had subsequently applied for the return of the child pursuant to the *Convention*: at *ibid.*, [29]–[30].

[163] *Neulinger v Switzerland* (2012) 54 EHRR 31, [131].   [164] *Ibid.*, [135]. See also at [49]–[56].

[165] *Ibid.*, [134], [138].

best interests of the child must be a primary consideration when conducting the art 8(2) proportionality assessment.[166]

The Strasbourg jurisprudence has been particularly influential in the United Kingdom, where it has coincided with the government's withdrawal of its reservation relating to immigration matters under the CRC and the subsequent coming into force of s 55 of the *Borders, Citizenship and Immigration Act 2009*, c 11.[167] This has resulted in a significant shift in emphasis in the domestic art 8 jurisprudence, with decision-makers paying greater attention to the best interests of any child affected by an immigration decision.

One of the earliest cases to afford more prominence to the best interests principle was *LD v SSHD*,[168] an appeal against a decision to remove a Zimbabwean man with three young children who were lawfully resident in the United Kingdom. Drawing on the principles set out in the Strasbourg jurisprudence, Blake J held that 'there can be little reason to doubt that the interests of the child should be a primary consideration in immigration cases' and that '[a] failure to treat them as such will violate Article 8 as incorporated directly into domestic law'.[169] In the context of a removal decision, Blake J took the view that '[v]ery weighty reasons are needed to justify separating a parent from a minor child or a child from a community in which he or she had grown up and lived for most of her life'.[170] He considered that both principles were engaged in the case and that, given the absence of any strong reasons to support the removal of the children's father, the appellant's removal would constitute a violation of art 8.[171]

---

[166] See also *IAA v UK* (2016) 62 EHRR SE19, [41]; *Jeunesse v Netherlands* (2015) 60 EHRR 17; *Nunez v Norway* (2014) 58 EHRR 7; *Omojudi v UK* (2010) 51 EHRR 10; *AA v UK* [2012] INLR 1; *Maslov v Austria* [2009] INLR 47. In *Maslov* and *AA v UK*, the applicants were young adults who were each subject to a deportation order because of offences committed as a minor, the respective governments reasoning that the interference with the applicants' art 8 rights were legitimate for the prevention of disorder or crime. In both cases the Court held that, 'where offences committed by a minor underlie an exclusion order, regard must be had to the best interests of the child. In particular, the obligation to take the best interests of the child into account includes an obligation to facilitate his reintegration, an aim that the Court has previously held will not be achieved by severing family or social ties through expulsion': *AA v UK*, [60]; see also *Maslov*, [72], [82]–[83]. Although not referring to the best interests principle, in *Jakupovic v Austria* (2004) 38 EHRR 595, [29], the Court held that 'very weighty reasons' would be required 'to justify the expulsion of a young person (16 years old), alone, to a country which has recently experienced a period of armed conflict with all its adverse effects on living conditions and with no evidence of close relatives living there'.

[167] See *supra* text accompanying n 119.

[168] *LD v SSHD* [2010] UKUT 278. Although earlier decisions in the UK had pointed to the relevance of the interests of a child when applying art 8, this was never explicitly done by reference to art 3of the CRC. For example, in *EB (Kosovo) v SSHD* [2009] 1 AC 1159, [12], Lord Bingham acknowledged that 'it will rarely be proportionate to uphold an order for removal of the spouse if there is a close and genuine bond with the other spouse and that spouse cannot reasonably be expected to follow the removal spouse to the country of removal, or if the effect of the order is to sever a genuine and subsisting relationship between parent and child'.

[169] *Ibid.*, [28].   [170] *Ibid.*, [26].

[171] *Ibid.*, [29]. The following month Blake J issued his decision in *R (MXL) v SSHD* [2010] EWHC 2397 (Admin), which (at [83]) outlined a similar set of principles: 'Once Article 8 is engaged, the exercise of judgment in a case falling within its ambit must comply with the principles identified by Strasbourg. In a case where the interests of children are affected this means that other principles of international law binding on contracting states should be complied with. In the case of children those principles are reflected in Article 3(1) of the [CRC] to which the UK is now a party without any derogation in respect of immigration decision making.'

The issue was revisited the following year in the now oft-cited decision of the Supreme Court in *ZH (Tanzania) v SSHD*. This case involved an appeal against a decision to remove a Tanzanian woman who had two children born in the United Kingdom: a daughter aged 12 and a son aged 9. Before the case was heard, the Secretary of State conceded that, on the particular facts, removing the appellant would be a disproportionate interference with the art 8 rights of the children; however, the case proceeded to allow the Supreme Court to deliver guidance on the general principles which should apply in future cases.[172] In the majority opinion, Baroness Hale drew on the Strasbourg jurisprudence and underlined that the best interests principle is relevant 'not only to how children are looked after in this country while decisions about immigration, deportation or removal are being made, but also to the decisions themselves'.[173] Accordingly, '[i]n making the proportionality assessment under article 8, the best interests of the child must be a primary consideration'.[174]

The decisions of the Supreme Court in *ZH (Tanzania) v SSHD* and the Upper Tribunal in *LD v SSHD* each arose in the context of an appeal against the removal of a child's parent where the parent had no right to be or to remain in the country. Courts have, however, sensibly taken the view that the general principles set out in these cases apply wherever an art 8 right is engaged. As Lord Kerr stated in *H (H) v Deputy Prosecutor of the Italian Republic, Genoa*, 'the intrinsic value of the [art 8] right cannot alter according to context'.[175] Accordingly, although the interests that a state invokes to justify the interference will differ depending on the context, the approach to the application of art 8 remains the same.[176] A review of decisions in the United Kingdom over the past five years reveals that the best interests principle has been incorporated into the art 8 proportionality assessment in a wide range of contexts, including cases involving the extradition of a parent,[177] the removal of children who are part of a family unit,[178] the return of a child pursuant to the *Convention on the Civil Aspects of International Child Abduction*,[179] the deportation of a parent following

---

[172] *ZH (Tanzania) v SSHD* [2011] 2 AC 166, [13]. For an excellent discussion on the decision in *ZH* and its background, see J Fortin, 'Are Children's Best Interests Really Best? *ZH (Tanzania) (FC) v Secretary of State for the Home Department*' (2011) 74 *Modern Law Review* 947.

[173] *Ibid.*, [24] (Baroness Hale). Indeed, this point was conceded by the Secretary of State in *ZH*: *ibid.* The UKUT has since re-emphasised that the best interests obligation is both procedural *and* substantive: *AA (unattended children) Afghanistan CG* [2012] UKUT 00016, [33] ('[I]t is not helpful to attempt to analyse the duty ... as being either procedural or substantive in effect. It applies to the procedures involved in the decision-making process; but it will also apply to those aspects of the substantive decision to which it is relevant').

[174] *ZH (Tanzania) v SSHD* [2011] 2 AC 166, [33].

[175] *H (H) v Deputy Prosecutor of the Italian Republic, Genoa* [2013] 1 AC 338, [141].   [176] *Ibid.*

[177] *Ibid.*; *H v Lord Advocate* [2013] 1 AC 413. In *H (H)*, Lord Kerr held (at [146]) that '[i]n the field of extradition, as in every other context, ... the importance of the rights of the particular children affected falls to be considered first. This does not impair or reduce the weight that will be accorded to the need to preserve and uphold a comprehensive charter for extradition. That will always be a factor of considerable importance, although ... the weight to be attached to it will vary according to the nature and seriousness of the crime or controls involved.'

[178] *Zoumbas v SSHD* [2013] 1 WLR 3690; *IE v SSHD* [2013] CSOH 142; *JW (China) v SSHD* [2013] EWCA Civ 1526; *AAN (Malawi) v SSHD* [2012] CSOH 151; *R (Meaza Asefa) v SSHD* [2012] EWHC 56 (Admin).

[179] *Convention on the Civil Aspects of International Child Abduction*, opened for signature 25 October 1980, 1343 UNTS 89 (entered into force 1 December 1983). See *Re E (Children) (Abduction: Custody Appeal)* [2012] 1 AC 144 and the decision below in *Eliassen v Eliassen* [2011] EWCA Civ 361.

a criminal conviction,[180] the removal of an unaccompanied child,[181] the admission of a child applying from outside the United Kingdom,[182] the detention of a parent[183] and the denial of permanent residence to a parent and her children.[184]

The infusion of the best interests principle into the art 8(2) proportionality assessment is a welcome development. As the discussion above demonstrates, the general principles set out by the ECtHR and subsequently developed in the domestic sphere have enhanced the visibility of children in the immigration context, with a clear acknowledgement that the presence of a child requires a decision-maker to adopt a more child-focused approach to decision-making.[185] It is clear, however, that the jurisprudence remains embryonic, with regional and domestic decision-makers only just beginning to map the consequences of the integration of the best interests principle into the art 8 decision-making process. As this area of law develops there is value in reflecting on two related concerns that have been raised in relation to the jurisprudence.

First, it has been suggested that art 8 decisions retain an 'adult-oriented dimension' because the majority of the decisions focus on the art 8 rights of the parent rather than the child's stand-alone art 8 rights.[186] Fortin laments that 'recent case law often makes no direct mention of the child's status as an article 8(1) rights holder in his or her own right'.[187] Although this oversight may ultimately give rise to little substantive difference, this approach fails to 'raise children's profile as rights holders'.[188]

The second concern derives from the restricted scope of art 8, which requires an interference with an individual's private life or family life. This requirement may cause difficulties for children in migration cases where the art 8 right is not engaged. For example, in a case involving the removal of an unaccompanied child there will generally be no interference with the child's family life and, depending on the length of time that the child has been in the host state, potentially no interference with the child's private life.

---

[180] *CW (Jamaica) v SSHD* [2013] EWCA Civ 915; *AJ (Bangladesh) v SSHD* [2013] EWCA Civ 493; *SS (Nigeria) v SSHD* [2014] 1 WLR 998; *Ogundimu v SSHD* [2013] UKUT 00060; *Sanade v SSHD* [2012] UKUT 00048; *Lee v SSHD* [2011] EWCA Civ 348; *Omotunde v SSHD* [2011] UKUT 00247; *T v SSHD* (SIAC, Appeal No SC/31/2005, 22 March 2010).

[181] *R (AA) v Upper Tribunal* [2012] EWHC 1784 (Admin); *FM (Afghanistan) v SSHD* (Upper Tribunal, AA/01079/2010, 10 March 2011), [159]–[161].

[182] *Mundeba v Entry Clearance Officer, Nairobi* [2013] UKUT 00088; *Muse v Entry Clearance Officer* [2012] EWCA Civ 10; *Entry Clearance Officer v T* [2011] UKUT 00483; *R (SS) v SSHD* [2011] EWHC 3390 (Admin). These cases demonstrate that in the UK, although s 55 of the *Borders, Citizenship and Immigration Act 2009*, c 11, does not apply to children outside the UK, the broader obligation imposed under art 3 of the *CRC* continues to inform the art 8(2) proportionality assessment.

[183] *R (MXL) v SSHD* [2010] EWHC 2397 (Admin).

[184] *R (Tinizaray) v SSHD* [2011] EWHC 1850 (Admin). Although the denial of permanent residence did not automatically give rise to removal or deportation, the Court considered that that did 'not reduce or minimise the [Secretary of State's] duty to take account of the best interests of any child directly affected by that applicant and its possible refusal': at [12].

[185] 'The evolution of the United Kingdom's attitude to the rights of children when immigration decisions fall to be taken has thus been from a position in which the maintenance of immigration control was expressly preserved as the primary consideration by the reservation entered by the United Kingdom to the Convention to a position now in which the United Kingdom must treat the best interests of a child as "a primary consideration" when an immigration decision is to be taken affecting him or her': *R (Reece-Davis) v SSHD* [2011] EWHC 561 (Admin), [22].

[186] Fortin, *supra* n 172, 960.

[187] *Ibid.*   [188] *Ibid.*

Similarly, the removal or deportation of a parent where the child will accompany the parent will, again, generally not constitute an interference with family life, although it may interfere with the parent and/or child's private life.[189] The question that arises is this: if there is no interference with a parent or child's private or family life, can the best interests principle still prevent the removal of a parent and/or a child? Does the best interests principle have a role to play independently of art 8? As a matter of international law the answer must be yes. Although the Strasbourg court is jurisdictionally tied to the provisions of the *ECHR* – albeit interpreting those provisions taking into account the wider international human rights framework – at the international level the best interests principle in art 3 of the *CRC* has an independent existence and may apply in cases where there has been no interference with an art 8 right.

As the jurisprudence on art 8 continues to develop in the United Kingdom, decision-makers are beginning to acknowledge the wider application of the best interests principle.[190] The independent operation of art 3 was acknowledged by the Supreme Court in the case of *Re E (Children) (Abduction: Custody Appeal)*, where Baroness Hale held that the circumstances undoubtedly engaged the applicants' 'article 8 rights, as well as the obligation under article 3.1 of [the *CRC*] to make [the child's] welfare a primary consideration'.[191] In *SS (Sri Lanka) v SSHD*, the Court of Appeal acknowledged that the removal of a mother and her two children would not infringe the applicant's art 8 rights, but determined that the tribunal had nevertheless erred by failing to 'consider the best interest of the children'.[192] In the case of *DS (Afghanistan) v SSHD*, the Court of Appeal noted that the statements of principle regarding the best interests principle set out in *ZH (Tanzania) v SSHD* 'cannot [be] read . . . as being confined to article 8(2) considerations'.[193] The High Court of England and Wales has been particularly explicit:[194]

> In the three cases relied upon . . . the consideration of the best interests principle took place in the context of Article 8 ECHR. That is hardly surprising given that section 55 was not in force; no doubt when Article 8 is raised on behalf of a particular child that will continue notwithstanding the enactment of section 55. It does seem to me to be clear, however, that the obligation arising under section 55 of the Act to have regard to the need to safeguard and promote the welfare of the child arises independently of whether Article 8 is relied upon in a particular case.

---

[189] See, e.g., *MK (best interests of child) India* [2011] UKUT 00475, [36] ('[t]here is no issue of separation: the whole family goes or the whole family stays; that is fully agreed by the SSHD and the claimant. That means in this case that if removed, the return of the claimant and his family would not involve any disruption of their family life'); *R (EM) (Eritrea) v SSHD* [2013] 1 WLR 576, [66].

[190] See, e.g., Blake (2011) *supra* n 101, 10.

[191] *Re E (Children) (Abduction: Custody Appeal)* [2012] 1 AC 144, [50].

[192] *SS (Sri Lanka) v SSHD* [2012] EWCA Civ 945, [19].

[193] *DS (Afghanistan) v SSHD* [2011] EWCA Civ 305, [22].

[194] *R (TS) v SSHD* [2010] EWHC 2614 (Admin), [56]. See also *FM (Afghanistan) v SSHD* (Upper Tribunal, AA/01079/2010, 10 March 2011), [108] ('[w]hilst this case is about the expulsion of a lone child who is separated from his family, it is unlikely that his best interests are to be treated as of less importance or significance in law than those of a child whom it is proposed to expel accompanied by a family member or members'); *HS v SSHD* [2010] CSIH 97, [8], [12] (the argument that art 3 has autonomous operation was raised by the applicant, but the court considered that the 'question of whether [CRC] Article 3 provides a person with a "stand alone" legal remedy' did not arise); *JO and others (section 55 duty) Nigeria* [2014] UKUT 00517, [7] (noting that art 8 and s 55 of the *Borders, Citizenship and Immigration Act 2009*, c 11, have 'separate juridical identities'); *MK (section 55 – Tribunal options) Sierra Leone* [2015] UKUT 00223, [22]; *RA v SSHD* [2015] UKUT 00242; *RA v SSHD* [2015] UKUT 00292.

In the majority of cases little will turn on whether a decision-maker applies art 3 directly or indirectly via art 8, as either route will achieve the same result. There will, however, be situations involving the removal of a child that will not engage art 8. For those cases, the judicial acknowledgement that art 3 has an autonomous existence, and may provide an independent basis for affording protection, is significant.

6.3.3 The Removal of a Parent Where the Child Has a Right to Remain

The best interests principle has also played a critical role outside of Europe in cases involving the removal of a parent where the child has the legal right to remain. One of the first decisions to discuss the role of the best interests principle in this context was the decision of the High Court of Australia in *MIEA v Teoh*.[195] The case involved a Malaysian citizen with an Australian-citizen wife, three Australian-born children and four Australian-born stepchildren. Mr Teoh's application for residency status was rejected on character grounds because he had been convicted of drug offences. He sought judicial review of that decision. The High Court held that the primary decision-maker had committed an error of law by failing to treat the best interests of Mr Teoh's children as a primary consideration. The majority of the High Court considered that Australia's ratification of the *CRC* generated a legitimate expectation that decision-makers would act in conformity with it, including art 3.[196] According to Mason CJ and Deane J, '[a] decision-maker with an eye to the principle enshrined in the [*CRC*] would be looking to the best interests of the children as a primary consideration, asking whether the force of any other consideration outweighed it'.[197] The High Court concluded that in refusing to grant Mr Teoh residency status the primary decision-maker had treated the government's character policy, rather than the best interests of Mr Teoh's children, as the primary consideration.

Subsequent decisions have confirmed that the reasoning in *MIEA v Teoh* applies both to the situation where the removal of a parent will force the separation of the child and parent, as was the scenario in *MIEA v Teoh*, and to the situation where the child is constructively deported because she will voluntarily accompany the parent upon departure. Thus, in *Vaitaiki v MIEA*,[198] the Full Court of the Federal Court of Australia held that the primary decision-maker had erred in failing to give regard to the fact that, by accompanying their father to Tonga, the Australian-citizen children 'would have to leave the community in which they had lived all of their respective lives, start a new life in a new land, and lose the many benefits available to them as citizens of Australia'.[199] This decision was followed in

---

[195] *MIEA v Teoh* (1995) 183 CLR 273. [196] *Ibid.*, 291 (Mason CJ and Deane J). [197] *Ibid.*, 292.
[198] *Vaitaiki v MIEA* (1998) 150 ALR 608.
[199] *Ibid.*, 631 (Branson J). See also at 614 (Burchett J): 'This leaves out of account that the children, as citizens, would be deprived of the country of their own and their mother's citizenship under our law ... and of its protection and support, socially, culturally and medically, and in the many other ways evoked by, but not confined to, the broad concept of lifestyle. It ignores the social and linguistic disruption of their childhood, as well as the loss of their homeland. It ignores educational problems ... And it ignores the fact that these young children would not only be transported to a foreign environment, very different from that in which they have grown up thus far, but would also be isolated there from the normal contacts of children with their mother's family, who live in Sydney, and their father's mother and sisters, who also live here.'

Wan v MIMA, where the Full Court provided a list of factors to be considered where it is likely that the child will accompany her parent to their home country.[200]

> (a) the fact that the children, as citizens of Australia, would be deprived of the country of their own and their mother's citizenship, 'and of its protection and support, socially, culturally and medically, and in the many other ways evoked by, but not confined to, the broad concept of lifestyle' (*Vaitaiki* per Burchett J . . .);
> (b) the resultant social and linguistic disruption of their childhood as well as the loss of their homeland;
> (c) the loss of educational opportunities available to the children in Australia; and
> (d) their resultant isolation from the normal contacts of children with their mother and their mother's family.

In *Wan v MIMA*, the Court acknowledged that the identification of what the best interests of Mr Wan's children required would 'not have led inexorably'[201] to a decision in conformity with those interests, so long as the decision-maker did 'not treat any other consideration as inherently more significant than the best interests of Mr Wan's children'.[202]

The decision of the High Court in *MIEA v Teoh*, and its subsequent application in *Vaitaiki v MIEA* and *Wan v MIMA*, has been endorsed widely both within Australia[203] and internationally.[204] In Australia, the jurisprudence has been supplemented with the publication of a series of ministerial directions that stipulate that the best interests of any child must be a primary consideration in deciding whether to refuse or cancel a parent's visa.[205]

In Canada, the leading decision is *Baker v Canada (MCI)*, which involved a Jamaican national who had been served with a deportation order after it was established that she had worked illegally in Canada and overstayed her visitor's visa. Ms Baker applied for humanitarian protection under what was then s 114(2) of the *Immigration Act*,[206] principally on the basis that her deportation would be contrary to the best interests of her children. The certified question for the Supreme Court was whether, in the absence of express reference to the *CRC* in domestic immigration legislation, decision-makers were required to treat the best interests of children as a primary consideration in assessing an application

---

[200] *Wan v MIMA* (2001) 107 FCR 133, [30] (citations omitted).   [201] *Ibid.*, [32].   [202] *Ibid.*

[203] See, e.g., *Santhirarajah v Attorney-General* [2012] FCA 940; *Tauariki v MIAC* [2012] FCA 1408, [48]; *Lesianawai v MIAC* [2012] FCA 897, [32]–[36]; *Nweke v MIAC* [2012] FCA 266, [10]–[16]. The Australian government has, with some success, attempted to limit the reach of *MIEA v Teoh* (1995) 183 CLR 273: see, e.g., *Re MIMIA; Ex parte Lam* (2003) 214 CLR 1; *Basile v MIAC* (2011) 193 FCR 329, [46]; *Baker v MIAC* [2012] FCAFC 145, [56].

[204] See, e.g., *ZH (Tanzania) v SSHD* [2011] 2 AC 166, [26], citing *MIEA v Teoh* (1995) 183 CLR 273, 292, and *Wan v MIMA* (2001) 107 FCR 133, [32].

[205] See, e.g., MIAC, *Direction No 55 – Visa Refusal and Cancellation under s 501* (25 July 2012), [9.3(1)], [11.2(1)]), which directs that '[d]ecision-makers must make a determination about whether [cancellation/removal] is, or is not, in the best interests of the child'. The *Direction*, at [9.3(4)] and [11.2(4)], lists a number of factors which must be considered in assessing the best interests of the child: '(a) The nature and duration of the relationship between the child and the person . . .; (b) The extent to which the person is likely to play a positive parental role in the future . . .; (c) The impact of the person's prior conduct, and any likely future conduct, . . . on the child; (d) The likely effect [of] separation . . .; (e) Whether there are other persons who already fulfill a parental role in relation to the child; (f) Any known views of the child . . .; (g) Evidence that the person has abused or neglected the child . . .; and (h) Evidence that the child has suffered or experienced any physical or emotional trauma arising from the person's conduct.'

[206] RSC 1985, c I-2.

for humanitarian protection. The majority of the Supreme Court answered affirmatively. Although the majority held that the *CRC* had no direct application in Canadian law, it considered that 'the values reflected in international human rights law may help inform the contextual approach to statutory interpretation and judicial review'.[207] Specifically,[208]

> [t]he values and principles of the [*CRC*] recognize the importance of being attentive to the rights and best interests of children when decisions are made that relate to and affect their future ... The principles of the [*CRC*] and other international instruments place special importance on protections for children and childhood, and on particular consideration of their interests, needs, and rights. They help show the values that are central in determining whether this decision was a reasonable exercise of the [humanitarian and compassionate] power.

Applying this reasoning, the Supreme Court determined that in assessing an application for humanitarian protection 'the decision-maker should consider children's best interests as an important factor, give them substantial weight, and be alert, alive and sensitive to them'.[209] The Court emphasised that the best interests will not always be determinative, but considered that 'where the interests of children are minimized, in a manner inconsistent with Canada's humanitarian and compassionate tradition and the Minister's guidelines, the decision will be unreasonable'.[210]

The requirement specified in *Baker v Canada (MCI)* has since been codified in s 25(1) of the *Immigration and Refugee Protection Act*,[211] which mandates that in exercising the discretion to grant humanitarian protection the Minister must 'tak[e] into account the best interests of a child directly affected'.[212] The provision has been supplemented by departmental guidelines, which provide guidance on the matters which decision-makers ought to consider in assessing a child's best interests.[213] The Supreme Court's decision in *Baker v Canada (MCI)* and its subsequent codification have given rise to a considerable body of case-law on the application of the best interests principle in decisions involving the deportation of a child's parent[214] and, as the discussion below demonstrates, more generally.[215] Similar to the

---

[207] *Baker v Canada (MCI)* [1999] 2 SCR 817, [70].   [208] *Ibid.*, [71].   [209] *Ibid.*, [75].   [210] *Ibid.*
[211] SC 2001, c 27.
[212] A child may also apply directly for humanitarian protection under s 25(1) of the *Immigration and Refugee Protection Act*, SC 2001, c 27: see *infra* text accompanying n 231. Section 25(1) is bolstered by s 3(3)(f), which provides that the Act is to be construed and applied in a manner that 'complies with international human rights instruments to which Canada is signatory'. In *De Guzman v Canada (MCI)* [2006] 3 FCR 655, [82]–[83], the Federal Court of Appeal confirmed that s 3(3)(f) 'attaches more than mere ambiguity-resolving, contextual significance' to international human rights instruments, requiring the Act to be 'interpreted and applied consistently with an instrument to which paragraph 3(3)(f) applies, unless, on the modern approach to statutory interpretation, this is impossible'.
[213] CIC, *IP 5: Immigrant Applications in Canada Made on Humanitarian or Compassionate Grounds* (1 April 2011), [5.12]. For example, these guidelines provide that '[t]he relationship between the applicant and "any child directly affected" need not necessarily be that of parent and child, but could be another relationship that is affected by the decision. For example, a grandparent could be the primary caregiver who is affected by an immigration decision and the decision may thus affect the child.'
[214] See, e.g., *Denis v Canada (MCI)* 2015 FC 65; *Mangru v Canada (MCI)* [2011] FCJ No 978; *Okoloubu v Canada (MCI)* [2008] FCJ No 1495; *Kolosovs v Canada (MCI)* [2008] FCJ No 211; *Raposo v Canada (MCI)* [2005] FCJ No 157; *Cordeiro v Canada (MCI)* [2004] FCJ No 179; *Hawthorne v Canada (MCI)* [2003] 2 FC 555; *Legault v Canada (MCI)* [2002] 4 FC 358; *Garasova v Canada (MCI)* (1999) 177 FTR 76.
[215] See *infra* text accompanying n 243–53.

Australian case-law, the Canadian jurisprudence makes clear that in cases involving the deportation of a parent, the decision-maker must consider both 'the benefit to the child of the parent's non-removal from Canada as well as the hardship the child would suffer from either her parent's removal from Canada or her own voluntary departure should she wish to accompany her parent abroad'.[216] According to the Federal Court of Appeal, '[s]uch benefits and hardships are two sides of the same coin, the coin being the best interests of the child'.[217]

In New Zealand, recourse to the best interests principle is mediated via the *Immigration Act 2009* (NZ), which allows a parent to appeal against deportation on humanitarian grounds where '[t]here are exceptional circumstances of a humanitarian nature that would make it unjust or unduly harsh for the appellant to be deported from New Zealand' and '[i]t would not in all the circumstances be contrary to the public interest to allow the appellant to remain in New Zealand'.[218] In *Ye v Minister of Immigration*[219] – a case involving two families, each containing New Zealand-born children and Chinese national parents at risk of removal – the New Zealand Supreme Court held that New Zealand's immigration legislation must be interpreted in a way that is consistent with New Zealand's obligations under the *CRC* and, in particular, the requirement that 'in all actions concerning children, by public and administrative authorities, the best interests of the child shall be a "primary consideration"'.[220] This means that in considering a parent's humanitarian appeal it is necessary to consider 'who will care for the child, and the nature and extent of the difficulties the child may face in remaining in New Zealand without parents' or, if the child is to leave New Zealand, 'the nature and extent of any problems the child may face if returned to the parent's home country'.[221]

In the United States, the best interests principle has played a more limited although not inconsequential role in decisions involving the removal of a parent. The principal route for challenging removal is on the basis that removal will cause 'exceptional and extremely unusual hardship to the [non-citizen's] spouse, parent, or child, who is a citizen of the United States or [a non-citizen] lawfully admitted for permanent residence'.[222] Although the statutory criterion directs the decision-maker to consider the impact that a parent's removal will have on a child, the 'exceptional and extremely unusual hardship' threshold

---

[216] *Hawthorne v Canada (MCI)* [2003] 2 FC 555, [4].   [217] *Ibid.*

[218] *Immigration Act 2009* (NZ) s 207. A child may also apply directly for protection under s 207: see *infra* text accompanying n 232.

[219] *Ye v Minister of Immigration* [2009] NZSC 76. See also *Huang v Minister of Immigration* [2009] NZSC 77, handed down concurrently.

[220] *Ye v Minister of Immigration* [2009] NZSC 76, [24]; see also at [25] ('[i]t is appropriate, in the light of New Zealand's obligations under art 3(1), to interpret the relevant provisions of the Immigration Act so that the interests of New Zealand citizen children are always regarded as an important consideration in the decision-making processes'). The Supreme Court thus affirmed the decision of the High Court (*Ding v Minister of Immigration* (2006) 25 FRNZ 568) and Court of Appeal (*Ye v Minister of Immigration* [2008] NZCA 291). This accords with the approach taken in earlier New Zealand authority: see, e.g., *A v Chief Executive, Department of Labour* [2001] NZAR 981; *Puli'uvea v Removal Review Authority* (1996) 14 FRNZ 322 (leave to appeal to the Privy Council refused in *Puli'uvea v Removal Review Authority* [1996] 3 NZLR 538); *Elika v Minister of Immigration* [1996] 1 NZLR 741; *Tavita v Minister of Immigration* [1994] 2 NZLR 257.

[221] *Ye v Minister of Immigration* [2009] NZSC 76, [42].   [222] 8 USC §1229b(b)(1).

is difficult to satisfy.[223] Moreover, US courts have generally proven reluctant to draw on international human rights standards in adjudicating removal decisions.[224] There are exceptions, although they are few and far between. In *Beharry v Reno*, a US District Court held that the absence of a best interests assessment in removal proceedings violated international law and, in particular, the requirement that 'the best interests of the child must be considered where possible'.[225] That conclusion is grounded in a more far-reaching ruling that the *CRC* should be read as customary international law[226] and that immigration legislation should be interpreted in a way that does not violate that customary law.[227]

More recently, the Court of Appeals for the Ninth Circuit considered the application of the best interests principle in *Cabrera-Alvarez v Gonzales*. The petitioners in that case argued that the 'exceptional and extremely unusual hardship' standard in 8 USC §1229b(b) should be interpreted 'consistently with the "best interests of the child" principle by giving the child's best interests extra weight in balancing the factors relevant to evaluating a hardship'.[228] Although the Court of Appeals accepted that the best interests principle was applicable to proceedings involving the deportation of a parent,[229] it considered that §1229b(b) was compatible with art 3 of the *CRC* on the basis that 'the child's interests are *already* a primary consideration in the agency's decision whether to grant cancellation of

---

[223] See, e.g., the discussion in *Re Monreal-Aguinaga*, 23 I & N Dec 56, 59 (BIA, 2001), citing the legislative history which makes clear that the standard was intended to emphasise that 'the alien must provide evidence of harm to his spouse, parent, or child *substantially beyond that which ordinarily would be expected to result from the alien's deportation*' (emphasis in original). For one of very few published examples of a case that did satisfy the threshold, see *Re Recinas*, 23 I & N Dec 467 (BIA, 2002), a case involving a single mother with six children, including four US-citizen children. The four citizen children had never been to Mexico, were unfamiliar with the Spanish language, and the applicant had no family or support structure in Mexico. The BIA considered that the case fell 'on the outer limit of the narrow spectrum of cases in which the exceptional and extremely unusual hardship standard will be met': at 470. See, generally, D Thronson, 'Thinking Small: The Need for Big Changes in Immigration Law's Treatment of Children' (2010) 14 *UC Davis Journal of Juvenile Law and Policy* 239; P Glen, 'The Removability of Non-Citizen Parents and the Best Interests of Citizen Children: How to Balance Competing Imperatives in the Context of Removal Proceedings?' (2012) 30 *Berkeley Journal of International Law* 1.

[224] The failure of the United States to routinely assess the best interests of the child in removal decisions has been challenged before the Inter-American Commission on Human Rights, which concluded that 'removal proceedings for non-citizens must take due consideration of the best interests of the non-citizens' children and a deportee's right to family, in accordance with international law': *Smith v US*, Case 12.562, IACHR (Ser C) No 81/10, 12 July 2010 [57].

[225] *Beharry v Reno* 183 F Supp 2d 584, 604 (ED NY, 2002).

[226] *Ibid.*, 601 ('[g]iven its widespread acceptance, to the extent that it acts to codify longstanding, widely-accepted principles of law, the CRC should be read as customary international law').

[227] *Ibid.*, 604. The Second Circuit Court of Appeals reversed the District Court's decision on procedural grounds, but declined to discuss its treatment of international law: *Beharry v Ashcroft*, 329 F 3d 51 (2nd Cir, 2003). However, in subsequent cases the Second Circuit has rejected the reliance on international human rights law promoted in *Beharry v Reno*: see, e.g., *Guaylupo-Moya v Gonzales*, 432 F 3d 121 (2nd Cir, 2005).

[228] *Cabrera-Alvarez v Gonzales*, 423 F 3d 1006, 1010 (9th Cir, 2005).

[229] In so finding, the Court relied on the decisions in *MIEA v Teoh* (1995) 183 CLR 273 and *Baker v Canada (MCI)* [1999] 2 SCR 817: see *Cabrera-Alvarez*, 1011. As regards the status of the *CRC* in the United States, the Court 'assum[ed], without deciding, that the [CRC] ha[d] attained the status of "customary international law"': at 1007.

removal' and the Court did 'not see how the terms of the [CRC] dictate the amorphous "extra weight" that Petitioner contends is required'.[230]

6.3.4 The Discretionary Grant of Protection to Children on Humanitarian Grounds

An increasing number of states have introduced discretionary humanitarian protection schemes that require decision-makers to apply the best interests principle in any removal decision involving a child. This includes cases where the child is the principal applicant. By way of illustration, and as already touched upon above, Canadian legislation mandates that in exercising the discretion to grant humanitarian protection the Minister must 'tak[e] into account the best interests of a child directly affected'.[231] The comparable New Zealand statutory humanitarian protection scheme has been interpreted to require the decision-maker to treat the best interests of the child as a primary consideration.[232] In Australia the process is less transparent, with the Minister retaining a non-compellable and non-reviewable discretion to grant protection '[i]f the Minister thinks it is in the public interest to do so'.[233] Published guidelines provide that, in exercising the discretion, the Minister should take into account circumstances that may enliven Australia's obligations under the CRC, including art 3.[234] Several European states have legislated to mandate that the best

---

[230] *Cabrera-Alvarez v Gonzales*, 423 F 3d 1006, 1011-12 (9th Cir, 2005) ('When an alien parent seeks cancellation of removal because of exceptional and extremely unusual hardship to a qualifying child … that child's "best interests" are precisely the issue before the agency, in the sense that "best interests" are merely the converse of "hardship." In other words, the agency's entire inquiry focuses on the qualifying children, making their interests a "primary consideration" in the cancellation-of-removal analysis').

[231] *Immigration and Refugee Protection Act*, SC 2001, c 27, s 25(1). See *supra* text accompanying n 211–12.

[232] See generally *supra* text accompanying n 218–21. For examples see *AD (Nigeria)* [2012] NZIPT 500451, [52] (allowing the humanitarian appeal of a Nigerian mother and three Nigerian children on the basis that it would be contrary to their best interests to 'face an entirely uncertain future in Nigeria with [their mother], a person with limited intellectual and emotional skills'); *BP (Iran)* [2012] NZIPT 500965 (allowing the humanitarian appeal of a ten-year-old Iranian girl, where her parents had been recognised as refugees and it was in her best interests to remain with them); *BL (Iran)* [2012] NZIPT 500963 (allowing the humanitarian appeal of a five-year-old Iranian boy, where his parents had been recognised as refugees and it was in his best interests to remain with them); *AD (Czech Republic)* [2012] NZIPT 500876 (allowing the humanitarian appeal of a seven-year-old girl from the Czech Republic, where her parents and brother had been recognised as refugees and it was in her best interests to remain with them); *AH (South Africa)* [2011] NZIPT 500228 (allowing the humanitarian appeal of a South African mother and her five-month-old son in circumstances where they were both at risk of harm from an ex-boyfriend and his gang associates); *AH (Iran)* [2011] NZIPT 500395 (allowing the humanitarian appeal of a ten-year-old Iranian boy, where his parents had been recognised as refugees and it was in his best interests to remain with them).

[233] *Migration Act 1958* (Cth) ss 351, 417, 501J. For a discussion on this 'public interest' power, which has been the subject of extensive criticism, see Foster and Pobjoy (2009) *supra* n 33.

[234] MIAC, *Minister's Guidelines on Ministerial Power (s 345, s 351, s 391, s 417, s 454 and s 501J)* (P A098, 24 March 2012), [12]. See also MIAC, *Administration of Ministerial Powers* (P A124, 24 March 2012), [15.3], which sets out further detail on factors to be considered in assessing the best interests of a child. As a matter of practice, the RRT may, where a child is ineligible for refugee protection, refer cases to the Minister for consideration: see, e.g., *1206440* [2013] RRTA 102, [45]–[50]; *1113067* [2012] RRTA 982, [95]–[96]; *1201414* [2012] RRTA 410, *1201414* [2012] RRTA 410, [50]; *1103115* [2011] RRTA 434, [32]–[33]; *1102118* [2011] RRTA 415, [63]; *1100862* [2011] RRTA 291, [50]–[51].

interests of the child be considered in assessing whether a child should be granted a humanitarian protection status, including Sweden,[235] Finland[236] and Norway.[237]

The discussion that follows briefly examines two case studies: Norway and Canada.

In Norway, the best interests principle plays an increasingly central role in the assessment of humanitarian protection claims involving children. Section 38 of the *Immigration Act*,[238] which came into force in January 2010, provides that '[i]n cases concerning children, the best interests of the child shall be a fundamental consideration' and that '[c]hildren may be granted a residence permit [on humanitarian grounds] even if the situation is not so serious that a residence permit would have been granted to an adult'. Prior to the passage of the reformulated *Immigration Act*, the best interests principle already played a significant role in humanitarian protection decisions as a result of the incorporation of the CRC into national human rights legislation in 2003.[239] In a study published in 2009, Vitus and Lidén identify a number of patterns in the assessment of humanitarian claims concerning children, observing that humanitarian protection is granted primarily in cases where a child has serious health problems or where there will be insufficient care for the child in their country of origin.[240] The authors suggest that protection has also typically been granted in cases involving single mothers without significant family networks in their home country, where the child will be returned to a country in conflict, or where there is a risk of a harmful traditional practice such as FGC.[241] Decision-makers have also taken into account the child's attachment to Norway and the child's need for stability.[242]

The legislative framework in Canada provides the Minister with discretion to grant permanent residence on humanitarian and compassionate grounds (often referred to as 'H&C protection'). In exercising that discretion, the Minister must 'tak[e] into account the best interests of a child directly affected'.[243] The Canadian Supreme Court has made clear that '[b]ecause children may experience greater hardship than adults faced with

---

[235] See ch 1 s 10 of the Swedish *Aliens Act* (2005:716), which provides that '[i]n cases involving a child, particular attention must be given to what is required with regard to the child's health and development and the best interests of the child in general'. This provision was introduced in 1997 following Sweden's ratification of the CRC. See generally Lundberg (2011) *supra* n 106; M Eastmond and H Ascher, 'In the Best Interest of the Child? The Politics of Vulnerability and Negotiations for Asylum in Sweden' (2011) 37(8) *Journal of Ethnic and Migration Studies* 1185.

[236] See s 6 of the Finnish *Aliens Act* (301/2004), which provides that in any decision concerning children 'special attention shall be paid to the best interests of the child and to circumstances related to the child's development and health'. This direction applies to applications for residence on humanitarian grounds. See generally A Parsons, *The Best Interests of the Child in Asylum and Refugee Procedures in Finland* (2010).

[237] See s 38 of the *Act of 15 May 2008 on the Entry of Foreign Nationals into the Kingdom of Norway and Their Stay in the Realm (Immigration Act)*.

[238] *Act of 15 May 2008 on the Entry of Foreign Nationals into the Kingdom of Norway and Their Stay in the Realm (Immigration Act)*.

[239] By way of amendment to the Norwegian *Act No 30 of 21 May 1999 Relating to the Strengthening of the Status of Human Rights in Norwegian Law (The Human Rights Act)*.

[240] K Vitus and H Lidén, 'The Status of the Asylum-Seeking Child in Norway and Denmark: Comparing Discourses, Politics and Practices' (2010) 23(1) *Journal of Refugee Studies* 62, 74.

[241] *Ibid.*

[242] *Ibid.* See also H Lidén and H Rusten, 'Asylum, Participation and the Best Interests of the Child: New Lessons from Norway' (2007) 21 *Children and Society* 273.

[243] *Immigration and Refugee Protection Act*, SC 2001, c 27, s 25(1).

a comparable situation, circumstances which may not warrant humanitarian and compassionate relief when applied to an adult, may nonetheless entitle a child to relief.[244]

The Minister has issued departmental guidelines to guide decision-makers in the assessment of a child's best interests,[245] which, as noted in Section 6.3.3, have been supplemented by a considerable body of case-law. The guidelines make clear that the phrase 'child directly affected' is to be construed broadly, capturing a 'Canadian or foreign-born child' in addition to 'children outside Canada'.[246] The humanitarian route may thus apply to a child in a range of situations, including cases involving the deportation of the parent of a citizen-child,[247] cases where a child has no legal right to remain and is herself at risk of removal[248] and cases where a child, presently outside of Canada, seeks entry into Canada in order to be reunited with parents and/or siblings.[249] The departmental guidelines state that in assessing a child's best interests it is necessary to take into account the child's 'emotional, social, cultural and physical welfare',[250] providing a non-exhaustive list of relevant factors.[251] The guidelines also emphasise that the codification of the best interests principle into legislation '*does not mean* that the interests of the child outweigh all other factors in a case.'[252] Rather, '[w]hile factors affecting children should be given substantial weight, the best interests of a child is only one of many important factors that officers need to consider'.[253]

---

[244] *Kanthasamy v Canada (MCI)* [2015] 3 SCR 909, [41].

[245] CIC, *IP5, supra* n 213, [5.12]. See also CIC, *OP 4: The Processing of Applications That Include a Request for Humanitarian and Compassionate or Public Policy Consideration* (26 February 2013). There is uncertainty as to whether 'child' should also be construed broadly, so as to include adults in child-like states (for example, due to ongoing dependency or a disability). A series of decisions of the Federal Court favour such a wider reading: see *Naredo v Canada (MCI)* [2000] FCJ No 1250; *Swartz v Canada (MCI)* 2002 FCT 268; *Yoo v Canada (MCI)* 2009 FC 343; *Ramsawak v Canada (MCI)* [2009] FCJ No 1387; *Noh v Canada (MCI)* [2012] FCJ No 774. This line of authority has, however, been challenged in *Leobrera v Canada (MCI)* [2010] FCJ No 692, *Moya v Canada (MCI)* 2012 FC 971 and *Norbert v Canada (MCI)* 2014 FC 409.

[246] CIC, *IP5* (2011) *supra* n 213, [5.12].   [247] See *supra* Section 6.3.3.

[248] See, e.g., *Lu v Canada (MCI)* 2016 FC 175; *Kanthasamy v Canada (MCI)* [2015] 3 SCR 909; *Lauture v Canada (MCI)* 2015 FC 336; *Kaneza v Canada (MCI)* 2015 FC 231; *Sun v Canada (MCI)* [2012] FCJ No 218; *Noh v Canada (MCI)* 2012 FC 529; *EB v Canada (MCI)* [2011] FCJ No 134; *Duka v Canada (MCI)* [2010] FCJ No 1334; *Toney v Canada (MPSEP)* [2009] FCJ No 1128; *Hinzman v Canada (MCI)* [2009] FCJ No 521; *Ferrer v Canada (MCI)* [2009] FCJ No 440; *Diakité v Canada (MCI)* [2009] FCJ No 217; *Joe v Canada (MCI)* [2009] FCJ No 176; *Makias v Canada (MPSEP)* [2008] FCJ No 1534; *Patel v Canada (MCI)* [2005] FCJ No 1305; *Ek v Canada (MCI)* [2003] FCJ No 680; *Koud v Canada (MCI)* 2001 FCT 856.

[249] See, e.g., *Kobita v Canada (MCI)* [2012] FCJ No 1580; *Kisana v Canada (MCI)* [2009] FCJ No 713; *Gill v Canada (MCI)* [2008] FCJ No 780.

[250] CIC, *IP5* (2011) *supra* n 213, [5.12].

[251] 'The age of the child; the level of dependency between the child and the H&C [humanitarian and compassionate] applicant or the child and their sponsor; the degree of the child's establishment in Canada; the child's links to the country in relation to which the H&C assessment is being considered; the conditions of that country and the potential impact on the child; medical issues or special needs the child may have; the impact to the child's education; and matters related to the child's gender': *ibid.*

[252] *Ibid.* (emphasis in original).

[253] CIC, *IP5, supra* n 213, [5.12]. The 'substantial weight' language derives from the decision of the Supreme Court in *Baker v Canada (MCI)* [1999] 2 SCR 817, [75]. The Canadian case-law evinces some confusion as to the appropriate weight to be accorded to the best interests of children: see Canadian Council for Refugees, United Church of Canada and International Bureau for Children's Rights, 'The Understanding and Application of "Best Interests of the Child" in H & C Decision-Making by Citizenship and Immigration Canada' (Report, September 2008) 19.

6.3.5 Special Protection Measures for Unaccompanied Children

As a response to the distinct challenges presented by the increase in the arrival of unaccompanied children, a number of jurisdictions have introduced special protection measures specifically targeted at this subset of children. The EU has been particularly proactive in this area. In 2010 the European Commission published the four-year *Unaccompanied Minors Action Plan*,[254] which was followed by the adoption of Council Conclusions on the same issue.[255] Both are underpinned by the best interests principle.[256] The *Action Plan* recommends that 'where return is not possible or integration in the country of residence is considered in the best interests of the child, a legal status should be granted to unaccompanied minors' and these children 'should be supported in their path toward successful integration in the host society'.[257] The Council Conclusions encourage member states to 'adopt a decision on the future of each [unaccompanied minor] ... taking into account the importance of finding durable solutions based on an individual assessment of the best interests of the child'. According to the Conclusions, those solutions could consist of 'return and reintegration in the country of origin or return, granting international protection status or granting other status according to national law of the Member States'.[258]

A number of European states have now introduced special protection statuses for unaccompanied children, which incorporate a requirement to consider the best interests of the child.[259] By way of illustration, in the United Kingdom an unaccompanied child will not be removed unless the Secretary of State is satisfied that there are 'adequate reception arrangements' in place in the child's home country.[260] These children are granted a form of limited leave until they are seventeen-and-a-half years of age, at which point in time the leave to remain lapses. In assessing whether discretionary leave ought to be granted,

---

[254] European Commission, *Communication from the Commission to the European Parliament and the Council: Action Plan on Unaccompanied Minors (2010-2014)*, COM(2010)213. For an earlier review of EU policies on unaccompanied children, see S Ruxton, *Separated Children and EU Asylum and Immigration Policy* (2003).

[255] Council of the European Union, *Council Conclusions on Unaccompanied Minors – 3018th Justice and Home Affairs Council Meeting* (3 June 2010). See also Parliamentary Assembly, Council of Europe, 'Unaccompanied Children in Europe: Issues of Arrival, Stay and Return' (Report, Doc 12539, 21 March 2011). For developments, see European Commission, *Report from the Commission to the Council and the European Parliament: Mid-Term Report on the Implementation of the Action Plan on Unaccompanied Minors*, COM(2012)554, and the accompanying working document, European Commission, *Commission Staff Working Document on the Implementation of the Action Plan on Unaccompanied Minors*, SWD(2012)281.

[256] 'This common approach should be based on the respect for the rights of the child as set out in the EU Charter of Fundamental Rights and the [CRC], in particular the principle of "the best interests of the child" which must be the primary consideration in all action relating to children taken by public authorities': European Commission (2010) *supra* n 254, 2.

[257] *Ibid.*, 14.   [258] EU Council, *Conclusions on Unaccompanied Minors* (2010) *supra* n 255, [12].

[259] Two comparative studies provide a comprehensive overview of the policies on unaccompanied children adopted in each of the EU member states: France Terre D'Asile, *Right to Asylum for Unaccompanied Minors in the European Union: Comparative Study in the 27 EU Countries* (2012); European Migration Network, *Policies on Reception, Return and Integration Arrangements for, and Numbers of, Unaccompanied Minors – An EU Comparative Study* (2010).

[260] UKBA, *Asylum Process Guidance*, [17.7] and Home Office, *Processing Children's Asylum Claims*, 55, now incorporated into UK, *Immigration Rules*, para 352ZC.

decision-makers are instructed that 'the best interests of the child must be taken into account as a primary consideration in the decision'.[261]

The majority of unaccompanied children arriving in the United Kingdom are granted limited leave to remain rather than refugee or subsidiary protection status.[262] A number of commentators have suggested that these figures demonstrate an over-reliance on the grant of limited leave to remain, in circumstances where refugee status or another form of complementary protection would be more appropriate.[263] This is problematic in circumstances where children granted discretionary leave are afforded a more limited set of rights than beneficiaries of refugee or subsidiary protection status, and where the grant of limited leave limits a child's right to appeal against an unsuccessful refugee determination.[264]

In the United States an unaccompanied child may apply for a bespoke form of protection: special immigrant juvenile status ('SIJS'). In order to be eligible for SIJS a child (less than 21 years of age) must first be declared the dependent of a juvenile court or placed in the care of a child welfare agency. A state court must then decide that the child cannot be reunited with one or both parents because of abuse, abandonment, neglect or a similar reason, and that it is not otherwise in the child's best interests to return to her home country.[265] Critically, SIJS is the only form of protection in US immigration law that expressly incorporates the best interests principle as an eligibility requirement. For this subset of children, the SIJS creates a 'hybrid system' where non-immigration child welfare experts make the best interests determinations, and immigration officers address immigration matters such as inadmissibility and waivers.[266]

---

[261] UKBA, *Asylum Process Guidance*, [17.8]; Home Office, *Processing Children's Asylum Claims*, 57.

[262] In 2012, 870 decisions were reached for unaccompanied children: 332 children were granted discretionary leave to remain and 160 children were granted refugee status: see Home Office data table (vol 3) available at www.gov.uk/government/publications/immigration-statistics-october-to-december-2012/immigration-statistics-october-to-december-2012#asylum-part-2-appeals-unaccompanied-asylum-seeking-children-age-disputes-and-dependants.

[263] 'The research has shown that far too many legal representatives and local authorities do not take into account the implications of the difference between being granted limited leave and being granted refugee status and assume that as a separated child has been given discretionary leave to remain, he or she has partially succeeded in his or her application. Therefore, they do not advise or encourage the child to appeal against a refusal to grant him or her asylum': N Finch, 'Seeking Asylum Alone' in H Andersson et al. (eds), *The Asylum Seeking Child in Europe* (2005) 57, 59. See also Bolton (2012) *supra* n 106.

[264] See generally *FA (Iraq) v SSHD* [2010] 1 WLR 2545; *DS (Afghanistan) v SSHD* [2011] EWCA Civ 305; *TN v SSHD* [2011] EWHC 3296 (Admin); *KA (Afghanistan) v SSHD* [2013] 1WLR 615; *EU (Afghanistan) v SSHD* [2013] EWCA Civ 32; *TN (Afghanistan) v SSHD* [2014] 1 WLR 2095.

[265] 8 USC §1101(a)(27)(J) (2012). The findings of the state court do not bestow immigration status on an SIJS application, with the final decision resting with the USCIS. For a discussion on the legislative framework, see *Re the Welfare of DAM* (Minn Ct App, No A12-0427, 10 December 2012). That case involved an 18-year-old national of Honduras who had lived in the United States since he was five or six years old. His living situation was unstable: his parents had separated, both abused alcohol, and his father was physically violent towards him. The applicant applied for SIJS. The District Court accepted that the child had been placed in the custody of a state agency or department and that it would not be in the best interests of the child to return to Honduras because of his lack of ties there; however, it considered that reunification with his mother was possible. The Court of Appeals of Minnesota considered that the District Court had erred on the basis that the legislation only requires a finding that reunification with *one* of the child's parents is not viable – so it was sufficient that reunification with the applicant's father was not possible.

[266] Dalrymple (2006) *supra* n 106, 165.

The preceding overview of state practice demonstrates the capacity of art 3 to limit a state's ability to remove a child and/or a child's parent from its jurisdiction. Although states may have initially resisted the idea that art 3 may give rise to an independent source of protection status, the above discussion makes clear that the best interests principle is playing an increasingly central role in decisions involving the removal of children. The application of the best interests principle in a range of migration contexts and across multiple jurisdictions illustrates that the argument advanced in this chapter – that the best interests principle may give rise to an independent protection status – is not merely a theoretical aspiration but finds support in a fast-evolving body of regional and domestic jurisprudence that engages with art 3 to provide effective protection to children and their parents. That jurisprudence provides an important source of guidance for decision-makers tasked with considering the application of art 3 as an independent source of protection.

6.4 The Application of Article 3 as an Independent Source of Protection

How, then, should a decision-maker determine what is in the best interests of the child and whether those interests preclude the removal of the child from a host state? Although there is clear value in providing a general framework for the application of the best interests principle as an independent source of protection, it is important to emphasise that the best interests principle is, by its very design, a flexible and dynamic concept.[267] A best interests assessment must take place on a case-by-case-basis, taking into account the specific circumstances of the individual child.[268] There are, however, a number of signposts that are capable of guiding decision-makers in the application of art 3 of the *CRC* to situations where a child is at risk of removal. This section offers a detailed, though certainly not exhaustive, guide to the implementation of art 3 as an independent basis for international protection. These general principles derive principally from the jurisprudence developed in the various migration-related contexts discussed in Section 6.3.

Article 3 will be engaged wherever a child may be affected by an immigration decision.[269] In certain circumstances, art 3 will require a decision-maker to look beyond the claim

---

[267] UNCRC, *GC14*, [11]. As noted by McLachlin J of the Supreme Court of Canada, '[t]he multitude of factors that may impinge on the child's best interests make a measure of indeterminacy inevitable. A more precise test would risk sacrificing the child's best interests to expediency and certainty': *Gordon v Goertz* [1996] 2 SCR 27, [20]. See also *Kanthasamy v Canada (MCI)* [2015] 3 SCR 909, [35], noting that the best interests principle must 'be applied in a manner responsive to each child's particular age, capacity, needs and maturity'.

[268] 'These circumstances relate to the individual characteristics of the child or children concerned, such as, inter alia, age, sex, level of maturity, experience, belonging to a minority group, having a physical, sensory or intellectual disability, as well as the social and cultural context in which the child or children find themselves, such as the presence or absence of parents, whether the child lives with them, quality of the relationships between the child and his or her family or caregivers, the environment in relation to safety, the existence of quality alternative means available to the family, extended family or caregivers, etc': UNCRC, *GC14*, [48]. As UK Upper Tribunal has explained, '[e]very case will be intensively fact sensitive': *MK (section 55 – Tribunal options) Sierra Leone* [2015] UKUT 00223, [17].

[269] Although not without controversy, this may also require a decision-maker to take into account the prospective best interests of an unborn child. Although it is generally accepted that, subject to domestic law providing otherwise, the *CRC* does not apply to unborn children (P Alston, 'The Unborn Child and Abortion under the Draft Convention on the Rights of the Child' (1990) 12 *Human Rights Quarterly* 156), there is a compelling argument that in the case of a pregnant mother the refugee decision-maker

and/or evidence formally put forward by the applicant. As Gaudron J of the High Court of Australia has observed, any reasonable person 'would assume or expect that the interests of the child would be taken into account ... *as a matter of course* and without any need for the issue to be raised with the decision-maker'.[270] Decision-makers are thus under an obligation to 'be *proactive* in identifying [the child's best interests] so that they can be properly taken into account'.[271]

An assessment of a child's best interests involves a two-stage process. The first stage requires a decision-maker to determine what is in the best interests of the child. The second stage requires a decision-maker to assess whether those interests are outweighed by any countervailing factor. The two stages are set out by the Australian Federal Court in *Wan v MIMA*:[272]

> [The decision-maker is] required to identify what the best interests of Mr Wan's children required ... *and then* to assess whether the strength of any other consideration, or the cumulative effect of other considerations, outweighed the consideration of the best interests of the children understood as a primary consideration.

The two stages are distinct and should not be conflated. In *ZH (Tanzania) v SSHD*, the UK Supreme Court stressed the importance of considering the child's best interests *first*.[273] The reason for this is straightforward: a failure first to determine what is in the best interests of the child makes it impossible to assess whether any countervailing considerations outweigh those interests. As the Australian Federal Court has explained:[274]

> Given this balancing exercise, where the children's best interests were left at the level of mere hypothesis, it is hardly surprising that the positive finding of a risk of harm to the Australian community from even the small risk of the applicant re-offending outweighed the hypothesis of possible harm to the best interests of the applicant's children should his visa be cancelled.

In this case the Federal Court quashed the Minister's decision on the basis that the Minister had never addressed the 'central question of what the best interests of the children required'

---

ought to consider the best interests of the unborn child, on the basis that if the child is born she or he will have rights under the *CRC*: see, e.g., *Li v Canada (MPSEP)* 2016 FC 451; *CA v SSHD* [2004] EWCA Civ 1165; *Griffiths v Minister for Immigration* [2003] FMCA 249. Contra *SZRLY v MIAC* [2012] FCA 1459.

[270] *MIEA v Teoh* (1995) 183 CLR 273, 304 (emphasis added). This insightful assumption is made 'because of the special vulnerability of children, particularly where the break-up of the family unit is, or may be, involved, and because of their expectation that a civilized society would be alert to its responsibilities to children who are, or may be, in need of protection.' In *Garasova v Canada (MCI)* (1999) 177 FTR 76, [41], Lemieux J similarly stated that art 3 requires 'close attention to the interests and needs of children because children's rights and attention to those interests are central humanitarian and compassionate values in Canadian society'.

[271] *Ye v Minister of Immigration* [2009] NZSC 76, [50] (emphasis added). See also *Uelese v MIBP* [2015] HCA 15, [64]–[68]; *SS (Sri Lanka) v SSHD* [2012] EWCA Civ 945, [20]. In certain circumstances, this may require a decision-maker to undertake further inquiries: see, e.g., *Jones v Canada (MCI)* 2015 FC 419, [29]–[30].

[272] *Wan v MIMA* (2001) 107 FCR 133, [32] (emphasis added). This passage was approved by Baroness Hale in *ZH (Tanzania) v SSHD* [2011] 2 AC 166, [26]; see also at [29].

[273] *ZH (Tanzania) v SSHD* [2011] 2 AC 166, [33]. See also *MK (best interests of child) India* [2011] UKUT 00475, [19]; *ALJ and A, B and C's Application for Judicial Review* [2013] NIQB 88, [96].

[274] *Nweke v MIAC* [2012] FCA 266, [20].

and was thereby unable to 'assess whether any other consideration outweighed the best interests of the children understood as a primary consideration'.[275] A similar point has been made by the UK Upper Tribunal, which explained that the balancing exercise mandated by art 3 'cannot realistically or sensibly be undertaken unless and until the scales are properly prepared'.[276]

6.4.1 Stage One: Determining the Best Interests of the Child

As explained above, it is imperative that a decision-maker determines what is in the best interests of the child as a distinct and separate stage. This is made clear by the express language of art 3(1): the use of the word 'shall' reflects the mandatory nature of the obligation, while the term 'consideration' makes clear that the child's interests must actually be taken into account.[277] Alston has underlined that the 'consideration' mandated by art 3 must be 'genuine rather than token or merely formal' and must 'ensure that all aspects of the child's best interests are factored into the equation'.[278] This point has been recognised in case-law, with the Canadian Supreme Court emphasising that a decision-maker must be 'alert, alive and sensitive' to the best interests of an affected child.[279] It is insufficient for a decision-maker simply to state that they have taken into account the interests of the child without identifying with adequate particularity what those interests are.[280] Similarly, it is insufficient for a decision-maker to simply speculate as to what *may* be in the best interests of a child.[281] The best interests of the child must be 'well-identified and defined',[282] with the decision-maker undertaking 'a careful and sympathetic assessment of the children's interests'.[283] The UK Upper Tribunal has similarly explained that 'being adequately informed and conducting a scrupulous analysis are elementary prerequisites to the inter-related tasks of identifying the child's best interests and then balancing them with other material considerations'.[284]

---

[275] *Nweke v MIAC* [2012] FCA 266, [21]. See also *Spruill v MIAC* [2012] FCA 1401, [12]–[19]; *Lesianawai v MIAC* [2012] FCA 897, [37]–[51]; *Tauariki v MIAC* [2012] FCA 1408, [33]–[44]. In Canada, see, e.g., *Williams v Canada (MCI)* [2012] FCJ No 184, [63]; *Ferrer v Canada (MCI)* [2009] FCJ No 440, [6].

[276] *JO and others (section 55 duty) Nigeria* [2014] UKUT 00517, [11].

[277] 'The words "shall be" place a strong legal obligation on States and mean that States may not exercise discretion as to whether children's best interests are to be assessed and ascribed the proper weight as a primary consideration in any action undertaken': UNCRC, *GC14*, [36].

[278] P Alston, 'The Best Interests Principle: Towards a Reconciliation of Culture and Human Rights' in P Alston (ed), *The Best Interests of the Child: Reconciling Culture and Human Rights* (1994) 1, 13.

[279] *Baker v Canada (MCI)* [1999] 2 SCR 817, [75]. For a detailed discussion on the substantive content of the 'alert, alive and sensitive' phrase, see *Kolosovs v Canada (MCI)* [2008] FCJ No 211, [8]–[12]; *PGS v Canada (MCI)* [2012] FCJ No 10, [60]–[66].

[280] *Li v Canada (MPSEP)* 2016 FC 451, [25]; *Lu v Canada (MCI)* 2016 FC 175, [45]–[54]; *Kanthasamy v Canada (MCI)* [2015] 3 SCR 909, [39]; *Hawthorne v Canada (MCI)* [2003] 2 FC 555, [32]; *AA (AP) v SSHD* [2014] CSIH 35, [16].

[281] *Lesianawai v MIAC* [2012] FCA 897, [50].

[282] *Legault v Canada (MCI)* [2002] 4 FC 358, [12]; *Kanthasamy v Canada (MCI)* [2015] 3 SCR 909, [39].

[283] *Ahmad v Canada (MCI)* [2008] FCJ No 814, [30]. See also *Taylor v Canada (MCI)* 2016 FC 21, [31].

[284] *JO and others (section 55 duty) Nigeria* [2014] UKUT 00517, [11]. See also *MK (section 55 – Tribunal options) Sierra Leone* [2015] UKUT 00223, [32]; *RA v SSHD* [2015] UKUT 00242, [8].

A best interests assessment requires decision-makers to consider the long-term effects that a decision or action may have on a child's welfare and development, including those effects that may be felt after a child has reached her eighteenth birthday.[285] This need for a forward-looking examination is difficult to reconcile with the approach adopted by some states of granting children temporary protection status solely for the duration of childhood. For example, as discussed above, unaccompanied children arriving in the United Kingdom are granted a form of limited leave until they are seventeen-and-a-half years of age, at which point in time the leave to remain lapses and the child may be removed.[286] This approach gives rise to an enforced state of limbo, requiring children to live with a constant fear and anxiety that they will be removed as soon as they reach adulthood.[287] As the High Court of England and Wales has observed:[288]

> I am unable to see how the welfare of a 16 year old youth is best promoted by forcing him to anxiously face the prospect or spectre of removal from the UK … The stress of this constant re-appraisal of his life is hardly conducive to the promotion of his best interests … The claimant has been forced into a form of limbo by the decision of the SSHD. I fail to see how this can be suggested to advance the best interests of a 16 year old youth. He is entitled – is he not – to have some notion of what his future holds?

A mechanistic approach such as that adopted in the United Kingdom – which mortgages off a permanent solution to some future point in time (or, more cynically, serves only to postpone removal) – is incompatible with the object and purpose of the *CRC* which, at its core, is concerned with *developing* a child to their fullest potential and *preparing* a child for a responsible life in a free society.[289] A child cannot be expected to postpone her growth and development.[290] The best interests principle requires a decision-maker to consider a child's future protection and development needs. In certain circumstances this may require the implementation of an *immediate* and *permanent* solution, such as the grant of an indefinite form of protection.

There are three factors that must be taken into account in making an assessment as to what is in the best interests of a child.[291] The first factor is the views of the child. Article 12(1) of the *CRC* imposes a positive obligation on states to give due weight to the views of the child

---

[285] This argument has been made by Goodwin-Gill, who argues that 'what is in the best interests of the child must necessarily be understood also as including those decisions and actions, the effects of which will continue or be felt *after* the age of eighteen': Goodwin-Gill (2012) *supra* n 1, 227. See also *R (AA) v Upper Tribunal* [2012] EWHC 1784 (Admin), [44].

[286] See *supra* text accompanying n 260–1.   [287] Bolton (2012) *supra* n 106.

[288] *R (ABC) (a minor) (Afghanistan) v SSHD* [2011] EWHC 2937 (Admin), [58].

[289] See *CRC*, Preamble, arts 6(2), 23(3), 27(1), 29(1)(a), 29(1)(d). See further Goodwin-Gill (2012) *supra* n 1, 227.

[290] 'Solutions for children in flight cannot be mortgaged to some future time and place; on the contrary, as the child will not postpone his or her growth or development, so the need to implement elements of a durable solution is immediate': Goodwin-Gill (2012) *supra* n 1, 227. An obvious parallel can be found in the context of adoption, where decision-makers are generally required to reach a decision that will be in the long-term best interests of the child. For example, in the UK 'the paramount consideration of the court or adoption agency must be the child's welfare, *throughout his life*': *Adoption and Children Act 2002*, c 38, s 1(2) (emphasis added).

[291] The factors discussed here derive in part from the framework set out in: J Tobin, 'Judging the Judges: Are They Adopting the Rights Approach in Matters Involving Children' (2009) 33 *Melbourne University Law Review* 579; J Tobin, 'Justifying Children's Rights' (2013) 21 *International Journal of Children's Rights* 395.

in accordance with her age and level of maturity. Article 12(2) stipulates that children have a right to be heard in 'any judicial and administrative proceedings affecting the child'. Although a child's views may not be determinative, they represent a critical ingredient in undertaking the best interests assessment. This has been affirmed by the UNCRC, which considers that 'there can be no correct application of article 3 if the components of article 12 are not respected'.[292] The recast *EU Qualification Directive* also expressly notes that, in assessing the best interests of the child, member states should in particular take into account 'the views of the minor in accordance with his or her age and maturity'.[293]

Senior appellate courts have recognised the importance of seeking a child's views when determining the best interests of a child in the immigration context. The United Kingdom Supreme Court has drawn expressly upon art 12 of the *CRC* in affirming that an important part of determining a child's best interests is 'discovering the child's own views'.[294] This is regarded as important because a child's views and interests will not always coincide with their parents' and, in some cases, a parent may not be able to properly put the child's views before the court.[295] According to Baroness Hale, '[t]he important thing is that everyone, the parties and their representatives, but also the courts, is alive to the need to obtain the information necessary in order to have regard to the best interests of the children as a primary consideration, and to take steps accordingly'.[296] The New Zealand Supreme Court[297] and the Canadian Federal Court of Appeal[298] have similarly acknowledged the right of children to express their views in the context of an art 3 best interests assessment.

The second factor that must be taken into account is the specific situation and circumstances of the child, including the child's age, level of maturity and any particular vulnerabilities or needs that that child may have.[299] For example, has the child been the subject of physical or psychological abuse? Does the child suffer from a disability or other medical condition? What, if any, language does the child speak? Is the child unaccompanied or accompanied by a family member? What it the child's level of integration in the host country? What is the strength of the child's relationship with family members in the host country? What is the child's stage of education? To what extent would the child have linguistic, medical or other difficulties in adapting to life in another country? The best interests of a child in a specific situation of vulnerability will not be the same as a child who is

---

[292] UNCRC, *GC12*, [74]. See also UNCRC, *GC14*, [43], [53]–[54].   [293] Recital 18.

[294] *ZH (Tanzania) v SSHD* [2011] 2 AC 166, [34].

[295] *H (H) v Deputy Prosecutor of the Italian Republic, Genoa* [2013] 1 AC 338, [85], citing largely from the *amicus curiae* submissions of the CORAM Children's Legal Centre: CORAM Children's Legal Centre, 'Case for the CORAM Children's Legal Centre', filed in *H (H) v Deputy Prosecutor of the Italian Republic, Genoa* (undated) (copy on file with author); CORAM Children's Legal Centre, 'Note for the CORAM Children's Legal Centre', filed in *H (H) v Deputy Prosecutor of the Italian Republic, Genoa* (7 March 2012) (copy on file with author).

[296] *H (H) v Deputy Prosecutor of the Italian Republic, Genoa* [2013] 1 AC 338, [86]. See also *JO and others (section 55 duty) Nigeria* [2014] UKUT 00517, [14].

[297] *Ye v Minister of Immigration* [2009] NZSC 76, [53]; *Ye v Minister of Immigration* [2008] NZCA 291, [134]–[146] (Glazebrook J).

[298] *Hawthorne v Canada (MCI)* [2003] 2 FC 555, [33]; see also *Khader v Canada (MCI)* [2013] FCJ No 359, [33]–[34]; *Vasquez v Canada (MCI)* 2002 FCT 413, [14].

[299] 'A determination of what is in the best interests of the child requires a clear and comprehensive assessment of the child's identity, including her or his nationality, upbringing, cultural and linguistic background, particular vulnerabilities and protection needs': UNCRC, *GC6*, [20]. See also UNCRC, *GC14*, [48]; *Rights and Guarantees of Children in the Context of Migration and/or in Need of International Protection*, Advisory Opinion OC-21/14, 19 August 2014, IACHR (Ser A) No 21, [71].

not in the same situation. As the UNCRC has apprised, decision-makers must 'take into account the different kinds and degrees of vulnerability of each child' in order to accommodate the reality that 'each child is unique and each situation must be assessed according to the child's uniqueness'.[300]

The third factor is the extensive catalogue of rights protected under the *CRC*. The best interests principle is self-evidently indeterminate. It has been suggested that such imprecision gives rise to a risk that the best interests principle will be used as 'an alibi for individual arbitrariness'.[301] This criticism, however, is premised on an interpretation of art 3 that fails to take into account the balance of the *CRC*. The international rules of treaty interpretation make clear, however, that art 3 must be read within the context of the *CRC* as a whole, including each of the rights protected under it.[302] The latter construction injects substantive content into art 3, and thus provides a critical bulwark against the risk of subjective arbitrariness. As Alston explains,[303]

> the [*CRC*] as a whole goes at least some of the way towards providing the broad ethical or value framework that is often claimed to be the missing ingredient which would give a greater degree of certainty to the content of the best interests principle. It provides a carefully formulated and balanced statement of values to which some [now, 196] States Parties have formally subscribed.

The argument is developed further by Tobin:[304]

> While the best interests principle remains a fluid and flexible concept it is not unfettered or entirely subject to the personal whims of a decision-maker. Rather it remains informed and constrained by the rights and principles provided for under the Convention ... Put simply, a proposed outcome for a child cannot be said to be in his or her best interests where it conflicts with the provisions of the Convention.

In other words, it is in a child's best interests to enjoy the rights and freedoms provided for in the *CRC*. This integrative construction of art 3 is endorsed by the UNCRC, which affirms that '[t]he concept of the child's best interests is aimed at ensuring both the full and effective enjoyment of all the rights recognized in the Convention and the holistic development of the child'.[305]

Critically, there is no principled basis for importing any additional hardship threshold into the best interests analysis. As explained by the Canadian Federal Court, '[t]here is no basic needs minimum which if "met" satisfies the best interest test', and there is no 'hardship threshold, such that if the circumstances of the child reach a certain point on the hardship

---

[300] UNCRC, *GC14*, [76]. See, e.g., *Akyol v Canada (MCI)* 2014 FC 1252, [23], where the Federal Court of Canada was appropriately critical of the primary decision-maker for failing to give sufficient regard to a child applicant's learning difficulties.

[301] I Thèry, '"The Interest of the Child" and the Regulation of the Post-Divorce Family' in C Smart and S Sevenhuijsen (eds), *Child Custody and the Politics of Gender* (1989) 78, 82. See P Alston and B Gilmour-Walsh, *The Best Interests of the Child: Towards a Synthesis of Children's Rights and Cultural Values* (1996) 2, for a summary of the key criticisms of the indeterminacy of the provision.

[302] *VCLT*, art 31(1)–(2).   [303] Alston (1994) *supra* n 278, 19.

[304] Tobin (2006) *supra* n 55, 287. See also M Freeman, *A Commentary on the United Nations Convention on the Rights of the Child: Article 3 – The Best Interests of the Child* (2007) 9; Alston and Gilmour-Walsh (1996) *supra* n 301, 39.

[305] UNCRC, *GC14*, [4]. The approach has also been approved by UNHCR and UNICEF: UNHCR, *Child's BID Guidelines* (2008) *supra* n 88, 15, 67; UNICEF, *Implementation Handbook for the CRC* (2007) *supra* n 69, 38.

scale only then will a child's best interests be so significantly "negatively impacted" as to warrant positive consideration'.[306] As the Federal Court recognises, '[t]he question is *not*: "is the child suffering enough that his 'best interests' are not being 'met'?["] The question at the initial stage of the assessment is: "what is in the child's best interests?"'[307] The Canadian Federal Court of Appeal has similarly noted that a hardship threshold is ill-suited when assessing the claims of children, given that '[c]hildren will rarely, if ever, be deserving of any hardship'.[308]

A principled construction of art 3 thus requires a decision-maker to consider the extent to which a child seeking international protection will enjoy each of the rights protected under the CRC, giving regard to both the personal circumstances of the child and the conditions prevailing in the home country. That assessment should be based on empirical evidence that relates to both the specific child and the human rights conditions in the destination country. This is because the best interests assessment 'requires a judgment to be made on a rational basis taking into account all relevant factors' and not just 'on the basis of how these matters are perceived by the child and/or parent(s)'.[309] By anchoring the best interests assessment in both a principled (rights-based) and objective (evidence-based) framework, the risk of subjective and/or speculative arbitrariness in the application of the best interests principle is considerably reduced.[310]

A broad range of CRC rights may be relevant to the best interests assessment.[311] As acknowledged by UNHCR, 'the best interests of the child determination must take account of the full range of the child's rights, and ... is rarely determined by a single, overriding factor'.[312] Although by no means an exhaustive list, decision-makers have considered the following substantive rights in determining whether removal is in a child's best interests: the right to an education (arts 28 and 29);[313] the right to protection against

---

[306] *Williams v Canada (MCI)* [2012] FCJ No 184, [64].   [307] *Ibid.* (emphasis in original).
[308] *Hawthorne v Canada (MCI)* [2003] 2 FC 555, [9]. See also *Taylor v Canada (MCI)* 2016 FC 21, [22]; *Kanthasamy v Canada (MCI)* [2015] 3 SCR 909, [41]; *Akyol v Canada (MCI)* 2014 FC 1252, [15]–[19]; *Etienne v Canada (MCI)* 2014 FC 937, [8]–[11], [24]; *Alcocer v Canada (MCI)* [2013] FCJ No 2, [13]; *Judnarine v Canada (MCI)* [2013] FCJ No 61, [45]–[47]; *Santhirarajah v Attorney-General* [2012] FCA 940, [320]; *Sebbe v Canada (MCI)* [2012] FCJ No 842, [15]–[16]; *Sun v Canada (MCI)* [2012] FCJ No 218, [43]–[48].
[309] *MK (best interests of child) India* [2011] UKUT 00475, [20].   [310] Tobin (2009) *supra* n 291, 589–92.
[311] There have been suggestions (*MK (best interests of child) India* [2011] UKUT 00475, [21]; *R (Tinizaray) v SSHD* [2011] EWHC 1850 (Admin), [19]–[20]) that decision-makers assessing claims involving the removal of a child may benefit from the provision of a checklist, similar to that which is sometimes provided to decision-makers in the family law arena (see, e.g., *Children Act 1989*, c 41, s 1(3)). Although the UNCRC (see, e.g., UNCRC, GC6, [84]), UNHCR (see, e.g., UNHCR, *Child's BID Guidelines, supra* n 88, 67–76) and a number of states (see, e.g., MIAC, *Direction No 55, supra* n 205, [9.3], [11.2] (Australia); UKBA, *Asylum Process Guidance*, [17.8] and Home Office, *Processing Children's Asylum Claims*, 51–2 (UK)) have made efforts to identify those factors that a decision-maker ought to take into account, the CRC itself ultimately provides the most principled 'interpretation tool' to give meaning to the content of the best interests principle (*FM (Afghanistan) v SSHD* (Upper Tribunal, AA/01079/2010, 10 March 2011), [152]).
[312] UNHCR, *Child's BID Guidelines* (2008) *supra* n 88, 67, approved in *MK (best interests of child) India* [2011] UKUT 00475, [21]; *R (Meaza Asefa) v SSHD* [2012] EWHC 56 (Admin), [47].
[313] See, e.g., *Wan v MIMA* (2001) 107 FCR 133, [30], approved in *ZH (Tanzania) v SSHD* [2011] 2 AC 166, [30]; *Cebreros v MIMIA* [2002] AATA 213, [119]–[121]; *MK (best interests of child) India* [2011] UKUT 00475, [41]–[51]; *R (TS) v SSHD* [2010] EWHC 2614 (Admin), [75]; *LD v SSHD* [2010] UKUT 278, [30]; *Ye v Minister of Immigration* [2008] NZCA 291, [253]–[269] (Glazebrook J), affirmed in *Ye v Minister of Immigration* [2009] NZSC 76; *Diakité v Canada (MCI)* [2009] FCJ No 217, [87]–[92]. In assessing

discrimination (art 2);[314] the right to the highest attainable standard of health, including access to medical care and treatment (arts 24 and 25);[315] the right to life, survival and development (art 6);[316] the right to protection from all forms of physical or mental violence (arts 19, 34, 35, 36, 37 and 38);[317] the right to be registered and acquire a nationality, and to preserve an identity, including a nationality (arts 7 and 8);[318] the right to privacy and home life, based on the child's level of integration in the host country (art 16);[319] and the right to an adequate standard of living, based, among other things, on the availability of care arrangements for the child in the country of origin (arts 20 and 27).[320]

a child's ability to access education in the destination country, courts have underlined the need to 'ascertain[] the child's mother tongue and other languages spoken and written (and degree of fluency)' and to consider '[h]ow this would affect [the child's] integration in the community and their participation in the education system in the destination country': *Ye v Minister of Immigration* [2008] NZCA 291, [181] (Glazebrook J); see also at [249]–[255]. For similar reasoning, see *Kim v Canada (MCI)* [2007] FCJ No 1399, [18]–[22]. See generally UNCRC, *GC14*, [79].

[314] See, e.g., *Ye v Minister of Immigration* [2008] NZCA 291, [256]–[269] (Glazebrook J), affirmed in *Ye v Minister of Immigration* [2009] NZSC 76; *CR (Iran)* [2013] NZIPT 500795, [46]–[47]; *FM (Afghanistan) v SSHD* (Upper Tribunal, AA/01079/2010, 10 March 2011), [108]; *Kanthasamy v Canada (MCI)* [2015] 3 SCR 909, [50]–[59].

[315] *Kanthasamy v Canada (MCI)* [2015] 3 SCR 909, [46]–[49]; *R (TS) v SSHD* [2010] EWHC 2614 (Admin), [31]–[32]; *Kolosovs v Canada (MCI)* [2008] FCJ No 211, [14]; *Williams v Canada (MCI)* [2012] FCJ No 184; *Canada (MCI) v Patel* 2008 FC 747. See generally UNCRC, *GC14*, [77]–[78].

[316] See, e.g., *FM (Afghanistan) v SSHD* (Upper Tribunal, AA/01079/2010, 10 March 2011), [108], [132].

[317] See, e.g., *Diakité v Canada (MCI)* [2009] FCJ No 217; *AA (unattended children) Afghanistan CG* [2012] UKUT 00016, [89]–[93]; *Awolope v Canada (MCI)* [2010] FCJ No 645. See generally UNCRC, *GC14*, [71]–[74].

[318] See, e.g., *ZH (Tanzania) v SSHD* [2011] 2 AC 166, [30], affirmed in *H (H) v Deputy Prosecutor of the Italian Republic, Genoa* [2013] 1 AC 338; *H v Lord Advocate* [2013] 1 AC 413, [12]. See also *Sanade v SSHD* [2012] UKUT 00048, [65]; *Omotunde v SSHD* [2011] UKUT 00247, [38]; *Wan v MIMA* (2001) 107 FCR 133, [30]; *Vaitaiki v MIEA* (1998) 150 ALR 608, 614 (Burchett J); *Ye v Minister of Immigration* [2008] NZCA 291, [110]–[115] (Glazebrook J); and, for a European perspective, *Zambrano v Office national de l'emploi*, C-34/09, EU:C:2011:124 (8 March 2011). Significantly, each of these cases involved children that had been born in the host state. Articles 7 and 8 of the CRC may give rise to distinct considerations where the affected child is a national of another country. As the Upper Tribunal sensibly recognised in *MK (best interests of child) India* [2011] UKUT 00475, [25], 'factors such as citizenship and immigration status can sometimes strengthen, [or] sometimes weaken the argument that the best interests of the child lie in remaining in the [host country]'. In that case, the Tribunal noted that 'the fact that [the claimant] and the children are Indian citizens demonstrates that they have another country to go to and one in which, absent special circumstances, they can legitimately expect to enjoy the benefits of that country's citizenship'. See generally UNCRC, *GC6*, [20], [84]; UNCRC, *GC14*, [56]; UNHCR, *Child's BID Guidelines* (2008) *supra* n 88, 67.

[319] See, e.g., *ZH (Tanzania) v SSHD* [2011] 2 AC 166, [29] (noting the relevance of 'the level of the child's integration in [the host country] and the length of absence from the other country'); *LD v SSHD* [2010] UKUT 278, [27] ('substantial residence as a child is a strong indication . . . of what the best interests of the child requires'); *FM (Afghanistan) v SSHD* (Upper Tribunal, AA/01079/2010, 10 March 2011), [108]. See also CRC, art 20; UNCRC, *GC6*, [84].

[320] *ZH (Tanzania) v SSHD* [2011] 2 AC 166, [29] (noting the need to consider 'where and with whom the child is to live and the arrangements for looking after the child in the other country'); *AJ (Bangladesh) v SSHD* [2013] EWCA Civ 493, [31] ('[w]hen considering the child's best interests, it must be in the context of the particular circumstances of the child's family'); *R (TS) v SSHD* [2010] EWHC 2614 (Admin), [31]–[32]; *ALJ and A, B and C's Application for Judicial Review* [2013] NIQB 88, [102]. See also UNCRC, *GC6*, [85], recognising that '[i]n the absence of the availability of care provided by parents or members of the extended family, return to the country of origin should, in principle, not take place without advance secure and concrete arrangements of care and custodial responsibilities upon return to

An additional right critical to the best interests assessment in the immigration context is the child's right to be with her family.[321] In the majority of cases involving unaccompanied children, if the child's family can be located the best interests of the child will generally be best served by reuniting the child with her family.[322] This is consistent with the protection against arbitrary interference with the family (art 16), the obligation to respect the responsibilities, rights and duties of parents (art 5), and the duty of non-separation (art 9). Yet the principle of family unity is not absolute, and it is critical that family reunification is not invoked as an automatic trump card to justify a child's removal where that removal will be contrary to the child's best interests.[323] This is inherent in the structure of art 9(1), which specifies that a child may be separated from her parents where this is necessary for her best interests. Although art 9(1) expressly includes certain circumstances that may necessitate separation – most relevantly, cases 'involving abuse or neglect of the child by the parents' – the UNCRC has made clear that the list is not comprehensive and that other considerations may dictate that family reunion is not in the best interests of the child:[324]

> Family reunification in the country of origin is not in the best interests of the child and should therefore not be pursued where there is a 'reasonable risk' that such a return would lead to the violation of fundamental human rights of the child ... Where the circumstances in the country of origin contain lower level risks and there is concern, for example, of the child being affected by the indiscriminate effects of generalized violence, such risks must be given full attention and balanced against other rights-based considerations, including the consequences of further separation. In this context, it must be

the country of origin'. This is reflected, for instance, in the UK's policy on unaccompanied minors: see UKBA, *Asylum Process Guidance*, [17.7]; Home Office, *Processing Children's Asylum Claims*, 55.

321 See, e.g., *ZH (Tanzania) v SSHD* [2011] 2 AC 166, [29]; *LD v SSHD* [2010] UKUT 278, [26]; *Wan v MIMA* (2001) 107 FCR 133, [30].

322 'In order to pay full respect to the obligation of States under article 9 of the Convention to ensure that a child shall not be separated from his or her parents against their will, all efforts should be made to return an unaccompanied or separated child to his or her parents except where further separation is necessary for the best interests of the child, taking full account of the right of the child to express his or her views': UNCRC, *GC6*, [81]. See also UNHCR, *Child's BID Guidelines* (2008) *supra* n 88, 72; European Commission, *Unaccompanied Minors Action Plan* (2010) supra n 254, 12.

323 '[S]ometimes a parent may do a child more harm than good and it is in the child's best interests to find an alternative home': *H (H) v Deputy Prosecutor of the Italian Republic, Genoa* [2013] 1 AC 338, [33] (Baroness Hale). See, e.g., *Ek v Canada (MCI)* [2003] FCJ No 680, [33], where the Canadian Federal Court held that the immigration officer had erred in their conclusion that a child should be returned to Cambodia in order to be reunited with her parents and family. The Court considered that the officer had 'almost completely failed to analyse what hardship would be faced by [the child] if she were forced to leave Canada', giving only 'cursory mention to her establishment in Canada and her wishes' and '[n]o real consideration ... to her schooling or the bond she had with her aunt, uncle and cousins whom the evidence reveals are her current family'. More generally, see UNCRC, *GC6*, [81]–[83]; UNHCR, *Child's BID Guidelines* (2008) *supra* n 88, 71–2; UNICEF, *Implementation Handbook for the CRC* (2007) *supra* n 69, 316. For academic support, see McAdam (2007) *supra* n 26, 181–2; J Bhabha, '"Not a Sack of Potatoes": Moving and Removing Children across Borders' (2006) 15 *Boston University Public Interest Law Journal* 197, 204–5.

324 UNCRC, *GC6*, [82]. The Committee goes on to state (at [83]) that where family reunification is not possible in the destination country (for example, because of country conditions), a state's obligations under art 10(1) of the *CRC* will be triggered. This article provides that 'application by a child or his or her parents to enter or leave a State party for the purpose of family reunification shall be dealt with by States parties in a positive, humane and expeditious manner'.

recalled that the survival of the child is of paramount importance and a precondition for the enjoyment of any other rights.

In assessing whether family reunification is appropriate, the decision-maker must take into account the views of the child and, consistent with art 5 of the *CRC*, the views of the child's parent or other interested party.

The best interests assessment is generally more complex in cases involving children accompanied by their parents. The more straightforward scenario is where the child's parents are eligible to remain in the host state – for instance, because the parents qualify for refugee status. In this situation it will almost always be in the best interests of the child to remain with their family. For instance, in *BP (Iran)* an Iranian girl, aged ten, was at risk of being removed to Iran alone after both her mother and father, also citizens of Iran, had been recognised as refugees in New Zealand. The child was granted humanitarian protection on the basis that it was in her best interests 'to be with both parents who are the people with responsibility for her day-to-day care' and that '[g]iven that the parents will remain in New Zealand, it is in the ... child's best interests that she too be permitted to remain'.[325]

The more difficult scenario is where neither the parents nor the child has any right to remain in the host state. In this situation there has been a tendency for decision-makers to start from an assumption that the parents will be removed and then assess the best interests of the child off the back of that assumption. This typically results in a finding that it is in the best interests of the child to remain with their family and therefore be removed.[326] A more principled approach, consistent with art 3 and the wider rights framework protected under the *CRC*, is to assess the child's best interests without reference to the immigration status of the child's parent. As recognised by the Court of Appeal for England and Wales, '[t]he best interests of the child are to be determined by reference to the child alone without reference to the immigration history or status of either parent'.[327] The Federal Court of Canada has similarly recognised that the decision-maker must 'have regard to the child's circumstances, *from the child's perspective*',[328] and accordingly 'it is the child that must, first and foremost, be considered when analyzing [the best interests of the child], rather than whether the child could adapt to life in another country, accompany parents, or otherwise fit might be in someone else's fate'.[329]

---

[325] *BP (Iran)* [2012] NZIPT 500965, [16]. For a similar result, see *AD (Czech Republic)* [2012] NZIPT 500876, [12]–[15]; *BL (Iran)* [2012] NZIPT 500963.

[326] See, by way of illustration, *IE v SSHD* [2013] CSOH 142, where the primary decision-maker's analysis of the best interests of the child was premised upon a factual assumption that the child's mother would be removed.

[327] *EV (Philippines) and another v SSHD* [2014] EWCA Civ 874, [33].

[328] *Etienne v Canada (MCI)* 2014 FC 937, [9] (emphasis added).

[329] *Bautista v Canada (MCI)* 2014 FC 1008, [20]; see too at [26]–[30]. See also MacDonald and Toal (2014) *supra* n 152, 632–3 ('In cases where the central issue is whether the parents are to be removed ... to assess the best interests of the child on the assumption that the parents will be removed is to pre-judge the outcome of the inquiry into that central issue'); *Inniss v Canada (MCI)* 2015 FC 567, [17] ('As a matter of law, the best interests of the child must be determined first. Thus, if the determination is made that the children should remain with their parents, then it should remain open for an officer to conclude that the children should remain in Canada with their parents'); *IE v SSHD* [2013] CSOH 142, [14] ('[I]t seems to me that as a matter of law, as well as logic, the respondent was not entitled to proceed upon a factual assumption that the [parent] would be removed when assessing what was in the best interests of the children'); *Jiminez v Canada (MCI)* 2015 FC 527, [27]–[30]; *Trach v Canada (MCI)* 2015 FC 282, [39]; *Joseph v Canada (MCI)* 2013 FC 993, [18]–[21]; *Chandidas v Canada (MCI)* 2013 FC 258, [63]–[69]; *Kambo v Canada (MCI)* [2012] FCJ No 936, [39]–[52].

In undertaking the best interests assessment the decision-maker must canvass the full range of options for the child, including the possibility of the entire family remaining in the host state, and then assess which of those options is best suited to securing the realisation of the child's rights.[330] In the event that there are separate issues raised by a family member remaining in the host state – for example, where the child's parent has been convicted of a crime and is considered to be a risk to the safety of the host state – these concerns are addressed in the second stage of the best interests process.[331]

A child's best interests are rarely determined by a single overriding factor. The best interests assessment can thus not be approached as a binary or overly formulaic exercise, but must entail consideration of a range of factors, including any view held by the child, the child's individual circumstances and the extent to which the child will be able to enjoy CRC rights in her home country.[332] As the UNCRC has explained, the relevance and weight to be afforded to each element 'will necessarily vary from child to child and from case to case, depending on the type of decision and the concrete circumstances'.[333] In cases where there is a tension or even a clear conflict between factors – for instance, where family reunification conflicts with the need to guarantee the child's survival and development or indeed with the child's or parent's own individual view – the decision-maker must weigh up the various factors in order to reach a determination as to what is in the child's best interests.[334]

Where a decision-maker determines that removal is not in the best interests of the child, it is important to keep in mind the cumulative strength of the factors that fed into that determination, as this will be relevant to the balancing exercise undertaken in the second stage of the best interests assessment.[335] For example, if all the factors relevant to the determination of the best interests of the child overwhelmingly support the child and/or the child's parents remaining in the host state, then strong countervailing factors will be required to justify an outcome that is inconsistent with the child's best interests. On the other hand, in a borderline case – where there are good arguments that support a determination that it is in the child's best interests to return to her home state – less will be required by way of countervailing factors.[336]

---

[330] UNHCR, *Child's BID Guidelines* (2008) *supra* n 88, 67.

[331] It may be the case that where a family member is a criminal it will not be in the child's best interests to remain with that family member. This will require an assessment of the specific situation and circumstances of the child: see *supra* text accompanying n 299. The point is made by Baroness Hale in *H (H) v Deputy Prosecutor of the Italian Republic, Genoa* [2013] 1 AC 338, [33]: '[T]here is . . . a strong public interest in ensuring that children are properly brought up. This can of course cut both ways: sometimes a parent may do a child more harm than good and it is in the child's best interests to find an alternative home for her. But sometimes the parents' past criminality may say nothing at all about their capacity to bring up their children properly.'

[332] *MK (best interests of child) India* [2011] UKUT 00475, [21] ('the best interests of the child consideration . . . is not to be approached as a simplistic or reductionist exercise').

[333] UNCRC, *GC14*, [80].

[334] *Ibid.*, [81]. See also UNHCR, *Field Handbook* (2011) *supra* n 118, 67; UNHCR, 'Quality Integration Project: Considering the Best Interests of a Child within a Family Seeking Asylum' (December 2013) 33–40.

[335] 'The need to keep in mind the "overall" factors making up the best interests of the child consideration must not be downplayed': *MK (best interests of child) India* [2011] UKUT 00475, [24].

[336] *MK (best interests of child) India* [2011] UKUT 00475. See also *EV (Philippines) and another v SSHD* [2014] EWCA Civ 874, [36]–[37]; *Zoumbas v SSHD* [2013] 1 WLR 3690, [13]; *Ye v Minister of Immigration* [2008] NZCA 291, [130]–[133].

6.4.2 Stage Two: The Balancing Exercise

Article 3 provides that in all actions 'concerning children ... the best interests of the child shall be *a primary* consideration'.[337] The adoption of the indefinite article ('a' rather than 'the') indicates that the child's best interests are 'not to be considered as the single overriding factor' and thus affords sufficient flexibility, 'at least in certain extreme cases', to enable decision-makers to take into account a broader range of interests.[338] Yet, while this means that identifying a child's best interests will not 'lead inexorably to a decision in conformity with those interests',[339] it does *not* mean that a decision that conforms with a child's best interests can be easily displaced by reference to some other interest.[340] As Alston explains, the formulation adopted by the drafters imposes a 'burden of proof on those seeking to achieve ... a non-child-centered result to demonstrate that, under the circumstances, other feasible and acceptable alternatives do not exist'.[341] Thus, in the context of a child seeking international protection, where removal of the child is contrary to the child's best interests, those interests must be afforded *substantial* weight[342] and the decision-maker must provide a compelling and evidence-based justification in any case where the decision-maker reaches a decision that is contrary to the child's best interests.[343]

The weight to be given to the child's best interests has been the subject of considerable debate in national courts and tribunals.[344] In *ZH (Tanzania) v SSHD*, Baroness Hale recognised that the child's best interests might be outweighed by 'the cumulative effect of other considerations',[345] but underlined that a decision-maker must not 'treat any other consideration as inherently more significant than the best interests of the children'.[346] In this particular case Baroness Hale considered that the competing interests relied upon by the government – a need to maintain immigration control, the mother's immigration history and the precariousness of her immigration status when the children were born – were insufficient to outweigh the fact that the children's best interests were plainly served by

---

[337] *CRC*, art 3(1) (emphasis added).

[338] Alston (1994) *supra* n 278, 13. For example, one of the drafters noted that 'the interests of the child should be a primary consideration in actions concerning children but were not the overriding, paramount consideration in every case, since other parties might have equal or even superior legal interests in some cases (e.g. medical emergencies during childbirth)': *Report of the Working Group on a Draft Convention on the Rights of the Child*, E/CN.4/L.1575 (1981), [24].

[339] *ZH (Tanzania) v SSHD* [2011] 2 AC 166, [26] (Baroness Hale).

[340] '[W]hilst the best interests of the child is a primary consideration, and not the only or the paramount consideration, it is much, much more than merely a consideration to which regard must be had': *R (Mansoor) v SSHD* [2011] EWHC 832 (Admin), [32]. In other words, '[w]hilst it has been judicially recognised that a primary consideration is not the same as a paramount or determinative consideration ... it must at least mean a consideration of the first importance': *R (MXL) v SSHD* [2010] EWHC 2397 (Admin), [84].

[341] Alston (1994) *supra* n 278, 13. See also Alston and Gilmour-Walsh (1996) *supra* n 301, 12; Tobin (2009) *supra* n 291, 588–9; McAdam (2007) *supra* n 26, 180.

[342] *Baker v Canada (MCI)* [1999] 2 SCR 817, [75].

[343] See generally CORAM Children's Legal Centre, 'Case for the CORAM Children's Legal Centre', filed in *H (H) v Deputy Prosecutor of the Italian Republic, Genoa* (undated).

[344] See, e.g., *H (H) v Deputy Prosecutor of the Italian Republic, Genoa* [2013] 1 AC 338, [11]–[15]; *R (Meaza Asefa) v SSHD* [2012] EWHC 56 (Admin), [65]; *R (Mansoor) v SSHD* [2011] EWHC 832 (Admin), [32]–[35]; *ZH (Tanzania) v SSHD* [2011] 2 AC 166, [25]–[28] (Baroness Hale), [46] (Lord Kerr); *Ye v Minister of Immigration* [2009] NZSC 76, [52]; *Ye v Minister of Immigration* [2008] NZCA 291, [59]–[79] (Glazebrook J); *Wan v MIMA* (2001) 107 FCR 133, [32].

[345] *ZH (Tanzania) v SSHD* [2011] 2 AC 166, [26].   [346] *Ibid.*

remaining in the United Kingdom with their mother.[347] In a separate concurring opinion, Lord Kerr similarly acknowledged that the best interests principle 'is not a factor of limitless importance in the sense that it will prevail over all other considerations'[348] but took the view that '[i]t is a factor ... that must rank higher than any other'.[349] According to Lord Kerr, '[w]here the best interests of the child clearly favour a certain course, that course should be followed unless countervailing reasons of considerable force displace them'.[350]

There has been judicial debate as to whether the decision of Lord Kerr goes further than the decision of the majority as regards the weight to be afforded to the best interests of the child.[351] It has been suggested that while Baroness Hale left open the possibility that there may be more than one primary consideration, Lord Kerr adopted a more hard-line view that the best interests of the child must rank higher than *any* other consideration. Lord Kerr has since clarified that he did intend to express the position more strongly than the majority, explaining that '[w]hat [he] was seeking to say was that ... no factor must be given greater weight than the interests of the child'.[352] The distinction may be semantic, but to the extent that there is any difference between the two positions, Baroness Hale's construction is more neatly aligned with the language of art 3.[353]

Both the UNCRC and UNHCR suggest that only rights-based interests can outweigh the best interests of a child.[354] Although certainly positive from a protection standpoint, such a strict interpretation does not sit comfortably with the language of art 3, which places no limitation on the range of interests that may be taken into account and balanced against the best interests of a child. In *ZH (Tanzania) v SSHD*, Baroness Hale observed that the distinction between rights-based and non-rights-based arguments was difficult to understand, particularly given that wider interests, such as protecting the economic well-being of a host country, are also concerned with protecting the rights of individuals.[355] It may simply be the case, as Baroness Hale suggests in *ZH (Tanzania) v SSHD*, that the approach adopted

---

[347] *Ibid.*, [33].   [348] *Ibid.*, [46].   [349] *Ibid.*

[350] *Ibid.* Lord Kerr went on to note that '[w]hat is determined to be in a child's best interests should customarily dictate the outcome of cases such as the present [involving the removal of a child from a host state], therefore, and it will require considerations of substantial moment to permit a different result'.

[351] See, e.g., *R (BN) v SSHD* [2011] EWHC 2367 (Admin) [130]–[132]; *Lee v SSHD* [2011] EWCA Civ 348, [15].

[352] *H (H) v Deputy Prosecutor of the Italian Republic, Genoa* [2013] 1 AC 338, [145] (emphasis in original). Lord Kerr notes that in suggesting that the child's interests should be 'given a primacy of importance' he was not seeking to 'stoke the debate about the distinction between "*a* factor of primary importance" and "*the* factor of primary importance". What [he] was seeking to say was that, in common with the opinion of the High Court of Australia [sic – Federal Court of Australia] in *Wan [v MIMA* (2001) 107 FCR 133] ... no factor must be given greater weight than the interests of the child.'

[353] Baroness Hale's construction has been preferred in subsequent UK decisions. See, in particular, *Zoumbas v SSHD* [2013] 1 WLR 3690, [10]–[13]; *R (Meaza Asefa) v SSHD* [2012] EWHC 56 (Admin), [65]; *EV (Philippines) and another v SSHD* [2014] EWCA Civ 874, [32]. But contra the recent observations of the UNCRC in its *GC14*, which states that '[t]he expression "primary consideration" means that the child's best interests may not be considered on the same level as all other considerations' (at [37]) and that 'a larger weight must be attached to what serves the child best' (at [39]). This 'strong position' is justified on the basis of the 'special situation of the child: dependency, maturity, legal status and, often, voicelessness' (at [37]).

[354] UNCRC, *GC6*, [86]; UNHCR, *Child's BID Guidelines* (2008) *supra* n 88, 76. See *ZH (Tanzania) v SSHD* [2011] 2 AC 166, [27]–[28] (Baroness Hale); *Sanade v SSHD* [2012] UKUT 00048, [65]; *R (Mansoor) v SSHD* [2011] EWHC 832 (Admin), [32].

[355] *ZH (Tanzania) v SSHD* [2011] 2 AC 166, [28].

by the UNCRC and UNHCR reflects the reality that an argument that a child and/or her parents remaining in a host country poses a specific risk to the community will more easily outweigh the best interests of a child than an argument that the child and/or her parent's continued presence poses a more general threat to the economic well-being of the host country.[356] The question is one of weight rather than admissibility.

The two interests most commonly relied upon to militate against what is in a child's best interests are the maintenance of immigration control and the protection of members of the host community as a result of criminal activity or other serious misconduct by the child or the child's family member. As regards the former, it is self-evident that '[i]mmigration control and child protection/making the best interests of a child a primary consideration do not always pull in the same direction'.[357] Although a legitimate consideration – given that maintaining the integrity of a system of immigration control is one of the means by which a state protects its economic well-being and national security[358] – decision-makers have appropriately recognised that a general concern about maintaining immigration control will on its own generally be insufficient to justify an outcome inconsistent with the best interests of a child.[359]

Although not dispositive, evidence that the continued presence of a child and/or a child's parent in a host state poses a risk to members of the community may more easily outweigh the best interests of a child. This interest is most commonly raised where a family member of the child has engaged in criminal or other serious misconduct. Although a child must not be punished for the conduct of her parents,[360] the criminal activity of a family member, and the attendant risk it may pose to the host community, may militate against a decision that is in the best interests of the child – for instance, keeping the family together in the host state – and necessitate the removal of that family member.[361] Critically, in this scenario it will not necessarily follow that the child will be removed from the host state. Rather, it is necessary to revisit the first stage of the best interests assessment and assess whether it would be in the child's best interests to join the family member overseas or to remain in the host state notwithstanding the parent's removal.

Other countervailing factors that have been relied upon by decision-makers in undertaking the balancing exercise include: the integrity of the international system of extradition;[362] deterrence of parents sending children to a host state as 'anchor

---

[356] *ZH (Tanzania) v SSHD* [2011] 2 AC 166; *H (H) v Deputy Prosecutor of the Italian Republic, Genoa* [2013] 1 AC 338, [141].

[357] *R (AN) (a child) v SSHD* [2012] EWCA Civ 1636, [91].

[358] *R (Mansoor) v SSHD* [2011] EWHC 832 (Admin), [34].

[359] *ZH (Tanzania) v SSHD* [2011] 2 AC 166, [28] (Baroness Hale), [46] (Lord Kerr); *Ye v Minister of Immigration* [2009] NZSC 76, [31]; *R (Mansoor) v SSHD* [2011] EWHC 832 (Admin), [35]. The UNCRC suggests that arguments relating to 'general migration control' are not rights-based and can therefore not override an outcome that is in the best interests of the child: UNCRC, GC6, [86]. See also UNCRC, 2012 *Discussion Day Report*, [73].

[360] *ZH (Tanzania) v SSHD* [2011] 2 AC 166, [44] (Lord Hope).   [361] See, e.g., *supra* n 180.

[362] Again, this generally arises where a family member of the child is the subject of an extradition request: see, e.g., *H (H) v Deputy Prosecutor of the Italian Republic, Genoa* [2013] 1 AC 338. In that case, Baroness Hale made clear that '[i]t is not enough to dismiss these cases in a simple way – by accepting that the children's interests will always be harmed by separation from their sole or primary carer but also accepting that the public interest in extradition is almost always strong enough to outweigh it. There is no substitute for . . . careful examination': at [34]. See also *Santhirarajah v Attorney-General* [2012] FCA 940.

children';[363] the integrity of the practical application of the Dublin regime;[364] and the deterrence of people-smuggling networks.[365] Decision-makers have, however, recognised that the art 3 balancing exercise should not be limited to a consideration of the interests that conflict with the child's best interests. Most critically, leading courts have accepted that there is an independent public interest in promoting the best interests of children. As the UK Supreme Court held in a case involving the extradition of a parent, '[i]t is not just a matter of balancing the private rights of children against the public interest in extradition, because there is also a wider public interest and benefit to society in promoting the best interests of its children'.[366] Children are, after all, 'a country's most valuable asset for the future'[367] and there is thus a strong public interest 'in ensuring that children are properly brought up'.[368] Decision-makers have also sensibly affirmed that there is an autonomous public interest in the preservation and protection of the family unit, underlining that 'the preservation and protection of the family is a matter of significant social importance'[369] and that '[o]bservance of the international obligation to protect the family unit is a matter of public interest'.[370]

How a decision-maker ultimately balances the best interests of the child with other relevant interests will depend on the circumstances of the individual child. This will always be a fact-sensitive inquiry. As explained above, it will, in particular, be important for the decision-maker to keep in mind the overall factors that make up the substantive determination as to the child's best interests, given that the cumulative strength of those factors is central to the balancing exercise.[371] As explained by the UK Upper Tribunal, if 'all the

---

[363] See, e.g., *Children's Aid Society of Toronto v MM* [2010] OJ No 2550, [19], where the Ontario Court of Justice noted that '[t]here is no question of encouraging in any fashion or manner whatsoever the act of sending and abandoning foreign children in Canada'. States have tended to rely on anecdotal evidence of this practice: see McAdam (2006) *supra* n 26, 182 n 70.

[364] *ALJ and A, B and C's Application for Judicial Review* [2013] NIQB 88, [98]; *R (Mozaffar) v SSHD* [2014] EWCA Civ 854, [42].

[365] See, e.g., recent policies in Australia: M Gordon, 'People Sent Offshore Will Include Children', *Sydney Morning Herald* (online), 22 August 2013. See generally M Foster and J Pobjoy, 'A Failed Case of Legal Refugee Status Determination in Australia's "Excised" Territories' (2011) 23 *International Journal of Refugee Law* 583.

[366] *H (H) v Deputy Prosecutor of the Italian Republic, Genoa* [2013] 1 AC 338, [25] (Baroness Hale). This argument is developed at length in CORAM Children's Legal Centre, Case in *H (H)* (2012) supra n 295, [8]: 'The special protection to be accorded to children and the obligation to implement the best interests principle are not merely matters of private individual rights to be balanced against a public interest in implementing extradition arrangements, they are as important as the maintenance of effective criminal justice systems and, it may justifiably be said, significantly more important than the public interest in the maintenance of [an] effective immigration control system and the public interest in international comity'.

[367] *Re X (a minor)* [1975] Fam 47, 52. As Freeman notes, 'giving greater weight to children's interests maximizes the welfare of society as a whole ... Putting children first is a way of building for the future': Freeman (2007) *supra* n 304, 41.

[368] *H (H) v Deputy Prosecutor of the Italian Republic, Genoa* [2013] 1 AC 338, [33] (Baroness Hale). See also *Helu v Immigration and Protection Tribunal and Minister of Immigration* [2015] NZSC 28, [172] (McGrath J).

[369] *Singh v Minister of Immigration* [2012] NZIPT 500067, [96].

[370] *Helu v Immigration and Protection Tribunal and Minister of Immigration* [2015] NZSC 28, [76] (Elias CJ), [171] (McGrath J). See also *DR (Iran)* [2015] NZIPT 502356, [27]; *Manase v Minister of Immigration* [2012] NZIPT 500522, [105]; *Loumoli v Minister of Immigration* [2012] NZIPT 500442, [99]–[102]; *Vaitaiki v Minister of Immigration* [2012] NZIPT 500060, [109]–[111]; *AH (South Africa)* [2011] NZIPT 500228, [33].

[371] See *supra* text accompanying n 335. See also *R (SG and others) v Secretary of State for Work and Pensions* [2015] 1 WLR 1449, [108].

factors weighed in the best interests of the child consideration point overwhelmingly in favour of the child and/or relevant parent(s) remaining in the United Kingdom, that is very likely to mean that only very strong countervailing factors can outweigh it'.[372] Conversely, in a borderline case, where there are factors that support a determination that it is in the child's best interests to leave the host state, less may be required to outweigh the child's best interests. In any cases where the decision-maker ultimately concludes that a child's best interests are outweighed by other countervailing facts, the decision-maker must provide an evidence-based justification explaining what other considerations of equal or greater priority justify overriding those interests, and demonstrate that no feasible and acceptable alternative outcome exists that would be more compatible with the child's best interests.[373]

Conclusions

This chapter has stepped outside the framework of the international refugee protection regime, and analysed the capacity of the CRC to provide an independent source of international protection. Section 6.1 examined the more traditional sources of complementary protection based on the obligation of *non-refoulement* implicit in, at the very minimum, arts 6 and 37 of the CRC. It demonstrated that these child-specific duties of *non-refoulement* – often neglected at the national level – cast a wider and more tailored net than the generic *non-refoulement* obligations under the CAT and ICCPR. Section 6.2 focused in on a more embryonic form of protection: art 3 of the CRC, which requires that the best interests of the child shall be a primary consideration in all actions concerning children. As the analysis in Sections 6.3 and 6.4 demonstrates, the best interests principle is playing an increasingly central role in decisions involving the removal of children, and may, in certain circumstances, proscribe the removal of a child notwithstanding the fact that she is ineligible for protection as a refugee. The application of art 3 in a range of migration contexts and across multiple jurisdictions demonstrates that the argument advanced in this chapter – that the best interests principle may give rise to an independent source of protection – is not merely a theoretical aspiration but finds support in a fast-evolving body of regional and domestic jurisprudence. That jurisprudence provides a valuable source of guidance for decision-makers tasked with considering the application of art 3 as an independent source of protection.

The CRC provides a legal and moral benchmark for the treatment of children both generally and within the asylum context. As Erika Feller, former Deputy High Commissioner for UNHCR, has observed, 'the CRC requires perhaps the most exacting standards for protection and assistance to minors under any international instrument' and provides 'a valuable frame ... for any consideration of asylum issues as they affect children'.[374] Although the Convention may well remain the cornerstone of the international refugee protection regime, it is becoming increasingly clear that the CRC provides a critical additional layer of protection, which may, in certain circumstances, provide a more appropriate and more child-friendly gateway for assessing the protection needs of a child seeking international protection.

---

[372] *MK (best interests of child) India* [2011] UKUT 00475, [24].   [373] See *supra* text accompanying n 341.
[374] E Feller, 'The Right to Be Heard for Separated Children Seeking Asylum in Europe' (Statement delivered to the EU Seminar on Children Affected by Armed Conflict and Forced Displacement – A Child Rights Perspective in Development Co-Operation and Migration Policies, Sweden, 1 March 2001).

CONCLUSIONS

The *Refugee Convention* – rightly characterised as the foundation and cornerstone of the international refugee protection regime – provides a robust and dynamic mechanism for the protection of refugee children. The *Convention* has, however, grown up within and now constitutes part of a broader international human rights legal framework, and it must be interpreted and applied within that context. In particular, the close of the twentieth century saw the international community come together and agree a treaty-based framework for the protection of children's rights.[1] The *CRC* now provides the most comprehensive and authoritative articulation of the minimum obligations that a state owes to a child, both generally and in the asylum context. Accepting as a starting point that refugee children benefit from both the *Convention* and the *CRC*, Chapter 1 examined the interaction between the two legal regimes in the context of the refugee status determination process. Chapter 1 then identified three modes of interaction where the *CRC* might be engaged to assist in determining the status of an at-risk child: as a *procedural guarantee* to inform the refugee determination process; as an *interpretative aid* to inform the interpretation of the *Convention* definition; and as an *independent source of status* outside the international refugee protection regime. In examining these three modes of interaction, the balance of the book has demonstrated the critical role of the *CRC* in both informing and supplementing the protection afforded under the *Convention*.

Chapter 2 examined the relevance of the *CRC* to the procedural dimension of the refugee protection regime and the extent to which the rights framework enshrined in the *CRC* might inform and strengthen the procedural guarantees afforded children throughout the refugee status determination process. In recognition of the reality that children, particularly accompanied children, are often rendered invisible in national refugee status determination processes, the focal point for Chapter 2 was art 12 of the *CRC*. This participatory right, together with the duty of *non-refoulement* protected under art 33 of the *Convention*, provides a compelling and principled basis for the proposition that the removal of a child without an independent assessment of refugee status will constitute a violation of international law. In circumstances where, as a consequence of the independent examination of a child's claim, a family unit ends up with mixed protection statuses, art 9 of the *CRC* will be engaged, affording a robust and largely unqualified safeguard to prevent the separation of a child from her parent(s).

Together, arts 12 and 9 have the capacity to significantly enhance the visibility of children in the refugee status determination process. However, as the chapter acknowledged, further

---

[1] See P Alston and J Tobin, *Laying the Foundations for Children's Rights: An Independent Study of Some Key Legal and Institutional Aspects of the Impact of the Convention on the Rights of the Child* (2005) 7.

procedural safeguards will be necessary to ensure that a child can effectively navigate the refugee status determination. The *CRC* will be relevant to those safeguards: in particular, the requirement that 'appropriate measures' are taken to 'ensure that a child who is seeking refugee status . . . receive appropriate protection and humanitarian assistance',[2] the require-ment that the best interests of the child shall be a primary consideration in all actions concerning children[3] and, in the context of unaccompanied children, the requirement to appoint a guardian or adviser and a legal representative.[4] Although an examination of each of these obligations was beyond the more limited scope of this book, the analysis of arts 9 and 12 demonstrated the capacity of the *CRC* to secure procedural guarantees not otherwise provided under the *Convention*, and confirmed the need for more sustained engagement with the *CRC* in the design and implementation of the procedural dimension of the refugee protection regime.

Chapters 3 to 5 examined the manner in which the *Convention* definition is interpreted and applied in assessing the refugee status of children. The chapters drew on contemporary developments in the interpretation of art 1A(2), informed where appropriate by the rights framework enshrined in the *CRC*, to test the capacity of the *Convention* to respond to the special protection needs of children. As demonstrated in Chapter 1, recourse to the *CRC* as an interpretative aid finds support in guidance provided by UNHCR and the UNCRC and is consistent with the rules of treaty interpretation. As the case-law review demonstrated, an interactive approach also finds support in the fast-evolving, albeit still underdeveloped, jurisprudence of courts and tribunals in the common law world, which are increasingly approaching the *Convention* definition from the optic of the child. The *CRC* has a particularly critical role to play in informing the definition of 'being persecuted', with the *CRC* providing a comprehensive and state-generated framework setting out a child's distinct and especially tailored set of human rights. In circumstances where there is general consensus that international human rights law is relevant to the identification of persecu-tory harm, and where, by way of ratifying the *CRC*, an overwhelming majority of states have acknowledged that children have a distinct set of human rights, it necessarily follows that the rights enshrined in the *CRC* must be considered when applying the 'being persecuted' standard to children. The principle of non-discrimination – one of the general principles underpinning the *CRC* – also has a role to play in informing the 'for reasons of clause', and provides a principled reference point for establishing the interests protected by the *Convention*'s nexus ground.

As acknowledged at the outset, this book is not an exhaustive treatise on the refugee definition. Rather than addressing every doctrinal obstacle that a child may face in demonstrating eligibility for refugee status, the case-law review was used to identify the key challenges that children have faced to date. There are certainly others. For instance, in what circumstances will it be appropriate to refuse a child refugee status on the basis that the child has an internal protection alternative?[5] In what, if any, circumstances will it be appropriate to remove a child to a 'safe third-country' for processing.[6] Does the transition from childhood to adulthood engage the cessation provision under art 1C of the

---

[2] *CRC*, art 22(1).   [3] *CRC*, art 3(1).   [4] CRC, arts 18(2), 20(1); UNCRC, *GC6*, [33]–[38].
[5] See, e.g., UNHCR, 2009 *Guidelines*, [53]–[57]; *EU Qualification Directive*, recital 27; *Ultima v Canada (MCI)* 2013 FC 81, [33]–[35]; *RA (AP) v SSHD* [2011] CSOH 68; *Elmi v Canada (MEI)* [1999] FCJ No 336; *T97-05827* (IRB, 16 July 1998), [8]; *T98-00366* (IRB, 18 January 1999), [8].
[6] See Chapter 6, *supra* n 99.

Convention?[7] When will a child be found to have re-availed herself of the protection of her country of nationality for the purposes of art 1C of the *Convention?*[8] In what circumstances will the exclusion provisions in art 1F apply to children?[9] The case-law review demonstrates that the *CRC* may have a role to play in informing the answer to each of these questions.[10]

Finally, Chapter 6 stepped outside the international refugee protection regime and examined the capacity of the *CRC* to provide an independent source of international protection. The chapter demonstrated that the child-specific duties of *non-refoulement*, implicit in (at the very least) arts 6 and 37 of the *CRC* cast a wider and more tailored net than the generic *non-refoulement* obligations under the *CAT* and *ICCPR*. The chapter then focused in on a more embryonic form of protection: art 3, which specifies that the best interests of the child shall be a primary consideration in all actions concerning children. Article 3, it was suggested, may preclude the removal of a child notwithstanding the fact that the child is not eligible for protection as a refugee or protection under the *non-refoulement* obligations in international human rights law. The relevant question in such a case is whether the removal of the child is in the child's best interests. If it is not, there will be a strong presumption against removing the child, subject only to a tightly circumscribed range of countervailing factors that may in certain circumstances override the child's best interests. Article 3 thus creates a new category of protected persons, whose interests need to be assessed against the applicable *CRC* standards.

The third mode of interaction – the *CRC* as an *independent source of status* – is both the most far-reaching and the least developed. The independent protection guarantees discussed in Chapter 6 are generally referred to as *complementary* protection in the sense that the human rights guarantees are complementary to and should be considered after a refugee status determination. This is justified on the basis that the *Convention* affords a more secure legal status, and confers a range of civil, political and socio-economic rights.[11] This logic has been challenged both generally[12] and specifically in the context of children.[13] Goodwin-Gill has asked what the *Convention* adds from a protection standpoint: 'What is better protected through the [*Convention*], than through the [*CRC*]? Is there any aspect of *need* that might otherwise be missed?'[14] The pragmatic answer must surely be the extent of the *Convention*'s domestic endorsement and implementation, which will generally mean that refugee status

---

[7] See, e.g., *Ixtlilco-Morales v Keisler*, 507 F 3d 651 (8th Cir, 2007); *Valcu v Attorney General*, 394 Fed Appx 884 (3rd Cir, 2010); Chapter 5, *supra* n 146.

[8] See, e.g., *Cadena v Canada (MPSEP)* 2012 FC 67, [27]–[32].

[9] See, e.g., UNHCR, 2009 *Guidelines*, [58]–[64]; *R (ABC) (a minor) (Afghanistan) v SSHD* [2011] EWHC 2937 (Admin); M Happold, 'Excluding Children from Refugee Status: Child Soldiers and Article 1F of the Refugee Convention' (2002) 17 *American University International Law Review* 1131.

[10] See, e.g., the potential role of the best interests principle: Chapter 6, text accompanying n 92–100.

[11] J C Hathaway and M Foster, *The Law of Refugee Status* (2nd edn, 2014) 2; M Foster, *International Refugee Law and Socio-Economic Rights: Refuge from Deprivation* (2007) 353. See also J McAdam, *Complementary Protection in International Refugee Law* (2007) 49–51.

[12] See, e.g., V Chetail, 'Are Refugee Rights Human Rights? An Unorthodox Questioning of the Relations between Refugee Law and Human Rights Law' in R Rubio-Marín (ed), *Human Rights and Immigration* (2014) 19.

[13] See, e.g., G S Goodwin-Gill, 'The United Nations Convention on the Rights of the Child and Its Application to Child Refugee Status Determination and Asylum Processes: Introduction' (2012) 26 *Journal of Immigration, Asylum and Nationality Law* 226.

[14] *Ibid.*, 228.

affords the most secure domestic route to protection.[15] A principled answer is more difficult to identify. Insofar as there are gaps in the protection afforded under the *Convention* vis-à-vis the *CRC*, there is a compelling argument that the principles of equality and non-discrimination – the core human rights values of the international system – mandate equal treatment between individuals eligible for refugee status and individuals eligible for a complementary form of protection.[16] A full examination of these issues is beyond the more modest scope of this book. The critical point must be that at-risk children benefit from both the *Convention* and the *CRC*, and where the latter affords greater protection it can and should be invoked.[17]

The book's central conclusion is that the *Convention* is capable of responding in a sophisticated and principled way to refugee claims brought by children, but that the *CRC* has an important role to play in both informing and supplementing the *Convention*. Today a refugee lawyer must also be a human rights lawyer.[18] In particular, in order to ensure that the *Convention* has enduring value and relevance, including for refugee children, the *CRC* must be used as a procedural guarantee to incorporate safeguards into the refugee status determination process, and as an interpretative aid to inform the interpretation of the *Convention* definition. The *CRC* also gives rise to an independent source of status outside the traditional refugee protection regime, which may, in certain circumstances, provide a more appropriate and more child-friendly gateway for assessing the protection needs of a child seeking international protection. Although debates will no doubt continue as to the contours of the relationship between the *Convention* and the *CRC*,[19] what is clear is that both the *Convention* and the *CRC* have a critical role to play in securing protection for children seeking international protection. It is only by embracing the mutually reinforcing relationship between the two legal regimes – responsive both to the difficulties associated with refugeehood and the distinct needs and vulnerabilities of childhood – that these children can be guaranteed the protection to which they are entitled under international law.

[15] 'Refugee law speaks to a world where international norms are realised through a carefully constructed status that many States are content to endorse and use': C Harvey, 'Time for Reform? Refugees, Asylum-Seekers, and Protection under International Human Rights Law' (2014) 33(4) *Refugee Survey Quarterly* 1, 4.

[16] See J Pobjoy, 'Treating Like Alike: The Principle of Non-Discrimination as a Tool to Mandate the Equal Protection of Refugees and Beneficiaries of Complementary Protection' (2010) 34 *Melbourne University Law Review* 181.

[17] Harvey makes a similar point in relation to human rights law generally: Harvey (2014) *supra* n 15.

[18] T A Aleinikoff, 'The Refugee Convention at Forty: Reflections on the IJRL Colloquium' (1991) 3 *International Journal of Refugee Law* 617, 625.

[19] See, e.g., Chetail (2014) *supra* n 12; Harvey (2014) *supra* n 15.

ANNEX 1 *CRC*, PREAMBLE AND ARTICLES 1 TO 41

Preamble

The States Parties to the present Convention,

Considering that, in accordance with the principles proclaimed in the Charter of the United Nations, recognition of the inherent dignity and of the equal and inalienable rights of all members of the human family is the foundation of freedom, justice and peace in the world,

Bearing in mind that the peoples of the United Nations have, in the Charter, reaffirmed their faith in fundamental human rights and in the dignity and worth of the human person, and have determined to promote social progress and better standards of life in larger freedom,

Recognizing that the United Nations has, in the Universal Declaration of Human Rights and in the International Covenants on Human Rights, proclaimed and agreed that everyone is entitled to all the rights and freedoms set forth therein, without distinction of any kind, such as race, colour, sex, language, religion, political or other opinion, national or social origin, property, birth or other status,

Recalling that, in the Universal Declaration of Human Rights, the United Nations has proclaimed that childhood is entitled to special care and assistance,

Convinced that the family, as the fundamental group of society and the natural environment for the growth and well-being of all its members and particularly children, should be afforded the necessary protection and assistance so that it can fully assume its responsibilities within the community,

Recognizing that the child, for the full and harmonious development of his or her personality, should grow up in a family environment, in an atmosphere of happiness, love and understanding,

Considering that the child should be fully prepared to live an individual life in society, and brought up in the spirit of the ideals proclaimed in the Charter of the United Nations, and in particular in the spirit of peace, dignity, tolerance, freedom, equality and solidarity,

Bearing in mind that the need to extend particular care to the child has been stated in the Geneva Declaration of the Rights of the Child of 1924 and in the Declaration of the Rights of the Child adopted by the General Assembly on 20 November 1959 and recognized in the Universal Declaration of Human Rights, in the International Covenant on Civil and Political Rights (in particular in articles 23 and 24), in the International Covenant on Economic, Social and Cultural Rights (in particular in article 10) and in the statutes and relevant instruments of specialized agencies and international organizations concerned with the welfare of children,

Bearing in mind that, as indicated in the Declaration of the Rights of the Child, 'the child, by reason of his physical and mental immaturity, needs special safeguards and care, including appropriate legal protection, before as well as after birth',

Recalling the provisions of the Declaration on Social and Legal Principles relating to the Protection and Welfare of Children, with Special Reference to Foster Placement and Adoption Nationally and Internationally; the United Nations Standard Minimum Rules for the Administration of Juvenile Justice (The Beijing Rules); and the Declaration on the Protection of Women and Children in Emergency and Armed Conflict, Recognizing that, in all countries in the world, there are children living in exceptionally difficult conditions, and that such children need special consideration,

Taking due account of the importance of the traditions and cultural values of each people for the protection and harmonious development of the child,

Recognizing the importance of international co-operation for improving the living conditions of children in every country, in particular in the developing countries,

Have agreed as follows:

Part I

Article 1

For the purposes of the present Convention, a child means every human being below the age of eighteen years unless under the law applicable to the child, majority is attained earlier.

Article 2

1. States Parties shall respect and ensure the rights set forth in the present Convention to each child within their jurisdiction without discrimination of any kind, irrespective of the child's or his or her parent's or legal guardian's race, colour, sex, language, religion, political or other opinion, national, ethnic or social origin, property, disability, birth or other status.
2. States Parties shall take all appropriate measures to ensure that the child is protected against all forms of discrimination or punishment on the basis of the status, activities, expressed opinions, or beliefs of the child's parents, legal guardians, or family members.

Article 3

1. In all actions concerning children, whether undertaken by public or private social welfare institutions, courts of law, administrative authorities or legislative bodies, the best interests of the child shall be a primary consideration.
2. States Parties undertake to ensure the child such protection and care as is necessary for his or her well-being, taking into account the rights and duties of his or her parents, legal guardians, or other individuals legally responsible for him or her, and, to this end, shall take all appropriate legislative and administrative measures.
3. States Parties shall ensure that the institutions, services and facilities responsible for the care or protection of children shall conform with the standards established by competent authorities, particularly in the areas of safety, health, in the number and suitability of their staff, as well as competent supervision.

Article 4

States Parties shall undertake all appropriate legislative, administrative, and other measures for the implementation of the rights recognized in the present Convention. With regard to economic, social and cultural rights, States Parties shall undertake such measures to the maximum extent of their available resources and, where needed, within the framework of international co-operation.

Article 5

States Parties shall respect the responsibilities, rights and duties of parents or, where applicable, the members of the extended family or community as provided for by local custom, legal guardians or other persons legally responsible for the child, to provide, in a manner consistent with the evolving capacities of the child, appropriate direction and guidance in the exercise by the child of the rights recognized in the present Convention.

Article 6

1. States Parties recognize that every child has the inherent right to life.
2. States Parties shall ensure to the maximum extent possible the survival and development of the child.

Article 7

1. The child shall be registered immediately after birth and shall have the right from birth to a name, the right to acquire a nationality and, as far as possible, the right to know and be cared for by his or her parents.
2. States Parties shall ensure the implementation of these rights in accordance with their national law and their obligations under the relevant international instruments in this field, in particular where the child would otherwise be stateless.

Article 8

1. States Parties undertake to respect the right of the child to preserve his or her identity, including nationality, name and family relations as recognized by law without unlawful interference.
2. Where a child is illegally deprived of some or all of the elements of his or her identity, States Parties shall provide appropriate assistance and protection, with a view to re-establishing speedily his or her identity.

Article 9

1. States Parties shall ensure that a child shall not be separated from his or her parents against their will, except when competent authorities subject to judicial review determine, in accordance with applicable law and procedures, that such separation is necessary for the best interests of the child. Such determination may be necessary in a particular case such as one involving abuse or neglect of the child by the parents, or one where the parents are living separately and a decision must be made as to the child's place of residence.
2. In any proceedings pursuant to paragraph 1 of the present article, all interested parties shall be given an opportunity to participate in the proceedings and make their views known.
3. States Parties shall respect the right of the child who is separated from one or both parents to maintain personal relations and direct contact with both parents on a regular basis, except if it is contrary to the child's best interests.
4. Where such separation results from any action initiated by a State Party, such as the detention, imprisonment, exile, deportation or death (including death arising from any cause while the person is in the custody of the State) of one or both parents or of the child, that State Party shall, upon request, provide the parents, the child or, if appropriate, another member of the family with the essential information concerning the whereabouts of the absent member(s) of the family unless the provision of the information would be detrimental to the well-being of the child. States Parties shall further ensure that the submission of such a request shall of itself entail no adverse consequences for the person(s) concerned.

Article 10

1. In accordance with the obligation of States Parties under article 9, paragraph 1, applications by a child or his or her parents to enter or leave a State Party for the purpose of family reunification shall be dealt with by States Parties in a positive, humane and expeditious manner. States Parties shall further ensure that the submission of such a request shall entail no adverse consequences for the applicants and for the members of their family.
2. A child whose parents reside in different States shall have the right to maintain on a regular basis, save in exceptional circumstances personal relations and direct contacts with both parents. Towards that end and in accordance with the obligation of States Parties under article 9, paragraph 1, States Parties shall respect the right of the child and his or her parents to leave any country, including their own, and to enter their own country. The right to leave any country shall be subject only to such restrictions as are prescribed by law and which are necessary to protect the national security, public order (*ordre public*), public health or morals or the rights and freedoms of others and are consistent with the other rights recognized in the present Convention.

Article 11

1. States Parties shall take measures to combat the illicit transfer and non-return of children abroad.
2. To this end, States Parties shall promote the conclusion of bilateral or multilateral agreements or accession to existing agreements.

Article 12

1. States Parties shall assure to the child who is capable of forming his or her own views the right to express those views freely in all matters affecting the child, the views of the child being given due weight in accordance with the age and maturity of the child.
2. For this purpose, the child shall in particular be provided the opportunity to be heard in any judicial and administrative proceedings affecting the child, either directly, or through a representative or an appropriate body, in a manner consistent with the procedural rules of national law.

Article 13

1. The child shall have the right to freedom of expression; this right shall include freedom to seek, receive and impart information and ideas of all kinds, regardless of frontiers, either orally, in writing or in print, in the form of art, or through any other media of the child's choice.
2. The exercise of this right may be subject to certain restrictions, but these shall only be such as are provided by law and are necessary:
   (a) For respect of the rights or reputations of others; or
   (b) For the protection of national security or of public order (*ordre public*), or of public health or morals.

Article 14

1. States Parties shall respect the right of the child to freedom of thought, conscience and religion.
2. States Parties shall respect the rights and duties of the parents and, when applicable, legal guardians, to provide direction to the child in the exercise of his or her right in a manner consistent with the evolving capacities of the child.
3. Freedom to manifest one's religion or beliefs may be subject only to such limitations as are prescribed by law and are necessary to protect public safety, order, health or morals, or the fundamental rights and freedoms of others.

Article 15

1. States Parties recognize the rights of the child to freedom of association and to freedom of peaceful assembly.
2. No restrictions may be placed on the exercise of these rights other than those imposed in conformity with the law and which are necessary in a democratic society in the interests of national security or public safety, public order (*ordre public*), the protection of public health or morals or the protection of the rights and freedoms of others.

Article 16

1. No child shall be subjected to arbitrary or unlawful interference with his or her privacy, family, or correspondence, nor to unlawful attacks on his or her honour and reputation.
2. The child has the right to the protection of the law against such interference or attacks.

Article 17

States Parties recognize the important function performed by the mass media and shall ensure that the child has access to information and material from a diversity of national and international sources, especially those aimed at the promotion of his or her social, spiritual and moral well-being and physical and mental health. To this end, States Parties shall:

(a) Encourage the mass media to disseminate information and material of social and cultural benefit to the child and in accordance with the spirit of article 29;
(b) Encourage international co-operation in the production, exchange and dissemination of such information and material from a diversity of cultural, national and international sources;
(c) Encourage the production and dissemination of children's books;
(d) Encourage the mass media to have particular regard to the linguistic needs of the child who belongs to a minority group or who is indigenous;
(e) Encourage the development of appropriate guidelines for the protection of the child from information and material injurious to his or her well-being, bearing in mind the provisions of articles 13 and 18.

Article 18

1. States Parties shall use their best efforts to ensure recognition of the principle that both parents have common responsibilities for the upbringing and development of the child. Parents or, as the case may be, legal guardians, have the primary responsibility for the upbringing and development of the child. The best interests of the child will be their basic concern.
2. For the purpose of guaranteeing and promoting the rights set forth in the present Convention, States Parties shall render appropriate assistance to parents and legal

guardians in the performance of their child-rearing responsibilities and shall ensure the development of institutions, facilities and services for the care of children.

3. States Parties shall take all appropriate measures to ensure that children of working parents have the right to benefit from child-care services and facilities for which they are eligible.

Article 19

1. States Parties shall take all appropriate legislative, administrative, social and educational measures to protect the child from all forms of physical or mental violence, injury or abuse, neglect or negligent treatment, maltreatment or exploitation, including sexual abuse, while in the care of parent(s), legal guardian(s) or any other person who has the care of the child.

2. Such protective measures should, as appropriate, include effective procedures for the establishment of social programmes to provide necessary support for the child and for those who have the care of the child, as well as for other forms of prevention and for identification, reporting, referral, investigation, treatment and follow-up of instances of child maltreatment described heretofore, and, as appropriate, for judicial involvement.

Article 20

1. A child temporarily or permanently deprived of his or her family environment, or in whose own best interests cannot be allowed to remain in that environment, shall be entitled to special protection and assistance provided by the State.

2. States Parties shall in accordance with their national laws ensure alternative care for such a child.

3. Such care could include, *inter alia*, foster placement, *kafalah* of Islamic law, adoption or if necessary placement in suitable institutions for the care of children. When considering solutions, due regard shall be paid to the desirability of continuity in a child's upbringing and to the child's ethnic, religious, cultural and linguistic background.

Article 21

States Parties that recognize and/or permit the system of adoption shall ensure that the best interests of the child shall be the paramount consideration and they shall:

(a) Ensure that the adoption of a child is authorized only by competent authorities who determine, in accordance with applicable law and procedures and on the basis of all pertinent and reliable information, that the adoption is permissible in view of the child's status concerning parents, relatives and legal guardians and that, if required, the persons concerned have given their informed consent to the adoption on the basis of such counselling as may be necessary;

(b) Recognize that inter-country adoption may be considered as an alternative means of child's care, if the child cannot be placed in a foster or an adoptive family or cannot in any suitable manner be cared for in the child's country of origin;

(c) Ensure that the child concerned by inter-country adoption enjoys safeguards and standards equivalent to those existing in the case of national adoption;

(d) Take all appropriate measures to ensure that, in inter-country adoption, the placement does not result in improper financial gain for those involved in it;

(e) Promote, where appropriate, the objectives of the present article by concluding bilateral or multilateral arrangements or agreements, and endeavour, within this framework, to ensure that the placement of the child in another country is carried out by competent authorities or organs.

Article 22

1. States Parties shall take appropriate measures to ensure that a child who is seeking refugee status or who is considered a refugee in accordance with applicable international or domestic law and procedures shall, whether unaccompanied or accompanied by his or her parents or by any other person, receive appropriate protection and humanitarian assistance in the enjoyment of applicable rights set forth in the present Convention and in other international human rights or humanitarian instruments to which the said States are Parties.

2. For this purpose, States Parties shall provide, as they consider appropriate, co-operation in any efforts by the United Nations and other competent intergovernmental organizations or non-governmental organizations co-operating with the United Nations to protect and assist such a child and to trace the parents or other members of the family of any refugee child in order to obtain information necessary for reunification with his or her family. In cases where no parents or other members of the family can be found, the child shall be accorded the same protection as any other child permanently or temporarily deprived of his or her family environment for any reason, as set forth in the present Convention.

Article 23

1. States Parties recognize that a mentally or physically disabled child should enjoy a full and decent life, in conditions which ensure dignity, promote self-reliance and facilitate the child's active participation in the community.

2. States Parties recognize the right of the disabled child to special care and shall encourage and ensure the extension, subject to available resources, to the eligible child and those responsible for his or her care, of assistance for which application is made and which is appropriate to the child's condition and to the circumstances of the parents or others caring for the child.

3. Recognizing the special needs of a disabled child, assistance extended in accordance with paragraph 2 of the present article shall be provided free of charge, whenever possible, taking into account the financial resources of the parents or others caring for the child, and shall be designed to ensure that the disabled child has effective access to and receives education, training, health care services, rehabilitation services, preparation for employment and recreation opportunities in a manner conducive to the child's achieving the

fullest possible social integration and individual development, including his or her cultural and spiritual development

4. States Parties shall promote, in the spirit of international cooperation, the exchange of appropriate information in the field of preventive health care and of medical, psychological and functional treatment of disabled children, including dissemination of and access to information concerning methods of rehabilitation, education and vocational services, with the aim of enabling States Parties to improve their capabilities and skills and to widen their experience in these areas. In this regard, particular account shall be taken of the needs of developing countries.

Article 24

1. States Parties recognize the right of the child to the enjoyment of the highest attainable standard of health and to facilities for the treatment of illness and rehabilitation of health. States Parties shall strive to ensure that no child is deprived of his or her right of access to such health care services.

2. States Parties shall pursue full implementation of this right and, in particular, shall take appropriate measures:
   (a) To diminish infant and child mortality;
   (b) To ensure the provision of necessary medical assistance and health care to all children with emphasis on the development of primary health care;
   (c) To combat disease and malnutrition, including within the framework of primary health care, through, *inter alia*, the application of readily available technology and through the provision of adequate nutritious foods and clean drinking-water, taking into consideration the dangers and risks of environmental pollution;
   (d) To ensure appropriate pre-natal and post-natal health care for mothers;
   (e) To ensure that all segments of society, in particular parents and children, are informed, have access to education and are supported in the use of basic knowledge of child health and nutrition, the advantages of breastfeeding, hygiene and environmental sanitation and the prevention of accidents;
   (f) To develop preventive health care, guidance for parents and family planning education and services.

3. States Parties shall take all effective and appropriate measures with a view to abolishing traditional practices prejudicial to the health of children.

4. States Parties undertake to promote and encourage international co-operation with a view to achieving progressively the full realization of the right recognized in the present article. In this regard, particular account shall be taken of the needs of developing countries.

Article 25

States Parties recognize the right of a child who has been placed by the competent authorities for the purposes of care, protection or treatment of his or her physical or mental health, to a periodic review of the treatment provided to the child and all other circumstances relevant to his or her placement.

Article 26

1. States Parties shall recognize for every child the right to benefit from social security, including social insurance, and shall take the necessary measures to achieve the full realization of this right in accordance with their national law.
2. The benefits should, where appropriate, be granted, taking into account the resources and the circumstances of the child and persons having responsibility for the maintenance of the child, as well as any other consideration relevant to an application for benefits made by or on behalf of the child.

Article 27

1. States Parties recognize the right of every child to a standard of living adequate for the child's physical, mental, spiritual, moral and social development.
2. The parent(s) or others responsible for the child have the primary responsibility to secure, within their abilities and financial capacities, the conditions of living necessary for the child's development.
3. States Parties, in accordance with national conditions and within their means, shall take appropriate measures to assist parents and others responsible for the child to implement this right and shall in case of need provide material assistance and support programmes, particularly with regard to nutrition, clothing and housing.
4. States Parties shall take all appropriate measures to secure the recovery of maintenance for the child from the parents or other persons having financial responsibility for the child, both within the State Party and from abroad. In particular, where the person having financial responsibility for the child lives in a State different from that of the child, States Parties shall promote the accession to international agreements or the conclusion of such agreements, as well as the making of other appropriate arrangements.

Article 28

1. States Parties recognize the right of the child to education, and with a view to achieving this right progressively and on the basis of equal opportunity, they shall, in particular:
    (a) Make primary education compulsory and available free to all;
    (b) Encourage the development of different forms of secondary education, including general and vocational education, make them available and accessible to every child, and take appropriate measures such as the introduction of free education and offering financial assistance in case of need;
    (c) Make higher education accessible to all on the basis of capacity by every appropriate means;
    (d) Make educational and vocational information and guidance available and accessible to all children;
    (e) Take measures to encourage regular attendance at schools and the reduction of drop-out rates.

2. States Parties shall take all appropriate measures to ensure that school discipline is administered in a manner consistent with the child's human dignity and in conformity with the present Convention.
3. States Parties shall promote and encourage international cooperation in matters relating to education, in particular with a view to contributing to the elimination of ignorance and illiteracy throughout the world and facilitating access to scientific and technical knowledge and modern teaching methods. In this regard, particular account shall be taken of the needs of developing countries.

Article 29

1. States Parties agree that the education of the child shall be directed to:
   (a) The development of the child's personality, talents and mental and physical abilities to their fullest potential;
   (b) The development of respect for human rights and fundamental freedoms, and for the principles enshrined in the Charter of the United Nations;
   (c) The development of respect for the child's parents, his or her own cultural identity, language and values, for the national values of the country in which the child is living, the country from which he or she may originate, and for civilizations different from his or her own;
   (d) The preparation of the child for responsible life in a free society, in the spirit of understanding, peace, tolerance, equality of sexes, and friendship among all peoples, ethnic, national and religious groups and persons of indigenous origin;
   (e) The development of respect for the natural environment.
2. No part of the present article or article 28 shall be construed so as to interfere with the liberty of individuals and bodies to establish and direct educational institutions, subject always to the observance of the principle set forth in paragraph 1 of the present article and to the requirements that the education given in such institutions shall conform to such minimum standards as may be laid down by the State.

Article 30

In those States in which ethnic, religious or linguistic minorities or persons of indigenous origin exist, a child belonging to such a minority or who is indigenous shall not be denied the right, in community with other members of his or her group, to enjoy his or her own culture, to profess and practise his or her own religion, or to use his or her own language.

Article 31

1. States Parties recognize the right of the child to rest and leisure, to engage in play and recreational activities appropriate to the age of the child and to participate freely in cultural life and the arts.
2. States Parties shall respect and promote the right of the child to participate fully in cultural and artistic life and shall encourage the provision of appropriate and equal opportunities for cultural, artistic, recreational and leisure activity.

Article 32

1. States Parties recognize the right of the child to be protected from economic exploitation and from performing any work that is likely to be hazardous or to interfere with the child's education, or to be harmful to the child's health or physical, mental, spiritual, moral or social development.
2. States Parties shall take legislative, administrative, social and educational measures to ensure the implementation of the present article. To this end, and having regard to the relevant provisions of other international instruments, States Parties shall in particular:
    (a) Provide for a minimum age or minimum ages for admission to employment;
    (b) Provide for appropriate regulation of the hours and conditions of employment;
    (c) Provide for appropriate penalties or other sanctions to ensure the effective enforcement of the present article.

Article 33

States Parties shall take all appropriate measures, including legislative, administrative, social and educational measures, to protect children from the illicit use of narcotic drugs and psychotropic substances as defined in the relevant international treaties, and to prevent the use of children in the illicit production and trafficking of such substances.

Article 34

States Parties undertake to protect the child from all forms of sexual exploitation and sexual abuse. For these purposes, States Parties shall in particular take all appropriate national, bilateral and multilateral measures to prevent:
(a) The inducement or coercion of a child to engage in any unlawful sexual activity;
(b) The exploitative use of children in prostitution or other unlawful sexual practices;
(c) The exploitative use of children in pornographic performances and materials.

Article 35

States Parties shall take all appropriate national, bilateral and multilateral measures to prevent the abduction of, the sale of or traffic in children for any purpose or in any form.

Article 36

States Parties shall protect the child against all other forms of exploitation prejudicial to any aspects of the child's welfare.

Article 37

States Parties shall ensure that:

(a) No child shall be subjected to torture or other cruel, inhuman or degrading treatment or punishment. Neither capital punishment nor life imprisonment without possibility of release shall be imposed for offences committed by persons below eighteen years of age;

(b) No child shall be deprived of his or her liberty unlawfully or arbitrarily. The arrest, detention or imprisonment of a child shall be in conformity with the law and shall be used only as a measure of last resort and for the shortest appropriate period of time;

(c) Every child deprived of liberty shall be treated with humanity and respect for the inherent dignity of the human person, and in a manner which takes into account the needs of persons of his or her age. In particular, every child deprived of liberty shall be separated from adults unless it is considered in the child's best interest not to do so and shall have the right to maintain contact with his or her family through correspondence and visits, save in exceptional circumstances;

(d) Every child deprived of his or her liberty shall have the right to prompt access to legal and other appropriate assistance, as well as the right to challenge the legality of the deprivation of his or her liberty before a court or other competent, independent and impartial authority, and to a prompt decision on any such action.

Article 38

1. States Parties undertake to respect and to ensure respect for rules of international humanitarian law applicable to them in armed conflicts which are relevant to the child.

2. States Parties shall take all feasible measures to ensure that persons who have not attained the age of fifteen years do not take a direct part in hostilities.

3. States Parties shall refrain from recruiting any person who has not attained the age of fifteen years into their armed forces. In recruiting among those persons who have attained the age of fifteen years but who have not attained the age of eighteen years, States Parties shall endeavour to give priority to those who are oldest.

4. In accordance with their obligations under international humanitarian law to protect the civilian population in armed conflicts, States Parties shall take all feasible measures to ensure protection and care of children who are affected by an armed conflict.

Article 39

States Parties shall take all appropriate measures to promote physical and psychological recovery and social reintegration of a child victim of: any form of neglect, exploitation, or abuse; torture or any other form of cruel, inhuman or degrading treatment or punishment; or armed conflicts. Such recovery and reintegration shall take place in an environment which fosters the health, self-respect and dignity of the child.

Article 40

1. States Parties recognize the right of every child alleged as, accused of, or recognized as having infringed the penal law to be treated in a manner consistent with the promotion of the child's sense of dignity and worth, which reinforces the child's respect for the human rights and fundamental freedoms of others and which takes into account the child's age and the desirability of promoting the child's reintegration and the child's assuming a constructive role in society.

2. To this end, and having regard to the relevant provisions of international instruments, States Parties shall, in particular, ensure that:

   (a) No child shall be alleged as, be accused of, or recognized as having infringed the penal law by reason of acts or omissions that were not prohibited by national or international law at the time they were committed;

   (b) Every child alleged as or accused of having infringed the penal law has at least the following guarantees:

      (i) To be presumed innocent until proven guilty according to law;

     (ii) To be informed promptly and directly of the charges against him or her, and, if appropriate, through his or her parents or legal guardians, and to have legal or other appropriate assistance in the preparation and presentation of his or her defence;

    (iii) To have the matter determined without delay by a competent, independent and impartial authority or judicial body in a fair hearing according to law, in the presence of legal or other appropriate assistance and, unless it is considered not to be in the best interest of the child, in particular, taking into account his or her age or situation, his or her parents or legal guardians;

    (iv) Not to be compelled to give testimony or to confess guilt; to examine or have examined adverse witnesses and to obtain the participation and examination of witnesses on his or her behalf under conditions of equality;

     (v) If considered to have infringed the penal law, to have this decision and any measures imposed in consequence thereof reviewed by a higher competent, independent and impartial authority or judicial body according to law;

    (vi) To have the free assistance of an interpreter if the child cannot understand or speak the language used;

   (vii) To have his or her privacy fully respected at all stages of the proceedings.

3. States Parties shall seek to promote the establishment of laws, procedures, authorities and institutions specifically applicable to children alleged as, accused of, or recognized as having infringed the penal law, and, in particular:

   (a) The establishment of a minimum age below which children shall be presumed not to have the capacity to infringe the penal law;

   (b) Whenever appropriate and desirable, measures for dealing with such children without resorting to judicial proceedings, providing that human rights and legal safeguards are fully respected. 4. A variety of dispositions, such as care, guidance and supervision orders; counselling; probation; foster care; education and vocational training programmes and other alternatives to institutional care shall be available to ensure that children are dealt with in a manner appropriate to their well-being and proportionate both to their circumstances and the offence.

Article 41

Nothing in the present Convention shall affect any provisions which are more conducive to the realization of the rights of the child and which may be contained in:

(a) The law of a State party; or

(b) International law in force for that State.

Preamble

The High Contracting Parties,

Considering that the Charter of the United Nations and the Universal Declaration of Human Rights approved on 10 December 1948 by the General Assembly have affirmed the principle that human beings shall enjoy fundamental rights and freedoms without discrimination,

Considering that the United Nations has, on various occasions, manifested its profound concern for refugees and endeavoured to assure refugees the widest possible exercise of these fundamental rights and freedoms,

Considering that it is desirable to revise and consolidate previous international agreements relating to the status of refugees and to extend the scope of and the protection accorded by such instruments by means of a new agreement,

Considering that the grant of asylum may place unduly heavy burdens on certain countries, and that a satisfactory solution of a problem of which the United Nations has recognized the international scope and nature cannot therefore be achieved without international co-operation,

Expressing the wish that all States, recognizing the social and humanitarian nature of the problem of refugees, will do everything within their power to prevent this problem from becoming a cause of tension between States,

Noting that the United Nations High Commissioner for Refugees is charged with the task of supervising international conventions providing for the protection of refugees, and recognizing that the effective co-ordination of measures taken to deal with this problem will depend upon the co-operation of States with the High Commissioner,

Have agreed as follows:

Chapter I General Provisions

Article 1 Definition of the Term 'Refugee'

A. For the purposes of the present Convention, the term 'refugee' shall apply to any person who:

   (1) Has been considered a refugee under the Arrangements of 12 May 1926 and 30 June 1928 or under the Conventions of 28 October 1933 and 10 February 1938, the Protocol of 14 September 1939 or the Constitution of the International Refugee Organization;

Decisions of non-eligibility taken by the International Refugee Organization during the period of its activities shall not prevent the status of refugee being accorded to persons who fulfil the conditions of paragraph 2 of this section;

(2) As a result of events occurring before 1 January 1951 and owing to well-founded fear of being persecuted for reasons of race, religion, nationality, membership of a particular social group or political opinion, is outside the country of his nationality and is unable or, owing to such fear, is unwilling to avail himself of the protection of that country; or who, not having a nationality and being outside the country of his former habitual residence as a result of such events, is unable or, owing to such fear, is unwilling to return to it.

In the case of a person who has more than one nationality, the term 'the country of his nationality' shall mean each of the countries of which he is a national, and a person shall not be deemed to be lacking the protection of the country of his nationality if, without any valid reason based on well-founded fear, he has not availed himself of the protection of one of the countries of which he is a national.

B. (1) For the purposes of this Convention, the words 'events occurring before 1 January 1951' in article 1, section A, shall be understood to mean either

(a) 'events occurring in Europe before 1 January 1951'; or

(b) 'events occurring in Europe or elsewhere before 1 January 1951'; and each Contracting State shall make a declaration at the time of signature, ratification or accession, specifying which of these meanings it applies for the purpose of its obligations under this Convention.

(2) Any Contracting State which has adopted alternative (a) may at any time extend its obligations by adopting alternative (b) by means of a notification addressed to the Secretary-General of the United Nations.

C. This Convention shall cease to apply to any person falling under the terms of section A if:

(1) He has voluntarily re-availed himself of the protection of the country of his nationality; or

(2) Having lost his nationality, he has voluntarily reacquired it; or

(3) He has acquired a new nationality, and enjoys the protection of the country of his new nationality; or

(4) He has voluntarily re-established himself in the country which he left or outside which he remained owing to fear of persecution; or

(5) He can no longer, because the circumstances in connection with which he has been recognized as a refugee have ceased to exist, continue to refuse to avail himself of the protection of the country of his nationality;

Provided that this paragraph shall not apply to a refugee falling under section A (1) of this article who is able to invoke compelling reasons arising out of previous persecution for refusing to avail himself of the protection of the country of nationality;

(6) Being a person who has no nationality he is, because the circumstances in connection with which he has been recognized as a refugee have ceased to exist, able to return to the country of his former habitual residence;

Provided that this paragraph shall not apply to a refugee falling under section A (1) of this article who is able to invoke compelling reasons arising out of previous persecution for refusing to return to the country of his former habitual residence.

D. This Convention shall not apply to persons who are at present receiving from organs or agencies of the United Nations other than the United Nations High Commissioner for Refugees protection or assistance.

    When such protection or assistance has ceased for any reason, without the position of such persons being definitively settled in accordance with the relevant resolutions adopted by the General Assembly of the United Nations, these persons shall *ipso facto* be entitled to the benefits of this Convention.

E. This Convention shall not apply to a person who is recognized by the competent authorities of the country in which he has taken residence as having the rights and obligations which are attached to the possession of the nationality of that country.

F. The provisions of this Convention shall not apply to any person with respect to whom there are serious reasons for considering that:

    (a) He has committed a crime against peace, a war crime, or a crime against humanity, as defined in the international instruments drawn up to make provision in respect of such crimes;

    (b) He has committed a serious non-political crime outside the country of refuge prior to his admission to that country as a refugee;

    (c) He has been guilty of acts contrary to the purposes and principles of the United Nations.

ANNEX 3 *FINAL ACT OF THE CONFERENCE OF PLENIPOTENTIARIES*, RECOMMENDATION B (PRINCIPLE OF FAMILY UNITY)

B

The Conference,

Considering that the unity of the family, the natural and fundamental group unit of society, is an essential right of the refugee, and that such unity is constantly threatened, and

Noting with satisfaction that, according to the official commentary of the *ad hoc* Committee on Statelessness and Related Problems (E/1618, p 40), the rights granted to a refugee are extended to members of his family,

Recommends Governments to take the necessary measures for the protection of the refugee's family, especially with a view to:

(1) Ensuring that the unity of the refugee's family is maintained particularly in cases where the head of the family has fulfilled the necessary conditions for admission to a particular country;
(2) The protection of refugees who are minors, in particular unaccompanied children and girls, with special reference to guardianship and adoption.

BIBLIOGRAPHY

Books, Articles and Papers

Abram, E F, 'The Child's Right to Family Unity in International Immigration Law' (1995) 17 *Law and Policy* 397

Albert, M, 'Governance and *Prima Facie* Refugee Status Determination: Clarifying the Boundaries of Temporary Protection, Group Determination, and Mass Influx' (2010) 29 (1) *Refugee Survey Quarterly* 61

Aleinikoff, T A, 'The Refugee Convention at Forty: Reflections on the IJRL Colloquium' (1991) 3 *International Journal of Refugee Law* 617

Alston, P, 'The Unborn Child and Abortion under the Draft Convention on the Rights of the Child' (1990) 12 *Human Rights Quarterly* 156

Alston, P, 'The Best Interests Principle: Towards a Reconciliation of Culture and Human Rights' in P Alston (ed), *The Best Interests of the Child: Reconciling Culture and Human Rights* (1994) 1

Alston, P, (ed), *Non-State Actors and Human Rights* (2005)

Alston, P, and Gilmour-Walsh, B, *The Best Interests of the Child: Towards a Synthesis of Children's Rights and Cultural Values* (1996)

Alston, P, and Tobin, J, *Laying the Foundations for Children's Rights: An Independent Study of Some Key Legal and Institutional Aspects of the Impact of the Convention on the Rights of the Child* (2005)

Anker, D, 'Refugee Status and Violence against Women in the "Domestic" Sphere: The Non-State Actor Question' (2001) 15 *Georgetown Immigration Law Journal* 391

Anker, D, 'Boundaries in the Field of Human Rights: Refugee Law, Gender and the Human Rights Paradigm' (2002) 15 *Harvard Human Rights Journal* 133

Anker, D, 'Refugee Law, Gender, and the Human Rights Paradigm' (2002) 15 *Harvard Human Rights Journal* 133

Anker, D, *Law of Asylum in the United States* (2015)

Anker, D, Kelly, N, and Willshire, J C, 'Mejilla-Romero: A New Era for Child Asylum', 12–09 *Immigration Briefings* (September 2012) 1

Aust, A, *Modern Treaty Law and Practice* (3rd edn, 2013)

Bennion, F, *Bennion on Statutory Interpretation* (5th edn, 2008)

Benvenisti, E, 'Reclaiming Democracy: The Strategic Use of Foreign and International Law by National Courts' (2008) 102 *American Journal of International Law* 241

Berliner, L, et al., 'Children's Memory for Trauma and Positive Experiences' (2003) 16 *Journal of Traumatic Stress* 229

Bhabha, J, 'Minors or Aliens? Inconsistent State Intervention and Separated Child Asylum-Seekers' (2001) 3 *European Journal of Migration and Law* 283

Bhabha, J, '"More Than Their Share of Sorrows": International Migration Law and the Rights of Children' (2003) 22 *Saint Louis University Public Law Review* 253

Bhabha, J, 'The "Mere Fortuity" of Birth? Are Children Citizens?' (2004) 15(2) *Differences: A Journal of Feminist Cultural Studies* 91

Bhabha, J, '"Not a Sack of Potatoes": Moving and Removing Children across Borders' (2006) 15 *Boston University Public Interest Law Journal* 197

Bhabha, J, 'Un "Vide Juridique"? – Migrant Children: The Rights and Wrongs' in C Bellamy et al. (eds), *Realizing the Rights of the Child* (2007) 206

Bhabha, J, 'Independent Children, Inconsistent Adults: Child Migration and the Legal Framework' (Innocenti Discussion Paper No IDP-2008-02, UNICEF, May 2008)

Bhabha, J, *Child Migration and Human Rights in a Global Age* (2014)

Bhabha, J, and Crock, M, *Seeking Asylum Alone: A Comparative Study* (2007)

Bhabha, J, and Schmidt, S, *Seeking Asylum Alone: United States* (2006)

Bhabha, J, and Young, W, 'Not Adults in Miniature: Unaccompanied Child Asylum Seekers and the New US Guidelines' (1999) 11 *International Journal of Refugee Law* 84

Bierwirth, C, 'The Protection of Refugee and Asylum-Seeking Children, the Convention on the Rights of the Child and the Work of the Committee on the Rights of the Child' (2005) 24(2) *Refugee Survey Quarterly* 98

Bjorge, E, *The Evolutionary Interpretation of Treaties* (2014)

Blake, N, 'Current Problems in Asylum and Protection Law: The UK Judicial Perspective' (Paper presented at the Ninth World Conference of the International Association of Refugee Law Judges, Slovenia, 7 September 2011)

Blake, N, and Husain, R, *Immigration, Asylum and Human Rights* (2003)

Bolton, S, et al., 'Vulnerable Persons Working Group' (Workshop Discussion Paper, International Association of Refugee Law Judges, World Conference, Slovenia, 2011)

Bolton, S, 'Promoting the Best Interests of the Child in UK Asylum Law and Procedures' (2012) 26 *Journal of Immigration, Asylum and Nationality Law* 232

Bossin, M, and Demiradache, L, 'A Canadian Perspective on the Subjective Component of the Bipartite Test for "Persecution": Time for Re-Evaluation' (2004) 22(1) *Refuge* 108

Boyle, A, 'Some Reflections on the Relationship of Treaties and Soft Law' (1999) 48 *International & Comparative Law Quarterly* 901

Brennan, S, and Noggle, R, 'The Moral Status of Children: Children's Rights, Parents' Rights, and Family Justice' (1997) 23 *Social Theory and Practice* 1

Bronstein, I, and Montgomery, P, 'Psychological Distress in Refugee Children: A Systematic Review' (2011) 14 *Clinical Child and Family Psychology Review* 44

Carr, B, 'We Don't Need to See Them Cry: Eliminating the Subjective Apprehension Element of the Well-Founded Fear Analysis for Child Refugee Applicants' (2006) 33 *Pepperdine Law Review* 535

Carr, B, 'Incorporating a "Best Interests of the Child" Approach into Immigration Law and Procedure' (2009) 12 *Yale Human Rights and Development Law Journal* 120

Chetail, V, 'Are Refugee Rights Human Rights? An Unorthodox Questioning of the Relations between Refugee Law and Human Rights Law' in R Rubio-Marín (ed), *Human Rights and Immigration* (2014) 19

Clapham, A, *Human Rights in the Private Sphere* (1993)

Clapham, A, *Human Rights Obligations of Non-State Actors* (2006)

Cohen, C P, 'The Human Rights of Children' (1983) 12 *Capital University Law Review* 369

Cohen, J, 'Questions of Credibility: Omissions, Discrepancies and Errors of Recall in the Testimony of Asylum Seekers' (2001) 13(3) *International Journal of Refugee Law* 293

Cohn, I, 'The Convention on the Rights of the Child: What It Means for Children in War' (1991) 3(1)*International Journal of Refugee Law* 100

Cohn, I, and Goodwin-Gill, G S, *Child Soldiers: The Role of Children in Armed Conflict* (1994)

Crawley, H, 'Child First, Migrant Second: Ensuring That *Every* Child Matters' (Policy Paper, ILPA, February 2006)

Crawley, H, ILPA, *When Is a Child Not a Child? Asylum, Age Disputes and the Process of Age Assessment* (2007)

Crawley, H, '"Asexual, Apolitical Beings": The Interpretation of Children's Identities and Experiences in the UK Asylum System' (2011) 37 *Journal of Ethnic and Migration Studies* 1171

Crisp, J, 'Meeting the Needs and Realizing the Rights of Refugee Children and Adolescents: From Policy to Practice' (1996) 15(3) *Refugee Survey Quarterly* 1

Crock, M, 'Lonely Refuge: Judicial Responses to Separated Children Seeking Refugee Protection in Australia' (2005) 22(2) *Law in Context* 120

Crock, M, *Seeking Asylum Alone: Australia* (2006)

Crock, M, 'Re-Thinking the Paradigms of Protection: Children as Convention Refugees in Australia' in J McAdam (ed), *Forced Migration, Human Rights and Security* (2008) 155

D'Andrea, W, et al., 'Understanding Interpersonal Trauma in Children: Why We Need a Developmentally Appropriate Trauma Diagnosis' (2012) 82(2) *American Journal of Orthopsychiatry* 187

Dalrymple, J K, 'Seeking Asylum Alone: Using the Best Interests of the Child Principle to Protect Unaccompanied Minors' (2006) 26 *Boston College Third World Law Journal* 131

Dauvergne, C, and Millbank, J, 'Forced Marriage as a Harm in Domestic and International Law' (2010) 73 *The Modern Law Review* 57

Detrick, S, *The United Nations Convention on the Rights of the Child: A Guide to the 'Travaux Préparatoires'* (1992)

Detrick, S, *A Commentary on the United Nations Convention on the Rights of the Child* (1999)

Doná, G, and Veale, A, 'Divergent Discourses, Children and Forced Migration' (2011) 37 *Journal of Ethnic and Migration Studies* 1273

Dorevitch, A, and Foster, M, 'Obstacles on the Road to Protection: Assessing the Treatment of Sex-Trafficking Victims under Australia's Migration and Refugee Law' (2008) 9(1) *Melbourne Journal of International Law* 1

Eastmond, M, and Ascher, H, 'In the Best Interest of the Child? The Politics of Vulnerability and Negotiations for Asylum in Sweden' (2011) 37(8) *Journal of Ethnic and Migration Studies* 1185

Edwards, A, 'Age and Gender Dimensions in International Refugee Law' in E Feller, V Türk and F Nicholson (eds), *Refugee Protection in International Law: UNHCR's Global Consultations on International Protection* (2003) 46

Edwards, A, 'Transitioning Gender: Feminist Engagement with International Refugee Law and Policy 1950–2010' (2010) 29(2) *Refugee Survey Quarterly* 21

Edwards, A, *Violence against Women under International Human Rights Law* (2010)

Eekelaar, J, 'The Emergence of Children's Rights' (1986) 6 *Oxford Journal of Legal Studies* 161

Eekelaar, J, 'The Interests of the Child and the Child's Wishes: The Role of Dynamic Self-Determinism' in P Alston (ed), *The Best Interest of the Child: Reconciling Culture and Human Rights* (1994)

Farmer, A, 'A Commentary on the Committee on the Rights of the Child's Definition of Non-Refoulement for Children: Broad Protection for Fundamental Rights' (2011) 80 *Fordham Law Review Res Gestae* 39

Feller, E, Assistant High Commissioner – Protection, UNHCR, 'Rule of Law 60 Years On' (Statement, 61st Session of the UNHCR ExCom, 6 October 2010)

Feller, E, 'The Right to Be Heard for Separated Children Seeking Asylum in Europe' (Statement delivered to the EU Seminar on Children Affected by Armed Conflict and Forced Displacement – A Child Rights Perspective in Development Co-Operation and Migration Policies, Sweden, 1 March 2001)

Feller, E, 'Statement by Erika Feller' (2004) 23(2) *Refugee Survey Quarterly* 329

Finch, N, 'Seeking Asylum Alone' in H Andersson et al. (eds), *The Asylum Seeking Child in Europe* (2005) 57

Fortin, J, *Children's Rights and the Developing Law* (2009)

Fortin, J, 'Are Children's Best Interests Really Best? ZH (Tanzania) (FC) v Secretary of State for the Home Department' (2011) 74 *Modern Law Review* 947

Foster, M, *International Refugee Law and Socio-Economic Rights: Refuge from Deprivation* (2007)

Foster, M, 'Non-Refoulement on the Basis of Socio-Economic Deprivation: The Scope of Complementary Protection in International Human Rights Law' [2009] *New Zealand Law Review* 257

Foster, M, 'The "Ground with the Least Clarity": A Comparative Study of Jurisprudential Developments Relating to "Membership of a Particular Social Group"' (UNHCR Legal and Protection Policy Series Paper, August 2012)

Foster, M, and Pobjoy, J, 'A Failed Case of Legal Exceptionalism? Refugee Status Determination in Australia's "Excised" Territories' (2011) 23 *International Journal of Refugee Law* 583

Fredman, S, *Discrimination Law* (2nd edn, 2011)

Freeman, J M and Huu, N D, *Voices from the Camps: Vietnamese Children Seeking Asylum* (2003)

Freeman, M, *A Commentary on the United Nations Convention on the Rights of the Child: Article 3 – The Best Interests of the Child* (2007)

Freeman, M, 'Why It Remains Important to Take Children's Rights Seriously' (2007) 15 *International Journal of Children's Rights* 5

Freeman, M, 'The Human Rights of Children' (2010) 63 *Current Legal Problems* 1

Freeman, M, 'The Value and Values of Children's Rights' in A Invernizzi and J Williams (eds), *The Human Rights of Children* (2011) 21

French, D, 'Treaty Interpretation and the Incorporation of Extraneous Legal Rules' (2005) 55 *International and Comparative Law Quarterly* 281

Fullerton, M, 'The Law of Refugee Status by James C. Hathaway and Michelle Foster' (2015) 109(4) *American Journal of International Law* 908, 915–17.

Gardiner, R, *Treaty Interpretation* (2nd edn, 2015)

Gates, C, 'Working toward a Global Discourse on Children's Rights: The Problem of Unaccompanied Children and the International Response to Their Plight' (1999) 7 *Indiana Journal of Global Legal Studies* 299

Glen, P, 'The Removability of Non-Citizen Parents and the Best Interests of Citizen Children: How to Balance Competing Imperatives in the Context of Removal Proceedings?' (2012) 30 *Berkeley Journal of International Law* 1

Goodman, R, 'The Incorporation of International Human Rights Standards into Sexual Orientation Asylum Claims: Cases of Involuntary "Medical" Intervention' (1995) 105 *Yale Law Journal* 255

Goodwin-Gill, G S, *The Refugee in International Law* (1983)

Goodwin-Gill, G S, 'Unaccompanied Refugee Minors: The Role and Place of International Law in the Pursuit of Durable Solutions' (1995) 3 *International Journal of Children's Rights* 405

Goodwin-Gill, G S, 'Who to Protect, How ..., and the Future?' (1997) 9 *International Journal of Refugee Law* 1

Goodwin-Gill, G S, 'Part II: Final Report and Draft Declaration on Minimum International Standards for Refugee Procedures' in International Law Association, *Delhi Conference – Committee on Refugee Procedures* (2002) 18

Goodwin-Gill, G S, 'Refugees and Their Human Rights' (Working Paper No 17, Refugee Studies Centre, August 2004)

Goodwin-Gill, G S, 'The Search for the One, True Meaning ... ' in G S Goodwin-Gill and H Lambert (eds), *The Limits of Transnational Law: Refugee Law, Policy Harmonization and Judicial Dialogue in the European Union* (2010) 204

Goodwin-Gill, G S, 'The Challenge of the Child Soldier' in H Strachan and S Scheipers (eds), *The Changing Character of War* (2011) 410

Goodwin-Gill, G S, 'The United Nations Convention on the Rights of the Child and Its Application to Child Refugee Status Determination and Asylum Processes: Introduction' (2012) 26 *Journal of Immigration, Asylum and Nationality Law* 226

Goodwin-Gill, G S, and Lambert, H (eds), *The Limits of Transnational Law: Refugee Law, Policy Harmonization and Judicial Dialogue in the European Union* (2010)

Goodwin-Gill, G S, and McAdam, J, *The Refugee in International Law* (3rd edn, 2007)

Grahl-Madsen, A, *The Status of Refugees in International Law* (1966)

Griffin, J, *On Human Rights* (2008)

Guggenheim, M, *What's Wrong with Children's Rights* (2005)

Gupta, A, 'The New Nexus' (2014) 85 *University of Colorado Law Review* 377

Hafen, B, and Hafen, J, 'Abandoning Children to Their Autonomy: The United Nations Convention on the Rights of the Child' (1996) 37 *Harvard International Law Journal* 449

Happold, M, 'Excluding Children from Refugee Status: Child Soldiers and Article 1 F of the Refugee Convention' (2002) *17 American University International Law Review* 1131

Happold, M, *Child Soldiers in International Law* (2005)

Harrell-Bond, B, 'Are Refugee Camps Good for Children?' (Working Paper No 29, New Issues in Refugee Research, UNHCR, August 2000)

Hart, H L A, *The Concept of Law* (3rd edn, 2012)

Harvey, C, 'Is Humanity Enough? Refugees, Asylum Seekers and the Rights Regime' in S Juss and C Harvey (eds), *Contemporary Issues in Refugee Law* (2013) 68

Harvey, C, 'Time for Reform? Refugees, Asylum-Seekers, and Protection under International Human Rights Law' (2014) 33(4) *Refugee Survey Quarterly* 1

Hathaway, J C, 'The Evolution of Refugee Status in International Law: 1920-1950' (1984) 33 *International and Comparative Law Quarterly* 348

Hathaway, J C, 'A Reconsideration of the Underlying Premise of Refugee Law' (1990) 31(1) *Harvard International Law Journal* 129

Hathaway, J C, 'Reconceiving Refugee Law as Human Rights Protection' (1991) 4 *Journal of Refugee Studies* 113

Hathaway, J C, *The Law of Refugee Status* (1991)

Hathaway, J C, 'The Relationship between Human Rights and Refugee Law: What Refugee Judges Can Contribute' in International Association of Refugee Law Judges, *The Realities of Refugee Determination on the Eve of a New Millennium: The Role of the Judiciary* (1998) 80

Hathaway, J C, 'A Forum for the Transnational Development of Refugee Law: The IARLJ's Advanced Refugee Law Workshop' (2003) 15 *International Journal of Refugee Law* 418

Hathaway, J C, *The Rights of Refugees under International Law* (2005)

Hathaway, J C, 'Leveraging Asylum' (2010) 45 *Texas International Law Journal* 503

Hathaway, J C, and Foster, M, 'International Protection/Relocation/Flight Alternative as an Aspect of Refugee Status Determination' in E Feller, V Türk, and F Nicholson (eds), *Refugee Protection in International Law: UNHCR's Global Consultations on International Protection* (2003) 353

Hathaway, J C, and Foster, M, 'The Causal Connection ("Nexus") to a Convention Ground' (2003) 15 *International Journal of Refugee Law* 461

Hathaway, J C, and Foster, M, *The Law of Refugee Status* (2nd edn, 2014)

Hathaway, J C, and Hicks, W S, 'Is There a Subjective Element in the Refugee Convention's Requirement of "Well-Founded Fear"?' (2004) 26 *Michigan Journal of International Law* 505

Hathaway, J C, North, A M, and Pobjoy, J, 'Supervising the Refugee Convention: Introduction' (2013) 26 *Journal of Refugee Studies* 323

Hathaway, J C, and Pobjoy, J, 'Queer Cases Make Bad Law' (2012) 44 *New York University Journal of International Law and Politics* 315

Hazeldean, S, 'Confounding Identities: The Paradox of LGBT Children under Asylum Law' (2011) 45 *UC Davis Law Review* 373

Herlihy, J, and Turner, S W, 'The Psychology of Seeking Protection' (2009) 21(2) *International Journal of Refugee Law* 171

Holborn, L W, *The International Refugee Organization: A Specialized Agency of the United Nations – Its History and Work, 1946–1952* (1956)

James, A, and Prout, A, *Constructing and Reconstructing Childhood* (1990)

Jastram, K, 'Economic Harm as a Basis for Refugee Status and the Application of Human Rights Law to the Interpretation of Economic Persecution' in J Simeon (ed), *Critical Issues in International Refugee Law* (2010) 143

Jastram, K, and Newland, K, 'Family Unity and Refugee Protection' in E Feller, V Türk and F Nicholson (eds), *Refugee Protection in International Law: UNHCR's Global Consultations on International Protection* (2003) 555

Jayawickrama, N, *The Judicial Application of Human Rights Law: National, Regional and International Jurisprudence* (2002)

Joseph, S, and Castan, M, *The International Covenant on Civil and Political Rights* (3rd edn, 2013)

Joseph, S, Schultz, J and Castan, M, *The International Covenant on Civil and Political Rights: Cases, Materials, and Commentary* (2nd edn, 2004)

Kagan, M, 'Is Truth in the Eye of the Beholder? Objective Credibility Assessment in Refugee Status Determination' (2003) 17 *Georgetown Immigration Law Journal* 367

Kagan, M, 'Refugee Credibility Assessment and the "Religious Imposter" Problem: A Case Study of Eritrean Pentecostal Claims in Egypt' (2010) 43(5) *Vanderbilt Journal of Transnational Law* 1179

King, M, et al., 'A Systematic Review of Mental Disorder, Suicide, and Deliberate Self Harm in Lesbian, Gay and Bisexual People' (2008) 8 *PMC Psychiatry* 70

Kirby, M, 'Transnational Judicial Dialogue, the Internationalisation of Law and Australian Judges' (2008) 9 *Melbourne Journal of International Law* 171

Kohli, R K S, and Mitchell, F, 'An Analysis of the Coverage of Issues Related to Children in COI Reports Produced by the Home Office' (Paper prepared for the Advisory Panel on Country Information, April 2008)

Kohli, R K S, Mitchell, F, and Connolly, H, 'An Analysis of the Coverage of Issues Related to *Children* in Country of Origin Reports Produced by the Home Office' (Paper prepared for the Independent Advisory Group on Country Information, October 2012)

Krappmann, L, 'The Weight of the Child's Views (Article 12 of the Convention on the Rights of the Child)' (2010) 18 *International Journal of Children's Rights* 501

Lambert, H, 'The European Court of Human Rights and the Rights of Refugees and Other Persons in Need of Protection to Family Reunion' (1999) 11(3) *International Journal of Refugee Law* 427

Lambert, H, 'The Conceptualisation of "Persecution" by the House of Lords: *Horvath v SSHD*' (2001) 13 *International Journal of Refugee Law* 16

Langlaude, S, *The Right of the Child to Religious Freedom in International Law* (2007)

Lauterpacht, E, and Bethlehem, D, 'The Scope and Content of the Principle of Non-Refoulement' in E Feller, V Türk and F Nicholson (eds), *Refugee Protection in International Law: UNHCR's Global Consultations on International Protection* (2003) 87

Legomsky, S H, 'Second Refugee Movements and the Return of Asylum Seekers to Third Countries: The Meaning of Effective Protection' (2003) 15 *International Journal of Refugee Law* 567

Lidén, H, and Rusten, H, 'Asylum, Participation and the Best Interests of the Child: New Lessons from Norway' (2007) 21 *Children and Society* 273

Lipsky, G A, (ed), *Law and Politics in the World Community: Essays on Hans Kelsen's Pure Theory and Related Problems in International Law* (1953)

Löhr, T, *Die kinderspezifische Auslegung des völkerrechtlichen Flüchtlingsbegriffs* (2009)

Löhr, T, 'Der Flüchtlingsbegriff im Lichte der Kinderrechtskonvention' in K Barwig, S Beichel-Benedetti and G Brinkmann (eds), *Hohenheimer Tage zum Ausländerrecht* (2010) 300

Lowe, V, *International Law* (2007)

Lundberg, A, 'The Best Interests of the Child Principle in Swedish Asylum Cases: The Marginalization of Children's Rights' (2011) 3 *Journal of Human Rights Practice* 49

MacDonald, A, *The Rights of the Child: Law and Practice* (2011)

Macdonald, I A, and Toal, R, *Immigration Law and Practice in the United Kingdom* (9th edn, 2014)

Marouf, F, 'The Emerging Importance of "Social Visibility" in Defining a "Particular Social Group" and Its Potential Impact on Asylum Claims Related to Sexual Orientation and Gender' (2008) 27 *Yale Law and Policy Review* 47

Martin, D, 'The Refugee Concept: On Definitions, Politics, and the Careful Use of a Scarce Resource' in H Adelman (ed), *Refugee Policy: Canada and the United States* (1991) 30

Martin, D, 'Review of *The Law of Refugee Status*' (1993) 47 *American Journal of International Law* 348

Mathew, P, Hathaway, J C, and Foster, M, 'The Role of State Protection in Refugee Analysis' (2003) 15 *International Journal of Refugee Law* 444

McAdam, J, 'Seeking Asylum under the Convention on the Rights of the Child: A Case for Complementary Protection' (2006) 14 *International Journal of Children's Rights* 251

McAdam, J, *Complementary Protection in International Refugee Law* (2007)

McAdam, J, 'Individual Risk, Armed Conflict and the Standard of Proof in Complementary Protection Claims: The European Union and Canada Compared' in J C Simeon (ed), *Critical Issues in International Refugee Law: Strategies for Interpretative Harmony* (2010) 59

McAdam, J, 'Australian Complementary Protection: A Step-By-Step Approach' (2011) 33 *Sydney Law Review* 687

McAdam, J, 'Interpretation of the 1951 Convention' in A Zimmermann (ed), *The 1951 Convention Relating to the Status of Refugees and Its 1967 Protocol: A Commentary* (2011) 75

McCorquodale, R, 'Non-State Actors and International Human Rights Law' in S Joseph and A McBeth (eds), *International Human Rights Law* (2009) 97

McCorquodale, R, (ed), *International Law Beyond the State: Essays on Sovereignty, Non-State Actors and Human Rights* (2011)

McLachlan, C, 'The Principle of Systemic Integration and Article 31(3)(c) of the Vienna Convention' (2005) 54 *International and Comparative Law Quarterly* 279

Mégret, F, 'Nature of Obligations' in D Moeckli, S Shah and S Sivakumaran, *International Human Rights Law* (2nd edn, 2014) 96

Melo, L, 'When Children Suffer: The Failure of US Immigration Law to Provide Practical Protection for Persecuted Children' (2010) 40 *Golden Gate University Law Review* 263

Melzac, S, 'The Emotional Impact of Violence on Children' in V Varma (ed), *Violence in Children and Adolescents* (1996) 1

Messineo, F, 'Non-Refoulement Obligations in Public International Law: Towards a New Protection Status?' in S Juss (ed), *Research Companion to Migration Theory and Policy* (2012)

Millbank, J, 'From Discretion to Disbelief: Recent Trends in Refugee Determinations on the Basis of Sexual Orientation in Australia and the United Kingdom' (2009) 13(2) *International Journal of Human Rights* 391

Minow, M, 'Children's Rights: Where We've Been and Where We're Going' (1995) 68 *Temple Law Review* 1573

Mullally, S, 'Separated Children in Ireland: Responding to "Terrible Wrongs"' (2011) 23(4) *International Journal of Refugee Law* 632

Muller, M, Anker, D, and Rosenberg, L, '*Escobar v Gonzales*: A Backwards Step for Child Asylum Seekers and the Rule of Law in Particular Social Group Asylum Claims' (2006) 10(1) *UC Davis Journal of Juvenile Law and Policy* 243

Myers, J E B, et al., 'Psychological Research on Children as Witnesses: Practical Implications for Forensic Interviews and Courtroom Testimony' (1996) 28 *Pacific Law Journal* 3

Nillson, E, 'A Child Perspective in the Swedish Process: Rhetoric and Practice' in H E Anderson et al. (eds), *The Asylum-Seeking Child in Europe* (2005) 73

Nolan, A, *Children's Socio-Economic Rights, Democracy and the Courts* (2011)

Noll, G, 'Evidentiary Assessment under the Refugee Convention: Risk, Pain and the Intersubjectivity of Fear' in G Noll (ed), *Proof, Evidentiary Assessment and Credibility in Asylum Procedures* (2005) 141

Noll, G, 'Seeking Asylum at Embassies: A Right to Entry under International Law?' (2005) 27 *IJRL* 542

Noll, G, 'Asylum Claims and the Translation of Culture into Politics' (2006) 41 *Texas International Law Journal* 491

Nowak, M, *Article 6: The Right to Life, Survival and Development* (2005)

Nowak, M, and E McArthur, *The United Nations Convention Against Torture: A Commentary* (2008)

Nykanen, E, 'Protecting Children? The European Convention on Human Rights and Child Asylum Seekers' (2001) 3 *European Journal of Migration and Law* 315

O'Donnell, D, 'Resettlement or Repatriation: Screened out Vietnamese Child Asylum Seekers and the Convention on the Rights of the Child' (1989) 6(3) *International Journal of Refugee Law* 382

O'Donnell, D, 'The Rights of Children to Be Heard: Children's Right to Have Their Views Taken into Account and to Participate in Legal and Administrative Proceedings' (Innocenti Working Paper No IWP-2009–04, UNICEF, April 2009)

Orakhelashvili, A, 'Restrictive Interpretation of Human Rights Treaties in the Recent Jurisprudence of the European Court of Human Rights' (2003) 14 *European Journal of International Law* 529

Parsons, A, *The Best Interests of the Child in Asylum and Refugee Procedures in Finland* (2010)

Pask, E D, 'Unaccompanied Refugee and Displaced Children: Jurisdiction, Decision-Making and Representation' (1989) 1(2) *International Journal of Refugee Law* 199

Pauwelyn, J, 'The Role of Public International Law in the WTO: How Far Can We Go?' (2001) 95 *American Journal of International Law* 535

Pauwelyn, J, *Conflict of Norms in Public International Law: How WTO Law Relates to Other Rules of International Law* (2003)

Plattner, D, 'Protection of Children in International Humanitarian Law' (1984) 24(240) *International Review of the Red Cross* 140

Pobjoy, J, 'Treating Like Alike: The Principle of Non-Discrimination as a Tool to Mandate the Equal Protection of Refugees and Beneficiaries of Complementary Protection' (2010) 34 *Melbourne University Law Review* 181

Pobjoy, J, 'A Child Rights Framework for Assessing the Status of Refugee Children' in S Juss and C Harvey (eds), *Contemporary Issues in Refugee Law* (2013) 91

Pobjoy, J, 'The Best Interests of the Child Principle as an Independent Source of Protection' (2015) 64(2) *International Comparative Law Quarterly* 327

Pobjoy, J, 'Article 22' in P Alston and J Tobin (eds), *The UN Convention on the Rights of the Child: A Commentary* (2017) (forthcoming)

Pobjoy, J, and Tobin, J, 'Article 10' in P Alston and J Tobin (eds), *The UN Convention on the Rights of the Child: A Commentary* (2017) (forthcoming)

Price, M E, 'Persecution Complex: Justifying Asylum Law's Preference for Persecuted People' (2006) 47(2) *Harvard International Law Journal* 413

Reinisch, A, 'The Changing International Legal Framework for Dealing with Non-State Actors' in P Alston (ed), *Non-State Actors and Human Rights* (2005) 37

Rodley, N, *The Treatment of Prisoners under International Law* (2009)

Rossi, E, 'A "Special Track" for Former Child Soldiers: Enacting a "Child Soldier Visa" as an Alternative to Asylum Protection' (2013) 31 *Berkeley Journal of International Law* 392

Ruxton, S, *Separated Children and EU Asylum and Immigration Policy* (2003)

S, Peers et al., *The EU Charter of Fundamental Rights: A Commentary* (2014) 661–91

Sadoway, G, 'Refugee Children before the Immigration and Refugee Board' (1996) 15(5) *Refuge* 17

Sands, P, 'Treaty, Custom and the Cross-Fertilization of International Law' (1998) 1 *Yale Human Rights and Development Law Journal* 85

Schabas, W, *The Abolition of the Death Penalty in International Law* (3rd edn, 2002)

Scott, C, and Alston, P, 'Adjudicating Constitutional Priorities in a Transnational Context: A Comment on Soobramoney's Legacy and Grootboom's Promise' (2000) 16 *South African Journal on Human Rights* 206

Seugling, C, 'Toward a Comprehensive Response to the Transnational Migration of Unaccompanied Minors in the United States' (2004) 37 *Vanderbilt Journal of Transnational Law* 861

Shacknove, A, 'Who Is a Refugee' (1985) 95 *Ethics* 274

Simmons, B A, *Mobilizing for Human Rights* (2009)

Sinclair, I, *The Vienna Convention on the Law of Treaties* (1984)

Slaughter, A, 'A Typology of Transjudicial Communication' (1994) 29 *University of Richmond Law Review* 99

Smyth, C, *European Asylum Law and the Rights of the Child* (2014)

Spijkerboer, T, *Gender and Refugee Status* (2000)

Steiner, H J, Alston, P, and Goodman, R, *International Human Rights in Context: Law Politics Morals* (3rd edn, 2007)

Storey, H, 'The Right to Family Life and Immigration Case Law at Strasbourg' (1990) 39 *International & Comparative Law Quarterly* 328

Sweeney, J A, 'Credibility, Proof and Refugee Law' (2009) 21(4) *International Journal of Refugee Law* 700

Thèry, I, '"The Interest of the Child" and the Regulation of the Post-Divorce Family' in C Smart and S Sevenhuijsen (eds), *Child Custody and the Politics of Gender* (1989) 78

Thronson, D, 'Kids Will Be Kids? Reconsidering Conceptions of Children's Rights Underlying Immigration Law' (2002) 63 *Ohio State Law Journal* 979

Thronson, D, 'Choiceless Choices: Deportation and the Parent-Child Relationship' (2006) 6 *Nevada Law Journal* 1165

Thronson, D, 'You Can't Get Here from Here: Toward a More Child-Centered Immigration Law' (2006) 14 *Virginia Journal of Social Policy and the Law* 58

Thronson, D, 'Thinking Small: The Need for Big Changes in Immigration Law's Treatment of Children' (2010) 14 *UC Davis Journal of Juvenile Law and Policy* 239

Thronson, D, 'Clashing Values and Cross Purposes: Immigration Law's Marginalization of Children and Families' in J Bhabha (ed), *Children without a State: The Scope of Child Statelessness in the 21st Century* (2011) 237

Tobin, J, 'Parents and Children's Rights under the Convention on the Rights of the Child: Finding Reconciliation in a Misunderstood Relationship' (2005) 7(2) *Australian Journal of Professional and Applied Ethics* 31

Tobin, J, 'Beyond the Supermarket Shelf: Using a Rights Based Approach to Address Children's Health Needs' (2006) 14 *International Journal of Children's Rights* 275

Tobin, J, 'Judging the Judges: Are They Adopting the Rights Approach in Matters Involving Children' (2009) 33 *Melbourne University Law Review* 579

Tobin, J, 'Seeking to Persuade: A Constructive Approach to Human Rights Treaty Interpretation' (2010) 23 *Harvard Human Rights Journal* 1

Tobin, J, 'Assessing GLBTI Refugee Claims: Using Human Rights Law to Shift the Narrative of Persecution within Refugee Law' (2012) 44 *New York University Journal of International Law and Politics* 447

Tobin, J, *The Right to Health in International Law* (2012)

Tobin, J, 'Justifying Children's Rights' (2013) 21 *International Journal of Children's Rights* 395

Tuitt, P, 'The State, the Family and the Child Refugee' in D Fottrell (ed), *Revisiting Children's Rights: 10 Years of the UN Convention on the Rights of the Child* (2000) 149

Türk, V, 'Introductory Note to UNHCR Guidelines on International Protection' (2003) 15 *International Journal of Refugee Law* 303

Van Bueren, G, 'Opening Pandora's Box: Protecting Children against Torture or Cruel, Inhuman and Degrading Treatment or Punishment' (1995) 17 *Law and Policy* 378

Van Bueren, G, *The International Law on the Rights of the Child* (1998)

Van der Kolk, B A, 'The Complexity of Adaptation to Trauma: Self-Regulation Stimulus Discrimination, and Characterological Development' in B A van der Kolk et al. (eds), *Traumatic Stress: The Effects of Overwhelming Experience on Mind, Body, and Society* (1996) 182

Verdirame, G, 'A Friendly Act of Socio-Cultural Contestation: Asylum and the Big Cultural Divide' (2012) 44 *New York University Journal of International Law and Politics* 559

Verdirame, G, and Pobjoy, J, 'The End of Refugee Camps?' in S Juss (ed), *Ashgate Research Companion on Migration Theory and Policy* (2013) 91

Vernant, J, *The Refugee in the Post-War World* (1953)

Vitus, K, and Lidén, H, 'The Status of the Asylum-Seeking Child in Norway and Denmark: Comparing Discourses, Politics and Practices' (2010) 23(1) *Journal of Refugee Studies* 62

Waibel, M, 'Demystifying the Art of Interpretation' (2010) 22 *European Journal of International Law* 571

Watters, C, *Refugee Children: Toward the Next Horizon* (2008)

Weis, P, 'The Concept of the Refugee in International Law' (1960) 87 *Journal du droit international* 928

Wouters, K, *International Legal Standards for the Protection from Refoulement* (2009)

Wyness, M, Harrison, L and Buchanan, I, 'Childhood, Politics and Ambiguity: Towards an Agenda for Children's Political Inclusion' (2004) 38(1) *Sociology* 81

Young, K, 'The Minimum Core of Economic and Social Rights: A Concept in Search of Content' (2008) 33 *Yale Journal of International Law* 113

Zimmerman, A, (ed), *The 1951 Convention Relating to the Status of Refugees and Its 1967 Protocol: A Commentary* (2011)

Zimmermann, A, and Mahler, C, 'Article 1A, Para 2' in A Zimmermann (ed), *The 1951 Convention Relating to the Status of Refugees and Its 1967 Protocol: A Commentary* (2011) 281

UN Materials

General

Ad Hoc Committee on Statelessness and Related Problems, *Memorandum from the Secretariat of the International Refugee Organization*, E/AC.32/L.16 (1950)

Ad Hoc Committee on Statelessness and Related Problems, *Provisional Draft of Parts of the Definition Article of the Preliminary Draft Convention Relating to the Status of Refugees, Prepared by the Working Group on This Article*, E/AC.32/L.6 (1950)

Ad Hoc Committee on Statelessness and Related Problems, *United States of America: Memorandum on the Definition Article of the Preliminary Draft Convention Relating to the Status of Refugees (and Stateless Persons) (E/AC.32/2)*, E/AC.32/L.4 (1950)

Bustamante, J, *Report of the Special Rapporteur on the Human Rights of Migrants*, A/64/213 (2009)

Bustamante, J, *Report of the Special Rapporteur on the Human Rights of Migrants*, A/HRC/11/7 (2009)

Economic and Social Council, *Progress and Prospect of Repatriation, Resettlement and Immigration of Refugees and Displaced Persons – Resolution of 24 August 1948*, ECOSOC Res 157 (VII), E/1027 (1948)

Holy See: Draft Recommendations for Inclusion in the Final Act of the Conference, E/CONF.2/103 (1951)

ILC, 'Law of Treaties' [1964] (2) *Yearbook of the International Law Commission* 5

ILC, 'Reports of the Commission to the General Assembly' [1966] (2) *Yearbook of the International Law Commission* 169

ILC, *Report of the International Law Commission – Fifty-Third Session*, A/56/10 (2001)

ILC, *Fragmentation of International Law: Difficulties Arising from the Diversification and Expansion of International Law – Report of the Study Group of the International Law Commission*, A/CN.4/L.702 (2006)

Koskenniemi, M, ILC, *Fragmentation of International Law: Difficulties Arising from the Diversification and Expansion of International Law – Report of the Study Group of the International Law Commission*, A/CN.4/L.682 (2006)

Machel, G, *Impact of Armed Conflict on Children*, A/51/306 (1996)

Note Verbale Dated 5 October 1979 Addressed to the Division of Human Rights by the Permanent Representation of the Polish People's Republic to the United Nations in Geneva, E/CN.4/1349 (1979)

Question of a Convention on the Rights of the Child – Report of the Working Group, E/CN.4/L.1468 (1979)

Report of the Ad Hoc Committee on Statelessness and Related Problems, E/AC.32/5 (1950)

Report of the Independent Expert for the United Nations Study on Violence against Children, A/61/299 (2006)

Report of the Informal Open-Ended Working Group on the Rights of the Child, E/CN.4/1982/30/Add.1 (1982)

Report of the International Law Commission – Fifty-Eighth Session, A/61/10 (2006)

Report of the Sixty-First Session of the Executive Committee of the High Commissioner's Programme, A/AC.96/1095 (2010)

Report of the Working Group on a Draft Convention on the Rights of the Child, E/CN.4/L.1575 (1981)

Report of the Working Group on a Draft Convention on the Rights of the Child, E/CN.4/1984/71 (1984)

Report of the Working Group on a Draft Convention on the Rights of the Child, E/CN.4/1988/28 (1988)

Report of the Working Group on a Draft Convention on the Rights of the Child, E/CN.4/1989/48 (1989)

Summary Record of the Thirty-Fourth Meeting, E/CONF.2/SR.34 (1951)

Summary Record of the 1438th Meeting, E/CN.4/SR.1438 (1978)

Summary Record of the 216th Meeting, CRC/C/SR.216 (1995)

Summary Record of the 53rd Meeting (Second Part), E/CN.4/1985/SR.53/Add.1 (1985)

Summary Record of the 54th Meeting, E/CN.4/1989/SR.54 (1989)

Summary Record of the 56th Meeting, E/CN.4/1988/SR.56 (1988)

UN, *Children Deprived of a Normal Home Life*, E/CN.5/271 (1952)

UNGA, International Conference on Indo-Chinese Refugees, Office of the UNHCR, *Report of the Secretary General*, A/44/523 (1989)

UNGA, *A World Fit for Children*, A/RES/S-27/2 (2002)

UNGA, *Assistance to Refugees, Returnees and Displaced Persons in Africa*, A/RES/47/107 (1993)

UNGA, *Assistance to Refugees, Returnees and Displaced Persons in Africa*, A/RES/48/118 (1994)

UNGA, *Assistance to Refugees, Returnees and Displaced Persons in Africa*, A/RES/49/174 (1995)

UNGA, *Assistance to Unaccompanied Refugee Minors*, A/RES/49/172 (1995)

UNGA, *Assistance to Refugees, Returnees and Displaced Persons in Africa*, A/RES/50/149 (1996)

UNGA, *Assistance to Unaccompanied Refugee Minors*, A/RES/50/150 (1996)

UNGA, *Assistance to Refugees, Returnees and Displaced Persons in Africa*, A/RES/51/71 (1997)

UNGA, *Assistance to Unaccompanied Refugee Minors*, A/RES/51/73 (1997)

UNGA, *Assistance to Refugees, Returnees and Displaced Persons in Africa*, A/RES/52/101 (1998)

UNGA, *Assistance to Unaccompanied Refugee Minors*, A/RES/52/105 (1998)

UNGA, *Assistance to Refugees, Returnees and Displaced Persons in Africa*, A/RES/53/126 (1999)

UNGA, *Assistance to Unaccompanied Refugee Minors*, A/RES/53/122 (1999)

UNGA, *Assistance to Refugees, Returnees and Displaced Persons in Africa*, A/RES/54/147 (2000)

UNGA, *Assistance to Unaccompanied Refugee Minors*, A/RES/54/145 (2000)

UNGA, *Assistance to Refugees, Returnees and Displaced Persons in Africa*, A/RES/55/77 (2001)

UNGA, *Assistance to Refugees, Returnees and Displaced Persons in Africa*, A/RES/56/135 (2002)

UNGA, *Assistance to Unaccompanied Refugee Minors*, A/RES/56/136 (2002)

UNGA, *Assistance to Refugees, Returnees and Displaced Persons in Africa*, A/RES/57/183
    (2003)
UNGA, *Assistance to Refugees, Returnees and Displaced Persons in Africa*, A/RES/58/149
    (2004)
UNGA, *Assistance to Unaccompanied Refugee Minors*, A/RES/58/150 (2004)
UNGA, *Assistance to Refugees, Returnees and Displaced Persons in Africa*, A/RES/59/172
    (2005)
UNGA, *Assistance to Refugees, Returnees and Displaced Persons in Africa*, A/RES/60/128
    (2006)
UNGA, *Assistance to Refugees, Returnees and Displaced Persons in Africa*, A/RES/61/139
    (2007)
UNGA, *Assistance to Refugees, Returnees and Displaced Persons in Africa*, A/RES/62/125
    (2008)
UNGA, *Assistance to Refugees, Returnees and Displaced Persons in Africa*, A/RES/63/149 (2009)
UNGA, *Assistance to Refugees, Returnees and Displaced Persons in Africa*, A/RES/64/129 (2010)
UNGA, *Guidelines for the Alternative Care of Children*, A/RES/64/142 (2010)
UNGA, *Study of the Office of the United Nations High Commissioner for Human Rights on
    Challenges and Best Practices in the Implementation of the International Framework for
    the Protection of the Rights of the Child in the Context of Migration*, A/HRC/15/29 (2010)
UNGA, *Assistance to Refugees, Returnees and Displaced Persons in Africa*, A/RES/65/193
    (2011)
UNGA, *Office of the United Nations High Commissioner for Refugees*, A/RES/65/194 (2011)
UNGA, *Report of the Human Rights Council: Report of the Third Committee*, A/62/434
    (2011)
UNGA, *Assistance to Refugees, Returnees and Displaced Persons in Africa*, A/RES/67/150
    (2012)
UNGA, *Rights of the Child*, A/HRC/19/L.31 (2012)
UNGA, *Assistance to Refugees, Returnees and Displaced Persons in Africa*, A/RES/68/143 (2013)
UNGA, *Assistance to Refugees, Returnees and Displaced Persons in Africa*, A/RES/69/154
    (2014)
UNGA, *Rights of the Child*, A/RES/68/147 (2014)
UNGA, *Rights of the Child*, A/RES/69/157 (2014)
United Nations Rules for the Protection of Juveniles Deprived of their Liberty, A/RES/45/113
    (1990) Annex
*United Nations Standard Minimum Rules for the Administration of Juvenile Justice
    ('The Beijing Rules')*, A/RES/30/33 (1985) Annex
Vienna Declaration and Programme of Action, A/CONF.157/23 (1993)
Written Statement Submitted by the Women's International Democratic Federation, E/CN.4/
    NGO/244 (1979)

HRC

HRC, *General Comment No 6: Article 6 (Right to Life)*, HRI/GEN/1/Rev.8 (1982)
HRC, *General Comment No 13: Equality before the Courts and the Right to a Fair and Public
    Hearing by an Independent Court Established by Law*, HRI/GEN/Rev.8 (1984)
HRC, *General Comment No 15: The Position of Aliens under the Covenant*, HRI/GEN/1/
    Rev.8 (1986)

HRC, *General Comment No 17: Rights of the Child*, HRI/GRN/1/Rev.7 (1989)

HRC, *General Comment No 18: Non-Discrimination*, HRI/GEN/1/Rev.8 (1989)

HRC, *General Comment No 19: Protection of the Family, the Right to Marriage and Equality of the Spouses (Article 23)*, HRI/GEN/1/Rev.8 (1990)

HRC, *General Comment No 20: Article 7 (Prohibition of Torture, or Other Cruel, Inhuman or Degrading Treatment or Punishment)*, HRI/GEN/1/Rev.8 (1992)

HRC, *General Comment No 31: The Nature of the General Legal Obligation Imposed on States Parties to the Covenant*, HRI/GEN/1/Rev.8 (2004)

UNCEDAW

UNCEDAW, *General Recommendation No 19: Violence against Women*, HRI/GEN/1/Rev.8 (1992)

UNCERD

UNCERD, *General Recommendation XXVII on Discrimination against Roma*, HRI/GEN/1/Rev.8 (2000)

UNCESCR

UNCESCR, *General Comment No 3: The Nature of States Parties' Obligations (Art 2, Para 1 of the Covenant)*, HRI/GEN/1/Rev.8 (1990)

UNCESCR, *General Comment No 11: Plans of Action for Primary Education (Art 14)*, HRI/GEN/1/Rev.8 (1999)

UNCESCR, *General Comment No 12: The Right to Adequate Food (Art 11)*, HRI/GEN/1/Rev.8 (1999)

UNCESCR, *General Comment No 13: The Right to Education (Art 13)*, HRI/GEN/1/Rev.8 (1999)

UNCESCR, *General Comment No 14: The Right to the Highest Attainable Standard of Health (Art 12)*, HRI/GEN/1/Rev.8 (2000)

UNCESCR, *General Comment No 15: The Right to Water (Arts 11 and 12 of the Covenant)*, HRI/GEN/1/Rev.8 (2002)

UNCESCR, *General Comment No 16: The Equal Right of Men and Women to the Enjoyment of All Economic, Social and Cultural Rights (Art 3)*, HRI/GEN/1/Rev.8 (2005)

UNCESCR, *General Comment No 18: The Right to Work (Art 6)*, HRI/GEN/1/Rev.8 (2005)

UNCESCR, *General Comment No 20: Non-Discrimination in Economic, Social and Cultural Rights (Art 2, Para 2 of the International Covenant on Economic, Social and Cultural Rights)*, E/C.12/GC/20 (2009)

UNCRC

UNCRC, *Report on the Seventh Session*, CRC/C/34 (1994)

UNCRC, Discussion Day: State Violence against Children (2000)

UNCRC, *General Comment No 1: Article 29(1) – The Aims of Education*, CRC/GC/2001/1 (2001)

UNCRC, *Report of the Twenty-Eighth Session*, CRC/C/111 (2001)

UNCRC, *Concluding Observations: United Kingdom of Great Britain and Northern Ireland*, CRC/C/15/Add.188 (2002)

UNCRC, *General Comment No 3: HIV/AIDS and the Rights of the Child*, CRC/GC/2003/3 (2003)

UNCRC, *General Comment No 5: General Measures of Implementation of the Convention on the Rights of the Child (Articles 4, 42 and 44(6))*, CRC/GC/2003/5 (2003)

UNCRC, *General Comment No 6: Treatment of Unaccompanied and Separated Children outside Their Country of Origin*, CRC/GC/2005/6 (2005)

UNCRC, *General Comment No 7: Implementing Child Rights in Early Childhood*, CRC/C/GC/7/Rev.1 (2006)

UNCRC, *Report on the Fortieth Session*, CRC/C/153 (2006)

UNCRC, *Report on the Forty-Third Session*, CRC/C/43/3 (2006)

UNCRC, *General Comment No 8: The Right of the Child to Protection from Corporal Punishment and Other Cruel or Degrading Forms of Punishment*, CRC/C/GC/8 (2007)

UNCRC, *General Comment No 9: The Rights of Children with Disabilities*, CRC/C/GC/9 (2007)

UNCRC, *General Comment No 10: Children's Rights in Juvenile Justice*, CRC/C/GC/10 (2007)

UNCRC, *General Comment No 12: The Right of the Child to Be Heard*, CRC/C/GC/12 (2009)

UNCRC, *General Comment No. 13: The Right of the Child to Freedom from All Forms of Violence*, CRC/C/GC/13 (2011)

UNCRC, '2012 Day of General Discussion: The Rights of All Children in the Context of International Migration' (Background Paper, August 2012)

UNCRC, *Consideration of Reports Submitted by States Parties under Article 44 of the Convention – Concluding Observations: Australia*, CRC/C/AUS/CO/4 (2012)

UNCRC, *General Comment No 14 on the Right of the Child to Have His or Her Best Interests Taken as a Primary Consideration (Art 3, Para 1)*, CRC/C/GC/14 (2013)

UNCRC, *Report of the 2012 Day of General Discussion: The Rights of All Children in the Context of International Migration* (2013)

UNHCR

Standing Committee of the UNHCR ExCom, *Family Protection Issues*, EC/49/SC/CRP.14 (1999)

UNHCR ExCom, *Determination of Refugee Status*, No 8 (XVIII) (1977) (reproduced in UNHCR, *Conclusions Adopted by the Executive Committee on the International Protection of Refugees* (2009) 9)

UNHCR ExCom, *Follow-Up on Earlier Conclusions of the Sub-Committee of the Whole on International Protection on the Determination of Refugee Status, Inter Alia, with Reference to the Role of UNHCR in National Refugee Status Determination Procedures*, No 28 (XXXIII) (1982) (reproduced in UNHCR, *Conclusions Adopted by the Executive Committee on the International Protection of Refugees* (2009) 36)

UNHCR ExCom, *The Problem of Manifestly Unfounded or Abusive Applications for Refugee Status or Asylum*, No 30 (XXXIV) (1983) (reproduced in UNHCR, *Conclusions Adopted by the Executive Committee on the International Protection of Refugees* (2009) 39)

UNHCR ExCom, *General*, No 41 (XXXVII) (1986) (reproduced in UNHCR, *Conclusions Adopted by the Executive Committee on the International Protection of Refugees* (2009) 53)

UNHCR ExCom, *Refugee Children*, No 47 (XXXVIII) (1987) (reproduced in UNHCR, *Conclusions Adopted by the Executive Committee on the International Protection of Refugees* (2009) 61)

UNHCR ExCom, *Refugee Children*, No 59 (XL) (1989) (reproduced in UNHCR, *Conclusions Adopted by the Executive Committee on the International Protection of Refugees* (2009) 79)

UNHCR ExCom, *General*, No 71 (XLIV) (1993) (reproduced in UNHCR, *Conclusions Adopted by the Executive Committee on the International Protection of Refugees* (2009) 97)

UNHCR ExCom, *UNHCR Policy on Refugee Children*, EC/SCP/82 (1993)

UNHCR ExCom, *General*, No 74 (XLV) (1994) (reproduced in *UNHCR, Conclusions Adopted by the Executive Committee on the International Protection of Refugees* (2009) 103)

UNHCR ExCom, *General*, No 81 (XLVII) (1997) (reproduced in UNHCR, *Conclusions Adopted by the Executive Committee on the International Protection of Refugees* (2009) 121)

UNHCR ExCom, *Conclusion on Refugee Children and Adolescents*, No 84 (XLVIII) (1997) (reproduced in UNHCR, *Conclusions Adopted by the Executive Committee on the International Protection of Refugees* (2009) 125)

UNHCR ExCom, *Conclusion on International Protection*, No 85 (XLIX) (1998) (reproduced in UNHCR, *Conclusions Adopted by the Executive Committee on the International Protection of Refugees* (2009) 127)

UNHCR ExCom, *Conclusion on the Protection of the Refugee's Family*, No 88 (L) (1999) (reproduced in UNHCR, *Conclusions Adopted by the Executive Committee on the International Protection of Refugees* (2009) 135)

UNHCR ExCom, *Conclusions on the Provision of International Protection Including through Complementary Forms of Protection*, No 103 (LVI) (2005) (reproduced in UNHCR, *Conclusions Adopted by the Executive Committee on the International Protection of Refugees* (2009) 177)

UNHCR ExCom, *Conclusion on Women and Girls at Risk*, No 105 (LVII) (2006) (reproduced in UNHCR, *Conclusions Adopted by the Executive Committee on the International Protection of Refugees* (2009) 183)

UNHCR ExCom, *Conclusion on Children at Risk*, No 107 (LVIII) (2007) (reproduced in UNHCR, *Conclusions Adopted by the Executive Committee on the International Protection of Refugees* (2009) 190)

UNHCR ExCom, *Conclusion on Refugees with Disabilities and Other Persons with Disabilities Protected and Assisted by UNHCR*, No 110 (LXI) (2010) (reproduced in *Report of the Sixty-First Session of the Executive Committee of the High Commissioner's Programme*, A/AC.96/1095 (2010) [13])

UNHCR, *Handbook on Procedures and Criteria for Determining Refugee Status under the 1951 Convention and the 1967 Protocol Relating to the Status of Refugees*, HCR/IP/4/Eng/REV.1 (1979, re-edited 1992)

UNHCR, *Note on Refugee Children*, EC/SCP/46 (1987)

UNHCR, *Guidelines on Refugee Children* (1988)

UNHCR, *Note on International Protection (Submitted by the High Commissioner)*, A/AC.96/728 (1989)

UNHCR, *Refugee Children: Guidelines on Protection and Care* (1994)

UNHCR, *Guidelines on Policies and Procedures in Dealing with Unaccompanied Children Seeking Asylum* (1997)

UNHCR, 'Progress Report on Refugee Children and Adolescents, including UNHCR's Strategy for Follow-Up to the Report of the Impact of Armed Conflict on Children', EC/47/SC/CRP.19 (9 April 1997)

UNHCR, 'Note on Burden and Standard of Proof in Refugee Claims' (16 December 1998)

UNHCR, *Interpreting Article 1 of the 1951 Convention Relating to the Status of Refugees* (2001)

UNHCR, *Guidelines on International Protection: Gender-Related Persecution within the Context of Article 1A(2) of the 1951 Convention and/or Its 1967 Protocol Relating to the Status of Refugees*, HCR/GIP/02/01 (2002)

UNHCR, *Guidelines on International Protection: 'Membership of a Particular Social Group' within the Context of Article 1A(2) of the 1951 Convention and/or Its 1967 Protocol Relating to the Status of Refugees*, HCR/GIP/02/02 (2002)

UNHCR, 'Background Note on the Application of the Exclusion Clauses: Article 1 F of the 1951 Convention Relating to the Status of Refugees' (4 September 2003)

UNHCR, *Procedural Standards for Refugee Status Determination under UNHCR's Mandate* (2003)

UNHCR, *Guidelines on International Protection: Religion-Based Refugee Claims under Article 1A(2) of the 1951 Convention and/or the 1967 Protocol Relating to the Status of Refugees*, HCR/GIP/04/06 (2004)

UNHCR, *Guidelines on International Protection: The Application of Article 1A(2) of the 1951 Convention and/or 1967 Protocol Relating to the Status of Refugees to Victims of Trafficking and Persons at Risk of Being Trafficked*, HCR/GIP/06/07 (2006)

UNHCR, 'Position on Claims for Refugee Status under the 1951 Convention Relating to the Status of Refugees Based on a Fear of Persecution due to an Individual's Membership of a Family or Clan Engaged in a Blood Feud' (17 March 2006)

UNHCR, 'Advisory Opinion on the Extraterritorial Application of Non-Refoulement Obligations under the 1951 Convention relating to the Status of Refugees and its 1967 Protocol' (Opinion, 26 January 2007)

UNHCR, *UNHCR Guidance Note on Refugee Claims Relating to Sexual Orientation and Gender Identity* (2008)

UNHCR, *UNHCR Guidelines on Determining the Best Interests of the Child* (2008)

UNHCR, *UNHCR Handbook for the Protection of Women and Girls* (2008)

UNHCR, 'Brief of the United Nations High Commissioner for Refugees as *Amicus Curiae* in Support of the Petitioner', filed in *Valdiviezo-Galdamez* (14 April 2009)

UNHCR, 'Brief of the United Nations High Commissioner for Refugees as Amicus Curiae in Support of the Petitioners and Reversal of the BIA's Decision', filed in *Orellana-Monson v Holder* (7 May 2009)

UNHCR, *Conclusions Adopted by the Executive Committee on the International Protection of Refugees* (2009)

UNHCR, *Guidance Note on Refugee Claims Relating to Female Genital Mutilation* (2009)

UNHCR, *Guidelines on International Protection: Child Asylum Claims under Article 1A(2) and 1 F of the 1951 Convention and/or 1967 Protocol Relating to the Status of Refugees*, HCR/GIP/09/08 (2009)

UNHCR, UNICEF and Save the Children, Separated Children in Europe Programme, *Statement of Good Practice* (4th revised edn) (2009)

UNHCR, 'Brief *Amicus Curiae* of The United Nations High Commissioner for Refugees in Support of Respondent Fancis Gatimi', filed in *Matter of Gatimi* (25 March 2010)

UNHCR, 'Brief of the United Nations High Commissioner for Refugees as Amicus Curiae in Support of Petitioner', filed in *Gaitan v Attorney General* (13 June 2010)

UNHCR, 'Brief *Amicus Curiae* of the United Nations High Commissioner for Refugees in Support of Petitioner's Petition for Rehearing En Banc', filed in *Mejilla-Romero* (18 June 2010)

UNHCR, 'Brief *Amicus Curiae* of the Office of the United Nations High Commissioner for Refugees in Support of Respondent X', filed in *Matter of X* (17 August 2010)

UNHCR, 'Brief of the United Nations High Commissioner for Refugees as Amicus Curiae in Support of Petitioner', filed in *Rivera-Barrientos* (18 August 2010)

UNHCR, 'Brief of the United Nations High Commissioner for Refugees as Amicus Curiae in Support of the Petitioner', filed in *Bueso-Avila* (9 November 2010)

UNHCR, *Guidance Note on Refugee Claims Relating to Victims of Organized Gangs* (2010)

UNHCR, *Field Handbook for the Implementation of UNHCR BID Guidelines* (2011)

UNHCR, *Ministerial Communique*, HCR/MINCOMMS/2011/6 (8 December 2011)

UNHCR, *Guidelines on International Protection No 9: Claims to Refugee Status Based on Sexual Orientation and/or Gender Identity within the Context of Article 1A(2) of the 1951 Convention and/or Its 1967 Protocol Relating to the Status of Refugees*, HCR/GIP/12/09 (2012)

UNHCR, 'The United Nations High Commissioner for Refugees' *Amicus Curiae* Brief in Support of Petitioner', filed in *Henrique-Rivas v Attorney General* (23 February 2012)

UNHCR, 'Quality Integration Project: Considering the Best Interests of a Child within a Family Seeking Asylum' (December 2013)

UNHCR, 'Case for the First Intervener', filed in *HJ* (undated)

UNHCR and UNICEF, *Safe & Sound: What States Can Do to Ensure Respect for the Best Interests of Unaccompanied and Separated Children in Europe* (2014)

UNHCR, 'Submission from the United Nations High Commissioner for Refugees (UNHCR) to the legal representatives in case numbers XXX, XXX and XXX before the Danish Refugee Appeal Board' (2015)

UNHCR, *The Heart of the Matter: Assessing Credibility when Children Apply for Asylum in the European Union* (2014)

UNHCR, *Global Trends 2014* (2015)

UNHCR, *Global Trends 2015* (2016)

UNICEF

UNICEF, *Annual Report on Child Protection* (2014)

UNICEF, *Hidden in Plain Sight: A Statistical Analysis of Violence Against Children* (2014)

UNICEF, *Implementation Handbook for the Convention on the Rights of the Child* (3rd edn, 2007)

UNICEF, *Progress for Children: A Report Card on Child Protection* (2009)

UNICEF, *The State of the World's Children: Celebrating 20 Years of the Convention on the Rights of the Child* (2009)

UNICEF, *The State of the World's Children 2014 in Numbers: Every Child Counts* (2014)

UNICEF, *The State of the World's Children* (2015)

Domestic Guidelines, Manuals, Directions, Forms and Other Administrative Documents

Australia

DIAC, 'Refugee Law Guidelines' (March 2010)

DIAC, 'Application for a Protection (Class XA) Visa' (Form 866, July 2013)

DIAC, *Procedures Advice Manual 3 – Policy and Procedural Instructions for Officers Administering Migration Law* (1 January 2015)

MIAC, *Administration of Ministerial Powers* (P A124, 24 March 2012)

MIAC, *Minister's Guidelines on Ministerial Power (s 345, s 351, s 391, s 417, s 454 and s 501J)* (P A098, 24 March 2012)

MIAC, *Direction No 55 – Visa Refusal and Cancellation under s 501* (25 July 2012)

MRT and RRT, *Guidance on the Assessment of Credibility* (March 2012)

Refugee and Humanitarian Division, 'Protecting the Refugee's Family (The Final Act of the 1951 United Nations Conference of Plenipotentiaries): An Australian Perspective' in DIMIA, *Interpreting the Refugees Convention: An Australian Contribution* (2002) 175

Canada

CIC, *IP 5: Immigrant Applications in Canada Made on Humanitarian or Compassionate Grounds* (1 April 2011)

CIC, *OP 4: The Processing of Applications That Include a Request for Humanitarian and Compassionate or Public Policy Consideration* (26 February 2013)

IRB, *Guidelines Issued by the Chairperson Pursuant to Section 65(3) of the Immigration Act: Guideline 3: Child Refugee Claimants: Procedural and Evidentiary Issues* (30 September 1996)

IRB, *Interpretation of the Convention Refugee Definition in the Case Law* (31 December 2010)

New Zealand

Immigration New Zealand, *Immigration New Zealand Operational Manual: Refugees and Protection* (2011)

United Kingdom

Home Office, *Processing Children's Asylum Claims* (ver 1.0, 12 July 2016)

Joint Committee on Human Rights, *Human Rights of Unaccompanied Migrant Children and Young People in the UK*, House of Lords Paper No 9, House of Commons Paper No 196, Session 2013–14 (2013)

UKBA, *Every Child Matters: Statutory Guidance to the UK Border Agency on Making Arrangements to Safeguard and Promote the Welfare of Children* (November 2009)

UKBA, *Asylum Process Guidance: Processing an Asylum Application from a Child* (ver 6, 16 April 2013)

United States

Memorandum from Jeff Weiss, Acting Director, Office of International Affairs, INS, 'Guidelines for Children's Asylum Claims' (File No 120/11.26, 10 December 1998)

USCIS Asylum Division, 'Asylum Officer Basic Training Course: Guidelines for Children's Asylum Claims' (21 March 2009)

Other

General

Blake, N, and Drew, S, 'In the matter of the United Kingdom Reservation to the UN Convention on the Rights of the Child' (Opinion, 30 November 2001)

Canadian Council for Refugees, United Church of Canada and International Bureau for Children's Rights, 'The Understanding and Application of "Best Interests of the Child" in H & C Decision-Making by Citizenship and Immigration Canada' (Report, September 2008)

Comprehensive Plan of Action for Indo-Chinese Refugees adopted by the International Conference on Indo-Chinese Refugees held in Geneva on 13 and 14 June 1989, International Conference on Indo-Chinese Refugees, Office of the UNHCR, *Report of the Secretary General*, A/44/523 (1989) Annex pt II

Council of the European Union, *Council Conclusions on Unaccompanied Minors – 3018th Justice and Home Affairs Council Meeting* (3 June 2010)

ECRE, 'Position on Refugee Children' (Policy Statement, November 1996)

Email from T Bridge, Publications Team, RRT, 7 May 2012 (on file with author)

Explanations Relating to the Charter of Fundamental Rights [2007] *Official Journal of the European Union* C 303/17

European Commission, *Communication from the Commission to the European Parliament and the Council: Action Plan on Unaccompanied Minors (2010–2014)*, COM (2010)213

European Commission, *Commission Staff Working Document on the Implementation of the Action Plan on Unaccompanied Minors*, SWD(2012)281

European Commission, *Report from the Commission to the Council and the European Parliament: Mid-Term Report on the Implementation of the Action Plan on Unaccompanied Minors*, COM(2012)554

European Migration Network, *Policies on Reception, Return and Integration arrangements for, and Numbers of, Unaccompanied Minors – An EU Comparative Study* (2010)

France Terre D'Asile, *Right to Asylum for Unaccompanied Minors in the European Union: Comparative Study in the 27 EU Countries* (2012)

Gordon, M, 'People Sent Offshore Will Include Children', *Sydney Morning Herald* (online), 22 August 2013

ICRC, *Inter-Agency Guiding Principles on Unaccompanied and Separated Children* (2004)

ILPA, *Working with Refugee Children: Current Issues in Best Practice* (2012)

JCHR, *The Treatment of Asylum Seekers*, HL 81-I, HC 60-I, Session 2006–07 (2007)

Memorandum from Bo Cooper, General Counsel, INS to Doris Meissner, Commissioner of INS, 3 January 2000 (on file with author)

Michigan Guidelines on the International Protection of Refugees, 'The Michigan Guidelines on Well-Founded Fear' (2004)

Parliament of Australia, Explanatory Memorandum, Migration Amendment (Complementary Protection) Bill 2011 (Cth)

Parliamentary Assembly, Council of Europe, 'Unaccompanied Children in Europe: Issues of Arrival, Stay and Return' (Report, Doc 12539, 21 March 2011)

Refugee Women's Legal Group, *Gender Guidelines for the Determination of Asylum Claims in the UK* (1998)

Report to US HICOG on IRO, US Zone of Germany (22 October 1951) (reproduced in L W Holborn, *The International Refugee Organization: A Specialized Agency of the United Nations – Its History and Work, 1946–1952* (1956) 500)

Michigan Guidelines on the International Protection of Refugees, 'The Michigan Guidelines on Nexus to a Convention Ground' (2002)

Treaty Reservations and Declarations

'Germany', 1669 UNTS 475

'Japan', 1775 UNTS 447

'Netherlands', 1855 UNTS 420

'New Zealand', 1719 UNTS 495

'Singapore', 1890 UNTS 526

'Switzerland', 1965 UNTS 505

'United Kingdom of Great Britain and Northern Ireland', 1658 UNTS 682

Briefs and Submissions

Appellant, 'Case for the Appellant', filed in *ZH (Tanzania) v SSHD* (undated)

Appellant-Petitioner, 'Initial Brief Filed by the Appellant-Petitioner', filed in *Kholyavskiy v Mukasey* (15 June 2007)

Center for Gender and Refugee Studies et al., 'Brief of *Amici Curiae* in support of Petitioner's Petition for Rehearing or Rehearing *En Banc*', filed in *Mejilla-Romero* (21 June 2010)

CORAM Children's Legal Centre, 'Case for the CORAM Children's Legal Centre', filed in *H (H) v Deputy Prosecutor of the Italian Republic, Genoa* (undated)

CORAM Children's Legal Centre, 'Note for the CORAM Children's Legal Centre', filed in *H (H) v Deputy Prosecutor of the Italian Republic, Genoa* (7 March 2012)

Foster, M, and Pobjoy, J, Submission No 9 to Senate Legal and Constitutional Affairs Legislation Committee, Parliament of Australia, *Inquiry into the Migration Amendment (Complementary Protection) Bill 2009* (28 September 2009)

Harvard Immigration Refugee Clinical Program, 'Brief of *Amici Curiae* Harvard Immigration and Refugee Clinical Program and Other Immigration Rights Advocates in Support of Petitioner', filed in *José Fuentes-Colocho v United States Attorney General* (19 November 2013)

Human Rights Law Resource Centre, Submission No 5 to Senate Legal and Constitutional Affairs Legislation Committee, Parliament of Australia, *Inquiry into the Migration Amendment (Complementary Protection) Bill 2009* (September 2009)

Goodwin-Gill, G S, and Hurwitz, A, 'Memorandum' reproduced in House of Lords Select Committee on the European Union, *Defining Refugee Status and Those in Need of International Protection*, House of Lords Paper No 156, Session 2001–02 (2002) ('Minutes of Evidence Taken before the European Union Committee (Sub-Committee E)' (10 April 2002) 1–3)

Sadoway, G, 'Applicants' Further Memorandum of Argument', filed in *KH v Canada (MCI)* (9 January 2008)

United States Attorney, 'Brief', filed in *Gonzalez v Reno* (24 April 2000)

INDEX

Abandoned children, social group membership, 179–80
Abduction of children
    under CRC, 21, 127–8
    family separation and, 146–7
    nexus to Convention ground and, 159–60
    as persecutory harm, 117
Abram, E.F., 73, 74
Accompanied children
    best interests of child principle and, 232
    child eligible but parent ineligible, 76–7
    claims of, 27
    individual assessment requirement, 44–5, 62–9
    invisibility of child refugees, 45, 47, 49–52
    non-alignment of interests, 59, 86
    non-refoulement obligation and, 62, 68
    parent eligible but child ineligible, 76
Accountability theory, 110
Actual identity, nexus to Convention ground, 165
Adoption, 19, 46
Afghanistan
    country of origin information and, 92
    unaccompanied children from, 148
African Charter on the Rights and Welfare of the Child, 124–5, 196
Age
    cessation provisions, as basis for engaging, 240–1
    Convention, age-sensitive interpretation of, 11, 80–1
    as critical factor in adjudication of claims, 116
    as indicator of ability to experience or communicate fear, 87
    risk assessment, age-sensitive (*See* Age-sensitive risk assessment)
    social group membership
        age-based group, 176–8
        age plus other characteristics, 176, 178–82, 185
        as immutable characteristic, 176–7, 180–1
Age-sensitive risk assessment
    overview, 11–12, 79, 99–100
    burden of proof, 90
    definition of refugee and, 79–81
    evidentiary challenges
        generally, 79
        overview, 89–90
        country of origin information, 91–2
        credibility of evidence (*See* Credibility of evidence)
        fact-finding, shared duty of, 90–1

liberal benefit of doubt, 93–9
similarly situated persons, 93
forward-looking assessment of risk, 82, 89–90
homosexuality and, 94
incorrect assessment, 79
persecutory harm and, 123
well-founded fear/genuine risk requirement
generally, 81
overview, 79, 81–2
ability to understand, 83
bipartite understanding of, 82–4
difficulty in articulating, 83–4
dispensing with subjective element, 86–9
forward-looking assessment of risk, 82, 89–90
imputation of fear from parent to child, 85–6
Michigan Guidelines on Well-Founded Fear, 156
objective element, 81–2, 86–9
past persecution, relevance of, 82–3
"predicament" approach and, 161
rationale for requiring children to establish, 84–9
subjective element, 81–2
Alienage, 14, 15, 52, 188, 217
Alleviation of risk theory, 110–11, 114–16
Alston, Philip, 107, 112–13, 225, 228, 234
American Convention on Human Rights, 149–50
Anker, Deborah, 29, 102, 111
Arbitrary detention under CRC, 46
Assembly, freedom of, 19–20, 55
Association, freedom of, 19–20, 55
At-risk children defined, 2
Australia
best interests of child principle in
application of CRC Article 3, 223–5
determination of best interests, 225
discretionary grant of protection on humanitarian grounds, 218
as independent source of protection, 201, 202–3
removal of parent and, 213–14, 218
country of origin information in, 93–4
Department of Immigration and Citizenship, Guidelines, 69, 122, 125
determination of refugee status in, 50, 53, 62
family unity in, 69
government guidelines in, 27
individual assessment requirement in, 53, 61–2
interplay between Convention and CRC in, 8
liberal benefit of doubt in, 98
Migration Amendment (Complementary Protection Act) 2011, 191
Minister for Immigration and Citizenship, Guidelines, 214, 218
nexus to Convention ground in
causal link, 160
intention requirement, 160
political opinion, 169
"predicament" approach, 161–2
religion, 171
social group membership, 174, 176–7, 178
non-refoulement obligation in, 190–1
non-separation duty in, 76

Australia (cont.)
  persecutory harm/being persecuted in
    generally, 102
    alleviation of risk theory, 114–15
    definition of "being persecuted," 121–2, 125, 129–30
    domestic child abuse, 134
    education, 141, 142
    human rights framework, 104
    protection theory, 111–12
    psychological harm, 153
    state protection, 111, 112, 115
  similarly situated persons in, 93
  well-founded fear/genuine risk requirement in, 85, 86

Balancing of interests in best interests determination, 234–8
  generally, 224
  crime prevention and, 236
  immigration control and, 236
  rights-based interests, 235
Being persecuted. *See* Persecutory harm/being persecuted
Bennion, F., 172–3
Best interests of child principle
  generally, 7, 12, 20–1, 80–1, 187, 196, 238, 241
  overview, 187, 196–203
  application of CRC Article 3, 223–5
  complementary protection, applicability of, 187
  under CRC, 20–1, 46
  discretionary grant of protection on humanitarian grounds, 218–20
  ECHR and, 206–13
  education and, 229–30
  family unity and, 73, 231–2
  first country of arrival rules, 198–9
  flexibility of, 223
  as independent source of protection, 199–203, 223–5
  as informing definition of refugee, 197–8
  internal protection alternative, 198–9, 240
  International Refugee Organization and, 203–5
  medical care and, 229–30
  nationality and, 229–30
  non-discrimination/equality and, 229–30
  non-refoulement obligation and, 198
  non-separation duty and, 146
  persecutory harm/being persecuted and, 124
  as primary consideration, 8, 31
  privacy and, 229–30
  proactivity in, 223–4
  removal of parent and, 213–18
  right to life and, 229–30
  safe third-country rules, 198–9, 240
  Stage 1: determination of best interests, 225–33
    generally, 224
    accompanied children, 232
    catalogue of rights, 228, 229–30
    deterrence and, 236–7
    Dublin regime and, 236–7
    extradition and, 236–7

family unity/reunification, 231–2
genuine, 225
long-term effects, 226
mandatory, 225
no additional hardship threshold, 228–9
preservation of family unit, 237
principled and objective determination, 229
promotion of best interests of children, 236–7
right to be heard/views of child, 226–7
specific situation and circumstances, 227–8
Stage 2: balancing exercise, 234–8
  generally, 224
  immigration control and, 236
  protection of host community, 236
  rights-based interests, 235
standard of living and, 229–30
state practice regarding, 203
  discretionary grant of protection on humanitarian grounds, 218–20
  ECHR and, 206–13
  international models, 203–5
  removal of parent and, 213–18
  unaccompanied children and, 221–3
state protection and, 198–9
as two-stage process, 224
unaccompanied children and, 221–3
unborn children, 223–4
UNHCR, Guidelines on Determining the Best Interests of the Child, 2
Bethlehem, D., 41, 54
Bhabha, Jacqueline, 2, 6, 14, 17, 46, 48, 50, 95, 129, 198
Bierwerth, Christoph, 193
Bipartite understanding of well-founded fear/genuine risk requirement, 82–4
Bolton, Syd, 202
Boys, social group membership, 179–80
Buchanan, I., 167
Bullying as persecutory harm, 142
Burden of proof in age-sensitive risk assessment, 90
Byelorussia (Soviet SSR), best interests of child principle in, 203–4

Canada
age-sensitive risk assessment in, 91, 93, 96, 97–8
best interests of child principle in
  generally, 196
  balancing of interests, 237
  determination of best interests, 223, 224, 225, 227, 228–9, 231, 232
  discretionary grant of protection on humanitarian grounds, 218–20
  as independent source of protection, 202–3
  removal of parent and, 214–16, 220
derivative protection in, 50
determination of refugee status in, 47, 50, 64–5
fact-finding in, 91
government guidelines in, 27
Immigration Act, 68, 214
Immigration and Refugee Protection Act, 64, 68, 82–3, 215
Immigration and Refugee Protection Regulations, 76, 77
individual assessment requirement in, 62, 64–8
interplay between Convention and CRC in, 8

Canada (cont.)
  interpretation of Convention in, 35
  IRB, Guidelines, 56–7, 64, 84, 97, 98, 125
  liberal benefit of doubt in, 96–7
  nexus to Convention ground in
      generally, 165
      intention requirement, 159
      political opinion, 168
      "predicament" approach, 163, 164
      religion, 170
      social group membership, 173, 176, 182
  non-refoulement obligation in, 189, 190
  non-separation duty in, 76, 77
  persecutory harm/being persecuted in
      generally, 101, 132, 156
      definition of "being persecuted," 116, 118, 123, 125–6, 128, 129, 130
      domestic child abuse, 132, 135, 137–9
      education, 141, 142, 143–4
      family separation, 146, 147–8, 149
      protection theory, 111–12
      psychological harm, 151–2, 153, 155
      state protection, 109
  right to be heard/views of child in, 56–7
  well-founded fear/genuine risk requirement in, 82, 84–5, 88
Cartagena Declaration on Refugees, 186
CAT. See Convention against Torture (CAT)
Causal link to Convention ground
  overview, 157–8
  domestic child abuse, 163–4
  intention requirement, 158–60
  nature of, 157–8
  "predicament" approach, 164
  socio-economic deprivation, 163
  standard of, 158
  trafficking of children, 164
CEDAW. See Convention on the Elimination of All Forms of Discrimination against Women (CEDAW)
CERD. See International Convention on the Elimination of All Forms of Racial Discrimination (CERD)
Cessation of refugee status, 16, 81, 177–8, 240–1
Charter of Fundamental Rights (EU), 196, 202, 221
Child abuse. See Domestic child abuse
Childhood, social group membership, 179–80
Child labor
  under CRC, 21, 127–8, 131–2
  as domestic child abuse, 132–3
Child pornography
  as domestic child abuse, 132–3
  Optional Protocol on the Sale of Children, Child Prostitution and Child Pornography (OPSC), 11, 22, 29, 41, 43, 106, 133, 187
  as persecutory harm, 117
Child refugees
  age-sensitive risk assessment (See Age-sensitive risk assessment)
  challenges facing, 3, 4–5
  as child and refugee, 14–15
  complementary protection under CRC (See Complementary protection under CRC)
  defined, 2
  determination of refugee status (See Determination of refugee status)

gender-based persecution compared, 4–5
  incorrect assessment of, 3–4, 5, 79
  in international law (*See* International law, child refugees in)
  invisibility of (*See* Invisibility of child refugees)
  lesser form of protection for, 45
  nexus to Convention ground (*See* Nexus to Convention ground)
  persecutory harm/being persecuted (*See* Persecutory harm/being persecuted)
  special protection
    generally, 19
    under CRC, 21–2, 46
    unaccompanied children, 221–3
  statistics on, 1
  vulnerabilities of, 21–2
Children seeking international protection defined, 2
Child rights framework
  overview, 5–8, 27, 239
  complementary protection under CRC and, 30–1
  interpretive aid within, 28–30
  procedural guarantee within, 27–8
Child soldiers. *See* Military recruitment of child soldiers
China
  nexus to Convention ground and, 165
  one-child policy, 85, 86, 121–2, 165, 166–7
  persecutory harm/being persecuted and, 121–2, 129–30, 141
  well-founded fear/genuine risk requirement and, 82–3, 85, 86
Clapham, A., 113
Cohn, I., 127
Complementary protection generally
  overview, 186
  CAT and, 186–7
  ICCPR and, 186–7
  non-refoulement obligation, 186–7
Complementary protection under CRC
  overview, 186–7, 238, 241–2
  Article 3, applicability of, 187
  best interests of child principle, applicability to, 187
  within child rights framework, 30–1
  non-refoulement obligation as
    generally, 12
    overview, 186–7, 188–92, 238
    cruel, inhuman or degrading treatment or punishment, protection against, 193–5
    development, right of, 192–3
    liberty, right to, 193–5
    life, right to, 192–3
    military recruitment of child soldiers, protection against, 30–1, 195–6
    survival, right of, 192–3
    torture, protection against, 193–5
  temporary protection and, 186
Comprehensive Plan of Action for Indo-Chinese Refugees (1989), 205–6
Constructive deportation, 52
Convention. *See* Refugee Convention (Convention)
Convention against Torture (CAT)
  generally, 149–50, 238
  complementary protection generally, 186–7
  non-refoulement obligation and, 186–7, 188–92, 196

Convention grounds
  overview, 165, 240
  ejusdem generis approach, 172–4, 176–8, 183
  nationality as, 3, 25–6, 108–9, 157, 165, 172–3
  political opinion as, 166–9
    generally, 3, 25–6, 108–9, 172–3
    adult-centric definition of political activity, 167
    gangs and, 169
    independent or imputed opinion, 165, 166–7
    parents or family members, opinions of, 166–7
    social group membership versus, 166
    unlikelihood of targeting children, 167–8
  race as, 3, 25–6, 108–9, 157, 165, 172–3
  religion as, 169–72
    generally, 3, 25–6, 108–9, 158, 172–3
    child's own religious beliefs, 170–1
    family members, religious beliefs of, 169–70
    female children, 171–2
    IHRL and, 171
  social group membership as (*See* Social group membership)
Convention on the Civil Aspects of International Child Abduction, 208, 210–11
Convention on the Elimination of All Forms of Discrimination against Women (CEDAW), 29, 104, 106
Convention on the Rights of the Child (CRC). *See also specific topics*
  abduction of children under, 21, 127–8
  adoption of, 13–14, 19–20
  adoption under, 46
  applicability of, 6, 14, 19–20
  arbitrary detention under, 46
  Article 1, 1, 6, 175–6, 240–1, 244
  Article 2
    generally, 14, 20
    non-discrimination/equality and, 197, 229–30
    persecutory harm/being persecuted and, 130
    social group membership and, 183
    text of, 244
  Article 3
    best interests of child principle (*See* Best interests of child principle)
    discretionary grant of protection on humanitarian grounds, 218–20
    as independent source of protection, 7, 12, 80, 239, 241–2
    removal of parent, 213–18
    special protection for unaccompanied children, 221–3
    text of, 244
  Article 4, 17, 245
  Article 5, 14, 58–9, 245
  Article 6
    generally, 7, 12, 30–1, 238, 241
    family separation and, 148
    non-refoulement obligation and, 186–7, 188–92
    persecutory harm/being persecuted and, 130–1
    right to life and, 192
    text of, 245
  Article 7, 145, 150, 229–30, 245
  Article 8, 229–30, 245
  Article 9
    generally, 11, 239–40
    determination of refugee status and, 45, 46, 59

family separation and, 145, 146, 147
family unity and, 70, 72–8
non-separation duty and, 72
text of, 246
Article 10, 70, 145, 246
Article 11, 247
Article 12
  generally, 19–20, 239–40
  best interests of child principle and, 227
  determination of refugee status and, 46, 55–9, 61–2
  family separation and, 146
  family unity and, 75
  political opinion and, 164, 168
  text of, 247
Article 13, 134–5, 247
Article 14, 170–1, 247
Article 15, 164, 168, 248
Article 16, 73, 145, 229–30, 248
Article 17, 17, 248
Article 18, 145, 147, 248–9
Article 19
  domestic child abuse and, 133, 134–8
  family separation and, 147
  psychological harm and, 149–50, 152
  text of, 249
  violence, protection against, 229–30
Article 20, 6, 145, 148–9, 229–30, 249
Article 21, 249–50
Article 22
  generally, 14, 17, 20, 21–2
  determination of refugee status and, 54, 59
  non-discrimination/equality and, 197
  persecutory harm/being persecuted and, 124
  text of, 250
Article 23, 143–4, 250–1
Article 24, 143–4, 152, 193, 229–30, 251
Article 25, 229–30, 251
Article 26, 131, 147, 252
Article 27, 130–1, 147, 193, 229–30, 252
Article 28, 140, 143–4, 193, 229–30, 252–3
Article 29, 140, 143–4, 229–30, 253
Article 30, 253
Article 31, 253
Article 32, 192, 254
Article 33, 192, 254
Article 34, 192, 229–30, 254
Article 35, 192, 229–30, 254
Article 36, 192, 229–30, 254
Article 37
  generally, 7, 12, 30–1, 238, 241
  determination of refugee status and, 59
  domestic child abuse and, 138
  non-refoulement obligation and, 186–7, 188–92
  persecutory harm/being persecuted and, 127, 128, 129
  psychological harm and, 149–50, 152
  text of, 254–5

Convention on the Rights of the Child (CRC) (cont.)
    violence, protection against, 229–30
  Article 38, 9, 31, 189, 195–6, 229–30, 255
  Article 39, 155–6, 255
  Article 40, 127, 129, 255–6
  Article 41, 127, 256
  assembly, freedom of, 19–20, 55
  association, freedom of, 19–20, 55
  best interests of child principle (*See* Best interests of child principle)
  child defined, 1, 175–6
  child labor under, 21, 127–8, 131–2
  complementary protection under (*See* Complementary protection under CRC)
  consensus regarding, 27
  Convention, interplay with, 5–8, 10, 123, 124–5, 239
  cruel, inhuman or degrading treatment or punishment, protection against, 193–5
  deprivation of family environment under, 46
  economic exploitation under, 192
  education under, 193, 229–30
  expression, freedom of, 19–20, 55
  family separation under, 127–8
  female genital cutting under, 192
  forced marriage under, 192
  gangs under, 131–2
  honour killings under, 192
  ICCPR versus, 20–1, 127
  ICESCR versus, 20–1, 127
  IHRL and, 6, 28–30, 123, 124–5, 239
  as independent source of protection, 7, 12, 80, 239, 241–2 (*See also* Best interests of child principle and
    complementary protection generally)
  international human rights law and, 6, 123, 124–5, 239
  as interpretive aid (*See* Interpretive aid, CRC as)
  jurisdictional scope, 14, 19–20
  liberty under, 193–5
  medical care under, 193, 229–30
  military recruitment of child soldiers under, 21, 127–8, 131–2, 195–6
  narcotics under, 192
  nationality under, 229–30
  near-universal ratification of, 31
  non-discrimination/equality under, 229–30
  non-refoulement obligation under, 30
  Optional Protocol on a Communications Procedure (OPCP), 11, 22, 29, 41, 106, 189
  Optional Protocol on the Involvement of Children in Armed Conflict (OPAC), 11, 22, 31, 41, 43, 195–6
  Optional Protocol on the Sale of Children, Child Prostitution and Child Pornography (OPSC), 11, 22, 29, 41, 43,
    106, 133, 187
  participation, right of, 55
  parties to, 187
  play and recreation under, 21, 127–8
  Preamble, 243–4
  privacy under, 229–30
  as procedural guarantee (*See* Procedural guarantee, CRC as)
  refugees, provisions regarding, 21–2
  rehabilitation under, 46
  religion, freedom of, 19–20, 55
  reservations to, 14–15
  right to be heard/views of child, 20, 45, 55–9, 146, 239–40

right to life under, 192, 229–30

sexual exploitation under, 21, 127–8, 192

socio-economic deprivation under, 131–2

special protection of child refugees under, 21–2, 46

standard of living under, 193, 229–30

Survival and development, 1, 131, 141, 148, 150, 188, 191, 192–196, 230, 233, 236, 245

text of, 243–56

torture, protection against, 193–5

traditional practices under, 21, 127–8, 131–2, 192, 219

trafficking of children under, 21, 127–8, 131–2, 192

Travaux Préparatoires, 74, 136

upbringing of children under, 21

violence under, 192, 229–30

vulnerabilities of children, 21–2

war under, 131–2

Cooper, Bo, 48

Corporal punishment as persecutory harm, 117, 118, 142

Country of origin information, 91–2

CRC. *See* Convention on the Rights of the Child (CRC)

Credibility of evidence

adverse credibility findings, 93–4

age assessments, 94

corroborating evidence, 96–7

demeanour of child, 98

evidential concessions, 96, 99–100

implausibility of evidence, 97–8

inconsistencies or gaps in stories, 97–8

liberal benefit of doubt, 93–9

Crime prevention, balancing of interests and, 236

Crisp, J., 24

Crock, Mary, 2, 14, 17, 46, 47, 48

Cruel, inhuman or degrading treatment or punishment

as persecutory harm, 117, 126

protection against under CRC, 193–5

as psychological harm, 149–51

Cumulative approach to social group membership, 174–5

Custody of children

family separation and, 145

persecutory harm and, 117

Customary international law, 32, 40

Death penalty, 129, 192

Debt bondage

as domestic child abuse, 132–3

as persecutory harm, 118

Declaration of the Rights of the Child, 19

Definition of refugee

adult focus of, 80

age-sensitive risk assessment and, 79–81

alienage, 14, 15, 52, 188, 217

cessation of refugee status, 16, 81, 177–8, 240–1

in Convention, 3, 12, 16, 68, 257–8

CRC Article 3 versus, 198

exclusion of refugees, 16, 50, 81, 198–9, 240–1

interplay between Convention and CRC, 80–1

by IRO, 18

Definition of refugee (cont.)
    nexus to Convention ground (*See* Nexus to Convention ground)
    persecutory harm/being persecuted (*See* Persecutory harm/being persecuted)
    separate treatment of constituent elements, 81
    well-founded fear/genuine risk requirement (*See* Well-founded fear/genuine risk requirement)
Denmark, proposals regarding CRC, 21
Deprivation of family environment
    under CRC, 46
    family separation as persecutory harm, 148–9
    nexus to Convention ground and, 162
Derivative protection, 50–2
Derogation, 20–1, 74–5, 108, 128–9, 209
Design of study, 8–12
Determination of best interests, 225–33
    generally, 224
    accompanied children, 232
    catalogue of rights, 228, 229–30
    deterrence and, 236–7
    Dublin regime and, 236–7
    extradition and, 236–7
    family unity/reunification, 231–2
    genuine, 225
    hardship threshold, 228–9
    long-term effects, 226
    mandatory, 225
    no additional hardship threshold, 228–9
    no right to remain, 232
    preservation of family unit, 237
    principled and objective determination, 229
    promotion of best interests of children, 236–7
    right to be heard/views of child, 226–7
    specific situation and circumstances, 227–8
Determination of refugee status
    overview, 11, 44–6, 78
    child-specific harm, 50
    disabled children, 50–1
    domestic child abuse and, 65
    education, deprivation of, 50
    family unity and
        generally, 70
        overview, 45, 69–70
        best interests of child principle, 73
        child eligible but parent ineligible, 76–7
        family separation versus, 144, 145
        non-separation duty, 45, 67, 69–70, 72–8
        parent eligible but child ineligible, 76
        Recommendation B, 71–2, 260
        reunification versus, 70
    female genital cutting and, 50, 51
    gangs, 50
    human shields, 65
    illegitimate children, 50
    individual assessment requirement
        overview, 45, 52–4
        accompanied children, 44–5, 62–9

child-centered framework, 60
   non-refoulement obligation and, 45, 54–5, 60, 62, 68
   right to be heard/views of child, 55–9
   unaccompanied children, 44–5, 60–2
  invisibility of child refugees
   overview, 44–5, 46–7
   accompanied children, 45, 47, 49–52
   derivative protection, 50–2
   unaccompanied children, 47–9
  military recruitment of child soldiers, 50, 65
  non-discrimination/equality and, 65
  prima facie determination, 10
  sexual abuse and, 65
Disability Convention, 144, 196
Disabled children
  determination of refugee status, 50–1
  persecutory harm and, 130
  social group membership, 179–80
Discretionary grant of protection on humanitarian grounds, 218–20
Discrimination. *See* Non-discrimination/equality
Domestic child abuse
  child labor as, 132–3
  child pornography as, 132–3
  debt bondage as, 132–3
  determination of refugee status and, 65
  female genital cutting as, 132–3, 138
  forced marriage as, 132–3
  incest as, 132–3
  neglect as, 132–3
  nexus to Convention ground and, 159–60, 162, 163–4
  by non-state actors, 133
  persecutory harm/being persecuted and, 117, 130, 132–9
  prostitution as, 132–3
  psychological harm as, 132–3
  sexual abuse as, 132–3
  state protection and, 132–9
  traditional practices as, 132–3
  trafficking of children as, 132–3
Drafting history. *See* Travaux Préparatoires
Dublin II (EU), 199
Dublin III (EU), 199
Due diligence standard of protection, 114

Economic exploitation under CRC, 192
ECOSOC (United Nations Economic and Social Council), 204
Education
  best interests of child principle and, 229–30
  under CRC, 193, 229–30
  deprivation of, 50, 117
  persecutory harm/being persecuted and, 139–44
   bullying as, 142
   corporal punishment as, 142
   de facto denial of, 141, 143
   expulsion or suspension, 141
   non-discrimination/equality and, 140–1, 142, 143–4

Education (cont.)
    primary education, 140, 142–3
    quality of education, 140, 143–4
    secondary education, 140
    UNCESCR and, 139, 140–2, 143
  progressive implementation, 74
  religion and, 171
Ejusdem generis approach to social group membership, 172–4, 176–8, 183
Equality. *See* Non-discrimination/equality
European Convention on Human Rights (ECHR)
  generally, 188
  adult focus of, 211
  Article 3, 134, 149–50, 188
  Article 8, 73, 146, 206–13
  best interests of child principle and, 206–13
  domestic child abuse and, 134
  interference with private life or family life requirement, 211–12
  persecutory harm/being persecuted and, 105
  proportionality and, 211
  psychological harm and, 151
European Council on Refugees and Exiles (ECRE), 52
European Court of Human Rights (ECtHR)
  best interests of child principle and, 208–9
  psychological harm and, 151
  relevance of age and, 151
European Union
  Charter of Fundamental Rights, 196, 202, 221
  Dublin II, 199
  Dublin III, 199
  Qualification Directive
    best interests of child principle and, 227
    CRC Article 3 as independent source of protection and, 199–200
    family separation and, 149
    non-refoulement obligation and, 190
    persecutory harm/being persecuted and, 117–18, 120, 123
    social group membership and, 175
  unaccompanied children in, 221
  Unaccompanied Minors Action Plan, 221
Evidentiary challenges regarding age-sensitive risk assessment
  generally, 79
  overview, 89–90
  country of origin information, 91–2
  credibility of evidence (*See* Credibility of evidence)
  fact-finding, shared duty of, 90–1
  liberal benefit of doubt, 93–9
  similarly situated persons, 93
Exclusion of refugees, 16, 50, 81, 198–9, 240–1
ExCom Conclusions (UNHCR)
  generally, 7, 11, 23–5
  accompanied children and, 64
  determination of refugee status, 54–5, 64, 72
  family unity and, 72
  independent source of protection, 201
Expression, freedom of, 19–20, 55
Extrajudicial killing, family separation and, 146–7

Fact-finding
  non-refoulement obligation and, 90–1
  shared duty of, 90–1
Falun Gong, 122
Families, social group membership, 182–5
Family separation as persecutory harm/being persecuted, 144–9
  generally, 117
  abduction of children and, 146–7
  alternative parental care and, 145
  under CRC, 127–8
  custody of children and, 145
  deprivation of family environment, 148–9
  extrajudicial killing and, 146–7
  family unity versus, 144, 145
  identity and, 145
  illegitimate children and, 146–7
  incarceration and, 146–7
  institutionalisation and, 146–7
  non-separation duty
    generally, 145, 146
    overview, 239–40
    best interests of child principle and, 146
    family unity and, 45, 67, 69–70, 72–8
    non-refoulement obligation and, 75
  parental responsibilities and, 145
  privacy and, 145
  prostitution and, 148
  rape and, 148
  removal of child, 146–7
  right to be heard/views of child and, 146
  sexual abuse and, 148
  sexual exploitation and, 148
  state protection and, 148–9
  street children, 147–8, 149
Family unity
  generally, 70
  overview, 45, 69–70
  best interests of child principle, 73, 231–2
  child eligible but parent ineligible, 76–7
  family separation versus, 144, 145
  non-separation duty, 45, 67, 69–70, 72–8
  parent eligible but child ineligible, 76
  Recommendation B, 71–2, 260
  reunification versus, 70
Fear requirement. *See* Well-founded fear/genuine risk requirement
Feller, Erika, 2, 238
Female genital cutting (FGC)
  generally, 30, 165
  under CRC, 192
  determination of refugee status and, 50, 51
  as domestic child abuse, 132–3, 138
  non-separation duty and, 77
  as persecutory harm, 117, 118
  unaccompanied children and, 60
  well-founded fear/genuine risk requirement and, 82–3, 85
Finch, N., 222

Finland
    Aliens Act, 219
    best interests of child principle in, discretionary grant of protection on humanitarian grounds, 218–19
First country of arrival rules, 198–9
Forced marriage
    under CRC, 192
    as domestic child abuse, 132–3
    as persecutory harm, 117
Former status, social group membership, 179–80
"For reasons of." *See* Convention grounds; Nexus to Convention ground
Foster, Michelle, 2, 5, 22–3, 38–9, 41, 105, 106, 108, 109, 159, 160, 178
Freeman, M., 237

Gangs
    under CRC, 131–2
    determination of refugee status, 50
    nexus to Convention ground and, 159–60
        political opinion, 169
        social group membership, 179–80
Gardiner, R., 34, 40–1
Gender-based persecution, 4–5
General Comments (UNCRC)
    generally, 7–8, 11, 31
    best interests of child principle, 227, 231, 235, 236
    complementary protection, 187
    determination of refugee status, 56–7, 58
    domestic child abuse, 134–6, 137
    education, 144
    GC6
        generally, 7–8, 26, 95
        best interests of child principle and, 187, 188, 190, 193, 194, 196, 200, 227, 230–1, 236
        definition of refugee and, 125
        right to be heard/views of child and, 56–7
        unaccompanied children and, 86–7, 128
    GC7, 144
    GC8, 137, 150
    GC12, 19–20, 55, 56–7, 58
    GC13
        domestic child abuse and, 134–6, 137
        education and, 140–1
        psychological harm and, 150
    GC14
        generally, 23, 124
        best interests of child principle and, 196–7, 198, 223, 225, 235
        independent source of protection, 196–7, 200, 223
        non-refoulement obligation, 190, 193, 195–6
        persecutory harm/being persecuted, 124, 125
        psychological harm, 150
        unaccompanied children, 26
        weight afforded to, 22–3
Geneva Conventions (1949), 17, 19, 70, 188
Geneva Declaration of the Rights of the Child (1924), 13–14, 19–20
Genuine risk requirement. *See* Well-founded fear/genuine risk requirement
Germany, reservations to CRC, 14–15
Girls, social group membership, 179–80
González, Elián, 48–9, 60–1

Good faith interpretation, 33–4
Goodman, Ryan, 112–13
Goodwin-Gill, Guy, 6, 70, 80, 83, 102, 111, 173, 186, 195, 199–200, 226, 241
Grahl-Madsen, A., 53, 66–7, 69, 87–8, 101, 143
Gross, L., 29–30
Guardianship, 19, 146

Haines, Rodger, 106–7
Harrison, L., 167
Hart, H.L.A., 102
Harvey, C., 242
Hathaway, James C., 5, 10, 22–3, 28–9, 32, 36, 42, 54, 87, 88, 98, 102, 103, 105–6, 108, 109–10, 111, 112, 127, 151, 173, 178
Hicks, W.S., 87, 88
HIV/AIDS, social group membership and, 179
Holborn, L.W., 17, 204
Holy See, Recommendation B and, 71
Homosexuality
    age-sensitive risk assessment and, 94
    psychological harm and, 154
    social group membership and, 172, 179–80
Honour killings under CRC, 192
HRC. See United Nations Human Rights Committee (HRC)
Humanitarian grounds, discretionary grant of protection on, 218–20
Human rights law. See International human rights law
Human shields, determination of refugee status and, 65
Hurwitz, Agnès, 199–200

ICCPR. See International Covenant of Civil and Political Rights (ICCPR)
ICESCR. See International Covenant of Economic, Social, and Cultural Rights (ICESCR)
ICJ (International Court of Justice), 40, 41
IHRL. See International human rights law
ILC. See International Law Commission (ILC)
Illegitimate children
    family separation and, 146–7
    non-discrimination/equality, 50
    persecutory harm and, 117
    social group membership, 179–80
Immigration control, balancing of interests and, 236
Imputed identity, nexus to Convention ground, 165
Incarceration, family separation and, 146–7
Incest as domestic child abuse, 132–3
Incorrect assessment of child refugees
    generally, 3–4, 5
    age-sensitive risk assessment, 79
Independent source of protection, CRC Article 3 as, 7, 12, 80, 239, 241–2. See also Best interests of child principle and complementary protection generally
Individual assessment requirement
    overview, 45, 52–4
    child-centered framework
        overview, 60
        accompanied children, 44–5, 62–9
        unaccompanied children, 44–5, 60–2
    non-refoulement obligation and, 45, 54–5, 60, 62, 68
    right to be heard/views of child, 55–9

Infanticide as persecutory harm, 117
Institutionalisation, family separation and, 146–7
Intention requirement for nexus to Convention ground, 158–60
Inter-American Commission on Human Rights, 217
Internally displaced persons, 13
Internal protection alternative, 198–9, 240
International Bill of Rights, 103, 105, 107–8, 126–7
International Conference on Indo-Chinese Refugees (1989), 205–6
International Convention on the Elimination of All Forms of Racial Discrimination (CERD), 29, 104, 106
International Court of Justice (ICJ), 9, 32, 40, 41
International Covenant for the Protection of All Persons from Enforced Disappearance, 188
International Covenant of Civil and Political Rights (ICCPR)
    generally, 11, 19, 20–1, 106, 126–8, 188
    aliens, 188
    best interests of child principle and, 202
    complementary protection generally, 186–7
    CRC versus, 20–1, 127
    non-refoulement obligation and, 186–7, 188–95, 196
    non-separation duty, 73
    persecutory harm/being persecuted and
        generally, 29
        definition of "being persecuted," 126–9, 130
        human rights framework, 104
        human rights on own terms, 108
        psychological harm, 149–50
        widely supported norms, 106
    religion and, 171
    social group membership and, 177
International Covenant of Economic, Social, and Cultural Rights (ICESCR)
    generally, 11, 19, 20–1, 106, 126–8
    CRC versus, 20–1, 127
    persecutory harm/being persecuted and
        generally, 29
        definition of "being persecuted," 126–9, 130
        education, 140
        human rights framework, 104
        human rights on own terms, 108
        unaccompanied children, 128
        widely supported norms, 106
International humanitarian law
    best interests of child principle and, 218–20
    discretionary grant of protection on humanitarian grounds, 218–20
International human rights law
    Convention and, 6, 28–30, 123, 124–5, 239
    CRC and, 6, 28–30, 123, 124–5, 239
    nexus to Convention ground and, 168
    persecutory harm/being persecuted and
        generally, 102
        core/margin approach, 106
        hierarchical approach, 106–7
        human rights framework, 103–4
        human rights on own terms, 107–9
        overinclusiveness, 107–9
        psychological harm, 151
        regional human rights law versus, 105
        seriousness of violation, 106–7

soft law, 105
    widely supported norms, 105–6
  refugees and, 28–9
  VCLT and, 103, 106
International law, child refugees in
  overview, 10–11, 13–16, 43
  Convention (*See* Refugee Convention (Convention))
  CRC (*See* Convention on the Rights of the Child (CRC))
  domestic practice compared, 14–15
International Law Commission (ILC), 34, 36, 37, 38, 40, 42
International Refugee Organization (IRO), 17–19, 203–5
Interpretation of Convention
  overview, 31–2
  age-sensitive interpretation, 11, 80–1
  CRC as interpretive aid (*See* Interpretive aid, CRC as)
  CRC as relevant rule
    overview, 37–9
    "applicable in the relations between the parties," 41–3
    "relevant" rules, 40–1
    "rules of international law," 40
    "take into account," 39–40
    VCLT and, 37–9, 40–3
  in domestic fora, 32–3
  general rule, 33–5
  human rights object and purpose, 35–7
  ILC and, 34, 36, 37, 38, 40, 42
  lex specialis and, 32
  as "living instrument," 4, 36–7
  pacta sunt servanda and, 31–2
  separate treatment of constituent elements, 12
  systemic approach, 37–9
  transnational judicial conversation, 9
  VCLT and
    overview, 32
    CRC as relevant rule of international law, 37–9, 40–3
    in domestic fora, 32–3
    general rule, 33–5, 39
    good faith interpretation, 33–4
    human rights object and purpose, 35–7
    systemic approach, 34–5
Interpretive aid, CRC as
  overview, 6–7, 11–12, 239, 240–1
  age-sensitive risk assessment (*See* Age-sensitive risk assessment)
  within child rights framework, 28–30
  legal basis for, 32
  nexus to Convention ground (*See* Nexus to Convention ground)
  persecutory harm/being persecuted (*See* Persecutory harm/being persecuted)
Interracial marriage, social group membership, 179–80
Invisibility of child refugees
  overview, 3–4, 5
  in determination of refugee status
    overview, 44–5, 46–7
    accompanied children, 45, 47, 49–52
    derivative protection, 50–2
    unaccompanied children, 47–9
Involuntary confinement as persecutory harm, 117

IRO. *See* International Refugee Organization (IRO)
IRO Constitution, 17–19
Italy, Recommendation B and, 71

Japan
   adoption of CRC, 22
   reservations to CRC, 14–15
Jastram, K., 69, 108

Kidnapping
   under CRC, 21, 127–8
   family separation and, 146–7
   nexus to Convention ground and, 159–60
   as persecutory harm, 117
Krappmann, L., 55

Lauterpacht, E., 41, 54
Lex specialis, Convention and, 32
Liberal benefit of doubt, 99
Liberty under CRC, 193–5
Lidén, H., 219
Life, right to, 192–3
Lowe, V., 105
Lundberg, A., 62–3

Machel, G., 1
Martin, D., 107–8
McAdam, Jane, 2, 15, 66, 83, 111, 186, 189, 190, 200
McLachlan, C., 37, 39
Medical care
   best interests of child principle and, 229–30
   under CRC, 193, 229–30
Meeting on Refugees and Displaced Persons (1979), 205
Membership of a particular social group. *See* Social group membership
Messineo, F., 191
Methodology of study, 8–12
Michigan Guidelines on Well-Founded Fear, 156
Military recruitment of child soldiers
   determination of refugee status, 50, 65
   Optional Protocol on the Involvement of Children in Armed Conflict (OPAC), 11, 22, 31, 43, 195–6
   as persecutory harm, 117
   protection against under CRC, 21, 127–8, 131–2, 195–6
Modification of behaviour as psychological harm, 154

Nationality
   best interests of child principle and, 229–30
   as Convention ground, 3, 25–6, 108–9, 157, 165, 172–3
   under CRC, 229–30
Neglect as domestic child abuse, 132–3
Newland, K., 69
New Zealand
   best interests of child principle in
      determination of best interests, 227, 232
      discretionary grant of protection on humanitarian grounds, 218

as independent source of protection, 202–3
    removal of parent and, 216, 218
Immigration Act 2009, 216
individual assessment requirement in, 62, 67–8
interplay between Convention and CRC in, 8
nexus to Convention ground in
    political opinion, 169
    "predicament" approach, 162, 163–4
    religion, 170–1
    social group membership, 176, 183, 184–5
non-refoulement obligation in, 190
non-separation duty in, 76, 77
persecutory harm/being persecuted in
    alleviation of risk theory, 114
    definition of "being persecuted," 126, 131
    education, 142–4
    family separation, 145
    psychological harm, 152–3, 155, 156
reservations to CRC, 14–15
right to be heard/views of child in, 56–7
well-founded fear/genuine risk requirement in, 89
Nexus to Convention ground
    generally, 81, 108
    overview, 11–12, 157, 165, 185, 240
    abduction of children and, 159–60
    actual identity and, 165
    causal link
        overview, 157–8
        domestic child abuse, 163–4
        intention requirement, 158–60
        nature of, 157–8
        "predicament" approach, 164
        socio-economic deprivation, 163
        standard of, 158
        trafficking of children, 164
    China, one-child policy and, 165
    deprivation of family environment and, 162
    domestic child abuse and, 159–60, 162
    gangs and, 159–60
    imputed identity and, 165
    international human rights law and, 168
    nationality and, 3, 25–6, 108–9, 157, 165, 172–3
    non-discrimination/equality and, 157, 161, 185
    political opinion and, 166–9
        generally, 3, 25–6, 108–9, 172–3
        adult-centric definition of political activity, 167
        gangs and, 169
        independent or imputed opinion, 165, 166–7
        parents or family members, opinions of, 166–7
        social group membership versus, 166
        unlikelihood of targeting children, 167–8
    race and, 3, 25–6, 108–9, 157, 165, 172–3
    religion and, 169–72
        generally, 3, 25–6, 108–9, 158, 172–3
        child's own religious beliefs, 170–1
        family members, religious beliefs of, 169–70

Nexus to Convention ground (cont.)
    female children, 171–2
    IHRL and, 171
  social group membership and (*See* Social group membership)
  trafficking of children and, 159–60, 162, 164, 185
Nillson, E., 62–3
Non-discrimination/equality
  generally, 242
  best interests of child principle and, 229–30
  child-specific harm and, 65, 130–1
  China, one-child policy, 86
  under CRC, 229–30
  determination of refugee status and, 65
  education and, 140–1, 142, 143–4
  illegitimate children, 50
  nexus to Convention ground and, 157, 161, 185
  persecutory harm and, 117, 130–1
  psychological harm and, 153
  refugees generally, 20, 35–6
  religion and, 158
  social group membership and, 36, 177, 183
Non-refoulement obligation
  overview, 241
  accompanied children and, 62, 68
  best interests of child principle and, 198
  CAT and, 186–7, 188–92, 196
  complementary protection generally, 186–7
  as complementary protection under CRC, 12
      generally, 12
      overview, 186–7, 188–92, 238
      cruel, inhuman or degrading treatment or punishment, protection against, 193–5
      development, right of, 192–3
      liberty, right to, 193–5
      life, right to, 192–3
      military recruitment of child soldiers, protection against, 30–1, 195–6
      survival, right of, 192–3
      torture, protection against, 193–5
  Convention and, 45, 54–5, 189–90
  under CRC, 30
  fact-finding and, 90–1
  ICCPR and, 186–7, 188–92, 196
  individual assessment requirement and, 45, 54–5, 60, 62, 68
  non-separation duty and, 75
  pacta sunt servanda and, 54
  procedural guarantee, CRC as, 11, 239
  risk of irreparable harm, 30
  standard of proof, 189
  unaccompanied children and, 60
Non-separation duty
  generally, 145, 146
  overview, 239–40
  best interests of child principle and, 146
  family unity and, 45, 67, 69–70, 72–8
  non-refoulement obligation and, 75
Non-state actor doctrine, 133
Non-state actors

domestic child abuse by, 133
persecutory harm/being persecuted by, 110, 112–14, 115–16
Norway
    best interests of child principle in, discretionary grant of protection on humanitarian grounds, 218–19
    Immigration Act, 219
    persecutory harm/being persecuted in, 118
Nykanen, E., 58

OAU Convention Governing the Specific Aspects of Refugee Problems in Africa, 186
Object and purpose of Refugee Convention, 1–2, 35–7, 103, 111
Objective element, well-founded fear/genuine risk requirement, 81–2
Optional Protocol on a Communications Procedure (OPCP), 11, 22, 29, 41, 106, 189
Optional Protocol on the Involvement of Children in Armed Conflict (OPAC), 11, 22, 31, 41, 43, 195–6
Optional Protocol on the Sale of Children, Child Prostitution and Child Pornography (OPSC), 11, 22, 29, 41, 43,
    106, 133, 187
Orakhelashvili, A., 40
Orphans, social group membership, 179–80
Ostracism as psychological harm, 153

Pacta sunt servanda
    Convention and, 31–2
    non-refoulement obligation and, 54
Parents defined, 44
Participation, right of, 55
Particular social group. *See* Social group membership
Past persecution
    psychological harm, relevance to, 155, 156
    well-founded fear/genuine risk requirement, relevance to, 82–3
Persecution of child as persecution of parent, 51–2
Persecutory harm/being persecuted
    generally, 81
    overview, 11–12, 101–2, 156, 240
    abduction of children as, 117
    absence of definition, 101
    adult-centric understanding of, 116
    age-sensitive risk assessment and, 123
    "being persecuted" standard, 101, 102–3
    best interests of child principle and, 124
    case studies
        generally, 102
        overview, 131–2
        domestic child abuse, 132–9
        education, 139–44 (*See also* Education)
        family separation, 144–9 (*See also* Family separation as persecutory harm/being persecuted)
        psychological harm, 149–56 (*See also* Psychological harm as persecutory harm/being persecuted)
    child pornography as, 117
    child-specific persecution, 124–5
    corporal punishment as, 117, 118, 142
    cruel, inhuman or degrading treatment or punishment as, 117, 126
    cumulative impact of harm, 132
    custody of children and, 117
    debt bondage as, 118
    definition of "being persecuted"
        generally, 101–2
        overview, 116

Persecutory harm/being persecuted (cont.)
    appropriate protection, 124
    benchmark, CRC as, 123–6
    child-specific harm, 117–18, 127–8
    CRC as benchmark for persecutory harm, 126–31
    discrimination, 130–1
    female genital cutting, 118, 138
    harm not persecution in case of adults but persecution in case of children, 117, 118–22
    higher standard of protection, 130–1
    non-state actor doctrine, 133
    physical harm, 120
    psychological harm, 120–1
    strengthening of rights, 128–30
    symbolic function of CRC, 131
  disabled children and, 130
  domestic child abuse and, 117, 130, 132–9
  education, 139–44 (*See also* Education)
  family separation, 117, 144–9 (*See also* Family separation as persecutory harm/being persecuted)
  female genital cutting as, 117, 118
  forced marriage as, 117
  illegitimate children and, 117
  infanticide as, 117
  international human rights law and
    generally, 102
    core/margin approach, 106
    hierarchical approach, 106–7
    human rights framework, 103–4
    human rights on own terms, 107–9
    overinclusiveness, 107–9
    psychological harm, 151
    regional human rights law versus, 105
    seriousness of violation, 106–7
    soft law, 105
    widely supported norms, 105–6
  involuntary confinement as, 117
  military recruitment of child soldiers as, 117
  modification of behaviour as, 154
  non-discrimination/equality and, 117
  by non-state actors, 110, 112–14, 115–16
  persecution of child as persecution of parent, 51–2
  prosecution as, 129
  prostitution as, 117
  protection theory, 114
  psychological harm, 149–56 (*See also* Psychological harm as persecutory harm/being persecuted)
  punishment as, 129
  rape as, 122
  sexual abuse as, 117
  socio-economic deprivation as, 121
  state protection and, 109–16
    accountability theory, 110
    alleviation of risk theory, 110–11, 114–16
    best interests of child principle and, 198–9
    as bifurcated theory, 110
    domestic child abuse, 132–9
    due diligence standard of protection, 114
    family separation and, 149

futility of, 138
outstanding questions, 115–16
protection theory, 110, 111–14, 115–16
torture as, 117, 126
Physical harm, persecutory harm/being persecuted and, 120
Play and recreation under CRC, 21, 127–8
Pobjoy, Jason, 151
Poland, best interests of child principle in, 203–4
Political opinion, 166–9
adult-centric definition of political activity, 167
as Convention ground, 3, 25–6, 108–9, 157, 172–3
gangs and, 169
independent or imputed opinion, 165, 166–7
parents or family members, opinions of, 166–7
social group membership versus, 166
unlikelihood of targeting children, 167–8
Poverty
generally, 1
social group membership, 179–80
"Predicament" approach to nexus to Convention ground, 164
Privacy
best interests of child principle and, 229–30
under CRC, 229–30
family separation and, 145
Procedural guarantee, CRC as
overview, 6, 11, 44–6, 78, 239–40
within child rights framework, 27–8
family unity
generally, 70
overview, 45, 69–70
best interests of child principle, 73, 231–2
child eligible but parent ineligible, 76–7
family separation versus, 144, 145
non-separation duty, 45, 67, 69–70, 72–8
parent eligible but child ineligible, 76
Recommendation B, 71–2, 260
reunification versus, 70
individual assessment requirement
overview, 45, 52–4
accompanied children, 44–5, 62–9
child-centered framework, 60
non-refoulement obligation and, 45, 54–5, 60, 62, 68
right to be heard/views of child, 55–9
unaccompanied children, 44–5, 60–2
invisibility of child refugees
overview, 44–5, 46–7
accompanied children, 45, 47, 49–52
derivative protection, 50–2
unaccompanied children, 47–9
non-refoulement obligation and, 11, 239
Prosecution as persecutory harm, 129
Prostitution
as domestic child abuse, 132–3
family separation and, 148
Optional Protocol on the Sale of Children, Child Prostitution and Child Pornography (OPSC), 11, 22, 29, 41, 43, 106, 133, 187

Prostitution (cont.)
  as persecutory harm, 117
  social group membership and, 179–80
Protection theory, 110, 111–14, 115–16
Protocol Relating to the Status of Refugees (1967), 16, 22, 32, 53, 187
Psychological harm as persecutory harm/being persecuted, 149–56
  generally, 120–1
  cruel, inhuman or degrading treatment or punishment as, 149–51
  as domestic child abuse, 132–3
  family members, risk to, 151–2
  homosexuality and, 154
  individual circumstances and vulnerabilities, 151
  modification of behaviour as, 154
  non-discrimination/equality and, 153
  ostracism as, 153
  past persecution, relevance of, 155, 156
  past trauma, effect of, 154–6
  sexual orientation and, 154
  violence, threats of, 151–3
Punishment as persecutory harm, 129

Qualification Directive (EU)
  best interests of child principle and, 227
  CRC Article 3 as independent source of protection and, 199–200
  family separation and, 149
  non-refoulement obligation and, 190
  persecutory harm/being persecuted and, 117–18, 120, 123
  social group membership and, 175

Race as Convention grounds, 3, 25–6, 108–9, 157, 165, 172–3
Rape as persecutory harm, 122, 148
Refugee Convention (Convention). See also specific topic
  Ad Hoc Committee on Statelessness and Related Problems, 71
  adoption of, 13–14
  age-sensitive risk assessment (See Age-sensitive risk assessment)
  applicability to children, 3, 4–5, 25–6
  Article 1, 186–7, 188, 257–8
  Article 1A
    generally, 3, 4, 16, 25–6
    domestic child abuse and, 133
    nexus to Convention ground and, 157–8, 161, 162, 164
    persecutory harm/being persecuted and, 110, 114–15
    social group membership and, 172, 173–4, 185
    well-founded fear/genuine risk requirement and, 81, 88–9
  Article 1C, 154, 178
  Article 1F, 25–6, 50
  Article 5, 32, 35
  Article 33, 11, 45, 54, 188, 189–90, 239
  Article 35, 23
  carve-out provisions, 16
  cessation provisions, 16, 81, 177–8, 240–1
  Convention grounds (See Convention grounds)
  as cornerstone of international refugee protection regime, 6
  CRC, interplay with, 5–8, 10, 123, 124–5, 239
  determination of refugee status (See Determination of refugee status)

exclusion provisions, 16, 50, 81, 198–9, 240–1
Final Act of the United Nations Conference of Plenipotentiaries on the Status of Refugees and Stateless Persons, 19, 71
IHRL and, 6, 28–30, 123, 124–5, 239
international human rights law and, 28–30
interpretation of (*See* Interpretation of Convention)
national enforcement, necessity of, 9
nexus to Convention ground (*See* Nexus to Convention ground)
non-refoulement obligation and, 45, 54–5, 189–90
object and purpose of, 1–2, 35–7, 103, 111
parties to, 187
persecutory harm/being persecuted (*See* Persecutory harm/being persecuted)
Preamble, 257
Protocol Relating to the Status of Refugees (1967), 16, 22, 32, 53, 187
Recommendation B, 19, 71–2, 260
refugee defined, 3, 12, 16, 68, 257–8
rights of refugees, 16
supranational enforcement body, lack of, 9
as surrogate national protection, 1–2, 103, 111
Travaux Préparatoires, 53, 71
well-founded fear/genuine risk requirement (*See* Well-founded fear/genuine risk requirement)
Refugee rights, 10, 15
Refugee Women's Legal Group, 109
Rehabilitation under CRC, 46
Religion
  as Convention ground, 3, 25–6, 108–9, 172–3
  education and, 171
  freedom of, 19–20, 55
  nexus to Convention ground, 169–72
    generally, 3, 25–6, 108–9, 158, 172–3
    child's own religious beliefs, 170–1
    family members, religious beliefs of, 169–70
    female children, 171–2
    IHRL and, 171
  non-discrimination/equality and, 158
Removal of parent, best interests of child principle and, 213–18
Reservations to Convention on the Rights of the Child, 14–15
Right to be heard/views of child, 20, 45, 55–9, 146, 226–7, 239–40
Right to life
  best interests of child principle and, 229–30
  under CRC, 192–3, 229–30
Risk assessment. *See* Age-sensitive risk assessment
Robinson, Mary, 133
Roma children, 143–4

Safe third-country rules, 198–9, 240
Sands, P., 37, 38, 39
Scott, C., 107
Separated children. *See* Unaccompanied children
Separation from family as persecutory harm/being persecuted. *See* Family separation as persecutory harm/being persecuted
Serious harm. *See* Persecutory harm/being persecuted
Sexual abuse and violence
  determination of refugee status and, 65
  as domestic child abuse, 132–3
  family separation and, 148

Sexual abuse and violence (cont.)
  as persecutory harm, 117
Sexual exploitation
  under CRC, 21, 127–8, 192
  family separation and, 148
Sexuality-based persecution, 4–5
Sexual orientation. *See* Homosexuality
Shacknove, A., 109
Shared duty of fact-finding, 90–1
Similarly situated persons, 93
Simmons, B.A., 43
Singapore, reservations to CRC, 14–15
Slavery. *See* Forced marriage; Trafficking of children
Social group membership
  overview, 172
  abandoned children, 179–80
  age as immutable characteristic, 176–7, 180–1
  age-based group, 176–8
  age plus other characteristics, 176, 178–82, 185
  boys, 179–80
  children as social group, 175–82
  as Convention ground, 3, 25–6, 108–9
  cumulative approach, 174–5
  disabled children, 179–80
  ejusdem generis approach, 172–4, 176–8, 183
  family as social group, 182–5
  former status, 179–80
  gangs and, 179–80
  girls, 179–80
  HIV/AIDS and, 179
  homosexuality, 172, 179–80
  illegitimate children, 179–80
  interracial marriage and, 179–80
  lack of temporal bright line, 176
  least clarity, as Convention ground with, 172
  MPSG Guidelines, 174–5, 182
  non-discrimination/equality and, 36, 177, 183
  orphans, 179–80
  particularity requirement, 169, 181–2
  political opinion versus, 166
  poverty and, 179–80
  prostitution and, 179–80
  social perception approach, 174, 181
  social visibility requirement, 169, 181–2
  street children as group, 179–81
  unaccompanied children, 179–80
  UNHCR approach, 174–5
Social perception approach to social group membership, 174, 181
Socio-economic deprivation
  under CRC, 131–2
  nexus to Convention ground and, 163
  as persecutory harm, 121
Soft law, 40, 105
Somalia
  failure to ratify CRC, 6, 41–2
  signing of CRC, 43

South Africa, invisibility of child refugees and, 47

Soviet Union, best interests of child principle in, 203–4

Special protection of child refugees
  generally, 19
  under CRC, 21–2, 46
  unaccompanied children, 221–3

Special Rapporteur on the Human Rights of Migrants, 201

Standard of living
  best interests of child principle and, 229–30
  under CRC, 193, 229–30

State practice regarding best interests of child principle, 203
  discretionary grant of protection on humanitarian grounds, 218–20
  ECHR and, 206–13
  international models, 203–5
  removal of parent and, 213–18
  unaccompanied children and, 221–3

State protection, persecutory harm/being persecuted and, 109–16
  accountability theory, 110
  alleviation of risk theory, 110–11, 114–16
  best interests of child principle and, 198–9
  as bifurcated theory, 110
  domestic child abuse, 132–9
  due diligence standard of protection, 114
  family separation and, 149
  futility of, 138
  outstanding questions, 115–16
  protection theory, 110, 111–14, 115–16

Statute of the International Court of Justice, 9, 40

Street children
  family separation and, 147–8, 149
  social group membership, 179–81

Subjective element, well-founded fear/genuine risk requirement, 81–2

Sudan
  country of origin information and, 92
  nexus to Convention ground and, 165

Surrogate national protection, 1–2, 103, 111

Survival and development, 1, 131, 141, 148, 150, 188, 191, 192–196, 230, 233, 236, 245

Sweden
  Aliens Act, 56, 219
  best interests of child principle in, discretionary grant of protection on humanitarian grounds, 218–19
  individual assessment requirement in, 62–3

Switzerland, reservations to CRC, 14–15

Temporary protection, 186

Thronson, D., 47, 49, 50, 69

Tobin, John, 6, 44, 115, 134, 228

Torture
  as persecutory harm, 117, 126
  protection against under CRC, 193–5

Torture Convention. *See* Convention against Torture (CAT)

Traditional practices
  under CRC, 21, 127–8, 131–2, 192, 219
  as domestic child abuse, 132–3
  female genital cutting (*See* Female genital cutting (FGC))

Trafficking of children
  under CRC, 21, 127–8, 131–2, 192

Trafficking of children (cont.)
  as domestic child abuse, 132–3
  nexus to Convention ground and, 159–60, 162, 164, 185
Transnational judicial conversation, 9
Travaux Préparatoires
  of Convention, 53, 71
  of CRC, 74, 136
Tuitt, P., 46–7, 48

UDHR. *See* Universal Declaration of Human Rights (UDHR)
Unaccompanied children
  best interests of child principle and, 221–3
  capacity to apply for refugee status, 60
  defined, 2
  female genital cutting and, 60
  individual assessment requirement, 44–5, 60–2
  International Refugee Organization and, 203–5
  invisibility of child refugees, 47–9
  non-refoulement obligation and, 60
  social group membership, 179–80
  special protection, 221–3
  World War II, following, 203–5
Unaccompanied Minors Action Plan (EU), 221
Unborn children, best interests of child principle, 223–4
UNCEDAW (United Nations Committee on the Elimination of Discrimination against Women), 113
UNCESCR. *See* United Nations Committee on Economic, Social and Cultural Rights (UNCESCR)
UNCRC. *See* United Nations Committee on the Rights of the Child (UNCRC)
Underage military recruitment. *See* Military recruitment of child soldiers
UNHCR. *See* United Nations High Commissioner for Refugees (UNHCR)
UNHCR Guidance Notes/Policy
  ExCom Conclusions
    generally, 7, 11, 23–5
    accompanied children and, 64
    determination of refugee status, 54–5, 64, 72
    family unity and, 72
    independent source of protection, 201
  Guidelines on Determining the Best Interests of the Child, 2
  Guidelines on International Protection
    generally, 11, 22–3, 25
    MPSG Guidelines, 174–5, 182
  Guidelines on Refugee Children (1998), 24
  Note on Proof, 94–5
  Policy on Refugee Children (1993), 7, 24–5
  Refugee Children: Guidelines on Protection and Care (1994), 7, 15, 24, 95, 121
  2009 Guidelines on Child Asylum Claims
    generally, 7, 25–6
    age-sensitive risk assessment, 79, 90, 92, 94–5, 97
    determination of refugee status, 54, 56, 63–4
    education and, 142
    persecutory harm/being persecuted, 104, 118–19, 120, 122, 124–5, 147
    political opinion, 171
    political opinion as Convention ground, 168
    social group membership, 176, 178, 179, 180
    unaccompanied children and, 48
    weight afforded to, 22–3
    well-founded fear/genuine risk requirement, 84, 85–7

Unaccompanied Children Guidelines (1997), 124–5, 201
UNHCR Handbook
   generally, 3, 11, 25
   age-sensitive risk assessment, 93, 94–5
   determination of refugee status, 53, 63
   family unity, 71
   persecutory harm/being persecuted, 118
   well-founded fear/genuine risk requirement, 83, 86–7
UNICEF. *See* United Nations Children's Fund (UNICEF)
United Kingdom
  best interests of child principle in
   generally, 197–8, 202
   application of CRC Article 3, 224–5
   balancing of interests, 234–6, 237–8
   determination of best interests, 225, 226, 227, 230, 232, 233
   ECHR and, 207, 209–11, 212–13
   following World War II, 204
   as independent source of protection, 201–2, 204
   unaccompanied children and, 221–2
  Border Agency, Guidelines, 90, 91, 96, 98, 168, 176–7, 197–8, 202, 230–1
  Borders, Citizenship and Immigration Act 2009, 202, 209, 211
  country of origin information in, 92
  derivative protection in, 50
  determination of refugee status in, 57, 66
  fact-finding in, 90–1
  government guidelines in, 27
  immigration control in, 211
  interplay between Convention and CRC in, 8
  interpretation of Convention in, 33, 36–7
  liberal benefit of doubt in, 95–6
  nexus to Convention ground in
   generally, 157
   causal link, 158
   political opinion, 166, 167, 168, 169
   "predicament" approach, 161, 164
   social group membership, 173, 176, 177, 184–5
  non-refoulement obligation in, 189
  non-separation duty in, 74–5, 76–7
  persecutory harm/being persecuted in
   alleviation of risk theory, 114
   definition of "being persecuted," 118, 119, 126
   domestic child abuse, 134, 138
   family separation, 144, 146, 148
   human rights framework, 104
   persecution of child as persecution of parent, 51–2
   protection theory, 111–12, 114
   psychological harm, 154
  Recommendation B and, 71
  reservations to CRC, 14–15
  right to be heard/views of child in, 58
  similarly situated persons in, 93
  state protection in, 110
  well-founded fear/genuine risk requirement in, 87
United Nations Children's Fund (UNICEF), 58, 92, 201
United Nations Committee on Economic, Social and Cultural Rights (UNCESCR)
  definition of "being persecuted," 127

United Nations Committee on Economic, Social and Cultural Rights (UNCESCR) (cont.)
 education and, 139, 140–2, 143
 state protection and, 113
United Nations Committee on the Elimination of Discrimination against Women (UNCEDAW), 113
United Nations Committee on the Rights of the Child (UNCRC)
 best interests of child principle and, 196–7, 198, 200–1, 223
  balancing of interests, 235, 236
  determination of best interests, 227–8, 231–2, 233
 complementary protection and, 187
 Concluding Observations, 31
 country of origin information and, 92
 determination of refugee status, right to be heard/views of child, 56
 Discussion Days, 6, 26, 31
 General Comments (*See* General Comments (UNCRC))
 interpretive aid, CRC as, 240
 liberal benefit of doubt and, 94–5
 non-refoulement obligation and, 30, 188–9, 190, 191–2, 193–6
 persecutory harm/being persecuted and
  definition of "being persecuted," 124, 125, 130–1
  domestic child abuse, 133, 134–6, 137
  education, 140, 142
  family separation, 144, 147
  psychological harm, 150
 state compliance and, 187
 well-founded fear/genuine risk requirement and, 83
United Nations Department of Social Affairs, 203
United Nations Economic and Social Council (ECOSOC), 204
United Nations General Assembly, 13
United Nations High Commissioner for Human Rights
 best interests of child principle and, 201
 Special Committees, 205–6
 unaccompanied children and, 205–6
United Nations High Commissioner for Refugees (UNHCR). *See also* UNHCR Guidance Notes/Policy
 best interests of child principle and
  balancing of interests, 235
  CRC Article 3 as independent source of protection, 198–9, 201
  determination of best interests, 229–30
 on challenges facing child refugees, 3
 country of origin information and, 92
 Department of International Protection, 25
 determination of refugee status and
  individual assessment requirement, 45, 52–3, 63–4
  invisibility of child refugees, 47
  non-refoulement obligation, 54–5
  right to be heard/views of child, 56
 domestic child abuse and, 135
 Executive Committee of the High Commissioner's Programme, 16
 fact-finding and, 90
 on interpretation of Convention, 35
 interpretive aid, CRC as, 240
 liberal benefit of doubt and, 94–5, 97–8, 99
 nexus to Convention ground and
  political opinion, 168, 169
  "predicament" approach, 161, 164
  social group membership, 174–5, 176, 177, 178, 179, 180, 182
 persecutory harm/being persecuted and

definition of "being persecuted," 118–19, 120, 121, 122, 124–5, 128
    family separation, 147
    human rights framework, 104
    psychological harm, 151, 153
  similarly situated persons and, 93
  well-founded fear/genuine risk requirement and, 82, 83, 84, 85–7
  Working Group on Refugee Children at Risk, 23–4
United Nations Human Rights Committee (HRC)
  determination of refugee status and, 59
  non-refoulement obligation and, 188
  non-separation duty and, 73
  persecutory harm/being persecuted and
    international human rights law, 107
    protection theory, 113
    psychological harm, 150–1
United Nations Special Representative of the Secretary-General for Children and Armed Conflict, 92
United States
  age-sensitive risk assessment in, 93, 96, 97, 98
  Attorney General, 61
  best interests of child principle in
    following World War II, 204
    as independent source of protection, 198, 202–3
    removal of parent and, 216–18
    unaccompanied children and, 222
  Citizenship and Immigration Service (USCIS), 119–20
  comparative law, use of, 9–10
  derivative protection in, 50–2
  determination of refugee status in, 49, 50, 51, 52
  failure to ratify CRC, 6, 8, 41–2
  government guidelines in, 27
  Immigration and Nationality Act, 82–3
  Immigration and Naturalization Service (INS)
    generally, 48–9, 60–1
    Guidelines, 8, 43, 53–4, 66, 86, 96, 99, 138, 198
  individual assessment requirement in, 60–1
  interplay between Convention and CRC in, 8
  liberal benefit of doubt in, 95–6
  nexus to Convention ground in
    generally, 165
    intention requirement, 159, 160
    political opinion, 166–9
    "predicament" approach, 162–3, 164
    religion, 169–70, 171–2
    social group membership, 172–3, 175, 178, 179–80, 181–2, 183, 184–5
  non-refoulement obligation in, 189, 190
  non-separation duty in, 76, 77
  persecutory harm/being persecuted in
    generally, 101, 102
    definition of "being persecuted," 117, 118, 119–21, 122, 125, 126, 128, 130
    domestic child abuse, 132, 135
    education, 139, 141
    family separation, 148
    human rights framework, 104
    persecution of child as persecution of parent, 51–2
    psychological harm, 151–2, 153, 154–5
  Recommendation B and, 71

United States (cont.)
  signing of CRC, 43
  special immigrant juvenile status in, 222
  well-founded fear/genuine risk requirement in, 82–3, 85
Universal Declaration of Human Rights (UDHR)
  generally, 19, 20–1, 105
  CRC and, 20–1
  interpretation of Convention and, 35, 36
  persecutory harm/being persecuted and
    generally, 29
    human rights framework, 104
Upbringing of children under CRC, 21

Van Bueren, G., 19–20, 131
Verdirame, Guglielmo, 103
Vernant, Jacques, 102
Vienna Convention on the Law of Treaties (VCLT)
  "applicable in the relations between the parties," 41–3
  Article 18, 43
  Article 31(1), 33–4
  Article 31(2), 19, 33–4, 35
  Article 31(3)(c), 34, 39–43, 106, 208
  best interests of child principle and, 208
  as customary international law, 32
  drafting history, 40
  good faith interpretation, 33–4
  international human rights law and, 103, 106
  interpretation of Convention and
    overview, 32
    CRC as relevant rule of international law, 37–9, 40–3
    in domestic fora, 32–3
    general rule, 33–5, 39
    good faith interpretation, 33–4
    human rights object and purpose, 35–7
    systemic approach, 34–5
  "relevant" rules, 40–1
  "rules of international law," 40
  "take into account," 39–40
Vietnam, unaccompanied children from, 205–6
Views of child. See Right to be heard/views of child
Violence, protection against under CRC, 192, 229–30
Vitus, K., 219

War
  generally, 1
  persecutory harm/being persecuted and, 131–2
Well-founded fear/genuine risk requirement
  generally, 81
  overview, 79, 81–2
  ability to understand, 83
  bipartite understanding of, 82–4
  difficulty in articulating, 83–4
  dispensing with subjective element, 86–9
  forward-looking assessment of risk, 82, 89–90
  imputation of fear from parent to child, 85–6

Michigan Guidelines on Well-Founded Fear, 156
objective element, 81–2, 86–90
past persecution, relevance of, 82–3
"predicament" approach and, 161
rationale for requiring children to establish, 84–9
subjective element, 81–2, 89–90
Women's International Democratic Federation, 21
World Trade Organization Panel, 40, 42
World War II
  children during, 203
  unaccompanied children following, 203–5
Wyness, M., 167

Xue Hanquin, 37

Young, W., 6, 95, 129, 198